THE GERMANIC LANGUAGES

Germanic – one of the largest subgroups of the Indo-European language family – comprises 37 languages with an estimated 470 million speakers worldwide. This book presents a comparative linguistic survey of the full range of Germanic languages, both ancient and modern, including major world languages such as English and German (West Germanic), the Scandinavian (North Germanic) languages, and the extinct East Germanic languages. Unlike previous studies, it does not take a chronological or a language-by-language approach, organized instead around linguistic constructions and subsystems. Considering dialects alongside standard varieties, it provides a detailed account of topics such as case, word formation, sound systems, vowel length, syllable structure, the noun phrase, the verb phrase, the expression of tense and mood, and the syntax of the clause. Authoritative and comprehensive, this much-needed survey will be welcomed by scholars and students of the Germanic languages, as well as linguists across the many branches of the field.

WAYNE HARBERT is Professor and Director of Undergraduate Studies in the Department of Linguistics, Cornell University. He has published extensively on syntactic topics, with a particular emphasis on historical syntax. His work on Germanic languages covers a wide range of problems in historical Germanic syntax and phonology, drawing on data from Gothic, Old English, Old High German, Old Saxon, Old Norse, and Modern German.

CAMBRIDGE LANGUAGE SURVEYS

General editors
P. Austin *(SOAS, London)*
J. Bresnan *(Stanford University)*
B. Comrie *(Max Planck Institute for Evolutionary Anthropology, Leipzig)*
S. Crain *(University of Maryland)*
W. Dressler *(University of Vienna)*
C. Ewen *(University of Leiden)*
R. Lass *(University of Cape Town)*
D. Lightfoot *(University of Maryland)*
K. Rice *(University of Toronto)*
I. Roberts *(University of Cambridge)*
S. Romaine *(University of Oxford)*
N. V. Smith *(University College, London)*

This series offers general accounts of the major language families of the world, with volumes organized either on a purely genetic basis or on a geographical basis, whichever yields the most convenient and intelligible grouping in each case. Each volume compares and contrasts the typological features of the languages it deals with. It also treats the relevant genetic relationships, historical development, and sociolinguistic issues arising from their role and use in the world today. The books are intended for linguists from undergraduate level upwards, but no special knowledge of the languages under consideration is assumed. Volumes such as those on Australia and the Amazon Basin are also of wider relevance, as the future of the languages and their speakers raises important social and political issues.

Volumes already published include
Chinese Jerry Norman
The Languages of Japan Masayoshi Shibatani
Pidgins and Creoles (Volume I: Theory and Structure; Volume II: Reference Survey) John A. Holm
The Indo-Aryan Languages Colin Masica
The Celtic Languages edited by Donald MacAulay
The Romance Languages Rebecca Posner
The Amazonian Languages edited by R. M. W. Dixon and Alexandra Y. Aikhenvald
The Languages of Native North America Marianne Mithun
The Korean Language Ho-Him Sohn
Australian Languages R. M. W. Dixon
The Dravidian Languages Bhadriraju Krishnamurti
The Languages of the Andes Willem Adelaar with Pieter Muysken
The Slavic Languages Roland Sussex and Paul Cubberley
The Germanic Languages Wayne Harbert

THE GERMANIC LANGUAGES

WAYNE HARBERT

CAMBRIDGE UNIVERSITY PRESS
Cambridge, New York, Melbourne, Madrid, Cape Town, Singapore, São Paulo

CAMBRIDGE UNIVERSITY PRESS
The Edinburgh Building, Cambridge CB2 2RU, UK

Published in the United States of America by Cambridge University Press, New York

www.cambridge.org
Information on this title: www.cambridge.org/9780521015110

© Wayne Harbert 2007

This publication is in copyright. Subject to statutory exception
and to the provisions of relevant collective licensing agreements,
no reproduction of any part may take place without
the written permission of Cambridge University Press.

First published 2007

Printed in the United Kingdom at the University Press, Cambridge

A catalogue record for this publication is available from the British Library

ISBN-13 978-0-521-80825-5 hardback
ISBN-10 0-521-80825-1 hardback
ISBN-13 978-0-521-01511-0 paperback
ISBN-10 0-521-01511-1 paperback

Cambridge University Press has no responsibility for the persistence or accuracy of URLs for external or third-party internet websites referred to in this publication, and does not guarantee that any content on such websites is, or will remain, accurate or appropriate.

to Myrlyn, Diane, and Jenny

CONTENTS

List of tables x
List of language abbreviations xi
Acknowledgments xii

1 Introduction 1
   1.1 Some remarks on the organization of this volume 1
   1.2 Divergence and convergence in the Germanic languages 6
      1.2.1 Germanic languages and Standard Average European 9
      1.2.2 Typological classification 12
   1.3 A survey of the Germanic languages 13
      1.3.1 East Germanic 14
      1.3.2 West Germanic 15
      1.3.3 The North Sea Coast languages 17
      1.3.4 North Germanic 19

2 The Germanic lexicon 21
   2.1 Loanwords 22
   2.2 Derivation 26
      2.2.1 Compounding 29
   2.3 Discourse particles 32
   2.4 Phrasal verbs 36

3 The sound systems of Germanic: inventories, alternations and structures 41
   3.1 Segmental inventories and alternations 41
      3.1.1 The obstruents: place and manner of articulation 41
      3.1.2 The sonorants 53
      3.1.3 The vowels 56
   3.2 The suprasegmental phonology of the Germanic languages 65
      3.2.1 Syllable structure and sonority 65
      3.2.2 Length 74
      3.2.3 Lexical stress and the foot in Germanic phonology 79
      3.2.4 Word tone in Germanic 84

viii   Contents

4   The Germanic nominal system: paradigmatic and syntagmatic variation   89
   4.1   Nominal inflection   89
      4.1.1   Historical prelude: Indo-European heritage and Germanic innovation   89
      4.1.2   Inflectional categories of the noun   91
   4.2   The internal structure of the nominal phrase   122
      4.2.1   Nominal phrases without nominal heads   122
      4.2.2   Nominal phrases with pronoun heads   124
      4.2.3   Nominal phrases headed by lexical nouns   126
   4.3   Determiners   137
      4.3.1   Weak quantifiers   137
      4.3.2   Definite articles   141
   4.4   Genitive phrases   148
      4.4.1   Genitive phrases and determiners   150
      4.4.2   Proper name possessors and pronominal possessors   155
      4.4.3   The English 'double genitive' construction   158
      4.4.4   The prenominal periphrastic possessive (*Jan se boek*) construction   158
      4.4.5   Special developments of the genitive in possessive constructions   161
      4.4.6   Meronymic constructions   164
   4.5   Predeterminers   167
   4.6   Discontinuous nominal phrases   168
   4.7   Adjective phrases   171
      4.7.1   Comparison   174
   4.8   Pronouns in the Germanic languages   175
      4.8.1   Personal pronouns   175
      4.8.2   The referential properties of pronouns   196
   4.9   The external syntax of noun phrases: subjects   214
      4.9.1   Subject agreement   214
      4.9.2   The typology and distribution of "expletive" arguments   224
      4.9.3   Subjects in imperative clauses   236
      4.9.4   Derived subjects and the syntax of voice   237
      4.9.5   Raising constructions   256

5   The verbal systems of Germanic: paradigmatic and syntagmatic comparison   270
   5.1   Historical prelude: the Indo-European heritage and Germanic innovations   270
      5.1.1   Types of verbal inflection   270
      5.1.2   Categories of verbal inflection: the Germanic tense/mood system and its Indo-European antecedents   272
   5.2   Modal auxiliaries   285
   5.3   Developments in the expression of tense in Germanic   292
      5.3.1   Identifying periphrastic tense/aspect constructions   293
      5.3.2   Future   297

    5.3.3   Perfect tenses and past tenses   301
    5.3.4   The meaning of the (present) perfect and the past   307
    5.3.5   Progressive   315
5.4 Voice inflections and voice auxiliaries   316
    5.4.1   Passive   317
    5.4.2   Middle voice   322
    5.4.3   The Scandinavian *s*-passive   327
5.5 Nonfinite verbal forms   329
    5.5.1   The infinitive   329
    5.5.2   The present participle and the English gerund   341
    5.5.3   The past participle and the supine   345
5.6 Verbal valency   347
5.7 Head, complement and adjunct placement in the verb phrase   350
    5.7.1   The relative order of the verb and its complements within the VP   353
    5.7.2   The order of objects   362
5.8 Phrasal verbs   366

6 The syntax of the clause   369
6.1 Sentence adverbs   370
6.2 The syntax of negation   376
    6.2.1   Some definitions: negation, scope and polarity   376
    6.2.2   Scope, polarity and syntactic position   377
    6.2.3   Polarity items, negative concord and multiple negation   379
    6.2.4   Negative complementizers and pleonastic negation   382
    6.2.5   Constituent negation with sentential scope   383
    6.2.6   On formal differences between sentential negators and constituent negators   392
    6.2.7   On the typology of sentential negation in Germanic   394
6.3 The syntax of the left periphery: topics, verb-second and subject/verb inversion   398
    6.3.1   Main-clause/subordinate clause asymmetries in verb position   400
    6.3.2   The triggers of verb-second order and the typology of V-2   404
6.4 Complementizers   415
    6.4.1   That-clauses   415
    6.4.2   Infinitive complements   417
6.5 Relative clauses, questions and other fronting constructions   420
    6.5.1   A typology of Germanic relative constructions   420
    6.5.2   Questions   473
    6.5.3   Topic constructions and left dislocation constructions   478

References   482
Index   505

TABLES

4.1 Adjective endings in selected Germanic languages   99
4.2 Definite articles/demonstrative adjectives in selected Germanic languages   106
4.3 Second person pronouns in selected Germanic languages   193
5.1 Inflectional endings of active strong verbs in selected Germanic languages   285

LANGUAGE ABBREVIATIONS

AF	Afrikaans		ME	Middle English
BN	Bokmål Norwegian		MHG	Middle High German
DA	Danish		NF	North Frisian
DU	Dutch		NN	Nynorsk Norwegian
EF	East Frisian		NO	Norwegian
EME	Early Middle English		OE	Old English
EN	English		OHG	Old High German
FA	Faroese		ON	Old Norse
FR	Frisian		OS	Old Saxon
GE	German		PG	Pennsylvania German
GMC	Germanic		SAE	Standard Average European
GO	Gothic		SW	Swedish
IC	Icelandic		WF	West Frisian
IE	Indo-European		YI	Yiddish

ACKNOWLEDGMENTS

I would like to thank Abby Cohn, Sarah Fagan, Roger Lass and Paul Roberge for their willingness to read and comment on portions of this work. It has benefitted substantially from their attention and advice. Thanks are also due to Jessica Bauman for her valuable assistance in the early stages, and to Steve Barganski for his thorough and expert copy-editing. I owe a special debt of gratitude to Diane Harbert, who, in addition to her constant support throughout this long project, devoted many hours to proofreading the manuscript, catching a multitude of errors in the process. I gladly accept responsibility for the probably numerous errors which remain.

1

Introduction

1.1 Some remarks on the organization of this volume

No single volume can adequately address a topic area as broad as "The Germanic Languages" in all of its aspects. It is necessary to single out a particular dimension on which to focus. Languages can be looked at in their societal context, for example, with attention to such questions as their use and significance in the communities of speakers who employ them, their relationship with the associated cultures (including, for example, literary uses), their demographics and their variation along geographical and demographical dimensions. One can alternatively regard language from a historical perspective, as chronological sequences of divergences and convergences, states and transitions. Each of these points of view has provided the organizational framework for successful volumes on the subject. It is also possible, abstracting away from their social, geographical, cultural and temporal contexts, to examine the languages of the family as assemblages of grammatical units, rule systems and constructions. This is the perspective which I will adopt here. The present volume is aimed primarily at those who are interested in how the Germanic languages are put together – what they have in common in terms of their linguistic organization and how they differ from each other structurally. That choice in turn determines several other features of the organization of the volume. In particular, I will not adopt the standard and often successful approach of covering the territory by means of a series of self-contained descriptions of individual languages. That encyclopedic approach is an ideal format for describing languages in their socio-cultural setting, since the demographic, historical, cultural and geopolitical situation of every language is unique. When the focus is on the grammatical structures, patterns and inventories of the languages, though, such an organizational model becomes less ideal. For one thing, it necessarily leads to a large amount of repetition. The Germanic languages are, after all, more alike than they are different, and this becomes increasingly true the farther one descends the genetic tree. Once one has read about the structure of the noun phrase in Swedish, for example, a description of the noun phrase in Danish will present few surprises. Such a format is also not conducive to side-by-side comparison of the ways in which the languages accomplish particular tasks, and so does not present a ready picture of structural commonalities and differences across the family. I have therefore decided to organize the discussion according to linguistic constructions and subsystems, rather than by languages. For example, there is a section on vowel systems, a section on the expression of future tense, and a section on relative clause formation, in each of which an individual Germanic language may be mentioned or not, depending on whether it offers something of particular interest in connection with the grammatical phenomenon under investigation. These decisions will no doubt make the volume less useful for readers with certain purposes. In particular, since it does not include chapters on individual Germanic languages, it does not provide a sense of how the grammars of individual languages work as integrated systems. Fortunately, there are other volumes suited to the interests of readers who want to inform themselves about the shape of individual Germanic languages. König and van der Auwera 1994 is particularly to be recommended. There are also volumes which approach these languages from a historical perspective – most notably, the recent volume by Howell, Roberge and Salmons (forthcoming). It is hoped that what is lost in the present treatment in terms of coherent pictures of individual languages is compensated for by a clearer family portrait.

A further practical consideration in favor of the present format is that it allows us to sidestep the thorny question of how many Germanic languages there are, and which varieties to devote chapters to. In volumes on language families in which the main aim is the exhaustive description of particular languages it is usual to single out a particular variety of each language as the object of that description. Most often, the written standard variety is chosen (even though linguists recognize the privileged position of standard languages to be largely a matter of historical accident), and nonstandard dialects are given relatively short shrift. Such an a priori limitation would simply not work in a study in which the main focus is the range of grammatical phenomena found in the Germanic languages, since, as we will be seeing, the family abounds in highly interesting and sometimes widespread linguistic developments which happen only to be found in nonstandard varieties. The standard languages show a relatively high degree of homogeneity, in part the result of their centuries of contact with each other and other Western European standard languages as languages of high culture and literature. The range of structural variation among these varieties is thus relatively small in comparison with that found when nonstandard varieties are taken into account. The division of the territory into, for example, a chapter on Dutch (represented by standard Dutch) and a chapter on German (represented by standard German) is arbitrary not only because of the substantial variation that exists within the individual languages, but also because of the famous fuzziness of the boundaries between languages in some cases. The Germanic languages include two notable dialect continua – the West Germanic dialect continuum, encompassing Belgium, the Netherlands, Germany, Switzerland and Austria, and the Scandinavian dialect continuum, encompassing Denmark, Sweden, Norway and parts of Finland – in which it is impossible to draw non-arbitrary language boundaries between neighboring varieties at any point (see Crystal 1987: 25).

There are also some more theoretical reasons for adopting the construction-by-construction approach followed here. While I have attempted as much as possible to keep linguistic theory in the background, this book is very much informed by the spirit of recent "principles and parameters" approaches to linguistic variation – the idea that languages are not free to differ from each other arbitrarily and without limit, but rather that linguistic variation is constrained by general parameters of variation, and that therefore structural differences across the languages of the family may be expected to be patterned, rather than random. The construction-by-construction, side-by-side format of the volume serves to highlight such patterns of variation as are found.

Once the decision was made to organize the presentation around patterns, paradigms and constructions, rather than around languages, no principled reason remained for including only the modern members of the family. If the book were an examination of languages in context, partitioning the Germanic languages according to the salient demographic property of having or lacking native speakers might make sense. Once the focus is on structure, though, separating them on the basis of this criterion seems plainly more arbitrary, since few structural differences correlate with this distinction. Whether a particular variety belongs to early Germanic or modern Germanic is not entirely unrelated to its structural characteristics; there are several features which unite the postmedieval members of the family, and distinguish them from the early medieval varieties. Some such differences arise by virtue of the fact that the later languages, but not the earlier ones, were around to participate in pan-European diffusions of such features as the distinction between formal and familiar forms of second person pronouns and indefinite articles. Others arise because the later languages, but not the earlier ones, participated in late parallel developments such as open syllable lengthening or the rise of medial negators. More often, though, the linguistic features which turn out to have general predictive value – whether a language is O(bject) V(erb) or VO, for example, or whether it has lexically case-marked arguments or not – are ones which crosscut the early Germanic/modern Germanic distinction. Therefore, it was decided for present purposes to treat both the pre-modern members of the family and the living members of the family on a par, to the extent possible – as different variants on a common theme. In treating Gothic and Old High German, for example, side-by-side with Afrikaans and Faroese, this volume differs from most other treatments of the Germanic languages.

The descriptions offered here are not theory-neutral; I doubt that it is possible to do linguistic description in a truly theory-neutral way. My particular training and inclination as a syntactician (working within the Government-Binding/Principles and Parameters tradition) necessarily informs my descriptions of particular phenomena, the kinds of explanations I offer for instances of variation (in which the assumption of parameters will play a prominent role, for example), and even, to an extent, the kinds of structures and phenomena singled out as worthy of description and explanation, as well as those left out of consideration. A scholar with a different theoretical orientation would imaginably have produced a somewhat different work. Nonetheless, an effort has been made to keep theoretical assumptions in the background in order to make the descriptions accessible to all readers with a background in linguistics, and to deploy theory-specific terminology only when it substantially contributes to the efficiency of the description.

The goals of the work are fundamentally synchronic: to identify and describe structural similarities and differences across the Germanic family. Nonetheless, it will be seen that discussion of linguistic history intrudes with some frequency. There are various reasons for this. For one thing, many of the accounts offered for the distribution of features across these languages are typological in nature. Many claims are made of the following sort: languages in a subgroup of the Germanic languages share a feature Y because they share a linked property Z from which the presence of Y follows. The validity of such typological linkages is supported by showing that they vary together over time – that when Y arises by historical change, Z appears too. Second, there are some shared features of the family or subgroups within it whose appearance and distribution can only be explained in historical terms: features which exist only because of historical facts of inheritance or borrowing. Some of the more interesting cases involve differences in the uses to which inherited "junk" (Lass 1988) are put. See, for example, the discussion of the weak/strong adjective contrast in Section 4.2.3.3 and the discussion of the development of the reflexive/nonreflexive possessive distinction in German (Section 4.8.2.1.1).

Discussions of phonology and the lexicon are accorded less space than the discussion of morphology and syntax. The particular choices made with respect to how much attention to give to each of these topics reflect, besides space limitations and the particular interests of the author, the fact that morphosyntactic aspects of the grammar are more amenable to the systematic contrastive treatment adopted here; their side-by-side investigation holds out the most promise of helping us to answer one of the central questions of the volume: In what systematic ways are the Germanic languages alike and in what ways different? Aside from prosodic phonology, it is difficult to make typological statements about the sounds or the vocabulary of the Germanic languages of comparable generality to those possible for the morphosyntax of these languages.

This book does not separate the treatment of morphology (or "accidence") from the treatment of syntax in the way that is familiar from most handbooks of Germanic languages. This fact, too, is related to its central goal of systematic, side-by-side comparison of the Germanic languages; there are numerous cases in which some languages in the family use inflectional morphology to encode particular structural relations among elements, while others avail themselves of syntactic means for this purpose. So, for example, Gothic and some of the Scandinavian languages have passive affixes – a matter of morphology – but these are functionally equivalent to the periphrastic passive markers of other languages in the family, which are syntactic in nature since they are free morphemes. Similarly, some of the languages of the family exhibit case inflections – a matter of morphology – but the same grammatical relationships which are encoded by means of these are encoded by means of free morphemes (in the form of prepositions) in other languages. Treating the two separately because one is a morphological phenomenon and the other a syntactic phenomenon would, of course, obscure the fundamental point of their functional equivalence. Instead, I have chosen a different organizational scheme, based on lexical classes. Chapter 4, for example, treats the morphosyntax of nouns and the other lexical categories (adjectives, determiners and pronouns) with which they are associated, and the syntax of the phrases in which these categories participate. Chapter 5 is devoted to verbs and their phrases. Within each of these discussions, there is a secondary division into a discussion of the paradigmatic properties of these lexical items followed by a discussion of their syntagmatic properties. Paradigmatic relationships are the relationships obtaining between an expression and other expressions which are substituted for it in different contexts. Case paradigms, and their prepositional phrase equivalents in languages without case (e.g., *the man, to the man, of the man*...) are instances of paradigmatic relationships. The syntagmatic relationships of a linguistic expression are the relationships which hold between it and non-equivalent expressions with which it is concatenated in forming larger linguistic expressions. The relationship between a subject and a verb, for example, is of this type. To a certain extent, this distinction overlaps with that between morphology and syntax, since, for example, case paradigms are a matter of morphology, and putting together a noun phrase and a verb phrase to form a sentence is a matter of syntax, but the two are not entirely isomorphic.

By its nature, a survey of this sort consists largely of reports of previous scholarship. This work owes a great debt to the centuries-long tradition of description of Germanic languages, and, in particular, to a recent spate of reference grammars and grammatical sketches of high quality for individual languages. The reader may find the following to be of particular interest: Allan *et al.* 1995; Bandle 2002, 2005; Booij 1995, 2002b; Braunmüller 1991; Collins and Mees 1996; Donaldson 1981, 1993; Engel 1988; Haugen 1982; Holmes and Hinchcliffe 1994; Jacobs 2005; Katz 1987; König and van der Auwera 1994; Kristoffersen 2000; Lass 1994; Lindow *et al.* 1998;

Lockwood 1995; Mitchell 1985; Tiersma 1999; Zifonun *et al.* 1997. However, the exercise of creating a construction-by-construction comparison of all of the Germanic languages (and attempting to fill in the considerable gaps in the available descriptions of the older languages in particular, as required by that exercise) has turned up occasional patterns and generalizations which had not been observed before.

1.2 Divergence and convergence in the Germanic languages

Germanic (hereafter, GMC) is, in the first order, a genetic concept. The GMC languages share many properties and constructions by virtue of common ancestry. Common inheritance is the reason, for example, that they signal inflectional contrasts by a mixture of suffixation and alternations in root vowel. It is also the reason that they have only a single inflectional past tense, and do not distinguish between preterite and imperfect, for example. The GMC languages share the first of these characteristics with other languages with which they are more remotely related, including the neighboring Celtic and Romance languages. The second, however, is a GMC innovation, which sets GMC apart from these other branches of Indo-European (IE), the larger family to which it belongs, including Celtic and Romance. Among the other distinguishing characteristics of the GMC languages which set them apart from their IE ancestor are:

- the fixing of the accent on the root or first syllable of the word (Section 3.2.3) and the possibly related tendency to reduce final syllables
- the incorporation of verbal nouns and verbal adjectives into the verbal paradigms as infinitives and participles
- the reduction of the system of inflectional tenses to a simple contrast between non-past and past and the possibly related tendency to introduce new periphrastic constructions for the expression of tense and aspect
- the introduction of a class of weak verbs, with "dental preterites"
- the systematization and restructuring of vowel alternations (ablaut) in the signaling of tense contrasts in the inherited strong verbs (Section 5.1)
- the reduction of the IE inventory of moods by conflation of the subjunctive and optative (5.1.2.2.1)
- the reduction of the inherited system of inflections for verbal voice and the consequent introduction of periphrastic passives (Section 5.4)
- the introduction of a strong/weak inflectional distinction in adjectives (4.2.3.3)
- the introduction of definite articles

1.2 Divergence and convergence in the Germanic languages

    the reduction of the IE case system to four core cases (nominative, accusative, dative, genitive, with occasional survivals of other cases) (4.1.2.3.1)
    the development of a productive class of so-called weak nouns, based on IE *n*-stems
    the introduction of relative pronouns (6.5.1.1) based on demonstrative and (secondarily) interrogative pronoun paradigms
    the introduction of verb-second word order (Section 6.3).

In some cases, the common inheritance of the GMC languages has taken the form of an inherited dilemma, to which the individual languages have responded with individual and original solutions. This is illustrated in the interesting example of the varied treatment of weak and strong adjective endings, for example, as discussed in 4.2.3.3.

Some of the GMC languages are more closely related than others. The precise nature of these genetic relationships has historically been a matter of dispute (see Nielsen 1989 for an overview of early GMC), but a very widely accepted hypothesis is that GMC first split into a Northwest GMC branch and an East GMC branch (represented almost solely by Gothic). The differences between the East GMC group and the Northwest GMC group are partly matters of regional variation. So, for example, IE final *-ō became -a in Gothic (*giba* 'I give'), but -u in Northwest GMC (Old High German *gibu* 'I give'). To some extent, though, they are matters of chronology. Many differences between East GMC and Northwest GMC reflect the fact that East GMC separated from the rest of GMC early and was recorded early, and so retains archaic features lost in the remaining languages (such as passive inflections and reduplicated verbs), and fails to participate in the later innovations in which those other languages took part.

Northwest GMC in turn is hypothesized to have split into a North GMC and a West GMC branch. The existence of a North GMC subgroup is beyond dispute, given the strong familial resemblance of its member languages to each other; these languages are the products of a very robust heritage of common innovation in all areas of grammar, which sets them apart from the rest of GMC, and the resemblances have been further reinforced by subsequent sustained contacts, with the result that there is still today a high degree of mutual intelligibility among them. The evidence for a West GMC genetic subgroup is more problematic, and has been called into question (though see Voyles 1971). On surer ground is the existence of a strongly innovative subgroup of West GMC languages, the North Sea Coast, or Ingvaeonic group, consisting of Anglo-Saxon, Frisian and Old Saxon, which share a number of features to the exclusion of German, their sister West GMC language. Among these features, perhaps the ones with the greatest systematic significance are the loss of person distinctions in the

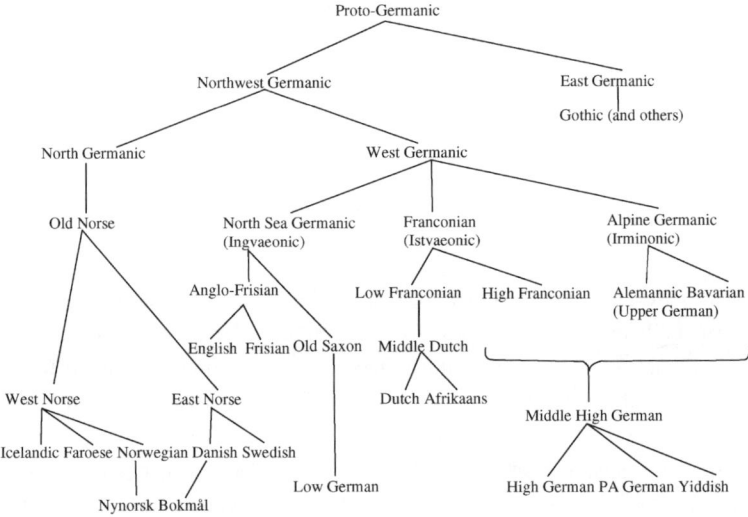

Figure 1.1 *The Germanic Family Tree*

plural verb, loss of case contrasts in part of the pronominal paradigms, and loss of GMC reflexive pronouns. Each of these will be discussed in Chapter 4.

The tree shown in Figure 1.1 gives a widely accepted, though not uncontroversial, picture of the genetic relationships among the GMC languages.

This tree sets forth a hypothesis about genetic relatedness, its branches graphically representing the order of divergence from a common ancestor ("the tree model"). Such tree diagrams do not give a complete picture of the interrelationships among them, though, and must be supplemented by another graphic device, such as the curly brackets used here. Similarities between languages are not always the result of common ancestry. Rather, originally separate varieties can converge over time through borrowing/areal spread of linguistic features across geographical space and linguistic boundaries (the "wave model"). In addition to shared ancestry, the GMC languages have remained geographically contiguous, creating the constant possibility of linguistic borrowing, mutual influence, and consequent convergence. For example, note that there is no single branch of the tree which dominates "German"; the German language (to the extent that it is a unitary language at all) is the product of centuries of mutual influence between originally separate West GMC linguistic groups. In a similar way, the varieties that we label "Low German," regarded now (in part for political reasons) as a variety of German, originated as a variant of Ingvaeonic West GMC – Old Saxon – which originally had more in common with Old English, but which has been

"Germanized" by successive waves of linguistic influence from the south. For early GMC, Rosel (1962) and Nielsen (1989) have reconstructed a complex history of periods of waxing and waning linguistic and cultural affinity between GMC subgroups, in order to account for the pattern of shared features. In later GMC, besides the interactions which gave rise to modern German, we can mention the mutual influence among the Scandinavian languages (particularly during the period of Danish hegemony beginning in the fourteenth century and lasting, in the case of Norwegian and Faroese, into the twentieth century), which resulted in a high degree of homogeneity at all levels, the possibly profound Norse influence on English beginning in the Old English period, which has been implicated in many of the features of Modern English but whose effect on the grammar of English is still awaiting a full evaluation, and the strong influence of Low German in late medieval times on the Scandinavian languages during the period of the Hanseatic league. The effect of the latter appears to been particularly strong in Danish, which in some respects (including phonology (Section 3.2.2) and syntax (Sections 4.9.4.1.2.2 and 4.9.5.2), for example) resembles German more than the other Scandinavian languages. In some cases, the effect of contact has been claimed not to be limited to direct borrowing, but to appear in grammar simplification/constructional loss, as a result of disrupted transmission of the language between generations (e.g., Norde 2001: 243; McWhorter 2002).

1.2.1 Germanic languages and Standard Average European

Such convergence by diffusion of linguistic features across boundaries is possible even when the languages in question are not related, or only remotely related. Vennemann, in a series of papers (Vennemann 2003a,b,c), has hypothesized such external influences from the very earliest period of GMC prehistory (see also Schrijver 2003). As a result of such contacts with neighboring languages, the GMC languages in modern times have been claimed to have become, in greater or lesser degrees, part of a group of "Standard Average European (SAE) languages," which share with other languages of north central Europe (notably Romance languages) a cluster of linguistic constructions to the exclusion of geographically more distant languages on the European periphery. Haspelmath (1998) discusses the eleven most compelling features of SAE, though suggesting that there are other, weaker ones. These are:

    a.   Definite and indefinite articles. This is, in fact, problematic as an SAE feature. While the GMC languages all exhibit definite articles, at least in an embryonic form (see Section 4.3), they share these not only with Romance, but with the Celtic languages, which are not part of the SAE cluster. On the other hand, while most of the modern GMC languages have indefinite articles in common with the Romance languages, these are demonstrably of late origin. They are not found in the earliest attested versions of these languages, nor yet in Modern Icelandic.

b. *Have*-perfects. All of the extensively attested GMC languages except Gothic have a periphrastic perfect formed with *have* plus a past participle – which they share with all of the Romance languages, as well as Czech and some Balkan languages.

c. All GMC languages, including Gothic, have a periphrastic passive formed with the past participle plus a verb of being or becoming (Section 5.4.1). They share this feature exclusively with the Romance and Slavic languages, according to Haspelmath.

d. Anticausative prominence. Languages make use of various means for deriving verbs from other verbs while changing their valency. In Gothic, for example, transitive/causative verbs sometimes involve additional morphology, relative to their intransitive counterparts (*wakan* 'to be awake' / *wak-j-an* 'to waken someone'), but sometimes intransitives are morphologically more complex than their transitive/causative counterparts. Included here are inchoatives with the inherited *-nan* suffix (*gaskaidnan* 'to divorce (intrans)' ~ *skaidan* 'to separate (trans)') and the apparently innovated reflexive middle verbs (*sik laisjan* 'to learn' – literally, 'to teach oneself'). Haspelmath claims that the derivation of intransitives from transitives (through the addition of "anticausative" morphology) is most frequent in German, French, Romanian, Russian, Greek and Lithuanian, while "causativization" – the derivation of transitives from intransitives – is more usual in neighboring non-SAE languages.

e. Nominative experiencers. In some languages the semantic argument roles of agent or actor are assigned to nominative subjects, and for semantic roles other than agent/actor (including roles such as experiencer and possessor) are represented by non-nominative nominal phrases (see Section 4.2.1.4.2). Thus, for example, in Scottish Gaelic, *I have a book* is expressed as *Tha leabhar agam* 'Is a book with-me', and *I like the book* is expressed as *Is toil leam an leabhar* 'Is pleasing with-me the book'. According to Haspelmath, the SAE languages, to a greater extent than neighboring languages, tend to realize these experiencer and possessor arguments, too, as nominative subjects, as English does. The fit of this feature with other hypothesized SAE features is quite loose, however. On the one hand, Basque and Turkish – not SAE languages by other standards – have a high proportion of nominative experiencers. On the other hand, Icelandic and Faroese have low ratios, and are thus excluded from the SAE fold.

f. Dative external possessors. In Romance, continental West GMC, Gothic, Balto-Slavic, Hungarian, Greek and Armenian, the possessor is expressed as a dative in certain kinds of possessive constructions (Gothic *afmaimait imma auso* 'he-cut-off him-Dat ear'). This construction is missing in non-SAE languages, but also in Modern English (see Section 4.4.6 and McWhorter 2002). Among the IE languages, it is lacking only in English and Insular Celtic, according to Vennemann (2003b: 356).

g. Many of the SAE languages, including Romance languages, GMC and Albanian, allow negated nominal phrases to carry the force of sentential negation (Gothic *ni waihts im* 'I am nothing'). The distribution of this possibility in GMC is explored in Section 6.2.5. It is found in all GMC languages except Old Saxon. Non-SAE languages tend to require a sentential negator, typically attached to the verb.

h. Particle comparatives. The SAE languages – including GMC (Section 4.7.1), Romance, Balto-Slavic, Balkan languages, Hungarian, Finnish and Basque, according to Haspelmath – characteristically make use of a "comparative particle" which is not a preposition, and thus does not affect the case of the following nominal (Gothic *frijondans wilja seinana mais þau guþ* 'loving their own will more than God-Acc'). Non-SAE languages use a variety of different devices.

i. A-and-B conjunction. Most European languages, according to Haspelmath, including the SAE languages, make use of an A-and-B construction for conjunction, as opposed to a variety of other devices (e.g., A-and B-and, A B-and) found elsewhere.

j. Relative clauses. Among the many strategies available for forming relative clauses (Section 6.5.1.5.1), the use of a strategy involving relative pronouns which occur at the front of the relative clause and encode the case number and person features of the relativized argument (Gothic *sunus meins, in þuzei waila galeikada* 'my son, in whom I am well pleased') is claimed by Haspelmath to be unique to SAE languages.

k. Verb fronting in polar questions. In GMC, Romance and Slavic languages and modern Greek, yes/no questions are formed by fronting the verb (Section 6.3.2), rather than by intonation or the use of a question particle.

This SAE hypothesis must be regarded with caution for a number of reasons. First, it is clear that the different hypothesized SAE features do not pick out the same subsets of languages. Second, they are attributable to widely different time periods. One of them – the external dative construction – is probably of IE date, as Haspelmath notes.

Others date from different prehistoric eras (Gothic, for example, has a periphrastic passive but no periphrastic perfect), while at least some others date from postmedieval times. This is true, for example, of indefinite articles, and the events which led to Icelandic and Swedish being on opposite sides of the fence with respect to nominative experiencers. The SAE constructions also sometimes differ in detail in the languages that share them, in ways which undermine the likelihood of common origin. GMC, for example, uses 'become' as the cardinal passive auxiliary, while Romance uses 'be', and it is not unimaginable that the two could have originated independently, starting out from copular sentences in which the predicate was a participle functioning as a stative adjective. Similarly, the core GMC relative pronouns are based on demonstrative pronouns while the relative pronouns of Romance are based on interrogative pronouns, and the syntactically comparable relative pronouns of ancient Greek appear to have been relative pronouns from the beginning (Fortson 2004: 130). Thus, we might be dealing here with three independent responses to the breakdown of the inherited correlative syntax of IE (see Section 6.5.1), especially in view of the difficulty of defending on other linguistic or historical evidence the existence of one or more eras of contact sufficient for diffusion of the construction to have taken place.

Other attempts have been made as well to account for features of subgroups of GMC, by diffusion of constructions across major language boundaries. Lindstedt (2000: 371) claims that the loss of simple past tense in some varieties of spoken German and the extension of present perfect to the expression of (imperfective) past tense is an areal development, encompassing southern German as well as northern Italian and spoken French.

1.2.2 Typological classification

In addition to genetic groupings, it is sometimes profitable to group the GMC languages typologically, according to structural properties – groupings which often crosscut genetic groupings, as well as each other. For example, it is proposed in Section 4.9.5 that those GMC languages which have developed V(erb)–O(bject) syntax have a wider range of "noun-phrase raising" constructions than OV languages, and in Section 5.7.1.1 it is observed that "verb-raising" is characteristic of the OV languages of GMC. It also appears that those languages which have lost morphological case contrasts in the noun phrase, whether VO (English, Swedish, Danish, Norwegian) or OV (Dutch, West Flemish, Frisian, Afrikaans), also have some properties in common to the exclusion of GMC languages with richer morphological case (see Section 5.7.2.1). Such instances are often viewed as the results of implicational linkages between grammatical properties, of the sort pursued in "principles-and-parameters" models of linguistic variation. Thus, in addition to sharing features by virtue of common inheritance, and by virtue of language contact/areal spread, some features shared by subsets of the GMC languages arguably arise as by-products of other typological commonalities.

English is in many respects a typological outlier in the GMC family. McWhorter (2002: 265) claims that "where a subset of GMC languages have departed sharply from the original GMC 'typology,' English never fails to be a member," and enumerates ten features with respect to which English deviates from all or virtually all the rest of GMC. These include the loss of inherent reflexives (in middle voice constructions, for example), the absence of external possessors (Section 4.4.6), the absence of gender (Section 4.1.2.2), the loss of GMC prefixes, the absence of a perfect construction with 'be', the absence of passives with 'become', differences in verb-second syntax (Section 6.3), the absence of a distinctively singular form of the second person pronoun (Section 4.8.1.5), and the loss of the indefinite pronoun *man*. McWhorter attributes these changes to disruption of intergenerational transmission during the Danish conquest.

1.3 A survey of the Germanic languages

Another dimension along which the GMC languages can be divided is the distinction between state and non-state languages. The GMC languages, relative to other language families of the world, include a high proportion of national languages. These include some varieties of English (hereafter EN), German (GE), Dutch (DU), Swedish (SW), Danish (DA), Norwegian (NO), Faroese (FA), Icelandic (IC), Afrikaans (AF) and Luxembourgish, as well as some English-based creoles (Tok Pisin in Papua New Guinea and Bislama in Vanuatu). Other GMC languages are non-state languages. These include Yiddish (YI), Pennsylvania German (PG), Schwyzertütsch, East Frisian (EF) and all of the varieties regarded as nonstandard "dialects" of the state languages (including some sufficiently remote from the standard variety that they would count as separate languages under different political circumstances). Intermediate in status is West Frisian (WF), which is officially the second language of the Netherlands, though according to Gorter *et al.* (2001: 111), this status has "only entailed moderate promotion by the state." Some varieties, such as Limburgisch in the Netherlands and North Frisian (NF) in Schleswig-Holstein, have official standing as "regional languages."

This accidental distinction between state and non-state languages is not unconnected with the internal shape of the language, since official recognition as a standard for public purposes usually brings with it greater normalization and regulation, the development of varying degrees of stylistic divergence between written and spoken varieties, and the articulation of the vocabulary in certain domains (e.g., technology and bureaucracy). It is also, of course, of very profound importance for their external histories and their viability over the long term; all of the non-state languages mentioned above are at considerable risk of extinction. With few exceptions (YI and PG), the situation of non-state GMC languages is made yet more problematic by the fact that they are sufficiently similar to the surrounding dominant languages that they tend to be dismissed as "mere dialects" of those languages, and denied recognition as independent languages, along with such prestige and consideration as comes with that status.

1.3.1 East Germanic

East GMC has no surviving members. It is represented mainly by Gothic (GO), preserved in sixth-century manuscripts of portions of a fourth-century Bible translation, eight leaves of a piece of biblical exegesis (named the *Skeireins* by its first editor) and scattered minor documents.[1] GO apparently survived as a liturgical language along the Danube into the ninth century, and a quite remarkable survival of GO into modern times was documented in the 1560s by Ferdinand Ogier de Busbecq, a Flemish diplomat, who recorded a word list of about a hundred items from informants from the Crimea (see Stearns 1978). GO is written in its own alphabet, based largely on that of Greek with possible influence from Latin and GMC runes, apparently devised by the bishop Wulfila, to whom the Bible translation is also attributed. Other East GMC languages are known only through meager onomastic evidence. The received view is that since the GO corpus consists mainly of highly faithful translations from Greek originals, it is of no value for the recovery of GMC syntax – a view which the present discussion will call into question.

Antonsen (1975: 24ff.) takes the position that Northwest GMC is recorded at roughly the same time (starting in the third century) in a broad area of northern continental Europe and southern Scandinavia, in the earliest GMC runic writing, though the identification of the language of these inscriptions as Northwest GMC has been disputed. Runic writing slightly antedated the first GO writing, and it is possible that Wulfila was familiar with it and made marginal use of it in devising his alphabet. The runic writing system, known as the *futhark* because of the canonical order of its first six characters, was based on western Mediterranean models. The corpus of inscriptions in the earliest runic writing system, the older *futhark*, though scant, is of great importance for our understanding of GMC. Although GO is frequently cited for its archaic nature, it has in fact deviated from common GMC relatively far in comparison to the roughly contemporary language recorded in the

---

[1] In the present work, all citations from the Gothic Bible, as well as their Greek equivalents, are taken from the edition of Streitberg 1960.

brief epigraphic documents in the older *futhark* – particularly with respect to the preservation of vowels in unstressed syllables. I will cite here where possible only examples in the earliest period of the older *futhark*, which Antonsen labels Northwest GMC, though I will refer to them more neutrally as Runic GMC. The runic *futhark* writing tradition persisted long after the separation of the Northwest GMC languages, surviving in modified forms in the Anglo-Saxon *futhorc* in which the earliest EN literature is recorded, and the younger *futhark*, which remained in use in Scandinavian countries until modern times.

1.3.2 West Germanic

The individual languages of the West GMC group are the next attested, Old English (OE) and Old High German (OHG) being documented from roughly the eighth century, and Old Saxon (OS) in the ninth century, Frisian (FR) and DU from still later periods.

1.3.2.1 *German and its siblings*

Standard GE is conventionally referred to as (New) High GE. The qualifier 'High' is a topographical term, referring to those varieties spoken in the relatively higher elevations of the south, as opposed to the low-lying plains of northern Germany. Linguistically, the two varieties are most saliently distinguished by the fact that High GE varieties participated in all or part of the consonant changes known as the High German consonant shift (Section 3.1.1.3). In fact, the various dialects of GE can be arrayed on a cline according to the degree to which they participated in these changes. They are most fully implemented in the Alpine dialects in Swabia, Bavaria, Austria and Switzerland, but carried through less consequently in the Franconian dialects, and not at all in the Low GE dialects. Thus, dialectologists speak broadly of Upper GE, Middle GE, and Low GE dialects. Standard GE is based largely on Middle GE (Franconian) dialects, whose phonology it reflects. The Upper GE dialects and the Franconian dialects were originally separate branches of West GMC, which have coalesced over the centuries into a (partial) linguistic unity through mutual linguistic influence. Low GE arose from OS, a North Sea Coast language, and still reflects this origin in some ways – for example, in the single form of verb endings for all persons in the plural. Partly in consequence of its heterogeneous origins, GE is much more dialectally diverse than any of the other modern GMC languages. Gordon (2005) reports that the Mainfrankish dialect and the Swabian dialect, for example, are only about "40% inherently intelligible with Standard GE."

GE is conventionally divided into three chronological periods: Old High German (OHG), from the earliest attestation (eighth century) to the end of the eleventh century,

Middle High German (MHG), from the eleventh century to the end of the sixteenth century, and Modern GE (NHG), from the end of the sixteenth century. The original literature for the first of these is relatively small, becoming quite voluminous in later periods. The various varieties of GE have about 100,000,000 speakers, constituting the largest linguistic community in Western and Central Europe. Standard GE is the official language in Austria (7.5 million), Germany (78 million), Liechtenstein, one of four official languages in Switzerland (4 million), where a majority speaks Swiss GE (Schwyzertütsch), and one of four official languages in Luxembourg. It is also spoken among minority populations in central and eastern Europe and northern Italy. The largest number of GE speakers outside Europe is in the USA, where there are as many as 1.5 million speakers.

Two other West GMC languages, YI and PG are basically of Middle GE origin, as demonstrated by the degree of their participation in the High German Consonant shift, though the facts of YI are complex. The precise date and dialect of the GMC source of YI, and the question of whether it is most appropriately characterized as a West GMC language or as a "fusion language" are addressed in Jacobs 2005: 9ff. A main dialect division arose between those varieties spoken in GMC-speaking countries (Western YI) and those spoken in the Slavic countries to the east (Eastern YI). Western YI declined due to linguistic assimilation to GE, and the vast majority of YI speakers speak Eastern varieties. There are four major modern dialects of YI: Western, Central, Northeastern and Southeastern, Standard YI reflecting features of the latter two (Jacobs *et al.* 1994: 390). YI is written in the Hebrew alphabet, and is thus the only modern GMC language not written in Roman letters. (Examples in the present work are given in transliteration, following the conventions of the particular source from which the examples are cited.) YI is spoken by about 5 million people, in New York, Israel, Melbourne, Montreal, Mexico City and Buenos Aires (Jacobs 2005: 3). It is not an official language in any of the countries in which it is spoken, and not a majority language in any geographical area larger than individual neighborhoods, though it has achieved stable bilingualism in many of these areas, as the language of ultraorthodox Jewish communities (Fishman 2001).

PG (Pennsylvanisch, sometimes referred to in EN colloquially and inaccurately as Pennsylvania Dutch) was introduced into North America beginning in the early eighteenth century. It has maintained itself most robustly as the community language of Old Order Mennonite and Old Order Amish communities, in which spheres it has also achieved a relatively stable bilingualism. It resembles most the Frankish dialects of GE. There are 2 to 3 million speakers of PG in Canada, the United States, Central and South America.

Luxembourgish (Luxembourgeois, Letzeburgisch), also a Moselle Franconian dialect in origin, is the national language in Luxembourg, and spoken natively by a large majority there (300,000), with small populations in Belgium and France. It is not much used for written communication, in which domain French and GE are used instead.

Limburger, or Limburgs Plat, a Middle Franconian language, more or less mutually intelligible with Ripuarian dialects of GE, according to Gordon (2005), is spoken by around 1.5 million people in the provinces of Limburg in the Netherlands and Belgium, having official status as a regional language in the former.

1.3.2.2 Dutch and its siblings

DU (Nederlands) is the descendant of Old Low Franconian – that is, that portion of Franconian West GMC which did not undergo the High German consonant shift – though it also shows the effects of contact with Ingvaeonic languages. Reflecting the linguistic complexity of northwestern coastal Europe, DU has a wide range of dialects, with sometimes rather low mutual intelligibility. Chronologically, DU is divided into Old DU (to 1150), of which only scant records exist, Middle DU, from 1150 to 1500, which is represented by a very substantial original literature, and Modern DU, since 1500. DU is currently spoken by about 21 million people in Europe – 15 million in the Netherlands and 6 million in Belgium. The variety spoken in Belgium is often called Vlaams (Flemish), and listed by Gordon (2005) as a separate language, though it is not generally so treated. DU is also an official language in former DU colonies in Surinam and the DU Antilles, and is spoken in Indonesia as well.

AF originated from DU dialects, transplanted to southern Africa in the seventeenth century, though it has been transformed by massive effects of language contact, and is, besides EN, the GMC language which deviates grammatically the farthest from the others. It is spoken by about 6 million people, and is one of the official languages of the Republic of South Africa (co-official with EN, Ndebele, Southern and Northern Sotho, Swazi, Tsonga, Tswana, Venda, Xhosa and Zulu), and Namibia.

1.3.3 The North Sea Coast languages

FR (Frysk), an Ingvaeonic or North Sea Coast language closely akin to EN in its origins, is spoken by about 750,000 people in the Netherlands and Germany, constituting the language of about 4% of the inhabitants of the former (Gorter *et al.* 2001: 103). FR has four dialects with low mutual intelligibility. WF, in northern coastal Holland, is spoken by about 400,000 people, and has a literary standard (Hoekstra and Tiersma 1994: 506). Northern FR is spoken in Schleswig-Holstein and adjacent islands in northern Germany by about 10,000 people. Eastern FR is spoken in a small region in northwestern Germany near the Dutch border by a very few speakers (1000, according to Hoekstra and Tiersma 1994: 505, though Gordon (2005) gives a much higher figure). The three varieties are not mutually intelligible, and, for that matter, there is not full mutual intelligibility among the various dialects of NF. The earliest FR texts are from the second half of the thirteenth century. FR is officially recognized as the second language of the Netherlands, where it has status in law and education. Northern FR has some official status as a regional language in Schleswig-Holstein.

OS is represented by the important ninth-century epic poem *Heliand*, based on the New Testament, and a probably related fragmentary poetic retelling of Genesis, as well as minor documents. In the Middle Ages, one of the successors of OS, Middle Low GE, developed considerable prestige as the language of the Hanseatic League, and had significant linguistic influence on the continental Scandinavian languages. It has, however, declined quite markedly in status since then; none of the modern offshoots of OS is a state language, and they are, in fact, now widely regarded as dialects of the surrounding dominant languages, in spite of their separate origin and the fact that they are often not intelligible to speakers of the standard varieties of those dominant languages. Because of the lack of official status and perception as autonomous languages, they are highly subject to attrition in favor of the surrounding language. According to Lindow *et al.* (1998: 20), the ability to speak Low GE (Niederdeutsch, Plattdüütsch) ranges from 46% to 64% in different areas of Low GE territory. The "Low Saxonian" varieties of northeastern Holland, in which Ingvaeonic was historically a major constituent, are also regarded as DU dialects (de Schutter 1994: 441), though there has been an effort to achieve official recognition for them like that accorded to Limburger (see the listings for Stellingwerfs, Twents and Veluws in Gordon 2005).

EN, also a West GMC language in origin, stands out from the rest of the family in a number of ways, lexically, grammatically and demographically. In the lexicon, EN has absorbed massive amounts of non-native vocabulary, particularly from Romance languages (French and Latin), and it has developed a habit of forming neologisms from non-native elements to a much greater extent than other languages of the family (see Chapter 2). In terms of grammar, as noted in Section 1.2.2, it has also innovated to a much greater extent than other GMC languages. EN also holds a unique demographic position within the family and, indeed, among the languages of the world, in that it is more widely spoken than any other language (though exceeded by Mandarin Chinese in the number of native speakers). Exact numbers are hard to come by. According to one estimate, 350 million people speak EN natively, and another 350 million make significant use of it as a second language. Other estimates are provided in McArthur 2002: 3. It is also a global lingua franca in a number of domains. For example, air traffic controllers use EN as their common language of communication worldwide. Crystal (2003: 109) lists seventy-five countries in which EN plays an important role, as the majority language, an official language or as a major language in education, commerce or some other domain.

1.3.4 North Germanic

The North GMC languages have remained relatively homogeneous for a longer time than West GMC languages, and differences tend to be gradual, rather than abrupt. Haugen (1982: 3) expresses the view that "Scandinavia may be looked on as a single speech continuum." Characteristics of Common Scandinavian, distinct from those of West GMC, begin to emerge around 550 AD, according to Haugen (1982: 5), and the linguistic differentiation of the individual dialects begins to be evident from around 1150 AD, the earliest division being between a West Norse group, represented by IC, FA and NO, and an East Norse group, represented by SW and DA. The linguistic separation of SW and DA began as recently as 1300 AD. Though Scandinavian manuscripts are relatively late compared to those of West GMC, the runic inscriptions in the older *futhark* after c. 550 AD and the younger *futhark* after c. 800 AD provide a continuous though scant record of linguistic development. In later medieval times, the North GMC branch is represented by the very rich original literature of Old Norse (ON) (a normalized version of Old IC and Old NO), which, in spite of its name, is contemporary with the middle period of such West GMC languages as EN and GE. On typological grounds, the modern North GMC languages can be divided into a conservative Insular North GMC group, represented by IC and FA, and an innovative group, represented by the continental Scandinavian languages – SW, NO and DA. This classification crosscuts the earlier division into Western and Eastern North GMC; NO, which, like IC, is a Western North GMC language in origin, has come to show a marked typological resemblance to SW. The continental group in general has converged to a remarkable degree, and investigators remark on the high degree of mutual intelligibility among them (Haugen 1982: 18), though Haberland (1994: 316) notes that the sound system of DA presents something of an obstacle to this possibility of "inter-Scandinavian semi-communication."

IC (Íslenzka), the official language of Iceland, with 250,000 speakers, is the most grammatically conservative of the modern North GMC languages – indeed, of the modern GMC languages in general. Such dialect differences as exist are very slight.

FA (Føroysk) is spoken by 50,000 people in the Faroe Islands, where it is an official language, joining DA in that status in 1948. It resembles IC more than any other language, though it has changed phonologically and inflectionally to a greater extent than the former. It is also much more varied in its spoken forms.

SW (Svensk) is the native language of over 8 million people in Sweden, and 300,000 in southern and western parts of Finland. It is an official language in both countries, sharing that status with Finnish in Finland.

NO (Norsk) has two different, co-official written standard varieties – Bokmål 'book language' (hereafter, BN) or Riksmål (earlier Dano-Norwegian (Haugen 1982: 16)) and Nynorsk 'New Norwegian', or Landsmål (hereafter, NN) – the former based on written DA and the DA-influenced speech of NO upper classes and the latter on rural dialects of NO little influenced by DA (Haugen 1982: 16). 83% of Norwegians receive primary education in BN, and 17% in NN (Askedal 1994: 221). The total population of NO speakers is about 4 million. All NO dialects are mutually intelligible (Askedal 1994: 221).

DA (Dansk) is an official language in Denmark, the Faroe Islands (together with FA) and Greenland (together with Kalaallisooq), with about 5 million speakers. Gordon (2005) attributes the view to Norbert Strade that the Jutish dialect, spoken in Jutland near the GE border, is sufficiently different from Standard DA that "from the viewpoint of intelligibility, it could be considered a separate language."

2

The Germanic lexicon

The focus of this chapter is in fact considerably narrower than the title might suggest. The study of the lexicons of languages is a multifaceted pursuit. The words of a language are the interface between its internal aspect, as a cluster of linguistic systems, and its external aspect, as a way of encoding and cataloguing the experiences of its speakers (Lass 1994: 178). Study of the lexicon thus straddles the study of purely linguistic aspects of language and the more general study of culture, since the vocabularies of languages are shaped by and reflect the intellectual and material culture in which their speakers function. Both of these are worthwhile undertakings. Much can be learned about the developmental histories of societies by studying the ways in which their vocabularies change over time. Indeed, in the case of cultures no longer extant, language often provides prospects for a reconstruction of the life of the mind which is finer-grained and more nuanced than what is possible through the more ambiguous and indirect evidence of physical remains and artifacts. The GMC languages in particular possess rich and multilayered lexicons which, when carefully examined, can generate an intricate picture of contacts, events, influences and cultural trends spanning millennia, even in the absence of a direct historical record. However, the focus of the present volume is on the GMC languages as systems and structures, and in keeping with that focus I will forego discussion of the possibilities for linguistic archaeology which the GMC lexicon affords, and concentrate exclusively on its more purely linguistic aspects – on the processes of word formation and the ways in which the shape of the lexicon and changes in the lexicon affect the other linguistic subsystems of the language. Loanwords, for example, will be of interest here not for their cultural and historical import, but for the ways in which the linguistic systems of individual languages have responded to them – the degree to which they are integrated into the phonological and morphological patterns of the language, the degree to which they carry over characteristics of their origin, and, in the latter case, the effects they have had on the shape of the language (for example, in adding new segments to the sound system, in altering patterns of stress assignment, or in disrupting the transparency, productivity or generality of word-formation processes).

Even within this narrowly defined domain, only certain word classes and word-formation processes have been singled out for description, selected on the basis that they are in some way typical of the family. A thorough examination of the structure of the lexicon in GMC languages would take far more space than is available here. Instances of one particular kind of lexical development, that of "grammaticization" (the rise of grammatical function words), are treated severally under the appropriate chapters on morphosyntax. So, for example, case-marking prepositions, definite and indefinite articles are treated in the chapter on nouns and noun phrases, while modal verbs and infinitive markers are treated in the chapter on verbs and verb phrases.

The chapter will conclude with a discussion of two categories of lexical items particularly characteristic of the GMC languages: discourse particles and phrasal verbs.

2.1 Loanwords

Much of the core vocabulary of the GMC languages is of IE origin, as are their basic modes of word formation. However, from the beginning, borrowing from other languages has been among the ways in which the GMC languages have acquired new words. A substantial portion of the common GMC vocabulary is not transparently of IE origin. A partial list of such words is given in Lass 1994: 181–182. It is possible that some of these words simply have non-obvious IE etymologies (see, for example, Orel 2003), but several of them belong to specific areas of endeavor (*boat*, *sea*, *sail*, *ship*, *sheep*, *lamb*, *calf*, *plow*) and may mark the borrowing of new words along with technologies. These words, if in fact they are borrowings, were fully integrated into inherited inflectional paradigms. The verb *drink*, for example, listed by Lass as non-IE, nonetheless assumed the inherited mode of tense formation through alternation in internal vowels (ablaut). See Bammesberger 1986, 1990, Heidermanns 1993 and Casareto 2004 for a discussion and exhaustive listing of the membership of major word classes in Common GMC.

From the time of these early loans, all of the GMC languages have continued to take new vocabulary from neighboring languages, at different rates, in different forms and from different sources. Main episodes of borrowing have included the following:

    a. Common GMC adopted a number of words from its Italic and Celtic neighbors in prehistoric times, and the individual languages adopted relatively large amounts of Latin vocabulary in early medieval times with the rise of monastic culture. The GO Bible contains numerous words taken from Greek, though it is unclear to what extent these in fact achieved the status of loanwords.

2.1 Loanwords 23

b. OE adopted large numbers of Scandinavian vocabulary items during the period of Danish invasions beginning in the ninth century, though these do not usually appear in writing until the Middle English (ME) period because of the way they were distributed geographically. These Scandinavian loans are unusual in that they involve items which are not typically borrowed – everyday, low-prestige terms, and even some function words and grammatical formatives.

c. Subsequent to the Norman Conquest, vast numbers of Norman French words entered the EN lexicon. Other GMC languages, too, including GE, have drawn heavily on French, beginning in medieval times. The items in question are typically high-prestige vocabulary. Belonging to a different register are the numerous French borrowings for everyday words appearing in West Flemish, as discussed in Haegeman 1992 and the references discussed there, which, like the Scandinavian loans in EN, evidence a different sort of language-contact situation.

d. The Scandinavian languages drew heavily on Middle Low GE vocabulary beginning in the late twelfth century and reaching a peak during the period of the Hanseatic League, from approximately the thirteenth to the sixteenth centuries (including a number of Latinate words which came into these languages through Middle Low GE) – see especially Bandle *et al.* 2002: 955. This was followed during the Renaissance by a period of borrowing from High GE, under the influence of the Reformation.

e. FA has adopted large numbers of DA words. This tendency is resisted officially; the DA borrowings are discouraged in writing and not recognized by dictionaries, for example, giving rise to a wide discrepancy in vocabulary between spoken and written registers (Barnes 1994: 216; Bandle *et al.* 2005: 1583).

f. YI has drawn extensively on the vocabularies of Hebrew and Slavic languages.

g. All of the GMC languages have taken part in the diffusion of the increasingly international vocabulary of such fields as technology, commerce and politics.

h. In the twentieth and twenty-first centuries, all of the other GMC languages have been under the expanding influence of the EN lexicon.

Particularly in modern times, the borrowing of foreign vocabulary has become ideologically loaded, leading to alternating periods of receptiveness to direct borrowing and resistance to it. Representing the poles of the spectrum among the modern languages are EN, on the one hand, which has developed a vocabulary considerably more extensive than that of the other GMC languages by massive overt borrowing, and which seems inclined to build its neologisms by using formatives from the classical languages (Greek and Latin), and, on the other, IC, in which there is strong resistance to the introduction of foreign elements into the lexicon. Thráinsson (1994: 188) characterizes the IC situation as follows:

> The Modern Icelandic lexicon is relatively free of unassimilated loanwords . . . there is a strong and conscious effort to create new words from Icelandic for new concepts, for example in science and technology. Many professional societies have their own language committees that meet regularly to discuss proposed neologisms or to try to come up with new ones.

> The methods used in coining new words include translation of the foreign word bit by bit, compounding of existing nouns, derivation by productive derivational affixes, creation of new roots and assimilation of foreign words to the Icelandic sound and inflectional systems. Sometimes old words are also given new meanings.

In the latter category, Thráinsson cites *sími* 'telephone'←*síma* 'thread', *tölva* 'computer'←*tala* 'number', *útvarp* 'radio'←*út* 'out' + *varpa* 'throw'.

It should be pointed out that the cases just cited from IC do in fact involve a type of borrowing; languages need to add new vocabulary as new concepts come to require linguistic expression, and among the strategies deployed at various times in the GMC languages by way of balancing this need for new words with the resistance to foreign elements has been such covert borrowing – borrowing the lexical concept, as IC, has done, but not the phonological shape of the word which would identify it as foreign. Such covert borrowing takes the form of calques, or loan translations, in which the template for formation of the word is adopted, but native morphemes substituted for foreign ones. This phenomenon has existed (side-by-side with straightforward borrowing) from the earliest times. So, for example, GO borrows *aiwaggeli* 'gospel' and *aiwlaugia* 'benefaction' directly from Greek *eu-angélion* and *eu-logía*, but translates *eu-genés* 'well born' as *goda-kunds*. OE (and other early GMC languages) had a decided preference for loan translations. This can be seen by comparing the OE and the Modern EN counterparts to the following Latin words (examples in part from Lass 1994).

(2.1)

	Latin	OE	Mod EN
	misericordia	mildheortness 'mildheartness'	mercy
	circumcidere	ymbsníþan 'around-cut'	circumcise
	illuminatiō	inlīhtnis 'inlight-ness'	illumination/enlightenment
	trinitas	þrīnis 'three-ness'	trinity
	longanimus	long-mōd 'long-mood'	patience
	unanimus	āñ-mōd 'one mood'	unanimous

Other languages, too, exhibit historical fluctuation between direct borrowing and covert borrowing. GE, for example, which borrowed extensively from French in previous eras, experienced a period of relative linguistic purism in the seventeenth and eighteenth centuries, borrowing the names of new chemical elements during that era, for example, as loan-translations (*Wasserstoff* 'water-stuff', from French/neo-Greek *hydrogène*, *Sauerstoff* 'sour-stuff', from French *oxygène*). In Modern DA the EN terms *landslide victory*, *nuclear family* and *think tank* are calqued as *jordskredssejr*, *kernefamilie* and *tænketank* respectively (Allan *et al.* 1995: 556).

Calquing is one of the means languages make use of for nativizing borrowings, by integrating them into native lexical, phonological and inflectional patterns. In addition, direct borrowings containing non-native sounds are typically remade by way of substituting the closest native sound ("phonological nativization," Hock 1986: 390). Hock, for example, cites the substitution of /k/ for /x/ in EN borrowings from GE. The /u:/ of GO *Rumoneis*, from Latin *Rōmāni* is claimed to result from the fact that, at the time of the borrowing, GO had no closed /o:/ sound like that of Latin, and the GO /u:/ was perceived as the closest substitute. Phonological nativization also manifests itself in the adaptation of borrowings to the prosodic patterns of the language, as reflected, for example, in the accent shift which has taken place in IC *stúdent*, *prófessor*. Borrowed forms are also typically nativized inflectionally, by combining them with the (least marked) inflectional affixes of the language. Aside from possible early instances like *drink*, for example, which form their tenses by ablaut, verbs are almost invariably borrowed into the GMC languages as weak verbs, which form their past tenses by the more usual means of adding a dental suffix. Inflectional nativization is normally quite systematic; among inflectional affixes, only plural markers are sometimes carried over from the source language, as in EN *stratum~strata*, GE *Thema~Themata*, SW *gangster~gangsters*, DU *museum~musea*. Even in these cases, the borrowed plural formation tends to be replaced by an unmarked native one in time. Thus, GE also has *Themen*, SW also has *gangstrar-na* 'the gangsters' (Holmes and Hinchcliffe 1994: 27), and DU also has *museums* (Booij 2002b: 29).

One particular problem faced in the nativization of nouns borrowed into some GMC languages is what gender to assign to them. This problem has been particularly thoroughly studied with respect to loanwords in GE (Reed 1942; Arndt 1970; Carstensen 1980; Gregor 1983; Schlick 1984; Köpke and Zubin 1995; Hickey 2000). Some general strategies emerge. Interestingly, even when the source language has a system of grammatical gender, the gender of the noun in the source language does not seem to play a role in determining its gender in the borrowing language. Hock (1986: 402), for example, notes that GE *Garage* is feminine (as are all nouns ending in *–age*), even though its French source is masculine. Typically, borrowed nouns are assigned their gender on the basis of the gender of semantically similar native nouns. Berger *et al.* (1972: 206) cite GE

Chanson, feminine in French but neuter in GE because of the synonymous *das Lied* 'the song', *High Society*, feminine in GE because of *die Gesellschaft*, and *der Star*, masculine because of *der Stern*. Holmes and Hinchcliffe (1995: 12) cite SW *ett team, ett jobb, ett game*, all neuter because of the neuter gender of the synonymous native nouns *ett lag, ett arbete, ett spel*. In other cases, the assignment is based on the shape of the noun, not always in a way that has a basis in native principles of gender assignment. For example, in SW, foreign loans ending in *-ek, -em* and *-iv* are neuter (*ett bibliotek* 'the library', *ett system, ett adjektiv*) (Holmes and Hinchcliffe 1995: 6). In GE, nouns in *-age* or *-tion* are feminine (*die Frustration*), while nouns in *-ing* are neuter (*das Happening*). Where none of these strategies leads to a single result, there can be uncertainty and fluctuation in gender assignment (GE *der* or *das Joghurt, der, die* or *das Dschungel*), though there seems to be some evidence for default gender preferences, which may vary across the GMC languages (see Section 4.1.2.2).

On the other hand, borrowings are sometimes not fully nativized, particularly in instances in which they are very numerous, or where the retention of foreign features is favored by prestige. Such cases can lead to importation of non-native linguistic features, and consequent modification of the linguistic system. Most of these effects have involved marginal, local introductions of new sounds. GO, for example, exhibits a high front rounded vowel, represented as <w>, but only in Greek words (*swnagoge* 'synagogue', *hwssopon* 'hyssop-Dat'). ME adds /ʒ/ from French, as does MHG. GE /dʒ/ also occurs only in foreign loans (*Dschungel*), and some varieties of YI have adopted palatalized consonants from Slavic (Jacobs *et al.* 1994: 394). Most of the time, these sorts of developments remain restricted to the forms with which they are borrowed.

Borrowing of foreign words has also introduced new derivational affixes into the GMC languages. While many of these too remain confined to the non-native vocabulary, they can on occasion become more productive, combining with native roots. This is the case with the GE verbal suffix *-ieren*, as in *buchstabieren* 'to spell' and the GO agent noun suffix *-areis*, from Latin *-arius*, as in *bokareis* 'scribe'.

Some of the effects of wide-scale borrowing are less specific. In EN, for example, Romance influence (on literary tradition, as well as word formation) is linked to the loss in ME of the metaphorical compounds (*kennings*) which so characterized OE literary language. To the massive borrowing of Romance forms may also be traced the current preference for borrowing or building new words from foreign elements, rather than native elements, with the consequent loss of the transparency in the lexicon to which Lass has alluded (see the next Section).

2.2 Derivation

The inherited devices for word derivation in GMC consisted of prefixes and suffixes, sometimes working in conjunction with internal modifications of the root (ablaut – see

Section 5.1.1). Since words in GMC (and IE) are right-headed, suffixes determine the category of the word. Thus we use suffixes to effect a change of lexical category – for example, from a verb to a noun. Prefixes can be grammatically active too, though, in the sense that they can change the valency and case-government of the forms to which they are attached. So, for example, GO *gaggan* 'to go' is an intransitive verb, while *miþgaggan* 'to accompany' takes a dative object. In GE, the prefix *be-* is found frequently as a transitivizer (*leben* 'to live', *beleben* 'to animate').

In general, the inherited derivational prefixes of GMC have survived better than the suffixes, in large part for phonological reasons connected with the fixing of the stress accent of GMC on syllables at the beginning of the word (see Section 3.2.3). Thus, for example, most of the prefixes found in GO (*ga-, fra-, un-*, as well as a large inventory of prepositions which function as prefixes) are cognate to prefixes still found in modern GE and DU. The North GMC languages and EN, however, for reasons that probably do not have to do with phonological change, have lost many of these; as Heusler (1967: 40) points out, true (unstressed) prefixes were generally lost in ON. McWhorter (2002: 232) observes that in EN the former prefixes *be-, ge-*, and *for-* (as in OE *sēon* 'to see', *besēon* 'to look at', *winnan* 'to toil', *gewinnan* 'to win') whose counterparts in other West GMC languages are frequent and partly productive (AF *verafrikaans* 'to Afrikaansify'), have been given up as well.

IE had a very extensive inventory of derivational suffixes. These were added to roots, rather than to words. That is, the base-forms to which they were attached did not appear in an unaffixed form as independent words. The subsequent history of this inventory in the GMC languages, as Lass (1994: 199) notes, has been one of fairly steady decline. Suffixes have undergone phonological reduction and modification, which, even when not resulting in total loss, have often rendered them unrecognizable as derivational morphemes. This effect has often been reinforced by the loss of contrasting, derivationally related forms whose existence would have served to make it easier to identify the affixes. The fact that *mind, birth, seed, need, deed, gift, might* all share a common (pre-)GMC suffix, for example, and *death, flood, ground, greed, lust, thought, thirst* another one (Casaretto 2004: 496ff., 522ff.) is no longer part of our sense of relatedness among lexical items.

Among verbs, at least, the system of inherited derivational affixes, if no longer productive, was at least partially transparent in the earliest attested GMC.[1] In GO, for example, there were such clear alternations as that among a strong durative verb *wakan* 'to be awake', the intransitive inchoative weak verb *(ga-)wak-nan* 'to become awake' and the transitive causative weak verb *(us-)wak-jan* 'to wake someone'. A similar

---

[1] Clear evidence for productivity, such as might be provided by the extension of these suffixes to recent borrowings, is slight; Gothic does borrow Latin *accumbere* 'to recline' as *anakumb-jan*, with a native affix.

triplet is found in the paired verbs *ga-qiu-nan* 'to come to life', *ga-qiu-jan* 'to vivify' and their root adjective *qiu-s* 'alive'. Such transparent correspondences are much less in evidence in later medieval GMC languages, however; the inchoative *-nan* verb class is entirely lost in West GMC, though still in evidence in Scandinavian (SW *mörkna* 'become dark' from *mörk* 'dark'), and the causative *-jan* verbs, while still a distinct class, are no longer identifiable by virtue of containing a single suffix with a particular shape. We recognize the OHG counterpart to GO *wakjan*, for example, as a member of the class of '*–jan*-verbs' because it exhibits a geminate consonant in the present (*weckit* 'he wakes s.o.') and a preterite (*wahta*) in which the past tense ending is added directly to the root, without a linking vowel. In still other verbs of this class, the causative affix shows up as a linking element *-i-* between the root and the past tense marker: *dhecch-i-dôn* 'they covered'. But after the late medieval simplification of geminates and the elimination of contrasts in unstressed vowels, even these characteristics can no longer be relied upon. Resultantly, the class largely loses its coherence, and verbs of this former class are identifiable only in cases such as GE *röten* 'redden' from *rot* 'red', *stärken* 'strengthen' from *stark* 'strong' by virtue of the umlauting effect of the former *-jan* suffix on the root vowel. Here, we are no longer dealing so much with a verb class as with a word-formation rule.

Lass (1994: 191ff.) notes that one of the consequences of this long-term trend has been a progressive erosion in the speaker's sense of relatedness among forms in the lexicon. He cites the fact (p. 199) that there are 139 noun- and adjective-forming suffixes of IE or GMC date which are identifiable in Old GMC words, of which only 42 remain reasonably productive in OE. That is, about two-thirds of them had been lost or had become opaque by the time of late medieval GMC. For all of that, the lexicon of OE is still characterized by relatively highly productive use of affixes in the derivation of new vocabulary, in comparison with some modern languages. Lass states that

> One of the most striking features of the Old English lexicon is the extensive involvement in [word formation], not only of transparent affixation, compounding, and conversion, but of other devices of varying ages: ancient ones like ablaut, and newer ones like i-umlaut. This results in what Kastovsky (1992: 294) calls "large morphologically related word-families"; considerable portions of the lexicon "cohere" in a rather special way, characteristic of older IE and to some extent more archaic modern languages like German, but quite alien to Modern English.
>
> (Lass 1994: 191)

The history of derivational morphology in GMC, however, has not been only one of loss. Also in evidence is a countervailing tendency to introduce new derivational affixes. In place of the obsolete and opaque inherited suffixes for nominal derivation has arisen a new set of more salient suffixes which derive from originally independent lexical items. Kluge (1913: 227), who refers to these as "Kompositionssuffixe" (roughly, "compound-suffixes"), notes that they are more numerous and more usual in West GMC than in GO, which lacks *-haid* '-hood', *-dōm* '-dom' and *-skapi* '-ship', though it has *-leiks* '-like' and *-sams* '-some'. He concludes that this sort of formation was only in its beginning stages in common GMC. Many of these new suffixes belong to the class of "non-cohering" suffixes, which form their own prosodic domains, separate from that of the root (Kristoffersen 2000: 43).

This development seems to have been limited to nouns and adjectives, no similar developments being found in verbs – no doubt connected with the fact that compounds headed by verbs are uncommon in GMC. Of the new verbal derivational affixes arising to replace the inherited ones which had been lost or become opaque, only one, the (Middle) EN *-en* in *redden, blacken*, is in part a native development. Even this one is apparently also partly borrowed, reflecting the influence of Scandinavian *-nan* verbs, according to the *OED*. The majority of new verb-deriving affixes in the GMC languages are borrowings from Greek or the Romance languages, as in GE *-ieren*, DA *-ere*, EN *-ate*, *-ize* and *-ify*. Some of these have come to be sufficiently native to attain productivity and be usable with native as well as foreign roots (e.g., GE *stolzieren* 'to swagger', based on *stolz* 'proud', and EN *bowdlerize*).

Forms like *freedom* and *friendship* also reflect a typological departure from the mode of word formation in early GMC. These new suffixes are of a different sort from the earlier ones, in that they do not attach to stems but to words – that is, to forms which are able to appear independently. Lass (1994: 200) sees in this typological shift from a stem-based to word-based lexicon "a major evolutionary direction" in GMC. A late phenomenon which can perhaps be regarded as the ultimate outcome of this trend is the employment of category shift or zero-derivation in modern EN – the frequent and prescriptively decried tendency to create new verbs, for example, by using nouns as verbs with no derivational affixes (*to impact, to interface*).

2.2.1 Compounding

Compounding is the process of forming new words by conjoining two or more root morphemes. Compounds in GMC, like other words, are right-headed, in the sense that it is the rightmost element in the compound which determines the category of the whole, as well as such grammatical features as gender and the choice of plural affixes.[2]

---

[2] English *passers-by* represents a possible counterexample. If it is a compound, it is clearly the leftmost element which is the head, since the whole is understood to be a (plural) noun. Jacobs (2005: 146) observes that YI has, in addition to compounds formed on the GMC model, with

In principle, members of almost any lexical category can serve as the first element of the compound, and any of the major categories, noun, adjective or verb, can appear as the second element. In fact, compounds headed by verbs are not common in GMC, and not equally possible in all of the modern languages. Booij (2002b: 141) reports them to be unproductive in DU, while Josefsson (1998: 68) reports that they are reasonably productive in SW. There is some direct evidence of their non-productivity in early GMC: as Eythórsson (1995: 24) points out, GO 'resolves' such Greek compounds as *hydropotéō* 'water-drink' into a separate verb plus object (*driggkan wato*). Noun- and adjective-headed compounds, on the other hand, have from the beginning been markedly productive, and figure prominently as a poetic device in older GMC poetry, in the form of the frequent metaphorical compounds known as *kennings* (Later Runic *walha-kurna* 'foreign corn' = 'gold', Tjurkø bracteate, Antonsen 1975: 79).

The development from a stem-based lexicon to a word-based lexicon discussed in the preceding section is also visible in the history of compound formation in GMC. Lass (1994: 194) notes that a distinction is traditionally made between "genuine compounds," in which the first element is a stem (a root plus the associated noun-class marker) and "non-genuine" compounds, in which it is not. The former is the older of the two, and the one inherited from IE. Lass cites GO *fot-u-baurd* 'foot-board (stool)' as an example, and formations of this sort are abundant in the compound names of the older runic inscriptions (*Hle-wa-gastiz* 'Fame-Guest'). In each case, the first element contains a noun root and a noun class marker (*-u*, *-wa*) but it is not a free-standing form, lacking a case affix. There can be other differences as well between the first element of a compound and the same lexical item in its free-standing form. Kluge (1913: 229) cites such examples as GO *mana-seþs* 'man-seed', but *mann* 'man'.

These stem compounds later became increasingly less frequent, according to Lass, in consequence of the breakdown of the noun-class system, and were replaced increasingly by newer "non-genuine" compounds. These new types of compounds come in three varieties. The earliest of them, apparently, are what we may characterize as "root" compounds, differing from stem compounds in that the first element consists solely of a lexical root without an accompanying class marker. These are reflected in a

the modifying element preceding the head (and bearing stress), a second model, patterned after Hebrew, in which the head is first and the modifier second, the main stress falling on the latter. Both of these patterns are highly productive, and either may combine elements of Hebrew and GMC origin (*sóf zàc* 'final sentence', *sòf zác* 'end of sentence'). Booij (2002b: 143) points out that compounds like *redskin*, sometimes characterized as "exocentric," or headless, are in fact right-headed compounds. It is the right-hand member which determines the category of the whole. What sets them apart is the fact that they are used as metonyms, referring in this case, for example, to 'someone who has red skin'. On the other hand, Booij points out some more complex cases of metonymic compounds in DU in which the rightmost element does not fully determine the grammatical properties of the whole. *Het oor* 'the ear' is neuter, but *de domoor* 'the dumb-ear' = 'idiot' is common gender.

small number of cases even in GO, for example, *gud-hus* 'temple ('God-house'), *þiu-magus* 'servant-boy', *hauh-þuhts* 'high-seeming' (Braune 1973: 69), and become increasingly frequent in later GMC. The second type of innovative compound, the genitive type, in which the first element is a noun with a genitive case suffix, is apparently of later occurrence. According to Kluge (1913: 229) and Lass (1994: 195), it is uniquely represented in GO by *baurg-s-waddjus* 'city's wall'. It is also rare in other early GMC languages, according to Kluge, appearing first in names for the days of the week (*Wodnes-dæg*) as a calque on the Latin names, but it becomes more frequent later.

It is not clear that such genitive compounds are still in use in the modern GMC languages. There are indeed some in which the two nouns are separated by a morpheme which stems from, and looks like, a genitive suffix. Such an element, for example, is found in GE forms like *Liebe-s-gedicht* 'love poem' and *liebe-s-krank* 'lovesick'. Lass (1994: 195) notes that the *-s-* cannot be analyzed synchronically as a genitive marker even though it is one by origin since, among other things, *-(e)s* as a genitive case marker appears only on masculine and neuter nouns in GE, and *Liebe* 'love' is a feminine noun. These compounds thus represent yet a third type of innovative compound, in which the two components are joined by a fixed and meaningless "linking" morpheme. Lass cites as an early instance, the OE *stān-e-gella* 'stone-yeller (kestrel)', in which the *-e-* appears as a semantically empty linking element. Each of the modern languages, in addition to "root" compounds, has a small inventory of such linking elements. DU, for example, has three such elements (Booij 2002b: 178): *-s-*, of genitive origin *(schaap-s-kop* 'sheep's head'), *-er-*, of plural origin, and [-ə] (sometimes written <en> in official orthography) *(schaap-e(n)-vlees* 'sheep-flesh' = 'mutton'), which in some instances is a case marker in origin and in others a word-final *-e-* which was apocopated in non-compound forms. The inventory in DA is similar (*dreng-e-skole* 'boys' school', *dag-s-rejse* 'daytrip').

Booij (2002b: 179f.) presents a number of arguments for viewing such elements as "stem-extensions" of the first member of the compound, rather than as linking elements which are just inserted between two members of the compound. First, he notes that they belong to the first constituent prosodically, as evidenced by syllabification. Second, in constructions involving "gapping," such as *schap-en- of vark-en-vlees* 'mutton or pork' (lit., sheep-EN or pig-EN meat), in which two conjoined first constituents of the compound share a final constituent which occurs only after the second of them, each of them is nonetheless equipped with its own "linking element." Further, it is always the first element of the compound which determines whether a particular linking element can occur in the compound. Finally, some of these linking elements can occur outside of compounds, in instances of derivation involving certain non-cohering suffixes, as in *arbeid-s-loos* 'work-less (unemployed)'. Booij concludes that they are therefore suffixes on the first member of the compound (see also Josefsson 1998: 61). Viewed in this way, these compounds bear a certain resemblance to the original stem compounds of GMC. In languages offering a choice of such stem extensions, there are typically some partial generalizations about which ones can be used in a given instance – all of them making reference, as noted, to properties of the first noun. These are described for DU by Booij (2002b: 180) and for DA by Allan *et al.* (1995: 544), for example. Josefsson (1998: 60) reports a partial generalization in SW about the distribution of compounds with the linking element *-s* and those without: the linking element must be used if the lefthand member of the compound is itself a compound: *barn+bok+klubb* 'book club for children,' but *barn+bok+s+klubb* 'club for children's books'.

The linking element, or stem extension, can sometimes have the same shape as plural morphemes.[3] In most such cases, however, the morpheme has no plural force. There are, though, occasional compounds in the GMC languages in which the first element of the compound is semantically as well as formally plural. Allan *et al.* (1995: 33) cite in DA, for example, such cases as *børnebørn* 'grandchildren', plural of *et barnebarn* 'the grandchild', either *barnefødsler* or *børnefødsler* 'childbirths' as the plural of *en barnefødsel*, and *mødrehjem* 'home for mothers'. For DU, Booij (2002b: 147) cites *huiz-en-rij* 'row of houses' and notes such contrasts as that between *bedrijf-s-terrein* 'company area' and *bedrijv-en-terrein* 'companies' area' (2002b: 179).

2.3 Discourse particles

One highly distinctive word category shared by (perhaps) all of the GMC languages and apparently rare outside that family, is a class of short, unstressable, typically monosyllabic words with at most vague propositional meaning which signal something about the speaker's relation to the utterance or to the hearer. These can, for example, indicate the degree of the speaker's commitment to the truth of the proposition, the source for the speaker's knowledge, the assumptions the speaker makes about the degree to which his/her knowledge or belief is shared or not shared by the hearer, and (particularly in the case of commands) the degree of imperative force the hearer is invited to see in the utterance. Particles fitting this description have been reported for all of the modern GMC languages. For example, they are described for GE by Abraham (1991, 2000, 2001b) and Zifonun *et al.* (1997: 903ff., 1206ff.), for DU by Foolen (1995), for DA by Davidsen-Nielsen (1996), for SW by (Aijmer 1996),

---

[3] Booij (2002b: 179) notes that the officially promoted practice of spelling the stem extension [-ə] as <en> in DU just in cases where the plural suffix of the first element would also be *-en* reinforces such an identification.

for IC by Thráinsson (1994: 188), for NO by Andvik (1992), for FR by Hoekstra and Tiersma (1994: 528), for YI by Jacobs (2005: 207) and for AF by Donaldson (1993: 213). The particles in question are sometimes referred to generally as "modal particles" (e.g., Arndt 1960; Abraham 2000; Foolen 1995), while others (Aijmer 1996) seem to restrict this label to the subset of them which convey epistemic modality (that is, information about the speaker's beliefs concerning the proposition). Other labels attached to them are "discourse particles" or "discourse markers," "metacommunicative particles," "filler words" and "shading particles" (*Abtönungspartikeln*: Zifonun *et al.* 1997). In the present treatment, I will refer to them as "discourse particles" (glossed as PART in the examples).

Discourse particles can be categorized in a variety of different ways, and the reader is referred to the references cited for various categorization schemes. Davidsen-Nielsen (1996: 285) distinguishes between a group of particles in DA which are oriented toward the hearer (2.2a) and a second set, illustrated in (2.2b), which are oriented toward the speaker, "in the sense that they reflect the speaker's conception of, or attitude to, his own knowledge of the state of affairs referred to" (Davidsen-Nielsen 1996: 285).

(2.2)   a.   John er da/ jo/ nu/ skam en flink fyr   (DA)
             John is PART   a nice guy
            (DA, Davidsen-Nielsen 1996: 285)

           b.   John er nok/ vel/ vist en flink fyr
             John is PART   a nice guy

In the first case (2.2a), that of hearer-oriented particles, *jo* signals the speaker's expectation that the knowledge expressed in the proposition is shared and accepted by the hearer, while *da* and *nu* signal, to varying degrees, the speaker's expectation that the hearer does not accept or agree with the truth of the proposition. *Skam* is used to reassure the hearer of the truth of the proposition. In the second group (2.2b), the speaker-oriented particles *nok*, *vel* and *vist* serve to distance the speaker from a commitment to the truth of the proposition, and to convey information about the source of the knowledge. *Vel*, for example, expresses uncertainty and invites confirmation from the hearer, functioning more or less equivalently to tag questions. *Vist* suggests that the knowledge is not direct, but based on report. *Nok* suggests that the probability of the truth of the proposition is a conclusion of the speaker himself. This group is the one that Aijmer (1996), writing on SW, labels "modal particles," and she compares them with the "evidential" morphemes used in other languages of the world to convey information about the source and reliability of the knowledge embodied in the proposition.

The discourse particles of the other GMC languages overlap in functions with these examples from DA. Hearer-oriented particles are, for example, reflected in GE (2.3a),

34   2 *The Germanic lexicon*

where the *ja* signals the assumption that the knowledge is shared and agreed to by the hearer, and (2.3b), where the *doch* signals that the hearer is being reminded of something known but forgotten. To this class may perhaps be added particles which serve as instructions to the hearer about how to interpret requests or commands, rendering them softer and more polite in some instances, as in SW (2.3c), GE (2.3d.), DU (2.3e.) ("down-graders" or "down-toners"), and more emphatic in others, as in GE (2.3f) (Abraham's "up-graders"). In commands, as Zifonun *et al.* (1997: 1219) note, such particles anticipate the degree of receptiveness on the part of the hearer to the command, reflecting the speaker's assumption about the extent to which the hearer is prepared to carry out the requested action. A further instance of a discourse particle affecting illocutionary force is the YI example in (2.3g), in which the presence of the *den* signals that the question is offered rhetorically, and a negative answer is presupposed.

(2.3)   a. Wir sind ja alle Freunde
           we are PART all friends [as you know]
           (GE, Wauchope 1991: 1)
        b. Er war doch lange krank gewesen
           he was PART long sick
           'He was sick for a long time [don't you remember?]'
           (GE, Karagjosova 2003: 339)
        c. Men du kan väl köpa litte köttfärs hos Märta
           but you can PART buy some mince at market
           (SW, Aijmer 1996: 402)
        d. Könntest du mal eben'n bißchen rücken?
           could you PART PART a bit move
           'Couldn't you move over just a bit?'
           (GE, Wauchope 1991: 14)
        e. Komm maar binnen!
           come PART in
           'Please come in'
           (DU, Foolen 1995: 59)
        f. Hör' schon auf!
           PART
           'Stop that [for God's sake]'
           (GE, Abraham 2000: 335)
        g. Ikh hob den gelt?
           I have PART money?
           (YI, Lockwood 1995: 61)

Further subject-oriented cases are given in (2.4). AF *glo* in (2.4a) indicates that the proposition is merely opinion. SW *visst* in (2.4b) signals an inference.

(2.4)   a. Hy het glo   nie 'n sent van   die erfenis   gekry nie
            he has PART not a cent from the inheritance gotten not
            'Apparently, he didn't get a cent of the inheritance'
            (AF, Donaldson 1993: 214)
    b. Han förstår   visst   allt man säjer till honom
            he   understands PART all one says to him
            'He seems to understand everything one says to him'
            (SW, Aijmer 1996: 394)

Traditionally, these particles are treated as adverbs and it is often the case that they are translational equivalents of full lexical adverbs with clear propositional meaning, as in (2.4a). However, they differ from such adverbs in a number of respects, enumerated in Wauchope 1991: 48, for example. They are typically monosyllabic, weakly stressed, indeclinable (that is, lacking comparative forms), unable to stand alone as an utterance (as adverbs like *apparently* can), and have a fixed position of occurrence, after the finite verb (never initial) but before the rheme of the sentence. Etymologically, they often differ from lexical adverbs in being related to/homophonous with function words – such as conjunctions, answering particles and interjections – rather than adjectives. Thus, for example, GE *denn*, *aber* function as both conjunctions and discourse particles, and *ja* is at once a discourse particle and a question-answering particle ('yes'). They also differ semantically from more canonical adverbs, providing information that is sometimes quite hard to state propositionally about how the sentence is situated in context, including the speaker's presuppositions, expectations of the hearer, attitudes toward the truth of the utterance or its illocutionary intent.

Among the modern languages, EN makes far less extensive use of such discourse particles than the others. It has a few: *just*, for example, functions as one such particle with a variety of contextually determined meanings, ranging from softening of commands to expression of the fact that the state of affairs described in the utterance is contrary to the speaker's expectations. EN does not have the extensive system of discourse particles found in the others, though, and typically employs other means, such as lexical adverbs, tags and parentheticals instead. Davidsen-Nielsen (1996: 287) notes in particular that DA hearer-oriented discourse particles are often rendered in EN with tags like 'You know', 'You see', while speaker-oriented ones are often rendered with parentheticals such as 'I guess', 'I suppose', 'It seems'. Andvik gives the following EN translational equivalents for NO modal particles.

(2.5)   nok 'all right, probably, to be sure'
             vel 'I suppose, no doubt, of course'
             da 'certainly'
             jo 'you know'
             nå 'after all, really'
             visst 'surely, I believe'
             (NO, Andvik 1992: 3)

All of the other modern languages have elaborated systems of discourse particles. The status of such particles in early GMC awaits fuller exploration. In GO, only two possible cases emerge. These are the forms *ibai*, which in its occurrence in questions presupposes a negative answer (Streitberg 1920: 219), and *an*, which appears to invite an affirmative response, both of them having the effect of making the questions rhetorical:

(2.6)   a. ibai   mag blinds   blindana tiuhan
                PART can the-blind the-blind lead?
                (GO, Luke 6:39)
             b. an   nuh   þiudans is þu?
                PART now-and king   are you?
                'So you are a king, then?'
                (GO, John 18:37)

At least some of the modal particles of modern GMC languages are of demonstrably late origin (Wauchope 1991: 1). On the other hand, Wauchope argues that at least some of them, including *thoh*, *ia* and *thanne*, had such functions already in OHG times, and since the cognates of these forms also function as discourse particles in modern continental Scandinavian languages, it is possible that the discourse particle system reaches in its roots at least back to common Northwest GMC.

(2.6)   c. Thes nu   gidua thu nu   unsih wis, wer thoh   manno thu sis
                Of   this make you now us   wise, who PART of-men you are
                'Make this known to us, just who you are among men'
                (OHG, Otfrid I:27-35-37, cited in Wauchope 1991: 82)

2.4 Phrasal verbs

Another highly (and increasingly) characteristic lexical type in the GMC languages is the class of so-called phrasal verbs.[4] These verbs, represented by GE *nachschlagen*

---

[4] These are also variously known as particle verbs, verb-particle combinations, separable-prefix verbs and stressed-prefix verbs (Dehé *et al.* 2002: 1). The label separable-prefix verb is used in describing them in the verb-final languages, such as GE and DU, where, as a side-effect of the

'look up (a word/fact)', EN *look up*, for example, consist of a lexical verb plus a "particle," the two of them forming a semantic unit, conveying a single verbal meaning. The present section will focus on their lexical properties. Their syntactic properties, also a matter of considerable interest, will be discussed in Section 5.8.

Such two-part verbs are often used where other languages would use a single, morphologically complex verb. So, for example, in GO, phrasal verbs with the directional particles *inn* and *ut* are often used in combination with a verb of motion or transfer to convey the meaning of a Greek verb with a directional prefix, such as *eis-* 'in' or *ex-* 'out', as in the following examples:

(2.7) a. atgaggands inn
          going in = Greek eis-elthṑn
          (GO, Matt. 9:25)
       b. saei inn ni atgaggaiþ þairh daur
          who in not goes   through door
          = Greek ho mḕ eis-erchómenos 'the one not entering'
          (GO, John 10:1)
       c. atiddja ut Peilatus
          went out Pilate = Greek ex-êlthen
          (GO, John 18:29)
       d. biþe ut usiddjedun eis
          as out departed they = Greek ex-erchoménōn
          (GO, Matt. 9:32)

Both the GO particle and the Greek prefix convey the same meaning, but they have different morphological status. The prefix is a bound morpheme, always occurring in a fixed position in the word, whereas the particle in the GO examples is an autonomous morpheme, variously preceding and following the verb, and even occurring separate from it, as in (2.7b). The inclination to prefer such phrasal verbs over verbs with directional prefixes is no doubt connected with the general preference in GMC for packaging motion and manner together in lexical verbs, to the exclusion of direction (French *entrer dans la maison en courant* vs. EN *run into the house*), as discussed in Section 5.6.

---

fact that nonfinite verbs, including infinitives, occur in final position, the verbal particle precedes the infinitive. The infinitive is used as a citation form in dictionaries (GE *anrufen* 'call up'), and therefore in the citation form the particle looks like a prefix. The view that they are a sort of prefix is also conveyed in the orthography. It is nonetheless clear that they are not prefixes in the usual sense, on phonological or morphological grounds. They have their own stress, and they are separable from the associated verb in a way prohibited to genuine affixes. They in fact exhibit effectively the same degree of syntactic autonomy that particles do in such VO languages as SW and EN.

In GO and other early GMC languages, phrasal verbs seem to have been limited to this directional type, and modern GMC still reflects this history, the most common sort of verbal particle typically being homophonous with directional prepositions. This homophony makes the identification of phrasal verbs in languages like GO somewhat uncertain. Since *inn* and *ut* have fixed directional meanings, and since they are clearly not bound morphemes, one might alternatively suppose that these constructions involve two separate lexical items, and that *inn* and *ut* are not instances of a special class of verbal particles but are simply directional adverbs or intransitive prepositions with spatial meanings, in free association with the verb, rather than forming a single lexical item with it. Compelling evidence distinguishing these two views is hard to come by for the historical languages. However, the fact that *inn* and *ut* occur in GO exclusively in association with such verbs is consistent with an identification as verbal particles. Clear syntactic evidence that directional particles are not just adverbs/ intransitive prepositions is found in the modern languages, where they are distributionally distinct from these other types of elements. For example, Dehé *et al.* (2002: 2) note that, while adverbials in SW and EN (including some which seem to be functionally identical to particles) are prohibited from intervening between a verb and its direct object, particles belonging to phrasal verbs may do so freely:

(2.8)   a. I carried in/ off/ *inside/ *into the house the boxes
          b. Johan skrev upp   numret
             Johan wrote down number-the
             (SW, Dehé *et al.* 2002: 3)
          c. *Johan ställer dar   glaset
             Johan puts   there glass-the
             (SW, Dehé *et al.* 2002: 3)

Thus, they have privileges of distribution not shared by adverbs. Conversely, Dehé *et al.* note that in verb-final languages, such as GE, adverbs can appear in positions which are prohibited to particles.

(2.9)   a. wenn ein Licht aufleuchtet / *wenn auf ein Licht leuchtet
            if   a light up-lights   *if up a light lights
          b. wenn ein Licht plötzlich leuchtet/ wenn plötzlich ein Licht....
            if   a light suddenly shines   if suddenly a light ....
           (GE, Dehé *et al.* 2002: 4)

The identification of phrasal verbs has also become easier in some instances on semantic grounds beginning in late medieval times, with the development of some new types of particle verbs which appear not to have existed earlier. While the core cases of verbal particles are directional prepositions in origin, and had transparent directional interpretations in the early languages (Elenbaas 2003), they have in many instances lost their original lexical semantic content entirely, and are only interpretable in combination with the verb. We may distinguish two subtypes. In one of them, idiomatic verb-particle combinations, the combination has a noncompositional meaning. That is, the meaning of the whole cannot be computed from the meanings of its component parts. In cases like GE *nach=schlagen* (literally, 'after-strike') or EN *look up*, the meaning 'consult a reference source for' is simply assigned to the whole phrasal verb, and no component of it can be specifically attributed to *up*, for example. In this feature, idiomatic phrasal verbs are like compounds, whose meanings also tend toward noncompositionality (*egghead, flatfoot*), and it is clear at this point that we are dealing with items which constitute a single lexical item in some sense, in spite of their apparent syntactic complexity. Since it is not computable from its parts, as Jackendoff (2002: 73) notes, the meaning of *look up* must be listed as an entry in our mental lexicons. The second innovative type of phrasal verb is of a more regular sort; the verbal particle has again lost its original directional meaning, but has developed a new meaning relating to the shape of the action described by the verb. Denison (1981) identifies as a cardinal instance of this type the "completive *up*," represented in *eat up, break up, fill up*, for example. Denison notes that this use belongs to the semantic domain of *Aktionsart*, or verbal aspect; the particle alters the contour of the action denoted by the simplex verb, indicating in this case that that action took place up to the point of logical, irreversible conclusion. Wedel (1997) refers to this as "complexive aspect." Denison notes that the aspectual use of verbal particles is also exemplified, though less productively, by the particles in *kill off, chatter away*. Jackendoff (2002: 77) observes that in some instances the addition of an aspectual particle also has the effect of changing the valency of the verb; durative phrasal verbs with the particles *on* or *away* cannot take direct object arguments, even though formed from transitive verbs: *fight* (**the army*) *on*, for example.

Both the idiomatic type of phrasal verb construction and the aspectual type seem to have their roots in the later medieval languages. The development of completive *up*, for example, is discussed in detail in Denison 1981, who assigns it to the twelfth century in EN and notes that it appears to have arisen earlier yet in the Scandinavian languages (ON *brjóta upp* 'break up') from which in fact the EN construction may derive (cf. also Kastovsky 1992: 320). It finds only isolated representation in the continental West GMC languages (GE *aufessen* 'eat up', *aufgeben* 'give up'), where Denison assigns a later date. Some observers have noted that this development reflects a basic change in the way the categories of *Aktionsart* found expression in the GMC lexicon. In earlier GMC, *Aktionsart* had been encoded either by means of derivational suffixes or by means of prefixes. As an example of the role of suffixes in signaling aspectual contrasts, we can cite GO *dreiban* 'drive', a primary strong verb, and the corresponding derived, iterative/ intensive weak verb *draibjan* 'to plague' (or perhaps, 'to drive to distraction'), the new semantic element of repeated action being contributed by the suffix. The role of prefixes in encoding aspect is exemplified by GO *itan* 'eat', *fra-itan* 'eat up, devour'. A number of prefixes, in particular, had the effect of marking the verb for complex aspect (see Wedel 1997 for a discussion of the scholarship in this area). By the time of medieval GMC, however, the suffixal encoding of contrasts in verbal aspect, already unproductive for hundreds of years, had also become morphologically opaque. This left only the prefixal strategy. The lower receptivity of GE to the development of the complexive *up* construction, Denison suggests, may be connected with the fact that, unlike EN and the Scandinavian languages, GE has retained more of the true, inseparable prefixes which convey the same concept of complexive action (e.g., *erdenken* 'to think out/up', *verhüllen* 'to wrap up', *zerfetzen* 'to tear up').

More generally, Denison (1981: 52) suggests that the early development of the particle construction in the Scandinavian languages may be linked to the early and general loss of GMC prefixes in North GMC described in Heusler 1967: 40–41 – information previously encoded in the prefix coming to be encoded instead by the verbal particle. The nature of the connection has been variously interpreted. Faarlund (1994: 70) proposes that the phrasal-verb strategy arose in Scandinavian as a way of remedying the information loss occasioned by the disappearances of prefixes: ON *lúka* had come to mean both 'close' (cf. OE *belūcan*) and 'open' (OE *onlūcan*) in consequence of prefix-loss, and the development of verbal particles, for example, in *lúka upp* 'open up', resolved such ambiguity. However, Samuels (1972: 84f.) seems to advance the rise of particles as the cause of, not the response to, the loss of prefixes; prefixes were replaced by the verbal particles as part of the implementation of a general preference which he also sees reflected in the shift from prenominal to enclitic definite articles, for example.

While other languages have elements like the verbal particles of GMC phrasal verbs (besides other IE languages, Booij (2002a: 23) cites Hungarian and Estonian), there seem to have been no developments quite comparable to the proliferation of phrasal verbs in some recent GMC languges, in which original directional adverbs (or intransitive prepositions) have become dissociated from their original spatial meanings and assumed a massive role in the derivation of new words. Jackendoff (2002: 74) cites the case of *out*-formations in recent American EN, for example (*black out, chicken out, zone out, flip out, veg out, chill out, burn out*).

3

The sound systems of Germanic: inventories, alternations and structures

3.1 Segmental inventories and alternations

3.1.1 The obstruents: place and manner of articulation

3.1.1.1 *Stops*

The GMC languages have relatively rich, though not particularly exotic, inventories of obstruent consonants (stops, affricates and fricatives). The inventory which we can reconstruct for common GMC is given in (3.1), though not all of these oppositions were distinctive.[1] This inventory is distinguished from the system found in IE by the relatively large number of fricatives it contains. It is distinguished from the inventories of many of the later GMC languages in lacking affricates. Some of the GMC languages also have long (geminate) variants of these obstruents. Consonant length, as well as vowel length, will be treated later, as a suprasegmental feature.

(3.1) The proto-GMC obstruents

	Labial	Coronal	Dorsal	
Stops	p, b	t, d	k, g (k^w, h^w)	
Fricatives	f, β	θ, ð	x, ɣ	h
		s, z		

---

[1] In particular, [b, d, g] did not contrast with the voiced fricatives [β, ð, ɣ]. The former arose as contextual variants of the latter according to standard views. As Moulton (1954) points out, comparative evidence dates the phonetic split between the two to the Germanic period, since all of the daughter languages exhibit the stop variants at least after nasals and in gemination, but the difference remained allophonic. Similarly, [h] arose as a contextual variant of [x], in syllable onset position. Moulton again dates this to the Germanic period, since all of the daughter languages have [h] in syllable onsets. In this case, though, he assigns them to different phonemes, in spite of their complementarity, because of the degree of phonetic difference.

Some of the developments leading to this inventory are staples of any introduction to historical linguistics because of their early discovery and their importance for the development of the methodology of historical/comparative linguistics. These include such events as the First and Second Consonant Shifts (the former more commonly known as "Grimm's Law," though Grimm's formulation subsumed both of these shifts) and Verner's Law. Interestingly, certain aspects of these sound changes have remained refractory in spite of having been examined and reexamined over generations. Within the last few years there has been a renewal of interest in them, as recent developments in phonetics and phonological theory give us new ways of regarding them, and a new picture is emerging of these GMC hallmarks.

Common GMC, and most of the languages descending from it, exhibit paired sets of stop consonants, {/p, t, k/ /b, d, g/} which contrast with respect to laryngeal features – that is, the activity of the glottis during their articulation. The two sets are not represented equally in all environments; the /b, d, g/ set appears in some languages only in certain environments, alternating with fricatives in other environments, as discussed below. In DU and AF the /g/ is lacking except in loanwords, and DU/AF words whose cognates in other GMC languages have a stop /g/ exhibit dorsal fricatives instead (Booij 1995: 7).

For GMC, the features [labial], [coronal] and [dorsal] are sufficient to characterize the place contrasts in this inventory. [Coronal] sounds are, roughly, those produced by raising the blade of the tongue to the roof of the mouth, and are distinguished from [labial] sounds, articulated with the lips, and [dorsal] sounds, articulated with the back of the tongue. Later GMC languages exhibit a contrast between two types of coronal sounds: dental/alveolar and palatal. We can accommodate this by further subdividing the [coronal] consonants into [±anterior] varieties. In the GMC languages, this feature is of importance only for fricatives; none of these languages has a contrastive set of palatal ([coronal, –anterior]) stops, though these do arise as contextual variants of velar stops in certain environments, as discussed in Section 3.1.1.5. A further distinction is required by the fact that some Scandinavian languages, including NO and dialects of SW (Andersson 1994: 272; Bandle *et al.* 2005: 1123), have developed an additional pair of coronal stops, /ṭ, ḍ/ which arose from /rt, rd/ sequences. These consonants are articulated with "retroflexion" – that is, they are [–anterior] sounds which are formed with the tip, rather than the blade of the tongue, and an additional feature is required for their characterization (perhaps the feature [–distributed] of Chomsky and Halle 1968). Whether the labiovelars /k^w/ and /h^w/ in GO constitute yet another place of articulation, or whether they are sequences of consonants, is discussed in note 10.

This set of place features works better in many cases in accounting for the systematic patterning of sounds than do more specific articulatory labels like "bilabial," "labiodental," "interdental," "dental," "alveolar" and so on. It predicts, for example, that for the purpose of systematic patterning of sounds, interdental, dental and alveolar sounds should all pattern together, since they are all [coronal, anterior] – a prediction which seems to be correct. (The [coronal] stops of GMC are realized phonetically variously as alveolar stops (EN, GE, DA) or as dental stops (SW (Granberry 1991: 7) and FA (Lockwood 1964: 7), for example. Some languages show internal variation on this point (Kress 1937: 86; Jacobs et al. 1994: 395; Jacobs 2005: 109).)[2]

Views concerning the nature of the glottal feature responsible for the distinction between the series /p, t, k/ and the series /b, d, g/ have shifted in recent times. In traditional grammars as well as some scholarly treatments of EN and GE it is usual for the feature in question to be identified as [voice]. See Jessen (1996: 199) for a list of investigators who have taken this view. Rendering this characterization problematic – at least in its extension to the whole family – is the fact that members of the series /b, d, g/ are either contextually or generally unvoiced in many GMC languages. Jessen (1996) points out that the series /b, d, g/ in GE is not systematically voiced, tending to be unvoiced except in intervocalic position (see also Jessen and Ringen 2002: 190). Barnes (1994: 193) states that in FA "the voicing is at best weak and sometimes absent." In DA (Haberland 1994: 320) and IC, both series are uniformly unvoiced, contrasting only in aspiration. Iverson and Salmons (1999, 2003) claim, though more controversially, that the /b, d, g/ series is not uniformly voiced in EN, either, asserting that, unlike the voiced stops of French, which are thoroughly voiced, the /b, d, g/ of EN are not voiced at all at the beginnings of words (2003: 3).

Reservations about calling the feature in question [voice] are reflected in some earlier accounts, which speak of "fortis" and "lenis," though sometimes without

---

[2] The feature set [labial], [coronal] and [dorsal], based on articulators, supplants an earlier feature system (Chomsky and Halle 1968), in which consonantal place was characterized with a pair of binary features, [±anterior, ±coronal]. A crucial difference between this feature set and the more recent one has to do with the fact that, under the former, labial and velar sounds were characterized as a natural class, sharing in common the feature [–coronal]. No such prediction follows under the new system, with its three privative features. Remaining to be seen is whether this system is sufficient to characterize the cases in GMC in which labials and velars do seem to pattern together, to the exclusion of coronals. There are some sound changes in the GMC languages for which the noncoronal consonants of GMC – /p, b, f, b, g, k/ – do seem to pattern together. So, for example, in Old Upper GE, lowering of the second element of /eu/ to /o/ under the influence of /a/ was blocked by an intervening [–coronal] segment.

(i) a-umlaut of *eu in Old Upper GE (Braune 1963: 46f.)
    a. *liug-u*   'I lie'   : *liug-an*   'to lie'
    b. *chliub-u*   'I cleave'   : *chliub-an*   'to cleave'
    c. *biut-u*   'I offer'   : *beot-ames*   'we offer'

Similar facts are found in ON. There are, moreover, instances in which the labial fricative /f/ changes into velar fricative /x/ – Old DU /ft/ becoming /xt/, for example (DU *lucht* 'air'/ GE *Luft*) – or vice versa – in ME, for example, "skipping over" the intervening coronal consonants. See Bonebrake (1979).

precise characterization of the phonetic content of these notions. (Moulton 1954: 12 describes fortis consonants as "articulated with relatively great muscular energy.") The more recent investigators mentioned have converged on the view that what sets the two series apart most saliently in the languages in question is the acoustic effect of "aspiration," associated with widely separated vocal bands [spread glottis], or, in the view of Jessen (1996), the feature [tense], of which aspiration is the basic (though not the only) acoustic manifestation. Members of the series /p, t, k/ in GMC languages tend to be articulated with a spread glottis, and therefore strong aspiration (Jessen 1996, 1998; Iverson and Salmons 1995, 1999, 2003; Jessen and Ringen 2002 and others). According to these accounts, to the extent that /b,d,g/ are voiced at all in such languages as GE, it is a matter of "passive voicing" in voiced surroundings of segments which have no inherent voicing or other laryngeal specification. (Iverson and Salmons 2003: 52n observe, but do not explain, the fact that some languages but not others exhibit such passive voicing. Moulton 1954: 13 notes, for example, that the /b, d, g/ series are typically voiced in northern GE, but normally voiceless in southern GE.)

Thus, for some GMC languages, at least, the basic contrast in stops appears to be between a series specified for [spread glottis] and a series unspecified for laryngeal features, which may or may not get voicing from neighboring sounds. Iverson and Salmons (2003) project this onto the parent language, arguing that the addition of [spread glottis] to the laryngeally unmarked consonants /p, t, k/ of IE was a GMC innovation, which they label the "Germanic Enhancement," and they identify it as the main departure of GMC from IE consonantism, and a central and persistent characteristic of GMC consonantism which played an important role in many subsequent developments, including Grimm's Law.

In still other GMC languages, on the other hand, such as DU, the /p, t, k/ set is unaspirated or only weakly aspirated, so aspiration cannot be the significant feature. Iverson and Salmons (1999) claim that in DU, the distinctive feature is in fact [voice]. DU /b, d, g/ are specified for [voice], while /p, t, k/ are unspecified for laryngeal features. Iverson and Salmons claim that the consonant system of DU, in which voice, rather than aspiration, is the feature systematically distinguishing the two series, is "to a great extent Romance-like," and go on to suggest that this may reflect Romance influence in the prehistory of DU (1999: 20). These proposals invite investigation of the other dialects of West GMC, including AF, FR and Eastern YI, in which the /p, t, k/ series is also unaspirated.

An important feature of the account of Iverson and Salmon is that in the majority group of the GMC languages, it is the /p, t, k/ series which is marked with a laryngeal specification ([spread glottis]), while in DU it is the /b, d, g/ series which is marked ([voice]). Among the supporting arguments for this claimed difference between DU and EN/GE are "biases" in the direction of voicing assimilation in sequences of obstruents. In DU, a voiceless obstruent may assume the voice of a neighboring voiced obstruent (/s+d/→/zd/), while in EN and GE, voicing assimilation works uniformly in the other direction. In each case, it is the marked feature which spreads. In this connection, the discussion in Jacobs *et al*. 1994: 396 and Jacobs 2005: 129ff. of voicing assimilation in different dialects of YI is particularly interesting.

In IC and FA, /p, t, k/ have come to be "preaspirated" when they precede another consonant, including cases of (present or former) gemination: IC *brekka* [brɛʰk:a] 'slope', *happ* [haʰp] 'luck', *vatn* [vaʰtn] (Einarsson 1945: 16, 22; Kress 1982: 30). (See also Page 1997; Ringen 1999.) Preaspiration is also found in scattered NO and SW dialects (Bandle *et al*. 2005: 1122).

3.1.1.2 *Fricatives*

All of the GMC languages have two series of fricatives as well, contrasting in laryngeal features. In the case of fricatives, voicing is among the stable features distinguishing the two series, even in languages like GE, where it is not a reliable distinguishing feature for stops (Jessen 1996: 233).

The fricative charts in individual GMC languages tend to have more gaps than the stop charts. GO and OE had inventories like that in (3.1), and OE even added a new fricative, /ʃ/, but other languages have smaller ones. Some places of articulation are represented in some inventories but not others, and unlike stops, the fricatives do not always come in pairs with the same place of articulation but differing glottal features. All of the GMC languages have /f/, but they do not all have a lenis labial fricative, /β/ or /v/. It is missing, for example, in southern OHG, at a point after GMC /β/ had become a stop and before the fricativization of /w/ in MHG. For many speakers of DU, voicing contrasts in fricatives are in the process of being lost, according to de Schutter (1994: 448). Gussenhoven (1999: 74) states that in southern varieties, /v, z, ɣ/ are found, but that in the western Netherlands the inventory is reduced to /v, z/ or even just /z/, and that even the latter is absent in some western varieties (see also Booij 1995: 7; Collins and Mees 1996: 53). Such contrasts are fully neutralized in AF, where only the voiceless variants remain, though the /f/ : /v/ contrast has been reintroduced by the fricativization of [w] to [v] (Roger Lass, p.c.). The Scandinavian languages uniformly lack /z/ (Haugen 1976: 73).

With respect to place of articulation, the velar and nonstrident coronal (dental) fricatives (/θ, ð/) of GMC have a tendency to disappear. Although found in all of the medieval varieties of GMC, /θ, ð/ have tended strongly toward elimination in one way or another in modern GMC. Only Modern EN and Modern IC exhibit both of them, and the /ð/'s of EN are of secondary origin, arising from contextual voicing of /θ/, since the inherited GMC /ð/ had been changed into a stop already in common West GMC. In the remainder of West GMC (DU, FR, GE and AF), all former occurrences of /θ/ have turned into /d/ (see below), so neither fricative exists. In some dialects of EN, including, for example, Shetlands EN, /θ, ð/ have occlusivized to /t, d/ respectively.[3] The same development took place in initial position in North GMC languages other than IC (see, for example, Haugen 1982: 66). In some cases, /θ/ developed into /h/ (Barnes 1994: 195) – a development also found in the Goedelic languages. Non-initially, only /ð/ occurred in early Scandinavian, due to postvocalic voicing of fricatives, and in modern Scandinavian it has tended to be either deleted or occlusivized to /d/ (IC *ráða* [rauːða], FA *ráða* [rɔːa] 'advise', NO *råa* 'advise', SW *råda* [roːda] 'advise'). It is retained as /ð/ only in a few dialects of modern Scandinavian (Haugen 1982: 66). According to Haberland (1994: 320) the /ð/ in DA, which arose secondarily through postvocalic lenition of apical stops (Section 3.1.1.5), is not now a fricative, but an "alveolar voiced sonorant".

Also of limited occurrence are the velar fricatives /x, ɣ/. /x/ did not occur initially in common GMC, having become /h/ in that context. All of the standard GMC languages retain this initial /h/. /x/ has been reintroduced in initial position in YI through borrowing (Jacobs *et al*. 1994: 395) and in southern GE dialects (for example, Swiss GE), where it develops from the velar affricate arising from the High GE Consonant Shift (3.1.1.3). Early GMC – including OE – had both /x, ɣ/ in non-initial environments, but they were eliminated on the way to modern Standard EN, primarily by vocalization (OE *dragan*, Modern EN *draw*, OE *niht*, Modern EN *night*), where they are not changed to /f/. Northern dialects have retained /x/. Standard DU retains /ɣ/ and /x/, whose realization varies across dialects in terms of position and energy of articulation (Collins and Mees 1996: 191), velar articulations being usual in the south, but post-velar or uvular articulations in the north (Gussenhoven 1999: 74). AF has only /x/ (Donaldson 1993: 13), voicing contrasts in fricatives having been neutralized there, as in some dialects of DU. /ɣ/ was occlusivized early on in most dialects of GE to /g/, though in some Low GE dialects it has remained a fricative (Keller 1961: 303). All dialects of GE still retain /x/, whose precise place of articulation also tends to vary. In Standard GE, it is velar (or sometimes uvular) in the environment of non-front vowels, but fronted to an alveopalatal [ç] in other environments. Whether the [x] : [ç] difference is distinctive or not is a matter of controversy in GE grammar (Eisenberg 1994: 354). Not all dialects of GE have developed this palatal variant of /x/ (Keller 1961: 164, 205), and it is also absent from YI. In still other dialects of GE, it has merged with the sibilant /ʃ/ (Keller 1961: 164). ON lost /x/ in all positions, though it has reemerged as a positional variant of velar stops in IC in the context of other

---

[3] Roger Lass (p.c.) observes that in some dialects of English the resultant dental stops contrast with the old alveolar stops, and that in still other dialects (London and vicinity), the dental fricatives have been replaced by the labial fricatives /f, v/.

voiceless obstruents (*slikt* [slixt] 'such'). IC also has /ɣ/, for example, in *sagði* [saɣði] 'said'. Other standard varieties of Scandinavian lack both /x/ and /ɣ/.

The incidence of /v, β/ has been increased in standard GMC languages other than EN by the fricativization of /w/ – a development which apparently took place independently in medieval times, even, apparently, in GO (Krause 1968: 109). This is not universal among nonstandard varieties, though – exceptions existing in at least northern GE dialects (Keller 1961: 190), PG (where /w/ alternates with /β/ (van Ness 1994: 424)) and SW (Haugen 1982: 64). See 3.3.1 for further discussion of this change. Collins and Mees (1996: 198) describe standard Netherlands DU <w> as a labiodental approximant /ʋ/, and Kristoffersen (2000: 25) describes the NO <v> in the same way, since it is articulated without aperiodic noise, noting, though, that for some phonological purposes it patterns as an obstruent.

3.1.1.3 Affricates and the High German consonant shift

A final type of obstruent, affricates (stops with homorganic fricative release), is represented most systematically in High GE, where they arose as a part of the High German consonant shift. This event, which gives High GE a consonantism quite different from that of other GMC languages, involved a series of interrelated changes. The aspirated stops /p, t, k/ of GMC developed into fricatives or affricates. In general, they became (long, or geminate) fricatives postvocalically, but affricates initially and postconsonantally. The latter includes the case of gemination, where, for example, /pp/ becomes /ppf/. These effects can be seen in the following comparisons of EN and OHG cognates. (OHG, as well as Modern GE, is cited here since the original pattern is obscured by later changes in Modern GE.)

(3.2)   a. *EN*   *OHG*   *Modern German*
            open   offan   offen [ɔfn]
            plant   pflanzôn   pflanzen
            help   helpfan   helfen
            OE scieppan   skeppfen   schöpfen 'shape'

The affricates so created were a previously unexemplified articulatory type in GMC. Other GMC languages have also developed them, though to a more limited extent, primarily by way of the palatalization processes discussed in the next section.

Whether or not a particular consonant was affected by this High German consonant shift was a complex function of the type of consonant ([coronal] consonants shifting more readily than others, and [dorsal] consonants least readily of all), the context of the consonant (postvocalic consonants shifting more readily than initial or postconsonantal ones), and geography (the shift being carried through more completely in the southernmost dialects than in the more northerly ones, resulting in the famous

"Rhenish Fan" pattern of isoglosses). Thus, there are dialects with only the [coronal] affricate /ts/, dialects with only [coronal] or [labial] affricates, /pf, ts/, and, finally, dialects with all three (/ts, pf, kx/).

The High German consonant shift also involved a complementary event, in which the unaspirated stop series /b, d, g/ turned into aspirated stops /p, t, k/. This is generally conceived of as being in a chain relationship with the first event, filling the gaps created by the change of the original aspirated series to affricates and fricatives. The second event is yet more restricted geographically than the first one, and represented in full generality only in the southernmost dialects. While the entire /b, d, g/ series shifted in early Bavarian, only the coronal consonant /d/ shifted in the Frankish dialects, to which Modern Standard GE owes its consonant system.

(3.2)   b. *Old Bavarian*   *Standard German*
                kot   Gott   'God'
                pluot   Blut   'blood'
                tac   Tag   'day'

3.1.1.4 *Sibilants and palatalization*

The GMC languages present an array of sibilants, or "groove" fricatives – sounds in which the flow of air is constrained to a narrow channel by the shaping of the articulators, creating a characteristic high-frequency energy, perceived as "hissing" – and affricates with sibilant releases. Cardinal among the former is the IE /s/ – the only inherited fricative, according to standard accounts. Other sibilants have arisen from a variety of sources. In GE, for example, a second /s(s)/ arose from postvocalic /t/ through the High German consonant shift. Interestingly, this /s/ did not fall together qualitatively with the inherited /s/ (as other consonant shift fricatives fell together with the corresponding inherited fricatives), but continued to be distinguished from it in rhyme and orthography well into the MHG period. Evidence involving the transcription of foreign words points to place of articulation as the difference between the two, the inherited /s/ tending toward palatal articulation (Braune 1874). This finds indirect support in its later development in some contexts (e.g., before a consonant in syllable-initial position) into a palatal groove fricative, /ʃ/.

Palatal sibilants and palatal affricates (e.g. /ʃ, tʃ/) have also arisen in EN and other Ingvaeonic languages and the Scandinavian languages, at various stages, by "palatalization" of velar or alveolar stops in the environment before front vowels or glides. Palatalization of velar stops apparently proceeded through several stages, each of which is still in evidence in word-initial position in one of the Scandinavian languages, as noted in Haugen 1976: 73. First, velar stops developed palatal offglides when they preceded front vowels, as in IC *gefa* 'give' ([gj-]). In pre-modern languages these palatal variants are sometimes indicated orthographically by diacritic use of a following vowel character, as in OS *k(i)ennian*. In some languages, velar stops in these environments further underwent assibilation – for example, in EN (*choose*) and in FA – developing into affricates with sibilant release.

(3.3) kemur [tʃēmʊr] 'comes'
       geva   [dʒēva]   'give'
       skip   [ʃɪp]   'ship'
       (FA, Haugen 1982: 71)

Finally, the voiced velar stop /g/ developed ultimately to a palatal glide in palatal environments in EN, NO and SW (EN *yield*, SW *giva* ([j-]). (On the other hand, DA has restored a velar stop here: *give* ([g]) (Haugen 1976: 73), though apparently only in early modern times (Haugen 1976: 368).) This whole sequence of developments is generally referred to elliptically simply as 'palatalization'. These instances of palatalization do not represent a single historical event; the assibilation in Ingvaeonic and that in Scandinavian belong to the historical periods of the individual languages. See Minkova 2003: 74ff. on the chronology of palatalization and assibilation in EN and Haugen 1982: 71ff. on the Scandinavian languages. Their occurrence was also dependent on environment. Thus, while */g/ did not assibilate in initial position in IC, it did so medially: IC *segi* [seiji] 'say'.

In EN and GE the cluster /sk/ has developed independently into a palatal fricative /ʃ/. In DU, this cluster has become /sx/. Some varieties of YI have developed palatal allophones of coronal sounds /t, d, s, z, n, l/ as a result of Slavic influence (Jacobs *et al.* 1994: 394; Jacobs 2005: 108).

3.1.1.5 *Alternations in laryngeal features and continuance*

The laryngeal features and continuance features of GMC obstruents often undergo contextual neutralization, resulting in morphophonemic alternations. The most famous of these alternations are the Verner's Law alternations which came to play a systematic role in strong verb paradigms in early GMC (with the notable exception of GO – see (5.1.1)). Verner's Law occurred in early GMC, before the elimination of moveable stress. According to the standard account, it involved the voicing of non-initial voiceless fricatives when they were not immediately preceded by the accent. In the early GMC/pre-GMC verb forms ancestral to the OHG forms in (3.4), for example, the /x/ of the root remained unvoiced in the present tense form, since the stress was on the root, but it was voiced to /ɣ/ in past plural form, which had suffix stress, yielding (with a few subsequent sound changes) the observed alternation.

(3.4) ih ziuhu 'I pull' wir zugum 'we pulled' (OHG)

50   3 *The sound systems of Germanic*

The question of why the position of the accent should interact in this way with the laryngeal feature of voice has been a difficult one. Among more recent analyses, that of Iverson and Salmons (2003) more or less stands the traditional account on its head, holding that it is the consonants which do not undergo Verner's law which require special explanation; they claim that Verner's Law reduces to yet another instance of "passive voicing"; the [voice] of a vowel or other sonorant spreads more or less automatically to laryngeally unmarked obstruents which follow them. However, if the vowel was accented, such voicing spread was retarded because the pitch accent which GMC inherited from IE was realized as a different laryngeal feature on the vowel, which was incompatible with voicing spread.

Contextual neutralization of both voice and continuance are also reflected in the alternations in (3.5), from GO. It is standardly assumed that the GMC voiced obstruents which derived from the IE "voiced aspirates" were uniformly fricatives ([β, ð, ɣ]) in early GMC, but then became stops under certain circumstances (though see Vennemann 1984 and Iverson and Salmons 2003: 58 for a contrary view). In GO, in any case, we know that they were fricatives after vowels, but stops after consonants. This difference is not directly reflected in the orthography of GO, where both the fricative and the stops are written in the same way, but it can be argued for as follows: GO had final devoicing of a subset of these obstruents – namely, those which appeared after vowels. In these environments, they appear as voiceless fricatives, as in (3.5a). (There is some vacillation in the orthographic representation of this devoicing, suggesting to some that it may have been introduced after the original Bible translation. See Roberge 1983 for discussion.) This final devoicing also affected the one unambiguous voiced fricative of the language, /z/, as in (3.5c). It did not happen to the obstruents in question when they occurred after consonants, however, as in (3.5b). Thus, the sound represented by <d> in (3.5b) must have differed in some way from the one represented as <d> in (3.5a) to account for this different treatment. Taking our lead from the clear case of (3.5c), we can accommodate the difference by assuming that it was a stop in (3.5b), and that final devoicing in GO affected only fricatives.

(3.5)   a. anabiud-a ~ anabauþ   (GO)
            I-command I-commanded

         b. land-is ~ land   (GO)
            land-Gen land-Nom

         c. waz-uh ~ was   (GO)
            was-and was

This conclusion is in turn supported by comparative evidence of various kinds. First of all, it conforms to the distribution of stop and fricative variants in other GMC languages, such as ON, where they are distinguished orthographically (as <d> and <ð> respectively). Second, we know of other instances of final devoicing in early GMC – in particular, OE – which affected fricatives but not stops. The OE change is still represented in *selves/self*, for example. See Moulton 1954 for detailed discussion of the development of these obstruents in early GMC.

The continental West GMC languages exhibit a still more general neutralization of laryngeal contrasts in final position, which affects not only fricatives, as in OE and GO, but stops as well. This general "final devoicing," known as *Auslautverhärtung* in GE, is found in GE, DU, AF and FR and in some dialects of YI (Jacobs 2005: 115), where the distribution is complex, and apparently obscured by paradigm leveling. See also King 1969: 46ff. and the references cited there.

(3.6)   a.   binde   band [bant^h]   (GE)
               I-bind   I-bound

          b.   reed [re:t]   reden [re:dən]
               road   roads
               (FR, Hoekstra & Tiersma 1994: 511)

          c.   raaf   raven
               raven   ravens
               (DU, de Schutter 1994: 448)

Among other things, 'final devoicing' here involves the neutralization of the contrast between the /b, d, g/ series and the /p, t, k/ series in final position, in favor of forms which are perceived as the latter. Still unsettled is the precise phonetic means by which this is achieved, and whether "final devoicing," has a different nature in GE (where the two series are claimed to differ with respect to tenseness/aspiration) and DU, where they are claimed to differ in voice. See Iverson and Salmons 1999 and Jessen 1996: 217ff. for some discussion.

In the Ingvaeonic languages, where, as we have seen, fricatives (and only those) are devoiced finally, voicing distinctions are also neutralized for fricatives between voiced sounds by intersonorant voicing. This yields alternations like the following:

(3.7)   uulf ~ uulƀos   (OS)
                wolf   wolves

The Scandinavian languages present a more complex picture of an early, general final devoicing of all obstruents (still reflected in such alternations as ON *binda* 'to bind' *batt* 'I bound'), followed by a second change, in which fricatives were voiced postvocalically in final, as well as medial positions. (In consequence of this voicing, the velar fricative, /x/, was lost in these positions, thus disappearing from the inventory.)

The Ingvaeonic and Scandinavian developments led to a total neutralization of the voice opposition in fricatives, though in two different ways. In the Ingvaeonic languages, the combination of intervocalic voicing and final devoicing of fricatives resulted in the voiced ones occurring only medially and the voiceless ones occurring initially and finally, with continuing consequences for distribution in the modern languages. Such voicing contrasts as exist in Modern EN fricatives are mostly due to borrowing after the OE period (*either*, *ether*), or effacement of the intervocalic environment in which the voiced fricatives arose (*breath*, *breathe*).[4] In FR, voiced fricatives still do not occur initially, even in loanwords, but the distribution of voiced and voiceless fricatives in final position has become complex (though predictable) (Visser 1997: 49f.). In ON, and in later Scandinavian languages, a slightly different distribution is found, voiceless fricatives occurring only initially, and the voiced ones postvocalically (Faarlund 1994: 42; Haugen 1982: 60).

More difficult to assess is the role of intervocalic/postvocalic fricative voicing in early GE. GMC /θ/ underlies both the <th> of *thaz* 'that' in the OHG of the Frankish Tatian translation and the <d> of *uuirdit* 'becomes'. We cannot imagine that /θ/ developed directly into /d/ in the latter. For one thing, we note that the /θ/ remains word-initially, while the /d/ appears medially, in voiced surroundings. Stops tend toward fricativization in medial environments, rather than the other way around. We must therefore suppose that this is an instance of intervocalic fricative voicing, of /θ/ to /ð/, and that the latter later occlusivized to /d/ in all environments, as happens elsewhere in West GMC. Thus, GE, too participated in intervocalic fricative voicing, though curiously restricted to the coronal fricative.

In other dialects of GE, including later varieties of Frankish OHG, though, historical /θ/ appears as /d/ not just in medial positions but in initial and final positions as well; the *thaz* of Tatian shows up as *das* in Standard GE. The change in initial position again seems to have involved a sequence of voicing and subsequent occlusivization, the intermediate stage perhaps being represented in the early South Rhenish Franconian text of Isidor, which has <dh> for initial */θ/.

This latter change of /θ/ to /d/ cannot be one of intervocalic voicing, of course, since it occurs in initial position. Rather, it appears as if it belongs, at least in terms of its systematic effect, to the events constituting the High German consonant shift; it fills the gap in the system created by the change of unaspirated stops to aspirated stops (t→ts/s, d→t, θ→d). If it is a part of the consonant shift, though, it is again one that was not carried through to the projected conclusion. There were no corresponding

---

[4] Other sources for the contrast in Modern EN include the late OE degemination of geminate fricatives, which, unlike simple fricatives, had not undergone intervocalic voicing in pre-OE, as in *offer* (←OE *offrian*) vs. *over* (←OE *ofer*) (Roger Lass, p.c.).

3.1 Segmental inventories and alternations 53

developments of */f/→/b/ or */x/→/g/. Once again, it is significant that the sole fricative affected was a coronal.

The change of /θ/→/d/ seems to have extended in late medieval times to DU and Low GE, which do not otherwise participate in the characteristic consonant changes of High GE. Given the cross-linguistic markedness of the interdental fricative, however, it is perhaps possible that this reflects an independent development.

Postvocalic lenition of the stops /p, t, k/ has also taken place in some Scandinavian languages, yielding lenis or voiced stops in some varieties of FA (Barnes (1994: 193) and in DA (the "Danish Consonant Shift" – Bandle *et al.* 2002: 904f.), where they later developed in part into voiced fricatives (Haugen 1976: 80; Goblirsch 1994; Bandle *et al.* 2005: 1858). Postvocalic lenition of stops, in the form of the deaspiration of aspirated stops and sometimes the fricativization of unaspirated stops, also took place in some dialects of MHG (Paul 1989: 131ff.). In some dialects of IC, too, the contrast between aspirated and unaspirated stops is neutralized postvocalically (Bandle *et al.* 2005: 1562).

3.1.2 The sonorants

Nasal consonants have been highly stable throughout the history of the GMC languages, aside from local assimilatory phenomena. All of the GMC languages have a [labial] nasal stop /m/ and a [coronal] stop /n/. Some of the modern languages also include a contrastive velar nasal /ŋ/, arising from simplification of the sequence */ŋg/. [ŋ] has not become distinctive in most dialects of YI, where the /g/ of /ŋg/ is preserved (Jacobs 2005: 113). In IC and in FA, the /g/ is preserved finally and prevocalically, rendering the preceding /ŋ/ predictable, but it is lost in front of consonants (IC *þing* [θɪŋg] 'assembly (Nom)' *þings* [þɪŋs] 'assembly-Gen'). In GE, /g/ is generally lost in this sequence. Standard EN exhibits the sequence morpheme-internally, but not morpheme-finally (*singer, banging* vs. *finger, angle, conga*). Curiously, the value /ŋ/ was assigned to a separate rune in the Runic *futhark*, <◊>, even though apparently not phonemicized (since the /g/ was also written in the earliest inscriptions: *birgŋgu* 'burial' (Opedal stone, Krause 1966: 176)). See Schwink 2000 for some speculation on this point. Some GMC languages, including IC, FA and YI, have a palatal [ɲ], which is sometimes contrastive (Jacobs *et al.* 1994: 394; Lockwood 1964: 19; Thráinsson 1994: 147).

Of the local assimilatory processes to which nasal consonants are subject, we may make note of the following. First, in IC and FA, nasals, as well as other sonorant consonants, are devoiced in the context of consonants of the /p, t, k/ series (see Thráinsson 1994: 151 and Lockwood 1964:18f. for discussion). Second, there seems to be a 'conspiracy' in some subgroups of GMC – particularly the Ingvaeonic and North GMC languages – to eliminate homorganic nasal-obstruent sequences in which the two consonants differ in voicing or continuance. Here we can enumerate the

Ingvaeonic/ON loss of /n/ before fricatives (GE *Gans* 'goose' vs. EN *goose*, SW *gås*), the assimilation of nasals to following voiceless stops in common Scandinavian (Haugen 1982: 61), reflected in IC *binda* 'bind', *ég batt* 'I bound', the common Scandinavian assimilation of /θ/ to a preceding nasal (IC *finna* 'to find', *fundum* 'we found'), the development of /nn/ to /ð/ before /r/ in West Scandinavian (Haugen 1982: 63) (IC *maður* 'man (Nom.)'/ *manns* 'man-Gen',) the development of epenthetic stops between nasals and fricatives in various languages (YI *gans→gandz*) and other similar changes. Some aspects of this "conspiracy" may reflect universal tendencies (see Padgett 1995).

Most of the standard GMC languages have only a single /l/ and a single /r/ at the level of contrastive phonology. That is, there are no distinctive contrasts between different kinds of /l/, or different kinds of /r/. Marginal exceptions are Eastern YI, which contrasts palatalized and unpalatalized /l/'s (Jacobs *et al.* 1994: 394), and NO, in which a retroflex flap /ɽ/, arising from postvocalic /l/ and /rð/, contrasts with the apical flap /r/ in a few forms (Kristoffersen 2000: 24). The phonetic realization of these liquids, however, varies quite widely crosslinguistically and in individual languages. /r/ sounds are particularly variable in GMC, as they are elsewhere, both in terms of place and manner. /r/ is variously realized in GMC languages as a dental, alveolar, velar, uvular or retroflex sound, with varying degrees of friction. It is often a tap, flap or trill, and in some varieties and some contexts a fricative – for example, some dialects of YI, where it is realized as /ɣ/ (Jacobs *et al.* 1994: 394), in GE (de Boor *et al.* 1969: 86) and in DA (Haberland 1994: 320). In EN, it is typically realized as an (apical, molar or retroflexed) approximant with no friction. In preconsonantal and final positions, it is not infrequently realized with vowel-like variants (see Eisenberg 1994: 355) and tends strongly toward vocalization or loss in this context in various GMC languages (see Howell 1991: 42ff.).

Many GMC languages include more than one variant of /r/. In some cases, they are complementarily distributed. Howell (1991: 18) cites cases in which apical and uvular /r/ both appear, but in different phonetic surroundings. In other cases, as in the case of GE apical and uvular rolled or flapped /r/, they are in free variation (Eisenberg 1994: 355). Booij (1995: 8) notes that the realization of DU /r/ as an alveolar flap, an alveolar roll, a uvular roll, a uvular approximant or a uvular fricative "is a matter of individual and regional variation." To this inventory of realizations, Collins and Mees (1996: 199) add alveolar and uvular voiced and voiceless fricatives and approximants. The uvular articulations are replacing the alveolar ones in the Netherlands, though not in Belgium, according to Collins and Mees. The contrast between uvular and apical /r/ is also a dialect distinction in AF (Donaldson 1993: 15). DA has a uvular [ʀ], apparently the result of GE influence, which has also spread to adjacent areas of Sweden and Norway (Haugen 1976: 73), while the rest of Scandinavian has an apical [r]. In some languages, including EN, /r/ tends to be articulated with lip rounding in initial positions (Heffner 1950: 149).

3.1 Segmental inventories and alternations

Clear evidence for an apical variant of /r/ in early GMC is provided by the fact that it merged with GMC */z/ in some instances. This was the invariable outcome in Northwest GMC, where */z/ 'rhotacized' to /r/, falling together completely with inherited /r/. (Crucially, this included the postvocalic, preconsonantal environment, as in GO *huzd* 'treasure' OE *hord*.) GO did not take part in this change, but, as Howell notes, there were cases in which a */z/ in GO assimilated to a neighboring /r/, as in **uz-rinnan → urrinnan* 'go out'. Interestingly, there was no such assimilation to a following /l/: **uz-laisjan → uslaisjan* 'educate'. These and other considerations which he discusses establish the likely existence of an apical /r/ in early GMC. Whether there was in addition a non-apical 'back' /r/ has been the subject of controversy. Numerous studies, summarized in Howell (1991), also propose a back /r/ of one sort or another, at least postvocalically, based on the observation that /r/ is among the triggers of a number of changes involving the lowering or backing of a preceding palatal vowel in early GMC, and that it generally shares this role with the uncontroversially back sounds /h∼x/ and /w/. Among the best-known changes are:

(3.8)   a. GO 'breaking' (lowering of /i, u/ to [ɛ, ɔ] before h, hʷ, r)
            *wurd → waurd [wɔrd] 'word'

    b. OHG lowering of [ai] to [ae] (later [ee]) before h, r, w
       GO laisjis Early OHG laeris 'you teach'

    c. OE 'breaking' (epenthesis of a back vowel between palatal vowel and a following /x/, /w/, /rC/, /lC/):

OS	fehu	OE	feoh 'cattle, goods' (Hogg 1992: 88)
OHG	sterro	OE	steorra 'star'
OS	trewe	OE	trēowe 'tree (DSg)'
OHG	elaho	OE	eolh 'elk'

Example (3.8b) is of special interest since it shows that even the originally apical /r/ that came from rhotacism of /z/ has these effects. As Howell notes, numerous investigators argue from these effects to the conclusion that the languages in question must have had a 'back' /r/ – variously identified as uvular, velar or retroflex – in these environments. The arguments are summarized in Howell 1991: 10ff. He goes on to demonstrate in detail, though, on the basis of the vowel-affecting properties of various types of /r/ in modern GMC languages, that "back" /r/'s do not in fact have any systematic and exclusive effects of this sort on preceding vowels, casting doubt on this sort of argument. Howell proposes that the vowel-modifying effects of postvocalic (and especially preconsonantal) /r/ in GMC are linked to its tendency to vocalize in that context.

On the other hand, King and Beach (1998) argue against the received view that the uvular [ʀ] in GE is a very late development, due to French influence in modern times.

It is present in YI, and the latter must have inherited it before it separated from GE, since none of the neighboring languages provide a source from which it could be borrowed. King and Beach locate this separation in the period 1500–1650.

/l/ sounds similarly vary across the family, primarily with respect to whether they are 'clear' or 'dark' (that is, articulated with concurrent pharyngealization or velarization). In (the standard dialects of) SW, GE and IC, for example, "clear," apical /l/ prevails in all contexts, while in the EN standards, and in standard Netherlands DU (Collins and Mees 1996: 197), they are complementarily distributed, "clear" /l/ appearing prevocalically and "dark" /ɫ/ appearing in syllable codas. Some dialects of EN have only dark /ɫ/ in all positions, while others have only clear /l/ in all positions (Collins and Mees 1996: 169), and, similarly, some DU dialects have only one or only the other (Collins and Mees 1996: 197).

3.1.3 The vowels

The history of the vowel systems in the GMC languages has been one of extravagant proliferation from an initially modest inventory. A comparison of the GO inventory with that of a Swiss GE dialect described by Moulton (1973), the short vowels of the DA dialect of Copenhagen (Bandle *et al.* 2005: 1862) and the vowels of the Sunnmøre dialect of western NO (Bandle *et al.* 2005: 1865) (where vowel length is not distinctive) gives a sense of the magnitude of this explosion in contrasts.

(3.9) a. Gothic short vowels

/i/   /u/
    [ɛ]   [ɔ]
          /a/

b. Gothic long vowels

/i:/   /u:/
    /e:/   /o:/
    (/ɛ:/)   (/ɔ:/)
          (/a:/)

c. Toggenburg Swiss German vowels

i	ü	u	ī	ǖ	ū	iə	üə	uə
i̯	ü̯	u̯	ī̯	ǖ̯	ū̯			
e	ö	o	ē	ȫ	ō	ei	öü	ou
ę	ö̧	ǫ	ę̄	ȫ̧	ǭ		ö̧i	
æ		a	ǣ		ā	æi	au	

d. Copenhagen Danish short vowels (Bandle *et al.* 2005: 1862)

i	y	u
e	ø	o
ɛ	œ	ɔ
a		ʌ
ɑ		ɒ

e. Sunnmøre Norwegian vowels (Bandle *et al.* 2005: 1865)

i	y	ʉ	u
ɪ	Y		
e	ø		o
æ	œ	a	ɔ

At the phonological level, the GO short vowels form a three-vowel system. The vowels /ɪ/ and /ʊ/ have mid-vowel allophones [ɛ] and [ɔ] respectively, occurring in the breaking environment illustrated in (3.8a). (Lehmann 1994: 23 claims that the contrast has been phonemicized, but the forms he cites are of questionable interpretation.) The long vowel system is somewhat richer, with high, mid and low vowels, and a further height (or tenseness) distinction among mid-vowels which is probably phonemic, depending on how one interprets various occurrences of the digraphs <ai> and <au>. The low vowel /a:/ is of marginal occurrence, having arisen only by way of compensatory lengthening of /a/ in cases of common GMC nasal loss /__x (/briŋgan/ 'bring'~bra:xta/ 'I brought'). GO vowels therefore constitute a rather modest but typical inventory. In the 317 languages of the original UCLA Phonological Segment Inventory Database (UPSID), as reported in Maddieson 1984: 126, the vast majority of languages have between five and seven vowels, and the five positions represented (at the allophonic level) in the GO short vowels are by far the most common type (Maddieson 1984: 136).

In this respect, the contrast between early GMC and the modern GMC languages is stark. GE and NO – the only GMC languages included in the 317 languages of the UPSID survey – exhibited more distinct vowel qualities than any of the other languages represented.[5] The inventory in some nonstandard varieties is even richer; Moulton (1973) identifies dialects of Swiss GE in which sets of vowels (short front vowels, for example) demonstrate a five-way contrast along the sole dimension of

---

[5] This is not to say that these are the languages with the largest number of vowels. As Maddieson points out (1984: 127), some languages have larger inventories of vowels even though they have smaller inventories of distinct vowel qualities – that is, vowels differing in the position of the oral articulators (tongue height, backness and lip rounding) – than the GMC languages do. This is because they contrast this smaller inventory of vowel types in a greater number of ways with respect to such features as length and such co-occurring articulatory gestures as nasalization and laryngealization.

vowel height.⁶ Contributing to the unusually large number of distinct vowel qualities in the modern GMC languages is the fact that there tend to be qualitative differences as well as quantitative differences between long and short vowels in the system. In general, long vowels tend to be higher and tenser than the short vowels, and tend toward diphthongal realizations. Because of this clustering of properties, it is often a matter of controversy whether it is the tense/lax opposition or the length contrast which is more basic (see Zonneveld *et al.* 1999: 517f. on GE, for example). In the Scandinavian languages where vowel length has ceased to be contrastive (see Section 3.2.2), the historical distinction between long and short vowels has been entirely superseded by qualitative differences. In IC, for example, former short /ɪ/ and former long /i:/ now contrast as tense and lax (or high and high-mid (Roger Lass p.c.)). They can both be long or short, depending on phonetic context:

(3.10) a. vita   [vɪːtʰa]   'know'   hitta   [hɪʰtːa]   'hit'
        b. ís   [iːs]   'ice'   ísnum   [isnYm]   'ice-the-Dat'
        (IC, Einarsson 1945: 7)

The modern GMC languages are, in any case, exceptionally vowel-rich languages, with many more contrasts than early GMC. It will not be possible to do more here than provide the broadest sketch of how this transformation took place.

3.1.3.1 *Umlaut and front rounded vowels*
One major source of enrichment of the GMC vowel inventory was the development in the Northwest GMC languages of front rounded vowels, primarily the products of "umlaut." Umlaut – regressive assimilation of the vowel of preceding syllables to the quality of the unstressed vowel of an immediately following syllable – is among the persistent hallmarks of the GMC languages, having occurred with different effects at various points in the history of the family. Some investigators (e.g., McCormick 1981) link this predisposition to the development of strong root stress and the consequent tendency toward reduction of unstressed syllables. McCormick points out analogous developments in other language groups, such as the Celtic languages, with the same features. Umlaut has been a substantial source for new vowels in the GMC languages.

---

⁶ On the other hand, Roger Lass points out (p.c.) that some very small vowel systems are to be found among the modern languages. Southeast Yiddish, for example, which lacks both length distinctions and front rounded vowels, has the following system:

(i)   I   ʊ   (Southeastern Yiddish, Roger Lass, p.c.)
              ɛ   ɔ
                 ɐ

Paul (1989: 48), for example, lists nine vowel or diphthong phonemes in MHG which arose through umlaut triggered by a palatal vowel or glide in the following syllable (<ę, ä, ō, ü, æ, œ, iu, ōu, üe>).

As many as three different phases of umlaut may be distinguished, all of which remain of synchronic importance because they gave rise to various kinds of morphophonemic alternations in the GMC languages. The earliest, attributable to common GMC, involved an interchange of high and mid short vowels in the root, depending on the height of the vowel of the following unstressed syllable. High (front) vowels and glides in an unstressed syllable raised an /e/ in a preceding syllable to /i/ ("i-umlaut"), while low vowels lowered an /i/ in a preceding syllable to /e/ and an /u/ to /o/ ('a-umlaut').[7]

(3.11) a. *esti   → OE is   'is'
        b. *wiraz → OE wer   'man'

This development resulted in one new segment /o/, filling the gap left by the pre-GMC change /o/→/a/. It also introduced some morphophonemic alternations, such as that in GE *ich helfe* 'I help', *du hilfst* 'you help'. We must place this phase of umlaut in the common GMC period because it must have preceded the early loss of the unstressed vowels which conditioned it in forms such as (3.11b). Its effects are not in evidence in GO, though, where they have been obscured by a radical restructuring in the distribution of [i] and [e], [u] and [o]. A second phase of umlaut, involving the raising of /a/ to /e/ when the following syllable contained a high front vowel or glide, on the other hand, took place only in Northwest GMC, not in GO: OHG *gast/gesti* 'guests'; GO *gasts/gasteis* [gastīs]. As the OHG examples show, this development also resulted in morphophonemic alternations. It also affected the segmental inventory marginally: the new /e/, while it fell together with inherited /e/ in some languages (OE, OS), remains qualitatively distinct from it in others – ON, SW and DA (Haugen 1982: 31) and OHG/MHG, as well as some modern GE dialects. In GE, the umlaut vowel is higher than the inherited /e/ (the subject of a famous note by Twaddell 1938), while in Scandinavian its reflexes are lower than those of the inherited vowel (SW *sex* 'six' *sälja* 'sell'←*saljan*).

This a→e umlaut is often called "primary umlaut," and I will adopt that term in order not to contribute unnecessarily to terminological proliferation, while noting that it was not the first such event in GMC. It shares with the still earlier e→i umlaut the

---

[7] The high back vowels and glides /u w/ did not have the same raising influence on the vowel of the root in this early GMC umlaut, though they did later in OHG, where *sie nemant* 'they take' alternates with *ih nimu* 'I take', as well as *er nimit* 'he takes'.

property of changing the height of a root vowel, by way of approximating (fully or partially) to the height of the conditioner in the following unstressed syllable. In this respect, these changes are quite different from a third phase of GMC umlaut, in which originally back vowels were fronted, under retention of their height and roundness features, by way of approximating the frontness of a following palatal glide or vowel (/i, j/) in the next syllable. The changes involved here yield the set of front rounded vowels which so greatly enlarge the inventories in (3.9c, d); for example, and changed the possibilities of combination for phonetic features. Prior to the introduction of front rounded vowels by umlaut, roundness was predictable from the values of the other two dimensions of vowel variation – frontness and height: all front vowels were unrounded, and all nonlow back vowels were rounded. This third phase of umlaut also resulted in extensive morphophonemic alternations, as in the examples in (3.12) from OE. (In these examples, the front alternant is not always rounded, because of subsequent unrounding, as discussed below.)

(3.12) a. bōc   'book'   bēc   'books'
        b. mūs   'mouse'   mȳs   'mice'
        c. þūhte   'seemed'   þyncan   'to seem'
        d. cuman   'to come'   cymð   'he comes'
        e. burg   'town(NSg)'   byrig   'town(DSg)'
        f. strong   'strong'   strengest 'strongest'
           (OE)

This set of changes shows up in all of the Northwest GMC languages, with the notable exception of Standard DU, some other DU dialects and certain dialects of southern GE. Moreover, it takes essentially the same shape in all of the languages in which it occurs. However, whether it is a common inheritance in these languages from their Northwest GMC parent or the convergence of later independent developments in the individual languages, and whether it is connected with or unconnected with the "primary umlaut" of /a/→/e/, and, if so, what the nature of the connection is, remain among the murkier questions in GMC historical linguistics. The centerpiece of this debate is the fact that, while the results of this fronting umlaut are given a distinct orthographic representation in some of these languages (OE and ON) from the very beginning, other languages do not begin to represent them in a way distinct from their source vowels for centuries after they came to be written languages. On this account, it is known as "secondary umlaut." So, for example, fronting umlaut is not represented in our OS manuscripts, as in (3.13a), even though it shows up in the Low GE which derives from OS, and it is wholly unrepresented in OHG manuscripts spanning more than three centuries until it finally began to be reflected in the writings of Notker at the end of the period, and more robustly in MHG, though not with full regularity until the end of the Early New High GMC period (Fertig 1996).

(3.13)   a. OS fullian 'fill'   LG füllen
                OS brûdigomo 'bridegroom'   LG brüme
           b. OHG brūtigomo   New High GE Bräutigam
               OHG fullen   New High GE füllen
                (Holthausen 1921: 42)

Two basic positions have been taken on the failure of OHG and OS to represent fronting umlaut. One of these, finding an early expression in Twaddell 1938 and advocated by later investigators including Penzl (1949) and Antonsen (1964), is that fronting umlaut did take place in the common ancestor of the Northwest GMC languages, contemporaneous with the /a/→/e/ umlaut, and that the front rounded variants were not written in OHG simply because they were subphonemic; their occurrence was predictable from the phonetic environment. In addition, their non-representation may have been influenced by the unavailability of convenient and obvious graphical symbols for representing them. The /e/ of primary umlaut was written, on the other hand, because it was split off from its source vowel owing to its similarity to a pre-existing phoneme.

Voyles (1992 as well as later work) finds this analysis problematic on three grounds. First, the explanation offered for the systematic failure to represent front rounded vowels in earlier OHG is questionable, since in numerous other cases, scribes in the early medieval languages, including OHG, do represent subphonemic variation, and since, in any case, the variation between front rounded vowels and their back rounded sources would have been rendered contrastive by early loss of the conditioner in such forms as *fullen* in OHG (3.13b). Second, if it were a common Northwest GMC innovation, rather than a series of parallel innovations in individual languages, it should be reflected in all of the daughter languages, yet the coastal dialects of DU, which have the /a~e/ alternations of primary umlaut, do not show secondary umlaut alternations between /u~y/, and it is also unrepresented in some dialects of Upper GE, where one finds, for example, /ʃdʊk/ for Standard GE *Stück* 'piece' (Howell and Salmons 1997). Finally, some GE forms originally containing a palatal glide which should have caused umlaut do not exhibit it (*glauben* 'believe'←*gelaubjan*, *suchen* 'look for'←*sōkjan*).

Voyles claims, as had some earlier scholars, that fronting umlaut ("secondary umlaut") is not a common Northwest GMC inheritance; rather, it is a late development in GE, dating only from the Late OHG period, and signaled in the orthography from its earliest occurrence. This accounts directly for the failure of representation in earlier GE. Forms like OHG *fullen* pose a problem for this account, too, though, since the /j/

which would have served as the phonetic conditioner of umlaut in these forms would have disappeared centuries before this hypothesized Late OHG umlaut event. The modern GE example shows that it has nonetheless undergone umlaut. Voyles accommodates this by claiming that fronting umlaut in GE was not a phonetic process, but a morphological one. *Füllen* is a member of a particular class of verbs – class 1 weak verbs – united by a number of inflectional characteristics; all of them had a suffix *-jan*, which early on was reduced to *-en*. The *-en* ending, distinct from the infinitival endings of other verb classes, as well as certain other features, served to distinguish class 1 weak verbs from other verb classes. In some class 1 weak verbs – those with a root vowel /a/ – there was also an alternation between /a/ in some forms and /e/ in others, as in (3.14a), created by 'primary umlaut' of /a/→/e/. The /e/ shows up in forms in which the suffix *-j-* was present, while /a/ appears in forms in which it had been eliminated before /a/→/e/ umlaut took place.

(3.14) a. zellen 'to tell' zalta 'told' (OHG)

These alternations, according to Voyles, served as the basis for the late OHG restructuring of other verbs of the same class by rule extension/analogy:

(3.14) b. zalta : zellan :: fulta : ? → füllen

GE front rounded vowels, according to Voyles, arise through these analogies. Other lexical classes, some of whose members included lexical alternation of /a~e/ in their paradigm, were similarly restructured, as this pattern was generalized to an alternation /V[+back]~V[–back]/, again yielding front rounded vowels and the appearance of fronting umlaut. As a morphological change, in the process of "lexically expanding," this development admits of lexical exceptions – an assumption which accommodates problematic forms like *glauben* and *suchen*. Crucial to this account, though, is the prediction that front rounded vowels, as the products of analogy, should appear only in forms belonging to a lexical class whose members also include some with /a~e/ alternations on which the analogy can be based. Problematic for Voyles' view that fronting umlaut was an analogical change, rather than a phonetic change, therefore, are cases of fronting umlaut in paradigmatically isolated forms, such as *übel* 'ill'←OHG *ubil*, *über* 'above'←OHG *ubir*, *Mönch* 'monk'←OHG *munih* (see Fertig 1996).

The accounts offered for the failure of secondary umlaut to be reflected in dialects of DU and some dialects of Upper GE cover a wide range. Antonsen (1969) proposes that the effects of umlaut in the Upper GE varieties in question have been eliminated by leveling under the influence of related forms. According to another suggestion, it had occurred as an allophonic change, but the two allophones merged again upon loss of the conditioner, not having become sufficiently distinct to allow for phonemic split.

3.1 Segmental inventories and alternations 63

A solution founded on language contact and interference is offered in Buccini 1988. Finally, Howell and Salmons (1997) connect the failure of secondary umlaut in DU and failure of umlaut to apply to /u/ in Upper GE dialects, claiming that both primary and secondary umlaut constituted a single historical process, common to Northwest GMC, but that it was a scalar process, the likelihood of whose application in a given instance was a function of the phonetic distance between the trigger and the affected vowel. The distance was greatest where the trigger was a high front vowel or glide and the affected vowel was a low back vowel /a/, and less where the affected vowel was itself a high vowel, /u/. Individual languages were thus less likely to implement the change in this case, and variation is to be expected. The failure of umlaut to take place in *glauben* and *suchen* has a phonetic basis, on this account.

Palatal umlaut is not the only source for front rounded vowels in GMC. Others include u-umlaut in ON, in which [round] spread from a /u/ of an unstressed syllable to the vowel of the preceding syllable, under retention of other features (**triggwz→ tryggur* 'faithful'), rounding of vowels in New High GE in the context of consonants with labial articulation (GE *leffel→Löffel* 'spoon'), and spontaneous fronting of /u(:)/, for example, in DU, SW and IC (*suður* [sY:ðYr] 'south', Haugen 1982: 42).

In some GMC languages, front rounded vowels have become unrounded. In OE, this took place in two stages, /ø, ø:/ turning into /e, e:/ very early on in the southern dialects (though <oe> writings for these persist in the north) (Hogg 1992: 125), while /y/ persisted until late OE. In many of the central Frankish dialects of GE (e.g., Luxembourgish and PG), as well as YI, front rounded vowels have also become unrounded. In IC, too, historical /y/ has lost its rounding, as in *yrki* [ɪrkɪ] 'work' (Haugen 1982: 42; Bandle *et al.* 2005: 1120). On the other hand, several varieties of British EN, as well as some varieties of colonial EN, have developed new front rounded vowels, typically by fronting [u:] (Lass 1992: 53). Similarly, the place of the unrounded high front vowel of Icelandic has been taken by fronting of /ʊ/.

SW and NO have four contrastive high vowels, of which three are rounded: /i(:), y (:), ʉ(:), u(:)/ (Kristoffersen 2000: 14). The phonetic difference between the two non-back rounded vowels, /y(:)/ and /ʉ(:)/, varies dialectally, involving in some of them a contrast between two distinctive lip shapes ("inward" and "outward" rounding; see Bandle *et al.* 2005: 1119, 1603 for discussion).

3.1.3.2 Diphthongs

GMC had the diphthongs /eu, ai, au/, consisting of non-high vowels followed by the glides /i, u/. The system is asymmetrical due to the early change of *ei→*ī. These diphthongs are falling diphthongs – diphthongs which begin with their most prominent component, the vowel, and end in a glide. They are also closing diphthongs – articulated with increasing tongue height. This inventory has been affected in the history of individual languages by monophthongization (of ai→ā in OE, ai, au→ē, ō in OS, for example). Conversely, new instances of closing diphthongs have arisen from long vowels through diphthongization. In ME, for example, this occurred as a part of the complex of vowel changes known as the Great Vowel Shift. A similar development took place beginning in MHG (OHG *zīt*, Modern GE *Zeit* 'time', OHG *hūs*, Modern GE *Haus* 'house'), and, in a somewhat different development, the long low and mid vowels of ON have become diphthongs in Modern IC: /e:, æ:, ø:/→/ai/, /a:, ɔ:/→/au/, /o:/→/ou/, for example. Other diphthongs have arisen from the vocalization of postvocalic consonants. This has been of importance in DA, for example, where there are as many as eleven distinct diphthongs (/ui, ɔi, ai, au, ɔu, æu, øu, yu, eu, ɛu, iu/, Bandle *et al.* 2005: 1862). In some cases, these changes occurred after orthographic practice was fixed, so they are variously represented in the orthography. Of still more systemic consequence have been the changes which have introduced centering diphthongs (those in which the transition is from less open to more open) in some GMC languages: in FA (Barnes 1994: 192; Haugen 1982: 45; Bandle *et al.* 2005: 1090), AF (Donaldson 1993: 8f.), Central YI (Jacobs 2005: 96), and most remarkably in FR, which has the inventory of centering diphthongs in (3.15a), according to Visser (1997), in part the result of a development of schwa-offglides after most GMC long vowels.[8]

(3.15)   a. FR centralizing diphthongs
/iə/   /yə/   /uə/
/ɪə/   /öə/   /oə/
(Visser 1997: 24)

These new diphthongs occur in monosyllables, and alternate with rising diphthongs (which begin with a glide and terminate with a vowel) when affixes are added, as in (3.15c) ("Modern FR Breaking", cf. Tiersma 1999: 17f.).

(3.15)   b. FR rising diphthongs
[jy]   [ju]   [wi]   [wo]
[jɪ]   [jö]   [jo]   [wɛ]   [wö]
[jɛ]   [jɔ]   [wa]
[ja]
(Visser 1997: 25)

         c. FR Breaking: foet /fuət/ 'foot'~fuotten /fwotən/ 'feet'

---

[8] A third type of diphthong, the 'height harmonic' type, developed in OE, where the height of the second member adjusted itself to that of the second (Hogg 1992: 101f.; Lass 1994: 50f.). Thus, GMC *[au] becomes OE [æa] and GMC *[eu] appears as [eo], for example.

Rising (glide-initial) diphthongs have also developed in the Scandinavian languages through a variety of individual changes, including the Scandinavian stress shift (Haugen 1982: 36), in which GMC *eu* becomes /jū/ (**freusan*→frjūsa 'freeze'), various instances of 'breaking' of vowels in specific phonetic environments (e.g., Northwest GMC **hert-a*→*hjarta* 'heart', under the influence of the back vowel in the following syllable), and the change of /e:/→/jɛ/ in Modern IC.

3.2 The suprasegmental phonology of the Germanic languages

Recent and comprehensive discussions of some aspects of the suprasegmental or prosodic phonology of the GMC languages – length, stress and tone – are to be found in van der Hulst 1999, particularly in the chapters by Lahiri *et al.*, Zonneveld *et al.* and Bruce and Hermans. The following sections rely heavily on these works, and the interested reader is referred to them for greater detail. For discussion of phonotactics in EN and other GMC languages, Lutz 1991 is an excellent source.

3.2.1 Syllable structure and sonority

The basic unit of hierarchical organization of sounds in the GMC languages, as elsewhere, is the syllable. The construction of syllables makes crucial reference to a ranking of sounds with respect to their relative sonority (roughly, "vowel-likeness"; see Clements 1990). Open vowels are the most sonorous sounds, while voiceless stops are the least sonorous. There are various formulations of this "Sonority Hierarchy," but for our purposes the following will suffice:

(3.16)   The Sonority Hierarchy
           Vowels
                   low vowels
                   high vowels/glides

           Sonorants
                   Liquids
                           r
                           l
                   nasal stops

           Obstruents
                   voiced fricatives
                   voiceless fricatives
                   voiced stops
                   voiceless stops

Syllables are built around a nucleus – a relative peak of sonority, more sonorous than the immediately surrounding sounds. In GMC stressed syllables, the nucleus must be a vowel. While IE allowed sonorants (liquids and nasals) to function as the nuclei of syllables, early GMC 'resolved' these inherited syllabic nasals and liquids into sequences of the vowel /u/ followed by a nonsyllabic sonorant (/n̥/→/un/).[9]

Neighboring sounds of lesser sonority attach to an adjacent nucleus. When they attach to a following nucleus, they become part of the syllable onset. When they attach to a preceding nucleus, they become part of the syllable coda. Nucleus and coda together constitute the 'rhyme' of the syllable: [$_{\text{SYLLABLE}}$ ONSET [$_{\text{RHYME}}$ NUCLEUS CODA]] (see Blevins 1995 for a general discussion of this architecture). The rhyme determines syllable weight, which is important for a number of phonological purposes, including, for example, defining the minimal word size allowable in a given language. In GO, we find a few function words like *sa* 'he, that one', *ni* 'not', whose rhyme consists only of a short vowel nucleus with no coda. In other languages, however, this possibility is excluded. In DU, for example (Booij 1995: 31), words and, for that matter, final syllables must have a rhyme consisting of two "morae," or units of length. That is, the nucleus must be a long vowel or a diphthong, or there must be a consonant in the coda. Booij refers to this as the minimal rhyme constraint.

Not all consonants are equally admissible in both onset and coda positions. The velar nasal /ŋ/, for example, never appears in the onset position in monosyllabic forms, while, in the modern GMC languages, /h/ does not appear in coda position. There are numerous other such asymmetries in individual languages. Unlike some languages, the GMC languages allow sequences of consonants, rather than just single consonants, to occur in the onset and in the coda of the syllable. Onsets may consist of two or, in highly restricted circumstances, three consonants. Not all possible pairs and permutations are allowed, however. Some sequences are ruled out by the way in which syllables are defined: more sonorous consonants cannot precede less sonorous consonants in an onset cluster because the first consonant would then constitute a peak of sonority relative to its surroundings, hence the nucleus of its own (defective) syllable. It follows that, while /pl/ may be an admissible onset, */lp/ will not be. Onsets are more narrowly constrained than this, however. Starting with GO, we observe the following general patterns.

---

[9] It is not clear to what extent liquids and nasals were disallowed as syllabic nuclei in all unstressed syllables in early GMC. Our principle of syllabification, under which each peak of relative sonority defines a separate syllable, would lead us to conclude that /r/ in GO *akrs* 'field' and /n/ in *razns* 'house' are syllabic nuclei of their own (quasi)-syllables, though see Ebbinghaus 1970 for a possible argument against this.

3.2 The suprasegmental phonology of the Germanic languages

a. GO has no onset clusters consisting of two obstruents, except where the first obstruent is /s/: /sp-, st-, sk-/. /s/ also combines freely with nasals, with /l/ but not with /r/, and with /w/ but not with /j/.
b. GO has no onset clusters consisting of two sonorants (e.g., */ml/), except that the glide /w/ can combine with the liquids /l, r/ (if these are in fact clusters – see below): /wl, wr/.
c. GO freely allows clusters of obstruents and liquids, or the glide /w/, except that /l/ does not combine with coronal stops, /s/ does not combine with /r/, and /w/ does not combine with labial obstruents. There were no onset clusters with /j/ in GO, though they arise in later languages from various sources.[10]

bl, br	pl, pr
*dl, dr	*tl, tr
gl, gr	kl, kr
	fl, fr
	þl, þr
	sl, *sr
	hl, hr
*bw	*pw
dw	tw
(k^w)[10]	[gw]
	*fw
	þw
	sw
	(h^w)

d. GO obstruents combine with nasals in onsets, but in a much more restricted way. Obstruent-nasal onset clusters first of all occur only with the coronal nasal /n/. There are no clusters /pm, tm, km/, for example.

---

[10] /k^w, h^w/ are parenthesized here, since they arose from IE monosegmental consonants with complex articulations (labio-velars), and are usually taken to be velar consonants with labial coarticulation in GO, as well. Krause (1968: 69) expresses uncertainty about whether they are monosegments or clusters. Lehmann (1994: 22) argues for unit phonemes, though the evidence is slight. That the originator of the GO alphabet may have regarded them as single segments is reflected in the fact that they are represented by separate alphabetic characters (though this is not true in other early orthographies: Runic *ehwu* 'mare' (Krause 1966: 244)). /gw←g^w/, on the other hand, also a labiovelar in origin (found only after nasals in GO, since it turned into /w/ or /g/ elsewhere in Common GMC), is written as a sequence.

(/pn/ is also unattested, but /p/ was a rare sound in early GMC in any case). /n/, moreover, does not combine with other coronal sounds in onsets. In this case, the restriction is narrower than it was with liquids. /*þn/, as well as /*tn, dn/, is non-occurring. There are also no cases of initial /gn/ in GO, but its widespread occurrence in other GMC languages makes it clear that this is an accidental gap. This is possibly also the case with /fn/, which is also found elsewhere in GMC, though in a very small number of words.

bn
*dn   *tn
(gn)   kn
        (fn)
        *þn
        hn

e. Triconsonantal onsets in GO consist solely of s + obstruent + r: /spr-, str-, skr-, *spl-, *skl- *stl-/.

The patterns of co-occurrence and non-co-occurrence of consonants in initial clusters here are in a way crosslinguistically typical. Other languages tend to show gaps in the same places as GO, and linguists at least since Trnka (1936) have noticed general trends in these patterns, which have been explored and analyzed in enormous detail over the decades. It is impossible to do more than skim the surface of that discussion here. The interested reader is referred especially to Vennemann 1988, Lutz 1991 (ch. 4, and the references cited there), as well as Booij 1995 and Visser 1997. We can divide the main restrictions into two types.

3.2.1.1 *Sonority-based restrictions*

a. Syllables cannot decrease in sonority from the left edge toward the nucleus (by definition). Note that this is apparently violated by the GO onset clusters *wl-*, *wr-*, which seem to begin with a glide followed by a liquid – a drop in sonority. Various possible accounts for this aberration suggest themselves, including the possibility that these are not clusters, but liquids articulated with lip rounding.[11] It is also apparently violated

---

[11] Uncertainty about the analysis of /w/ clusters recurs in historical GMC. The case of the GO labiovelars has been mentioned, and the status of /hw/ in pre-modern EN is similarly unclear. In some dialects, the reflexes of this sequence are still distinct, but they are pronounced as monosegments – as a labialized /h/, or as an aspirated /w/. The orthography gives no clue about when the monosegmental pronunciation arose.

3.2 The suprasegmental phonology of the Germanic languages 69

quite systematically by /s/ + stop clusters, which would also seem to involve a drop in sonority, and which are nonetheless crosslinguistically quite usual and diachronically stable. The exceptionality of s-clusters to sonority hierarchy generalizations is not fully understood, but a widespread view is that this results from the ability of /s/ to be extrasyllabic – that is, essentially, outside the structure of the syllable, hence not subject to sonority constraints, in such cases. Suzuki (1991) applies such an analysis to s-clusters in early GMC, and uses it to explain some otherwise puzzling differences between clusters like /st/ and clusters like /sl/ with respect to such things as reduplication in GO and alliteration in early GMC verse forms. Note in this context that /s/ (or /ʃ/ in some languages) is the only consonant allowed to begin triconsonantal onset clusters (see Lutz 1991: 205ff., Visser 1997: 90, 108 for additional discussion, references and suggested analyses).

b. Syllables preferentially increase in sonority toward the nucleus (and therefore, syllables with onsets are preferred over those without).

c. Syllables preferentially not only increase in sonority toward the nucleus, but must do so with a sufficiently steep gradient. As we will see, what 'sufficiently steep' means varies from language to language. GO disallows onsets consisting of two obstruents, aside from the s-cluster cases, and it disallows onsets consisting of two sonorants. In triconsonantal clusters, this requirement applies even more strictly; the third consonant in such clusters in GO can only be the most sonorous liquid, /r/.

3.2.1.2 *Place-based restrictions*

a. Onset clusters are preferentially composed of two consonants with different places of articulation. This accounts for such things as the gaps /*dl, *tl, *dn, *tn, *bw, *fw/, for example (and possibly /sr/, though note that /s/, unlike the coronal stops, does combine with /l/ and /n/).

b. In GMC, only coronal consonants can occur as non-initial members of onset clusters, except in the case where the first consonant is /s/. There are no clusters of the shape /Xm-/, where X≠/s/.

These same general restrictions are in evidence in the GMC languages besides GO, but with variation in their implementation. The following table (3.17) – based in part on Lutz 1991: ch. 4, and drawing on Visser 1997, Eisenberg 1994, Tiersma 1999 and Kristoffersen 2000 – shows how some later GMC languages have deviated from the pattern of GO with respect to the steepness of the sonority gradient in onset clusters. Because the focus is on what changed, I have only listed those clusters which

(a) appear in GO (or other early GMC languages) and (b) fail to appear in some modern GMC languages. Some onset clusters – those consisting of stops or fricatives (aside from the weak fricative /h/) plus liquids – are quite stable, and remain universally represented in GMC. Others – in particular, those consisting of obstruents plus nasals, and those consisting of weak fricatives plus liquids or nasals – have tended to disappear in some languages. We can characterize this as a change in the required steepness of the sonority gradient. Forms in angled brackets are unattested but assumed on the basis of comparative evidence. Forms in parentheses are marginal, occurring only in a handful of words in the language (GO /bn/, for example, occurs in *bnauan* 'rub', GE /dv/ only in the borrowed form *dwars* 'abeam', and EN /θw/ just in the borrowed word *thwart* and the imitative *thwack* – just enough to show that they are not phonotactic impossibilities). Square brackets are used where the cluster is retained, but with phonetic modification.

(3.17)

GO	IC	FA	DA/SW/NO	FR[12]	GE	EN
(bn)	–	–	–	–	–	–
<gn>	+	+	+	–	+	+
kn	+	+	+	+	+	–
<fn>	+	–	(+)	(+)	–	– (→sn)
hn	+	–	–	–	–	–
hl	+	–	–	–	–	–
hr	+	–	–	–	–	–
dw	[dv]	[dv]	[dv]	+	(+)	+
tw	[tv]	[tv]	[tv]	+	[tˢv]	+
kʷ	kv]	[kv]	[kv]	+	[kv]	+
þw	[þv]				(+)	
sw	[sv]	[sv]	[sv]	+	+	+
hʷ	[hv]	[hv]	–	–	–	[hʷ]
wl	–	–	–	–	–	–
wr	–	[vr]	[vr]	–	–	–

Many of the changes illustrated here between the early GMC situation and that in later GMC languages can be seen as serving to eliminate onset clusters with shallower sonority gradients, while retaining those with steeper gradients. EN, for example, has lost obstruent + nasal clusters, while retaining obstruent plus liquid clusters. Not all of

---

[12] In FR, onset clusters – even those consisting of /s/ + sonorant – can be split by epenthesis (Visser 1997: 258ff.)

3.2 The suprasegmental phonology of the Germanic languages

the changes serve that result, though. The change of /w/→/v/ in syllable onsets, widespread in North and West GMC languages, serves the sonority hierarchy by increasing the steepness of the sonority rise in words which begin with /w/, but creates less optimal onset clusters when it occurs after obstruents (/dw/→/dv/, for example). The elimination of clusters which are, from the standpoint of sonority restrictions, less ideal has progressed farther in EN than in other GMC languages. Lutz (1991:256) argues that the extent of loss of such clusters is a function of increasing prominence on the accented syllable – a development more advanced in EN than elsewhere. She notes (p. 249) that the loss of these clusters in EN took place over several centuries, that the order of loss is generally as predicted by the sonority difference between the two consonants (/g/ disappearing /__/n/ before /k/ did, for example), and that the clusters most widely retained in other languages were also the most recently lost in EN.[13]

GO exhibits a widely discussed local development which runs counter to the general expectation of dispreference for homorganic consonant onsets. In GO, GMC /fl/ has developed into /þl/ in a few instances, under uncertain phonetic and dialectal circumstances: *þliuhan* 'flee', OHG *fliuhan* (see Lehmann 1986: 363 and Davis and Iverson 1994, 1996 for discussion). Similarly typologically surprising developments occur in Northwestern British EN (Roger Lass p.c.), where EN /kl, gl/ have turned into /tl, dl/ respectively.

The modern GMC languages have also added a few onset clusters that were not present in early GMC; some of these, such as /pn/ and /sf/, are marginally represented in loanwords (the latter almost exclusively in *sphere* and its relatives). Unclear is whether affricates like /ts/, which arise in GE through the High German consonant shift, and in FR through palatalization, for example, are to be included in the list of new onset clusters. Interpreted as clusters, these are problematic from both the standpoint of the sonority restrictions and the standpoint of the preference for non-homorganic onset clusters. Nonetheless, they have been argued to be clusters, not unit phonemes, in at least some GMC languages (e.g., Visser 1997: 103ff.). In GE, they are standardly held to behave as single segments, rather than clusters. GE also developed new affricate plus sonorant clusters through the High German consonant shift, though fewer than it might have been expected to. /pfl/ and /pfr/ occur, arising from /pl/ and /pr/, but */tsr/ (from /tr/) does not.

---

[13] Even though FR has both obstruent + liquid and obstruent + nasal clusters, Visser (1997: 97) notes that they are treated differently by other phonological processes. In particular, word-internally, the obstruent and the nasal are separated by syllabification (*ak-ne* 'acne'), while the obstruent and the liquid are not (*se-kreet* 'secretion') – just as they would be syllabified in EN, which does not allow nasal plus obstruent clusters. This fact converges with the crosslinguistic and diachronic evidence to show that obstruent plus nasal is more marked as an onset cluster than obstruent plus liquid.

This notion of possible onset, partly language-specific and partly a reflection of crosslinguistic tendencies, also plays a role in the identification of syllable boundaries in multisyllabic forms. Vowels serve as syllable nuclei, and consonants adjacent to those vowels must normally be assigned to either the coda or the onset of the syllable. Where sequences of one or more consonants occur between two vowels, traffic rules are needed to determine which syllable they are assigned to. Generally assumed to be one of these is a principle "Maximize Onset," which requires that consonants be assigned to onsets, so long as the result is a possible onset in the language.[14] This insures, for example, that syllabification of a form like: re#frain will place the syllable boundary between the *e* and the *fr*, and not at any of the other a priori possible sites. Early GMC may have syllabified differently. Murray and Vennemann (1983: 59) and Lahiri *et al*. (1999: 357), following others, claim that in early GMC syllables were required to be bimoraic where possible – that is, to end with a long vowel, or with a short vowel and a consonant, so long as meeting this requirement would not leave a following syllable wholly without an onset (Lahiri *et al*. 1999: 408n). This requirement would override Maximize Onset in cases like **gas.tiz*. The most direct evidence we have for syllabification in early GMC – word division in certain GO manuscripts (cited in Murray and Vennemann 1983) – is in fact internally inconsistent on this point. Forms like *fa/dreinais*, *hwa/þro*, *þa/þro*, *wi/þra* are divided in a way consistent with Maximize Onset. *Fas/ta*, on the other hand, is split in a way consistent with a preference for bimoraic syllables (though see Booij 1995: 31 and Visser 1997: 97 for possibly comparable unexpected treatments of s-clusters in DU and FR). Other examples listed by Murray and Vennemann are consistent with either.

On the other hand, there is indirect evidence in favor of a syllabification like **gas.tiz*, in Common Scandinavian, for example, where, as Lahiri *et al*. (1999:57) note, the vowel of the unstressed syllable undergoes syncope (*gestz*), just as it does in words with clearly bimoraic initial syllables (*wul.faz→wulfz*), and unlike forms with a CV- initial syllable (*su.nuz→sunuz*). See also Russom 2002 for possible evidence from poetic metrics.

Jacobs (2005: 115ff.) notes that YI has a much larger inventory of initial clusters than the other GMC languages, due to extensive influence of Hebrew and Slavic languages. Some of these (/pt, ps, px, pk, tk, tf, xk/ and others) counterexemplify the GMC dispreference for obstruent-obstruent onset clusters. Some (/tn, tl, dn, dl/) counterexemplify the dispreference for homorganic onset clusters, and some (/kd, sd/)

---

[14] According to Booij (1995: 31), Maximize Onset requirement can come into conflict with another requirement, the Minimal Rhyme constraint, requiring that rhymes be of a certain minimal length. This conflict results in the phenomenon of ambisyllabicity, in which a single consonant, e.g., in a word like *adder*, is interpreted as both the coda of the first syllable and the onset of the second.

3.2 The suprasegmental phonology of the Germanic languages 73

appear to counterexemplify the prohibition against obstruent sequences whose elements differ in voice. Interestingly, as Jacobs (2005: 125) points out, such clusters are not preserved under syllabification; between vowels, a sequence of consonants (VC $CV) is split by a syllable boundary unless the second is a sonorant or the first is a sibilant – that is, only onset clusters of the types found in other GMC languages are left intact by syllabification.

Coda consonant sequences in the GMC languages are similarly, though less strictly, constrained by the sonority hierarchy; coda clusters must decline in sonority toward the right edge of the syllable, thus often being the mirror image of onset clusters. Steepness is not as important, though, and they are not subject to similar constraints against homorganic sequences. In fact, some GMC languages exhibit a dispreference for coda clusters consisting of sonorants followed by other consonants when these have *different* places of articulation. Where the sonorant is a nasal, these are often rendered homorganic by way of assimilation of the place of the nasal to that of the following obstruent as in GO *fimf* 'five'. Where the sonorant is a liquid, some dialects insert an epenthetic vowel between the two members of the cluster. While such epenthesis is not a feature of all of the GMC languages, its operation is relatively uniform in those where it does occur. In modern WF (Visser 1997: 263) and Old Upper GE, for example, it splits sequences of all liquids plus non-homorganic obstruents, as in Old Upper GE *wërah* for Frankish OHG *werk* 'work', FR /skɛlk~skɛlək/ 'apron'. It also splits sonorant/sonorant clusters, as in FR /tɛrm~tɛrəm/ 'intestine', Old Upper GE *charal* for Frankish OHG *karl* 'man', *horen* for Frankish OHG *horn* 'horn'. Further, in both OHG and FR (Visser 1997: 259n.), epenthesis is not restricted to coda position, but occurs (with restrictions) in cases where the two consonants belong to separate syllables, as in Old Upper GE *arapeit* for Frankish OHG *arbeit* 'work'. Collins and Mees (1996: 198) report similar facts about nonstandard dialects of DU, where *helpen* is pronounced as /hɛləpə/, for example. FR and Upper OHG differ, however, in that in FR, epenthesis does not occur between coronal sonorants and coronal obstruents (*wyld* [vilt] 'wild'). This does happen, though with much less frequency, in Old Upper GE, as in *garat* for Frankish *gart* 'sapling' (Braune 1963: 70), assuming that /r/ here was coronal. In none of these languages does epenthesis split up non-homorganic obstruent-obstruent clusters (Visser 1997: 265).

Place-based restrictions also manifest themselves in another way in codas, in a preference for coronal consonants in final positions. Final obstruent-obstruent clusters whose first member is not /s/ must end in a coronal. This is true, for example, in EN *apt, aft, act*, GE *acht* 'eight', *sanft* 'soft', *Klecks* 'blot', *Krebs* 'crab', and in GO *ahs* 'ear', *ansts* 'grace', *bairhts* 'bright', *gagrefts* 'decision', *gahugds* 'memory' (see also Booij 1995: 45 for DU). Even s-clusters occasionally metathesize by way of creating this preferred coronal-final order, as in OE *wæps* 'wasp', *axode* 'asked'. Booij offers

74   3 The sound systems of Germanic

an analysis in which final coronal obstruents in instances like these are not part of the coda, but a separate appendix, following the coda proper. Appendices may consist of as many as three coronal obstruents, as in DU *aardig-st* 'nicest', *bedaar-dst* 'calmest'.

3.2.2   Length

Vowel length, as reflected in (3.9) is an inherited feature of GMC. Consonant length is not. IE did not have long or geminate consonants. Geminate consonants arose in GMC from a variety of sources. Early sources of relatively minor importance include GMC assimilations in resonant clusters (IE **pḷnos* / GO *fulls*, Sanskrit *tasmai* / GO *þamma* 'that (Dat)' and so on (Prokosch 1938: 86)), the gemination of intervocalic glides in certain environments (Holtzmann's Law) and their subsequent development to stops in ON and GO (Verschärfung) (OHG *zweiio* 'of two'/ GO *twaddje*, ON *tveggja*), and "expressive gemination," for example, in intensive verbs like OE *treddian* 'tread' (Fagan 1989).

Three processes in the later medieval languages produced a much larger set of long consonants, and were of considerably more systematic importance. A main source of geminates in North GMC was a set of assimilations, similar in kind to the early GMC ones just illustrated, which occurred with particular robustness in North GMC languages at various points: ON *rann* 'house' (GO *razn*), ON *gull* 'gold' (GO *gulþs*), ON *finna* 'find' (GO *finþan*), ON *drakk* 'drank' (GO *drank*) are early instances, but succeeding rounds of such assimilations occurred later on in individual dialects (Haugen 1982: 64, 77, 79; Bandle *et al.* 2002: 878).

In the West GMC languages, coda consonants geminated before a following glide (or other sonorant). This is illustrated by OE *settan* 'set', OS *settian*, OHG *sezzen*, compared to GO *satjan*. This "West GMC gemination" led to new morphophonemic alternations, between geminate consonants and those which remained short because they did not precede /j/ (e.g., OE *ic fremme* 'I do' *du fremest* 'you do'). It appears to have been one of a number of events of a similar type; besides the gemination illustrated in these examples, of presumably common West GMC date, there is reason to think that OE underwent a second round of gemination at a later time, and there was an event in common Scandinavian which partly overlaps in its effects these West GMC events.

Gemination of this sort was sensitive to the nature of the affected consonant and the nature of the sonorant which triggered the change. In West GMC, the glide /j/ causes gemination most consistently, geminating all final consonants but /r/, originally (OHG *nerien* 'to save', though in some OHG texts one finds /rr/ (Braune 1963: 92)). /r/ and /l/ had a weaker effect as triggers of gemination than /j/, apparently causing gemination only of voiceless stops, and not with the same degree of consistency as gemination

/__/j/. Thus, we find in OE *bittor* 'bitter' alternating with *bitor*, corresponding to GO *baitrs*, *æppel* 'apple' alternating with *apul(dre)* 'appletree', and *æhher* 'ear of corn' alternating with *ear* (where the non-geminated /h/ has been deleted intervocalically). Gemination does not take place in OE in *fugel* (GO *fugls*), with a voiced consonant. Similarly, in OHG, we find gemination in *luzzil* 'little', *bitter*, *ackar* (GO *akrs*), but not in *fogal* (Sievers 1898: 116; Braune 1963: 92). A second round of gemination took place in later OE (Sievers 1898: 116), in which voiced stops were geminated /__r, yielding *blæddre* 'bladder', for example. In the ON version of this change, only velar stops geminate, and only before glides (/j, w/): *liggja*, *sløkkva* 'to extinguish'. Murray and Vennemann (1983) account for this array of facts in terms of a universal Syllable Contact Law which disprefers syllable contacts in which the onset of a following syllable is more sonorous than the coda of the preceding syllable. The likelihood of change occurring depends on the egregiousness of the violation (the degree of sonority difference between the two consonants).

Finally, geminate consonants resulted in GE from the High German consonant shift, through which, as we noted earlier, voiceless stops became geminate voiceless fricatives intervocalically, falling together, except in the case of sibilants, with the geminate fricatives resulting from the West GMC gemination. Thus, for example, corresponding to EN *open* we have OHG *offan*, and corresponding to EN *make* we have OHG *mahhôn*.

These changes resulted in a new phonological structure in the medieval languages, unexampled in earlier or later languages, in which length is a feature systematically shared by both vowels and consonants. It also seems to have occasioned a series of changes aimed at 'balancing' the relative length of co-occurring vowels and consonants (cf. Lass 1992: 70ff.). So, for example, in OHG, geminates from both the Consonant Shift and the West GMC gemination are shortened when the preceding vowel is long. We know that these consonants were geminated after long vowels, since they are represented as such in early texts, but they are degeminated soon after these early attestations. GMC **slāpan* is represented in early texts as *slāffan*, after the Consonant Shift, but later as *slāfan*. GMC **laidjan* 'to lead' appears in early OHG texts as *leittan* in the wake of West GMC gemination, but later as *leitan* (Braune 1963: 92f.). Similarly, the effects of first-round gemination do not appear in OE after long vowels (e.g., in *sēcan* 'seek'). It may be, as Murray and Vennemann (1983) claim, that it did not occur there, or we may alternatively imagine that, as in OHG, it did take place, but was followed by shortening. Sievers points out (1898: 116) that the second round of gemination in OE did take place in words that had long vowels in OE, such as *blæddre* 'bladder' and *næddre*, but which have short vowels in Modern EN, and surmises that the shortening occurred simultaneously with the gemination (see also Lahiri *et al.* 1999: 337f.).

We can view such geminate simplification as a part of a "conspiracy" (Lass 1992: 70), targetting syllable rhymes, and operating to prefer those which are bimoraic – that is, which have exactly two units of length. In nonfinal syllables, if the vowel of the nucleus is a long vowel or diphthong, then the preference for bimoraic syllables disfavors a coda consonant. Geminates are simplified in such cases so that the remaining consonant can syllabify with the next syllable. In cases involving consonant clusters, which cannot be shortened, it is the long vowel which is shortened in order to conform to the bimoraic template. If the vowel of the nucleus is a simple short vowel, then the coda of its syllable can contain a consonant, and geminates are retained in just those cases. By casting the phonological "target" in this way, one can also accommodate the other contexts in which degemination was usual in medieval GMC – finally and in preconsonantal position (OHG *mizzu* 'I measure'~*maz* 'I measured', *kunnan* 'to be able'~*konda* 'could'). Here again, if geminate simplification had not taken place in *mazz and *konnda, then the resultant rhyme (VCC) would violate the preference for a bimoraic syllable.

Lass (1992: 70ff.) points out that the two systematic effects of this shortening – the reduction of the number of contexts in which length contrasts occur, and the regulation of possible syllable types (in this instance, by preventing 'overlong' syllables) – are shared by a number of other changes beginning in about the same era, which collectively have the effect of more regular syllable shape and at least partly predictable vowel/consonant length. Already in early GMC, long vowels in monosyllabic forms tended to be followed by at most a single consonant (excluding coronal case affixes), while consonant clusters tended to be preceded by only a short vowel. We have numerous forms like GO *skalk-s* 'servant' and *land* 'land', for example, as well as *skōh-s* 'shoe' and *mēl* 'honey'. Forms like *leiht-s* [līxt-s] 'light', with both a long vowel and a consonant cluster were found too, though they were relatively infrequent. The appearance of degemination and vowel shortening before geminates in the medieval West GMC heralds the rise of an active dispreference for such overlong forms. Lass (1992: 70ff.) points out that other changes also conspired toward the elimination of such syllables, including vowel shortening in front of sequences of consonants at various points in the history of medieval EN (for example, EME closed-syllable shortening in *cēpte* 'I kept'→*cepte*).[15] Similar changes took place in Common Scandinavian (Haugen 1982: 25; Lahiri *et al*. 1999: 362) and in MHG (MHG *lieht*→ Modern GE *Licht* [lɪçt], Paul 1989: 77), but with much less regularity in the latter.

[15] Contravening this tendency to eliminate sequences of the shape VVCC is the OE process of lengthening of short vowels before clusters consisting of a sonorant and a homorganic voiced stop, variously known as Pre-Cluster Lengthening (Lass 1992: 71) and Homorganic Lengthening (e.g., Ritt 1994). This change, for example, turns *hund* 'dog' into *hūnd*, *cild* 'child' into *cīld*. This development is extensively discussed in Ritt 1994, and in Liberman 1992, but remains a problematic phenomenon. It has analogues in North GMC (Haugen 1982: 38).

3.2 The suprasegmental phonology of the Germanic languages

Conversely, all of these languages have shown some tendency to add weight to the rhymes of some shorter syllables. The earliest such event, which Lass (1992: 71) suggests could have occurred in Common Northwest GMC, lengthened vowels in absolute final position ('Foot-final Lengthening'). While GO has such forms as *sa* 'that one', these do not occur in Northwest GMC. The elimination of short syllables was most systematically carried through in North GMC, where, as a result of the "Great Quantity Shift" starting in DA in the thirteenth century (Haugen 1982: 25), all nonfinal stressed syllables came to have bimoraic rhymes of the shape -XX, either by lengthening the vowel (-V→VV), or by geminating the following consonant (-VC→VCC). Thus, *fara* 'go' turns up variously as *fāra* and *farra* (Haugen 1982: 25). Further, in monomorphemic forms with short vowels in closed syllables, the final consonant was geminated (Old SW *skip*→[skep:] Lahiri *et al.* 1999: 364). In SW (Andersson 1994: 274), as a result of these changes, long vowels are (virtually) excluded in front of long consonants, long consonants (almost) only occur after short vowels, and, except in Finland SW dialects, every stressed syllable must contain a long vowel or diphthong or a long consonant or consonant cluster (see Andersson 1994: 274 for the discussion of the few exceptions).

(3.18) a. *å* [oː]   'stream'
        b. *ås* [oːs]   'ridge'
        c. *oss* [osː]   'us'
        d. *ask* [ask]   'box'
        (SW, Andersson 1994: 274)

In IC too all vowels may be either long or short (Einarsson 1945: 4). They are long if followed at most by a single consonant, or if followed by clusters of the form /p, t, k, s/ + /j, r, v/ – that is, clusters which are possible onsets of a subsequent syllable.

(3.19) a. *hatur* [haːtYr] 'hate' *hattur* [hahtːYr] 'hat' *akrar* [aːkʰrar] 'fields'
        b. *líta* [liːtha] 'to look' *líttu* [lihtːY] 'Look!'
        c. *ef* [ɛːv] 'if' *eff* [ɛfː] 'the letter *f*' *lepja* [lɛːpʰja] 'lap up'
        (IC, Einarsson 1945: 4–5)

The acute accent in (3.19b), a former mark of vowel length, now encodes only vowel quality. In FA too (Lockwood 1964: 8), vowels are long when final, and before a single consonant, and before the consonant groups /kl, kn, pl, pr/, which are possible onsets, though not before /tl/, which is not. These languages thus represent the logical endpoint of Lass' hypothesized conspiracy toward regularization of syllable shape and the neutralization of tense contrasts. The pattern resulting from the quantity shift, however, is not wholly intact in all modern Scandinavian languages, due to paradigm leveling (Bandle *et al.* 2005: 1866).

This impulse toward syllable regulation did not take hold with such systematicity in other GMC languages. In the late medieval West GMC languages, short vowels of CV syllables came to be lengthened (open syllable lengthening), though these changes were carried through with varying degrees of regularity. Open syllable lengthening in DU and GE appears to have been a single event, beginning in DU territory and spreading southward (Lahiri *et al.* 1999: 350). The change resulted in length alternations within paradigms in both languages (DU *dag* 'day'~*dāgen* 'days'), but these were largely leveled in GE, by generalizing the long vowel throughout the paradigm (Lahiri *et al.* 1999: 352).

In EN, this open syllable lengthening belongs again to the EME period. OE [nama] 'name' became ME [na:m(ə)], for example. Numerous apparent exceptions and chronological complications have made a precise characterization of this event a very difficult matter. Primary among the problems is the fact that its effects show up with full regularity in EN only in forms ending in unstressed vowels in EME, which were later lost. Such forms include, for example, *ale, ape, bake, hate, mate, name* and so on. It appears much less regularly in forms which remain bisyllabic into Modern EN. Some of these (*acorn, bacon, beaver, gable, mason, raven*, for example) show lengthening, but most (*better, bottom, brother, cellar, desert, feather, hovel, moment, mellow, record, saddle*) do not (see the appendix in Ritt 1994 for an exhaustive list). Lahiri *et al.* (1999: 353) attribute this variability to the fact that the long vowel resulting from open syllable lengthening in these bisyllabic forms would be subject to shortening again when additional inflections were added, due to another of the quantity-adjustment rules of ME, trisyllabic shortening, which shortens long vowels in initial stressed syllables when they are followed by two or more syllables (the rule that underlies the *divine*~*divinity* alternation in EN). Trisyllabic shortening produced alternations between long vowels and short vowels in the paradigms of words like *beaver, brother*, and these were subsequently leveled in different directions in different forms.

All of these West GMC languages also gave up the length contrast in consonants by systematically degeminating them. Thus, among the modern languages long consonants are found only in North GMC. Nor are they universal there: DA is allied with the West GMC languages in having simplified geminate consonants, as well as in having a version of the quantity shift which shows resemblances to West GMC open syllable lengthening; like West GMC (and unlike other Scandinavian languages), it was always the vowel that was lengthened in DA, not the following consonant (Lahiri *et al.* 1999: 363). And like West GMC, short vowels in (nonfinal) CV syllables are lengthened in DA, but short vowels in CVC monosyllabic forms are not generally lengthened (Haugen 1982: 51). The degemination in these languages, as Lass (1992: 75) notes, largely negated the partial predictability of distribution of vowel length which resulted from open syllable lengthening, by introducing a new set of short vowels in front of singleton consonants. These languages have generally retained double writing of consonants as a way of signaling graphically that the preceding vowel is short.

The results of these events, as Lahiri *et al.* (1999: 340) point out, is that, with the exception of a few dialects of SW and NO, the modern GMC languages do not still preserve length in both the vowels and the consonants at the level of phonological contrasts. Consonant length is given up in the West GMC languages, but retained in most North GMC languages with the exception of DA. Vowels still vary in length in the North GMC languages, aside from DA (on which see Haugen 1976: 366), but predictably so.

3.2.3 Lexical stress and the foot in Germanic phonology

The GMC languages, like other Western European languages, have prosodically fixed word stress – that is, stress whose position is (mostly) predictable on the basis of the phonological shape of the word, and does not depend on grammatical information. In this respect, the GMC languages, like their Celtic and Italic neighbors, have departed from the pattern of accentuation in IE, in which accent was "free" – that is, not phonologically fixed and predictable, but able to appear on different syllables in different forms of a word, and therefore to signal meaning contrasts. This "free accent" is reflected, vestigially, at least, in the Greek examples in (3.20).

(3.20) patḗr 'father-NSg'
patr-ós 'father-GSg'
patér-a 'father-ASg'
páter 'father-VSg'
(Greek)

In early GMC, on the other hand, the accent came to occur invariably on the first syllable of the word in unprefixed forms, through the "Germanic Accent Shift." Rather than a simple shift in the position of accent, Iverson and Salmons (2003: 23) see in this accent shift "a profound change in the nature of accent itself." GMC has abandoned the lexical word tone of IE, implemented as a laryngeal feature associated with the nucleus of a syllable, and replaced it with rhythmically determined dynamic stress. The Greek accent is still a pitch accent, but in the GMC languages the primary correlates of stress are intensity and duration. Pitch is associated with stress only in a secondary way, and there is variation from one language to another, and even within languages, in the manner and degree in which the pitch of stressed syllables differs from that of neighboring syllables (see Lass 1992: 83; Lass 1994: 84; Haugen 1982: 22). In some languages, stressed syllables are higher in pitch than unstressed ones, while in others, they are lower in pitch.

The unit on the basis of which stress is assigned is held to be the metrical foot. Feet constitute a level of prosodic organization above the syllable. Feet are built up from syllables according to principles which differ across languages. The descriptive need for these larger units of prosodic organization is made evident in the phonology of many phenomena in the history of GMC whose description requires reference to a domain larger than a single syllable – e.g., where unstressed syllables tend to undergo reduction or not depending on whether the preceding syllable is "heavy," the processes in question serving to maintain overall "balance" in weight between the two successive syllables (see Dresher and Lahiri 1991 for some discussion of such processes). They include high vowel deletion in OE *wordu→word* 'words' but not *limu→limu* 'limbs', the "vowel balance" phenomenon in Scandinavian (Haugen 1982: 25; Bandle *et al.* 2005: 1109, 1858) and others. Feet are also the basis of stress assignment. One of the syllables within the foot is designated as its head, and serves as the locus of stress. Early GMC syllables are held to be assembled into feet from the left edge of the word rightward, the leftmost syllable in each foot serving as the head. The precise mode of foot formation in early GMC has been a matter of controversy. Lass (1992:85) proposes that OE feet were formed by grouping the syllables of a word into feet of two to three syllables, starting at the leftmost edge of the word, and marking the leftmost syllable in each foot as the strong syllable (the head), without regard to syllable count or syllable weight, yielding a factoring of the word into left-headed (trochaic) feet. Feet were then grouped together pairwise, the leftmost branch in each such pairing again being the strong branch. The notion of "head" is transitive; the leftmost syllable in the word, as the head of the leftmost foot, will be the head syllable of the word, and thus assigned the main word stress. Heads of feet further to the right have lesser prominence, and are thus assigned secondary stress. A competing account, advanced by Dresher and Lahiri (1991), holds that the GMC foot was assembled in a procedure sensitive to syllable weight; a heavy syllable – that is, a syllable whose rhyme was either a long vowel or a short vowel plus a final consonant – could constitute a foot by itself. A light, CV syllable could not, but would have to attach to a preceding, head-building heavy syllable where possible. Thus, a word like *ōperne* 'other-ASg' would have two feet: [ō] and [þer.ne]. As in Lass' account, in early GMC, the leftmost foot is always the most prominent, so that its head receives the main stress. In forms consisting of only light syllables, such as *fre-me-de* 'did', the first two syllables can combine to constitute a complex head ([fre.me]de]), the short vowels of each of these syllables adding up to the equivalent of a heavy syllable and constituting, therefore, a "resolved" head. The stress falls on the leftmost syllable of that complex head. Both of these accounts predict the same distribution of primary stress, but make different predictions about secondary stress – for example, in forms like *ōþerne*. In the account of Dresher and Lahiri, the syllable *þer* should receive secondary stress, since it is the head of its own foot, while in the account of Lass, it should not, since it forms the second syllable of the foot headed by /ō/. The two approaches also make different predictions with respect to the patterning of syncope processes, such as High Vowel Deletion, which were apparently sensitive to secondary stress. The interested reader is referred to Dresher and Lahiri 1991 and Lass 1994: 90ff.

In prefixed forms in the early GMC languages, stress becomes more complex. In verbs, prefixes are never stressed; the stress falls on the first syllable of the root, as in *us-léiþan* 'depart' (Prokosch 1938: 119). Two different positions have been assumed with respect to the history of this situation. Some claim that it arises because GMC stress was from the beginning not word-initial but root-initial. Others claim that stress was word-initial, but that prefixes were still separate lexical items at the time when stress was fixed, hence outside the reach of word stress. There is some evidence that the fusion of prefix and verb stem was not complete in early GMC, including the fact that they could be separated from the verb by intervening clitics, as in GO *ga-u-laubjats...?* 'Do you believe?' (Matt. 9:28) (see Lahiri *et al.* 1999: 336 for a summary of this debate, with references). In nouns and adjectives, on the other hand, stress generally falls on the prefix, as poetic alliteration shows us, for example, with the exception of the prefix *ge-/ga-*, which is never stressed: GO *ús-liþa* 'paralytic', OE *únrōt* 'sad'. The situation is complicated further by the fact that nouns and adjectives can be derived from verbs and the converse, carrying over the accentuation of the source, as in *forgífenis* 'forgiveness', for example (Hogg 1992: 100; Lass 1994: 92. See also Prokosch 1938: 199).

Word stress in the modern GMC languages is treated in detail in Zonneveld *et al.* 1999. Among these languages, only Insular Scandinavian (IC and FA) has remained true to the GMC preference for initial stress, and these languages have apparently even strengthened it, since prefixes are generally stressed in them. Lockwood notes that there are few exceptions in FA, of a systematic nature only in cases of words with three or more syllables which begin with the prefixes *ó-* 'un' or *sam-* 'together', for example, *sambærligur* 'agreeable' which is variably accented on the first or second syllable. Non-initial accent is making some inroads through borrowing, however, as in *studentur* 'student', accented on the second syllable.

Large-scale borrowings of Latinate vocabulary (from French and Latin, primarily) have led to radical change in the word stress of the other modern languages. Early borrowings from such sources were adapted to the native stress pattern, as in the case of OE *cándel←candéla* (Lass 1992: 86). Later loans, however, came in such numbers that the native stress rule was supplanted by one very much like that which applied in Latin (Zonneveld *et al.* 1999: 477), in which stress often falls on non-initial syllables.

As the latter functions in EN, if the penultimate syllable is heavy (has a long vowel or a consonantal coda), it is stressed: *volcáno/abándon*. If the penultimate is a light syllable (CV), the stress is typically shifted leftward to the antepenult (*Ámazon*). Stress does not occur further to the left than the antepenult (*antícipate*). This "three-syllable window" restriction (Zonneveld *et al.* 1999: 480) is shared with the rest of modern GMC, excluding Insular Scandinavian.

Another characteristic of these new stress patterns is that they are much less regular than the earlier one, and admit of more exceptions (involving primarily borrowed words). There are, for example, numerous exceptions to the general rule that light penults are not stressed (e.g., *vanílla, Kentúcky*), and that heavy final syllables are not stressed (*machíne, expéct, arrést, palisáde, ballóon*) (see Zonneveld *et al.* 1999: 482f.).

Interestingly, this change from GMC to Latinate stress patterns turns out to be less radical, both in terms of its effects and its analysis, than it might appear at first glance. In terms of effects, Lass (1992: 88f.) points out that the GMC stress rule is virtually subsumed as a special case of the new stress rule for native forms. Two-syllable words like *candle* are stressed on the first syllable under either rule. ME forms like *wúnede* 'dwelled' and *behólden* 'behold' are also both expected under either stress rule (the latter derivable under the GMC rule because of the prohibition of stress on verb prefixes). The differences emerge only in relatively few words of more than three syllables, and in unprefixed three-syllable words with heavy penults. In terms of analysis, the new rules still involve the forming of left-headed (trochaic) feet with heavy syllables at their head, the difference being that the prominent foot is at the right edge, rather than the left edge of the word (Zonneveld *et al.* 1999: 479).

As Zonneveld *et al.* point out, the stress rules found in continental West GMC, as well as in SW and NO, are of a type, with only modest variation among them. The pattern found in these languages resembles that of EN in, for example, yielding penultimate stress in bisyllabic words, and in polysyllabic words with heavy penultimate syllables. These parallels are reflected, for example, in the fact that EN, DU and NO all accent the words *kílo, sombréro, pásta, témpo, anacónda, súltan, r(h)ododénndron* in the same way (Zonneveld *et al.* 1999: 546f.). These other languages differ from EN, however, in a few ways. First, while the final syllable in EN is stressed only in exceptional cases, it is routinely stressed in the modern continental languages when "superheavy" – that is, consisting of a long vowel and a consonant, or of a short vowel followed by more than one consonant (see Zonneveld *et al.* 1999: 496, 522f. for discussion). So, for example, while EN has penultimate stress in *pírate, cóncert, antecédent, básalt*, and antepenultimate stress in *président* (because of the light penult), the final syllable is stressed in the corresponding words in DU, GE and NO. Further, while they share with EN the property that stress appears earlier than the penultimate syllable only when the penultimate is light, they apparently differ from

3.2 The suprasegmental phonology of the Germanic languages

EN in how light syllables are characterized. In EN, when the penult is an open syllable with a short vowel, the accent shifts to the antepenult (*Pánama*), but when it is an open syllable with a long vowel (*unrúly*) or a closed syllable with a short vowel and a coda consonant (*inférno*), the penult receives the accent. In the continental languages, only closed syllables count as heavy. Open syllables with long vowels in the penult do not prevent leftward shift of the accent. This difference is obscured by the orthography in many cases. EN *Pánama* is accented on the antepenult because the penult has a short vowel. The vowel of the penult in DU *Pánama*, on the other hand, is long (as are all vowels in open syllables in these languages), yet it does not prevent shift of the accent to the antepenult. This difference between the continental languages and EN is no doubt connected to the fact that in these languages, unlike EN, length is not contrastive in open syllables, since these languages do not allow short vowels in open syllables, and routinely lengthen them there (Lahiri *et al.* 1999: 365). These languages do have numerous forms in which the stressed penult has a short vowel which is not followed by a consonant cluster (DU *Apollo, Walhalla, libretto*, GE *Bazillus, Madonna*). In these, it is argued that the syllable is closed by the following consonant, which is ambisyllabic (Zonneveld *et al.* 1999: 498, 520). Open syllables with diphthongs do count as heavy in these languages: GE *Baláláika, Thesáurus* (Lahiri *et al.* 1999: 365; Zonneveld *et al.* 1999: 520). In all of these languages, though, the stress does fall on a penultimate open syllable with a long vowel if the vowel of the final syllable is /ə/, as in GE *Methode* 'method' (the "final-schwa rule," cf. Zonneveld *et al.* 1999: 521).

Again, statements about accent in these languages fall short of full generality. Zonneveld *et al.* (1999: 527ff.) list exceptions for GE, noting that the various generalizations differ in reliability, the preference for stress on superheavy final syllables being particularly violable. Some of these languages contain words with different meanings which seem to differ only in the position of stress, being otherwise of the same phonological shape. Zonneveld *et al.* (1999: 556), for example, list those in (3.21), among many others, from SW.

(3.21)   kórset 'the cross'   korsétt 'corset'
         fórmel 'formula'   forméll 'formal'
         módern 'the mother'   modérn 'modern'
         váran 'the ware'   varán 'kind of lizard'
         kántat 'edged'   kantát 'cantata'
         trúmpet 'sullenly'   trumpét 'trumpet'
         kánon 'canon'   kanón 'gun'
         krítiker 'critics'   kritíker 'critiques'
         (SW)

Many of these pairs, of course, involve one member which is not a lexical form but a syntactic compound, consisting of a noun and an enclitic definite article, and they are thus not straightforward minimal pairs. EN has a set of noun/verb pairs in which the accent contrast has been partially systematized in Latinate words according to lexical category, in such cases as *contrast* and *transfer*.

3.2.3.1 Stress in derived forms

A further legacy of the period of intense borrowing from Romance languages in the modern languages, excluding Insular Scandinavian, is some relatively complex interactions between stress and affixation. All of these languages distinguish between two sets of derivational suffixes, generally known as Class I suffixes and Class II suffixes. Class I suffixes are "stress-sensitive" – that is, they are counted as a part of the word in computing the position of stress. Resultantly, stress will appear on a different position in the base word when a Class I suffix is attached than when it is not (or even on the suffix, if the stress rules require). Examples of Class I suffixes are given in (3.22):

(3.22) a. séntiment   sentiméntal   (EN)
        b. éerzucht   eerzúchtig   (DU)
        c. Fínánz   finanziéll   (GE)
        d. príns   prinséssa   (SW)

Class II suffixes, on the other hand, are "stress-neutral"; they do not alter the stress patterns of the forms to which they are attached. Examples are given in (3.23):

(3.23) a. accómpany   accómpaniment (EN)
        b. hórizon   hórizonloos   (DU)
        c. geméin   Geméinschaft   (GE)
        d. främling   främlingskap   (SW)

See Zonneveld *et al.* 1999 for a discussion of this distinction and its complications.

As Zonneveld *et al.* (1999: 543) point out, in GE, DU, NO, SW and DA, there are also some instances in which inflectional affixes behave like Class II affixes, in causing stress shift. This is true specifically of some plural affixes on nouns, as in GE *Dóktor~Doktóren* 'doctors'.

3.2.4 Word tone in Germanic

Some GMC languages have reintroduced word level tonal contrasts, or "pitch accent" contrasts. These do not replace stress, but overlie and are partly dependent on it; only stressed syllables show pitch accent contrasts. The best-known case is the contrast between two word accents in most of the continental Scandinavian languages, excluding fringe areas, such as Finland SW, extreme Northern SW, North and West NO (Bruce and Hermans 1999: 607). Known respectively as Accent I (or acute) and Accent II (or grave), these contrast for the most part only in words of more than one syllable, and only when these are not stressed finally. All monosyllables and finally stressed polysyllables have only Accent I. Minimal pairs include SW *víner* 'it whizzes' and *vìner* 'wines'.

The phonetic realization of the distinction varies across languages of this group in complex ways (Bruce and Hermans 1999: 625), but in general, it appears that the difference is in how the pitch melody aligns with the stress of the word. Given a uniform rise-fall (Low-High-Low) melody for words, the peak (H) of the melody occurs earlier in Accent I words than in Accent II words; in Southern SW, for example, the alignment for Accent I is H*L (where * designates the word stress), yielding a pitch fall after the stress, but for Accent II, it is L*H, yielding a pitch rise after the main stress (Bruce and Hermans 1999: 624f.).

The polysyllabic words with Accent II were originally polysyllabic, while those with Accent I were originally monosyllabic in most cases, coming to be polysyllabic through such processes as attachment of an enclitic definite article, or epenthesis of a vowel between an obstruent and a (quasi-syllabic) final resonant, as in (3.24):

(3.24)   a. and-in → ánden
             duck-the
         b. akr→ áker 'field'
             (SW, Lahiri *et al.* 1999: 369)

Thus, to state one of the hypotheses of origin (that of Oftedal 1952) in a somewhat oversimplified way, pitch contours at the ends of phrases differed in shape when the phrase ended with a final stressed syllable from when it ended in an unstressed syllable. These contours were reinterpreted as tones, yielding one pattern for monosyllabic forms and other forms with final stress, and a second pattern for polysyllabic forms with unstressed final syllables. The forms in (3.24) were still monosyllabic forms at this time, becoming bisyllabic only later, and preserving their original pitch contours. Thus, Accent I words like those in (3.24) are polysyllabic forms with monosyllabic pitch contours (for a fuller discussion of this hypothesis, see Lahiri *et al.* 1999: 368ff).

The assignment of tonal accents interacts with affixation, in the case of monosyllabic roots. SW, for example, distinguishes between affixes which are "accent-neutral" – that is, with which the root retains its Accent I – and affixes which induce Accent II (Bruce and Hermans 1999: 613). The former include the clitic definite article and the present tense marker (*báck-en* 'the (football) back', *vín-er* 'it whizzes'). The latter include the plural marker *-ar/-er* (*bàck-ar* 'backs') and the infinitive suffix *-a*. The accent of polysyllabic forms is unaffected by affixation.

In some dialects of NO, apocope has resulted in the extension of this contrast to certain pairs of monosyllabic forms (e.g., *kóm* 'come-Imper' vs. '*kòm* 'come-Inf', the latter manifesting "circumflex" accent – an apocopated Accent II (Bruce and Hermans 1999: 617).

Of a common origin with the word tone contrast in other Scandinavian languages is the *stød* (literally, "thrust") phenomenon in DA, though it differs from that contrast in terms of its phonetic nature and distribution. Words with *stød* are articulated with a distinctive glottal gesture (creaky voice, Basbøll 2003) accompanying the rhyme of the stressed syllable. According to Riad (2000: 263), it is not the glottal gesture itself which is perceptually significant, but the fact that it is accompanied by a sharp lowering of frequency; *stød* is an artifact of compressing a circumflex (HL) accent into a single syllable, and thus basically a tonal phenomenon (but see Bruce and Hermans 1999: 627). For *stød* to occur, the syllable must be stressed and have a heavy rhyme with either a long vowel or a short vowel followed by a sonorant. The *stød* is realized during the articulation of the vowel if long, or on the sonorant if the vowel is short.

(3.25) a. sen   [se:'n]   'late'
        b. sind [sen']   'mind'
        (DA, Riad 2000: 264)

Riad attributes this condition to the requirement that the sonorant phase of the syllable rhyme be long enough to reach the low frequency required for creaky voice. He notes as well (p. 267) that the circumflex accent of NO dialects is in some instances subject to a sonority condition like that associated with *stød*. The tone contrast of the central Franconian dialects of DU and GE, to be discussed below, is similarly realized only in cases where a stressed syllable has either a long vowel or a short vowel followed by a sonorant (Bruce and Hermans 1999: 640).

Historically, forms with *stød* are related to forms with Accent I in other languages, while some forms without *stød* correspond to Accent II forms in other languages (though not all, since the non-occurrence of *stød* can also be conditioned by the shape of the syllabic rhyme). The historical direction of this relationship has been disputed (see Liberman 1982; Riad 2000). The correspondence is incomplete, however. While monosyllabic words, and words with final stress, can only have Accent I in the other languages, as discussed above, not all monosyllabic words or polysyllabic words with final stress have *stød* in DA (for a recent discussion, see Basbøll 2003). In polysyllables with non-final stress, *stød* does not appear if the final syllable consists

3.2 The suprasegmental phonology of the Germanic languages 87

of just schwa (Riad 2000: 265; Bruce and Hermans 1999: 622). This sets up DA morphophonemic alternations in cases like *gul* [gu:'l] 'yellow', *gule* [gu:lə] 'yellow-Pl' (Riad 2000: 264).

A second instance of word tone in GMC, also spanning linguistic boundaries, is the contrast found in a contiguous area of DU and GE dialects in northwestern Germany, Luxembourg, eastern Holland and eastern Belgium. This contrast (discussed in detail in Lahiri *et al.* 1999, Gussenhoven and Bruce 1999, Bruce and Hermans 1999, Gussenhoven 2000) is distinct in origin from the Scandinavian tone contrast, and phonetically different from it, though there are points of similarity. For example, as is true of Scandinavian, the contrast in some DU dialects requires stressed syllables with long vowels, or with short vowels followed by sonorants, for its realization (Gussenhoven 2000: 233). The two accents are known variously as Tone I/Accent I/push-tone (DU *valtoon*, GE *Stoβton*)/falling tone and Tone II/Accent II/drag-tone (DU *sleepton*, GE *Schleifton*) (Gussenhoven and Bruce 1999: 242). Accent I is realized as a HL melody, Accent II as a level high tone (or, in final position, as a falling-rising melody with vowel lengthening). Interestingly, Accent I is sometimes terminated with glottalization (Gussenhoven 2000: 219). The following examples of the phenomenon as it manifests itself in the DU dialect of Maasbracht are selected from a much longer list of minimal pairs in Bruce and Hermans (1999: 637f.).

(3.26)   Accent I (falling tone)   Accent II (drag-tone)
         bii 'bee'   bii 'at'
         piip 'to squeak'   piip 'pipe'
         wiis 'melody'   wiis 'wise'
         ʃiin 'appear'   ʃiin 'shine'
         baar 'pure'   baar 'give birth to'
         paater 'father'   waater 'water'
         værandaa 'veranda'   Jolandaa 'Yolanda'

Phonologically, the contrast has been analyzed as a lexical high tone (in Accent II) versus its absence (in Accent I) (Gussenhoven 2000: 221), the rest of the melodies of the two accents being filled in by general prosodic rules.

The origin of this contrast is not fully resolved. It is partially distributed according to the (present or former) segmental shape of the forms. For example, only Accent I appears in forms where the vowel is a high tense vowel /i, y, u/. However, as Gussenhoven points out, none of the environmental contrasts are of a sort usually associated with tonogenesis. For example, there are no reports of tonogenesis triggered by vowel height in other languages (Gussenhoven 2000: 233). In place of an account involving regular sound change, Gussenhoven suggests one based in part on language contact. He notes, to begin with, that a number of nouns distinguish their singulars and plurals solely by means of the accent difference, the former plural suffix having been apocopated, as in pairs like br<u>ii</u>f 'letters' br<u>ii</u>f 'letter', nøøt(ə) 'nuts' nøøt 'nut' from northeastern Belgium. In his account, after apocope of the plural suffix had taken place in such forms, the singular and plural forms would still have been distinguished by vowel length, the vowel in the latter having undergone open syllable lengthening. However, these border dialects of DU were under pressure from neighboring GE to level such paradigms in favor of a uniform long vowel. Caught between the impulse to imitate the neighboring prestige dialects and the impulse to resist morphological neutralization of an inherent morphological contrast, they compromised by lengthening the short vowel of the singular under retention of high pitch, to keep it distinct from the vowel of the plural. This high pitch was then reinterpreted as the high tone characteristic of Accent II.

4

The Germanic nominal system: paradigmatic and syntagmatic variation

4.1 Nominal inflection

4.1.1 Historical prelude: Indo-European heritage and Germanic innovation

Affixes in GMC, as elsewhere, serve one of two functions. Derivational affixes are applied to derive new words. Thus, *locate, relocate, relocation* are distinct words, and each might be expected to be listed separately in a dictionary. On the other hand, *locate, locates* and *located*, distinguished from each other by inflectional affixes, are in an intuitively clear sense simply variant forms of the same word, and would accordingly not be listed separately in the dictionary. Derivational affixes were discussed briefly in Chapter 2. The paradigmatic and syntagmatic relationships among inflectional morphemes in the GMC languages (or their analytic equivalents – see below) will be treated in the next two chapters.

Synchronically, few typological generalizations can be made about the shape of inflectional morphology across the GMC languages, except that suffixes are by far the most frequent and productive type of inflection. This is in part a reflection of their IE heritage. Suffixes were the prevailing (though not the exclusive) device for signaling grammatical contrasts in IE as well. Inflectional prefixes are only marginally present in GMC (see Section 5.1.1), and infixes play no role in GMC (though IE had one). However, another type of word-internal inflectional morphology – replacives, in which one segment or string of segments within a root is replaced with another – is encountered quite frequently. Some GMC replacive morphemes – the ablaut patterns of strong verbs (*sing, sang, sung*) – are of IE origin. Others are of later origin. In noun alternations like *foot~feet, mouse~mice*, and in verb alternations like GE *ich gebe* 'I give' *du gibst* 'you give', or *wir müssen* 'we must' *ich muß* 'I must', they are the results of the historical process of umlaut – the influencing of the quality of the vowel of the stem by the vowel of an inflectional suffix (e.g., **fōt~*fōt-ī→*fēt (-ī)*). Syllable-based lengthening and shortening processes of later medieval GMC resulted in still other similar internal alternations, such as that in *keep/kept*, for example.

89

The history of inflectional morphology in the GMC languages has been largely one of loss of inflectional distinctions and even of entire inflectional categories. This process of "deflection," to borrow a term from Weerman (1989), though evidenced in all GMC languages, has progressed unevenly across the family. So, for example, IC and GE have preserved more of the inventory of inflectional affixes than EN and AF, which have eliminated the inflectional categories of gender and (except in pronouns) case, among other things. It has also proceeded unevenly across inflectional categories. So, for example, while many of the modern GMC languages have ceased to signal case on nouns, all of them still retain ways of marking nouns plural. In this connection, it is important to distinguish between two functionally different types of inflection. Returning to our examples, we note that the *-ed* of *located* contributes in a specific way to the interpretation of the form, adding the meaning "past." On the other hand, the *-s* of *locates* does not appear to make an independent semantic contribution. Rather, it simply encodes the relationship between the word and others in construction with it, signaling (redundantly) that the subject of the verb is third person singular. Booij (2002b: 19f., citing Kuryłowicz 1964) refers to these two types of inflection as "inherent" and "contextual," respectively. Plural marking on nouns is another example of inherent morphology. On the other hand, plural marking on adjectives is contextual, serving only to encode the fact that they are in construction with a plural noun. Booij proposes that this distinction plays an important role in characterizing the distribution of morphemes in at least a couple of (possibly interdependent) ways. First of all, inherent morphemes tend to come closer to the root to which they are attached. Thus, for example, in such GE forms as *kauf-t-en* 'bought (1st/3rd person plural)' the (inherent) past tense suffix precedes the (contextual) plural agreement morpheme. Second, contextual inflection tends to be lost more readily over time. According to Booij, "this is to be expected since contextual inflection does not express independent information" (2002b: 20). So, for example, languages such as EN and DU, which have largely abandoned inflection for such contextually determined contrasts as case on nouns, and person/number agreement on verbs and adjectives, still inflect verbs for tense and nouns for number. Stated as a fact about typological distribution, inflection of nouns for number (where it is an inherent feature) should be more widespread than the inflection of verbs or adjectives for number.[1]

---

[1] These cases raise the interesting question of whether sound changes like the loss of unstressed final syllables in GMC can be constrained by semantic or categorial or other grammatical information (applying differentially to two phonetically identical strings when one of them but not the other happens to be a plural suffix, for example), or whether sound changes apply across the board, without regard to such considerations, seeming exceptions being the result of analogical restoration. For an interesting discussion of some disputed cases, see van Coetsem *et al.* 1981, Gussenhoven 2000.

Deflection has worked in tandem with two other partially related tendencies to reduce the range of variation within and across paradigms: syncretism of inflectional contrasts through extension of one member of a paradigm at the expense of others (for example, the extension of the second person singular verb ending in ON to third person, which, through borrowing, also gave us the EN -s in *locates*), and regularization of affixes by extending an affix from one paradigm to others (e.g., the generalization of EN -s as a plural marker beyond the noun classes in which it was original). Deflection is traditionally held to be the result of sound change; as the endings are reduced or eliminated by phonological processes, the inflectional categories they encoded disappear. While such sequences of events were prominent in the development of GMC, things do not always progress in this way. After a certain threshhold has been reached, the remaining affixes in a paradigm can lose their functional significance before they disappear. This possibility is illustrated, for example, by the retention of the former dative case -e marker on nouns in ME after it had ceased to signal dative, or the similarly defunctionalized attributive adjective endings of AF.

In general, the more phonologically substantial the ending, the better it resisted the processes of phonological reduction underlying deflection. So, for example, while GO had nominative case endings in both the singular and the plural of *a*-stem nouns, only the plural ending, where the vowel was long, survives in OHG.

(4.1) a. dag-s (←*dag-az) dag-ōs (←dag-ōz) (GO)
       b. tag   tag-a   (OHG)

This results in a paradigm in which some forms are endingless. Kastovsky (1994) sees in this development a shift in morphological typology, from a "stem-based" morphological system, in which all of the forms in the paradigm are derived by adding affixes to an abstract stem (which thus never appears as an actual word) to a "word-based" morphology, in which some forms in the paradigm are identical to the stem itself (see also Bloomfield 1933: 225, cited in Booij 2002b: 4, and Wurzel 1987: 47ff.).

4.1.2   Inflectional categories of the noun

4.1.2.1 *Number*

Number is the only inherent category for which nouns are inflected in all of the GMC languages, and the majority of nouns in all of these languages have plural forms which are distinct from those of the singular. There are accidental exceptions, in which singular and plural forms of individual nouns happen to have converged phonetically through ending loss (as in the case of early GMC neuter *a*-stems like OHG *wort* 'word/words'), but some groups of nouns have only singular, or only plural, forms for reasons that are linked to their meanings. Among these are non-count nouns which lack plural forms because they do not refer to enumerable entities. These include nouns denoting abstract properties (*goodness*), substances (*wool*) and collective terms (*cattle*). Under some circumstances, these can be used with plural morphology, but not without introducing an added sense of individuation. For example, it is possible to say "his many kindnesses," but *kindnesses* is understood here to refer elliptically to 'acts of kindness'. Conversely, there are nouns which have only plural forms (*pluralia tanta*). In EN, these include such nouns as *scissors*, *tweezers* and *odds* which refer to objects consisting of two identical components. The singulars of these nouns are simply nonexistent. For others, however, including, *contents*, *damages* and the like, the corresponding singular form has a different meaning. To a certain extent, we are dealing with point of view in all of these cases, and there are crosslinguistic differences in the use of singular and plural forms here. So, for example, EN uses *ashes*, *contents*, *wages* and *looks* as plurals, while the corresponding nouns (*aske*, *indhold*, *løn*, *udseende*) in DA are singular (Allan *et al.* 1995: 44). Similarly, the DA counterparts to *scissors*, *tweezers*, *scales* and *pliers* are singular (*en saks*, *en pincet*, *en vægt*, *en knibtang*). Conversely, in EN *furniture*, *information*, *knowledge* are non-pluralizable nouns, while their counterparts in DA (*møbler*, *oplysninger*, *kundskaber*) are plural, whose singular forms again denote 'a particular instance of X'.

In early GMC, and still in some relatively richly inflected modern languages (IC, FA), number has no morphological expression in the noun independent of case. So, for example, every different case ending for the plurals of the *a*-stem declension has a different shape in GO and IC:

(4.2)   GO   IC   (Einarsson 1945: 35)

	GO	IC (Einarsson 1945: 35)
Nom Pl	dag-ōs 'days'	smið-ir 'smith'
Acc Pl	dag-ans	smið-i
Dat Pl	dag-am	smið-um
Gen Pl	dag-ē	smið-a

This is of course no longer true of those languages which have lost case distinctions. However, even in modern GE, which retains vestigial case inflection in the plural, in the form of a dative plural *-(e)n*, the expression of number and case has been sequentialized; in *Kind-er-n* 'to the children (Dat)', there are separate number and case morphemes (though the two are conflated where the plural ending is also *-en*).

Besides signaling plural number on the noun itself, the GMC languages typically signal it on accompanying articles/demonstrative adjectives. In the most richly inflected languages (e.g., GO and IC), plural articles are distinct from the corresponding singulars for all genders and cases. Gradual deflection in the other languages, however, has again led to loss of distinctions. At the extreme pole are DU, which now has only a distinction between singular neuter article *het* and an invariant *de* for all other genders and numbers, and EN and AF, which have an invariant article for both singular and plural (*the, die*).

4.1.2.1.1 **Dual** IE had dual as well as singular and plural forms. The dual has disappeared in GMC in the inflection of nouns, though it persists as an inflectional category in GO verbs (see Section 4.9.1.1), and in pronouns in a variety of medieval GMC languages. Among the modern GMC languages, dual has survived as an inflectional category (in pronoun paradigms) only in North FR (see 4.8.1.1).

4.1.2.2 *Gender: inflectional category or lexical classification?*

Gender, while important as a means of classifying nominals, had at most a marginal status as a category of inflection in early GMC, and it is not until some modern GMC languages that we find inflectional morphemes emerging which signal gender exclusively. Gender has never been an inflectional category, as such, of the GMC noun. On the one hand, there are no inflectional endings which exclusively mark gender. The gender-particular endings in GMC paradigms also invariably encode other grammatical information, such as number and case, and are therefore so-called *portmanteau* morphemes. So, for example, the GO masculine and neuter are at most distinguished in some paradigms (e.g., the GMC *a*-stems) by having different forms for nominative singular, and nominative and accusative plural (4.3a). In all other cases, they are nondistinct (4.3b):

(4.3)   a. NSg   dag-s   waurd
                            'day-Masc'   'word-Neut'
              NPl   dag-ōs   waurd-a
              APl   dag-ans   waurd-a

             b. GSg   dag-is   waurd-is
              DPl   dag-am   waurd-am

Even here, one cannot identify *-s* as masculine singular nominative, since it also marks feminine singular nominative in other noun classes (e.g., *anst-s* 'grace', *handu-s* 'hand').

The closest one comes to a specific gender marker which encodes nothing but gender on the noun is the /a∼o:/ which appears in feminine ō-stems:

(4.3)   c. NSg gib-a   'gift'
               GSg gib-ō-s
               NPl gib-ō-s
               DPl gib-ō-m

All of these forms are distinctly feminine, and it may seem arguable that the /a~o:/ is a marker of feminine gender here, since the case/number is signaled by the consonant which follows it. Even here, however, it would be wrong to identify /a~o:/ as a gender marker, for reasons relating to productivity and predictability. With respect to the former, we note that the /a~o:/ alternation is restricted to a particular subset of feminine nouns: those that derive from the IE *ā*-stems. In the IE noun inflections which underlie the GMC ones, inflectional endings were typically not added directly to the noun root, but rather were linked to the root by a thematic suffix, which identified the inflectional class of the noun. So, for example, EN *father, mother, sister* all come from IE *r*-stems, so called because the thematic suffix was -(*e*)*r*-. It happened that one of these classes, whose thematic suffix in IE was -*ā* (from an earlier sequence of vowel plus laryngeal consonant (*$*eH_2$*)), included only feminine nouns. Nouns like GO *giba* are reflexes of this class of "ā-stems," which is why all of the nouns with the /a~o:/ termination are feminine.[2] In other inherited declension classes, though, there is no such consistent signal of feminine gender, and for some (e.g., the *u*-declension), there is no difference at all between masculine and feminine forms.

(4.3) d. Gothic u-stem nouns

	Masculine	Feminine
NSg	sun-us	hand-us
ASg	sun-u	hand-u
GSg	sun-aus	hand-aus
DSg	sun-au	hand-au
NPl	sun-jus	[hand-jus]

A similar situation arises in the GMC "weak" nouns, whose inflections derive from IE *n*-stems. In GO, for example, masculine *n*-stems are consistently distinct from feminine *n*-stems, the latter systematically exhibiting an <ō> or an <ei> before the case endings.

(4.3) e.
NSg	gum-a	tugg-ō	manag-ei
	'man-Masc'	'tongue-Fem'	'multitude-Fem'
GSg	gum-i-ns	tugg-ō-ns	manag-ei-ns
DPl	gum-a-m	tugg-ō-m	manag-ei-m

Again, the -*ō* and the -*ei* of the latter cannot be interpreted as gender morphemes, encoding feminine gender, independently of case and number. They are limited to nouns of these particular inflectional classes, and they are fixed and non-contrasting;

---

[2] Somewhat confusingly, these are referred to in GMC grammars as ō-stems, since IE /ā/ changed to /ō/ in GMC. Similarly, reflexes of IE o-stems are referred to as a-stems in GMC grammars, since IE short /o/ became GMC /a/.

a noun cannot be given a different gender simply by changing the suffix. These considerations suggest an alternative account: /a~o:/, ō and *ei* in these examples are not inflectional morphemes encoding gender, but derivational affixes signaling noun class. The association of these with gender is a matter of class membership. The class of *an*-stems contains masculine nouns, while the /a~o:/, *ōn-* and *-ein* classes contain only feminine nouns, the association with gender thus resulting from the fact that all of the members of this class happen to be feminine. They are thus not unlike the GE noun ending *-ung* in *Zeitung* 'newspaper', for example, which appears exclusively on feminine nouns, but which we would not wish to characterize as a gender morpheme.

Nouns are crucially different in this respect from adjectives. Formally, the endings of weak adjectives are identical to those of *n*-stem nouns, from which they derive historically. Masculine weak adjectives inflect just like *an*-stem nouns, while feminine weak adjectives inflect just like *ōn*-stem nouns (and present participles in the feminine like *ein*-stem nouns).

(4.4)   NSg   blind-a   blind-ō   giband-ei
              'blind-Masc'   'blind-Fem'   'giving-Fem'
        ASg   blind-a-n   blind-ō-n   giband-ei-n
        GSg   blind-i-ns   blind-ō-ns   giband-ei-ns
        DPl   blind-a-m   blind-ō-m   giband-ei-m

However, the endings here differ in two fundamental respects from the corresponding noun endings. First of all, "weak adjective," or "feminine adjective," unlike "weak noun" or "feminine noun," is not a lexical classification with fixed membership, but a matter of syntactically determined inflection. Any adjective may be assigned weak feminine endings under the appropriate syntactic circumstances. Adjectives acquire their gender by agreement with nouns with which they are in construction, and thus there are gender contrasts in the paradigms of individual adjectives. Note that it is the gender of the associated noun, not the noun-class marker, which determines the shape of the adjective inflection. Thus, for example, an accusative singular form like *aiweinōn* 'eternal' can be used to modify any feminine noun, under appropriate syntactic conditions, regardless of the morphological shape of the noun:

(4.5)   a.   balwein   aiweinōn
             punishment   eternal
             (GO, Matt. 25:46)

        b.   fralust   aiweinōn
             ruination   eternal
             (GO, 2 Thess. 1:9)

Therefore, the ō of *blindōm*, for example, unlike the ō of *tuggōm*, must be regarded as productive inflectional morphology.

For nouns, therefore, gender is not an inflectional category, but rather an abstract system of classification without morphological exponence. It is a selectional feature, important for conditioning the morphological realizations of other forms with which the noun appears in a syntagmatic or paradigmatic relationship. We may identify four ways in which the gender feature of nouns affects the shape of co-occurring forms. First, in the morphology-rich GMC languages, gender plays a (marginal) role in determining the shape of case/number affixes applied to the noun itself. So, for example, in GO, neuter nouns differ from feminine and masculine nouns, even when they belong to the same inflectional class, in never having -*s* in the nominative singular or plural. Compare, for example, the nominative singular *u*-stems *sunus* 'son' (Masc), *handus* 'hand' (Fem) with neuter *faihu* 'cattle'. This holds across all classes of nouns containing neuters, and is a reflection of the fact that neuter nouns in IE had systematically different nominative case endings from the other genders. Among the modern languages, neuters still retain their inflectional distinctiveness in IC, as the following examples show:

(4.6)

	Masc	Fem	Neut
NSg	smið-ur	heið-i	borð
NPl	smið-ir	heið-ar	borð
	'smith'	'heath, mountain'	'table'

(IC, Einarsson 1945: 35ff.)

Second, in all of the GMC languages with grammatical gender, the gender of the noun affects the choice of agreement morphology on (some subset of) adjectives. In some of them, both attributive adjectives and predicate adjectives agree in gender with associated nouns. In others, only attributive adjectives do, and in some cases even attributive adjective agreement is quite minimal, as in DU for example, where all of them end in -*e* (/ə/) except those modifying singular indefinite neuter nouns:

(4.7) a. een mooi boek 'a nice book (Neuter)'
  b. een mooie pen 'a nice pen (Common)'
   (Booij 2002b: 43)

Third, and still more robustly, in those GMC languages which still have gender, the gender of a noun determines the form of articles appearing with it.

Finally, the gender of nouns plays a role in determining the gender of pronouns of which the NPs they head are antecedents. This too is a general feature of all of the languages in which gender exists as a grammatical category, but there is some interesting variation. Pronouns are less likely than determiners or attributive adjectives to have their gender determined purely by the grammatical gender of an associated nominal (Corbett 1991: 225). Two different types of agreement are found across languages between a pronoun and its linguistic antecedent. Sometimes the gender of the pronoun is determined by the grammatical gender of the antecedent, but sometimes it is determined by the natural gender of the referent of that antecedent. Corbett calls these two types "syntactic" agreement and "semantic" agreement respectively (1991: 225). In a language without gender as an inflectional category, of course, only the latter is possible: a masculine pronoun is used if the referent is a male animate being, feminine if a female animate being, and a neuter pronoun if the referent of the antecedent is not animate.

(4.8)   a. The girl got up and she walked out

On the other hand, in languages with full grammatical gender systems, a pronoun may agree with the grammatical gender of its antecedent, rather than with the natural gender of the referent, and in some of these languages, including present-day GE, this is preferred, though "semantic" agreement is not precluded (cf. Corbett 1991: 228):

(4.8)   b. Schau dir dieses Mädchen an, wie gut   sie/es Tennis spielt
           Look this girl-Neut   at, how good she/it tennis plays
        (GE, Corbett 1991: 228)

Thus, there are so far two patterns in GMC with respect to gender assignment to pronouns. In languages without inflectional gender, pronoun gender is semantically determined. In languages with grammatical gender, such as GE and IC, it can be (and is sometimes preferred to be) determined by the grammatical gender of the antecedent noun. These two types of pronoun/antecedent agreement have been in competition since the earliest times, natural gender tending to override grammatical gender with animate antecedents. In OE, for example, the pronoun *hē* 'he' rather than *hit* 'it' is often used to refer back to neuter nouns with male referents (*ðæt cild . . . hē*) (Mitchell 1985: I, 35ff.).

SW and DA have developed a means of accommodating both of these impulses – toward grammatical agreement with inanimate nouns, but natural agreement with nouns which have animate reference (see Corbett 1991: 247; Braunmüller 2000; Andersson 2000). The personal pronouns *han* 'he' and *hun* 'she' (DA) are now restricted to reference to animates, with natural gender concord, while a different form, *den* 'that one (common gender)', has been drawn from the demonstrative paradigm to serve as the pronoun for referring back to inanimate antecedents with common gender. As noted in Hellan and Platzack 1999: 123, this development has occurred in those Scandinavian languages in which former masculine and feminine nouns have merged into common gender, eliminating the possibility of a contrast between *han* and *hun* based on grammatical gender. In NO, Bandle *et al.* (2005: 1590) report a split between NN and BN; in the former, pronouns agree in grammatical gender, irrespective of natural gender or animacy, while the latter observes a system like that described for DA.

One of the two main trends in gender morphology in GMC has been increasing syncretism in inflectional paradigms – that is, a reduction in the numbers of positions in adjective and determiner paradigms in which gender contrasts are signaled. Even in GO, gender distinctions are not made for all genders in all cases and numbers for both weak and strong adjectives. Syncretisms tend to occur along certain axes. In general, gender distinctions are richer in direct cases (nominative and accusative) than in oblique cases (dative and genitive). They also tend to be richer in singular than in plural. These axes interact with each other, and with the weak/strong adjective distinction, to be discussed below, in rather complex ways. So, for example, in GO, neuter and masculine adjective forms are distinct from each other only in direct cases, in both singular and plural. In oblique cases, they are the same. (This state of affairs has its antecedents in IE, and holds true of all GMC languages except IC, where a secondary distinction has arisen in the dative singular of strong adjectives between masculine *göml-um* 'old' and neuter *göml-u*.) Feminine adjectives in GO are distinct from masculine and neuter except in the dative plural of the strong paradigm.

(4.9)		*Weak*	*Strong*
	ASg	blindan (M)	blindana (M)
		blindō (N)	blind/-ata (N)
		blindōn (F)	blinda (F)
	DSg	blindin (M, N)	blindamma (M, N)
			blindai (F)
	APl	blindans (M)	blindans (M)
		blindōna (N)	blinda (N)
		blindōns (F)	blindōs (F)
	DPl	blindam (M, N)	blindaim (M, N, F)
		blindōm (F)	

Later GMC languages signal gender contrasts in fewer contexts than GO, and retrenchment, when it occurs, tends to be along combinations of these same axes (see Table 4.1). In particular, gender distinctions tend to be lost in plural and in oblique cases. They are also leveled out more readily in weak than in strong adjectives. So, for example, the facts of OHG are essentially like those of GO, except that OHG no longer makes gender distinctions in the genitive plural. Further, OE and ON, like GO and OHG, still make gender distinctions in the direct cases of the plurals of strong adjectives, but no longer in the plurals of weak adjectives.

Table 4.1 Adjective endings in selected Germanic languages

GO

	Strong			Weak		
	M	N	F	M	N	F
NSg	s	0[1]	a	a		ō
ASg	ana		ai	an	ō	
DSg	amma		ai		in	
GSg	is		aizōs	ins		ōns
NPl	ai	a	ōs	ans	ōna	ōs
APl	ans					
DPl	aim			am		ōm
GPl	aizē		aizō	anē		ōnō

OHG

	Strong			Weak		
	M	N	F	M	N	F
NSg	0[2]	0[3]	0[4]	o		a
ASg	an	a	a	on	a	ūn
DSg	emu		eru	en		
GSg	es		era			
NPl	e	iu	o	on	un	ūn
APl						
DPl	ēm			ōm		
GPl	ero			ōno		

OE

	Strong			Weak		
	M	N	F	M	N	F
NSg	0	0	u	a	e	
ASg	ne		re	an		an
DSg	um		es			
GSg						
NPl	e	u	a		an	
APl						
DPl	um			um		
GPl	ra			ena		

GE

	Strong			Weak		
	M	N	F	M	N	F
NSg	er	es	e	e	e	
ASg	en				en	
DSg	em		er			en
GSg	es					
NPl	e			en		
APl						
DPl	en					
GPl	er					

DA

	Strong		Weak	
	Com	Neut	Com	Neut
Sg	0	t	e	e
Pl	e		e	

FR

	Strong		Weak	
	Com	Neut	Com	Neut
Sg	e	0	e	e
Pl	e		e	

1 Alternates with -ata
2 Alternates with -ēr
3 Alternates with -az
4 Alternates with -iu

Modern GE no longer makes gender distinctions in the plural. In the singular, gender distinctions are signaled in most positions in strong adjective paradigms though neuter and masculine are identical in oblique cases, but among the weak adjective endings, gender distinctions have been neutralized except in the accusative singular, where masculine adjectives have *-en* but neuter and feminine adjectives have *-e*.

(4.10) a. NSg gute (M, N, F)
ASg guten (M), gute (N, F)
DSg guten (M, N, F)
GSg guten (M, N, F)

In continental Scandinavian, where case contrasts have disappeared, and where masculine and feminine have merged into a single "common gender," as discussed below, gender contrasts on adjectives are now restricted to the single instance of common gender *-0* vs. neuter gender *-t* in the strong endings:

(4.10) b. en ung pige
'a young girl'

c. et stor-t hus,
'a big house'
(DA, Allan *et al.* 1995: 95)

It is interesting to note that in this highly reduced type of adjective agreement, gender has finally emerged into its own, as a fully productive inflectional category whose morphological expression is no longer conflated with that of case.

Besides this reduction of the number of forms on which gender is encoded morphologically, a second major development, affecting a subset of the modern GMC languages, has been a reduction in the number of grammatical genders themselves. IE had three, masculine, feminine and neuter, though there is some evidence suggesting that the latter two are of later origin (see Beekes 1995: 174). This was also true of all of the older GMC languages, and is still true of GE, Standard YI, IC, FA and NN.

(4.11) a. der oivn 'the stove'

b. di śif 'the ship'

c. dus guulys 'the Exile'
(Std. YI, Birnbaum 1979: 227)

The remaining modern languages have fewer genders than this. Among standard languages, the inventory is most radically reduced in EN and AF, where grammatical gender has ceased to exist, as it has in some Western DA dialects:

(4.11)   d. en man / en hus
'the man' / 'the house'
(West Jutish, Braunmüller 2000: 28)

For a detailed consideration of possible causes for radical loss of gender as a grammatical category, see Kastovsky 2000 and Jones 1988 on gender loss in late OE, as well as McWhorter 2002. McWhorter points out (2002: 230) that it is not a consequence of phonetic erosion of the forms in question.

DU and FR, as well as the standard dialects of the continental Scandinavian languages, have only partially collapsed the gender system, from three genders to two.

(4.12)   a. en hånd (hånden)   (DA)
'the hand' (common gender)

b. et hus (huset)
'the house' (neuter gender)

c. de postbode   (DU)
'the mailman' (common gender)

d. het meisje
'the girl' (neuter gender)

e. de man   (FR)
'the man' (common gender)

f. it hus
'the house' (neuter gender)

In these languages, the former masculine and feminine have fallen together, into a "common gender," which now contrasts with neuter gender.[3] Sandström (2000) attempts to sort out the staging of this change from three genders to two by reference to some complex cross-dialectal variation in dialects of SW spoken in Finland, some of which retain three genders, some of which have only two, and some, interestingly, which seem to observe a three-gender system for some purposes (choice of clitic definite articles) but a two-gender system for other purposes (bound pronoun choice) (Sandström 2000: 798). NO, too, for historical reasons, presents a complex situation, in which the masculine/feminine/neuter system and the common/neuter system coexist, and sometimes compete, within different varieties (Bandle et al. 2005: 1593). Because

---

[3] Masculine gender continues to be encoded in a marginal way in SW morphology. Weak adjectives modifying nouns which denote male individuals may take the standard weak ending -a or they may take the alternative ending -e (Bandle et al. 2005: 1612).

of the circumstances of origin of common gender, nouns with common gender substantially outnumber neuter nouns in these languages; 75 percent of DA nouns (Allan *et al.* 1995: 4) and 80 percent of simplex DU nouns (Booij 2002b: 38) have common gender.

In all of the GMC languages with grammatical gender, the gender of individual nouns is sometimes predictable on the basis of formal and semantic subregularities. The most robust of these involve the genders of nouns derived by suffixes. Thus, for example, DA nouns in *-dom* are always common gender, GE nouns in *-ung* are always feminine, and GO nouns in *-areis* are always masculine.

There are some apparent crosslinguistic differences in the frequency with which nouns are assigned to the different genders. Steinmetz (2001: 206ff.) compares GE with two other languages with three-gender systems. He observes that in pairs of cognates like those in (4.13), representing "hundreds, perhaps thousands of cognate nouns, both inherited and borrowed," the GE noun is masculine, while the IC noun is neuter.

(4.13)   GE   IC
           Lauf   hlaup   'run, course'
           Name   nafn   'name'
           Kohl   kál   'cabbage'
           Apfel   epli   'apple'
           Gummi   gummi   'rubber'
           Haß   hatur   'hatred'
           Sommer   sumar   'summer'
           Regen   regn   'rain'
           Tee   te   'tea'
           Brief   bréf   'letter'
           (Steinmetz 2001: 208)

Steinmetz concludes that neuter is the default gender in IC, assigned where no formal or semantic principle favors a different gender assignment, while masculine is the default gender in GE. The first of these claims is supported by the numerous loanwords which appear as neuters in IC, including *ginn* 'gin', *gips* 'plaster', *salat* 'lettuce', *bréf* 'letter', but which have common gender in continental Scandinavian (Steinmetz 2001: 208).

In general, the neuter gender was the original one in (4.13), and Steinmetz posits a gender shift in the West GMC languages away from neuter gender. This trend, unfolding at different rates in the different West GMC languages, leads to such non-correspondences in gender as those in (4.14) between GE neuter nouns and their cognates in Standard YI, which are masculine or feminine. In almost all such cases, the neuter was the original gender of these cognates.

(4.14)
German	Yiddish	
Ziel	der tsil	'goal'
Zimmer	der tsimer	'room'
Loch	der/di lokh	'hole'
Wetter	der veter	'weather'
Salz	di zalts	'salt'
Ende	di end	'end'

(Steinmetz 2001: 207)

These correspondences suggest that the shift away from neuter is more advanced in YI than GE, and indeed, Northeastern YI has lost neuter altogether and has only a two-gender, masculine/feminine system (a reduction in the gender inventory of a different sort from those in the other two-gender languages of GMC).

4.1.2.3 The expression of case: synthetic and analytic

4.1.2.3.1 Case suffixes All of the GMC languages, aside from creoles, have some manifestations of case, however vestigial. (Late) IE had eight cases: nominative, vocative, accusative, genitive, dative, ablative, locative and instrumental, though some of the oblique cases already had defective paradigms. This system underwent further reduction in GMC (as in other branches), largely through the conflation of the oblique cases, so that in the most richly inflected GMC languages we find a core case system with four members: nominative, accusative, dative and genitive.

(4.15)

	GO		OHG	
	Sg	*Pl*	*Sg*	*Pl*
N	sa dags	þai dagōs	der tag	dia taga
A	þana dag	þans dagans	den tag	dia taga
D	þamma daga	þaim dagam	demo tage	dem tagum
G	þis dagis	þize dagē	des tages	dero tago
V	dag	—	—	—
I	— —	— —	diu tagu	— —

	Modern GE		IC	
N	der Tag	die Tage	dag-ur-inn	dag-ar-nir
A	den Tag	die Tage	dag-inn	dag-a-na
D	dem Tag-(e)	den Tage-n	degi-num	dögu-num
G	des Tag-es	der Tage	dag-s-ins	dag-a-nna

In addition, there are occasional regional retentions of a few other cases. The IE vocative is still retained in GO, where it is distinguished (by virtue of its endinglessness) from the nominative, but only in masculine singular *a*-stems. The early West GMC languages retain the IE instrumental, though again only in singular *a*-stems among nouns, and in pronoun forms like OHG *hwiu* 'by what means?' (the latter also surviving in GO (*hʋe*).

Among the languages which retain part of this case inventory there are some differences in terms of the contexts in which case is morphologically expressed. In the West GMC languages, exemplified by the OHG paradigm in (4.15), for instance, the nominative/accusative contrast is not signaled on the noun; only the article signals the distinction (and this only in the masculine and feminine singular). In the plural, the contrast is not marked on either the article or the noun in OHG (or other West GMC languages), and thus has been lost here altogether. These tendencies have continued, so that in Modern GE, one of the two modern West GMC languages retaining a four-case system, case inflection on nouns is now restricted to the genitive singular *-es* in masculine and neuter nouns, and the dative plural *-n*. (The dative singular termination *-e*, used into recent times, is now moribund.) Case has thus come to be signaled primarily by the articles and adjectives accompanying the noun.

YI is the other modern West GMC language preserving a four-case system, but the contexts in which case contrasts are visible are much fewer; genitive case is marked only on nouns (as *-(e)s* or *-ns*), and only in the instance of a small set of animate nouns and proper names (see Jacobs *et al*. 1994: 403; Lockwood 1995: 9). In the determiner system, the genitive has been lost and replaced by the originally dative form of the article. The three-way contrast among the remaining cases is not recoverable from the paradigm of any single noun, but can only be concluded by a pairwise comparison of the determiner plus noun paradigms for nouns of different genders, as (4.16) shows; all of the genders partially collapse the three-way contrast, but they do so in different ways. Dative forms have replaced accusative forms in the masculine singular, so that the dative/accusative distinction is now signaled only in feminine and neuter noun phrases, where the accusative is identical to the nominative. The nominative/accusative distinction can only be seen in the paradigms of masculine nouns. In the plural, the historical accusative determiner *di*, already homophonous with the nominative, has replaced the dative, and case contrasts are no longer found.

(4.16)
			M	F	N
Sg	N		der guter shiler	di gute tir	dos gute bukh
			'the good student'	'the good door'	'the good book'
	A		dem gutn shiler	di gute tir	dos gute bukh
	D		dem gutn shiler	der guter tir	dem gutn bukh
Pl	NAD		di gute shilers/tirn/bikher		

(YI, Jacobs *et al*. 1994: 405)

(Corresponding conflation of the dative/accusative distinction in the personal pronouns, by generalizing dative forms, has taken place in some dialects, Lockwood 1995: 64.)

In general, articles retain distinct case forms more robustly than nouns, and in general, pronouns retain case distinctions more robustly than either determiners or nouns. So, for example, in EN and in the continental Scandinavian languages, the nominative/accusative (or, more properly, subjective/objective) case distinction is not marked on nouns or determiners, but is retained in pronouns (DA *jeg/mig*).

Besides the successive reduction in the number of contexts in which contrasts are signaled, there has also been a tendency since prehistoric times toward reduction in the number of cases in the inventory itself. The inventory has changed, for that matter, between OHG and Modern GE, with the loss of the marginal instrumental case. Spoken FA has lost the genitive case. One vanishing case distinction in particular, however (that between dative and accusative case) may have been of special importance in propelling a subgroup across a significant typological threshhold, since its disappearance seems to be linked in some way to the loss of the lexical case/structural case contrast in those languages (cf. Allen 1995; Polo 2002), which had played an important role in the morphosyntax of early GMC (and still does in the other modern languages). The syntax of lexical case is a central topic of Section 4.1.2.4. Languages in which the accusative/dative distinction has disappeared include Middle and Modern EN, continental Scandinavian, Modern DU,[4] FR and AF, and (sectarian or "plain") PG. In general, in all of those languages where the nominative/accusative /dative distinction persists (early GMC, GE, YI, IC and FA), the definite article is still inflected for case, whereas in most of the languages where the dative/accusative distinction has been lost, case distinctions are signaled only in the pronoun – no longer in the definite article. This is true, for example, of NO, EN, AF, DU and plain PG:[5]

(4.17)   a. *Nominative*   *Objective*

eg	meg	'I/me'	(NN)
han	han/honom	'he/him'	(NN)
ik	my	'I/me'	(FR)
hy	him	'he/him'	(FR)
ich	mich	'I/me'	(Plain PG)
er	en	'he/him'	(Plain PG)
ek	my	'I/me'	(AF)
hy	hom	'he/him'	(AF)

---

[4] Donaldson (1981: 53) talks about a distinction, artificially introduced and rarely used outside of writing, between 'them (third person plural accusative)' *hen* and 'them (third person plural dative)' *hun* in DU.
[5] Non-sectarian PG continues to distinguish dative and accusative in personal pronouns (van Ness 1994: 430) and continues to inflect the definite article for case (van Ness 1994: 425).

Table 4.2 *Definite article/demonstrative adjectives in selected Germanic languages*

GO

	M	N	F
NSg	sa	þata	sō
ASg	þana	þata	þō
DSg	þamma	þamma	þizai
GSg	þis	þis	þizōs
NPl	þai	þō	þōs
APl	þans	þō	þōs
DPl	þaim	þaim	þaim
GPl	þizē	þizē	þizō

OHG

	M	N	F
NSg	der	daz	diu
ASg	den	daz	dea
DSg	demu	demu	deru
GSg	des	des	dera
NPl	dea	diu	deo
APl	dea	diu	deo
DPl	dêm	dêm	dêm
GPl	dero	dero	dero

OE

	M	N	F
NSg	sē	ðæt	sēo
ASg	ðone	ðæt	ðā
DSg	ðǣm	ðǣm	ðǣre
GSg	ðæs	ðæs	ðǣre
NPl	ðā	ðā	ðā
APl	ðā	ðā	ðā
DPl	ðǣm	ðǣm	ðǣm
GPl	ðāra	ðāra	ðāra

GE

	M	N	F
NSg	der	das	die
ASg	den	das	die
DSg	dem	dem	der
GSg	des	des	der
NPl	die	die	die
APl	die	die	die
DPl	den	den	den
GPl	der	der	der

YI

	M	N	F
NSg	der	dos	di
ASg	dem	dos	di
DSg	dem	dem	der
Pl	di	di	di

DA

	Com	Neut
Sg	den / -en	det / -et
Pl	de / -ne	

FR

	Com	Neut
Sg	de	it
Pl	de	de

The correlation does not hold across all GMC languages, however; in Low GE (Lindow *et al.* 1998: 151), the article continues to inflect for case even in those varieties in which dative and accusative have merged.

The radical loss of case inflection in the noun phrase is seen in a comparison between these paradigms from Middle and Modern DU (Weerman 1997: 427).

(4.17)   b. *Middle Dutch*   *Modern Dutch*
            NSg   die man 'the man'   de man
            ASg   dien man
            DSg   dien manne
            GSg   die mans

4.1.2.3.2 **Other ways of encoding grammatical roles** When inflectional affixes are lost, the grammatical information they encoded sometimes simply ceases to be expressed, as in the case of gender distinctions in EN and AF, for example. More commonly, however, the information comes to be encoded in an alternative way – for example, by "analytic," or periphrastic constructions, in which a free-standing morpheme, such as a preposition or an auxiliary, takes over the function of the bound affix in the earlier "synthetic" construction.[6] Instances of this type include:

(4.18)   a. The replacement of genitive and dative case in EN by *of*–NP and *to*–NP respectively

            b. The displacement of simple (inflectional) past tense in YI, AF, PG and other GE dialects by the periphrastic perfect

            c. The rise of periphrastic passives with passive auxiliaries

            d. The use of *ol* as an analytic plural marker in Bislama and Tok Pisin, EN-based pidgin languages, *ol haos* '(the) houses,'
            (Tryon 1987: 23)

The GMC languages have always made some use of analytic constructions for expressing some case-like notions. So, for example, they have always made extensive use of prepositions such as 'from' and 'with' to express notions that in more richly case-inflected languages are expressed exclusively by synthetic means, through ablative and comitative case affixes. The inflectional cases shared by all the early GMC

---

[6] Romaine (1994: 590), discussing similar developments in GMC creole languages, proposes that "Some morphem(e)s are... more robust than others. It has been suggested that grammatical morphemes fall in.o two classes: those which if lost will not be reconstituted...and those that if lost must be reconstituted." She provides lists of each.

languages are limited to nominative, accusative, dative and genitive, and each of these is associated with a core grammatical function – nominative for subjects, accusative for direct objects, dative for indirect objects and genitive for arguments of nominals – as well as more peripheral adverbial uses. In some of the modern GMC languages, as we have seen, the case system has been even further reduced, so that even some of the core grammatical relations have come to be expressed by prepositions instead. In the following, the information conveyed by OE genitive and dative case is conveyed by prepositions (*to* and *of* respectively) in Modern EN.

(4.19)
Ac þāra Terfinna land   wæs eal wēste...   Fela spella
but the Terfinn-Gen land was all deserted   Many stories-Gen

him   sǣdon þā Beormas (OE, Orosius)
him-Dat said the   Karelians

'But the land of the Terfinns was deserted.... The Karelians told many stories to him'

As a descriptive shorthand, we can refer to languages in which genitive and dative case are still signaled by case endings as "C-languages," and languages in which they have come to be encoded by prepositions as "P-languages."

In other instances, however, the adaptive re-encoding of the grammatical information involves mechanisms other than the simple substitution of a free morpheme for a bound affix. When the morphology marking the grammatical role of an argument is lost, that role may come to be signaled instead by fixed syntactic position instead ("positional licensing," Kiparsky 1997: 487). Thus, while GE allows the three phrases dependent on the verb to appear in any relative order in (4.20a), depending on the information structure of the sentence, in EN, where the nominal objects of the verb are not marked for case, only one relative order is possible.

(4.20)   a. Peter gab [zu Weihnachten] [dem Bruder] [das Buch] (any order)
          Peter gave for Christmas   the Brother-Dat the book-Acc

          b. Peter gave [his brother] [the book] [for Christmas]
          (Hawkins 1986: 39)

Kiparsky (1997: 461) states categorically that

> every GMC language which has lost case and agreement morphology, whether VO (EN, SW, DA, NO) or OV (DU, West Flemish, FR, AF) has imposed a strict mutual ordering requirement on its nominal arguments ... The order is always that subjects precede objects, and indirect objects (NPs, not PPs) always precede direct objects.

The specification "NPs, not PPs" in this quote is a concession to the fact that, as they lost the dative/accusative case distinction, the P-languages of the GMC family systematically availed themselves of both prepositional phrase constructions and fixed position for encoding the formerly dative marked objects in bitransitive constructions (that is, "indirect objects"), leading to alternations like the following:[7]

(4.21) a. I gave *the boy* the book
        b. I gave the book *to the boy*

(4.22) a. dat de vrouw...*de mannen* de film toont
           that the woman the men   the film shows
           (DU, Weerman 1997: 430)

        b. dat de vrouw de film *aan de mannen* toont
           that the woman the picture to the men   shows
           (DU, Weerman 1997: 444)

The traditional story that EN and other GMC languages lost case distinctions because the case morphemes had disappeared through phonetic erosion, and that they were forced to compensate for this loss by the introduction of prepositions, is not entirely correct. Allen (1995: 217), citing Mustanoja, makes the important point that in EN, genitive objects were given up quite early, even though genitive was the most robustly marked case, in terms of the size of the suffix, and that the switch to prepositions in EME in general was underway even in those dialects in which the means for morphological encoding of case were still intact. She proposes that this tendency was not so much a forced reaction to loss of endings as a part of an independent typological shift in the way grammatical relations were encoded. We may, in fact, see it as the natural culmination of a typological tendency traceable to early GMC.

Since the replacement of genitive and dative case morphology by prepositions took place well after the separation of the individual languages, it is not surprising that there is variation across them with respect to which prepositions came to be used in that way, and in what contexts. Holmes and Hinchcliffe (1994: 446) give a list of no fewer

---

[7] Such alternations raise at least questions of labeling. Are both of the italicized phrases in each of these pairs indirect objects? Weerman (1997) asserts that they both occupy the same IO grammatical role, just encoded in different ways, and the quote from Kiparsky crucially assumes this too. In other accounts, though, the bare NP arguments in (4.21a) and (4.22a) are analyzed as direct objects, and are sometimes claimed to be derived from their prepositional phrase counterparts in (4.21b) and (4.22b) by way of a process of "Dative Shift," or "Dative Movement," which converts indirect objects into direct objects, though see Dryer 1986 for a different proposal.

than nine different prepositions in SW which can serve as translational equivalents of EN *of* (*på, för, till, i, vid, över, av, om, från*). Nonetheless, there are common trends. This is unsurprising too, since prepositions as markers of grammatical roles arise through a process of grammaticalization, in which a preposition with lexical meanings takes on an additional function as a grammatical role marker on the basis of overlap between some subset of its lexical meanings and the meanings typically associated with the grammatical role. So, for example, EN *to*, DA *til* and SW *till*, as well as the *aan* of DU and the *oan* of FR which have come to function as markers of indirect objects in lieu of dative case, are all natively prepositions which can signal "goal-of-motion."

(4.23) a. Hun skrev et brev til mig
              she wrote a letter to me
              (DA, Allan *et al.* 1995: 422)

        b. Ik heb de boeken aan mijn vriend gezonden
           I have the books to my friend sent
           (DU)

This is not unexpected, given the overlap between the recipient role typically associated with indirect objects (e.g., of verbs like *give, say*) and "goal-of-motion" (e.g., with verbs like *send, bring*). AF has taken another path here, adapting a preposition *vir* 'for' for use as a marker of indirect objects – presumably because of the contiguity between benefactives and indirect objects. (SW, too, can use *för* for indirect objects: see Andersson 1994: 294.) Strikingly, AF has further extended this marker (variably) to direct objects as well, in which context its occurrence is conditioned by factors which include animacy (apparently under Portuguese influence; cf. Ponelis 1993: 272).

(4.24) a. Jan koop 'n boek vir haar
           Jan buys a book for her
           (AF, Ponelis 1993: 271)

        b. Jan gee 'n boek vir haar
           Jan gives a book VIR her
           (AF, Ponelis 1993: 271)

        c. hulle ken (vir) haar
           they know (VIR) her
           (AF, Ponelis 1993: 266)

Similarly, many of the prepositions which come to substitute for genitive (EN *of*, DA *af*, SW *av*, DU *van*, FR *fan*, for example) are prepositions with origin/source among their core lexical meanings.

(4.25)   a. de auto van mijn oom   (DU)
         the car of my uncle

         b. dit is van hout
            this is of wood

Much remains to be explained about the individual steps in such transitions from lexical preposition to grammatical role marker (see, for example, the discussion in Mitchell 1985: I, 506ff. on the problem of the OE antecedents of genitive *of*).

Functionally, these "grammatical" prepositions are the equivalents of case markers, but formally the distinction between the two is quite sharp. Unlike case suffixes, they precede the noun, and in fact are typically separated from it by determiners and adjectives. We are not dealing with a gradient change from case suffix to case particle to postposition of the sort found in some other language families (e.g., Masica 1991: 213). Nonetheless, some investigators, including Weerman (1997), have analyzed the "case prepositions" of GMC not just as functional equivalents to case morphology, but as case markers, with a different categorial status from lexical prepositions. There do seem to be some asymmetries, at least, between grammatical and lexical prepositions, which suggest possible structural differences. In EN, for example, just as direct objects must be strictly adjacent to their verbs, *of* phrases cannot be separated from their governing nouns by intervening lexical prepositional phrases.

(4.26)   a. the student of literature with the black mustache
         b. ??the student with the black mustache of literature

Similarly, Ponelis (1993: 269f.) concludes about AF *vir* that "the prepositional status of objective *vir* is not immediately clear," noting among other things that the *vir*-phrase has the same distribution as unmarked objects in that it is able to appear (apparently unlike benefactive PPs) in front of the direct object in bitransitive constructions:

(4.27)   Gee vir haar dit
         give *vir* her this
         (AF, Ponelis 1993: 271)

Furthermore, there are some asymmetries between objects of grammatical prepositions and objects of lexical prepositions with respect to their ability to antecede reflexives. In the following, the object of *to* can antecede a reflexive in the *about* phrase, but not the other way around.

(4.28)   a. I talked to the students about themselves
         b. ??I talked about the students to themselves

4.1.2.4 *Lexical case and structural case*

In the GMC languages, as elsewhere, noun phrases holding particular grammatical roles tend to appear in certain specific "default" cases characteristic of those roles. So, for example, subjects of finite clauses are characteristically nominative, and objects of transitive verbs are characteristically accusative:

(4.29)   a.   ik   qimands gahailja   ina
               I-Nom coming   will-heal him-Acc
               (GO, Matt. 8:7)

In those languages where dative is distinct from accusative, indirect objects characteristically appear in the dative case.

(4.29)   b.   jah atta   þeins... usgibiþ   þus   in bairhtein
               and father your   gives   to-you-Dat in brightness
               (GO, Matt. 6:6)

Genitive, in addition to possessors, marks subjects and objects of "action nouns":

(4.29)   c.   gaumei   saggwa boko
               attend-to singing scriptures-Gen
               'Attend to the singing of scriptures'
               (GO, 1 Tim. 4:13)
               (cf. usstoþ siggwan bokos
               he-stood to-sing scriptures-Acc)
               (GO, Luke 4:16)

            d.   und qum   fraujins unsaris
               until coming lords   our-Gen
               'until the coming of our Lord'
               (GO, 1 Tim. 6:14)

In addition to these core grammatical functions, the various cases have other marginal functions, often of a generally adverbial nature, some of which can be traced to the conflation of cases that gave rise to the GMC system. These are typically categorized in traditional grammars under labels like "genitive of separation," "instrumental genitive/dative," "accusative of time" and so on. They will not be treated further here. Nor will I discuss case choice on objects of prepositions.

There are, however, circumstances under which some non-canonical case replaces one of the default cases in the marking of a noun-phrase argument. Sometimes, this non-canonical case is in direct alternation with the default case, and choosing it is associated with a particular semantic effect. This is true, for example, with the so-called partitive genitive. Substitution of genitive for accusative on the objects of transitive verbs sometimes signals that the effect of the action on the object is less than total.

(4.30) a. jabai hʋas matjiþ þis hlaibis...
if someone eats this-bread-Gen.
'If someone eats of this bread'
(GO John 6:51)

b. saei matida miþ mis hlaib
who ate with me bread-Acc
'who ate bread with me'
(GO, John 13:18)

No doubt associated with this is the fact that many verbs of mental action/experience, in which the process described by the verb does not affect the object, also take genitive objects (though there is much more that could be said on this point; see Visser 1963: 366ff. for an exhaustive catalogue of OE verbs taking genitive objects, catalogued according to meaning types). In GO, these verbs include *gamaudjan* 'remind', *gamunan* 'remember', *hausjan* 'hear', *beidan* 'to await', *gairnjan* 'desire'.

(4.31) jah gamunda Paitrus waurdis Iesuis
and remembered Peter word-Gen of-Jesus
(GO, Matt. 26:75)

(Note that since in these instances the sense of "unaffected object" is inherent in the meanings of these verbs, the genitive objects do not alternate with objects in the default accusative case.) For an extensive discussion of the semantics of verbs taking oblique case objects in ON, see Bandle *et al.* 2002: 942ff. A similar instance of case alternation with consistent semantic import is the alternation – which GMC shares with other IE languages – between accusative and dative with prepositions like *in*, the former used with intransitive predicates signifying motion-toward-a-destination and the latter with predicates of position.

In other instances, the use of a case other than the default case for an object has less obvious semantic correlates, and may often be regarded as simply an idiosyncratic requirement of a particular verb. So, for example, in the following, *at-tekan* 'touch' and *andbahtjan* 'serve' require dative case on their sole objects.

(4.32) jah attaitok handau izos...jah urrais jah andbahtida imma
and he-touched hand-Dat her...and she-arose and served him-Dat
(GO, Matt. 8:15)

Assignment of a case other than the default case for a grammatical role on the basis of special requirements of a predicate is often referred to as "lexical case assignment," as opposed to the (default) "structural case assignment." The distinction between lexical case and structural case has syntactic significance. Lexically case-marked objects, for example, behave differently in a variety of ways from default accusative objects. The literature on this distinction is too large to be reviewed here, but the reader is referred to Freidin and Sprouse 1991 for some discussion and references. One of the central differences has to do with replaceability. One structural case may be "replaced" by another under appropriate syntactic circumstances. So, for example, the accusative object of a verb corresponds to a nominative subject in the related passive sentence, and to a genitive argument in the related action nominalization.

(4.33) a. Sie   verhafteten den Dieb
    they arrested   the thief-Acc

        b. Der Dieb   wurde von ihnen verhaftet
    the thief-Nom was   by them arrested

        c. die Verhaftung des Diebes
    the arrest   the thief–Gen
    (GE)

However, such substitutions are impossible for lexically case-marked objects, such as the dative object of *helfen* 'help', which cannot be replaced in this way.

(4.34) a. Sie halfen dem Kind
    they helped the child-Dat

        b. Dem Kind/*Das   Kind wurde von ihnen geholfen
    the   child-Dat/*the child-Nom   was by   them helped

        c. *Die Hilfe des Kindes/dem   Kind   von ihnen
    *the help the child-Gen/the child-Dat by   them
    (GE)

4.1.2.4.1 The loss of lexical case Lexical case is a universal feature of early GMC, and is still found in some of the modern languages (the C-languages), though it is losing ground in some of them. So, for example, genitive objects in GE are becoming fewer and more restricted in register, even though genitive continues to be robustly represented as a structural case. Lexical case generally does not exist in the case-poor P-languages. All of the latter started out as C-languages with lexical case, and a number of unresolved questions arise about this historical transition. One of these is whether there is an identifiable threshhold of morphological impoverishment in the case system at which lexical case ceases to be viable. Allen (1995: 217) makes the interesting point that the simplest imaginable answer ("when the case marking which could encode lexical case contrasts is lost") is not correct. In ME, lexical genitive case marking of objects disappeared at a point at which genitive was still robustly signaled in the morphology, its disappearance coinciding with the loss of the accusative/dative distinction. On the other hand, she adds that even in OE, where the accusative/dative distinction was "vigorous," genitive objects were increasingly falling out of favor and being replaced by accusative objects (Allen 1995: 218). That fact, reminiscent of the situation in Modern GE, suggests that perhaps the elimination of lexical case represents a typological shift that is not strictly linked to the availability of case contrasts. Lexically case-marked subjects, treated in the next section, seem to have persisted longer than lexically case-marked objects.

A second question is what replaces former lexical case marking, once this has been lost. It seems that the majority of verbs of Modern EN whose precursors took dative objects, including *help, forsake, forgive, hear, thank* and *withstand* (but not *listen*), continued to take bare objects in the objective case, which was the default case for sole objects of verbs. As Allen points out, though, verbs surviving into Modern EN which formerly took genitive objects now generally take prepositional objects (*yearn after*). Interestingly, though, this reflects an apparent change from ME, when many of these, too, took a bare object in objective case.

(4.35)　　　a. Ic hit ȝierne
　　　　　　　I it yearn
　　　　　　　(ME, Virtues and Vices, Allen 1995: 195)

Montgomery (2004: 272) reports that in older Appalachian EN, objects after verbs of smell, taste, feel, mental activity or sensation – that is, verbs whose objects would have tended to be genitive in early GMC – are introduced by *of*.

(4.35)　　　b. I can recollect of him a-going to school
　　　　　　　(Appalachian EN, Montgomery 2004: 272)

Similarly, as Abraham (1997: 34) points out, when lexical case is abandoned with verbs formerly taking genitive objects in GE, the objects sometimes emerge as bare accusative noun phrases, and sometimes as objects of prepositions (see also Bandle *et al.* 2005: 1151f. for Scandinavian languages).

(4.35)　　　c. eines Heimes begehren BECOMES　　ein Heim　　begehren
　　　　　　　　a home-Gen desire　　　　　　　　　a home-Acc desire

　　　　　　　d. der Gefallenen gedenken BECOMES　an die Gefallenen gedenken
　　　　　　　　the fallen-Gen to-think-of　　　　　　　on the fallen　　to-think

Allen (1995: 218) appears to suggest that the normal outcome in these cases (as in the case of former dative objects) is in fact for the formerly lexically case-marked object to revert to the default objective case, and that the constructions with prepositional phrases are not direct successors to the constructions with genitive objects, but reflect a separate selectional frame for the verb.

4.1.2.4.2 Lexical case and the syntax of experiencer constructions Lexical case assignment has received the most attention by far in the literature on GMC languages with respect to the phenomenon of non-nominative subject constructions. Again, the literature on this subject is far too extensive to be treated adequately here. The reader is referred to Andrews 1990, Cole *et al.* 1980, Zaenen and Maling 1990, Zaenen, Maling and Thráinsson 1990, Freidin and Sprouse 1991 and Allen 1995 for discussion. Only a relatively coarse-grained outline of the basic facts of the oblique subject constructions and their distribution in GMC is possible here. Case choice in these constructions is once again associated with the semantic roles assigned to the noun phrases in the sentence. In IC, for example (the language in which the phenomenon of oblique subjects has received the most attention), subjects of finite clauses, whether with other arguments as in (4.36a) or as sole arguments as in (4.36b), are normally nominative and they control verb agreement.

(4.36) a. Þeir   fóru   heim
           they-NomPl went-Pl home
           (IC)

       b. Egill   drap   Harald   í gær
          Egill-Nom killed Harald-Acc yesterday
          (IC, Freidin and Sprouse 1991: 403)

However, there are predicates whose sole noun phrase argument is in some other case than nominative. So, for example, the predicate *reka* 'drift' takes an accusative argument, and *líka* 'like' takes a dative argument.

(4.37) a. Drengi-na   rak   á   land
          boys-the-Acc drifted to land
          (IC, Andrews 1990: 169)

       b. Mér   líkar   vel   við hann
          me-Dat pleases well with him
          (IC, Kress 1982: 216)

Constructions of this sort are often referred to as "subjectless" or "impersonal," since they lack nominative subjects. However, it has long been observed that these non-nominative sole arguments in at least some GMC languages pattern in the same way as nominative subjects with respect to a number of distributional and referential properties that seem otherwise to hold only for subjects. For example, in general the missing argument in infinitive clauses – as in the 'control" case in (4.38a) or the "unspecified subject" case in (4.38b) – is understood to be the subject argument of the infinitive.

(4.38)   a. I want [ ] to see him (*I want for him to see [ ])
                b. It is good [ ] to see them

But by this criterion, an argument like the sole accusative argument of *reka* 'drift' in IC behaves like a subject, since it can be missing in such infinitive constructions:

(4.39)   hún vonast til að [ ] reka á land eina
                she hopes for to   drift to land alone-Acc
                (IC, Andrews 1990: 175)

That the missing argument is accusative is reflected by the fact that in example (4.39) the adverbial *eina* which "refers back" to it appears in accusative case.

Similarly, when verbs of personal experience (like 'like' or 'want') take two noun phrase arguments in IC, the experiencer argument appears in oblique case while the theme argument (unless assigned a lexical case of its own) appears in nominative case and (optionally) controls verb agreement, but it is again the non-nominative experiencer argument that behaves like a subject in, for example, disappearing in infinitive control constructions (4.40b), or in "unspecified subject constructions" like (4.40c), as well as with respect to numerous other diagnostics discussed in Zaenen *et al.* 1990.

(4.40)   a. Mig   vantar   peninga
                   me-Acc lacks-3Sg money-Nom
                   'I lack money'

                 b. Ég vonast til   að [ ] vanta ekki peninga
                   I   hope   for to   lack   not   money

                 c. Að [ ] vanta peninga er alltof   algengt
                   to   lack   money   is all-too common
                   (IC, Zaenen *et al.* 1990: 1068)[8]

---

[8] *Vanta* 'want' is one of a number of experiencer predicates in IC which takes accusative case experiencers. However, there is a tendency in colloquial IC to replace this accusative (or genitive) case with dative – a phenomenon referred to as "Dative Sickness." See H. Smith 1994, M. Smith 2001 and Eythórsson 2002.

Conversely, in spite of having the "coding properties" normally associated with subjects – nominative case and the ability to determine verb agreement – the nominative nominals here do not pattern with subjects, but rather with objects, with respect to this criterion (cf., e.g., Cole *et al.* 1980). Other diagnostics, involving word order and pronoun antecedence, point to the same conclusion. From this, it is concluded that the experiencer arguments here are subjects, though not nominative because they are assigned a lexical case. The reader is referred to the sources cited for details.

This oblique subject phenomenon is in evidence in ME as well (cf. Butler 1977; Cole *et al.* 1980). In EME texts like *Dame Sirith* and *Genesis and Exodus*, predicates like 'dream' and 'like' are used exclusively with objective case experiencers:

(4.41) a. a   foreward þat   þe   mai full well like
           an agreement that you-Obj may full well please
           'An agreement that may full well please you'
           (EME, *Dame Sirith* 255, 1275AD, in Cole *et al.* 1980: 729)

        b. Of þat him   drempte in prisun
           of that him-Obj dreamed in prison
           'He dreamed of that in prison'
           (EME, *Genesis and Exodus* 2116, 1250AD, in Cole *et al.* 1980: 729)

Nonetheless, these objective case experiencers again share with nominative subjects the ability to be the missing arguments in infinitival constructions:

(4.42) a. Him burþ [ ] to liken well his lif
           him befits   to like well his life
           'It befits him to like his life well'
           (EME, *Dame Sirith* 82, Cole *et al.* 729)

        b. Good is, quaþ Ioseph, [ ] to dremen of win
           good is   said joseph   to dream of wine
           (EME, *Genesis and Exodus* 2067, in Cole *et al.* 1980: 730)

Other types of evidence, including evidence from word order, lead Allen (1986, 1995: ch. 4) to conclude that these oblique experiencer arguments were subjects even in OE times. Oblique subjects are thus attested in at least two of the branches of GMC – North GMC and West GMC (GO provides no useful evidence). Whether it is a common GMC inheritance is a matter of contention, most recently revisited by Eythórsson and Barðdal (2005). GE has experiencer constructions which appear on the surface to be parallel to those in IC; the experiencer nominal appears in a case other than nominative, and the theme nominal appears in nominative case and controls the agreement morphology on the verb.

(4.43) Mir   gefallen diese Studenten
        me-Dat please-Pl these students-Nom
        'These students please me = I like these students'
        (GE)

In GE, however, it is the nominative argument, not the dative experiencer argument, which behaves like a subject with respect to its ability to be missing in infinitive control constructions. The experiencer does not behave like a subject here:

(4.44) a. Diese Studenten versuchten, [ ] mir zu gefallen
           these students tried   me to please
           'these students tried to please me'

        b. *Ich versuchte, diese Studenten [ ] zu gefallen
            I tried   these students   to please
            'I tried to like these students'
            (GE)

Similarly, in GE, unlike IC and ME, non-nominative experiencers cannot be the missing arguments in the "unspecified subject" construction:

(4.45) a. Mir ist übel
           me is bad
           'I feel sick'
           (GE, Zaenen *et al.* 1990: 127)

        b. *Übel   zu sein ist unangenehm
            [ ] bad to be   is unpleasant
            (GE, Zaenen *et al.* 1990: 127)

That is, in GE, unlike IC or ME, oblique experiencers do not appear to pattern with subjects. If this conclusion is correct, then the oblique subject construction crosscuts the branches of the GMC family tree. In their recent paper, however, Eythórsson and Barðdal (2005) contend that GE, too, has oblique subjects in experiencer constructions, and offer alternative explanations for the failure of the tests in (4.44) and (4.45). The interested reader is referred to that paper for discussion.

EN no longer has non-nominative experiencer subject constructions. For a very detailed discussion of the sequence of changes resulting in the disappearance of such constructions, the reader is referred especially to Elmer 1981 and Allen 1995. In the main, such constructions have been eliminated in one of two ways. On the one hand, some of the experiencer subjects have become simple objects, the subject role being assumed by a dummy subject 'it'. Schematically,

(4.46) a. us behoueþ BECOMES it behooveth us

This development occurred particularly often with predicates which, in addition to an experiencer object, also took a clausal argument (*seem, behoove, befit, grieve*).

On the other hand, many other experiencer constructions underwent change from an "impersonal" construction to a "personal" one, in which the former non-nominative experiencer subject has become a full-fledged nominative subject. This happened with *hunger, thirst, dream, rue, like, long, smart*, among other predicates. Schematically, this change can be represented as in (4.46b):

(4.46) b. him longs... BECOMES he longs...

This change is sometimes referred to as the "psych-shift." Interestingly, it seems not to have been unique to EN. Evans (1975), cited in Cole *et al*. 1980, observes that SW has undergone a shift in psychological predicates similar to the one observed in EN (see also Haugen 1976: 310, 371). Predicates which took non-nominative experiencers in ON but which have nominative subjects in Modern SW include:

(4.47) jag drömmer   'I dream'
        jag tycker   'I think'
        jag kommer i hug   'I remember'
        jag bör   'I ought'
        jag är varm   'I am warm'
        jag saknar   'I lack'
        jag längtar   'I miss'
        jag behöver   'I must'
        (SW, Evans 1975)

At least some of these predicates have become "personal" in NO and DA too:

(4.48) a. hun liker ham
          she likes him
          (NO, Mørck 1994: 162)

       b. mik þyrsti → eg var tyrst
          me thirsted   I was thirsty
          (NO, Bandle *et al*. 2005: 1156)

       c. drømde mik en drøm → jeg drømte en drøm
          dreamed me a dream   I dreamed a dream
          (DA, Haugen 1976: 310)

This psych-shift can be viewed as the result of the loss of the possibility for assigning lexical case to subjects. When lexical case is lost, subjects can only appear in the nominative structural case appropriate to that role. In such circumstances, a former oblique subject cannot remain such, but must be reanalyzed in one of two ways – either becoming a nominative subject, or assuming an object role appropriate to its non-nominative case. (There is, in fact, a third possible resolution; the predicate whose syntax had become problematic could simply be eliminated from the language. In this connection, it is surprising to note how many of the psychological predicates of Old and ME have disappeared from the language.) This leads to the question of why the possibility of lexical case on subjects should have been lost in Modern EN and SW, for example, but not in IC, leading to the psych-shift in just those languages. Again, it is natural to look for other typological commonalities shared by these languages (to the exclusion of IC) to which such developments might be linked. One such commonality is that they have lost the dative/accusative contrast, and it is tempting to see in this the crucial difference. Allen (1995: 219ff.) argues convincingly, though, against a direct typological connection between the ability of a language to maintain oblique subjects and the presence of a dative/accusative case distinction. She points out that in the history of EN, the non-nominative experiencer constructions ("Preposed Dative Experiencer Constructions") continued a robust and productive existence for centuries after the loss of the dative/accusative distinction, before eventually undergoing personalization. This being the case, the former cannot have been the direct cause of the latter. Rather, she proposes, lexical case was lost in stages. The loss of the dative/accusative contrast eliminated lexical case contrasts for objects, but it was still possible to have lexically case-marked subjects, since nominative and objective cases were still distinct, at least for pronouns. Thus, non-nominative subject constructions like (4.41) persisted in EN, until the gradual effects of declining frequency and transparency eventually led to obsolescence and reanalysis.

DU has also lost the dative/accusative distinction, and lexical case, but its experiencer predicates did not undergo psych-shift in the wake of these developments. Donaldson (1981: 179) lists a number of experiencer predicates which retain impersonal syntax in DU, in contrast to EN, including the following:

(4.49)   het bevalt me 'I like it'
         het spijt me 'I'm sorry'
         het lukte me 'I succeeded'
         het verwondert me 'I'm surprised'
         het verbaast me 'I'm amazed'
         (DU, Donaldson 1981: 179)

The experiencer arguments in these constructions, as in GE, also appear to pattern as nonsubjects with respect to such diagnostics as behavior in "unspecified subject" constructions, where, as in GE, it is the theme nominal, not the experiencer nominal, which can serve as the missing argument:

(4.50) a. [ ] Hem bevallen is niet moeilijk
    him to-please is not possible
   (DU, Zaenen 1987: 3)

Burridge (1993: 150ff.) argues, however, that these were in fact oblique experiencer subject constructions in Middle DU. If so, the state of affairs in Modern DU would reflect an alternative response to the loss of lexical case to that exemplified in English and continental Scandinavian. Burridge also points out a striking extension in productivity of oblique subjects in Middle DU; subjects which would normally be expected to be nominative, including even subjects of action verbs, could apparently take oblique case instead, in order to signal an instance of involuntary action by a non-agentive subject, as in (4.50b). This possibility no longer exists in Modern DU.

(4.50) b. Sinen pols sloech sterkeliic
    his pulse-Dat beats strongly
   (Middle DU, 1450, cited in Burridge 1993: 155)

For further discussion of the history of oblique subjects in Germanie, see Eythórsson and Barðdal 2005.

4.2 The internal structure of the nominal phrase

4.2.1 Nominal phrases without nominal heads

Nominal phrases (NPs) in the GMC languages typically contain a pronoun as in (4.51a) or a lexical noun (4.51b), which serve as the head of the NP.

(4.51) a. I saw [$_{NP}$ him]
   b. I saw [$_{NP}$ the old man]

However, some NPs appear to contain neither a pronoun or a noun, as in (4.52a–c).

(4.52) a. twai blindans
    two blind [ones]
   (GO, Matt. 9: 27)

   b. Ich sah zwei Blinde/die Blinden
    I saw two blind [ones] / the blind [ones]
   (GE)

   c. He drank the red wine and she drank the white [ ]

Constructions of this type could be regarded as involving nominalization of the adjective, so that they do, in fact, have noun heads (an analysis implicit in the capitalization of the adjective in the GE example, and explicitly suggested, e.g., by Behaghel 1923: I, 214f.). Alternatively, they could be held to be elliptical constructions, in which the adjective modifies an "understood" (or phonologically null) (pro-) nominal head. In fact, it appears probable that the different subcases in (4.52a–c) require different analyses. Most clearly involving nominalization are instances like the GO example in (4.52a) – examples of the type which Behaghel (1923: I, 215) refers to as "stehende Substantivierung." Here, *blindans*, though derived from an adjective, inflects like a noun, taking an invariant ending whose shape does not depend on the presence or absence of an article, as adjective endings do. It differs in this respect from what Behaghel refers to as "gelegentliche Substantivierung," illustrated by the GE examples in (4.52b), in which the "substantivized" adjectives are still inflectionally adjective-like, taking a weak or a strong ending depending on the presence and nature of the preceding determiner (see Section 4.2.2.3); for these, the ellipsis analysis would appear more defensible. Such an analysis is even more plausible for the EN cases represented by the EN example in (4.52c). These different types are found elsewhere in GMC – in DA, for example, as in (4.53), though it is often difficult to distinguish between type (4.52a) and (4.52b) on grounds of inflection.

(4.53)   a. de gamles   sparepenge
               the old [people]'s savings
               (DA, Allan *et al.* 1995: 50)

            b. Som ung var   han køn
               as a young [man] was he handsome
               (DA, Allan *et al.* 1995: 101)

            c. Han foretrækker dansk mad for fremmed []
               he prefers   Danish food to foreign
               (DA, Allan *et al.* 1995: 100)

Note that in (4.53a), the apparent adjective inflects like a noun in admitting the nominal genitive suffix *-s*.

EN, unlike other GMC languages, admits the type in (4.52b) in only highly restricted cases. Specific, non-anaphoric uses of adjectives as nouns, as in the GE or GO examples in (4.52a) and (4.52b), are disallowed in EN. We cannot speak in EN of 'two blinds', or 'the blinds', or 'the young' (= 'the young man'), for example, as one can in GE or DA. This may be connected with the lack of adjective inflection in EN. In EN, except in contexts of anaphoric dependency like (4.52c), adjectives used as nouns are (a) uninflected, (b) inherently plural for the purposes of subject-verb agreement and (c) generic in interpretation, as in:

(4.54)   The requirements of the blind were not taken into account

There are a few exceptions, in which past/passive participles can be used without support to refer to a specific individual, as in *the accused, the deceased*. This is a lexically limited possibility, however – not possible with *the injured*, for example.

4.2.2 Nominal phrases with pronoun heads

As nominal elements, pronouns can serve as the heads of nominal phrases. In this role, however, they are much more restricted than are lexical nouns with respect to the possibilities for co-occurrence with such other NP-components as determiners, modifiers and complements. For example, unlike nouns, pronouns cannot occur with definite articles (**the he*). Demonstrative and personal pronouns do co-occur in GMC with what will be referred to as predeterminers, such as *all*, *both*. Unlike noun heads, however, the pronoun comes in front of the pre-determiner.

(4.55)   Hon överraskade oss alla
           she surprised   us all
           (SW, Holmes and Hinchcliffe 1994: 179)

Personal pronouns also resist modification, generally disallowing preposed adjectives, as in the following EN and GE examples:

(4.56)   *poor he/ *armer er[9]

Many of the GMC languages do allow apparent modification of pronouns by post-positioned adjectives, as in the following EN and GE examples:

(4.57)   a. wir kranken
              we sick
              (GE)

           b. jus fraqiþanans
              you condemned
              (GO, Matt. 25:41)

---

[9] EN allows only a limited, formulaic premodification of pronouns by adjectives, but (a) the pronouns must be in their absolute forms (*poor me*/**poor I*) and (b) the admissible adjectives are highly restricted (**sick him*).

4.2 The internal structure of the nominal phrase

However, given the order here, it is at least likely that these are pronouns followed by substantivized adjectives functioning as appositives. Supporting such an interpretation is the fact that EN, where substantivized adjectives with specific reference are disallowed, also does not admit this construction.

(4.58) *we sick

Nominal phrases headed by personal pronouns are also highly restricted in their ability to contain (complement or modifying) prepositional phrases:

(4.59) a. *I put it of poetry on the shelf. (Cf. I put the book of poetry...)
b. *I read it by Chomsky

These restrictions apply only to personal pronouns in EN. There are other pronominals, such as the -*thing*-compounds (*something, anything, everything*) which do allow modification by adjectives and prepositional phrases (*anything white, anything by Chomsky*). Note again that in these cases, unlike those headed by lexical nouns, the adjectives obligatorily follow the head.

Relative modification of personal pronouns, on the other hand, both restrictive and non-restrictive, is generally possible:

(4.60) a. we(,) who are left

b. jus juzei simle wesuþ fairra
you who once were far
(GO, Eph. 2:13)

Hestvik (1990) proposes that the admissibility of modifiers in NPs headed by personal pronouns varies across the GMC languages. Thus, for example, a PP modifier on a pronoun in NO is deemed much more acceptable than in EN.

(4.61) a. han med røtt hatt
(NO, Hestvik 1990: 163)

b. ??He with the red hat

Compare also

(4.61) c. hende på cyklen har travlt
??she on the bicycle is in a hurry
(DA, Allan *et al.* 1995: 168)

4.2.3 Nominal phrases headed by lexical nouns

By contrast with pronouns, nominal phrases headed by lexical nouns admit a full range of complements, modifiers and determiners. In the following sections, the syntax of these components within the noun phrase will be considered individually, starting "at the bottom" – that is, with the ones which are most closely associated with the head.

4.2.3.1 Complements and modifiers of nouns

Noun phrases may contain, besides the head noun, other phrases. Some of these are arguments, thematically related to the head noun, and others are "modifiers," or "adjuncts." The distinction is harder to pin down for nouns than for verbs, for example, and there is disagreement about the extent to which nouns have argument structures like those of verbs. Grimshaw (1990), for example, claims that argument structures are limited to a restricted class of complex event nominals. For one thing, complements of nouns are in general optional, even when they are required by the lexically related verb, as the following examples illustrate.

(4.62)   a. Der Brand zerstörte das Gebäude
           the fire destroyed the building
           (GE)

           b. Die Zerstörung (des Gebäudes) (durch Brand)
           the destruction (of the building) (by fire)
           (GE)

When they do occur, arguments and adjuncts characteristically follow the head noun, in all of the GMC languages. Where a verb takes an accusative object complement, the corresponding nominal either takes a genitive case object in C-languages, or its prepositional equivalent in P-languages (see Section 4.1.2.3.1). Genitive NP complements of nouns, or their PP equivalents, are typically required to be closer to the head noun than are other complements or adjuncts:

(4.63)   a. der libhobər fun bejsbol fun bruklin
           the fan of baseball from Brooklyn

           b. *der libhobər fun bruklin fun bejsbol
           (YI, Jacobs 2005: 245)

Otherwise, arguments and adjuncts of nouns appear to be relatively freely ordered within the NP, even in languages which lack "scrambling" (cf. Section 5.7.2.1).

(4.64)   a. the discussion last summer about the peace negotiations

           b. the discussion about peace negotiations last summer

4.2.3.2 The position of adjectives in the nominal phrase

Descriptive adjectives in GMC appear predominantly to the left of the head noun, and appear to have done so throughout the history of the language (cf. Smith 1971 for statistics on adjective placement in the older dialects). When they appear in front of the noun, different semantic classes of descriptive adjectives tend to occur in more or less constant, though not rigidly fixed, relative order, which appears to be more or less uniform across (at least) the GMC languages. Thus, color adjectives tend to appear closer to the noun than quantity adjectives, and adjectives describing permanent attributes tend to occur closer to the noun than those describing temporary/modifiable attributes.

4.2.3.2.1 The problem of postnominal adjectives

In the older languages especially, however, N–Adj existed as a not infrequent alternative order. (This may in fact have been the only order in the archaic language of the older runic inscriptions; Antonsen (1981) observes that the corpus contains not a single instance of a descriptive adjective preceding the noun.)

(4.65)   a. gudea gimeinun
             combat common
             (OHG, Hildebrandslied)

           b. herron goten
             lord   good
             (OHG, Hildebrandslied)

           c. konung ólifþan
             king   lifeless
             (ON, Heusler 1967: 117)

           d. een ridder goet
             a   knight good
             (Middle DU, De Vooys, 1949: 310)

There are considerations supporting the view that this order is not just the mirror image of the Adj–N order, and that postnominal adjectives are not modifying adjectives, but appositive or predicative (see Kress 1982: 182, for example). In IC and ON, for instance, the adjective not only follows the noun but also the postnominal possessive pronoun.

(4.66)   a. Hann stóð við   húsdyr hennar lokaðar
             he   stood before house-door her   locked
             (IC, Kress 1982: 182)

(4.66) b. segl várt et forna
sail our the old
(ON, Heusler 1967: 127)

Converging with this is the observation that in certain respects postnominal adjectives are closer to predicate adjectives in their interpretation. We observed above that adjectives modifying -*thing*-pronouns in EN must follow the noun, but, as noted by Quirk *et al.* (1985: 418) adjectives which cannot appear as predicate adjectives (e.g., *main*, *mere* and *poor* on its "evaluative" reading) also cannot appear postnominally here:[10]

(4.67) a. something free/*main/*mere
(Cf. Quirk *et al.* 1985: 418)

b. This is free/*main/*mere

Finally, consider how Greek constructions like (4.68a) were treated in GO. In the Greek construction, a noun with an article is followed by an appositive adjective which has a definite article of its own.

(4.68) a. tò pneûma autoû tò hágion
the spirit his the holy
= 'The spirit of his, the holy (one)'
(Greek, 1 Thess. 4:8)

A construction very similar to the Greek one is found in Modern YI, possibly reflecting Semitic influence (see Jacobs *et al.* 1994: 408; Plank 2003: 345):

(4.68) b. di oygn di grine
the eyes the green
(YI, Jacobs *et al.* 1994: 408)

c. a meydl a sheyne
a girl a pretty
(YI, Jacobs *et al.* 1994: 408)

The GO translator sometimes rendered such constructions word-for-word, as in (4.68d), retaining both articles, but most often, according to Streitberg, omitted the first article and left the second as in (4.68e) (cf. also Luke 9:35, Mark 1:26, Matt. 5:29):

---

[10] EN, apparently uniquely, has a class of adjectives (with the *a-* prefix, such as *afloat*, *alive*) which can only appear after the noun (or in predicate adjective position). Roger Lass (p.c.) points out that this may reflect the fact that they are etymologically prepositional phrases.

(4.68)   d. sa   hundafaþs   sa   atstandands   in andwairþja is
                 the centurion   the   standing-there in presence   his
                 (GO, Mark 15:39)

                e. wigs sa   brigganda in   fralustai
                 way the   bringing   into   destruction
                 (GO, Matt. 7:13)

Importantly, the least frequent translation involved the omission of the article in front of the adjective, with or without the first article, yielding an order (Det)-N-Adj, as in (4.68g), for example – the translation of the Greek (4.68a):

(4.68)   f. in þamma daga ubilin
                 in the   day   evil
                 (GO, Eph. 6:13)

                g. ahman   seinana   weihana
                 spirit   his   holy
                 (GO, 1 Thess. 4:8)   (Cf. John 6:69)

The decided preference for retaining the article in front of these postposed adjectives suggests strongly that they were most naturally interpreted as appositive phrases, rather than as postposed modifying adjectives.

Postnominal position of an adjective phrase is forced in EN when the adjective itself has a complement:

(4.69)   a. A proud father

                b. *A proud of his children father~a father proud of his children

Some other GMC languages allow adjective-plus-complement constructions equivalent to the one in (4.69b) to appear prenominally. Constructions of this type, sometimes referred to as "extended attributive constructions," are typical in formal registers of DU and GE.

(4.70)   a. de   op dat ogenblik   al erg   grote   oppositie
                 the at   that moment   already large   opposition
                 (DU, de Schutter 1994: 465)

                b. ein auf seine Kinder   stolzer Vater
                 an   of   his   children proud   father
                 (GE)

The reason for this difference is apparently that complements of adjectives in these languages, unlike EN, precede the adjective, and therefore do not intervene between it and the noun. There seems to be a crosslinguistic dispreference for allowing complements of modifying phrases to intervene between the heads of those modifying phrases and the head of the phrase which they modify (cf. Maling 1983: 284, for example). In EN, adjectives are generally prenominal except in cases in which they must occur after the noun in order to satisfy this principle. Note that in the DU example in (4.71b), the principle is apparently accommodated by rightward shifting of just that material which would otherwise follow the adjective within the AP.

(4.71)   a. ze is [groter dan ik]
         she is bigger than I
         (DU: de Schutter 1994: 465)

         b. een grotere man [dan ik]
            a   bigger man than I
            (DU)

A principle of this sort also correctly predicts the positioning of prepositional phrase modifiers of nouns (*the student with the backpack*) and (under the assumption that clauses are headed by complementizers) of relative clauses. These modifying phrases also appear after the noun, since in prenominal position their complements would intervene between their own heads and the head of the modifying phrase (*[[P NP]N]).

4.2.3.3 *Syntactic conditions on attributive adjective inflection*

In the great majority of the GMC languages, attributive adjectives alternate between two complementarily distributed sets of endings, traditionally known as "weak" and "strong" (or, alternatively, as "definite" and "indefinite"). This distinction is one of the characteristic innovations of early GMC (though, as Orr (1982) points out, it has a functional counterpart in Baltic and Slavic), and as a formal contrast, at least, it has been surprisingly persistent. Such contrasts are found both in the highly inflected languages, such as GO and IC, and in minimally inflected languages such as FR and DA, though in YI (Jacobs *et al.* 1994: 405) it has been largely obscured by syncretism between the two paradigms. Only in EN is the contrast wholly absent.

	Weak	*Strong*
(4.72) a.	ik im hairdeis **gods**	hairdeis sa **goda** saiwala seina lagjiþ...
	I am shepherd good	shepherd-the-good soul his lays down
	(GO, John10:11)	
b.	**rauður** hestur	**rauði** hesturinn hans Páls
	(a) red horse	red horse the 'his' Pauls =
		'Paul's red horse'
	(IC, Einarsson, 1945: 116)	

c. in **wyt** skiep   it **wite** skiep
   a white sheep   the white sheep
   (FR, Tiersma, 1999: 45)

d. **varmt** vand   det **varme** vand
   warm water   the warm water
   (DA, Allan et al. 1995: 72)

e. een **duur** boek   het **dure** boek
   an expensive book   the expensive book
   (AF, Ponelis 1993: 365)

The function of this contrast – its role in the signaling of semantic and morphosyntactic oppositions – is more transparent in (some of) the younger GMC languages than in the older ones. The diachronic developments indicate a tendency toward regularization and functionalization of an originally semi-regular distribution – a development which has taken a remarkable diversity of paths in the individual languages.

Behaghel (1923: I, 197) observes that adjectives following the indefinite article appear to have been inflected strong in early GMC.

(4.73)   a. ān micel ēa
            a big-Str island
            (OE, Orosius 17:3, Behaghel 1923: I, 197)

         b. einemo sconemo chinde
            to-a pretty-Str child
            (OHG, Orosius 17:3, Behaghel 1923: I, 197)

         c. ein armaz wib
            a poor-Str woman
            (OHG, Otfrid II 14:48, cited in Behaghel 197)

He proposes that this was because the strong ending itself was from the beginning a signal of indefiniteness, and that the indefinite article, having arisen much later, was simply added to this syntagm.

Correspondingly, the usual appearance of "weak" endings after definite articles, as in the examples in (4.72), can be explained in a parallel way by claiming that the weak endings themselves were the original carriers of definite meaning. In fact, in OE, noun phrases often appear in definite meanings with weak adjectives and no definite article (see Klaeber 1950: xcii). In this context, mention should be made of the usual occurrence of weak endings without definite articles in instances of direct address, for example, in IC and FA (IC *góða frú* 'Dear Mrs. X' Einarsson 1945: 118).

However, some facts are hard to reconcile with the idea that the strong endings originally "meant" indefinite. First, the use of NPs with strong adjectives and no definite article to express definite meaning appears to be robust in the older languages. It is still the norm, for example, in ON poetry, as in *konung óliffan* [AccStr] '[the] lifeless king' (Heusler 1967: 117). It is also instantiated in OHG and in OE (see Behaghel 1923: I, 181). Second, the original adjective endings employed after possessive pronouns/genitive pronouns in early GMC seem to have been exclusively strong ones (Behaghel 1923: I, 190), even when the NPs containing them were definite.[11] This is still the case in Modern IC, with both lexical genitive phrases and possessive pronouns, when not accompanied by an article (Kress 1982: 182):

(4.74) a. izwara   goda   waurstwa
           your   good-Str   works
           (GO, Matt. 5:16, cited in Behaghel 1923: I, 190)

        b. ic mīnne   can   glædne   Hrōþulf
           I my   know   noble-Str   Hrothulf
           (OE, Beow. 1180, cited in Behaghel)

        c. iro   gôdumu   hêrron
           to-their   good-Str   lord
           (OS, Heliand 2821, cited in Behaghel)

        d. árlegur   rekstrarkostnaður   bílsens
           yearly-Str cost   of-business
           (IC, Kress 1982: 182)

        e. barnlaust   heimili   þeirra
           childless-Str home   their
           (IC, Kress 1982: 183)

Such anomalies are compatible with an alternative view of the original form of the strong/weak opposition, articulated, for example, in Hodler 1969: 81, under which strong adjectives occurred in all functions, and in which weak adjectives were originally not adjectives but derived nouns – nominalizations of adjectives, which came to be associated with demonstratives through their use as appositives, for example, in structures like (4.75), and through that association came to be reinterpreted as definite adjectives, in which functions they gradually displaced the strong forms. (See also

---

[11] The possessive pronouns originally inflected only strong, even after the definite article.

(i)   thes   mines   heiminges
            the-Gen   my-GenStr   home
            (OHG, Otfrid III 1:43)

Krahe 1967: 109; Fortson 2004: 305; Orr 1982; Heinrichs 1954: 64ff. Heinrichs (1954: 67), in fact sees in the -*n* suffix of weak adjectives an original demonstrative particle.)

(4.75) sunus meins sa liuba
son mine the beloved
(GO, Luke 9:35)

Over time, the distribution of the two types of endings has changed in some of the remaining languages in a way that has increased the fit between form and meaning. In continental Scandinavian, for example, as well as in one Insular GMC language (FA),[12] the weak (definite) declension is now used with possessives. Thus, these endings do now uniformly, though redundantly, encode definiteness.

(4.76) a. Peters långa resa
Peter's long-Wk journey
(SW, Holmes and Hinchcliffe 1994: 93)

b. Gittes røde tørklæde
Gitte's red-Wk scarf
(DA, Allan *et al.* 1995: 97)

c. okkara fagra land~fagra land okkara
our fair-Wk land
(FA, Lockwood 1964: 111)

d. mammusar lítli skattur
mother's little-Wk treasure
(FA, Lockwood 1964: 111)

e. havsins sterka dun
the-ocean's mighty-Wk roaring
(FA, Lockwood 1964: 111)

Early GE appears to have been on its way toward a similar regularization; by the end of the OHG period, weak endings had become the rule after possessives.

(4.77) a. mîn liobo sun
my beloved-Wk son
(OHG, Tatian 14:5, cited in Behaghel 1923: I, 191)

---

[12] Note also that FA and IC differ with respect to the placement of the genitive phrase. Braunmüller (1991: 239) suggests that this reflects DA influence in FA.

(4.77) b. sine liebun   thegana
          his beloved-Wk thanes
          (OHG, Otfrid III 8:20, cited in Behaghel 1923: I, 191)

This development can again be seen as a step toward strengthening the correlation between the weak ending and semantic definiteness. Here, however, it was superseded by a competing refunctionalization along other lines. From MHG onward, the choice of adjective ending is dissociated from meaning; the endings on adjectives after possessives and the inflectionally similar indefinite article may be either strong or weak, depending on the nature of the ending of the preceding possessives:

(4.78) a. min erester sun
          my first-Str son
          (MHG, Exod. 855, cited in Behaghel 1923: I, 191)

        b. zuo miner lieben   muoter
           to my   dear-Wk mother
           (MHG, Nib. 345:2, cited in Behaghel 1923: I, 191)

In Modern GE, if an adjective is preceded by either a definite article or by an indefinite article or possessive whose ending is homophonous with that of the corresponding definite article (that is, any determiner with a "strong" ending) then the adjective takes the weak ending. Otherwise (including the case in which the noun phrase contains no determiner), the adjective takes the strong ending.

On the morphological side, this has involved a restructuring/reinterpretation of the endings themselves. The strong endings of the adjectives had always partially overlapped formally with those of the definite article, as a by-product of their histories. (The definite article in GMC arises from the demonstrative pronoun, and the strong adjective endings also derived in part from original pronominal endings.) In MHG, this overlap was maximized in various ways. For example, the masculine nominative pronominal ending *-er* was extended to the masculine nominative strong adjective (MHG *guoter* vs. OE *gōd*, GO *goþs*). The result of this leveling is that in GE, the strong adjective endings have become identical to the endings of the determiner/demonstrative pronoun. A unitary set of endings has thus emerged, which is indifferently attachable to either definite or indefinite articles or to adjectives.

(4.79) a. d**er** alte Mann/ ein alt**er** Mann
           the old man/   an old man

        b. mit ein**em** alten Wein/mit d**em** alten Wein/ mit alt**em** Wein
           with an   old wine / with the old wine / with old   wine
           (GE)

As pointed out by Esau (1972), the strong endings form a richer inventory than the weak ones, and provide more information about the case, gender and number of the NP. For the most part, nouns are not themselves inflected for case or gender. It is the determiners and adjectives in the noun phrase which carry this inflectional information. The GE system insures that in any NP containing one or more such elements, there will be at least one occurrence of an information-rich strong ending. (Serving this same goal is the extension of adjective endings to originally uninflected genitive pronouns, as discussed in Section (4.4).) In fact, Esau proposes further that this must be supplemented by an economy principle which limits the strong ending to exactly one occurrence per noun phrase. If it occurs on the determiner, it cannot also occur on the attributive adjective, which must in consequence be weak. He points out that this assumption also accounts for an otherwise anomalous case. In GE, when an adjective unpreceded by a determiner modifies a genitive masculine or neuter noun, it does not appear with the strong ending, but with the weak ending: *guten Weines* 'of good wine'/*gutes Weines. Esau points out that this exception follows from the economy principle, since it is precisely here that the noun itself bears an inflectional ending, identical to the strong genitive singular ending of determiners and adjectives.

Low GE has apparently created a tripartite distinction, by articulating the masculine and neuter strong ending into two separate forms – one used after indefinite articles, and one (a 0-ending) used when there is no article. Thus, we have contrasts like:

(4.80) ool Book   en ollt(~oll) Book   dat oole Book
        old book   an old   book   the old book
        (Low GE, Lindow *et al.* 1998: 191f.)

In summary, the original contrast between strong and weak in GMC seems to have been connected, albeit in a relatively loose way, to definiteness, and may have served to signal definiteness prior to the development of the article system, though this has not been demonstrated compellingly. Both continental Scandinavian and GE have regularized the contrast, though in different ways. In SW, where it has brought it fully into line with the definiteness/indefiniteness opposition, it is now wholly regular though also wholly predictable. In GE, it has lost all association with definiteness, becoming purely a means of allowing more salient encoding of case, number and gender.

A refunctionalization of a different sort is reported for IC by Thráinsson (1994: 166), Braunmüller (1991: 199) and Kress (1982: 181); adjectives co-occurring with the definite article are typically weak, but may alternatively take strong endings to signal non-restrictive modification:

(4.81)   ríki   maðurinn/ríkur   maðurinn
         rich-Wk   man-the/rich-Str man-the
         'the rich man'/'the (known) man, who also happens to be rich'
         (IC, Braunmüller 1991: 199)

The opposition has been subject to a refunctionalization in AF which is much harder to characterize (Lass 1988; Ponelis 1993: 365f.; Donaldson 1994: 486f.). The sole remaining adjective marker in AF, -e, historically a weak adjective suffix, has become an "attributive marker," which appears on attributive adjectives or not, regardless of the presence of preceding determiners, depending rather in a complex way on the phonological shape of the adjective (polysyllabic adjectives but not monosyllabic ones), their morphological complexity, and the register of the text (serving as a marker of more formal style). The relatively marginal instances in which it still participates in meaningful contrasts bear comparison to the IC cases discussed above.

(4.82)   a. die arm   man   die arme   man
            the poor (penniless) man   the poor (pitiable) man
            (AF, Ponelis 1993: 365)

         b. 'n enkel man   'n enkele man
            a   single man   a   solitary man
            (AF, Lass 1988: 47)

Similar to an extent is the situation in DU (de Schutter 1994: 463); while the ending -e has become general on attributive adjectives, as in AF, it may in some instances be omitted to signal a contrast in the "scope" of the adjective. In the examples he gives, the difference is that between an "intersective" reading (Larson 1995) (modifying the individual) and a "non-intersective" reading (modifying the event):

(4.83)   a. een goed leraar
            a   good teacher = 'someone who is good at teaching'

         b. een goede leraar
            a   good teacher = 'a teacher who has a good character'
            (DU, de Schutter 1994: 463)

and possibly

(4.83)   c. ons oud   huis
            our old   house = 'the one we used to live in'

         d. ons oude   huis
            our old   house = 'our house which is old'
            (DU, de Schutter 1994: 463)

See Fudeman 1999: 274ff. for discussion of an interestingly similar development in Bala, a West African language, in which noun-class suffixes have been redistributed in such a way as to signal a similar contrast.

4.3 Determiners

4.3.1 Weak quantifiers

In this category I include quantificational elements such as OE *fela* 'many', *sum* 'a certain', GE *etlich* 'some, several', *wenig* 'few', *mancher* 'many a', as well as the numerals. Alternative labels for such elements include "relative quantifiers" (de Schutter 1994: 469) and "postdeterminers" (Quirk *et al.* 1985: 253). Classifying them together is a matter of expository convenience, and is not intended to suggest that they are a unitary category; differences in distribution and inflection suggest that they are not, though semantically they are united by the fact that they all involve existential quantification. Rather, it is intended to highlight the fact that that they are as a group not of a kind with either descriptive adjectives nor determiners/ "strong" quantifiers. Though often classified as adjectives, they cannot switch places with descriptive adjectives, in the way that the latter can be reordered among themselves.

(4.84)   three big beautiful houses/three beautiful big houses/
                      *big beautiful three houses

These elements come in between determiners and attributive adjectives:

(4.85)   die wenigen alten Männer (GE)
            the few   old   men

By way of accounting for this, they are, in some Government-Binding accounts, assigned to a layer of phrasal structure (the "Number Phrase") intermediate between the NP headed by the lexical noun and the Determiner Phrase headed by the definite article.

In some of the GMC languages, the indeterminate status of some of these elements is reflected in their curiously mixed effects on following attributive adjectives. In GE, definite articles and strong quantifiers with strong endings cause a following descriptive adjective to appear with a weak ending (under the "one-per-noun phrase" principle mentioned in the preceding section). This is illustrated in (4.86a-c). On the other hand, a descriptive adjective with a strong ending does not cause another descriptive adjective following it to assume a weak ending. Rather, each member of a series of attributive adjectives is inflected in the same way as the first (4.86d). However, when a descriptive adjective follows a weak quantifier, such as *wenige* 'few', *einige* 'some', *etliche* 'some', *solche* 'such', *manche* 'many a', *viel* 'many', it sometimes behaves as if the latter were also an adjective and inflects in parallel with it, but sometimes behaves as if the preceding weak quantifier were a determiner, and assumes a weak ending since the strong ending occurs on the weak quantifier. A pair of representative examples is given in (4.86e) and (4.86f). The distribution of the two behaviors is quite complex, as a perusal of the relevant entries in Berger *et al.* 1972 reveals, conditioned not only by the particular quantifier involved, but also the gender, number and case of the noun, and seems diachronically to be still very much in flux (see also Esau 1972: 141).

(4.86)   a. die   jungen   Mädchen
               the-Str   young-Wk   girls
               (GE)

            b. beide/jene   jungen   Mädchen
               both-Str/those-Str   young-Wk   girls
               (GE)

            c. jedes   junge   Mädchen
               every-Str young-Wk girl
               (GE)

            d. junge,   intelligente   Studenten
               young-Str   intelligent-Str   students
               (GE)

            e. vieles   überflüssige   Verhandeln
               much-Str   superfluous-Wk   negotiation
               (GE, Berger *et al.* 1972: 708)

            f. viele   hohe   Häuser
               many-Str   high-Str   houses
               (GE, Berger *et al.* 1972: 708)

Weak quantifiers typically precede the noun, across the entire family apparently, though some of them – most particularly, numerals – could also follow. This was true in GO as well as in early (poetic) OHG, though not prose, and in Runic GMC.

(4.87)   a. jota ains aiþþau ains striks
               jot   one   or   one   stroke
               (GO, Matt. 5:18)

            b. maizo   fimf hlaibam, jah fiskos twai
               more-than   five   loaves   and fish   two
               (GO, Luke 9:13)

c. untar   heriun tuem
   between armies two
   (OHG, Hildebrandslied 3)
   but: dhero zuueiio heido
        of-the two persons
   (OHG, Isidor (Eggers) 203)

d. Þrijoz dohtriz
   three   daughters
   (Runic GMC, Tune Stone, Antonsen 1975: 44)

   but: stAbA þria
        staves three
   (Later Runic, Gummarp Stone, Antonsen 1975: 83)

However, there are inflectional differences between prenominal and postnominal numerals which may suggest that they had different categorial status in the two positions. The lower cardinal numbers (one to three or one to four, depending on the language) tended to be inflected for case and gender like adjectives in the medieval languages. Higher cardinal numbers, on the other hand (from four to nineteen in GO, for example) could either inflect like adjectives or remain uninflected, but the choice between these options seems to have depended on position: they inflected like adjectives when postnominal, and were uninflected when prenominal:

(4.87)   e. wintriwe   twalibe
               of winters-GPl twelve-GPl
               (GO, Luke 8:42, Braune 1973: 89)

            f. af   fidwor windam
               from   four   winds-DPl
               (GO, Mark 13:27, Braune 1973: 89)

The same is true of OHG (Braune 1963: 232f.). In the modern languages, numerals have lost the ability to appear postnominally.

4.3.1.1   *The indefinite article*

The indefinite article, while similar to weak quantifiers semantically, is distinct from them in various ways, inflectionally, semantically and distributionally. It is not found in most IE languages, nor for that matter in all of the GMC languages. GO lacks it, as does OE, OS and ON. Among the modern GMC languages, it is not found in IC. The other modern languages developed their indefinite articles in late medieval times, and therefore well after the point of separation, but it is unlikely that they all did so entirely independently. Indefinite articles have arisen in the neighboring Romance languages, as well as in Breton among the Celtic languages, while IC, Welsh and Gaelic – the more peripheral languages in their respective families – did not develop them, and it is most probable that we are dealing here with an instance of areal diffusion. In all cases, the indefinite articles have arisen from the numeral 'one', from which they have, in some languages, become distinct through the effects of phonological reduction, since they typically lack syntactic stress (compare EN *one* and *a(n)*, FR *in* [ən] and *ien* 'one', for example). The original homophony between 'one' and 'an' makes it in general difficult to pinpoint the time of emergence of the indefinite article function. For instance, we find in OHG examples of a relatively early date like the following, where the form preceding the noun could, but does not have to, be translated as an indefinite article.

(4.88)   a. Einan   kuning uueiz ih
                 a   king   know I
                 (OHG, Ludwigslied 1)

However, we can be certain that if it was an article at this time, it at least was not obligatory on indefinite count nouns, as it is in the modern language:

(4.88)   b. gab her imo...frōnisc githigini, stuol hier in Vrankōn...
                 gave he to-him lordly retinue, throne here in Franconia
                 (OHG, Ludwigslied 5–6)

Similarly, in Modern IC, generally considered to lack an indefinite article, there are occasional uses of the numeral 'one' which approximate the meaning of the indefinite article (Kress 1982: 109).

In the modern GMC languages, the indefinite article may be either nonspecific or specific in meaning. In the former case, the speaker does not have a particular referent in mind. In the latter, the speaker has a particular referent in mind, but assumes that the hearer does not have sufficient information to identify it.

(4.89)   Every half hour a man is run over in NYC.
             !Someone should stop him.

In those GMC languages that have not developed an indefinite article, nonspecific indefinites are typically expressed by a bare (undetermined) noun. However, these languages at least sometimes avail themselves of other means for marking a noun phrase as indefinite and specific. This is, for example, the apparent function of *sums*, *sum* 'a (certain)' in GO and OE (for both singular and plural) and of IC *nokkur*. Paul (1989: 388) notes that in MHG the indefinite article can be used with a plural noun phrase to mark the noun phrase as indefinite and specific.

(4.90)   so sint einu   liute   dabi,   haizant   Arimaspi
so are a-certain people there, are called the Arimaspi
(MHG, Himml. Jerusalem14:12, cited in Paul 1989: 388)

4.3.1.1.1 **Variation in the occurrence of indefinite articles** There is also a limited amount of variation across the GMC languages in the specific conditions under which the indefinite article appears. (The special case of non-occurrence of indefinite articles in predicate noun phrases will be considered, along with definite articles, in Section 4.3.2.2.) MHG, for example, unlike Modern GE or Modern EN, allowed the indefinite article with non-count nouns, in a meaning like 'a quantity of'.

(4.91)   dâ   legen uns   an ein gras
there lay ourselves on a grass
(MHG, Nibelungenlied 1623: 3)

This use of the indefinite article is still found in YI (Lockwood 1995: 112). DU (de Schutter 1994: 469) allows the indefinite article in the plural, in the meaning 'a great number of'. In SW, it conveys the sense of 'approximately' (Holmes and Hinchcliffe 1994: 65).

In the continental Scandinavian languages, indefinite object noun phrases may lack an indefinite article in contexts where they would have one in EN, when non-specific and not modified by adjectives – conditions familiar in cases of object incorporation in languages which have that process (see Pereltsvaig in press for a description of the syntax of these in Norwegian).

(4.92)   a. De   venter   barn
they are expecting child
(DA, Allan *et al.* 1995: 68)

b. De   går   på café
they are going to café
(DA, Allan *et al.* 1995: 68)

c. Vi   tog   taxi
we took taxi
(SW, Holmes and Hinchcliffe 1994: 64)

4.3.2   Definite articles

GMC is not the only branch of IE to have developed a definite article. Greek has them as well, from the earliest period, as does Armenian. However, other older IE languages, including Latin, do not. Within GMC, they are not attested in the older Runic inscriptions (though perhaps just for want of sufficient examples). They are, however, found in all of the other GMC languages from the earliest times. Etymologically, they are connected with the demonstrative pronouns, and they are standardly held to have arisen from the use of the latter as demonstrative adjectives.

(4.93)   a. daz *der* tiuval dar pi   kitarnit stentit.
                    der hapet in ruovu rahono uueliha
              'that *the* devil thereby stands hidden.
               That one has in account every punishment'
          (OHG, *Muspilli* 68–69)

The point at which this transition is completed is hard to pin down. Behaghel (1923: I, 33) asserts that they had already lost the deictic force of demonstratives by the time of OHG. On the other hand, Abraham (1997: 39) claims that in MHG neither the definite nor the indefinite article had yet developed its modern meaning, and speaks of OHG and MHG as belonging to a "pre-article" phase. Philippi (1997: 62) claims they were still demonstratives in GO, OHG, OS and OE, and that they only became true definite articles in late medieval times. The claim is based primarily on their non-obligatoriness in these languages, supplemented by other arguments of lesser force. Hale (1994) has demonstrated, in any event, that in the late OHG of Notker, who was scrupulous about indicating stress, these definite-articles-to-be at least did not have the same prosodic status as demonstrative adjectives. Notker did not write accent marks on the former, while otherwise homophonous demonstrative adjectives, pronouns and complementizers were always accented.

(4.93)   b. mít   temo fiure
           with the   fire
          (OHG, Notker, cited in Hale 1994)

The enclitic definite articles of the Scandinavian languages arose from a different demonstrative form, *hinn, hin, hið* (Heusler 1967: 125), which tended to appear postnominally. It alternates in these languages with a (prenominal) demonstrative of the *þ*-paradigm. Under circumstances described in the next section, the reflexes of both of these co-occur in some NPs in modern Scandinavian.

(4.93)   c. hali   hino
           stone this
          (Runic GMC, Strøm whetstone, Antonsen 1975: 54)

              d. þat   azino
                  that stone
              (Later Runic, By stone, Antonsen 1975: 80)

These postnominal demonstratives also lost deictic force and stress at some point, and now occur as clitics following the head noun. Similar developments are attested elsewhere, in Romanian and other Balkan languages, for example.

Their status as bound morphemes leads to the question of whether they are properly regarded as (clitic) definite articles or simply as definiteness markers on the noun – that is, as inflectional morphology. In the literature on the North GMC languages, they are variously treated as clitic determiners and as definiteness suffixes. The problem of distinguishing between clitics and inflectional morphemes is in general a complicated one (see Zwicky and Pullum 1983 for a presentation of some suggested criteria). Possible evidence in favor of treating these clitic forms as definite articles rather than a definiteness inflection on the noun, at least originally, is provided by the fact that in older IC and Old SW (Braunmüller 1991: 43), they occurred outside of case markers on the noun and carried their own case inflection, independent of that on the noun.

(4.94)   a. mann-s-in-s
           man-Gen-the-Gen
           (IC)

           b. fisk-s-in-s
           fish-Gen-the-Gen
           (Old SW, Braunmüller 1991: 43)

c.
N	mað-ur-inn	menn 0 -in-ir
	man-Nom-the-Nom	men-Nom-the-Nom
G	mann-s-in-s	mann-a-(i)nn-a
	man-Gen-the-Gen	men-Gen-the-Gen
D	mann-i-(i)n-um	mönn-u-n-um (mönum-in-um)
	man-Dat-the-Dat	men-Dat-the-Dat
A	mann-0-inn	menn-0-in-a
	man-Acc-the-Acc	men-Acc-the-Acc

(IC, Braunmüller 1991: 194)

However, Braunmüller argues that such forms are no longer analyzed by speakers as involving independent declension of two separate elements. He notes that in some positions haplology has introduced opacity into the paradigm. Thus, for dative plural, instead of an expected *mönn-um-in-um, we find mönn-un-um.

In modern continental Scandinavian, the "internal" case inflection has disappeared, and the genitive case marker appears only outside the definite article (DA *pig-en-s* 'the girl's'). However, what has changed here seems to be not the status of the postnominal definite article, but the genitive marker -*s*, which itself has come to behave as a clitic, rather than an inflectional suffix (see 4.4.5.3).

Cliticization of the definite article is also found elsewhere in GMC. In GE, in particular, the article has merged with a number of prepositions ending in vowels or nasal consonants, to yield definite forms of the prepositions (*zum, zur, beim, vom, im* ← *zu* 'to' + *dem, zu* + *der, bei* + *dem, von* + *dem, in* + *dem* respectively).[13]

4.3.2.1 *Double determination*

As noted in 4.2.2.3, it was usual in the archaic language of ON poetry for definite noun phrases to appear without definite articles (Heusler 1967: 125). Even here, however, articles did appear when the noun was preceded by an adjective.

(4.95) enn gamle maþr
    the old   man
    (ON, Heusler 1967: 126)

The intersection of this preference for articles preceding adjectives and the development of the enclitic definite article has led to the phenomenon of "double determination" in some Scandinavian languages – that is, the co-occurrence under certain circumstances of both a phrase-initial and a postnominal determiner, particularly in noun phrases which have prenominal adjectives. (Plank 2003, who discusses these constructions at length, refers to the phrase-initial determiner which precedes the adjective as the "adjective-article," and the clitic determiner attached to the noun as the "noun-article.") ON exhibits double determination, as do SW, BN, NN and literary Modern IC (to which register the preposed articles *hinn*, etc., belong exclusively), though optionally, according to Plank (2003: 357). DA, on the other hand, does not have double determination (4.96g). In FA, the clitic article can be omitted. In BN there is a tendency to omit the clitic article when the NP refers to a type, rather than a specific individual (Bandle *et al.* 2005: 1589).

---

[13] The contractions are not productive in Modern GE. Thus, for example, *bei* + *der* does not yield *beir, and *zu* + *den* does not yield *zun. Behaghel (1923: I, 34) dates them from the fourteenth century, but sees a possible precursor in such OHG constructions as:

(i)   ze imo [for ze demo] heilante
    to him   to the   savior
    (OHG, Tatian 92:8, cited in Behaghel)

(4.96) a. en litla ǿ-en
           the little river-the
           (ON, Heusler 1967: 127)

       b. hinn rauða hestinn
           the red horse-the
           (literary IC, Einarsson 1945: 117)

       c. tann svarti kettlingur(in)
           the black kitten-the
           (FA, Lockwood 1964: 106)

       d. det gamle hus-et
           the old house-the
           (NN, Braunmüller 1991: 161)

       e. den långe pojken
           the tall boy-the
           (SW, Holmes and Hinchcliffe 1994: 91)

       g. manden ~ den gamle mand
           man-the the old man
           (DA, Allan *et al.* 1995: 54)

The presence of the clitic determiner in other types of noun phrases which are independently characterized as definite is also variable. So, for example, in standard SW, it does not appear when the noun is preceded by a demonstrative, but in southern and western dialects it does (Holmes and Hinchcliffe 1994: 96). There is also variation in double determination in NPs with relative clauses (Plank 2003: 357).[14] The co-occurrence of clitic determiners and possessives will be taken up in the next section.

4.3.2.2 *Other contexts for omission of the article*

There is variation across the GMC languages in contexts in which the definite article is retained or omitted. Some of this variation involves lexical context. Some involves

---

[14] Plank (2003) also discusses some more exotic instances of double determination in GMC, such as that in the following example from Bavarian:

(i)   Hast   die bsuffane Sau die gesehng?
        have-you the drunken swine the seen?
        (Bavarian, Plank 2003: 374)

syntactic context. There is little which can be said systematically about the former kind of variation. Proper names tend not to occur with articles, though there is variation on this point; the Scandinavian languages exhibit a "proprial" definite article, identical to the third person pronoun, in front of proper names (obligatorily in some cases) (see Delsing 1998: 99ff.).

(4.97)   han Per
         the Peter
         (East NO, Delsing 1998: 101)

In Bavarian, characterized by Weiß (1998: 69) as a "radical article language," articles appear routinely on proper names.

The ability to appear without an article is extended variably to other unique reference nouns. Thus, for example, Behaghel (1923: I, 59) points out that 'God' occurs without an article in all GMC languages, though in EN and GO 'night', 'heaven', 'earth' and 'hell', 'life' and 'death' are used without determiners, whereas in GE they are used with the article. GO *sauil* 'sun' and *mena* 'moon' are used without the article (in spite of the systematic appearance of one in the Greek model), as they are in IC (Kress 1982: 177), while EN requires an article here. In FA, the article is not used with noun phrases describing entities of which only one example is of immediate relevance (Barnes 1994: 207), such as *kongur* 'the king', *prestur* 'the priest', but the article is required with 'life', 'death' and 'sin' (Lockwood 1964: 107). Behaghel (1923: I, 63) also notes that in GO, the article is normally missing in the plural, as in (4.98), where both EN and Greek would require the article.

(4.98)   apaustauleis   usspillodedun imma...
         (the) apostles told   him
         (GO, Luke 9:10)

There is, further, a tendency in evidence in all of the languages to omit articles in a class of hard to characterize fixed phrases of mostly formulaic (often adverbial) meaning, most often involving nouns after prepositions (EN *to heart, by ear, in response, by nature, by name*, GE *zu Hause* 'at home', *über See* 'over sea', *zu Fuß* 'by foot') even in cases in which the noun would require an article outside of these constructions (see Behaghel 1923: I, 49ff. for detailed discussion).

In addition to idiosyncratic cases of this type, however, there are more systematic contexts for omission of articles. Among the most salient of these is in predicate position; both definite and indefinite articles tend to be omitted in predicate nominals of certain sorts. In particular, omission of both appears to be normal in cases of predicate nouns denoting function/profession, nationality or religion (a generalization to which EN, AF and YI stand out as (partial) exceptions):

(4.99)   a. hij is arts   ze zegt dat als arts
         he is doctor she says that as doctor
         (DU, de Schutter 1994: 469)

In GE, the article is omitted with assertions of profession, as in (4.99b), but not in assertions of membership in other categories, as in (4.99c):

(4.99)   b. Er ist Bäcker, Pfarrer, Schmied
            he is baker, minister, smith
            (GE)

         c. Er ist ein Kind, ein Dieb, ein Mann
            he is a child, a thief, a man
            (GE, Behaghel 1923: I, 88)

In the following examples, the article is employed when a predicate noun normally designating profession is used figuratively, as a description of an attribute.

(4.99)   d. Olivier var skuespiller but: Din lille pige er en skuespiller
            Olivier was actor   your little girl is an actress
            (DA, Allan et al. 1995: 62)

Similarly, the article reemerges in GE and DA when a predicate noun of profession is modified by a descriptive adjective, bringing the descriptive force into salience.

(4.99)   e. Er ist ein großer Künstler
            he is a great artist
            (GE, Behaghel 1923: I, 89)

         f. Han er en dygtig læge
            he is a good doctor
            (DA, Allan et al. 1995: 67)

This effect is not universal; in FA, the article is still omitted with an adjective:

(4.99)   g. Snæbjørn var frílíkur   seyðamaður
            Snæbjørn was excellent shepherd
            (FA, Lockwood 1964: 109)

The construction appears to have been of at least some antiquity (though I have been unable to identify examples in GO or Runic GMC).

(4.99)   h. was gicoran te kuninge
            was chosen to king
            (OS, Heliand 60 (Behaghel))

148   4 The Germanic nominal system

It is not, however, found in all of the GMC languages. Behaghel lists numerous examples from MHG in which the indefinite article occurs in predicate NPs, in contexts where they could not occur in Modern Standard GE. This is still true of YI (4.99j):

(4.99) i. er sî   ein koufman
           he were a merchant
           (MHG, Parzival 358:13)

       j. Er iz a beker
          he is a baker
          (YI, Lockwood 1995: 112)

In AF, the indefinite article may either be omitted or included.

(4.99) k. Ek is ('n) Suid-Afrikaner
           I am (a) South African
           (AF, Donaldson 1993: 65)

The indefinite article is required in EN in copular sentences with predicate NPs. However, EN too omits the article just with nouns of profession and nationality in non-copular predicate NPs:

(4.100) a. He was elected (??the) president but:
             *He was considered fool

        b. He said that as president but:
             *He said that as young man

4.4 Genitive phrases

The syntax of genitive phrases within NPs in GMC is quite complex, and only a relatively simplified and superficial account of it is possible here. There are first of all a few terminological issues which must be dealt with. First of all, the phrases which I will refer to here as "genitive phrases" can be realized either as NPs marked with an inflectional affix/clitic (*the man's*), or as a prepositional phrase headed by a genitival preposition (*of the man*). The latter, according to Delsing (1998: 98), exist in all modern GMC languages except DA, Standard SW and IC. As will be seen in the following, however, the two types of genitive phrases are differently distributed within individual languages.

Second, "possessive pronouns" also come in two different shapes. All of them are formed on the genitive of the personal pronoun. In some cases, however – for example, the third person reflexive in GO (4.101a) – these pronominal forms take adjectival endings which encode the gender, number and case features of the head noun. These are often referred to as possessive pronouns, less commonly as possessive adjectives. In other cases, like the third person nonreflexive in (4.101b), adjective endings are not added to the genitive pronoun, which remains uninflected for agreement with the noun.

(4.101)   a. aiþein   seinai
                mother-3SgFemDat self's-3SgFemDat
                (GO)

            b. aiþein   is
                mother-3SgFemDat his
                (GO)

The two were originally complementarily distributed. Non-agreeing genitive pronouns occurred in all instances where the possessor was third person and nonreflexive, while the agreeing possessive pronouns occurred in all other cases (first and second persons, and third person reflexive). The difference has disappeared in some languages, through either loss of concordial inflections (as in EN) or the extension of such inflections to originally uninflected forms (e.g., in the case of GE *ihr* 'her, their', which was originally uninflected, but which now inflects for agreement with the noun). Aside from their inflectional differences, the two behave identically in all respects and I will not distinguish between them hereafter, but will apply the label "possessive pronouns" without further differentiation according to type.

A second source of complexity is the fact that a variety of different semantic relations can obtain between the head noun and the genitive phrase. Besides possession, the genitive can encode the relationships of subject and object in the case of "action" nouns (*the Romans' destruction of the city*), whole/part relations (*half of my wealth*), identity (*the sin of gluttony*) and quality (*a man of honor*), among others. These thematic differences, moreover, can be of syntactic consequence, and there is variation in their syntactic expression across the GMC languages. In SW but not EN, descriptive genitives can appear as genitive-marked NPs in front of the head.

(4.102)   a. medelålders   herrar
                men of middle age   (NOT: *middle-age's men)

            b. en ärans man
                a   man of honor   (NOT: *An honor's man)
                (SW, Holmes and Hinchcliffe 1994: 45)

Conversely, EN allows even time adjuncts to be realized as prenominal genitives:

(4.102)   c. yesterday's attempt to leave   (Mallén 1989: 239)

150   4 The Germanic nominal system

As a further illustration of asymmetrical possibilities for interpretation, note that *des Künstlers* 'the artist's' in the GE example in (4.102d) can be interpreted as possessor, agent or theme, but when both a preverbal and a postverbal genitive are present, the former can be interpreted as agent or possessor, and the latter as theme, but not the converse, as in (4.102e).

(4.102)   d. Das Bild   des   Künstlers
           the picture of the artist
           (GE)

          e. Pauls Bild   seiner Frau
           Paul's picture of his wife
           (GE)

4.4.1   Genitive phrases and determiners

In earlier GMC languages, at least, genitive phrases could either appear before or after the noun they modified, with at least a slight preference for pre-head position.[15] In the language of the older runic inscriptions, Antonsen (1981: 55) proposes that the choice depended on whether the head noun was animate or not – prenominal genitives being found in the former case, postnominal genitives in the latter. In neither case do these genitives co-occur with definite articles in the runic corpus, of course, since articles are not found in Runic GMC. In later GMC languages, however, such co-occurrence is conditionally possible: prenominal, but not postnominal genitivals are typically incompatible with the definite article, though this is a generalization which admits of exceptions in both directions. In SW, for example, where genitive phrases systematically precede the head of the NP, neither the independent nor the clitic definite article can co-occur with them.

(4.103)   a. Peters   långa resa   cf. den långa resan
           Peter's   long trip   the long trip-the
           (SW, Holmes and Hinchcliffe 1994: 93)

---

[15] As suggested, for example, in the statistics compiled by Smith (1971: 287). In his count of the GO Skeireins, the genitive precedes the head 23 percent of the time and follows it 57 percent of the time, and a roughly similar ratio is found in OS. Others of the medieval languages, on the other hand, exhibited a sharper preference for one or the other (95 percent N-Gen in ON versus 98 percent Gen-N in OHG). This may have depended on the nature of the genitive phrase as well, with personal genitives appearing more frequently in front of the head than others. See Lanouette 1996 and the references cited there.

4.4 Genitive phrases

However, this is not the case in some northern dialects of SW, where constructions like (4.103b) are allowed, which are "sharply ungrammatical in Standard SW, DA and NO" (Holmberg and Sandström 1996: 114):

(4.103)   b. Jannes   bilen
                  Janne's car-the
                  (Northern SW, Holmberg and Sandström 1996: 114)

In FA as well, where genitives in the colloquial language are largely restricted to proper names, the prenominal genitive again cannot co-occur with the definite article.

(4.103)   c. mammusar lítli   skattur
                  mother's   little treasure
                  (FA, Lockwood 1964: 111)

In GE, where both postposed and preposed genitive phrases are possible (with restrictions discussed below), the article must occur with postposed genitives, but does not occur with prenominal genitives. A comparable asymmetry is found in EN.

(4.104)   a Das Haus ihres Vaters
               the house her   father's
               (GE)

               b. Gottes heilige Gebote
                  God's   holy   commandments
                  (GE, Behaghel 1923: I, 181)

In the earliest GMC, possessive pronouns seem to have been basically postnominal, as shown in the following Runic GMC examples:

(4.105)   a. magoz   minas   staina
                  son-Gen my-Gen stone-Acc
                'my son's stone'
                (Runic GMC, Vetteland, Antonsen 1975: 38)

               b. swestar minu
                  sister   my
                  (Runic GMC, Opedal stone, Antonsen 1975: 40)

Again, these possessive pronouns did not appear with articles in the Runic GMC language, but elsewhere in the early GMC languages postposed possessive pronouns were able to to co-occur with prenominal definite articles, as in GO (4.106 a, b) (independent of the Greek model), OHG (4.106c) and MHG (4.106d).

(4.106) a. þana ligr þeinana
         the bed your
         (= Greek sou tḗn klínēn your the bed)
         (GO, Matt. 9:6, cited in Behaghel 1923: I, 119)

      b. þis   nahtamatis meinis
         of-the dinner   mine
         (= Greek mou toû deípnou my the dinner)
         (GO, Luke 14:24)

      c. thiu quena minu
         the wife mine
         (OHG, Otfrid I 4:50)

      d. die geste mine
         the guests mine
         (MHG, Kutr. 387:3)

Among the modern languages, postposed possessive pronouns are preserved in YI and Western Scandinavian (IC, FA, NN and northern dialects of SW – see Holmberg and Sandström 1996: 99). This is the unmarked order in the Insular Scandinavian languages. In IC and North SW (optionally) and NN, though not in FA, the possessive co-occurs with a (clitic) definite article.

(4.107) a. der bankrot   zeyerer
         the bankruptcy their
         (YI, Jacobs et al. 1994: 406)

      b bok-i   mi / den nye bok-i   mi
         book-the my   the new book-the my
         (NN, Braunmüller 1991: 164)

      c. hestur-inn minn
         horse-the my
         (IC, Einarsson 1945: 114)

      d. drongur mín
         boy   my
         (FA, Barnes 1994: 208)

In these Scandinavian languages, however, the possessive pronoun can be moved to the pre-head position for emphasis (or even without emphasis when there is an attributive adjective – Barnes 1994: 208), and when this occurs, the definite article once again disappears as in (4.108b, c) – a further demonstration of the connection between the position of the possessor and the admissibility of the definite article. A similar alternation is found in YI (4.108d, e).

(4.108) a. mín drongur
        my boy
        (FA, Barnes 1994: 208)

      b. hús-ið mitt   mitt hús   *mitt hús-ið
        house-the my   MY house
        (IC, Thráinsson 1994: 167)

      c. den gamle bilen   hans   hans gamle bil
        the old   car-the his   his   old   car
        (NO, Bandle *et al.* 2005: 1589)

      d. mayn zun
        my   son
        (YI, Lockwood 1995: 53)

      e. der bruder mayner
        the brother mine
        (YI, Lockwood 1995: 53)

When the possessor was not a pronoun but a full genitive phrase, however, a different behavior emerges. Even when they followed the head, they (unlike possessive pronouns) did not co-occur with definite articles. This is still true in Modern IC (4.109c).

(4.109) a. leg   Haralds
        Harald's lodging
        (ON, Heusler 1967: 125)

      b. āhton   wælstōwe   geweald
        they-owned battlefield's control
        (OE, Quirk and Wrenn 1955: 71)

      c. módir   Jóns
        mother Jon's
        (IC)

Interestingly, though, Kress (1982: 168) reports that the determiner is beginning to be used in IC with genitive phrases following the noun in colloquial speech, perhaps bringing these cases into line with those involving postnominal possessive pronouns.

(4.109)   d. það er mergurinn málsins
                that is core-the the matter's
                (IC, Kress 1982: 168)

Prenominal genitive phrases could co-occur with the definite article in one special case in medieval continental West GMC (OS, OHG, MHG and Middle DU). In (4.110), preposed genitive phrases co-occur with a definite article belonging to the head noun, intervening between that definite article and the head (Behaghel 1923: I, 104ff.; de Vooys 1957: 305). This possibility was apparently restricted to proper names (see the next section.)

(4.110)   a. an thera Dauides burg
                in the   David's city
                (OS, Heliand (Behaghel) 401)

             b. dher gotes forasago
                the   God's prophet
                (OHG, Isidor (Eggers) 107)

             c. die Judas vriende
                the Judas' friends
                (Middle DU, de Vooys 1949: 305)

             d. ein Kriemhilde man
                a   Kriemhild's man
                (MHG, Nibelungenlied 1642: 3)

Interestingly, Behaghel cites examples from exactly these languages showing that they also allowed possessive pronouns to occur between the determiner and the noun.

(4.111)   a. that thîn hord
                the your treasure
                (OS, Heliand (Behaghel) 3284)

             b. in dheru sineru heiligun chiburti
                in the   his   holy   birth
                (OHG, Isidor (Eggers) 102 and 6 similar exx)

             c. den mînen liben man
                the my   dear man
                (MHG, Nibelungenlied 901: 3)

In these languages, there seems to be a syntactic slot for prenominal possessors, in between the determiner and the head, which can only be occupied by proper names and possessive pronouns. As the following section will demonstrate, this is not the only context in which these two elements pattern together in the GMC languages.

4.4.2 Proper name possessors and pronominal possessors

The last examples complete the picture of the distribution of possessive pronouns in GMC. We have seen that in some languages (GO and the modern Insular Scandinavian languages), possessive pronouns are postnominal and co-occur with the definite article. In EN and continental Scandinavian, on the other hand, possessive pronouns precede the noun, and do not co-occur with the definite article. Finally, as we see in (4.111), possessive pronouns in medieval continental West GMC could precede the head *and* co-occur with the definite article. This three-part classification finds a strikingly close counterpart in the Romance languages, where possessive pronouns sometimes follow the noun and co-occur with the article, sometimes occur sandwiched in between the article and the noun, and sometimes precede the noun without an article.

(4.112)   a. la   casa   sua (Italian)
         the house his

b. la sua casa (Italian)

c. mi casa (Spanish)

(See Cardinaletti 1998 for discussion, though her account of these does not transfer unproblematically to the GMC cases, since in the Scandinavian languages the prenominal possessive pronouns are stressed, while in Romance they are clitics.)

However, note that in the cases from medieval continental GMC discussed at the end of the last section it is not just possessive pronouns that can be sandwiched between the definite article and the noun; possessors which are unmodified proper names can go there as well, though other lexical possessive phrases cannot. That is to say, proper names appear here in a position otherwise restricted to pronouns.

(4.113)   a. in dheru   christes   chiriihhun
         in the   Christ's   churches
         (OHG, Isidor (Eggers) 684)

b. in dheru   sineru   heilegun   chiburdi
   in the   his   holy   birth
   (OHG, Isidor (Eggers) 102)

Similarly, while in IC (and other Western Scandinavian languages), both possessive pronominals and lexical possessive phrases can be moved to the prenominal position when focussed, as in (4.114a, b), Thráinsson (1994: 167) points out that the latter possibility is restricted to cases in which the lexical possessive phrase is a proper name. Noun phrases with modifiers, for example, cannot be placed there, as in (4.114c).

(4.114) a. minn hestur
my horse
(IC)

b. Haraldar hús
Harald's house
(IC)

c. dúkkur tlu stelpnanna ~ ?*litlu stelpnanna dúkkur
dolls little girls'   little girls'   dolls
(IC)

Further, possessors in Modern GE, as we have seen, can be either prenominal or postnominal. However, in the contemporary language, the latter is allowed only if the possessor is a possessive pronoun or a proper name – that is, exactly the same elements that can precede the head in the IC focus cases.[16]

(4.114) d. mein Haus   Pauls Haus
(GE)

e. ??der alten Frau Haus ~ das Haus der alten Frau
??the old woman's house   the house of the old woman
(GE)

Holmberg and Sandström (1996: 110) observe the mirror-image of this situation in northern dialects of SW, where it is only possessive pronouns and proper name possessors which may follow the noun plus article, as in the following:

(4.114) f. boken hans/boken mormors/boken Jannes
book-the his/book-the Mommy's/book-the Janne's
(Northern SW, Holmberg and Sandström 1996: 110)

Thus, in four separate cases in a variety of GMC languages, we see that proper names behave in the same way as possessive pronouns. The parallelism in their distribution suggests that possessive pronouns and proper names must share some categorial property. Lindauer (1998) suggests that they are both categorially adjectives, and that the prenominal position in Modern GE is restricted to adjectives. This seems to work better

---

[16] Possessive phrases which precede lexical nouns, labeled "Saxon genitives" by Engel (1988: 609), such as the following, are still recognized as possible by some GE speakers, but are distinctly old-fashioned.

(i)   meines Bruders   Tochter
my-Gen brother-Gen daughter

for GE, however, where all possessive adjectives inflect as adjectives, than in other languages (IC, for example), where third person possessive pronouns show no adjectival properties. A more probable reason for the parallelism between possessive pronouns and proper names in these cases might be that the positions in question are restricted to pronouns, and that proper names are a sort of pronoun. Like pronouns, they typically consist of only a single element, and do not freely allow modifiers, determiners and so on. And like pronouns, they are "indexical," having the semantic property of pointing to specific individuals.

Booij (2002b: 35) claims that the proper name possessors with -*s* in DU are determiners, noting the non-co-occurrence of prenominal possessors and determiners. However, there is a somewhat similar construction in IC with respect to which possessive pronouns and proper name possessors once again pattern together, to the exclusion of other possessors, but in which the distinguishing characteristic which unites them is precisely that they do co-occur with the determiner. In IC, as we have seen, lexical possessive phrases occur postnominally without an article, while possessive pronouns occur postnominally, but with an article.

(4.115) a. árlegur rekstrarkostnaður bílsens
yearly costs of-business
(IC, Kress 1982: 182)

b. hestur-inn minn
horse-the my
(IC, Kress 1982: 182)

Proper names can, like other lexical possessive phrases, occur postnominally without an article, as in (4.115c). However, an alternative is also available, just for possessors which are proper names, as shown in (4.115d):

(4.115) c. moður Jóns
mother Jon's
(IC)

d. hesturinn hans Jóns
horse-the 'his' Jon's
(IC, Einarsson 1945: 114)

Here, the proper name possessor is preceded by a proprial article (see Section 4.4.5.1). Strikingly, unlike (4.115c), but like the pronominal case in (4.115b), the possessor co-occurs here with a definite article on the possessed noun. Thus, we see again that in positions where possessive pronouns are allowed but lexical possessor phrases are not, proper names in many cases at least have the same distribution as the pronouns.

4.4.3 The English 'double genitive' construction

In EN, prenominal genitive phrases are marked with *'s* (on which see Section 4.4.6.2), while postnominal genitives are marked with the preposition *of*. There are a number of differences between the two. The prenominal ones, for example, admit of a possessive interpretation, while the postnominal ones do not. The postnominal ones co-occur with the definite article, while the prenominal ones do not. However, EN also exhibits a third construction, in which the genitive NP is doubly marked, with both an *of* and an *'s*, which has properties in common with both of the other types.

(4.116)   a. the picture of John's

On the one hand, these admit a possessor/agent interpretation, like prenominal genitive phrases. (In fact, unlike both of the other types, they do not admit a thematic interpretation. This example, therefore, is unambiguous in a way that 'John's picture' is not.) Similarly, they may co-occur with other postnominal genitivals, but not with other prenominal genitives.

(4.116)   b. this picture of Florence of John's

            c. *Mary's picture of John's

Thus, their interpretation and co-occurrence possibilities suggest that they are of a kind with prenominal genitive phrases, yet, unlike these, they do co-occur with articles.

4.4.4 The prenominal periphrastic possessive (*Jan se boek*) construction

Widespread among the continental West GMC languages is a construction in which a prenominal possessive phrase headed by a lexical noun is followed by a "resumptive" possessive pronoun, which typically agrees with it in gender and number. It can be seen in the GE example in (4.117a) that the possessive NP in these cases is not in genitive but in dative case (on which account it is sometimes referred to as the possessive dative), though there was in earlier Modern GE a parallel construction in which the possessive phrase took genitive case (Grebe *et al.* 1966: 514). Following Delsing (1998), I will refer to this as the prenominal periphrastic possessive construction.

(4.117)   a. meinem Bruder   sein Zimmer
                my   brother-Dat his   room
            (GE, Grebe *et al.* 1966: 514)

In Modern GE and Modern DU, the construction is regarded as colloquial (cf. Donaldson 1981: 59). It is, on the other hand, standard in the other languages in which it occurs.

(4.117) b. de son se strale
         the sun its rays
         (AF, Ponelis 1993: 225)

      c. Jan z'n kleren
         Jan his clothes
         (DU, de Schutter 1994: 468)

      d. ús dochter har skoech
         our daughter her shoe
         (FR, Tiersma 1999: 48)

      e. se wascht een Mann sien Hemd
         she washes a man his shirt
         (Low GE, Lindow *et al.* 1998: 197)

      f. æ mand hans hus
         the man his house
         (West Jutlandic, Delsing 1998: 90)

      g. da Schwaiz sei Präsident
         the Switzerland its president
         (Bavarian, Weiß 1998: 77)

      h. dem Papp séng Vokanz
         the father-Dat his vacation
         (Luxembourgish, Holmberg and Rijkhoff 1998: 99)

As Norde (1995: 216) points out, there are some differences in the construction between DU and AF. In DU, but not AF, it is limited to animate possessors, and in DU the resumptive pronoun agrees in gender and number with the possessive phrase, while in AF an invariant *se* is used in all cases.

The construction also appears in EN, where, however, it does not become usual in written registers until quite late (after 1500, according to Görlach 1991: 81; see also the discussion in Fischer 1992: 231). In North GMC, the construction is found in some colloquial varieties of NN, where, however, it is apparently not native but has its origins in a Low GE substratum, according to Braunmüller (1991: 165). See also Bandle *et al.* 2005: 1589.

(4.117)   i. Olav sin bil
           Olav his car
           (NN, Braunmüller 1991: 165)

See Koptjevskaya-Tamm 2003: 665ff. for an extensive discussion of the syntax and distribution of these constructions. Collectively, these examples suggest that the possessed noun phrases in GMC must have at least two separate positions for possessors: an inner one, occupiable by possessive pronouns in place of determiners, and an outer one, in which full NPs may occur. This in turn accords well with the structure made available by the "DP-hypothesis," which claims that determiners head their own phrases, and that, like other phrases, these may contain a (phrasal) specifier position and a (non-phrasal) head position.

(4.118)

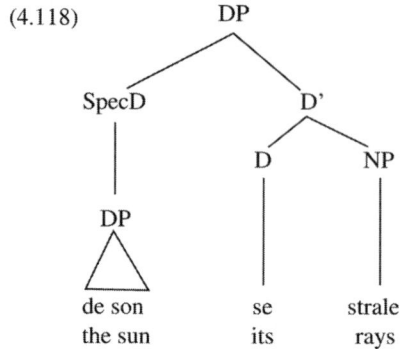

A still more articulated structure might be needed to accommodate constructions like the following in YI, in which a possessive pronoun precedes an (indefinite) article:

(4.119)   mayne   a   shvester
           mine   a   sister
           'a sister of mine'
           (YI, Jacobs *et al.* 1994: 406)

Delsing (1998: 100f.) finds similarities between the prenominal periphrastic possessive construction and the one found in Western Scandinavian (see Section 4.4.3) in which a proper name possessor occurs with a "proprial article," both following the noun, and occurring in a relative order which may be viewed as the mirror-image of the construction in (4.117). These constructions will be discussed further in the next section.

(4.120)   a. hesturinn hans Jóns
              horse-the his   Jon's
              (IC, Einarsson 1945:114)

           b. bilen   hans Olav
              car-the   his   Olav
              (NN, Braunmüller 1991: 165)

Delsing (1998) refers to this as the "postnominal periphrastic possessive construction," and suggests an analysis for it which unites it with the prenominal periphrastic possessive construction, noting, though, that there are some differences between the two (1998: 103). These include (a) the fact that the postnominal construction is apparently restricted to proper names, (b) that in the prenominal construction but not in the postnominal construction the linking pronoun is a reflexive pronoun (in those languages which have such a distinction), and (c) (most problematic for a claim of identity between them), that the prenominal construction does not admit a definite article on the head noun, but the postnominal construction requires it. This is especially striking in light of the fact that other postnominal possessive phrases in West Scandinavian languages do not allow definite articles:

(4.120) c. hús(*-ið)   Jóns   (IC)
          house (*-the) Jón's

4.4.5 Special developments of the genitive in possessive constructions:

4.4.5.1 *Proper name possessive markers*

The possessive marker -*s* is, historically, a genitive case suffix. There are reasons for thinking, however, that this is no longer its status in all cases in the modern GMC languages. On the one hand, in GE and DU constructions with prenominal proper name possessors and equivalent kinship terms, such as (4.121a), the -*s* behaves unlike the still productive genitive affix -*(e)s* which occurs on common nouns in two ways.

(4.121) a. Mutters   Schürze
           Mother's apron
           (GE)

        b. tantes   verjaardag
           aunt's   birthday
           (DU, de Vooys 1949: 305)

First, it is not (unlike genitive -*es*) restricted to masculine and neuter nouns. In both of these examples, it attaches to a feminine noun. Second, unlike the genitive -*es*, its form does not depend on the number of syllables in the noun (GE *des Tages* 'the day's'/ *des Wetters* 'the weather's', but *Pauls/Mutters*). These differences suggest that the -*s* of (4.121) has become a morpheme distinct from the genitive ending from which it originated. In being restricted to proper names (and a small set of kinship terms which are used as proper names), it is similar to a set of special genitive suffixes which have arisen in other modern GMC languages, to which I will apply the label "proper name possessive markers." Of the same type is the genitive suffix -*sa(r)* in FA, which also applies only to proper names and kinship terms (Lockwood 1964: 104; Koptjevskaya-Tamm 2003: 627). To this inventory can be added the FR -*e* which appears as a possessive marker only on kinship terms (Tiersma 1999: 49; Koptjevskaya-Tamm 2003: 627; Holmberg and Rijkhoff 1998: 100).

(4.121)   c. Jákup-sa(r)/mamu-sa(r) bók
Jakup's/mother's book
(FA, Lockwood, 1964: 106)

d. heit-e   piip
father's pipe
(FR, Tiersma 1999: 49)

The reason that these languages should have developed special markers for proper name possessors is no doubt that proper names are often unaccompanied by articles or adjectives on which case could be separately encoded. Similarly, Koptjevskaya-Tamm (2003: 629) points out that the previously discussed constructions in some Scandinavian languages in which proper names (and only those) are supplied with special proprial articles in genitive contexts can at least in some instances be regarded as motivated by the need to encode the genitive relation.

(4.121)   e. häns   Viktor heest
the-Gen   Victor horse
'Victor's horse'
(Northern SW, Koptjevskaya-Tamm 2003: 631)

These "proprial articles" can be viewed as the analytic counterpart to affixal proper name possessive markers like the GE -*s*.

4.4.5.2   *Associative NPs*

Braunmüller (1991: 204) links these proprial article constructions with proper names and another striking Scandinavian construction, found in ON (Heusler 1967: 120ff.) and IC, in which a proper name again appears in construction with an apparent pronoun. This is the use of a proper name after a plural pronoun to specify the individual who, along with speaker or hearer, is included in the set of individuals to which reference is intended:

(4.121)   f. þið   Ólafur
you-Pl   Olaf
'You and Olaf'
(IC, Braunmüller 1991: 204)

A similar construction is reported for AF by Donaldson (1993: 136), though with the noun in the first position. Den Besten (1996) labels these constructions "associative constructions," and provides a semantic analysis for them.

(4.121) g. Pa-hulle
Dad-they
'Dad and the others'
(AF, Donaldson 1993: 136)

4.4.5.3 Group genitives

EN possessive *'s*, like GE *-s*, has undergone a development from a genitive marker in certain noun classes to a generalized possessive marker. However, its behavior in the so-called "group genitive" construction indicates that EN *'s* is no longer an inflectional affix at all, but rather a clitic element, which does not attach to individual nouns, but to the right periphery of entire NPs, without regard to the category of the particular word to which it attaches.

(4.122) a. The man that I talked to's wife

This construction is found in some of the continental Scandinavian languages as well:

(4.122) b. det   er   pigen   Uffe   bor sammen meds   datter
that is   girl-the Uffe   lives   with's daughter
(DA, Haberland 1994: 325)

c. mannen med det hvite hårets kontor
the man with the white hair's office
(NO, Barnes 1994: 208)

d. ?han med hattens fru
he   with the hat's wife
(SW, Delsing 1998: 91)

Delsing (1998: 97) observes that the distribution of *'s* in these cases, following, as it does, the entire possessive NP, and attaching to whatever word happens to terminate that NP, can be captured by assuming that it is in fact a clitic variant of the "resumptive" pronoun in the prenominal periphrastic possessive construction discussed in the preceding section, of which the group genitive may therefore be considered a subcase. However, Norde (1995: 220) claims that this cannot be the origin of the SW construction, since SW lacks the hypothesized source construction.

4.4.6 Meronymic constructions

All of the GMC languages with the exception of EN (cf. McWhorter 2002) exhibit special constructions for the expression of "possession" in the cases in which the "possessed" noun is a part of the possessor – e.g., a body part. Following Mirto 1995, I will use the label "meronymic construction" for these (though the constructions he discusses are quite different from those of GMC). "Meronym" refers to the named part of the larger entity, the "holonym." What we can abstract as the core feature of meronymic constructions in the GMC languages appears to be that they do not make use of genitives or possessive pronouns to encode the holonym (as in *I broke my arm*). Rather, the meronym occurs with a definite article, or (in GO, OS and IC) is bare. The holonym may be unexpressed, particularly where it is identified with the subject of the clause.

(4.123)   a. Jeg har brækket armen
            I have broken arm-the
            'I have broken my arm'
            (DA Allan *et al.* 1995: 185)

         b. hafa hatt á höfði
            to have a hat on head-the
            (IC, Einarsson 1945: 115)

         c. Hon ska tvätta håret
            she shall wash hair-the
            (SW, Holmes and Hinchcliffe 1994: 66)

         d. Ek het pyn in die sy
            I have pain in the side
            (AF, Donaldson 1993: 141)

Where it is expressed, the holonym is treated in either of two ways. It appears as a dative NP, syntactically separate from the NP expressing the meronym, in all except the Scandinavian languages. This dative possessor is regarded by Haspelmath (1999: 116) as a European areal feature, belonging to "Standard Average European," and occurring not only in the central European members of the GMC family, but a number of geographically contiguous though remotely related or unrelated languages.

(4.123)   e. Em deit de Kopp ni mehr weh
            him does the head not more sore
            'His head no longer hurts'
            (Low GE, Lindow *et al.* 1998: 267)

f. Ni   galeiþiþ   imma in   hairto, ak in   wamba
    not goes   him   into heart, but into stomach
    'It does not go into his heart but into his stomach'
    (Greek has a definite article)
    (GO, Mark 7:19)

g. Usluknodedun imma   hliumans
    unlocked   to-him   ears-Nom   (Greek has a definite article)
    (GO, Mark 7:35)

h. Afmaimait imma auso taihswo
    he-cut-off him ear   right   (Greek has a definite article)
    (GO, John 18:10)

i. Legda im   êna bôk   an barm
    he-lay him   a   book on lap
    (OS, Heliand (Behaghel) 232)

j. Hē   ...sette his...hond him on þæt hēafod
    he   set   his hand   him on the head
    'He put his hand on his head'
    (OE, Quirk and Wrenn 1955: 68)

k. Hij heeft zich in de vinger gesneden
    he has   self in the finger cut
    (DU, Donaldson 1981: 60)

l. Di mame   hot em   gevasht di hor
    the mother has him washed the hair
    (YI, McWhorter 2002: 226)

The dative holonym in these cases is not in construction with the meronym NP, as evidenced by the fact that the two can be separated from each other by other constituents. Because of this, it is generally referred to as a "dative external possessor" (see McWhorter 2002 and the references cited there). The boundary between these "possessive datives" and other types of dative adjuncts, such as adversative datives (from which they may not be syntactically distinct in any case), is not absolutely sharp.

(4.124)   a. flêsk is unk   antfallan
             flesh is to-us fallen-away
             (OS, Heliand (Behaghel) 153)

(4.124) b. vvuo sint thir thiu   ougun íntanu
         how are to-you-Dat the eyes opened?
         (OHG, Tatian (Sievers) 132: 6)

         c. ni   lazet   faran   iu   thaz muat
            not let-you depart   you-Dat the courage
            (OHG, Otfrid II 21:19)

The similarity between dative holonyms and adversative datives is strengthened by the fact that the meronymic construction seems to be limited to affected objects. Compare the contrast observed by Thráinsson (1994) between the following examples.

(4.125) a. hún stakk þessu í   munn honum/hans
            she put   this in   mouth him-Dat/his-Gen
            (IC, Thráinsson 1994: 168)

         b. Þetta er munnur *honum/hans
            this is mouth *him-Dat/his

Moreover, in general, it appears to be admitted only in instances in which the meronym is affected by an action which is also understood to affect the holonym, by virtue of the part–whole relation (though the relationship often falls short of a true entailment):

(4.125) c. 'He touched X's hand' entails 'He touched X'

In cases where only the meronym, not the holonym, is affected by the action, we find a regular possessive construction.

(4.125) d. jah is ushafjands augona seina du siponjam
            and he raising   eyes   self's to disciples...
            (GO, Luke 6:20)

Constructions with this cluster of properties are generally absent from Modern EN. Thus, sentences like the following are impossible.[17]

(4.125) e. *I broke (to) myself the finger/washed (to) myself the hair

Otherwise, though, they are quite general in GMC. See McWhorter 2002: 225 for examples from other languages, as well as one possible account of the exceptionality

---

[17] EN does have a different meronymic construction of sorts in cases like (i):

(i)   He touched/ kissed/ hit/ cut me on the face

as an alternative to 'He touched my face' and the like. Here there is a strict entailment, such that if V(x, body-part of y) is true, then V(x, y) is also true. Compare the IC *skera sig í fingur* 'to cut self in finger' (Einarsson 1945: 115).

of EN. Vennemann (2003b: 356) sees in its absence from EN a Celtic, and ultimately Semitic, substratal influence.

McWhorter points out, though, that the Scandinavian languages depart from the others in expressing the holonym not as a bare dative NP, but as the object of a locative preposition:

(4.125) f. Það blæðir úr   munninum á   honom
     it   bleeds from   mouth-the on   him
     'He is bleeding from the mouth'
     (IC, Haspelmath 1999: 122)

In IC, the meronym can be expressed as a dative (4.125b) or as the object of a locative preposition, though Thráinsson (1994: 168) characterizes the first of these as quite formal. There is also some variation across GMC with respect to how obligatory these dative adjuncts are, and how acceptable the alternative genitive construction is.

4.5 Predeterminers

Following Quirk *et al.* (1985: 257), I will call elements which precede the definite article in nominal phrases "predeterminers." Membership in this category varies across the GMC languages, and within languages individual forms can belong to more than a single syntagmatic category. In EN, both *all* and *both* fit the definition of predeterminer, preceding the definite article or possessive pronouns. Here, though, as in other GMC languages, they can also appear in place of the definite article, with generic meaning. It appears, therefore, that they may function either as determiners or predeterminers. (EN, but not other languages, allows a third use, as pronouns taking genitival complements – e.g., *all of the children*).

(4.126) a. All/both the children All children/both children

    b. bēgen ðā   cyningas
     both   the   kings
     (OE, Bede 529:19, cited in Wülfing 1894: I, 304)

    c. alle mine venner
     all   my   friends
     (DA, Allan *et al.* 1995: 209)

    d. Alle dyr   bør   beskyttes
     all animals   should be   protected
     (DA, Allan *et al.* 1995: 208)

In GE, 'all' appears in the same two positions (with inflectional differences):

(4.126)   e. all die Kinder/alle Kinder
all the children/all children
(GE)

On the other hand, 'both' in GE never appears as a predeterminer in front of the definite article, and may in fact (unlike 'all') behave like a "postdeterminer," following the definite article:

(4.126)   f. *Beide die Kinder Die beiden Kinder
(GE)

It nonetheless does exhibit at least one characteristic behavior of predeterminers in the other GMC languages in that it may take a personal or demonstrative pronoun as a complement, in which case as in all of the other GMC languages it obligatorily precedes the pronoun.

(4.126)   g. wir beide
we both
(GE)

                 h. Chefen roste   os alle
boss-the praised us all
(DA, Allan *et al.* 1995: 210)

                 i. hy ealle
they all
(OE, Orosius 20:36, cited in Wülfing 1894: I, 464)

There is another class of predeterminers, which do not precede definite articles and possessives (with which they do not co-occur), but do precede the indefinite article:

(4.127)   a. sa'n   nuvere man
such a strange man
(FR, Tiersma 1999: 43)

                 b. Many an evening

4.6 Discontinuous nominal phrases

There are at least three distinct circumstances in which the subconstituents of NPs in the GMC language occur separated from each other by other constituents. The most

4.6 Discontinuous nominal phrases 169

generally occurring of these is the appearance of one of the predeterminers discussed in the foregoing section separate from the semantically associated NP.

(4.128)   a.   Vi är båda musiker
we are both musicians
(SW, Holmes and Hinchcliffe 1994: 197)

        b.   Eleverne bestod alle eksamen
pupils-the passed all-Pl exam-the
(DA, Allan *et al.* 1995: 210)

        c.   hī bēgen wæron...well gelǣred
they both were...well learned
(OE, Bede (Miller) 565: 11ff.)

In the generative literature, it has often been assumed that the NP and the associated 'both/all' are underlyingly a single constituent, and that they come to be separated by way of a movement operation, which either moves away the quantifier ("Q-Float") or moves the NP, leaving the quantifier in place ("Quantifier Stranding"). For a defense of the latter hypothesis see Sportiche 1988. Among the evidence supporting it is the fact that the positions in which "stranded" quantifiers may occur in a given language seem to depend on the types of NP movement the language has. Thus, for example, Giusti (1990) points out that GE and DU (to which we may add OE), but not Modern EN and NO, allow stranding of quantifiers associated with object NPs. She attributes this to the fact that GE and DU, but not EN and NO, have "Scrambling" (see Section 5.7.2.1), and can therefore strand the predeterminer by scrambling the object NP away from it.

(4.129)   a.   Der Lehrer hat die Schüler gestern alle gelobt
the teacher has the students yesterday all praised
(GE, Giusti 1990: 634)

        b.   Der Lehrer hat den Schülern gestern allen eine Fünf gegeben
the teacher has the pupils-Dat yesterday all a five given
(GE, Giusti 1990: 634)

        c.   Ik heb de kinderen gisteren allen gezien
I have the children yesterday all seen
(DU, Giusti 1990: 638)

        d.   nu hǣt hit mon eall Parthia
now calls it one all Parthia
'Now one calls it all Parthia'
(OE, Orosius 10:28, Wülfing 1894: I, 464).

(4.129) e. *The teacher has praised the students all

f. *Lareren gav elevene bøkene alle
teacher-the gave pupils-the books-the all
(NO, Giusti 1990: 639)

Some recent analyses, however, reject this "Q-stranding" approach, arguing that "floated quantifiers" are not to be identified with the corresponding predeterminers, but are, rather, independent adverbs.

Some of the GMC languages allow apparent discontinuities involving determiners of other sorts than predeterminers. GE and DU, for example, allow weak determiners such as *keine* 'no' to be separated from the rest of the noun phrase:

(4.130) Bücher hat er keine gelesen
books has he no read
(GE)

These cases are discussed by den Besten and Webelhuth (1990) under the label "DP-Split."[18] An opposite case, in which the determiner is fronted, leaving the noun behind, is represented in ON (Bandle *et al.* 2002: 948).

A final type of discontinuous NP, apparently restricted to the older languages (and shared by them with the other older IE languages (Fortson 2004: 139)) involves separation of genitive phrases or possessive pronouns from the NP they are understood to modify, typically by no more than a single verb. With possessive pronouns, the resulting order is typically Pron–V–NP, while with genitive NPs the order is typically NP–V–NP-Gen. That is to say, the two nominals exhibit the same relative order they would be expected to have if not separated:

(4.131) a. [baurgs] ist [þis mikilins þiudanis]
[city] is [the mighty king's]
'It is the city of the mighty king'
(GO, Matt. 5:35)

b. ainƕaþarammeh [seina] anafilhandam [daupein]
each [his] recommending [baptism]
'each one recommending his own baptism'
(GO, Sk III)

---

[18] The same languages exhibit "*was für*-split," as in (i). See den Besten and Webelhuth 1990.

(i) Was hat er für Bücher gelesen?
what has he for books read?
'What kind of books has he read?'

c. ac [sīo hand] gebarn // [mōdiges mannes]
   but [the hand] burned [brave man-Gen]
   'but the mighty man's hand burned'
   (OE, Beowulf 2697)

d. Nā þū [mīnne] þearft // [hafalan] hȳdan
   not you [my] need [head] to-hide
   'You do not need to hide my head'
   (OE, Beowulf 445)

Separation of the genitive phrase from the associated noun ("exbraciation," to borrow a term from Stockwell 1977) is also found in OE prose, but the separation of possessive pronouns and nouns appears to be restricted to poetic language (cf. Reskiewicz 1966: 325), where it serves to maintain preferred rhythmic structures.

(4.131) e. ðætte wē nū [ǣnigne onstal] habbað [lāreowa]
         that we now any supply have of-teachers-Gen
         'that we now have any supply of teachers'
         (OE, CP 4:1)

4.7 Adjective phrases

Adjective phrases in the GMC languages vary with respect to the category type and the position of the complements of the head adjective. Adjectives in all of the GMC languages admit clausal and prepositional phrase complements, as shown by the following GO examples and their EN glosses.

(4.132) a. ni im [wairþs [ei uf hrot mein inngaggais]]
         not I-am worthy that under roof my you-may-go
         (GO, Matt. 8:8)

b. [anahaimjaim] wisan [at fraujin]
   present to-be with the lord (Greek has endēmêsai)
   (GO, 2 Cor. 5:8)

However, NP complements of adjectives are restricted in distribution in ways that relate to the possibilities for case marking. Two rules of thumb may be isolated. First of all, in general, NP complements of adjectives appear only in dative, genitive or instrumental case, depending on the lexical requirements of particular adjectives. That is, NP complements of adjectives are lexically case-marked (see Section 4.1.2.3.1). There are, for the most part, no adjectives which take NP objects in the accusative – the unmarked, "structural" case for objects. Second, corollary to the first rule of thumb, in languages which do not have lexically case-marked objects in general (for example, which do not exhibit genitive or dative objects of specific verbs), adjectives do not generally allow NP complements at all (van Riemsdijk 1983b: 223; Weerman 1997: 438). When a language loses lexical case, therefore, former NP complements of adjectives are replaced by prepositional phrase complements with grammatical prepositions. So, for example, in the following, where the adjectives in GO or OE take bare NP complements in oblique cases, in Modern EN they take prepositional phrase complements.

(4.133)   a. [modags [broþr seinamma]]
            angry   brother his-DAT
            'angry with his brother'
            (GO, Matt. 5:22)

          b. [wairþs] sa waurstwa [mizdons is]
            worthy the worker   his-reward-GEN
            'The worker is worthy of his reward'
            (GO, 1 Tim. 5:18)

          c. þæs gefeohtes   georn
            the fighting-GEN eager
            'eager for fighting'
            (OE, Orosius 122:21, Mitchell 1985: I: 86)

          d. sīþes   wērig
            journey-GEN weary
            'weary of the journey'
            (OE, Beowulf 579, Mitchell 1985: I: 86)

The sole exception to the first rule of thumb seems to be Modern GE, in which a small set of adjectives appears to admit accusative objects (Abraham 1995; Engel 1988: 592). Abraham (1995: 247) lists fourteen such adjectives, including those in (4.134a), in comparison to twenty-seven which take genitive objects and sixty-seven which take dative objects.

(4.134)   a. *dick* 'thick', *gewärtig* 'expectant', *groß* 'large', *hoch* 'high',
            lang 'long', *leid* 'sorry', *los* 'free', *müde* 'tired', *satt* 'sated',
            schuldig 'guilty', *stark* 'strong', *überdrüssig* 'disgusted, weary',
            weit 'distant', wide', *wert* 'worth, worthy'.

Many of these are adjectives of quantity or dimension, moreover, which occur with accusative phrases representing units of measure, and it is at least arguable that the accusative phrases here are to be viewed as adverbial or specificational phrases of some sort, rather than as true complements. GE grammar books vary with respect to how they classify these accusative measure phrases. We note that phrases like *one foot tall* also occur in EN, for example, in which adjectives do not otherwise take NP complements. In the remaining, much smaller, set of cases of GE adjectives with accusative objects, the accusative occurs only sporadically and is regarded by some as resulting from confusion of genitive and accusative case forms (Grebe *et al.* 1966: 492).

(4.134)   b. Ich bin [[diesen Streit] müde]
              I   am   this quarrel-Acc   tired
              'I am tired of this quarrel'
              (GE, Berger *et al.* 1972: 467)

           c. Ich bin [[ihn]   überdrüssig]
              I   am him-Acc weary
              'I am weary of him'
              (GE, Grebe *et al.* 1966: 492)

Exceptions to the second rule of thumb – that adjectives will not take bare noun phrase complements if the language does not have lexical case – are also to be found. NO, even though it no longer has lexical case objects of verbs, allows prepositionless NP complements of adjectives, as in (4.135), apparently subject to the requirement that they be adjacent to the head (Maling 1983: 264). Again, though, these exceptions seem to be marginal; Åfarli (1992: 61) observes that the very few adjectives allowing such NP complements can usually take a PP complement instead.

(4.135)   a. Han er redd   (for) ulver
              he   is afraid   (of)   wolves
              (NO, Maling 1983: 264)

           b. Han er redd nok   for/*0 ulver
              he   is afraid enough of /*0 wolves
              (NO, Maling 1983: 264)

Weerman notes a handful of restricted, idiomatic exceptions in DU, as well, including:

(4.135)   c. Hij is het Frans   mahtig
              he   is the French able
              'He is capable of speaking French'
              (DU, Weerman 1997: 438)

Adjective phrases also vary with respect to the relative order of head and complement. Such variation parallels the relative order of objects and verbs; in OV languages like GE and DU, nonclausal complements of adjectives precede the adjectives of which they are dependents, while in VO languages such as EN and IC, they follow the adjective. For further discussion, see Section 4.2.2.2.1.

(4.136) a. tired of his studies

b. seines Studiums überdrüssig
   his studies-Gen tired
   (GE)

More specifically, it appears that in languages like GE, the complement of the adjective not only precedes the adjective but appears to the left of adverbial modifiers of the adjective (van Riemsdijk 1983b; Abraham 1995: 251).

(4.136) c. Ein [[seines Studiums] geradezu überdrüssiger] Student
   a his studies-Gen downright weary student
   (GE, van Riemsdijk 1983b: 229)

4.7.1 Comparison

Adjectives normally inflect for degrees of comparison in GMC by way of attachment of comparative/superlative suffixes. GMC had two variants of these suffixes, reflecting distinct IE ablaut grades, and they are distributed variously in the daughter languages. GO had both, and distributed them in a way partly determined by the inflectional class of the adjective. Thus, it has both *manag-iza* 'more' and *swinþ-ōza* 'stronger'. The forms with *-iz-* gave rise to umlaut alternations in other GMC languages, such as MHG *lanc/lenger*. In addition, the GMC languages have a highly characteristic persistent set of suppletive comparatives, such as GO *goþs, batiza, batists*/SW *god, bättre, best*. Competing with these affixal comparative forms in some of the GMC languages (e.g., EN, SW, DA, DU) are analytic constructions in which the positive degree of the adjective is used with the adverb 'more'. The choice between these is conditioned by the length of adjective, among other things.

Syntactically, the standard of comparison in comparative sentences in the GMC languages tends be marked by a particle (*þau* in GO, *än* in SW, *en* in IC, *as* in FR, *als* in GE, *þonne* in OE). In most of these languages, this is the exclusive way of expressing the standard. It competed in early GMC, however, with a second one, with which it was apparently in complementary distribution. In GO, the standard of comparison is always introduced by *þau* when the two things being compared are not (understood) subjects:

(4.137) a. frijondans wiljan seinana mais þau guþ
   loving will self's more than God
   'loving their own will more than [they love] God'
   (GO, 2 Tim. 3:4)

However, whenever the standard of comparison is the understood subject of an elided clause, the standard instead appears as a bare, dative-marked NP.

(4.137) b. nist skalks maiza fraujin seinamma,
not-is servant more lord-Dat self's
nih apaustaulus maiza þamma sandjandin sik
nor apostle more the one-Dat sending him
'The servant is not greater [than] his lord [is] nor an apostle
greater [than] the one sending him [is]'
(GO, John 13:16)

Both constructions still exist in (different registers of) IC, though they are no longer complementarily distributed in this way.

(4.137) c. Jón var eldri og reyndari en ég
Jon was older and more-experienced than I
(IC, Einarsson 1945: 120)

d. Jón var mér eldri og reyndari
Jon was me-Dat older and more-experienced
(IC, Einarsson 1945: 120)

4.8 Pronouns in the Germanic languages

4.8.1 Personal pronouns

4.8.1.1 *The basic contrasts*

In the category of personal pronouns I include non-demonstrative (unemphatic, non-deictic) third person pronouns, both reflexives and nonreflexives, as well as first and second person pronouns, while noting that this categorization is contrary to the usage of some traditional grammars, in which "personal pronoun" is limited to first and second persons. The personal pronouns in GMC have always inflected for the categories of person, number and case. In the third person, they also tend to contrast in gender and reflexivity. Consider the illustrative GO, FR and DA paradigms below.

(4.138) a. Gothic

		Nominative	Accusative	Dative	Genitive
1sg		ik	mik	mis	meina
2sg		þu	þuk	þus	þeina
3sg	masc	is	ina	imma	is
	fem	si	ija	izai	izōs
	neut	ita	ita	imma	is
	reflex	—	sik	sis	seina

		Nominative	Accusative	Dative	Genitive
1du		wit	ugkis	ugkis	—
2du		[cf.ON it]	igqis	igqis	igqara
1pl		weis	uns(is)	uns(is)	unsara
2pl		jus	izwis	izwis	izwara
3pl	masc	eis	ins	im	izē
	fem	[ijōs]	ijōs	im	izō
	neut	ija	[ija]	im	izē

(4.138) b. Danish

		Nominative	Objective	Possessive
1sg		jeg	mig	min
2sg	intimate	du	dig	din
2sg	polite	De	Dem	Deres
3sg	masc	han	ham	hans
	fem	hun	hende	hendes
	com	den	den	dens
	neut	det	det	dets
	reflex	—	sig	[sin]
1pl		vi	os	vores
2pl	intimate	I	jer	jeres
2pl	polite	De	Dem	Deres
3pl	non-reflex	de	dem	deres
	reflex	—	sig	deres

(4.138) c. (West) Frisian (simplified, from Howe 1996: 185, Tiersma 1999: 55)

		Nominative (weak/strong)	Objective (weak/strong)	Possessive (attrib/pred)
1sg		ik, 'k	my	myn/	mines
2sg	intimate	do, __, -sto	dy	dyn/dines
2sg	polite	jo,	je	jo(-wes)
3sg	masc	hy, __, er	him	syn/ sines
	fem	sy/(hja), se	har	har(-res)
	neut	it, t	it	syn/sines

ai (North FR only. Hardly used. Cf. Howe 1996: 193ff.)

1		wat/wët	unk/onk	unken, onkens
1		jat, jët	junk, jonk	junken, jonkens
1	(Sylt dialect)	jat	—	—
		wy, we	ús	ús/ uzes
		jimme, jim	jimme, jim	jimme(s)
		sy/(hja), se	harren, har	har(res)

It will be impossible to treat in detail the considerable variation in individual forms across the GMC languages. The reader is referred to the exhaustive discussion and extensive paradigms in Howe 1996. Suffice it to note that the third person is much more variable than the first and second persons – in large part a result of the long-standing tendency (in GMC and elsewhere) for demonstrative pronouns and deictic particles to be incorporated into the third person pronominal paradigms. This tendency continues even in postmedieval times, for example, in the incorporation of demonstrative *þit* (replacing earlier Old IC *it*) into the personal pronominal paradigms of Scandinavian, as in DA *det*.

Relative to nouns and verbs, pronouns tend to be conservative in their inflection. So, for example, dual inflection was retained in pronouns after it was lost in nominal and verbal paradigms in all of the older GMC languages. Similarly, case (in particular, the contrast between subject and object case) is retained for pronouns even in those languages (EN, FR, DU, AF, continental Scandinavian) which have lost case inflection on nouns and determiners. Howe (1996: 70) attributes this conservatism of pronouns in part to the fact that pronoun paradigms are largely suppletive, rather than segmentable, in the GMC languages. The accusative of YI *mir* 'we', for example, is not derived by adding an affix to the nominative; rather, it is expressed by a form (*undz* 'us') which shows no relation to the nominative. Thus, pronominal paradigms cannot be simplified simply by abandoning affixes.

From the earliest period, however, the pronoun system has also been characterized by syncretism. Note that, even in GO, reflexivity is expressed at the expense of gender and number, that there are no dual forms in the third person, and that gender contrasts are neutralized in the dative plural. Three major trends in syncretism can be identified in GMC pronoun paradigms. First, a number of languages have lost case distinctions among pronouns – particularly, between dative and accusative. Second, most of the modern languages have lost dual forms of the pronouns. Finally, there has been a tendency for reflexive forms to lose ground to nonreflexive forms.

With respect to the first of these tendencies, there has been a split in modern GMC between a group of languages (including DA, FR, SW, NO, DU, AF and EN), which have conflated dative and accusative into a single case among pronouns and a

178   4 *The Germanic nominal system*

group (IC, FA, some varieties of YI (see Howe 1996: 105) and GE), which have retained the distinction between dative and accusative. In the former languages, the surviving form sometimes derives from the dative (FR *him*) and sometimes from the accusative (DA *dig*). Howe (1996: 117) has proposed that in at least many such instances, the syncretism did not simply involve abandonment of one or another of the two case forms. Rather, the languages first developed a contrast between weak and strong, or stressed and unstressed, pronominal forms, and the original dative/accusative contrast was functionally reinterpreted as a contrast between stressed and unstressed forms, the datives taking over the expression of objects in stressed positions, and the former accusatives filling the office of unstressed object pronouns (cf. EN dialect *-en* as unstressed form of *him*). Subsequent generalization of the original stressed or the original unstressed forms could then result in complete leveling out of the contrast.

In some of the modern GMC languages, the nominative/accusative (or subjective/objective) distinction in pronouns, while not being lost, is undergoing something of a reinterpretation. In EN and DA, 'I' and 'me', for example, are still used as subjects and objects respectively, but the "objective" form is used for a variety of purposes other than marking the object, and its context of occurrence needs to be more broadly defined. In both languages, 'me' can be used as a free-standing form in one word responses to questions, even when resuming the subject of the question:

(4.139)   a. Parent: "Har du   spist kagen?"
                        have you eaten the cake?

            b. Child: "Mig?"
                       me?
                (DA, Allan *et al.* 1995: 145)

It is also used in topic position (4.139c), in predicate nominative position (4.139d), and (colloquially) in subject position when conjoined with another NP.

(4.139)   c. Me (/ *I), I don't like to go to the movies

            d. Hvem er anføreren? Det er jeg /   Det er mig
                who is captain-the? it is I   /   it is me
                (DA, Allan *et al.* 1995: 144)

            e. Min bror og mig er gode venner
                my brother and me are good friends
                (DA, Allan *et al.* 1995: 145)

As a first approximation to capturing the distribution of these forms, we may say that the subjective forms (*I, jeg*) are used only when the pronoun is the subject of the finite verb, while the objective forms (*me, mig*) are used in all other contexts. Miller (2002: 14) claims that objective in EN has become a default case. That approximation fails to cover instances like the following, though:

(4.140)   ham/ *han (der står) på   hjørnet,   er fra   uropatrjulen
          him-Acc/ *he-Nom (who stands) on corner-the is from riot-police-the
          (DA, Heltoft 2001: 178)

First and second person dual pronoun forms are found in the older GMC languages (GO, ON, OE, OS and (rarely) OHG (Howe 1996: 242) used with plural verbs everywhere except in GO), but the dual/plural distinction is given up in all modern languages except North FR (Howe 1996: 193ff.), where it still exists as a highly formal option (and is even extended to third person in one dialect). Formally, the leveling occurred in both directions, the former dual forms showing up in plural functions in (varieties of) YI, Bavarian and Low GE (Howe 1996: 279, 281) and NO (second person only) and, most robustly, in FA and IC, where original dual forms have supplanted plurals in both first and second persons (Compare DA *vi* 'we', FA *vit* 'we'.)

The tendency toward loss of reflexive forms is clearly exemplified in the FR paradigms above, where in contrast to DA and GO the specifically reflexive *s-* forms of GMC are not represented. This reflects a development common to all of the Ingvaeonic, or North Sea Coast, group of West GMC (Old FR, OE and OS), where the GMC *s*-reflexives were given up, and reflexivity was expressed by ordinary personal pronouns:[19]

(4.141)   a. and him   Hrōþgar gewāt   tō hofe   sīnum
             and him(self) H.   betook to court self's
             and Hrothgar betook himself to his (own) house
             (OE, Beowulf 1236)

This lack of specifically reflexive forms has been undone in the modern languages of the group in question, which have reintroduced reflexives from other sources in postmedieval times. Thus, ME introduced reflexives of the *himself* paradigm (for all persons), through affixing the originally emphatic adverb *self* to personal pronouns, while DU borrowed its new (third person) reflexives (*zich, zichzelf*) from Middle Low GE (which got it in turn from High GE – Stellmacher 1983: 274).

---

[19] This example was chosen to illustrate another curious fact about the reflexive forms of OE. While the dative and accusative *s*-reflexives were lost in OE, as a part of their general disappearance in Ingvaeonic, the reflexive possessive **sīn* was retained for some centuries, showing up in early OE poetry, only to be lost later on. See Harbert 1985.

(4.141) b. Jan wast   zich/zichzelf
Jan washes himself
(DU, Everaert 1991: 108)

FR appears to have undergone (or is undergoing) a development similar to that of EN. Reflexives are often still not distinguished (in any person) from the corresponding nonreflexive personal pronoun. So, for example, the following instance is ambiguous between reflexive and nonreflexive readings.

(4.141) c. se wasket har
she washes herself (or her)
(FR, Tiersma 1999: 60)

However, FR also has a morpheme *sels*, which as a free morpheme is used to emphasize an associated NP (corresponding to EN emphatic *himself*), as in (4.141d):

(4.141) d. ik seach de minister sels
I saw the minister himself
(FR, Tiersma 1999: 61)

It can also be added to pronouns in reflexive use, to make them emphatic and contrastive:

(4.141) e. se wasket harsels
she washes herself
(FR, Tiersma 1999: 60)

Harsels in (4.141e) is not merely emphatic and contrastive, though, but specifically reflexive. It can only refer back to the subject. Moreover, *har* and *harsels* in reflexive use stand in a partially complementary distribution, some contexts allowing only one and others allowing only the other (Tiersma 1999: 60f.; Everaert 1991), leading Everaert to claim that forms like *harsels* represent an independent paradigm of reflexive forms. (For discussion of the distributional differences between the two types of FR reflexives (as well as DU *zich/zichzelf*), see Section 4.8.2.2.) Therefore, it appears that all of the GMC languages which participated in the original Ingvaeonic reflexive loss have reconstituted their reflexive paradigms, in various ways. The EN and FR *self/sels*-reflexives in fact form a richer paradigm than the original GMC reflexives, since unlike the original they do allow for the simultaneous expression of both reflexivity and gender/number and extend the reflexive/nonreflexive distinction to first and second persons. Standard YI, on the other hand, has also extended the reflexive/nonreflexive distinction to the first and second person, but has accomplished this by extending the originally third person reflexive *zikh* to first and second person, resulting in the neutralization of expression of person and number in favor of the expression of reflexivity (cf. Birnbaum 1979: 250):

(4.142)   Ikh freg zikh   vos   es   hot emitser   gekoyft
          I   ask [my]self   what   there   has someone   bought
          (YI, Vikner 1995: 76)

The loss of the original reflexives (as well as their subsequent restoration) is reflected in more limited ways outside the Ingvaeonic group. OHG, for example, lost the dative reflexive (*sir*). Like Ingvaeonic, it used dative forms of the nonreflexive pronouns (e.g., *imo* 'him') in its stead. This paradigmatic gap was subsequently filled by extending the accusative reflexive *sich* to dative functions. DA has leveled out the reflexive/nonreflexive distinction in the plural possessive, as the paradigm shows; the same form, *deres*, is used in both functions.[20] (In this, DA differs from SW, where a distinction between *deras* 'their (nonreflexive)' and *sin* 'their (own) (reflexive)' is maintained.) GE and DU have restructured the contrast between reflexive and nonreflexive possessives still more radically, redeploying the formal distinction to signal gender/number contrasts, as discussed in Section 4.8.2.1.

4.8.1.2 *Strong, weak and clitic pronouns*

4.8.1.2.1 **Atonic pronouns and weak pronouns**

All of the GMC languages participate to one degree or another in contrasts involving pronoun "strength." Such contrasts are reflected, for example, in the fact that many of the slots in our sample paradigm from FR are occupied by two distinct forms. In the least interesting case, the strength contrast in question is a contrast between tonic pronouns, which can be stressed and therefore occur in such stressed positions as focus and topic positions, and atonic pronouns, which cannot be stressed, and therefore cannot appear in such positions. GE *es*, for example, always an atonic pronoun, can be clause-initial if a subject, but not if a topicalized object.

(4.143)   a. Es hat mich gesehen
             it has seen me
             (GE)

          b. *Es habe ich gesehen
             it I have seen
             (GE)

---

[20] Note also that when DA introduced the third person plural forms *De, Dem, Deres* into the second person as polite forms, it did not correspondingly begin using the third person reflexive object form as a polite second person form. Thus, 'yourself (polite)' is *Dem*, while 'themselves (third person plural)' is *sig*. This is in contrast with GE, where the third person reflexive *sich* was extended, along with other third person forms, to the polite second person: *Setzen Sie sich!* 'Seat yourself'.

For similar reasons, tonic but not atonic pronouns can be used as stand-alone answers. (In some slots in the paradigms of some languages, there are special emphatic forms reserved for this purpose – e.g., the *ekke* 'I' of AF (Ponelis 1993: 203; Donaldson 1993: 123) and the emphatic *ikke* 'I' of FR (Tiersma 1999: 55).)

(4.143) c. Was hast du gekauft? ??Es
what have you bought? It
(GE)

The same is true for DU, for example, where, moreover, there are differences in the phonological shape of the stressed and unstressed pronouns.

(4.143) d. Mij zag hij / *Me zag hij
me saw he
(DU, Cardinaletti 1999: 50)

The atonic forms often appear to be simply phonologically reduced forms of the corresponding tonic forms, with /ə/ in place of tense vowels (as seen in the DU examples), vowel elision (FR *ik/'k*), or loss of initial or final consonants (EN *him* vs. *'em*), though in Standard GE there is not even this degree of difference. In GE dialects the differences are much more pronounced, as illustrated in the tables in Weiß 1998: 92ff., and in Abraham and Wiegel 1993, but in most cases, the atonic forms can be derived from the tonic by way of similar phonological reductions. In Modern EN, where there are phonological alternations between *his* and *'is*, *them* and *'em*, *him* and *'im*, and in Appalachian EN between *hit* and *it* (Wolfram and Christian 1976: 58), all that can be said is that the full forms occur in stressed contexts and the latter in unstressed contexts. In other languages, on the other hand, there are some differences between tonic and atonic pronouns involving their shape, their syntactic distributions and their possible interpretations, which suggest that they are fundamentally distinct, rather than just contextual variants (weak pronouns arising through "underpronunciation" in unstressed contexts, for example). So, for example, Howe (1996: 31) and Cardinaletti (1999: 51) point out that atonic first and second person plural pronouns in DU, but not tonic ones, can have generic reference:

(4.144) a. In Amerika zie je/*jij de vreemdste dingen
in America see you the strangest things
(DU, Howe 1996: 31)

In DU and GE, moreover, third person atonic pronouns admit non-human, as well as human referents, while tonic third person pronouns admit only human referents (Howe 1996: 30; Cardinaletti 1999: 51). (Note that the pronoun has the same phonetic shape in both of the GE examples; it is nonetheless atonic in (4.144c) but tonic in (4.144d) because it is in a stressed topic position in the latter.)

(4.144) b. Kees zegt dat de fietsen daar nog staan,
Kees says that the bicycles there still stand,
maar zə/ *zij zijn weg
but they are gone
(DU, Cardinaletti 1999: 51)

c. *Sie hat er gestern gegessen
them [–hum] has he yesterday eaten
(GE, Cardinaletti 1999: 55)

d. Sie hat er gestern eingeladen
them [+hum] has he yesterday invited
(GE)

Howe (1996) attempts to relate these differences to the semantic effects of stress itself, but Cardinaletti (1999: 55) maintains that they demonstrate that the tonic/full and atonic/reduced pronouns are not simply variant forms, the latter occurring in a subset of the contexts of the former, but members of distinct lexical sets, with different meanings.

There are also sometimes formal differences between the two which involve more than phonological reduction. While the atonic pronouns are sometimes simply phonologically reduced forms of the tonic ones, sometimes, as in our FR paradigms (hy/er, do/sto (on which see Howe 1996: 29)), in DU (hun 'they (full form)'/ ze 'they (clitic)') and in West Flemish (eur 'her (full form)', ze 'her (clitic)') they are suppletive – that is, they have a form which is not related in an obvious way to the corresponding full pronoun forms.

There are, moreover, distributional differences between the two; in many (in fact, most) of the GMC languages, weak (atonic) pronouns appear leftward displaced relative to the position of non-pronominal NPs bearing the same role, and strong (tonic) pronouns. For instance, in SW (and elsewhere in Scandinavian) GMC weak pronouns, but not strong pronouns, undergo "object shift" to a position which is immediately to the right of the inflected verb (and the subject, where this is postverbal) but leftward of sentential negator.[21] Strong pronouns (as well as full NP objects) remain to the right of the sentential negator.[22]

---

[21] This object shift of weak pronouns, optional for some SW speakers and in some dialects of NO, and missing altogether in some dialects of SW (Hellan and Platzack 1999: 130), is obligatory in FA, DA, IC and NO (Hellan and Platzack 1999: 128). In all except IC, where it can apply to full NPs, object shift is restricted to weak pronouns.

(4.145) a. Igår   såg Anna den kanske inte
         yesterday saw Anna it   maybe not
         (SW, Cardinaletti 1999: 52)

    b. Igår   såg Anna kanske inte DEN
       yesterday saw Anna maybe not IT
       (SW)

Similar phenomena are found in the continental West GMC languages: weak object pronouns occur to the left of other arguments and adverbial phrases, appearing immediately to the right of the subject in embedded clauses, for example. Thus, while West Flemish generally observes a strict IO–DO order, a weak DO pronoun (but not a strong DO pronoun) can be reordered to the left of a non-pronominal IO:

SW is also more liberal than the other continental Scandinavian languages in yet another respect; only in SW can weak pronouns occur in between adverbial expressions, rather than preceding them all:

(i)   Igår   låste han ju alltså   dem, troligen inte
        yesterday read he as-you-know thus them probably not
        (SW, Hellan and Platzack 1999: 130)

Hellan and Platzack (1999: 128) note some circumstances in which weak pronouns are not fronted. They remain to the right of the nonfinite verbs in periphrastic constructions (ii), and they are not moved when they are the objects of prepositions (iii):

(ii)   Han hade inte träffat henne/ 'na
        he had not met   her-Wk/ her-Clitic
        (SW, Hellan and Platzack 1999: 128)
(iii)   Den lå   under 'a/ *Den lå 'a under
        it lay   under her
        (NO, Hellan and Platzack 1999: 128)

[22] In the case of bitransitive constructions, both objects shift to the left of negation when represented by weak pronouns, typically appearing in the order Indirect Object – Direct Object, though DA and SW allow the other order (Hellan and Platzack 1999: 131).

(i)   Ola ga   henne ikke appelsinen
        Ola gave her   not orange-the
(ii)   Ola ga   henne den ikke
        Ola gave her   it not
        (NO, Hellan and Platzack 1999: 126)

(4.145) c. da Valère ze /*under   Marie nie getoogd eet
that Valère them-Wk / *them-Str Marie not shown has
(West Flemish, Haegeman 1993: 142)

In Bavarian, according to Weiß, the primary determinant of the relative order of object pronouns is whether they are clitic (weak) or full (strong) pronouns; the former always precede the latter. Thus, masculine accusative weak pronoun *'n* 'it' must precede masculine dative strong *eam* (but see Abraham and Wiegel 1993).

(4.145) d. das'a'n eam geem hod (Bavarian, Weiß 1998: 89)
that he-Wk it-Wk to-him-Str given has

Only where both the IO and the DO are weak do their grammatical roles come into consideration, in which case they appear in the fixed order IO–DO. (See Section 5.7.2 for further discussion of the order of pronominal objects in GE.)

(4.145) e. das 'a   'm   'n   geem hod
that he-Wk to-me-Wk it-Wk given has

f. *das 'a 'n 'ma geem hod
(Bavarian, Weiß 1998: 89)

Thus, we apparently need to recognize at least two morphosyntactically distinct classes of pronouns, weak and strong, in some of the GMC languages – arguably all except EN and AF.[23] (Cf. also Tiersma 1999: 57; Haegeman 1993: 142; Cardinaletti 1999; Abraham and Wiegel 1993; Grohmann 1997: 171.)

4.8.1.2.2 **Weak pronouns and clitics** It is not clear that the foregoing division of GMC pronouns into strong and weak is sufficient. While the label "clitic" is sometimes used in place of "weak pronoun" in the sense of the preceding section – that is, a light, unstressed, often phonologically reduced pronoun which tends to occur further to the left in the clause than full NP arguments of the same type – some investigators claim that clitics and weak pronouns are distinct types of morphosyntactically

---

[23] Ponelis (1993: 196) observes that only the strong pronouns of DU survive in AF, and suggests that the loss of weak pronouns may be a creolization effect. See also Howe 1996: 230, however, who claims that "unaccented or reduced personal pronoun forms do occur in AF in unconnected speech." There is one context in which EN perhaps demonstrates the leftward displacement (relative to the position of full NP arguments) characteristic of GMC clitics – in particle shift constructions:

(i)   He picked up the chair (~He picked the chair up)
(ii)   He picked it up (~*He picked up it).

deficient pronouns, and that both are represented in the GMC languages. In the following, I will review some of the considerations on which such proposals are based. First, a comparison of the following example from NO with (4.145e) shows that it is possible to replace the weak pronouns of that example with still more phonologically minimal forms. That is, there are degrees of phonological reduction. Besides the atonic pronouns *henne* 'her', *den* 'it', NO also has the forms in (4.146a):

(4.146) a. Ola ga   a'n   ikke
             Ola gave her-it not
             (NO, Hellan and Platzack 1999: 126)

Second, clitics are, by definition, syntactically dependent on other elements in the sentence. In GMC, non-strong pronouns tend to appear after complementizers or verbs. Therefore, if any of them are clitics, they must be rightward clitics, attaching to the right of these elements. It follows that while it might be possible for a weak pronoun in a GMC language to be clause-initial, a clitic could not, since it would require an element to its left to which it could be attached. Some investigators have proposed just such contrasts in individual GMC languages. In FR, for example, the reduced form *'t* 'it' may begin a sentence (*'t wie in lang dei* 'it was a long day'), but the reduced form *er* 'he' cannot. It can only occur immediately after a verb, a relative pronoun or a complementizer (Tiersma 1999: 57f.). Tiersma categorizes the latter form as a clitic, but the former as a reduced pronoun. Similarly, in the Swiss GE dialect Olang Tirolese (Cardinaletti 1999), both the forms *es* 'it' and *se* 'they' are unstressable, but *es* can begin a sentence, whereas *se* must appear immediately after a verb or complementizer; Cardinaletti analyzes the former as a weak pronoun and the latter as a clitic. Subject clitics are also reported for a local dialect of British EN in Shorrocks 1996, though only in questions with verb preposing.

(4.146) b. Es isch toire
             it is   expensive
             (Olang Tirolese, Cardinaletti 1999: 58)

         c. *Se sain toire
             they are expensive
             (Olang Tirolese)

         d. daß ze toire   sain
             that they expensive are
             (Olang Tirolese)

Abraham and Wiegel (1993: 30), on the other hand, reject the idea that the ability of a pronoun to appear in sentence-initial position is probative for the distinction between weak pronouns and clitics, noting that DU *'k* 'I' can appear sentence-initially, as in (4.146e), while *ie* 'he' cannot, even though both of these forms behave like clitics with respect to another diagnostic – the requirement that clitics be adjacent to the complementizer in subordinate clauses.

(4.146)   e. 'k loop naar huis
              I   run   to   home

          f. *Ie belt   aan de deur
              he   rings at the door
              (DU, Abraham and Wiegel 1993: 30)

Abraham and Wiegel (1993: 30) point out that while in DU, *'k* 'I', *ie* 'he', *je* 'you', and *we* 'we' all appear to be reduced forms of the corresponding full pronouns (of *ik, hij, jij, wij* respectively), only the first two are clitics, according to the head-adjacency diagnostic, since the others can be separated from the preceding complementizer by an intervening adverb phrase.

(4.147)   a. dat, als alles goed gaat, ik/*-k   naar huis loop
              that, if all   well goes, I /+ I   to   home run
              (DU, Abraham and Wiegel 1993: 30)

          b. dat, als alles goed gaat, hij/ *ie aan de deur belt
              that, if all well goes,   he/ *he at the door rings
              (DU, Abraham and Wiegel 1993: 30)

          c. dat, als alles goed gaat, we de auto kopen
              that, if all   well goes, we the car buy
              (DU, Abraham and Wiegel 1993: 30)

Finally, we might expect to find differences between weak pronouns and clitics involving their different status as syntactic constituents. We would expect weak pronouns to count as clausal constituents, but not clitics, since they are, in effect, affix-like. In this context, it is interesting to observe that in YI, one and only one object of a bitransitive verb may appear in front of the lexical verb if both objects are NPs.

(4.147)   d. ???Er hot Soren dos bux   gegebn
              He   has Soren the book given
              (YI, den Besten and Moed-van Walraven 1986: 126)

This restriction does not apply, however, if one of the objects is a pronoun:

(4.147)   e. Er hot ir   dos bux gegebn
              He has to-her the book given
              (YI)

For further discussion of a need for a weak pronoun/clitic distinction see Cardinaletti 1999 and Cardinaletti and Starke 1999. If GMC does have clitics, they behave differently from those of the Romance languages in that they do not have to be hosted by the verb, and, when adjacent to the verb, they do not systematically precede it (Cardinaletti 1999: 57). Haegeman (1993: 145) also points out that, unlike Romance clitics, they need not occur in a single clitic cluster, but can be split up.

(4.147) f. da-t   Valère ze   nie gegeven eet
             that-it Valère to-them not   given   has
             (West Flemish, Haegeman 1993: 145)

4.8.1.3 Long object shift

In (4.145a), a non-strong pronominal object is seen shifted to a position immediately behind the subject. Hellan and Platzack (1999) point out, though, that among the Scandinavian languages SW and IC also allow "long object shift," in which (a subset of) weak pronouns appear immediately after the verb, and in front of a postverbal subject, rather than following it.

(4.148) a. Igår   kammade sig   Erik inte på hela   dagen
             yesterday combed   self Erik not on whole day-the
             'Yesterday Erik didn't comb his hair all day'
             (SW, Hellan and Platzack 1999: 132)

This possibility was apparently once general in Scandinavian (Hellan and Platzack 1999: 133), but is no longer possible except in SW. Grohmann (1997) reports similar variation in continental West GMC. GE but not DU allows a non-strong pronoun to occur to the left of the subject.

(4.148) b. daß-m die Professorin gestern   das Buch gegeben hat
             that-him the professor yesterday the book given   has
             (GE, Grohmann 1997: 179)

         c. *dat-m de professor gisteren   het boek gegeven heeft
             that-him the professor yesterday the book given   has
             (DU, Grohmann 1997: 179)

         d. dat de professor-m   gisteren het boek gegeven heeft
             that the professor-them yesterday the book given   has
             (DU, Grohmann 1997: 180)

West Flemish also allows such long object shift (Grohmann 1997: 179; Haegeman 1993: 146, 1992: 61):

(4.148)   e. da   ze-t /t-ze   Jan gegeeven eet
                that them-it/it-them Jan given   has
                (West Flemish, Haegeman 1993: 146)

In the languages that allow long object shift, the pronoun appears immediately after the verb in verb-second clauses, or after the complementizer in verb-final clauses. Since I will propose (Section 6.3) that the verb in a verb-second clause is actually in the slot usually reserved for the complementizer, we can generalize over these two cases.

4.8.1.4 On the antiquity of clitic pronouns in Germanic

The older GMC languages do not offer much orthographic evidence that could be used to argue for a contrast between strong and clitic pronouns. Nonetheless, there is distributional evidence that the pronouns in these languages had the properties of clitics in at least some contexts, assuming that the defining property of clitics is their morphosyntactic dependence on another element, to which they must be adjacent. Eythórsson (1995: 29ff.) makes note of the striking fact that in GO, while complements of verbs in general precede those verbs, pronouns generally follow them.[24]

(4.149)   a. ushaihah sik
               he-hanged himself
               (GO, Matt. 27:5)

Eythórsson points out that, given the tendency we have observed for pronouns elsewhere in GMC to occur further to the left than complements of other types, this state of affairs appears quite un-Germanic, taken at face value. He proposes, however, that it can be accounted for by assuming these object pronouns to be clitic-like elements, which, like clitics elsewhere, occur in a relatively leftward position in clausal structure, and require support by another element. In the absence of another such element, the verb moves to the complementizer position in order to provide support for the clitic, thereby coming to precede it. (Such V–C movement is independently established for GO.)

---

[24] In GO, of course, claims about grammaticality (particularly regarding word order) are well founded only when it can be demonstrated that the GO construction is independent of the Greek model for translation. Eythórsson's discussion of GO word order is a model of this methodology. He focusses on cases where the GO text "resolves" a Greek complex verb, such as *hydropótei* 'drink water' as a sequence of verb + complement (*drigkais. . .wato*) for lack of a single-word equivalent. In such cases, the order of the two is presumably dictated by the translator's own grammatical instincts.

There is support for this analysis elsewhere in early GMC. Eythórsson notes that in runic inscriptions in the older *futhark*, verbs normally follow their subjects, with one exception; the special first person singular pronominal form *eka* 'I' only occurs attached to the right of verbs.

(4.149)   b. ek erilaz   sawilagaz hat-eka
          I the Eril, Sawilagaz am-called-I
          (Runic GMC, Lindholm, Eythórsson 1995: 184)

Eythórsson's account for this is again that *eka* is a subject clitic, which occurs in a leftward position in clausal structure (adjoined to the complementizer position) and, as in GO, is supported by movement of the verb into the complementizer slot. Of substantially the same nature is a striking pattern that emerges in some (though not all) OE prose texts, for example, the OE translation of Bede's *Ecclesiastical History*. In that text, subject NPs typically precede their verbs:

(4.149)   c. Breaton ist garsegces   ēalond
          Britain is (an) ocean's island
          (OE, Bede (Miller) 24:29)

Overwhelmingly, however, when the subject is a personal pronoun which would otherwise be clause-initial, the order which appears is V–S.

(4.149)   d. Cwædon hēo tō him...
          said   they to him...
          (OE, Bede (Miller) 100:24)

          e. Cwōm hē tō þæm cycinge
          came he to the king
          (OE, Bede (Miller) 122:13)

          f. Fērde hē be þære ilcan stōwe
          went he to the same place
          (OE, Bede (Miller) 122:13)

Only when another, topicalized element precedes the subject pronoun, preventing it from being initial, does the verb remain behind that subject pronoun.

(4.149)   g. Eft   hē frægn
          again he asked
          (OE, Bede (Miller) 96:15)

Finally, Eythórsson (1995: 228) points out that subject pronouns in some cases exhibit clitic-like behavior in the archaic Old IC of the Poetic Edda, where they appear immediately to the right of fronted verbs or complementizers and, crucially, do not count as separate constituents for the purpose of the strict Verb-Second requirement which applied in both main and subordinate clauses in Old IC (4.149i).[25]

(4.149)   h. kallar-a-ðu síðan / til knía þinna
call-not-you then / to knees your
'You do not call to your knees'
(Early ON, Akv 37, cited in Eythórsson 1995: 227)

         i. er-at svá maðr hár / at þic af hesti taki
is-not so man tall / that you from horse he-might-take
'There is no man so tall that he can take you from a horse'
(Early ON, Akv 37, cited in Eythórsson 1995: 228)

Thus, we see evidence for the clitic status of subject pronouns in GO, OE and in Runic GMC.

Leftward displacement of object pronouns is similarly an old feature in West GMC, occurring in OS and OE (cf. Mitchell 1985: II, 978; Quirk and Wrenn 1955: 94), where pronominal objects tend to precede the verb in main clauses while full NP objects usually follow them:

(4.150)   a. and þā Engliscan hī hindan hetelīce slōgon
and the English them from behind fiercely struck
(OE, AS Chr. 1066)

         b. and Engle āhton wælstōwe geweald
and Angles possessed of-battlefield control
(OE, AS Chr. 1066)

---

[25] Note that in (4.149h), the clitic pronoun follows not only the verb but also the negative marker -*a*-. In the first person, on the other hand, a form -*k*-, clearly a reduced form of the first person pronoun, appears between the verb and the negative marker.

(i)   Loka ec qveð-c-a / lastastǫfom
to-Loki I speak-1Sg-not taunting-words
(Early ON, Ls18, Eythórsson 1995: 232)

Eythórsson claims that this is due to the fact that the -*c*- here is no longer a clitic pronoun, having further evolved into a subject agreement marker. Evidence of this is that it only appears attached to verbs, never to complementizers, and that it can co-occur with a separate subject pronoun, as in the present instance.

A similar asymmetry holds in prepositional phrases; personal pronoun objects of prepositions typically precede those prepositions, while full NP objects generally follow them. (For OE, see Quirk and Wrenn 1955: 90.)

(4.151)   that he [ina fram] uuerpa .... endi [ina āno] cuma up te himile
          that he [him from] throw [it] and [it without] come up to heaven
          'that he cast it from him and come up to heaven without it'
          (OS, Heliand (Behaghel) 1487–1489)

When the prepositional phrase is the complement of a verb in OE and OS its pronoun object typically occurs to the left of both the preposition and the verb.

(4.152)   a. Thô sprak im   iro   drohtin tô
             then spoke them their lord   to
             (OS, Heliand (Behaghel) 2925)

          b. and Tostig eorl him cōm tō
             and Tostig earl him came to
             (OE, AS Chr. 1066)

The OS example shows, in fact, that the object pronoun undergoes long object shift, occurring further to the left than the clausal subject. This was, in fact, the usual treatment of object pronouns in earlier West GMC:

(4.152)   c. thô hêt   ine mahtig Crist gangan imu tegegnes
             then commanded him mighty Christ to-go   him toward
             'Then the mighty Christ commanded him to go toward him'
             (OS, Heliand (Behaghel) 2938)

Thus, older GMC shows systematic leftward displacement of personal pronouns, and the requirement evidenced in at least some cases that they be supported by preceding heads supports an analysis specifically as clitics.

4.8.1.5 *New pronominal contrasts*

Postmedieval elaborations of the pronoun systems include GMC participation in the relatively late and pan-European introduction of an intimate/polite contrast in the second person (often referred to as the T/V system). We can distinguish two distinct levels in this development. In the first – attested in OHG as early as the ninth century (Bach 1965: 194), though not becoming general until much later (Lockwood 1968: 62), and in EN since the thirteenth century (Howe 1996: 170) – the second person

Table 4.3 Second person pronouns in selected Germanic languages

	Gothic T/V	LateME T	LateME V	Swedish T	Swedish V	MDutch T	MDutch V	Yiddish T	Yiddish V	W Frisian T	W Frisian V	Dutch T	Dutch V	Icelandic T	Icelandic V	German T	German V	Faroese T	Faroese V
Sg	þu	thou	Ye/you	du	ni	du	ghi	du	ir	do	jo	jij	u	þú	þér	du	Sie	tú	tygum
Pl	jus									jimme		jullie		þið		ihr		tit	

plural pronoun (OHG *ir*, ME *yē*, Middle DU *ghi*, SW *ni*[26]) is employed in addressing individuals of higher social rank, or for the maintainance of social distance, while continuing to be used for second person plural as well. In systems of this sort the polite/intimate distinction exists only in the singular. These uses of plurals as polite singulars were apparently based on the model of Latin *vos* and its descendants, which had undergone a similar development (Williams 1975: 248).

The second person pronouns in DU have undergone particularly complex developments (Howe 1996: 220ff). *Ghi*, originally plural, became a polite singular, and was supplanted as a plural by *jullie* (←*ghilieden* 'you people'). *Ghi* was supplanted in turn by *U* (of obscure etymology) as polite singular, and it became the new intimate form, displacing *du*, except regionally. Thus, the original plural 'you' is now restricted to intimate singular. In EN, too, the development of these pronouns has been relatively complex. *Ye*, later replaced by its objective form, *you*, came to be used as a polite singular (often with a singular verb), but by the beginning of the eighteenth century it had come to serve as a general pronoun of address in singular and plural, again neutralizing the polite/intimate distinction. Some dialects, including Shetlands EN (Robertson and Graham 1991: 4) and Yorkshire EN (Lass p.c.), retain the contrast between singular intimate *thou* and plural/ polite *ye*. Besides standard EN, the T/V distinction is disappearing in colloquial AF, where *U*, the polite second person pronoun, is often avoided by means of third person forms of address (Donaldson 1993: 124; Ponelis 1993: 207).

As of the seventeenth century, the use of second person plural forms as polite forms of address in GE was largely superseded by the use of third person plural *sie* (for detailed discussion, see Lockwood 1968: 62). Originally, this formal *Sie*, though formally a third person plural, was construed with a singular verb when addressing a singular individual. The third person singular masculine *Er* was also used in polite address with singular subjects. Both of these uses had fallen by the wayside in standard GE by the second half of the eighteenth century, replaced by a uniform *Sie* + plural verb, though they were retained longer in some dialects.

---

[26] *Ni* comes from second plural *I*, with the /n/ derived from a former verb ending, which became attached to the following clitic pronoun (Haugen 1976: 375). However, Haugen (1976: 82, 375f.) reports that the use of *ni* as a polite pronoun has never quite caught on, and is regarded as condescending, creating a dilemma that has been answered in part by the avoidance of pronouns altogether as forms of address.

YI still preserves the older system, using (originally second person plural) *ir* for polite address in the singular, or for neutral address in the plural, and *du* for singular intimate address, but in standard GE, *Sie* is used for polite address for both singular and plural, and the original second person plural *ihr* is reserved for intimate address in the plural. The polite/intimate contrast is thus now signaled in both singular and plural. Through the agency of GE influence in postmedieval times, this system has spread to DA, as well, where polite second person singular and plural pronouns are homophonous with the third person plural (*De, Dem, Deres*) except in their reflexive forms, as noted above. These replace an earlier plural-as-polite *I* 'you'.

IC makes use of still different means to instantiate this distinction. It uses the original dual form, *þið*, as the intimate form of address in the plural, and has reserved the original plural second person pronoun, *þér*, for polite address (singular and plural). The FA *tygum* 'you (polite singular)' is from a similar source, though presenting some formal problems (for which see Haugen 1982: 108). In IC, a corresponding distinction has arisen between *við* 'we' (originally dual but now neutral plural) and *vér* 'we' (originally plural and now plural honorific, equivalent, roughly, to the EN editorial/royal 'we').

As in other European languages, the contexts of appropriateness for polite and intimate forms of address have changed substantially since the 1960s, the latter becoming acceptable even among strangers under some circumstances. So, for example, Bandle *et al.* (2005: 1631) report that many Danes hardly ever use *De* anymore, and that in the second half of the twentieth century, *du* had become the unmarked form of address in NO (Bandle *et al.* 2005: 1595).

A further elaboration of the pronoun system in continental Scandinavian (DA, SW and BN, but not NN) is the one involving a bifurcation in the third person between a set of animate pronouns which do not agree with their antecedents in grammatical gender and a set of inanimate pronouns, which do. This development, discussed in detail in Section 4.1.2.2, can be regarded as a resolution to the ancient dilemma of whether agreement between third person pronouns and their antecedents should be based on natural or grammatical gender.

4.8.1.6   *Attributive and predicate possessive pronouns*

In some of the GMC languages, possessive pronouns have developed special forms for use in predicative positions. In Standard EN, the contrast has two distinct sources. For possessive pronouns which originally ended in -*n*, the -*n* was retained in the predicate form (*mine*), but lost in the attributive form (*my*). In other cases, the predicative form (*yours, ours*) but not the attributive form (*your, our*) adds a final -*s*, probably modelled on *his*. In Appalachian EN, the predicate possessives of all persons and numbers are formed with -*n* (*yourn, hisn, ourn*, etc.) (Toon 1982: 244). Similarly, FR, GE and AF have developed special endings for predicative possessives (in GE, largely homophonous with strong adjective endings):

(4.153)   a.   myn wiif   mines is thús
                 my wife   mine is at home
                 FR, Tiersma 1999: 59)

           b.   mein Auto   Das ist nicht meins
                 my   car   That is not   mine
                 (GE)

           c.   my/ jou /ons keuse   Die keuse is myne/joune/ons s'n
                 my/ your/our choice   The choice is mine/yours/ours
                 (AF, Ponelis 1993: 225)

4.8.2   The referential properties of pronouns

Most GMC languages exhibit a formal distinction between reflexive and nonreflexive pronouns. In GO (4.154a), *ina* 'him' and *im* 'them' are personal pronouns, while *sis* 'himself' is a reflexive.

(4.154)   a.   guþ$_i$ hauheiþ ina$_k$ in sis$_i$
                 God$_i$ glorifies him$_k$ in himself$_i$
                 (GO, John 13:32)

           b.   jah (is)$_i$ gafalh sik$_i$ faura im$_k$
                 and he   hid   himself from them
                 (GO, John 12:36)

In traditional usage, both the reflexives and the nonreflexives are classed together as "pronouns," and differentiated from each other, where necessary, by adding a qualifier (e.g., "personal," or "reflexive") and there is in fact morphological, syntactic and semantic justification for treating them as exponents of a common category. Semantically, they depend on (linguistic or extralinguistic) context for their referential interpretation; they "stand in for" full noun phrases. The two differ from each other in the conditions under which they are allowed to or are prevented from "picking up reference" from a co-occurring noun phrase. Reflexives like *sis* must find an antecedent within the sentence, and the relationship between the antecedent and the reflexive must meet certain syntactic requirements; the antecedent must be a subject[27], and the two must be sufficiently syntactically "close" to each other – in the case of GO, they must be inside the same minimal finite clause. Thus, it was not possible for the antecedent to be inside a main clause and the reflexive in a finite subordinate clause in GO:

(4.154) c. (eis$_i$) bedun ina ei   [(is) uslaubidedi im$_i$/(*sis$_i$)... galeiþan]
they$_i$ asked him that he allow them$_i$/*selves$_i$ to go
(GO, Luke 8:32)

In the following, I will refer to reflexive pronouns and other elements (reciprocals, for instance), which depend for their reference on a syntactic antecedent within the sentence, as anaphors, while nonreflexive pronouns, which can refer to individuals outside of the sentence, will be called pronominals. We will start our consideration of the crosslinguistic variation in the referential properties of pronouns in the GMC languages by considering pronominals, as exemplified by personal pronouns, and then we will turn to the rather richer and more complicated set of facts involving anaphors, as exemplified by reflexive pronouns.

4.8.2.1 *The referential properties of pronominals*

Pronominals, as I have defined them (including personal pronouns) have the property that they do not need an antecedent in the same clause. It seems to be the case generally that pronominals, so defined, also have the property that they cannot refer to an antecedent within the same minimal clause containing them. They can have an antecedent within the sentence, but only if it is separated from them by a sufficient syntactic distance – for example, if the pronominal is within a clause that does not also include the antecedent. The following set of EN sentences illustrates these properties:

(4.155) a. I$_i$ saw him$_j$

b. John$_i$ saw *him$_i$/himself$_i$

c. John$_i$ knows that Mary saw him$_i$/*himself$_i$

In (4.155b), the pronominal cannot refer to the subject, since they are too "close," and if coreference is intended, a reflexive must be used instead. On the other hand, it is

---

[27] A definition sufficiently broad to encompass the 'subjective genitives' with action nominals is required to accommodate the fact that these, too, could antecede reflexives:

(i) in quma fraujins...miþ allaim þaim weiham seinaim
in coming lord's-Gen with all the holy-ones self's
(GO, 1 Thess. 3:13)

198   4 *The Germanic nominal system*

possible for a pronominal to refer back to a subject if the two are in separate clauses, as in (4.155c). In these cases, the reflexive cannot be used in place of the personal pronoun. It is often the case that where a pronominal can refer back to the subject, the reflexive is excluded, and, conversely, where the pronominal is not able to refer back to the subject the reflexive can be used, though we will see that there are relatively many cases in the GMC languages where the two can overlap.

The main point of variation in GMC involving this "disjoint reference" requirement on pronominals has to do with the size of the syntactic space within which pronominals are prohibited from finding an antecedent. Such variation is in fact quite limited. All of the GMC languages are in agreement with GO, for example, that when the intended antecedent is in the main clause and a nonreflexive pronoun is in a subordinate clause with a finite verb, as in example (4.155c), the pronoun can refer back to that intended antecedent. The crosslinguistic differences seem to be limited to three environments. The first involves pronominals contained within nonfinite clauses. In GO, for example, when a personal pronoun is in a nonfinite clause (e.g., an infinitival or a participial clause), the personal pronoun cannot refer back to the subject of the main clause. Evidence of the impossibility of this interpretation is provided by that fact that, where the Greek text has a personal pronoun (e.g., *autón*) in such a construction, whose antecedent is the subject of the main clause, GO systematically renders this personal pronoun as a reflexive, as in the following examples, where underscores represent intended coreference:

(4.156)   a.   þai-ei ni wildedun   mik þiudanon ufar sis/(*im)
               who$_i$ not they-wanted me to-rule   over selves$_i$/*them$_i$
               'who didn't want me to rule over them'
               (GO, Luke 19:27)

          b.   jah bedun ina$_i$ allai gaujans...   [galeiþan fairra sis]
               and asked him all of the inhabitants$_i$ to go   from selves$_i$
               'And all of the inhabitants asked him to go from them'
               (GO, Luke 8:37)

          c.   (is) qaþ-uh   -þan ... þamma$_i$ [haitandin sik]
               he$_i$ said-and then   to-the-one inviting   self$_i$
               'And then he said to the one inviting him'
               (GO, Luke 14:12)

          d.   Þai frawaurhtans [þans frijondans sik]   frijond
               the sinners   those loving   selves love
               'The sinners love those loving them'
               (GO, Luke 6:32)

As the EN glosses indicate, though, the interpretation prohibited in GO is perfectly possible in EN; personal pronouns are possible (and reflexives are not) in reference to the main clause subject in these constructions in EN. The first parameter dividing the GMC languages, therefore, is whether a pronominal in a nonfinite (infinitive or participle) clause can be coreferent with the main clause subject. IC patterns with GO in disallowing the personal pronoun here and requiring the reflexive, as does MHG:

(4.157)   a. Hann$_i$ telur   mig hafa séð sig$_i$/*hann$_i$
               he   believes me to have seen him
              (IC, Andrews 1990)

           b. *Petur$_i$ bað   Jens að raka hann$_i$
              Peter$_i$ asked Jens to shave him$_i$
              (IC, Thráinsson 1991: 53)

           c. Diu künegîn   den sich küssen bat
              the queen that one self to-kiss asked
              'The queen asked that one to kiss her'
              (MHG, Parzival 806:28)

On the other hand, Modern GE patterns with EN. The pronoun is possible in such constructions.

(4.157)   d. Sie bat   mich, sie/*sich zu besuchen
               she asked me   to visit her/*herself
              (GE)

In the continental Scandinavian languages too, a personal pronoun can refer to the main clause subject from within the infinitive clause.

(4.157)   e. Jon$_i$ bad   oss   hjelpe ham$_i$
               John asked us to help   him
              (NO, Hellan 1983: 27)

           f. John hørte sin ven   beklage ham
              John heard his friend pity   him
              (DA, Allan et al. 1995: 165)

           g. Han bad   sjuksköterskan tvätta   honom
              he asked nurse-the   to-wash him
              (SW, Holmes and Hinchcliffe 1994: 143)

For a consideration of the historical relationship between these two patterns, see Harbert 1985, where it is argued that the GO-type pattern is the older one.

Second, there is variation in the GMC languages with respect to whether a personal pronoun occurring as the object of a locative preposition can refer to the subject of its clause or not. It apparently could not in GO, where a Greek personal pronoun referring to the subject was consistently translated as a reflexive:

(4.158) a. [is] galausida [_PP_ af sis/(*imma)] þos naudibandjos
he_i_ tore   from   self_i_ /(*him_i_) the chains
(GO, Mark 5:4)

b. gasaiƕands þan Iesus managans hiuhmans bi sik
seeing   then Jesus large   multitudes by him(self)
'Jesus then seeing a large multitude by him...'
(GO, Matt. 8:18)

EN does allow the personal pronoun here, as indicated by the glosses on these examples, and the reflexive is at least awkward here for some speakers. The majority of the GMC languages, however, including Scandinavian, GE and DU, pattern with GO in disallowing the personal pronoun here and requiring a reflexive:

(4.158) c. Franz sah eine Schlange neben sich/*?ihm
Franz saw a   snake   near *himself/him
(GE, Everaert 1980: 17)

d. Han lukkede døren efter   sig
he closed door-the behind self
(DA, Allan _et al._ 1995: 164)

e. Han stängde dörren efter   sig
he closed door-the behind self
(SW, Holmes and Hinchcliffe 1994: 143)

Finally, the GMC languages are divided with respect to the interpretation of personal pronouns occurring as possessors in nominal phrases. In some languages, including GO, a pronominal occurring as a possessive inside a nonsubject NP cannot refer back to the subject of the clause, and when possession by the subject is intended a reflexive possessive form must be used instead. We are able to tell this because New Testament Greek used genitive pronominal possessives (e.g., _autoû_) both in intended coreference and intended non-coreference with the clausal subject. The GO translator was thus free (and in fact required) to render this pronoun as either a personal pronoun or a reflexive according to the dictates of his own grammar. Wherever reference to the subject of the clause was intended, it was rendered as a reflexive, indicating again that the pronominal possessive could not corefer with that subject:

(4.159)   a. jah (is) qaþ   im   in [NP laiseinai seinai/(*is)]
          and he_i spoke to-them in teaching   self's_i/*his_i
          'And he spoke to them in his (own) teaching'
          (GO, Mark 4:2)

       b. qaþuh   þan Iesus_i bi [dauþau is_j]
          spoke-and then Jesus about his (John's) death
          (GO, John 11:13)

The Scandinavian languages agree with GO here. Pronominal possessives cannot be used in intended reference to the clausal subject, and reflexive possessives must be used instead where such coreference is intended:

(4.159)   c. Jón_i rétti   Haraldi [sin_i/*hans_i föt]
             Jon_i handed Harald self's_i/*his_i clothes
             (IC, Thráinsson 1976a)

       d. Hun læste [hendes nyeste roman]
          she_i read her*_i/j newest novel
          (DA, Allan et al. 1995: 174)

       e. Han kör   [hans bil]
          he_i drives his*_i/j car
          (SW, Holmes and Hinchcliffe 1994: 152)

On the other hand, in OE the pronominal possessive occurring in a nonsubject NP could refer back to the subject of the clause:

(4.159)   f. [he_i] sealde [NP his_i hyrsted sweord]...ombihtþegne
             he_i gave   his_i decorated sword to-servant
             (OE, Beowulf 672)

It is argued in Harbert 1985 that the GO/IC situation is the original one, and that OE here represents an innovative situation in which a pronominal possessive contained within an NP is no longer prevented from referring to an antecedent outside that NP. To put it another way, the domain D within which pronouns are prohibited from having an antecedent was, in GO, the minimal finite clause containing it, but in OE it came to be either the minimal finite clause *or* the minimal NP containing it. This in turn led to a loss of the reflexive/nonreflexive contrast in this context; since both coreference with the clausal subject and non-coreference with the clausal subject can now be expressed by means of the possessive form of the personal pronoun, the reflexive possessive now no longer has a distinctive function. Not surprisingly, while it remained as an apparent archaism in OE in poetic texts, as in (4.159g) (cf. Mitchell 1985: I, 119), it was lost from the language of prose.

(4.159)   g. and him   Hrōþgar gewāt tō [NP hōfe sīnum]
                 and himself Hrothgar betook to his house
                 (OE, Beowulf 1236)

Moreover, when EN later rebuilt its reflexive paradigm on the pattern of personal pronoun+self, genitives were notably excluded. Thus, we have no *hisself's* or *theirselves* in Modern (Standard) EN, and no systematic contrast between reflexive and pronominal possessors of the sort that existed in earlier GMC.

GE, too, has neutralized the pronominal/anaphoric possessive distinction for possessives. As in EN, it became possible for the former, as well as the latter, to refer back to the subject, rendering the distinction between reflexive and nonreflexive possessives superfluous. Unlike EN, GE has retained both forms which were formerly reflexive (*sein*) and forms which were formerly pronominal (e.g., *ihr*), but has refunctionalized them so that these now contrast only with respect to person and number – not with respect to their referential possibilities. The former reflexive *sein*, whose antecedent could originally be of any number or gender, was restricted to masculine and neuter singular antecedents, and the former masculine and neuter singular pronominal possessives were correspondingly eliminated, yielding a new complementarity, defined along axes of gender and number, between the surviving former possessive pronominals and the former reflexive possessives. The two sets of forms no longer contrast with each other with respect to reflexivity; former nonreflexives and former reflexives are both used either to refer back to the subject of the clause, or to a referent other than the subject of the clause:

(4.159)   h. Er$_i$ verkaufte [seinen$_{i,j}$ Wagen]
              he sold his   (own)/his (someone else's) car
              (GE)

            i. Sie$_i$ verkauften [ihren$_{i,j}$ Wagen]
              they sold their   (own)/their (someone else's) car
              (GE)

We may regard it as an instance of what Lass (1988) calls "exaptation" – the opportunistic assignment of new functional significance, unconnected with their original meanings, to formal oppositions which grammar change has rendered superfluous.

4.8.2.1.1 Other neutralizations of the pronominal/anaphor distinction
Burzio (1988) has proposed that the "disjoint reference" requirement on pronominals is only a

default, applying only when the pronominals have a distinctive reflexive counterpart with which to contrast. In the absence of such an opposition, the pronominal/anaphoric contrast is neutralized. This proposal works well for a number of cases in GMC. So, for example, for most of the GMC languages, the contrast between personal pronouns and reflexive pronouns exists only in the third person. In first and second persons, where distinctive reflexive forms do not exist (except in EN), personal pronouns are used in both reflexive and nonreflexive functions. Thus, in IC, such a form can occur in object position with the subject of its own clause as antecedent. In EN, on the other hand, which does have distinctive first person reflexives, the unmarked personal pronoun cannot be used to refer back to the subject:

(4.160)   a. Ég rakaði mig
　　　　　　　*I shaved me
　　　　　　　(IC, Thráinsson 1991: 63)

A still more extreme instance of such neutralization is found in OE and its immediate cousins, the Ingvaeonic languages. As noted, these languages lost even the GMC third person *s*-reflexives, and the personal pronouns appear in both reflexive and nonreflexive functions in all persons.

(4.160)   b. Þā wende hē hine　　　west
　　　　　　　then betook he him(self) west
　　　　　　　'Then he went west'
　　　　　　　(OE, AS Chr. 893)

This state of affairs was later undone in some of these languages by the creation or borrowing of new reflexive pronouns, but the Ingvaeonic lack of distinct reflexives is still reflected in FR (though see below for further discussion).

(4.160)   c. Hy$_i$ droege him$_{i/j}$　　　ôf
　　　　　　　he$_i$ dried　him$_j$/ him(self')$_i$ off
　　　　　　　(FR, Everaert 1991: 94)

In Middle DA, too, the third person plural objective reflexive was replaced by the third person personal pronoun (Haugen 1976: 310).

(4.160)   d. The hiØldo thØm　　　illa
　　　　　　　they kept　them[selves] badly
　　　　　　　(Middle DA, Haugen 1976: 310)

Though Haugen reports vacillation in dialects, Standard DA has restored the reflexive *sig* here (while keeping a historically nonreflexive form, *deres*, for the possessive).

4.8.2.2 *Short-distance and long-distance anaphors*

In the preceding section we noted that there is a difference between EN and GO, for example, with respect to the size of the syntactic space in which pronouns are prohibited from finding their antecedents. In GO, a nonreflexive pronoun inside an infinitival complement of a verb, for example, cannot refer back to the subject of the main clause. In EN, on the other hand, it can.

(4.161)   a. þai-ei ni   wildedun   mik þiudanon ufar <u>sis</u>/(*<u>im</u>)
              who$_i$ not they-wanted me to-rule   over selves$_i$/*them$_i$
              'who didn't want me to rule over them (/*themselves)'
              (GO, Luke 19:27)

This same example also illustrates a corresponding difference between the two languages with respect to reflexives. In GO, it is possible for the reflexive pronoun *sis* to refer back to the subject of the main clause from within the infinitive construction. In fact, it is the systematic use of the reflexive in such instances, translating the nonreflexive pronoun of the Greek model, which indicates to us that the personal pronoun is not possible here in GO. However, as the EN gloss shows, EN reflexives like *themselves* cannot occur inside infinitival constructions and have the subject of the main clause as their antecedents. We may say, therefore, following the terminology of Everaert (1991) (cf. also Thráinsson 1991), that GO *sis* is a long-distance (LD) anaphor, while EN *themselves* is a short-distance (SD) anaphor. In both cases (in fact, in all of the cases examined so far), the reflexives are in complementary distribution with the pronouns. Where the pronoun can be used to refer back to the subject, the reflexive cannot, and vice versa. However, such complementarity does not always hold. So, for example, in DA, reflexives may refer to the main clause subject from within an infinitive clause, but, as we have seen, pronouns contained within such clauses are not blocked from doing so:

(4.161)   b. Peter$_i$ bad   Jens om at barbere sig$_i$
              Peter$_i$ asked Jens to   shave him(self)$_i$
              (DA, Thráinsson 1991: 51)

One striking apparently convergent feature affecting a subset of the GMC languages is the development of a contrast between two formally distinct reflexives which are in virtual complementary distribution, conditioned at least partially by the long-distance/short-distance distinction just discussed. So, for example, DU has two different forms, *zich* and *zichzelf*, both of which translate as 'himself/herself/themselves', but which occur in largely non-overlapping contexts. First of all, DU allows LD-reflexives under some highly constrained circumstances. In particular, it is possible for a reflexive contained within an infinitive phrase to refer back to the main clause subject, but only if the reflexive is inside an adverbial prepositional phrase – not if it is a direct object, for example. This is shown in (4.162a):

(4.162)   a. Jan liet mij voor zich /*zichzelf/ hem werken
                Jan made me work for self/*himself'/him
                (DU, Everaert 1991: 91)

Note that the personal pronoun is also possible in these cases, so that the usual complementarity between reflexives and personal pronouns again breaks down here. However, as this example shows, only *zich*, not *zichzelf*, can be used to refer to the main clause subject. Everaert (1991: 80), as well as others, expresses the view that only morphologically simple anaphors can serve as LD-anaphors. This is consistent with the observation that reciprocals like *each other* are uniformly SD anaphors.

The following example would seem to suggest that, conversely, *zichzelf* but not *zich* can be a SD anaphor, referring to the subject of its own clause.

(4.162)   b. Jan verraste   zichzelf /*zich
                Jan surprised himself/*self
                (DU, Everaert 1991: 84)

In fact this is not quite correct, as Everaert points out. In cases like this, where the verb is semantically transitive, with both a subject and an object argument, only *zichzelf* is allowed. However, *zich* does occur as the reflexive object of "inherently reflexive verbs" – that is, verbs with non-transitive meanings which take semantically empty reflexive objects as a purely grammatical requirement. *Zichzelf* is not allowed here.

(4.162)   c. Jan schaamde zich /*zichzelf
                Jan was ashamed
                (DU, Everaert 1991: 84)

Note that in (4.162b), but not (4.162c), there is a reflexive in the EN gloss. Inherently reflexive verbs in those GMC languages which have them are generally translated as simple intransitives in EN, which has only a handful of inherently reflexive verbs (e.g., *behave oneself, perjure oneself*). Everaert (1980: 24) cites the following illustrative contrasts:

(4.162)   d. *Dutch*   *German*   *English*
                zich ophouden   sich aufhalten   to stay
                zich verheugen   sich freuen   to rejoice
                zich schamen   sich schämen   to be ashamed
                zich vergissen   sich irren   to be mistaken

The generalization to this point is therefore that *zich* cannot refer back to a subject which is its co-argument. That is, for example, it cannot refer back to the subject of the simple clause containing it if it is the thematic object of the verb and the subject is the agent of that verb. It can only refer back to the subject if the two are semantic arguments of separate verbs, as in the LD case, or if the reflexive is not associated with a semantic argument role at all (cf. Everaert 1986, 1991, in which these restrictions are implemented in different ways). There are some cases in which either *zich* or *zichzelf* can occur.

(4.162) e. Jan wast   zich/zichzelf
              Jan washes (himself)
              (DU, Everaert 1980: 3)

These can be accommodated by assuming that DU has both a transitive verb 'wash', whose object can be a reflexive *zichzelf*, and an inherently reflexive, semantically intransitive verb 'wash', which co-occurs with *zich*. Compare the two EN glosses to these examples.[28]

It is also *zich*, not *zichzelf*, which occurs as a complement to locative prepositions in DU.

(4.162) f. Martin   keek   voor   zich
              Martin   looked ahead of him(self)
              (DU, Everaert 1980: 3)

Note again that this is among the marked contexts for reflexives; EN prefers pronouns here, and DU allows them, so this is again a context where the usual complementarity between pronouns and reflexives breaks down.

In summary, then DU is a "two-reflexive language"; the two forms have in common the fact that they depend on a preceding nominal phrase for their reference. They differ in terms of their relationship to that antecedent, however. *Zich* can refer back to it from within an infinitive clause, or a locative prepositional phrase (in both of which contexts pronouns are also possible). As an object of a non-locative PP, or as a direct object, it cannot refer back to the subject of its own clause unless the verb of which it is the object is an "inherently reflexive" verb:

(4.162) g. Jan mopperde op zichzelf/ *zich
              Jan grumbled at himself
              (DU, Everaert 1991: 92)

This particular contrast cannot be old in DU, since both DU reflexive forms are borrowings from Middle Low GE and do not antedate the fourteenth century

---

[28] Whether the reflexive form in such inherently reflexive verb constructions is to be analyzed as a syntactic object, or just a voice marker on an intransitive verb, is a matter of dispute. Hestvik (1990: 98), for example, agues that the Norwegian equivalents of these Dutch examples are in fact syntactically intransitive verbs.

(Everaert 1980: 21). Strikingly, however, the DU two-reflexive system converges with that of other GMC languages. Vikner (1985) observes that DA maintains a distinction between *sig* and *sig selv* which overlaps with the distinction in DU to a surprising extent. Only *sig* is a LD anaphor, capable of referring back to the main clause subject from within an infinitive clause. *Sig selv* must refer to the closer subject:

(4.163) a. at Peter$_i$ hørte Anne$_j$ omtale sig$_i$/*$_j$
that Peter heard Anne mention himself/*herself
(DA, Vikner 1985: 8)

b. at Peter$_i$ hørte Anne$_j$ omtale sig selv$_j$/*$_i$
that Peter heard Anne mention herself/*himself
(DA, Vikner 1985: 8)

Taraldsen (1996) reports similar facts for IC. *Sjálfa sig* must be used to refer back to the subject of its own clause, as in (4.164a), but *sig* by itself can refer back to the subject of the main clause from within an accusative with infinitive construction:

(4.164) a. María elskar sjálfa sig/*sig
María loves self /*self
(IC, Taraldsen 1996: 203)

b. María taldi sig vera gáfaða
Maria believed self to be gifted
(IC, Taraldsen 1996: 203)

DA *sig* can, like DU *zich*, take the subject of its own clause as an antecedent just in the case of inherently reflexive verbs:

(4.164) c. Peter sov over sig
Peter overslept
(DA, Vikner 1985: 12)

Again, as in DU, both of the reflexives are possible in certain cases, and again, the EN glosses show that these are precisely the cases in which either a transitive or an intransitive interpretation is available for the verb.

(4.164) d. at Peter barbarede sig/sig selv
that Peter shaved (himself)
(DA, Vikner 1985: 13)

Thus, DA has counterparts to both DU *zich* and *zichzelf*, which are similarly distributed. This is also the case in NO, as reported by Hellan (1983: 17).

In fact, the Scandinavian languages add a third anaphor to the system. Appending the suffix 'self' to personal pronouns turns them into SD-anaphors, which must find antecedents within their own clause, but which, unlike their *s*-reflexive counterparts, cannot pick out a subject as an antecedent, and therefore must refer to an object.

(4.165) a. at   Susan$_i$ fortalte Anne$_j$ om hende selv$_{j/*i}$
             that Susan$_i$ told   Anne$_j$ about herself$_{j/*i}$
             (DA, Vikner 1985: 16)

         b   at   Susan$_i$ bad   Anne$_j$ om at [PRO$_j$ ringe til hende selv *$_{j/*i}$]
             that Susan$_i$ asked   Anne$_j$ to call her$_{j/i}$
             (DA, Vikner 1985: 16)

Similar facts are reported for NO by Hellan (1983). For a more detailed typology of the anaphors of the GMC languages, the reader is referred to the typological survey in Koster and Reuland 1991. The other authors in that volume offer a variety of suggestions for their theoretical analysis.

Setting the *hende selv* type aside, we see that at least a subgroup of GMC languages observes a distinction between two different reflexive forms. One of these (the *zich* type) may be separated from its antecedent by the boundary of an infinitive clause or a prepositional phrase, but can appear "closer" to its antecedent than that only if it is a syntactic argument of an inherently reflexive verb; the reflexive and its antecedent cannot be co-arguments of the same verb. The other reflexive (the *zichzelf* type) can never find its antecedent "at long distance," but it can have an antecedent which is a co-argument of the same verb. Since this distinction crosscuts the major subgroupings of GMC, it raises the question of how old/widespread it is. As noted, it cannot be very old in DU, at least in its present form, since both of the DU reflexives were borrowed from GE in early modern times. It is of course possible, however, that these borrowings were used to relexify a contrast that had existed earlier in the language. Everaert notes that FR, which, like DU, lost the GMC *s*-reflexives prehistorically, has a contrast between anaphoric *him* and *himsels* which mirrors that of *zich* and *zichzelf*. Where *zich* is found in DU, forms of the *him* paradigm are found in FR, and where DU has *zichzelf*, *himsels* is found in FR:

(4.166) a. Hy$_i$ skammet him$_i$/*himsels$_i$
            he is ashamed
            (FR, Everaert 1991: 94)

         b. Hy$_i$ beoardielet himsels$_i$/*him$_i$
            he judges   himself
            (FR, Everaert 1991: 94)

c. Hy$_i$ sette de faas foar him$_i$/*himsels$_i$
he$_i$ set the vase in front of him$_i$
(FR, Everaert 1991: 95)

d. Hy$_i$ rette him$_i$/himsels$_i$ ta foar syn opkommen
he prepared (himself) for his performance
(FR, Everaert 1991: 94)

In fact, possible evidence that such a two-reflexive system existed even in early GMC may be revealed by a close examination of the distribution of reflexive forms in the GO translations. The GO reflexive *sik/sis* occurs systematically independently of the Greek under two sets of circumstances. First, it is used whenever the GO text translates a Greek (nonreflexive) middle or passive verb as an inherently reflexive verb. Such cases are very numerous, including such verbs as *gawasida sik* 'washed (himself)', *ushof sik* 'rose', *ushahaih sik* 'hanged himself', *afskaiskaidun sik* 'departed', *atnehwida sik* 'approached', *inmaidida sik* 'was transfigured' and so on. In these cases, the reflexive has no counterpart in the Greek text.

(4.167) a. jah ohtedun sis
kaì ephobḗthēsan
and they were frightened
(GO, John 6:19)

b. Helias ataugida sik
Helías ephánē
Elias appeared
(GO, Luke 9:8)

c. galisand sik arans
synachthḕsontai hoi aetoí
gather (themselves) eagles = 'Eagles gather'
(GO, Luke 17:37)

d. jah warmidedun sik
kaì ethermaínonto
and they warmed (themselves)
(GO, John 18:18)

Second, it is used in cases of LD-reflexives, which find their antecedents across the boundaries of infinitive or participle clauses. In this case, it systematically translates the Greek pronoun *autón*, since the explicitly reflexive form of Greek, *heautón*, apparently could not function as a LD-reflexive. Note that these are all cases where *zich* would be used in DU. On the other hand, when the verb is a genuine transitive, used in a sentence describing action which happens to be directed by the subject toward itself, the reflexive *sik silban* seems to be used with general consistency. (An exception is Mark 5:5, where Gothic *sik* translates Greek *heautón*.)

(4.168) a. afaikai   sik silban
         let him deny   himself
         (GO, Luke 9:23)

      b. gakiusai   sik silban   manna
         examine   himself   man
         'Let a man examine himself'
         (GO, 1 Cor. 11:28)

      c. Xristus ...   sik silban atgaf faur þo
         Christ gave himself   for   it
         (GO, Eph. 5:25)

In corresponding cases in DU, *zichzelf* would be used. One possible interpretation of these facts is that *sik* and *sik silban* in GO were like DU *zich* and *zichzelf*, respectively, in their distribution, in which case the "two-reflexive" system would reach far back in GMC. Difficult to rule out is an alternative possibility, under which it is simply an artifact of translation. When the GO text uses *sik*, it is generally in translation of the (also monomorphemic) *autón*. When GO uses *sik silban*, it is generally in translation of the (bi-morphemic) *heautón*, which appeared to be a *zichzelf*-type reflexive in Greek. Thus, the possibility arises that what is reflected here is the author's translational choices for certain Greek forms, rather than a fact about the distribution of GO reflexives. Choosing between these alternative accounts would have to be based on a close examination of the (very few) cases where GO and Greek do not line up in this way. One interesting case of this sort is the following, where the GO translates the Greek *heautoîs* simply as *sis*, in a context where DU would have *zich* (cf. also Luke 1:24, Luke 20:20).

(4.169) d. ni   haband   waurtins   in sis
            not they-have roots   in selves = Greek *en heautoîs*
            (GO, Mark 4:17)

Also interesting from this perspective are instances like the following, in which *sik* is used as the subject of an accusative-with-infinitive construction to refer back to the matrix subject, even though the Greek model has the bimorphemic *heautoús*.

(4.169) e. taiknjandans   sik   garaihtans   wisan
            representing   themselves righteous   to be = Greek *heautoús*
            (GO, Luke 20:20)

(Cf. also Luke 13:29, Phil. 1:17). Compare the GO example with the analogous case in IC (4.164b), where an unreinforced reflexive is also used. The evidence on the whole, therefore, suggests that the two-reflexive system was present in early GMC.

4.8.2.3 *Very-long-distance anaphors or logophors?*

In a few GMC languages, reflexives are even allowed to pick out antecedents outside of the finite clause containing them, under some circumstances. These "truly long-distance reflexives," as Thráinsson (1991: 54) labels them, have received the most attention in IC (e.g., Thráinsson 1991; Sigurðsson 1986), but are also found in FA:

(4.170) a. Jón$_i$ sagði að ég hefði svikið   sig$_i$
Jon said that I had betrayed himself
(IC, Thráinsson 1991: 55)

b. Gunnvør$_i$ visti, at tey hildu lítið   um seg$_i$
G. knew that they had a poor opinion of herself
(FA, Lockwood 1964: 118)

c. segði kongur$_i$ við hann, at um hann blóðgaði   seg$_i$,
said king-the to-him that if he made-bleed self
skuldi hann missa lív
should he lose life
(FA, Lockwood 1964: 118)

Rather different from these are very-long-distance uses of *-self* reflexives in some dialects of EN, including Irish EN, which will be discussed below.

In most dialects of IC, reflexives whose antecedents occur outside the minimal clause containing them are restricted to subjunctive clauses: they cannot occur in indicative clauses (though Thráinsson 1991: 73n notes that some speakers of IC also allow these long distance reflexives in indicative complement clauses, of the verb *vita* 'know', for example, as do speakers of FA, apparently – cf. example (4.170b)).

(4.170) d. *Jón$_i$ veit   að þú hefur svikið   sig$_i$
Jon knows that you have betrayed him
(IC, Thráinsson 1991: 56)

Not just any subjunctive clause will suffice, however. Only subjunctive clauses expressing indirectly reported speech or thoughts admit such LD-reflexives. They may not, for example, occur in subjunctive counterfactual condition clauses and refer back to the subject of the main clause:

(4.170) e. *Jón$_i$ yrði   glaður ef þú hjálpaðir   sér$_i$
John would be glad if you helped-Subjunct self
(IC, Thráinsson 1991: 56)

Strikingly, the reflexive becomes possible here if this sentence is made into the complement of a verb of saying:

(4.170) f. Jón$_i$ sagði að hann yrði glaður ef þú hjálpaðir sér$_i$
Jon said that he would-be glad if you helped-Subjunct self
(Thráinsson 1991: 56)

Thráinsson (1991: 56) and others (e.g., Maling 1984) note that the choice of subjunctive or indicative in complements of verbs of speaking and thinking in IC (as elsewhere in GMC) is conditioned by point-of-view considerations. When indicative is used, the speaker is implying that s/he believes in the truth of the complement clause, whereas when s/he uses subjunctive, s/he is reporting the original utterance from the point of view of the individual who uttered it, and taking no position with respect to the truth of the utterance. The use of the reflexive in these instances is held to be conditioned by "point-of-view" considerations of a similar sort. Thus, no reflexive is possible in (4.170e) because it contains no report of Jón's speech or thoughts, whereas Jón's speech is being reported, from his point of view, in (4.170f), as signaled by both the subjunctive of indirect discourse and the reflexive.

In this respect, these uses of the reflexive resemble the uses of "logophoric pronouns" such as those found in Ewe, a Niger-Congo language (Clements 1975). Ewe has forms distinct from both the strict reflexives and the personal pronouns of that language which are used "to distinguish reference to the individual whose speech, thoughts, or feelings are reported or reflected in a given linguistic context, from reference to other individuals" (Clements 1975: 141). Clements notes that coreference with these forms seems to involve primarily such discourse notions as point of view, rather than particular syntactic requirements, such as subject antecedents. Thus, the logophor *ye* can, for some speakers, be anteceded by *Kofi* in (4.170g) but not by *Komi*, even though the latter is a subject, while the former is the object of a preposition. This is because *Kofi*, not *Komi*, is the individual whose speech is being reported.

(4.170) g. kɔmi$_k$ xɔ agbale tso kofi$_i$ gbɔ be wò-a-va
Kwami receive letter from Kofi side that Pro-T-come
me kpe na yè$_{i/*k}$
cast block for LOG
'Kwami got a letter from Kofi$_i$ saying that he should cast some blocks for him$_i$'
(Ewe, Clements 1975: 160)

Similarly, he points out (1975: 170) that the discourse antecedents for these logophors need not even co-occur with them in the same sentence. It has been recognized for a long time that the occurrence of long-distance reflexives in IC is also linked to point-of-view considerations of this type (Thráinsson 1976b), and that identifying them as logophors, rather than anaphors, provides a basis for accounting for a number of their properties. For example, like the logophors of Ewe, the long-distance reflexives of IC in fact need not find an antecedent in the same sentence at all, but may pick up their reference from a discourse antecedent as in (4.170h):

(4.170) h. Sigvaldi$_i$ neitaði því, að   þetta væri   vilja   þjóðarinnar
            Sigvaldi denied it   that this was   will the nation's

Að minnsta kosti væri það ekki sinn$_i$ vilji
At least   was it not self's will
(IC, Thráinsson 1991: 58)

(Compare also Bandle et al. 2005: 1581 for FA. For detailed discussion of the rather complex semantics of logophors, see Sigurðsson 1986; Sells 1987.)

For IC, though, this cannot be the whole story. While the "truly long-distance" reflexives of IC (like the logophors of Ewe) need not have an antecedent in the same sentence at all (and are therefore not anaphors at all, in the sense defined above), when they do have an antecedent in the same sentence, that antecedent has to meet some syntactic requirements, in addition to representing the originator of the speech or thoughts. In particular, when they have antecedents within the sentence, the antecedents of such reflexives in IC (unlike the logophor of Ewe) must be subjects. Some investigators (e.g., Clements 1975; Maling 1984) have posited that such restrictions represent a partial grammaticization of IC logophors.

Reflexive pronouns without antecedents also occur in some dialects of EN – most notably in Irish and Hebridean EN (Filppula 1999: 80ff.) – usually in cases where they are conjoined with other nominal phrases, and in the focal position in cleft constructions:

(4.170)   i. His brother was a shoemaker. And himself and his brother was
                                           up in the Orkney Isles
           (Hebridean EN, Filppula 1999: 85)

           j. And it's himself that told me that up in a pub
           (Irish EN, Filppula 1999: 86)

These are a quite different phenomenon from the Insular Scandinavian case. It appears to be emphasis, rather than point of view, which determines the occurrence of such reflexive forms. Filppula (1999: 84, 86), notes, along with others, that the distribution of reflexives in these cases is strikingly like that of the (nonreflexive) emphatic personal pronouns in the adjacent Goedelic languages of these areas, which are employed obligatorily in conjunction with other nominal phrases, and in cleft constructions.

4.9 The external syntax of noun phrases: subjects

In keeping with the fundamentally descriptive purpose of this volume, I will sidestep here a number of thorny issues having to do with the definition of the notion "subject," and will rely to a considerable extent on the reader's intuitions. Even picking out the subjects of particular sentences is occasionally problematic. In experiencer constructions like the following, for example, there is a mismatch between the "coding properties" of the underscored nominals, such as case and their (in)ability to control verb agreement on the one hand, and their syntactic "behavioral properties" on the other. These cases are discussed in Section 4.1.2.4.2:

(4.171) Mig   vantar   peninga
         me-Acc lacks-3Sg money-Nom
         'I lack money'
         (IC, Zaenen, Maling and Thráinsson 1990)

Questions also arise about whether one or the other of the underscored nominals in such "transitive expletive constructions" as (4.172), or both, are to be counted as subjects. These cases will be treated in Section 4.9.2.2.

(4.172) Það   luku   einhverjir stúdentar ekki þessu verkefni
         there finished   some students   not this   assignment
         (IC, Thráinsson 1996: 272)

4.9.1 Subject agreement

4.9.1.1 *Agreement between subject and verb*

As in other IE languages, the verb in the GMC languages is characteristically provided with a suffix which encodes grammatical features of its subject. In many of the modern languages, this inflection has tended to be reduced, and some of them no longer have any reflex of it, but in those where it is found, subjects are the only arguments which are encoded in the verb, in the usual case. GMC subject-verb agreement morphology takes the form of a single suffix which represents both the person and the number of the subject. In the present tense, and in the past tense of strong verbs, the morpheme in question is normally attached to the (present or past) inflectional stem of the verb, with no separate tense marker, as in (4.173a, b), from early OHG. In the past tense of weak verbs, the person/number morpheme co-occurs with a separate tense marker, as in (4.173c). In both cases, the person/number agreement suffixes also serve (redundantly) to signal tense, since a different set of agreement endings is used for past tense than for present tense.

(4.173) a. Subject agreement suffixes in Early OHG (Isidor)

Number: *Singular*   *Plural*

Person
1   ih gib-**u** (72)   uuir find-**emes** (51) / wir sculi-m (436)
2   dhu far-**is** (622)   er scul-**ut** (222)
3   ir send-**it** (285)   sie quhed-**ant** (431)

b. dhea angila stuond-un
the angels stood-3Pl
(Isidor (Eggers) 351)

c. ih chifrumi-d-a
I do-Past-1Sg
(Isidor (Eggers) 488)

There were originally distinct suffixes for each person/number combination. However, reduction of final syllables had led to some syncretism even in the earliest GMC:

(4.173) d. ih chifenc-0
I received
(OHG, Isidor (Eggers) 153)

e. ir ... quhad-0
he said
(OHG, Isidor (Eggers) 245)

The overall tendency has been toward further syncretism. At one end of the scale, the indicative present tense in GO exhibits seven formally distinct endings (including dual endings for first and second persons, but subtracting one for the systematic homophony of third person singulars and second person plurals). In other GMC languages, dual pronouns, where they are still found, are used with plural verbs.

(4.173) e. Gothic *nasjan* 'to save'

	Singular	*Dual*	*Plural*
1	nasj-a	nasj-os	nasj-am
2	nasj-is	nasj-ats	nasj-iþ
3	nasj-iþ		nasj-and

OE, on the other hand, has only four distinct agreement suffixes, Modern EN one, and continental Scandinavian none.

In the North GMC languages, the distinction between second and third person in the singular has been erased in most classes of verbs by extending the historical second person ending to the third person.[29] Thus, IC has:

(4.173) f. 1   ég kem   'I come'
              2, 3 þu, hann kem-ur   'You, he come(s)'

This is likely the source of EN third person -s as well, which arose in those parts of England subject to Norse influence; in Shetlands EN, which was under particularly strong Norse influence, both second and third person in the singular take the ending -s (Robertson and Graham 1991: 9).

Modern High GE and YI have neutralized the contrast between first and third person plural verb endings. In the North Sea subgroup of West GMC, person distinctions in the plural have been leveled out in all tenses and moods from the time of the earliest attestation, by extending the historical third person plural affix to the other persons. This state of affairs is still preserved for the most part in Modern DU:

(4.173) g. ik help   wij helpen
             jij helpt/ help je?   jullie helpen
             zij helpt/ helpt ze?   zij helpen
             (DU)

Note here that there is also partial conflation of second and third persons in the singular as well. However, a contrast re-emerges in question order, in which the subject follows the verb. Other languages in this subgroup have progressed still farther in the direction of elimination of endings. EN has now only the isolated -s of third person singular. Reduction of the paradigm has been carried still further in modern continental Scandinavian, where the -r suffix has been generalized throughout the paradigm, for all persons and numbers (e.g., DA *glemmer* 'I, you, he, she, we, they forget'). As a result, the suffix no longer conveys person/number information, but has become rather a tense marker – a major shift in the axis of agreement morphology. Number agreement outlasted person agreement in these languages (Bandle *et al*. 2005: 1142); written SW retained distinct plural forms as late as the early twentieth century (Holmes and Hinchcliffe 1994: 266). AF, like the continental Scandinavian languages, no longer has person inflection at all, but does not even retain former person markers as indicators of finiteness or tense. In this extreme case of deflection even the

---

[29] The contrast has been marginally reintroduced in monosyllabic verbs ending in vowels, /r/ and /s/: *þú ber-ð* 'you carry' (where the -ð derives from a clitic pronoun – a very usual phenomenon in GMC), versus *hann ber* 'he carries'.

contrast between finite and nonfinite has ceased to be encoded in the morphology (Ponelis 1993: 383).

In the main, person/number contrasts remain more robust in the verb 'be' than in other verbs. In IC, for example, the contrast between second and third persons is still signaled in the present indicative, and in GO the third person singular and the second person plural of 'be' are not identical in the present.

4.9.1.1.1 **Asymmetries in subject-verb agreement** As we saw in the preceding section, the form taken by agreement morphology in DU is affected by word order in one instance, different endings showing up on the verb depending on whether the subject precedes or follows it. Other languages exhibit similar asymmetries. For example in OE, all plural endings are reduced to a simple -e in the presence of a following subject.

(4.173) h. wē will-að ēow myningean
we want you to-remind
'We want to remind you'
(OE, Marsden 2004: 393)

i. nū will-e wē ēow gereccean
now want we you to-tell
'Now we want to tell you'
(OE, Marsden 2004: 393)

A more systematic instance of interaction between constituent order and agreement morphology is reflected in the following sets of examples from GO and OE:

(4.174) a. ik jah Barnabas ni habos
I and Barnabas not have-1Dual
(GO, 1 Cor. 9:6)

b. ik jah atta meins ain siju
I and father my one are-1Dual
(GO, John 10:30)

c. wairþiþ þus faheds jah swegniþa
become-3Sg to-you joy and rejoicing
(GO, Luke 1:14)

d. Þizeei ist frastisibja jah wulþus jah witodis garaideins
of-whom is-3Sg sonship and glory and of-law rule
(GO, Rom. 9:4)

(4.174) e. umb iii niht gefeaht   Æþered cyning ond Ælfred his brōþur
for 3 nights fought-3Sg. Æthered king   and Ælfred his brother
(OE, AS Chr. 871)

f. Æþered cyning ond Ælfred his brōþur ... gefuhton
Æthered king   and Ælfred his brother ...fought-3Pl.
(OE, AS Chr. 871)

As these examples show, in earlier GMC, when a conjoined subject appeared preverbally, the verb standardly exhibited dual or plural agreement, but when the conjoined subject appeared postverbally, the verb standardly showed singular agreement, though there are exceptions in both directions:

(4.174) g. malo   jah nidwa frawardeiþ
moths and rust   destroy-3Sg
(GO, Matt. 6:19)

This pattern is also found in Modern IC, as in (4.174h), and it may survive vestigially in colloquial EN presentational constructions such as (4.174i):

(4.174) h. sat   konungur og drottning í hásæti   og drukku saman
sat-Sg king   and queen in the high-seat and drank-Pl together
(IC, Einarsson 1945: 135)

i. There's a man and his wife at the door

Sometimes, plural subjects following the verb fail to control verb agreement even when they do not consist of conjoined singulars (Bandle *et al.* 2002: 942).

Finally, in at least one instance an agreement asymmetry depends on categorial properties of the subject; Irish EN (Filppula 2004: 88), Appalachian EN (Montgomery 2004: 247) and many varieties of northern British EN and southeastern American EN (Wolfram 2004) observe the "Northern Subject Rule," under which verbs with plural subjects take the ending *-s* except when the subject is a pronoun adjacent to the verb, in which case they take a -0 ending. (This distribution is similar in some respects to the agreement pattern found in Welsh.)

(4.174)   j. That's the way cattle feeds. They feed together.
(Appalachian EN, Mongomery 2004: 247)

4.9.1.2 *Agreement between subject and complementizer*
In addition to subject-verb agreement, some continental West GMC languages exhibit agreement between a subject pronoun and the complementizer of the clause. This possibility is differently limited in different languages, according to the person of the subject, the complementizers inflected and the features encoded by the agreement. In

Bavarian (Bayer 1984a; Kufner 1985) and FR (Hoekstra 1997), such inflection appears only in the second person, in which case it licenses omission of the subject pronoun. In some DU dialects, complementizers inflect only for the number of the subject (Haegeman 1992: 51, citing den Besten). Haegeman (1992: 51) characterizes West Flemish as the extreme case, in which agreement is found with all complementizers and all subjects. As (4.175a) shows, the subject from which the agreement features originate does not have to be adjacent to the complementizer in order for such inflection to occur.

(4.175)   a.   Kpeinzen dan-der   nie vele   mensen woaren
                 I-think   that-Pl-there   not   many   people   were
                 (West Flemish, Haegeman 1992: 50)

          b.   Jan   tinkt   dat-st   (do) jûn komst
                 Jan   thinks   that-2Sg   (you) tonight come-2Sg
                 (FR, Hoekstra 1997: 139)

4.9.1.3   *Concord between subjects and non-verbal predicates*

The GMC languages also exhibit various degrees of concord between subjects and adjective or noun phrases predicated of them. So, for example, in IC and GO predicate adjectives agree in case, gender and number with the clausal subject. Predicate nominals agree in case with the clausal subject.

(4.176)   a.   skipið   er gott
                 ship-the is good-NSgNom
                 (IC, Einarsson 1945: 133)

          b.   Kristján var   póstur
                 Kristján was a mailman-MSgNom
                 (IC, Einarsson 1945: 133)

          c.   [is] gredags   was
                 [he] hungry-MSgNom was
                 (GO, Mark 2:25)

          d.   ni   wairþaiþ   [jus]   airzjai
                 not become-3PlSubjunct [you] misled-3PlNom
                 (GO. Gal. 6:7)

That the nominative case on the predicate nominal or adjective in both of these languages is determined by subject concord is demonstrated by the fact that, when the nominal of which the adjective or nominal predicate phrase is predicated is in some case other than nominative, the predicate phrase occurs in the same case:

(4.177) a. so sunja frijans izwis briggiþ
 the truth free-APl you-APl will-bring
 'The truth will set you free' (independent of the Greek model)
 (GO, John 8:32)

 b. motarjos garaihtana domidedun guþ
 tax-collectors righteous-ASg judged God-ASg
 (GO, Luke 7:29, independent of the Greek model)

 c. hann kenndi mér, ungum, að skrifa
 he taught me-Dat, (being) young-Dat, to write
 (IC, Einarsson 1945: 133)

Predicate adjective and predicate nominal concord is variably distributed among the other GMC languages in a way that is independent of the extent to which they show subject-verb agreement. So, in DA, which, as noted, has no subject-verb agreement anymore, predicate adjectives still agree with their subjects in number or gender (though, of course, not case, since nouns and adjectives are not inflected for case in DA).

(4.178) a. Bilen er stor
 car-the is big-CSg
 (DA, Allan *et al.* 1995: 86)

 b. Huset er stort
 house-the is big-NSg
 (DA, Allan *et al.* 1995: 86)

 c. Romanerne er svære
 novels-the are difficult-Pl
 (DA, Allan *et al.* 1995: 86)

Allan *et al.* (1995: 88) note, however, a growing tendency for certain adjectives to abandon congruence. In Standard BN, passive participles do not agree with the subject of the clause, while in several dialects, and in the NN written standard, they do (Åfarli 1992: 11).

The earlier West GMC languages are characterized by a complex alternation between uninflected and inflected adjectives in predicate position, conditioned by the particular combination of number and gender involved, and by the type of adjective (non-derived adjectives versus past participles deployed as adjectives). For some discussion of this variability, see Behaghel 1923: I, 218. The modern West GMC languages have abandoned predicate adjective concord entirely, and now have systematically uninflected predicate adjectives. (Pivotal here was no doubt the fact that predicate adjectives typically had strong inflection, and the strong forms of West GMC in the nominative singular had become extensively endingless (MSg *blint~blintēr* 'blind' in OHG, *blind* in OE vs. GO *blinds*, ON *blindr*), leading to the possibility of interpreting predicate adjectives with strong nominative inflection as uninflected.) Since concord in the instance of predicate nominals involves only case, it also does not exist in those West GMC languages in which nominal phrases are not marked for case. In GE, where noun phrases show case in the form of the article and adjective endings, case concord is still found with predicate nominals, as in:

(4.179)   Laß deinen Geburtstag einen schönen Tag/ein schöner Tag werden
          let your birthday-MAcc [a beautiful day]-MAcc/MNom become
          (GE, Berger *et al.* 1972: 436)

However, it is increasingly retreating in favor of a default nominative in such cases, and the version with case concord no longer seems to be the standard form.

4.9.1.4 *Proposed syntactic correlates of agreement*
In recent syntactic work within the generative tradition, it has been claimed that the relative richness or paucity of subject agreement morphology on the verb in a particular language also plays a role in determining other syntactic properties of that language. The two major claims are (1) that rich agreement morphology is a necessary condition for the omissibility of subjects in finite clauses (hereafter, "pro-drop"), and (2) that the richness of agreement morphology determines whether or not lexical verbs can move to the left of clausal negators, frequency adverbials, and so on, by way of the V-to-T movement discussed in Section 6.3. The particular theoretical connection between phenomena in each case is beyond the scope of the present descriptive study, but to the extent that they involve empirical claims about the sorts of typological correlations which are a central focus of this study, they merit examination here. The following two sections will take up the hypothesized connections between agreement and pro-drop, and agreement and word order, in turn.

4.9.1.4.1 **Agreement and the distribution of null pronouns (the "pro-drop parameter")** Pro-drop – for present purposes, the omission of referential subject pronouns – is not a possibility in all languages. In languages like Ancient Greek, Spanish and Italian, referential subject pronouns may be "dropped" (unpronounced). Among the GMC languages, this possibility is genuinely represented only in GO. In GO, it was possible to omit referential subject pronouns, as in the following instances, where the missing pronouns have overt counterparts in the Greek model.

(4.180)   a. Þaruh þan swe **[0]** faridedun, anasaislep
and thence then as [they] sailed, [he] slept (Greek has overt pronoun)
(GO, Luke 8:23)

b. hausidedun ei **[0]** gatawidedi þo taikn
[they] heard that [he] made that sign (Greek has an overt pronoun)
(GO, John 12:18)

The other GMC languages do not in general allow dropping of referential subjects, as (4.180c) from Modern EN shows. This even seems to have been the case in the archaic language of the older runic inscriptions (Antonsen 1981: 53).

(4.180)   c. [He/*0] came yesterday

Referential subjects can be omitted to varying degrees in highly restricted contexts in some of these languages, where the identity of the missing subject is saliently recoverable from the discourse context. So, for example, Modern EN allows "diary drop" – omission of first person pronouns from initial positions in main clauses – in certain types of discourse. GE allows omission of second person singular pronouns under comparable circumstances (Prince 1997: 16), FR allows omission of second person subjects (Hoekstra 1997: 139) and YI allows omission of pronouns of any person and number from clause-initial position if they are discourse-salient (Jacobs et al. 1994: 408; Prince 1997: 3).

(4.180)   d. Q: vu   iz der mentsh?   A: [ ] iz in shtub
where is the person?   is in room
(YI, Jacobs et al. 1994: 408)

Only GO, however, allowed all subject pronouns to be omitted in all syntactic contexts. Syntacticians working in various generative theories have been concerned with identifying the conditions that must exist in a language in order for it to admit pro-drop, and most analyses have concluded that it is connected with the richness of agreement morphology in some way.[30] The correlation between richness of agreement and the omissibility of subject pronouns in GMC seems to accord well enough with the

---

[30] Or, alternatively, with "morphological uniformity." Pro-drop occurs in languages with rich agreement, such as Spanish, but also in languages with no agreement morphology, such as Japanese and Chinese (but not in EN, for example, which has agreement endings on some forms but not on others). This has led to the suggestion (Jaeggli and Safir 1989) that pro-drop requires not richness of inflection but uniformity of inflection – that is, endings on all forms, or on none. The requirement is satisifed by Japanese and Spanish, but not EN. Jaeggli and Safir (1989) note that continental Scandinavian languages are problematic for this alternative "morphological uniformity" proposal, since they have no agreement endings – hence are morphologically uniform – and yet do not allow pro-drop.

GO/Modern EN contrast, but breaks down elsewhere; early OHG, for example, as represented in the Isidor translation, is not a referential pro-drop language. The Latin model for translation routinely omits subject pronouns, but the OHG translation systematically restores them. So, for example, overt pronouns are supplied in the OHG version in forty-seven instances of clauses with first person singular subjects, though in the Latin text they are almost all unexpressed. This difference from GO is not attributable to relative richness of subject-verb agreement, however. GO agreement morphology is not richer in any plausibly relevant sense than the OHG of the Isidor translation, as a comparison of the paradigms in (4.173a) and (4.173e) indicates. The OHG paradigms are as rich as those of GO in the sense that there is a distinct verb agreement ending for each person/number distinction expressed in the (pro)nominal system. In fact, it is in this sense somewhat richer than GO, having six distinct endings in the present singular and plural, rather than only five. The same question arises for such modern GMC languages as IC and GE as well; why are they not pro-drop languages, in spite of having agreement morphology which is at least as rich as that of Spanish, for example? Jaeggli and Safir (1989), Rohrbacher (1994) and others claim that this is because rich morphology is only a necessary, not a sufficient, condition for strong pro-drop; in addition to the morphological requirement of rich agreement, there are syntactic restrictions on the occurrence of referential null pronouns which GE and IC fail to satisfy. Their failure to do so is connected in these analyses with yet another of their salient syntactic properties – the V-2 property. Modern GE and IC differ from Spanish and GO in that verbs in main clauses in the former languages occur systematically in second position, and the interaction of this property with the requirements for pro-drop is held to preclude the occurrence of pro-drop in the former. For details on how these ideas are implemented theoretically, see the discussion in Vance 1996. It is argued in Harbert 1999, however, that the claimed association between V-2 syntax and the absence of strong pro-drop is contradicted by the evidence in the early OHG of the OHG Isidor, which has not yet developed the strict V-2 syntax characteristic of later varieties of the language. The Isidor text demonstrates that the absence of pro-drop predates the emergence of V-2, and thus cannot depend on it.

4.9.1.4.2 **Agreement and verb position** There is some evidence supporting the conclusion that there is a typological correlation between richness of subject-verb agreement and the position of the lexical verb. Vikner (1995) and others claim that in languages with "rich" agreement, such as IC, the lexical verb moves into an empty Aux position ("V-to-I Movement"), while in languages with relatively impoverished agreement, such as EN and continental Scandinavian, the verb does not undergo such movement. Compare, for example, the following pair of sentences, where, in agreement-poor DA, the inflected verb of the subordinate clause follows the negative marker, but in relatively agreement-rich IC, it precedes. EN also lacks both rich agreement and V-to-I movement.

(4.181) a. Peter tvivler på at Marie ofte ryger disse cigarer
Peter doubts on that Marie often smoke these cigars
(DA, Vikner 1994: 123)

b. Ég spurði af hverju Helgi hefði oft lesið þessa bok
I asked why Helgi had often read this book
(IC, Vikner 1994: 127)

Jonas (1996a) notes that FA, intermediate in richness between IC and DA, has one dialect without V-to-I and another in which it is optional. Identifying a definite cross-linguistically valid "threshhold" of morphological richness for this purpose has proved elusive, though (see Vikner 1995; Thráinsson 1996; Jonas 1996a for discussion).

4.9.2 The typology and distribution of "expletive" arguments

As seen in the preceding section, GO and Modern EN represent opposite values of the "pro-drop parameter." GO omits argumental subjects freely while EN requires overt subjects in finite clauses. The two are also at opposite poles with respect to the representation of expletive, or dummy, subjects. In EN, all clauses must have overt subjects, and where that role is not assumed by a referential phrase, it must be assumed by a "dummy," or placeholder element. In fact, EN has two such "placeholder" forms: *it*, which appears in extraposition constructions and in meteorological expressions, and *there*, which appears in presentational constructions.

(4.182) a. It is impossible for a turtle to fly

b. There was a man in the garden

GO (as well as some other older GMC languages, including OHG) on the other hand, has no equivalent to either of these:

(4.182) c. ni skuld ist lagjan þans in kaurbaunan
not lawful is to-lay them in treasury
'[It] is not lawful to put them into the treasury'
(GO, Matt. 27:6)

d. Þan-uh was maurgins
then-and was morning
'And then [it] was morning'
(GO, John 18:28)

4.9 The external syntax of noun phrases 225

    e. wasuh þan fairra   im   hairda   sweine managaize haldana
        was-and then far from them a herd of-swine   many   kept
        'and [there] was then far from them a herd of many swine kept'
        (GO, Matt. 8:30)

The representation or nonrepresentation of such elements is often treated together with the omissibility or inomissibility of referential subjects, as another manifestation of parametric variation in pro-drop. And indeed, there seems to be some basis for claiming that they are typologically connected in some way. While there are languages which do not allow omission of referential subjects but which do allow the omission of such placeholder elements under some circumstances (e.g., Old and Modern GE), there are no languages which allow referential pro-drop but require overt expletives. This suggests an implicational relationship of some sort, and many recent theories of pro-drop are designed to yield such a result, by proposing one set of conditions which must be met to allow any pro-drop at all, and a still stricter set of requirements for the omission of referential subjects. Such two-part parameters yield a threefold classification of pro-drop languages – strong pro-drop languages like GO, which allow both missing expletives and missing referential subjects, non-pro-drop languages, like EN, in which both types of subjects must be overt, and a third set, which we may characterize as weak-pro-drop languages, such as Old and Modern GE and much of the rest of GMC, which allow expletive subjects, and only those, to be missing under some circumstances.

A closer examination of expletives in the GMC languages, however, demonstrates a range of variation in type and conditions for occurrence that largely negates a simple typology of this sort. In the following, I will sketch a rather different typology of expletive subjects, based largely on the detailed and comprehensive discussion of Vikner 1995 – especially chapters 6 and 7. The typology in question involves two main axes of variation. The first of these can be developed most straightforwardly by reference to a single example – that of GE. In GE, the pronoun *es* can function as an expletive in the broad sense of not having a particular extrasentential referent, in a number of different constructions (for discussion, see especially Leys 1979).

Impersonal passive constructions:

(4.183)   a. Es wird heute Abend getanzt
               It becomes   tonight danced
               (GE, Leys 1979: 28)

Presentational constructions:

(4.183)   b. Es steht eine Vase auf dem Tisch
               It stands a   vase on the   table
               (GE, Leys 1979: 28)

"Clausal subject extraposition constructions":

(4.183) c. Es überrascht mich, daß er kommt
It surprises me that he comes
(GE, Leys 1979: 28)

Meteorological constructions:

(4.183) d. Es regnet
it rains
(GE, Leys 1979: 28)

Leys points out, though, that this list of cases can be divided into two distinct groups on the basis of two apparently independent considerations. On the one hand, some of these instances of *es* persist even when they are non-initial – for example, when they are in subordinate clauses, or when the sentence begins with a topic. This is the case with the clausal subject extraposition *es* and the meterological *es*:

(4.184) a. Mich überrascht es nicht, daß er kommt
me surprises it not, that he comes
(GE)

b. Heute regnet es
today rains it
(GE)

c. Ich weiß nicht, ob es heute regnen wird
I know not if it today rain will
(GE)

The extraposition *es*, in fact, need not be in subject position in the clause; it also appears in cases of extraposition of clausal objects.

(4.184) d. Ich bedauere es, daß er kommt
I regret it that he comes
(GE, Leys 1979: 28)

On the other hand, the *es* in the two examples in (4.184e) and (4.184f) cannot appear in non-initial positions. When a topic is fronted in these sentences, or when the sentence is turned into a subordinate clause, the *es* obligatorily disappears.

(4.184) e. Heute Abend wird (*es) getanzt
this evening becomes (*it) danced
(GE)

4.9 *The external syntax of noun phrases*   227

   f. Auf dem Tisch steht   (*es) eine Vase
      on   the table stands (*it) a   vase
      (GE)

   g. Ich weiß nicht, ob (*es) auf dem Tisch eine Vase steht
      I   know not   if (*it) on the table a   vase stands
      (GE)

Leys notes further that the two types of *es* – those which disappear when non-initial and those which do not – have different translational equivalents in (Modern Standard) DU. The former translate as *er*, while the latter translate as *het*:

(4.184)   h. er   wordt   vanavond   getanst
             there becomes this evening danced
             (DU, Leys 1979: 29)

          i. er   staat een vaas op tafel
             there stands a   vase on table
             (DU, Leys 1979: 29)

          j. het verrast   me dat hij komt
             it surprises me that he comes
             (DU, Leys 1979: 29)

          k. het regent
             it rains
             (DU, Leys 1979: 29)

From this, Leys concludes that the crosslinguistic pairs

(4.185)   a. es~0 = er   b. es~es = het

represent two basically different types of "expletives." Note that (except for the case of the impersonal passive, which does not exist in EN), the two different types of *es* in GE also correspond respectively to two different forms in EN – *there* and *it*. Leys goes further to propose that only the first of these, es_1, is an expletive in the strict sense – a semantically empty element whose only function is as a placeholder for an obligatorily represented syntactic position, and which disappears when not needed for that purpose. The non-disappearing *es*, es_2 (the one in weather constructions and extraposition constructions) is, he claims, a true pronoun with referential properties and not an expletive at all. He further subclassifies this latter as either anaphoric, in the case of "extraposition-it," which gets its reference from the extraposed clause, or non-anaphoric, as in the case of "weather-it," which has general situational ("umweltbezogen") reference. A similar distinction is argued for in Vikner 1995: ch. 6, who characterizes the es_2 type as "quasi-arguments," following Chomsky, and proposes, as does Leys, that they are simply pronouns assigned a semantic role by the verb.

Extending this distinction across the family provides us with a first parameter of variation in GMC expletives. Some GMC languages, like EN and standard DU, distinguish formally between the two types, having both overt 'it'-type quasi-arguments and 'there'-type expletives. Here as well goes DA, which uses *der* as a true expletive and *det* in quasi-argument roles:

(4.186)   a. Der findes løver i Afrika
there are-found lions in Africa
(DA, Allan *et al.* 1995: 160)

b. Der sidder en dame på sofaen
there sits a woman on sofa-the
(DA, Allan *et al.* 1995: 161)

c. Det forekommer, at...
it happens that...
(DA, Allan *et al.* 1995: 159)

d. Det hagler
it hails
(DA, Allan *et al.* 1995: 160)

SW, on the other hand, is of the single-form type, using *det* as the translational equivalent of both 'it' (in extraposition structures and weather sentences) and 'there' (in presentational sentences and impersonal passives).[31]

---

[31] Wolfram and Christian (1976: 125f.) report that Appalachian EN, among younger speakers, also appears to be leveling out the distinction between the two by replacing the 'there'-type expletive *they* with *it* – a usage also reported in the *American Heritage Dictionary* (2000: 929) – though see Montgomery and Chapman (1992: 630f.).

(i)   a. They's copperheads around here
(Appalachian EN, older speakers, Wolfram and Christian 1976: 125)
b. It was a fly in it
(younger speakers, Wolfram and Christian 1976: 126)

(4.187) a. Det kan bli tråkigt att vara hemmafru
  it can get boring to be housewife
  (SW, Holmes and Hinchcliffe 1994: 139)

 b. Det blixtrar
  it lightnings
  (SW, Holmes and Hinchcliffe 1994: 142)

 c. Det bor många svenskar i England
  it lives many Swedes in England
  (SW, Holmes and Hinchcliffe 1994: 140)

 d. Nu ska det arbetas
  now shall it be-worked
  (SW, Holmes and Hinchcliffe 1994: 310)

GO and OHG belong in this category too, in a trivial way; they fail to distinguish between the two types of expletive pronouns by virtue of having no overt expletive pronouns at all.

The situation in GE is slightly different. GE uses *es* in both functions, but the two can be told apart in that the pure expletive *es* (required when sentence initial) disappears when the conditions for its occurrence are not met, but the weather-*es* and the extraposition-*es* do not similarly alternate with zero. Modern DU was also of this sort until the seventeenth century, using *het* in impersonal passives and presentational sentences, as well as in extraposition constructions, in which uses it was subsequently replaced by *er*. (Leys notes that the earlier situation still persists in West Flemish.)

(4.188) a. Het is gecloppet
   it is knocked
   (Middle DU, Burridge 1992: 165)

  b. Het quam te me die aer
   it came to me the eagle
   (fourteenth-c. DU, Burridge 1992: 166)

We can introduce our second parameter of variation by reference to the last of the SW examples above. As we saw in examples in (4.184f), the pure expletive in GE impersonal passive constructions or presentational constructions is obligatorily omitted when the clause is topic-initial or a subordinate clause. On the other hand, the *det* in corresponding SW constructions is retained even when non-initial, as is the EN *there*. Faarlund (1990: 64f.) and Vikner (1995:70), as well as others, have proposed that this is because in some GMC languages (GE, YI, FA and IC), the pure expletive pronoun is an expletive topic, rather than an expletive subject. It is a placeholder for the topic position (the specifier of CP, in our assumed tree structure), in case no other argument is fronted to that slot. When a topic occupies that position, *es* has no role, and is therefore omitted. The "presentational" expletive in these languages also disappears when the verb comes at the front of the sentence in questions.

(4.189)   a. *Eru það mýs i buðkerinu?
             are það mice in bathtub-the?
             (IC, Faarlund 1990: 65, citing Thráinsson)

           b. *Waren es Mäuser in der Badewanne?
             were es mice in the bathtub?
             (GE)

Similarly, in subordinate clauses, the *es* also disappears, since GE does not generally allow topics in subordinate clauses:

(4.189)   c. *Ich weiß, daß es ein Junge gekommen ist
             I know that es a boy come is
             (GE, Vikner 1995: 70)

IC and YI are like GE in that the expletive appears in main clauses just in case no other element occupies the topic position:

(4.190)   a. *Nekhtn iz es gekumen a yingl
             yesterday is es come a boy
             (YI, Vikner 1995: 69)

           b. *Í gær hefur það komið strákur
             yesterday has það come boy
             'Yesterday there came a boy'
             (IC, Vikner 1995: 70)

Vikner observes, however, that, unlike GE, such expletives can also occur freely in subordinate clauses.

(4.190)   c. Ikh veys az es iz gekumen a yingl
             I know that es is come a boy
             (YI, Vikner 1995: 70)

           d. Ég veit að það hefur komið strákur
             I know that það has come boy
             (IC, Vikner 1995: 70)

4.9 The external syntax of noun phrases

Vikner claims, however, that this is because these languages differ from GE in that they freely allow topics in embedded clauses:

(4.190) e. Jonas tsveyfelt az morgen vet Miriam fri oyfshteyn
             Jonas doubts   that tomorrow will Mary   early get up
             (YI, Vikner 1995: 72)

         f. Jón efast um að á morgun fari María snemma á fætur
             Jon doubts about that tomorrow will-go María early on feet
             (IC, Vikner 1995: 72)

He cites this correspondence as further evidence that the *es* of YI and GE and the *það* of IC are all topic expletives, and not subject expletives. Ottósson (1989: 95), however, has challenged the claimed parallel between the distribution of *það* and the distribution of topics in IC. He points out that there are some kinds of subordinate clauses (adverbial clauses with 'if' and 'when', for example) which do not allow initial topics but which nonetheless allow expletive *það*. Ottósson concludes therefore (as do many subsequent investigators, e.g., Thráinsson 1996 and Bobaljik and Jonas 1996) that *það* and comparable expletives are subject expletives, occupying a subject position, rather than a topic position (though this leaves open the question of why they uniformly disappear in main clauses when there is an initial topic phrase).

For present purposes, I will remain neutral between these two analyses of *það*-type expletives, referring to them simply as instances of "S-initial expletives." GE, YI, FA and IC have overt S-initial expletives. Modern EN, DA and SW have overt expletives with the distribution of ordinary subjects. Earlier GMC, as represented by GO, OHG, and ON, had neither. The following table summarizes these results:

(4.191)

	S-initial expletive	Expletive subject	Quasi-argument
GO	0	0	0
OE	0?	0	hit
GE	es	0	es
YI	es	0	es
SW	0	det	det
DA	0	der	det
IC	það	0	það
DU	er	0	het
Older DU	het	0	het
Std. EN	0	there	it
Appal. EN	0	they/it	it

There seem to be cases in which a clause-initial expletive has developed or is in the process of developing into an ordinary subject expletive (or subject quasi-argument), which does not automatically delete when non-initial. Such developments are not surprising, since subjects, as well as topics, tend to be clause-initial in the general case. A development of this sort is documented by Faarlund (1990) in the history of Dano-Norwegian. ON had no expletives, but these emerged (*þer/der*, *det*) in the fifteenth century, where for several centuries they were restricted to clause-initial position before becoming obligatory in non-initial positions, and in subordinate clauses as well – that is, developing the distribution of ordinary subject expletives:

(4.192) a. som   viser   at   det ennu er adskillige ting
             which shows that it   still is several   things
             (Dano-NO, Faarlund 1990: 68)

Similarly, a number of investigators (Leys 1979: 30; Faarlund 1990: 65; Burridge 1992: 167; Barbier 1996) make note of the fact that Standard DU *er* is obligatory in initial position, like an S-initial expletive, but that it is possible, though optional, in non-initial position in main clauses, and in subordinate clauses, though judgments vary widely.

(4.192) b. wordt   (er) nog gedanst?
             becomes (it) still danced?
             (DU, Leys 1979: 30)

Roughly the same thing appears to be true of AF *daar*, which is usually, but not always, omitted when non-initial:

(4.192) c. In Quaqua is (daar) baie   arm   swartes
             in Quaqua is (there) a-lot-of poor blacks
             (AF, Donaldson 1993: 133)

Variable realization is also found in some languages in the case of "quasi-argument" pronominals – extraposition *it* and weather-*it*. As Vikner points out, weather-*it* can, but need not be, omitted when not needed to occupy the sentence-initial position in some GMC languages (YI, FA), but not others (EN, GE), while in still others (IC), it cannot appear at all when non-initial.

(4.193) a. Gestern   regnete es
             yesterday rained   it
             (GE, Vikner 1995: 226)

         b. Nekhtn   hot (es) geregnt
             yesterday has (it) rained
             (YI, Vikner 1995: 226)

c. Í gjár   regnaði (tað)
    yesterday rained (it)
    (FA, Lockwood 1964: 115)

d. Í gær   rigndi (*það)
    yesterday rained
    (IC, Vikner 1995: 226)

e. morgnar
    dawns
    (IC, Kress 1982: 223)

Similar variability in the omissibility of extraposition 'it' (which was overt even in some early GMC languages, such as OE and ON) is noted in Faarlund 1990: 72 and Vikner 1995: 226.

Finally, Vikner (1995: 229) points out that, in some GMC languages, there are certain contexts in which expletives and (extraposition) quasi-arguments overlap, and where either is possible. For example, it is possible in DA and in DU, but not in EN. Such alternations are considered at substantial length by Vikner (1995: ch. 7).

(4.194) a. Der/ det vides ikke, om det   passer
             it   is-known not if that is true
             (DA, Allan *et al.* 1995: 161)

         b. Er/ Het wordt   gezegd dat Jan ziek is
             it   becomes said   that Jan sick is
             (DU, Vikner 1995: 229)

4.9.2.1 *Definiteness and expletives*

There is variation across the GMC languages with respect to whether the "co-argument" of the expletive – the postverbal nominal phrase with which the verb agrees, in the usual case – must be definite or not, and the valency of the verb plays a role in this variation. EN *there* constructions exhibit the definiteness effect:

(4.195) a. There is a deer in the garden

         b. *There is the deer in the garden

The second of these sentences is unacceptable in most contexts, on the interpretation where *there* is an expletive, rather than a locative adverb. A similar definiteness effect is found in DU and in SW, where the co-argument of an expletive must be indefinite (Boeckx 2002: 48):

(4.195)   c. *Det har bara Johan inte kommit
there has only John not come
(SW, Boekx 2002: 48)

d. *Er is alleen Jan nie gekommen
there is only John not come
(DU, Boekx 2002: 48)

IC allows exceptions to the definiteness effect with unaccusative verbs (see Section 4.9.4.1.2.5), but not with transitive verbs.

(4.195)   e. Það skín alltaf sólinn
there shone always sun-the
(IC, Boekx 2002: 48)

f. *Það hefur adeins Jón ekki lesið þessa bók
there has only John not read this book
(IC, Boekx 2002: 47)

In GE, on the other hand, the definiteness effect is absent even with transitive verbs.

(4.195)   g. Es kommt der Pfarrer
it comes the minister
(GE, Boekx 2002: 46)

h. Es hat nur Hans dieses Buch nicht gelesen
there has only Hans this book not read
(GE, Boekx 2002: 47)

4.9.2.2   Valency and expletives

The distribution of the expletive subject *there* in EN is particularly restricted. In Modern EN, it is fully natural only with the copula 'be' (but not the passive auxiliary 'be'). Its appearance with other unaccusative verbs (Section 4.9.4.1.2.5), primarily with 'coming into being' meanings (*arise, come, appear*) is archaic. In the remaining GMC languages with overt expletives, they occur relatively freely with both passive and unaccusative predicates:

(4.196)   a. at tað bleiv etið eitt súrepli
that there became eaten an apple
(FA, Vikner 1995: 202)

b. at der er kommet en dreng
that there is come a boy
(DA, Vikner 1995: 197)

However, these languages split on the point of whether expletives are allowed in active transitive sentences. IC and YI, for example, allow this possibility (as does one dialect of FA: Jonas 1996a, 1996b).

(4.196) c. az es hot imitser gegesn an epl
that there has someone eaten an apple
(YI, Vikner 1995: 189)

d. að það hefur einhver borðað epli
that there has someone eaten apple
(IC, Vikner 1995: 189)

On the other hand, DA, SW and a second dialect of FA do not allow this:

(4.196) e. *at der har nogen spist et æble
that there has someone eaten the apple
(DA, Vikner 1995: 189)

The occurrence or non-occurrence of the expletive across the GMC languages in constructions of different valency is discussed in detail in Vikner 1995: 187ff. and in Bobaljik and Jonas 1996. The possibility/impossibility of expletives in active transitive constructions like those above (that is, of "transitive expletive constructions" (TECs), as they have generally come to be known) has received particular attention in recent years, focussing on identifying and explaining its typological correlates. So, for example, Bobaljik and Jonas (1996), following Bures (1993), propose that TECs are possible only in those GMC languages with object shift of NPs (see Section 4.8.1.2.1), and develop a theoretical explanation for this. Jonas (1996b) relates the possibility of TECs to verb movement possibilities, and Thráinsson (1996) relates both to the verbal morphology – particularly to whether tense and agreement may be realized as separate morphemes attached to the verb, as in IC *reyk-t-i* 'smoke-Past-1Sg', or not, as in EN *smoke-s/smok-ed*, where we get agreement or tense, but not both at once. All of these investigators conclude that the TEC phenomenon exists in some languages but not others because in some languages the syntax makes available an inner and an outer layer of clausal structure, each of which has a subject position; the thematic subject of a transitive sentence occurs in the innermost of these, with an expletive as the "outer subject." In other languages, on the other hand, one of these subject positions is not available and expletive subjects cannot co-occur with thematic subjects in transitive structures. The interested reader is referred to the works cited for details of the various analyses.

4.9.2.3 *Agreement with expletives*

In intransitive passive constructions with expletive subjects, there are no other nominals in the sentence with which the inflected verb could agree, and the verb appears in

236   4 The Germanic nominal system

third person singular form, which is arguably either default agreement or agreement with the expletive. However, in constructions in which the expletive has a "co-argument" – the object of the passive or unaccusative verb (Section 4.9.4.1.2.5) or the thematic subject of a TEC – it is generally this co-argument, not the expletive, which controls agreement (Vikner 1995: 181f.).

(4.197)   Es   sind   drei   Autos   draußen
            there   are   three   cars   outside
            (GE, Vikner 1995: 181)

4.9.3 Subjects in imperative clauses

There are crosslinguistic differences, and even differences within languages, in whether the subject is expressed in imperative sentences. In GE, the second person singular familiar imperative typically has no overt subject, while the subject must be expressed in second person formal/plural imperatives:

(4.198)   a.   Komm!   Kommen Sie!
                 come! (FamSg)   come! (FormSg)

In IC, subjects are expressed in all imperatives except first person plural (Kress 1982: 142). When the subject is expressed, there are crosslinguistic differences in its position. It follows the verb in GE, IC, FR, DA and Irish EN, for example, but precedes in standard EN (aside from archaic formulae like "Hear ye!"). More generally, as König (1996: 33) notes, imperative verbs come later in the clause in EN than in other languages, being able to follow manner adverbs, for example.

(4.198)   b.   You wait here!
                 (EN)

            c.   harkje jo ris nei my
                 listen you to   me
                 (FR, Tiersma 1999: 98)

There are, however, dialects of EN, including Belfast EN, in which the subjects of imperative clauses follow even lexical verbs:

(4.198)   d.   Tell you the truth!
                 (Belfast EN, Henry 1996: 83)

            e.   Throw it you to me
                 (Belfast EN, Henry 1996: 84)

Note the order of object and subject in the last of these examples, which Henry interprets as involving object shift of the sort mentioned in Section 4.8.1.2.1. Haegeman (1995: 123) observes that in West Flemish, full pronominal subjects can occur in imperatives, but subject clitics cannot:

(4.198)   f.   Goa (*je)/ (gie) mo!
               go *clitic you but
               (West Flemish, Haegeman 1995: 123)

4.9.4   Derived subjects and the syntax of voice

The term "passive" is used in a systematically ambiguous way. On the one hand, it is a category of verbal inflection (or its periphrastic equivalent). I refer, for example, to passive forms of verbs. Those aspects of passive relating to how it is expressed in the verbal system are treated in Section 5.4.1. In addition to that status, however, passive can also be viewed as an operation affecting the ways in which the syntactic arguments of a predicate are realized in grammatical structure, and, in particular, the realization of its subject. It is this aspect of passive which warrants its discussion in the present section on subjects, where it will be considered alongside a number of other alternations in the realization of subjects, including the following:

Middle Voice Constructions:

(4.199)   a. He sells these books ~ These books sell well

Unaccusative Constructions:

(4.199)   b. She broke the glass ~ The glass broke

Raising Constructions:

(4.199)   c. That he is crazy is likely ~ He is likely to be crazy

"Tough-movement" constructions:

(4.199)   d. It is difficult to follow his ideas ~ His ideas are difficult to follow

4.9.4.1 *Passive*
Aside from function words, the following two sentences have the same lexical items, and they have the same truth value:

(4.200)   a. The house was destroyed by the earthquake

             b. The earthquake destroyed the house

The synonymy of these sentences, the fact that they contain the same lexical items, and the fact that they are representative of a vast number of similar pairs, related to each other in the same systematic way, has led most models of linguistic description to posit a "rule" of passive, which derives sentences like (4.200a) from sentences like (4.200b), or at least gives a general statement of the correspondences. In particular, we note three correspondences here. The subject of the active sentence is not the subject of the passive sentence. Rather, it is expressed, if at all, as the object of a preposition. Second, the direct object of the active sentence corresponds to the subject of the passive sentence. Finally, the passive sentence involves more morphology, including a passive auxiliary which is identical to the predicative verb 'be'.

Several decades of attempts at pinning down the exact nature of these operations and the relationships among them have not produced any universal agreement. Controversies have arisen about such questions as the extent to which the component operations are a lexical as opposed to a syntactic matter, the extent to which they are interdependent (that is, whether "demotion" of the subject of the active sentence and the "promotion" of the object of the active sentence necessarily co-occur), and why languages vary with respect to which arguments can be realized as the subjects of passive sentences, as we will see below. Again, given the basically descriptive goals of this work I will sidestep most of the theoretical questions and focus on the facts of structural correspondences and variation in passive sentences across the GMC languages. Also left out of the discussion will be stylistic questions involving crosslinguistic differences in the frequency of passive constructions, alternatives to the use of passives, and the like. I will take the case described above, in which the direct object of the passive sentence corresponds to the subject of its active counterpart and the subject of the active sentence corresponds to a prepositional agent phrase in the passive sentence, as the core case of passive, and discuss crosslinguistic variation around this core in the following sections.

4.9.4.1.1 **The expression of the passive agent** There is considerable variation in the prepositions used to mark the "logical subject" of passive sentences. The main parameter along which they differ involves whether there is a single, uniform preposition for all "logical subjects," regardless of their exact semantic roles, or whether preposition choice is conditioned by the semantic role of the logical subject. GO normally employs *fram* for agents and *þairh* for instrumental subjects. There are a few instances involving experiencer subjects with verbs of perception in which a bare dative NP is employed, without a preposition.

(4.201) a. ei   hauhjaidau   sunus gudis   þairh   þata
            that might-be-elevated son   of-God through that
            (GO, John 11:4)

b. ei gaumjaindau   mannam
   that they-might-be-noticed men-Dat
   (GO, Matt. 6:3)

The independence of these from the Greek model cannot be established. OE employs *mid, þurh, fram*, which were supplanted by *of/by* in ME (Visser 1963: 2176ff.). Modern EN, for the most part, uses *by*, without regard to the semantic role of the logical subject. Standard GE, prescriptively at least, distinguishes between *von* for logical subjects with agent and experiencer roles, *durch* for logical subjects with instrumental roles or secondary agent roles, and *mit* for logical subjects with instrumental roles.

(4.201)   c. (*)Das Schiff wurde von einem Torpedo versenkt
              the   ship   was   by a   torpedo sunk
              (GE, Berger *et al.* 1972: 505)

DU, on the other hand, uses *door* for agents as well as instruments.

(4.201)   d. Het raam   werd door hem gewassen
              the window was   by   him washed
              (DU, Donaldson 1981: 161)

Continental Scandinavian uses *av/af*, again without apparent sensitivity to the semantic role of the subject. IC also uses *af* (Sigurðsson 1989: 268), though agents are only rarely expressed in passive sentences, since passives are generally used in order to leave the actor unexpressed (Kress 1982: 150; Bandle *et al.* 2002: 943).[32]

4.9.4.1.2 **Passive voice and argument structure** In the canonical instance, represented in examples (4.200a-b) above, the predicate of a passive sentence is a transitive verb. The direct object of the active sentence corresponds to the subject of the passive sentence, while the subject of the active sentence is realized as the object of a

---

[32] So central is the non-expression of the agent in IC that Kress (1982: 150) refers to it as the "Anonymum" voice. Kress and Sigurðsson (1989: 268) report that IC passives imply agency and intentionality more strongly than other GMC passives, and are avoided when the action is not intentional. Thus, the IC equivalent of (i) is impossible (ii):

(i)   Peter wurde in einem Unfall   getötet
        Peter was   in an   accident killed
(ii)   ??Pétur var drepinn í slysi
        Peter   was killed in accident
        (IC, Sigurðsson 1989: 268)

preposition in the corresponding passive sentence. However, individual languages exhibit a more extensive range of correspondences.

4.9.4.1.2.1 *Passives of ditransitive sentences* Pairs of sentences like the following might give the impression that it is also possible for a (prepositionally marked) indirect object in an active sentence to correspond to the subject of the related passive sentence.

(4.202)   a. I gave the books to him ~ He was given the books

This appearance is illusory, however. In EN, such "indirect passives" are limited to those ditransitive verbs which can alternatively participate in double object constructions (DOCs) such as (4.202b). Thus, *donate* allows neither the DOC nor indirect passives (4.202c) (see Section 4.1.2.3.1).

(4.202)   b. I gave the boy a book

                c. They donated the money to the church

                d. *They donated the church the money

                e. *The church was donated the money

Similarly, NO has both DOCs and indirect passives (as do DA, with restrictions (Allan *et al.* 1995: 306, 315) and SW (Holmes and Hinchcliffe 1994: 497; Herslund 1986)).[33]

(4.202)   f. Jeg har gitt mannen en bok
                    I have given man-the a book

                g. Mannen ble gitt a bok
                    man-the is given a book

                h. En bok ble gitt mannen
                    a book is given man-the
                    (NO, Sprouse 1989: 259)

---

[33] NO offers yet another possibility: both objects may remain in place after the verb, and the subject position can be occupied by an expletive. Compare also Åfarli (1992: 60ff).

     (i)   Det ble gitt ham en bok
                 there was given him a book
                 (Sprouse 1989: 259)

The implicational relationship between DOCs and indirect passives holds in one direction only, though. In DA, for example, not all active double object sentences correspond to well-formed indirect passives:

(4.202)   i. *Jeg blev fortalt nyheden
              I   was told the news
              (DA, Allan *et al.* 1995: 315)

          j. *Hun blev givet et ur
              he   was given a watch
              (DA, Allan *et al.* 1995: 315)

Similarly, FR and DU have DOCs but no indirect passives (Tiersma 1999: 94, 101; Donaldson 1981: 163).

In languages such as IC, which maintain an accusative/dative case distinction, the two objects are differently marked. The IO receives dative case.

(4.203)   a. Ég gaf barninu   bókina
             I gave child-the-Dat book-the-Acc
             (IC, Sprouse 1989: 272)

In IC passive sentences involving such ditransitive verbs, either object can appear in clause-initial position.

(4.203)   b. Barninu   var gefin bókin
             child-the-Dat was given book-the-Nom
             (IC)

          c. Bókin   var gefin barninu
             book-the was given child-the-Dat
             (IC)

When the indirect object is fronted in such passive sentences, it does not assume the usual morphological markings of subjects. It remains dative and fails to control verb agreement. Nonetheless, Sprouse (1989) and many others (Andrews 1990; Cole *et al.* 1980; Zaenen, Maling and Thráinsson 1990, for example) have claimed that sentences like (4.203b) are in fact instances of indirect passive, and that *barninu* is a subject, in spite of its oblique case – a claim based on diagnostics like those advanced in Section 4.1.2.4. For example, such dative arguments can be the missing arguments in "unspecified subject" constructions like the following – a possibility characteristically restricted to subject arguments:

(4.203) d. [[] að vera gefnir ambáttir]   var mikill heiður
          to be   given   servants-NOM was great honor
          (IC, Zaenen, Maling and Thráinsson 1990: 113)

There is also a certain degree of variation with respect to whether the second object in DOCs can be made subject of the corresponding passive sentences. While some speakers of EN admit sentences like (4.203e), others do not. Sprouse (1989: 255) characterizes it as a distinction between American and British EN.[34] For an interesting analysis of this difference, see Dryer 1986: 832ff.

(4.203)   e. (*) The book was given Mary / her

4.9.4.1.2.2 *Prepositional passives* EN and continental Scandinavian (excluding DA, Vikner 1995: 246) deviate from the majority pattern in GMC in allowing objects of certain prepositions in active sentences to become the subjects of the corresponding passive sentences.

(4.204) a. Jon vart   tala   om/ Jon tales   om
            Jon became talked about/Jon is-talked about
            (NO, Åfarli 1992: 18)

         b. Marit blir glodd på
            Marit is   gazed at
            (Åfarli 1992: 19)

         c. This idea was argued about

         d. Han skrattas åt
            he is laughed at
            (SW, Haugen 1976: 379)

---

[34] Perhaps related to this is the fact that, in Modern GE, either of the two normally accusative objects of *lehren* 'teach' may become the subject of the passive sentence but, when the notional direct object is made into the subject, the notional indirect object shows up not in its usual accusative case, but in dative.

(i)   Ich   wurde die französische Sprache   gelehrt
          I-Nom   was   the French   language-Acc taught
          (Berger *et al.* 1972: 505)
(ii)   Mir   wurde die französische Sprache   gelehrt
          me-Dat was   the French   language-Acc taught
          (Berger *et al.* 1972: 505)

I will refer to these as prepositional passives, rather than adopt the widespread but infelicitous label "pseudopassive" for them.

In general, the prepositional phrase must be a complement of the verb, rather than an adverbial adjunct:

(4.204) e. *Operasjonen ble dødd etter
             operation-the 'became' died after
             (NO, Christensen 1986: 155)

There is crosslinguistic variation in whether it must also be adjacent to the verb:

(4.204) f. ??The book was paid twice for

         g. Boken ble betalt to ganger for
             book-the became paid twice for
             (NO, Christensen 1986: 156)

         h. Babyen blir skifta bleier på
             baby-the becomes changed nappies on
             (NO, Åfarli, 1992: 18)

These sorts of passives are not found elsewhere in GMC, even in languages (IC, DA and OE) which allow preposition stranding in other constructions such as relative clauses and topicalization constructions, for example.[35]

The fact that EN did not admit such passives until ME times, after it had lost object case distinctions and developed VO word order, coupled with the fact that NO and SW, which also allow prepositional passives, also exhibit these properties, lends some initial plausibility to the frequent claim that these characteristics are typologically connected to the possibility of prepositional passives, though as DA demonstrates, these are at best necessary, not sufficient conditions. See Vikner 1995: 246f. on this and related differences between DA and SW.

---

[35] For OE, see Thornburg 1984. Examples like the following from IC are not counterexamples; as Maling and Zaenen (1990) argue, it is topicalization of the object of the preposition, not passive, which strands the preposition here, since such constructions are systematically disallowed in contexts which do not allow topic-initial clauses.

(i) Þessa konu er oftast talað vel um
     that woman is often spoken well of
     (IC, Maling and Zaenen 1990: 155)

4.9.4.1.2.3 *Non-local passives* In all of the examples treated to this point, the subject of the passive clause is a semantic argument of the verb of the passive clause. In sentences like the following, however, the subject of the passive clause is not understood to be related semantically to the verb of that clause, but rather to be an argument of the infinitival verb. What is believed is not "he" but the proposition "He is a liar".

(4.205)   a. He is believed by many to be a liar

I will refer to these cases, in which the subject of a passive verb in a main clause is understood to be a semantic argument of the verb of the infinitive clause, as "non-local passives," since the passive subject is not part of the argument structure of the predicate of its clause. Descriptively, they are found only with those main verbs which admit "Accusative-with-Infinitive" (AcI) constructions of the sort discussed in Section 4.9.5.2.

(4.205)   b. Many believe him to be a liar

Thus, they are found only in languages which have such AcI constructions, like EN and IC (see Fagan 1992: 108f.), and not languages like GE, which lack AcI.

(4.205)   c. Komumenn sögðu konunginn   (vera) dauðan
           newcomers said   king-the-Acc to be dead
           (IC, Kress 1982: 246)

       d. Konungurinn var sagður (vera) dauður
          king-the-Nom was said   to be dead
          (IC, Kress 1982: 246)

       e. *Thomas wurde geglaubt am Leben zu sein
          Thomas was   believed alive to be
          (GE, Fagan 1992: 108)

One rather striking variant on this pattern is the so-called complex passive of NO (primarily BN – Bandle *et al.* 2005: 1592). These constructions, frequent in legal and bureaucratic styles, involve a "double passive"; the subject of the passive main verb is the logical object of a dependent past/passive participle of a transitive (4.205f, g) or unaccusative verb (4.205h). (See Section 4.9.4.1.2.5 for a discussion of unaccusatives.)

(4.205)   f. Møtet   ventes   holdt
             meeting-the is-expected held
             (NO, Engh 1984)

g. Boken ble forsøkt anbefalt oversatt
book the became attempted recommended translated
'It was attempted to recommend that the book be translated'
(NO, Christensen 1986: 136)

h. Fjellklatrerne ble meldt omkommet
mountain-climbers-the were reported perished
(NO, Christensen 1986: 161)

These constructions, dating back to at least the thirteenth century, according to Engh, are discussed in Engh 1984, Christensen 1985, 1986, Taraldsen 1984 and Hellan 1984.

4.9.4.1.2.4 *Impersonal passives* In the core case of passive described above, the object of an active sentence appears as the subject of the corresponding passive sentence. Some languages, though, admit passive sentences in which the object of the verb appears to remain in complement position, rather than becoming the subject, and the subject position is either unrepresented or represented by an expletive. This is in fact the normal case across the GMC languages when the object is a clause:

(4.206) a. Það var mér sagt, að þessi hjón hefðu tekið barnið
it was to-me said that this couple have taken child-the
af góðvilja
out-of kind-heartedness
(IC, Kress 1982: 238)

However, even nominal objects sometimes remain objects in passive sentences, rather than becoming subjects. This is the case, for example, in GE with lexically marked (dative or genitive) sole objects of verbs like *helfen* 'help':

(4.206) b. Es wurde dem Kind selten geholfen
it was the child-Dat seldom helped
(GE)

Compare also the following GO example:

(4.206) c. jah bajoþum gabairgada
and both-Dat save-Pass-3Sg
'and both will be saved' (Greek has nominative)
(GO, Matt. 9:17)

Passives of this sort, lacking a referential subject, are often referred to as impersonal passives. In GE, accusative objects cannot similarly remain accusative objects in passive constructions; rather, such objects must become the nominative subject of the passive construction. This is not universally true in GMC, however. Passives in which an object without lexical case remains an object in a passive sentence are described systematically for NO (BN and NN) by Åfarli (1992), but the phenomenon appears to exist in other continental Scandinavian languages (cf. Allan *et al.* 1995: 161 for DA; Thorell 1973: 202 for SW), and in IC (Barðdal and Molnár 2000). Thus, in NO, for example, a direct object may become the subject in a passive sentence, or it may remain postverbal, the subject position then being represented by the expletive *det*.

(4.206)   d. Ein mann vart sett
               a   man was seen
               (NO, Åfarli 1992: 81)

               e. Det vart sett ein mann
               it   was seen a   man
               (NO, Åfarli 1992: 80)

               f. Ein medalje vart gitt   soldaten
               a   medal   was given soldier-the
               (NO, Åfarli 1992: 86)

               g. Soldaten   vart gitt   ein medalje
               soldier-the was given a   medal
               (NO, Åfarli 1992: 86)

               h. Det vart gitt   soldaten   ein medalje
               it   was given soldier-the a   medal
               (NO, Åfarli 1992: 86)

There is a definiteness condition on the impersonal passive construction in NO: the direct object (in the case of ditransitive sentences such as (4.206e), the second object) must be indefinite (Åfarli 1992: 69). The non-movement passives of IC, on the other hand, seem not to be subject to such a condition (Barðdal and Molnár 2000: 110).

Åfarli points out that, in those varieties of NO with concord between the subject and the passive participle, the agreement evidence supports the claim that the expletive pronoun is indeed the subject of the impersonal passive construction, as the following examples show:

(4.207)   a. Ein mann   vart skoten
               a   man-MSg was shot-MSg
               (NN, Åfarli 1992: 91)

               b. Det vart skote/*skoten   ein mann
               it   was shot-NSg/*shot-MSg a   man
               (NN, Åfarli 1992: 92)

4.9.4.1.2.5 *Intransitive passives and the unaccusative hypothesis* A further deviation from the core case described above involves passives formed on apparently intransitive verbs which, in their active uses, do not appear with a nominal object at all. In these cases, the subject position, if realized at all, must once again be realized by an expletive, since there is no object to be turned into a subject by passive.

(4.208)   a. der waard hjir altyd dûnse
              there was here always danced
              (FR, Tiersma 1999: 100)

Intransitive passives of this sort are recent. They do not seem to have existed in older GMC, being attested for the first time in GE, for example, only from the end of the OHG period (Dal 1966: 130). They are nonetheless surprisingly widespread in West and North GMC – though notably absent in pre-modern and Modern EN, a state of affairs which leads one to suspect crosslinguistic diffusion. The following are some examples:

(4.208)   b. Það var barist
              it was fought
              (IC, Kress 1982: 151)

              c. Der festedes til kl. 2
              there was-partied until 2:00
              (DA, Allan *et al.* 1995: 315)

              d. Es wird hier nicht geschlafen
              it becomes here not slept
              (GE)

              e. Daar is gelag
              there is laughed
              (AF, Ponelis 1993: 256)

              f. Det sjöngs och dansades hela natten
              it was-sung and was-danced all night
              (SW, Holmes and Hinchcliffe 1994: 317)

              g. Jitz wird g' gässen u nid gschwätzt!
              now becomes eaten and not talked!
              (Bern GE, Hodler 1969: 473)

              h. Es vert gəzungən
              It becomes sung
              (YI, Jacobs 2005: 260)

4 *The Germanic nominal system*

The syntax of these intransitive passive constructions has been most extensively debated by reference to DU, because that happens to have been the language cited in an influential paper by Perlmutter (1978), who pointed out, as had others, that not all active sentences traditionally considered to be intransitive correspond to well-formed passive sentences. The examples in (4.209) are acceptable, while the ones in (4.210) are not.

(4.209) a. Door de kinderen wordt (er) op het ijs geschaatst
by the children becomes (there) on the ice skated
'It is skated by the children on the ice'
(DU, Perlmutter 1978: 157)

b. Er wordt hier door de jonge lui veel gedanst
it becomes here by the young people much danced
(DU, Perlmutter 1978: 168)

c. Er wordt in deze kamer vaak geslapen
it becomes in this room often slept
(DU, Perlmutter 1978: 168)

d. In de zomer wordt er hier vaak gezwommen
in the summer becomes it here often swum
(DU, Perlmutter 1978: 170)

(4.210) a. *In det weeshuis wordt er door de kinderen erg snel gegroeid
in this orphanage becomes there by the children very fast grown
(DU, Perlmutter 1978: 169)

b. *Er werd door het concert een hele tijd geduurd
it is by   the concert a long time lasted
(DU, Perlmutter 1978: 169)

c. *In de zomer wordt er hier vaak verdronken
in the summer becomes it here often drowned
(Perlmutter 1978: 171)

There seem to be some general semantic differences between those verbs which participate in intransitive passives and those which do not. Verbs in the former category include verbs describing willed, volitional actions, such as 'work', 'play', 'laugh', plus some involuntary bodily processes (e.g., 'sleep'). Verbs in the latter category include in the main verbs which describe non-volitional occurrences and states, including verbs whose sole argument has the semantic role of patient ('sink', 'float', 'fall', 'drown', 'roll', 'boil' and so on), and verbs which describe the coming into being or continuation of a state ('exist', 'come', 'happen', 'begin', 'disappear', 'remain' and so on). The difference between the two groups is brought out very saliently by the contrast between (4.209d) and (4.210c).

Similar contrasts are found in other languages with intransitive passives, as the following NO examples indicate:

(4.211)   a. Det blir   ropa   (frå skogen)
                it   becomes shouted (from wood-the)
                (NO, Åfarli 1992: 107)

            b. *Det vart   falle (av bladet)
                it   became fallen (by leaf-the)
                (NO, Åfarli 1992: 18)

Perlmutter's conclusion, however, is that the distinction between those apparent intransitive verbs which allow passivization and those which do not is not best characterized in semantic terms, but in syntactic terms. The sole arguments of verbs like 'fall', which bear the thematic role of patient, are not basic subjects. Rather, they start out as direct objects and are "promoted" into the subject role. Perlmutter labels these two groups of verbs "unergatives" and "unaccusatives" respectively, and calls the hypothesis of such a partitioning the "unaccusative hypothesis."

Providing general support for the unaccusative hypothesis is the fact that many of the verbs in the unaccusative category alternate with formally identical transitive verbs, and the argument which appears as the sole argument of the former shows up as the direct object of the latter:

(4.212)   a. The ball rolled down the hill

            b. The boy rolled the ball down the hill

(These sorts of alternations between transitives and intransitives with no difference in grammatical shape are a fairly recent development in the GMC languages, and thus another convergent feature. See Streitberg 1920: 191, though, for some isolated examples of intransitive uses of generally transitive verbs even in GO.)

Arguing more specifically for the unaccusative hypothesis in GMC is the following fact about NO. We have seen in Section 4.9.4.1.2.4 that in passives in NO involving transitive verbs, the direct object may remain in place, and the subject can be realized as an expletive *det*. Similarly, it turns out, the sole arguments of apparent intransitive verbs of the unaccusative type can also appear postverbally in the position typical of

250   4 *The Germanic nominal system*

direct objects, with *det* in the subject position. However, the sole arguments of verbs of the unergative type cannot:[36]

(4.213)　　a. Det veltar　　ein vase
　　　　　　　there overturns a　vase
　　　　　　　(NO, Åfarli 1992: 105)

　　　　　　b. Det brann　eit hus
　　　　　　　there burned a　house
　　　　　　　(NO, Åfarli 1992: 105)

　　　　　　c. *Det tenkte　berre ein mann
　　　　　　　there thought only one man
　　　　　　　(NO, Åfarli 1992: 89)

Moreover, as pointed out in Bandle *et al.* 2005: 1588, in NO, a nonfinite unaccusative verb and a following "subject" argument can move to the front of the clause as a single constituent – a possibility normally reserved for verbs and their objects.

(4.213)　　d. [Komme gjester] gjorde det aldri
　　　　　　　come　　guests　did　it　never
　　　　　　　'No guests ever came'
　　　　　　　(NO, Bandle *et al.* 2005: 1588)

Given this unaccusative hypothesis, the contrast between (4.209) and (4.210) can be stated, for our present descriptive purposes, as follows: unergative (basic intransitive) verbs can form intransitive passives, but unaccusative verbs (those whose subject originates as a object) cannot, since they are not intransitive.

Other diagnostics have been suggested as distinguishing between unaccusative verbs and unergative verbs. For example, the latter, but not the former, can form *-er* nominals in GE:

---

[36] This is not entirely unproblematic, as Åfarli (1992: 104) shows in the following correspondences. He claims (p. 130), though, that (ii) describes an event not an action, and suggests that the external argument (subject) of the transitive has been "internalized" (made into an object) here because it is understood as a theme (see also Askedal 1996).

(i)　　　　En bjørn angriper en sau
　　　　　a　bear attacks　a sheep
(ii)　　　　Det　angriper en bjørn
　　　　　there attacks　a　bear

(4.214) a. Arbeiter, Tänzer, Denker
worker, dancer, thinker
(GE, Grewendorf 1989: 22)

b. *Ankommer, *Faller, *Wachser
arriver, faller, grower

However, numerous researchers have pointed out "mismatches" in the results of the various proposed diagnostics. For detailed discussion of unaccusativity in GMC, the interested reader is referred to Hoekstra 1984, Grewendorf 1989, Shannon 1990, Fagan 1992: 118ff. and Askedal 1996. Some investigators have called into question Perlmutter's claim that the division between the two classes of single-argument verbs is a syntactic one, and semantically based alternatives to the unaccusative hypothesis have been advanced (see Zaenen 1985, Shannon 1987 and Fagan 1992: 122ff.)

4.9.4.2 Middle voice constructions

The term "middle voice" is used to refer to (at least) two semantically different types of construction: one expressing self-directed action (*I washed*) and one expressing (the possibility of) action on the subject by an implied but unexpressed agent (*These books sell well*). The two are very different in the distribution of their argument roles and in other respects. In the first example, the subject is understood to bear the thematic role of actor (as well as patient). In the second sentence, the subject is understood to bear the patient/theme role of the verb, and the actor is unexpressed – in fact, unexpressible. The use of the label "middle" to refer to two such different constructions is well established, and, in any case, the fact that they are expressed in similar ways across languages, and the fact that they arise historically by the same developments, both suggest that the two are connected in some way. (For one attempt at conflating them, see Kissock 1997.) So, for example, in IC, both types of "middle" constructions involve the use of the *-st* suffix, which arose from a reflexive pronoun:[37]

(4.215) a. Ég klæddist
I   dress-ST
'I dressed'
(IC, Sigurðsson 1989: 260)

---

[37] There are numerous other uses of the *-st* suffix too (according to Sigurðsson, "astonishingly many") which are catalogued in Sigurðsson 1989: 258–263. What seems to unite them is detransitivization/loss of a nominal theme argument.

(4.215)   b. úrið   týndist
           watch-the lose-ST
           'The watch got lost'
           (Sigurðsson 1989: 269)

For the sake of keeping them separate, I have designated these Type I and Type II middles respectively, the difference being whether the subject of the construction is understood as the logical subject and object of the base verb (Type I), or the logical object alone (Type II). Type I appears to be of GMC antiquity (see Streitberg 1920: 192 and Kemmer 1993: 182 for evidence from GO). Type II apparently emerges later, in individual languages. Of concern here will be primarily Type II. It will be seen, however, that this coarse typology greatly under-represents the diversity of middle constructions in GMC. The IC middle voice construction represented in (4.215a) has syntactic and semantic properties which are very different from those of EN middles. EN middles, in fact, represent a type with a number of characteristic semantic properties which are shared by middle constructions in GE and DU, but not found as a cluster elsewhere in GMC. I will refer to this special type as the West GMC middle construction, without wishing to imply any historical relation among its various instances. In fact, the cluster of properties defining the West GMC middle appears to be of rather late, postmedieval origin, not occurring in EN until the fifteenth century, for example. To the extent that these languages resemble each other, therefore, we seem to be dealing with yet another convergent feature. In the following section, I will discuss the properties of the West GMC middle. I will then go on to contrast its properties with the very different properties of IC middles, as described in Sigurðsson 1989.

4.9.4.2.1 Semantic and syntactic restrictions on West Germanic middles

West GMC middle voice constructions share with passives, and with the unaccusative predicates discussed in Section 4.9.4.1.2.5, certain common valency-changing properties. In core cases, a logical object of a transitive verb appears as its syntactic subject.

(4.216)   a. Diese Tür öffnet sich leicht
             this   door opens self easily
             'This door opens easily'
             (GE Middle)

          b. Diese Tür wird (leicht) geöffnet
             this   door becomes   opened
             (GE Passive)

          c. Diese Tür öffnet sich
             'This door opens'
             (GE Unaccusative)

The points of connection do not stop there. Middles and unaccusatives tend to be encoded formally in the same way in individual languages, as illustrated by examples (4.216a) and (4.216c). In languages like GE, where middle verbs have reflexives, unaccusatives tend to as well, while in languages like EN and DU, where middles are expressed as bare verbs, without reflexives, unaccusatives also lack reflexives. It also seems to be the case that those languages which allow passives of intransitive verbs also allow middle voice constructions to be formed from intransitive verbs. Sentences like (4.217a) and (4.217b) are possible, therefore, in GE and DU, though not in EN.

(4.217)   a. Hier lebt es sich gut
           here lives it self well
           'One can live well here'
           (GE Intransitive Middle)

          b. Het werkt prettig op deze kamer
           it works nicely in this room
           (Fagan 1992: 250)
           (DU Intransitive Middle)

The characteristics that set West GMC middle constructions apart from these other similar voice constructions include, saliently, first, that middle voice constructions never allow overt expression of the "demoted" subject as an "agent phrase" (in contrast with passives), and second, that on the other hand, the logical subject, though not overtly expressed, is implied in middle constructions but is not implied in unaccusative constructions. Middles can consequently be freely formed on verbs, such as 'read', which cannot occur spontaneously but require an animate actor/experiencer (4.218d) while such verbs resist unaccusative formation (4.218e):

(4.218)   a. The glass was broken by the vandals

          b. The glass breaks easily (*by the vandals)

          c. The glass broke

          d. The book reads easily

          e. *The book read

West GMC middle voice constructions exhibit a cluster of other characteristic semantic and syntactic restrictions, which are discussed in detail in Fagan 1992. First, in these languages, middle constructions are not reports of events, but predications of general properties of the subject. Example (4.218b), for example, attributes the property of fragility to the glass. It does not assert that it has been (or will be) broken. From this fact follow a number of individual properties. First, middles carry an implication of modality. That is, they can typically be paraphrased as passives with the modal 'can' ('These books read easily' = 'These books can be easily read') (Fagan 1992: 19). Second, the subject of the middle must have characteristics which facilitate carrying out the action described by the verb. As such, they are anomalous in cases where the possibility of carrying out the action of the verb on the subject is not subject to substantial influence by the characteristics of the subject. Thus, for example, 'The glass breaks/cleans easily' is well formed, because glass can have properties which affect its breakability or cleansibility, but '??The glass buys/admires easily' is odd because glass does not have obvious properties which would affect its buyability or admirability. Fagan (1992: 76) refers to this requirement of the subjects of middles as "responsibility." Thus, middles are restricted lexically in a way that passives are not.

Perhaps connected with this is the requirement that middle constructions contain, implicitly or explicitly, a manner element – an element which answers the question of how the action is carried out. This can be expressed by means of an adverb, like *well* or *easily*, for example, or it can be a *by*-phrase expressing means, as in (4.219a) or, as Fagan points out, it can be implicit in the verb, as in (4.219b), which is possible because *button* inherently describes a particular manner of fastening, which contrasts with others:

(4.219) a. This jar opens by pulling the tab

b. This dress buttons

Also connected with the fact that they express a general, timeless property of the subject is the fact that the implied actor/logical subject must be interpreted as arbitrary in reference, rather than referring to a specific unidentified individual.

In addition to these restrictions which are more or less organically linked to the meaning of the middle construction in these languages, Fagan proposes that the verbs which admit middle formation in GE, DU and EN are restricted in terms of verbal aspect. Verbs describing states (*know*, *own*, *hate* and so on) do not form middles:

(4.220) a. *This story believes easily

b. *Die Antwort weiß   sich   nicht leicht
the   answer   knows 'self' not   easily
(GE, Fagan 1992: 82)

Similarly, verbs falling into the lexical aspectual category of "accomplishment" (roughly, verbs describing instantaneous actions) do not form middles:

(4.221) a. *Diese Krankheit erkennt   sich   nicht leicht
             this   sickness recognizes 'self' not   easily
             (Fagan 1992: 85)

   b. *Gold finds easily in Africa

   c. *The pinnacle reaches easily

Fagan notes that there are no "prepositional middle constructions" even in languages that allow prepositional passives, such as EN:

(4.221) d. *John laughs at easily

   e. John was laughed at

and interprets this as evidence that middle constructions, unlike passive constructions, are created by lexical rules.

4.9.4.2.2 **The Icelandic middle construction** The IC middle construction with *-st*, originating from a reduced reflexive, is dated by Haugen (1982: 134) to early in the common Scandinavian period on the basis of its archaic morphological shape in some instances. Virtually none of the characteristics of West GMC middles are found in the IC constructions, as seen in (4.222).

(4.222) a. Við heyr-ð-um-st
             we hear-past-1Pl-ST
             'We were heard'
             (IC, Kissock 1997: 4)

   b. Í Afríku finnst gull
       in Africa gold   finds-ST (= can be found)
       (IC, Kress 1982: 144)

   c. Hesturinn fannst
       horse   found-ST
       'The horse got found'
       (IC, Sigurðsson 1989: 243)

On the one hand, (4.222b) shows that the IC middle can, like those in West GMC, be associated with the sense of potentiality. However, it also allows interpretation as a description of a specific event, as in (4.222c). A comparison of (4.222b) with EN (4.221b) shows, moreover, that it does not share the restrictions on verbal aspect that hold in EN. Note also that the IC construction, even when conveying a modal meaning, need not contain an adverb. It is also claimed by Sigurðsson (1989: 268) that IC middle constructions, unlike the West GMC middle, not only disallow the overt expression of the suppressed subject argument but also lack an implicit actor. Thus, in the following, the verb *drepa* 'kill' in its middle form means 'die', according to Sigurðsson, not 'be killed'.

(4.222)   d. Hundurinn drapst
dog-the   kill-ST
'the dog died'
(IC, Sigurðsson 1989: 268)

This absence of implied agency seems to make IC *st*-middles more like EN/GE/DU unaccusatives than like West GMC middles, and in many instances the most straightforward translation of the IC middle into one of these is as an unaccusative:[38]

(4.222)   e. Glugginn opnaðist
window-the opened-ST
'The window opened'
(IC, Sigurðsson 1989: 263)

However, they are not fully equivalent to unaccusatives, since the IC *st*-middles can be formed on verbs which do not describe potentially spontaneous events, but which require an animate actor/experiencer, as in (4.222a) and (4.222b).

4.9.5 Raising constructions

All of the GMC languages exhibit infinitive constructions in which nominal phrases appear to function as grammatical subjects or objects of the main verb, but are

---

[38] Sigurðsson (1989: 269) notes some overlap between -*st* middles and unaccusatives ("ergatives") in IC, but claims that they are formed by different operations. Paramount among the differences is the fact that (most) unaccusative constructions but not middle constructions preserve the oblique case assigning properties of their active counterparts:

(i)   Þeir hvolfa bátnum
they capsize boat-the-D
(Sigurðsson 1989: 279)
(ii)   Bátnum   hvolfir
boat-the-D capsizes
(iii)   Ég týndi úrinu
I lost watch-the-D
(Sigurðsson 1989: 269)
(iv)   úrið   týndist
watch-the-N lost-ST

4.9 The external syntax of noun phrases

understood to be logical subject (or object) arguments of the infinitive verb. These constructions often alternate with others in which the nominal phrase in question is a constituent of a subordinate clause. The following is an informal catalogue of the constructions in question, with illustrations from GO, and paired in each with examples showing the same predicate with a finite complement. Brief discussions of each of these (including explanations of the descriptive labels attached to them) will follow.

Subject Control Constructions:

(4.223) a. ibai jus wileiþ [þamma siponjos wairþan]?
perchance you want to-him disciples to-become?
(GO, John 9:27)

b. ƕa þus wileis [ei taujau]?
what to-you want-you that I-might-do?
(GO, Luke 18:41)

Object Control Constructions:

(4.223) c. [is] anabaud ahmin... [usgaggan af þamma mann]
he commanded spirit-Dat to-go from the man
(GO, Luke 8:29)

d. [is] anabauþ im [ei [eis] mann ni qeþeina]
He commanded them that they to-anyone not might say
(GO, Mark 7:36)

Subject-to-Subject Raising (nominativus cum infinitivo) Constructions:

(4.223) e. [eis] iohanne hausjan þuhtedun
they John to-hearken-to seemed
(GO, Skeireins VIa: 10)

f. þugkeiþ im... [ei in filuwaurdein seinai andhausjaindau]
seems to-them that in verbosity their they-may-be-heard
(GO, Matt. 6:7)

Subject-to-Object Raising (AcI) Constructions:

(4.223) g. ƕaiwa qiþand Xristu sunu Daweidis wisan?
how they-say Christ-Acc son-Acc David to-be?
(GO, Luke 20:41)

(4.223) h. qiþa izwis [ei [is] ni fraqisteiþ mizdon seinai]
I-say to-you that [he] not destroys reward his
'I say to you that he will not lose his reward'
(GO, Matt. 10:42)

Tough-Movement Constructions:

(4.223) i. weis ataugjan skuldai sijum faura stauastola
we to-reveal obliged are before the judgment seat
'We are obliged to be revealed before the judgment seat'
(GO, 2 Cor. 5:10)

j. skuld-u ist unsis [kaisaragild giban] þau ni-u?
lawful-Q is to-us tribute-to-Caesar to-give or not-Q?
'Is it lawful for us to give tribute or not?'
(GO, Mark 12:14)

In each of the control constructions, a nominal phrase occurs as the subject or object argument of the finite verb, with which it is also understood to be associated semantically, but that argument is also understood to bear a second semantic relationship to the infinitive verb – the semantic relationship normally associated with the subject of that verb. So, for example, in (4.223a), *jus* 'you' is the subject of 'want', as the verb agreement shows, and also a logical argument of that verb (the one who wants), but at the same time, it is understood to be the subject of the prospective proposition 'you will become disciples'. Similarly, in the 'object control' example in (4.223c), the argument *ahmin* 'spirit' is the object of the finite verb *anabiudan* 'command', as shown by the fact that it appears in the dative case normally associated with the nominal object of that verb. Moreover, it is also understood to bear a semantic relation to that verb – that of recipient of the command. On the other hand, it is also understood to bear a semantic relationship to the embedded clause verb – the entity which will 'go out' if the command is obeyed. In some grammatical models, this two-fold allegiance is accommodated by claiming that there are two different nominal expressions in the syntactic representation. The overt argument is an argument of the finite verb, but a second argument, in the form of a phonologically null pronominal (PRO), occurs as the subject of the infinitive. The fact that PRO in these examples is understood as having the same reference as the other argument is accommodated by assuming a relationship of "Control" which assigns to PRO the referential interpretation of the appropriate main clause nominal. Cases in which this "controller" NP is the object of the finite verb are called "object control constructions", and cases in which the controller is the subject of the main verb are called "subject control constructions". Both types of control constructions are commonplace in all of the GMC languages, old and new, and will not be dealt with further here. The other constructions in the catalogue are more variable across GMC, and will be the subject of the discussion in the remainder of this section.

4.9.5.1 *Subject raising constructions*

As (4.223e) and (4.223f) show, *þugkjan* 'seem' in GO, like its counterpart *seem* in EN, can appear with a finite clausal argument ('It seems (to me) *that he runs fast*'), or it can occur with a nominal subject and an infinitive complement ('*He* seems (to me) *to run fast*'). In the latter case, there is no semantic connection between 'seem' and its nominal subject. What 'seems' is the proposition 'he runs fast'. In traditional treatments this construction is sometimes referred to as the Nominative-with-Infinitive construction. It is accounted for in some analyses by assuming that the subject of 'seem' starts out as the subject of the infinitive, but that it is moved into the position of the subject of the finite verb by a transformational operation which, since it changes the clause membership of that nominal by moving it from a subordinate clause into a higher clause, is referred to as (Subject-to-Subject) Raising (SSR).

It is not clear whether the SSR construction can be reconstructed for GMC. There are a fair number of sentences like (4.223e) in the GO corpus, but they all occur with a single verb, *þugkjan* 'seem', and none of them is demonstrably independent of the Greek model. Moreover, the evidence from some other early GMC languages (and some modern ones) for the existence of SSR is slight and problematic. So, for example, in OE, while it has been claimed to exist with *þyncan* 'seem' on the basis of examples like:

(4.224) a. ðær   him   foldwegas   fægere þūhton
             where him-Dat earthways-Nom beautiful seemed-Pl
             'Where the earthways seemed beautiful to him'
             (OE, Beowulf 866, cited in Denison 1993: 221)

Denison (1993: 221) notes that this is for the most part restricted to cases in which there is no infinitive, and in which, therefore, we are not obviously dealing with a structure involving two separate clauses. Constructions like 'He seems to run fast' emerge productively only in ME, and most of the large set of SSR predicates in Modern EN (including such adjectives as *apt*, *bound*, *certain*, *likely*, and such verbs as *appear*, *happen*, *prove*, *see*, *turn out* – for a complete list, see Postal 1974: 292) either did not exist in EN or did not participate in raising constructions prior to ME times. Some investigators claim that the possibility for SSR first arose in ME, perhaps connected with the shift to VO syntax (see Denison 1993: 242ff. for a summary of various positions). In any case, it is undeniable that the construction developed robustly during ME, and that EN resultantly has a far larger set of SSR predicates than other GMC languages.

Similarly, the SSR construction in GE, if it exists at all, only occurs with the verb *scheinen* 'seem', and its existence as such has been called into question. Ebert (1975) notes that constructions with *scheinen* plus an infinitive do not have to involve a raised subject (as in (4.224b)), and proposes instead that these constructions involve verb-raising (Section 5.7.1.1.1) rather than SSR (see also Hawkins 1985: 75ff.).

(4.224)   b. Ihm scheint geholfen zu werden
        him seem helped to become
        'He seems to have been helped'
        (GE)

SSR appears more robustly in the Scandinavian languages, though with a smaller set of triggering predicates than in EN (most of which take the *-st/-s* suffix) (for discussion of IC, see Sigurðsson 1989: 96 and the references cited there).

(4.224)   c. hon þótti   mér   þat vel þekkjast
        she seemed to-me that well to-like
        (ON, Bandle *et al.* 2002: 941)

               d. Þeir sýnast vera gáfaðir
        they appear to-be gifted
        (IC, Sigurðsson 1989: 96)

               e. Hon tycktes inte veta   det
        she seemed not to-know that
        (SW, Holmes and Hinchcliffe 1994: 308)

The relative robustness of the construction in EN from ME on and in the Scandinavian languages again suggests a possible connection with VO-word order.

Some further remarks are warranted about the special status of 'seem'. We have seen that it is the only apparent raising predicate attested across the GMC languages – the only one found in GO and GE, for example. In that connection, it is worth noting that it is also syntactically quite different from the numerous other raising predicates in EN, as the following examples show. (For more detailed discussion of these differences between *seem* and other raising predicates, see Vikner 1995.)

(4.225)   a. Peter seems nice

               b. *Peter is likely nice
        (Vikner 1995: 263)

               c. *That he would come seemed

d. That he would come was likely
(Vikner 1995: 263)

e. Peter seems as if he is ill
(Vikner 1995: 264)

f. *Peter is likely as if he is ill
(Vikner 1995: 264)

4.9.5.2 Accusative-with-infinitive constructions

The GMC languages also exhibit similar constructions in which a nominal phrase appears to be the *object* of a finite verb with which it has no semantic affiliation. In (4.226a), for example, there is no entailment 'I believe him'. What is believed is the proposition 'He is a liar'. That is, *him* is not a semantic argument of *believe*.

(4.226) a. I believe him to be a liar

Nonetheless, *him* behaves as if it were a syntactic dependent of *believe*, in that it appears in the objective case which *believe* normally assigns to its nominal object. We can show that the objective case is dependent on the verb here, since if we passivize that verb, the pronoun can no longer appear in objective case:

(4.226) b. *It is believed him to be a liar

The most common labels for these constructions are bound to particular syntactic analyses. They are referred to sometimes as Subject-to-Object Raising (SOR) constructions, reflecting an analysis in which they are derived by raising the subject of the infinitive into the object position in the main clause, analogous to SSR, and sometimes as Exceptional Case Marking (ECM) constructions, reflecting an analysis in which the main clause verb assigns its case "down into" the infinitival clause. For present purposes, I will employ the more traditional and possibly more analysis-neutral label "accusative-with-infinitive" (AcI) construction, though it should be kept in mind that this label is also used for a rather different construction in Latin, for example.

Sigurðsson (1989: 81), following others, makes a useful distinction between L(et)-type and B(elieve)-type AcI constructions (see also Fischer 1990), which will be adopted in the following. The two have different syntactic properties in some languages, and a different distribution and developmental history across the family. So, for example, the L-type (which involves causatives like 'let', 'make' and verbs of perception like 'see', 'hear', 'feel') appears with bare infinitivals in Modern EN, and resists passivization, while the B-type (which involves epistemic verbs/verbs of mental process like 'believe', 'think', 'expect', 'consider' and verbs of saying like 'claim', 'report') takes infinitive phrases with *to* and allows passivization:

(4.227) a. We let him (*to) win

b. ??He was let win

c. We consider/think him to be a fool

d. He was thought to be a fool

DA and NO exhibit a similar contrast between the two types with respect to the admissibility of a prepositional infinitive marker (Sigurðsson 1989: 83), and this, in addition to other evidence, has led some investigators to conclude that B-type infinitive phrases are syntactically different from L-type infinitive phrases, containing more structure. With respect to their distribution, the L-type is found in all of the languages of the family, old and new, and its nativeness in GMC is beyond dispute. Examples like those in (4.228) from GO are easy to find in all the other GMC languages.

(4.228) a. waurkeiþ þans mans anakumbjan
         make   the   men   recline
         (GO, John 6:10)

b. þan   gasaiƕiþ   þata wairþan
   when   you-see   that become
   (GO, Mark 13:29)

c. ni   lailot þos   rodjan
   not let-he those speak
   (GO, Luke 4:41)

Less clear is the status of the B-type in early GMC. On the one hand, it is attested in GO with a wide range of verbs of saying and thinking, including *domjan* 'judge', *hugjan* 'think', *qiþan* 'say', *galaubjan* 'believe', *munan* 'think', *gatrauan* 'trust', *wenjan* 'hope', *witan* 'know', as in (4.229).

(4.229) a. ƕaiwa qiþand   Xristu sunu Daweidis   wisan?
         How   they-say   Christ son   of-David   to-be?
         (GO, Luke 20:41)

b. eis   allai gadomidedun ina skulan   wisan dauþau
   they all   judged   him deserving to-be of-death
   (GO, Mark 14:64)

c. hugjandona in gasinþjam ina wisan
   thinking   in company   him to-be
   (GO, Luke 2:44)

        d. galaubjand auk allai Iohannen praufetu wisan
           believe also all John prophet to-be
           (GO, Luke 20:6)

Moreover, it is even found in the absence of a model in the Greek text in a few instances, as in (4.229e), where the Greek has a subject control construction:

(4.229)   e. [ik] wenja mik... saljan at izwis
                I hope myself to stay with you
                (GO, 1 Cor. 16:7)

Taken at face value, these facts would suggest that B-type AcI was found even in early GMC. There are, however, some considerations which weigh against such a conclusion. First, it is counterindicated by the comparative evidence. B-type AcI was, according to Fischer (1990: 73), attested in OE only in slavish translations from Latin, and it did not emerge as a native (or nativized) possibility until ME (though see Miller 2002: 160f., 170, who claims that it was a part of the language by at least late OE, and perhaps earlier).[39] In GE (and in the rest of continental West GMC) it is still not possible:

(4.229)   f. *Ich glaube/erwarte ihn gut zu sein
                I believe/expect him good to be
                (GE)

Thus, B-type AcI is probably not to be reconstructed for GMC, and therefore, if it was a grammatical possibility in GO, then GO must have innovated, independent of the rest of GMC. A still more troubling consideration bearing on the interpretation of the GO data is that many of the verbs found in B-type AcI constructions in the GO text are also found elsewhere in subject-control constructions. Thus, next to AcI sentences like (4.229e) and (4.229d), we find sentences like (4.229g) and (4.229h) with the very same verb.

(4.229)   g. wenjands 0 qiman at þus sprauto
                hoping to-come to you soon
                (GO, 1 Tim. 3:14)

               h. sums raihtis galaubeiþ 0 matjan allata
                one indeed believes to-eat all
                (GO, Rom. 14:2)

---

[39] Fischer notes (1992: 120) that the verb *witan* 'know' also appears in AcI constructions early on in OE, even in native poetry, but suggests that this involves a specialized use in which it approximates perception verbs semantically (to which group it belongs from an etymological standpoint). However, see Miller 2002: 161.

Taken at face value, this would be a surprising state of affairs, based on what we know of the tendency toward mutual exclusiveness between these constructions in modern GMC. In EN, where *believe* is an AcI verb, the literal equivalent of a GE sentence like (4.229i) is quite bad. Conversely, in GE, where *glauben* 'believe' is a subject-control verb, the equivalent of the EN AcI construction is impossible:

(4.229) i. Er glaubt, das schon gemacht zu haben
             *He believes to have done that already
             (GE)

j. He believes himself to be intelligent
    *Er glaubt sich intelligent zu sein
    (GE)

This being the case, the coexistence of the two in GO is surprising, unless one can find a way to attribute them to distinct grammars. Indeed, it was noted as early as Apelt 1874 that, where GO diverges from the Greek construction on this point, it agrees with the contemporaneous Latin Vulgate. Subsequent investigators have also settled on Latin influence as an account of B-type AcI in GO (see Harbert 1978: 205 for some discussion). Therefore, we can imagine that AcI was not a possibility in GO at the time of the original translations, but that it worked its way into the texts under Latin influence later on in the transmission process.

If we do dismiss the GO evidence for B-type AcI in this way, we are left with the conclusion that it is found only in ME and Modern EN, and in the Scandinavian languages (SW and IC) – that is, once again in those languages which have undergone the shift to VO word order. Again, some investigators, including Fischer (1990: 128f.) have suggested a typological connection between these two features. DA also conformed to this expectation, up until recent times, but Platzack observes (1986: 129) that DA lost B-Type AcI in the eighteenth century (one suspects GE influence here), and now contrasts with SW in having subject control constructions in instances where SW has AcI:

(4.229) k. Albert har tilstået at være tyven
             Albert has confessed to be thief-the
             (DA, Platzack 1986: 130)

l. Albert har erkänt sig vara tjuven
    Albert has confessed self to-be thief-the
    (SW, Platzack 1986: 130)

4.9.5.3 *Tough-movement constructions*

In tough-movement constructions, the surface subject of the main clause is not semantically connected to the predicate of that clause, but is understood to correspond to the object of a dependent infinitive. For example, in (4.230a), there is no entailment that 'this test is tough'; the sentence is understood as equivalent in meaning to (4.230b).

(4.230)   a. This test is tough to fail

             b. It is tough [to fail this test]

On one analysis, sentences like (4.230a) are claimed to be derived by raising the object of *fail* in a string like (4.230b) into the position of subject of the main predicate *tough*, replacing the expletive. The process is conventionally referred to as tough-movement because predicates of 'ease' and 'difficulty' are typical of the main-clause predicates which appear in these constructions. The tough-movement operation, on this analysis, would be superficially analogous to subject-to-subject raising, except that it is an object rather than a subject which is displaced, but in fact there are some differences between the two which suggest that they are not comparable processes. Prominent among these is the fact that, unlike SSR constructions, in apparent subject-to-object raising, the surface position of the "raised" nominal can be separated from the associated infinitive by an arbitrarily long stretch of intervening syntactic material.

(4.230)   c. This test was easy for me to convince the principal to order the teachers to administer

Its "long-distance" properties have led other investigators to conclude that the process involved in linking the infinitive object position and the main subject position more closely resembles relative pronoun movement, and accordingly they posit the fronting of an abstract, relative-pronoun-like operator in these constructions.

There is reason to think that apparent tough-movement constructions (that is, constructions in which the subject of the main clause predicate is the understood object of its dependent infinitive, and not semantically connected to the main predicate) do not represent a unitary construction across the GMC languages. The construction meeting this definition in GO, in particular, is quite unlike those found elsewhere, though there is reason to think that it reflects native syntax. Consider the following pairs of Greek sentences and their GO translations.

(4.231)   a.ƕaiwa skuld ist in garda gudis usmitan
               how   proper is   in house God's to-behave
               (GO, 1 Tim. 3:15)

             b. pôs deî   en oíkōi theoû anastréphesthai
               how it-is-proper in house God's to-behave
               (Greek, 1 Tim. 3:1)

c. swe skuljau rodjan
   as I-should speak
   (GO, Eph. 6:20)

d. hōs deî   me   lalêsai
   as is-necessary me-Acc to-speak-ActiveInf
   (Greek, Eph. 6:20)

e. weis ataugjan skuldai   sijum
   we   to-reveal obliged-NPLMasc are-1pl
   'We are obliged to be revealed'
   (GO, 2 Cor. 5:10)

f. hēmâs phanerōthênai deî
   us-Acc to-be-revealed it-was necessary
   (Greek, 2 Cor. 5:10)

We see in the first pair of examples that when the Greek *deî* takes no nominal argument, but only an infinitive clause, GO translates the construction quite literally, as an impersonal construction. When in the Greek there is a nominal argument in accusative case ('It is necessary (for) us. . .'), as in (4.231d), GO personalizes the constructions, turning the accusative argument into the subject of the modal *skulan* 'should, be obliged to'. Finally, when the Greek construction involves an accusative nominal argument and a passive infinitive ('it was necessary (for) us to be revealed'), GO does not copy the Greek construction, using a passive infinitive. Rather, it uses the predicate *skuld wisan* 'be obliged', in place of *skulan*, with an infinitive which is not marked for passive. *Weis* 'we' is the subject (4.231e), as evidenced by the fact that it controls person/number agreement on the copula and nominative plural masculine agreement on the predicative adjective. This is an apparent tough-movement construction, as I have described them, since the subject of the main clause corresponds to the logical object of the infinitive. The same patterns are found with *maht* 'able', as well. There is no parallel to this in the other GMC languages. However, the systematicity of the alternations and the apparent absence of direct dependence on the Greek construction argue for nativeness.

There is, however, another possible analysis of these apparent tough-movement constructions. While *skuld* and *maht* are translatable as adjectives meaning 'obliged' and 'able' respectively, and are listed as such in some dictionaries, they are also, formally, the past/passive participles of the modals *skulan* 'should' and *magan* 'may, be able to' respectively. We might therefore alternatively take sentences like (4.231f) to be complex passive sentences with auxiliaries and infinitival main verbs, the passive morphology showing up on the former, rather than the latter (contrary to the pattern of all later GMC – that is, *'He is shoulded to arrest' rather than 'He should be arrested').

Other GMC languages exhibit constructions superficially resembling EN tough-movement constructions, whose predicates once again typically involve the notions of ease or difficulty of performing an action. IC is an exception, according to Holmberg and Rijkhoff (1998: 87).

(4.232) a. Han er umulig   at gøre tilpas
             he is impossible to please
             (DA, Allan *et al.* 1995: 279)

         b. ða stānas...bēoð earfoðe tō tōdǣlenne
             the stones are   difficult to divide
             (OE, Boethius 92:24, van der Gaaf 1928a: 129)

         c. Elephanten sind leicht zu transportieren
             elephants are easy   to transport
             (GE, Thiersch 1978: 148)

However, superficial similarities here may mask deeper syntactic divergence in some of these cases. Some investigators (Thiersch 1978; Hawkins 1986; Comrie 1995) have pointed out that tough-movement differs between GE and EN in at least a couple of significant ways. Among other things, in GE, the "long distance movement" property of the construction seems to be lacking.

(4.232) d. *Dieses Buch ist leicht für mich Heinrich zu lesen zu zwingen
             this   book is easy   for me Heinrich to read to force
             (GE, Hawkins 1986: 78)

There are also far fewer predicates which participate in the construction than in EN. Hawkins (1986: 78), citing König, counts only *leicht* 'easy', *einfach* 'simple', *schwer* 'difficult' and *interessant* 'interesting'. EN, on the other hand, exhibits a much larger inventory of tough-movement predicates.

(4.232) e. *Blumen sind nett zu finden
             flowers are nice to find
             (GE, Thiersch 1978: 154)

         f. *Er ist wichtig   zu erreichen
             he is important to reach
             (GE, Thiersch 1978: 155)

         g. *Die Linguistik ist langweilig zu studieren
             linguistics   is boring   to study
             (GE, Hawkins 1986: 78)

Thiersch (1978) asserts that the construction does not occur with true adjectives at all, but only with those apparent adjectives which also admit of an adverbial interpretation, an opinion which is seconded and argued for at length by Demske-Neumann (1994). What appear to be tough-movement constructions in GE are in fact special cases of what Demske-Neumann calls modal passive constructions. In these constructions, illustrated in (4.232h), a nominal phrase appears as the subject of a sentence with a copula and a prepositional infinitive, the whole being understood as having passive-like interpretation, with an element of modal meaning (possibility, necessity/obligation):

(4.232) h. Der Bericht ist (pünktlich/kaum/leicht)   zu lesen
             the report is (punctually/hardly/easily) to read
             'The report is (punctually/hardly/easily)   to be read'

Adverbs can be added to these, including modal adverbs such as *kaum* 'hardly'. Where the adverb is homophonous with an adjective, as is *leicht* 'easy/easily', the result resembles a tough-movement construction. The resemblance belies a fundamental structural difference. In the former, the infinitive is the predicate, and the adverb is a modifier. In tough-movement constructions, the adjective is the head of the predicate.

Demske-Neumann (1994) observes that both tough-movement constructions and modal passive constructions (or 'retroactive infinitives' – see Kageyama 1992: 114) existed in earlier GMC. Sentence (4.233a), for example, is clearly a modal passive construction, as is (4.233b), since *leohtsamo* is clearly an adverb on morphological grounds. On the other hand, in (4.233c), we are dealing with a tough-movement construction, since *suuâre* is clearly an adjective on inflectional grounds.

(4.233) a. in dhemu eristin ist   sunu zi archennanne
            in the   first   is (the) son to recognize
            'In the first one, the son is to be recognized'
            (OHG, Isidor 292, cited in Demske-Neumann 1994: 65)

         b. dhazs ist... so leohtsam-o zu firstandanne
            that is   so clearly   to understand
            'That is so clearly to be understood'
            (OHG, Isidor 173, cited in Demske-Neumann 1994: 65)

         c. er ist uns   suuâr-e ana zesehenne
            it is to-us difficult at to-look
            'It is difficult for us to look at'
            (OHG, Notker Ps. 133:10, cited in Demske-Neumann 79)

4.9 The external syntax of noun phrases

The breakdown of morphological distinctions between adverbs and predicate adjectives, however, precipitated reanalysis in some of these languages; GE gave up tough-movement constructions, while perpetuating the modal passive constructions which occasionally resemble them. In EN, the modal passive construction was virtually eliminated, and is restricted in Modern EN to a few conventionalized cases, like 'He is (hardly) to blame' (Demske-Neumann 1994: 11). For the most part, it has been eliminated by replacing the unmarked infinitive with a periphrastic passive infinitive, as documented in detail by van der Gaaf (1928a).

(4.233) d. This report is to be read by tomorrow

Curiously, as detailed by van der Gaaf, this same development came close to supplanting tough-movement constructions, and similar adjective + infinitive constructions. In (4.233), for instance, Early Modern EN uses an overtly passive infinitive where Old and Modern EN would use an unmarked infinitive (see also Fischer 1990; Miller 2002: 233f.). Thus, Modern EN tough-movement constructions appear to be a restoration, rather than a continuation, of the OE phenomenon (see Demske-Neumann 1994: 224ff.).

(4.233) a. whose feathers are beautiful to be worne
(Early Modern EN, van der Gaaf 1928a: 135)

b. a man is ... easie to be spoken unto
(van der Gaaf 1928a: 135)

c. they are much better to be eaten
(van der Gaaf 1928a: 135)

d. it is very sweet to be eaten
(van der Gaaf 1928a: 135)

SW and DA, according to Comrie (1995), have tough-movement constructions of the EN type, as in (4.234), while DU retains both constructions. Note the predicate adjective agreement in the SW example.

(4.234) Böckerna är svåra att läsa
books-the are hard-Pl to read
(SW, Comrie 1995: 20)

5

The verbal systems of Germanic: paradigmatic and syntagmatic comparison

5.1 Historical prelude: the Indo-European heritage and Germanic innovations

5.1.1 Types of verbal inflection

Verbal inflection in GMC tends to be more dynamic than nominal inflection. Verbs participate in more inflectional categories than nouns do, inflecting for tense, mood and voice as well as for agreement with the person and number of the subject, and the endings of verbs, as an accidental consequence of their phonological shape, have in general more successfully resisted the effects of final syllable reduction. So, for example, of the eight originally distinct case endings of the singular of masculine *o*-stem nouns in IE, only three (Genitive *tag-es*, Dative *tag-e* and instrumental *tag-u*) remain distinct in OHG, and only the first of these is still found in Modern GE. On the other hand, all of the three persons of the present tense verb, in both singular and plural, are distinct in OHG, just as they were in IE. OHG goes so far as to preserve both the thematic ending (-*u*) and the athematic ending (-*m*) of IE in the first person singular.

(5.1) *Singular*   *Plural*
    1. nimu   'I take'/sagem 'I say'   nemumēs
    2. nimis   nemet
    3. nimit   nemant

(OHG lacks the dual forms of IE, but their loss was not occasioned by phonological reduction of inflectional affixes.) The Modern GE paradigm is only marginally less rich than the OHG one, the first and third person plural forms having fallen together as -*en*, and the first person singular -*m* ending having been lost except in the verb 'be', where it is preserved as -*n*.

The GMC verbal system has also preserved much more of the internal inflection of IE than has the nominal system. In IE, word stress in both nouns and verbs was

5.1 Historical prelude

moveable, as discussed in Section 3.3.4, capable of falling either on the root or on a suffix. The presence or absence of stress affected the quantity and quality of the vowel, and led to the vowel alternations which we know as ablaut, still very much a part of verb inflection in many GMC languages. In general, the vowel /e/ appears in positions which received stress. One refers to such forms as *e*-grade forms. On the other hand, in unstressed positions, the vowel characteristically disappeared, yielding so-called zero-grade forms. An original alternation between a root-stressed form and an affix-stressed form is still reflected in Old Upper GE *ziuhan* 'to pull' *z[ ]ugum* 'we pulled'. The brackets indicate the position of the vowel which has been 'zeroed out' in the zero-grade form. Note also that the two forms differ with respect to the medial consonant. This is because of a secondary development in early GMC, Verner's Law, discussed in 3.1.2, in which a medial fricative consonant became voiced when not immediately preceded by stress. Given their common dependence on absence of accent, we expect the voiced Verner's Law fricatives to be found in zero-grade forms, and the corresponding voiceless fricative to be found in *e*-grade forms. The expected pattern is illustrated in the /h~g/ alternation of these examples. Still other forms exhibit a third ablaut variant of importance, the "o-grade." For discussion of its origin, see Beekes 1995: 166. This ablaut grade is also reflected in the paradigm of our example verb, though somewhat obscured by later sound changes, in the third person singular *zōh* 'I pulled' (from a GMC *zauh, short /o/ having become /a/ in GMC).

Such alternations in the vowels and consonants of the root have ceased to play any role at all in the inflection of GMC nouns. There are no GMC nouns which exhibit one ablaut grade in one case and a different ablaut grade in another case. There are similarly no nouns which exhibit Verner's law alternations within individual paradigms. It is only comparative evidence that allows us occasionally to recover former accent variation in GMC nouns and its phonetic effects. So, for example, we know that the /γ/ of OE *lagu* 'water, sea, ocean' is voiced because of Verner's Law (and that the form therefore must have had original suffix accent) only because of cognates such as Latin *lacus* (Bammesberger 1990: 156). Such paradigm-internal vowel-alternations as are found with GMC nouns (e.g., OHG *anst* 'grace-Nom/Acc': *ensti* 'grace-Dat/Gen') are due to the much later umlaut of the root vowel under the influence of the vowel of the suffix. These too have remained of marginal importance, tending to be leveled out over time. Ablaut alternations in verbal roots, on the other hand (and to a lesser extent the Verner's Law alternations that accompany them), have survived robustly as a device for signaling tense contrasts in the GMC verb. The so-called "strong" verbs of GMC preserve and systematize and even, to a degree, extend the inherited ablaut patterns. In fact, Vennemann (2003c: 569) claims that the use of ablaut in GMC verbs is more robust and systematic than in other IE languages, having undergone a revivification which he attributes to language contact.

272   5 *The verbal systems of Germanic*

It is also only in the verbal paradigms that inflectional prefixes are found, though even there they are a marginal phenomenon. Surviving from IE are the GO reduplicative prefixes in the preterites of a small set of strong verbs (Class 7 strong verbs, in the traditional classification system). A few of these are exemplified in (5.2):

(5.2)   haitan 'to be called'   haihait 'I was called'
         skaidan 'separate'   skaiskaiþ 'I separated'
         slepan 'to sleep'   saizlep 'I slept'

The prefix here is formed by copying the initial consonant or cluster to the left of the stem, and adding a linking vowel /e/ (written <ai>). Whether the initial cluster was copied, or only the first consonant of the cluster, depended in an interesting way on the nature of the cluster, as these examples reflect (see Section 3.3.1). Reduplicative prefixation is a relic here, though, and verbs of this class have been restructured in the other GMC languages, where a new root-internal vowel alternation has displaced reduplication as the signal of the past tense in this class of verbs. The continental West GMC languages have developed one new inflectional prefix, the *ge-* which characterizes past participles, through grammaticization of a derivational prefix with perfectivizing meaning.

(5.3)   a. shikn 'to send' geshikt 'sent' (YI)
         b. maken 'make' gemaakt 'made' (DU)

Overwhelmingly, though, in verbs, as well as in nouns, inflection in the GMC languages has been effected through suffixation, and this has become increasingly true over time. Both ablaut and reduplication are only relic means of marking past tense in the medieval languages, tending toward reduction, simplification or elimination in favor of the innovative suffixal past tense to be discussed below.

5.1.2 Categories of verbal inflection: the Germanic tense/mood system and its Indo-European antecedents

In this section, I will discuss the individual categories of verbal inflection, with the exception of person/number agreement morphology (subject-verb agreement), which is discussed in the preceding chapter. The inflectional categories of the GMC verb reflect considerable conflation of those found in IE. Most notably, GMC reduced the articulated aspect/tense system of IE, which simultaneously localized events in time and indicated something about the shapes of those events, to a simple tense system with a single binary opposition present/past. So, for example, the inflectionally distinct Greek imperfect (used to describe continuous events in the past), aorist (used to localize events in the past without indicating their extension or shape), perfect (used to describe a past event resulting in a state which continues into the present) and pluperfect (used to describe a past event resulting in a state which continued through some reference point in the past) all correspond to a single inflected form in GO – the simple past – as the following examples show:

(5.4) a. iþ   is   saislep
       but he   slept-3SgPast
       'But he was sleeping' = Greek imperfect
       (GO, Matt. 8:24)

       b. attaitok   imma
          touch-3SgPast   him
          'He touched him' = Greek aorist
          (GO, Matt. 8:3)

       c. ni   atiddja   nauhþan du im   Iesus
          not come-3SgPast yet   to them Jesus
          'Jesus had not yet come to them' = Greek pluperfect
          (GO, John 6:17)

The absence of a contrast between a simple past and an imperfective, continuous past still sets GMC apart from neighboring Celtic and Romance languages.

The loss of inflectional aspectual distinctions has been partly compensated for in some of the GMC languages by the development of periphrastic constructions, such as those to be discussed in sections on perfect (5.3.3) and progressive (5.3.5).[1]

GMC also (along with other IE languages) has reduced the inventory of moods, conflating the subjunctive and optative of IE (using forms which are etymologically the latter). For further developments in this category, see Section 5.1.5.1.

---

[1] Aspectual contrasts have also found occasional local expression. Among these, perhaps the most interesting is the distinction between "habitual" and "moment-of-speaking" present tenses – the former implying that the truth of the utterance is a matter of permanence, while the latter implies that its truth is temporary which is signaled by alternative choices of copula in some varieties of English.

(i)   a. He be's sick often (Irish English, Harris: 1993: 162)
      b. He's sick now (Harris 1993: 162)

A similar alternation (between habitual *be* and present *0*) is a salient characteristic of African-American English. The question of a historical connection between these two cases, and between them and the partially similar Old English *wesan* and *bēon* contrast (Mitchell 1985: I, 260), has been the subject of debate (cf. especially Rickford 1999). I am unaware of similar contrasts elsewhere in GMC, though they are present in the Romance languages, and, possibly more significantly, in Celtic.

(5.5)   a. qiþ þamma staina ei   wairþai   hlaibs
            tell to-the stone that it-become-PresSubjunct bread
            = Greek subjunctive
            (GO, Luke 4:3)

         b. nis-sijai!
            not-be-PresSubjunct
            'May it not be!' = Greek optative
            (Luke 20:16)

In the category of voice, GMC has only isolated relics of the inflectional middle voice of IE, primarily in the verb 'is called' (OE *hātte*). In place of this, GMC very early introduced a periphrastic middle involving a reflexive pronoun. For further discussion of such constructions, see Section 5.1.9.3.

(5.6)   ushahaih sik
         hanged   self
         'He hanged himself' = Greek aorist middle
         (GO, Matt. 27:5)

GO, alone among the older GMC languages, has an inflectional passive (based on the IE middle), but only in the present tense, as in (5.7a). Elsewhere, Greek passives are rendered as either analytic passives, consisting of the past participle plus the verb 'be' or as inchoative verbs with the derivational suffix *-nan*:

(5.7)   a. ei   hauhjaindau   fram mannam
            that praise-3PlPresPassSubjunct by   men
            'That they might be praised by men'
            (GO, Matt. 6:2)

         b. insandiþs was aggilus Gabriel fram guda
            sent   was angel   Gabriel by   God
            (GO, Luke 1:26)

         c. gahailniþ   sa þiumagus meins
            become-healed-3SgAct the servant   mine
            'My servant will be healed' = Greek 3FutPass
            (GO, Matt. 8:8)

5.1.2.1 *Germanic tense morphology and its antecedents*
The tense systems of individual modern GMC languages are considered in individual articles in the two volumes of Thieroff and Ballweg (1994/1995). The morphological

shape of the tense forms of many basic GMC verbs can be traced to IE sources. So, for example, non-derived verbs typically (though not exclusively) had *e*-grade vocalism and root accent in the IE present, and many of the basic verbs of GMC accordingly exhibit /e/ in the present tense. The inherited GMC past tense derived from the IE perfect, and exhibits a different vowel pattern. The perfect singular of IE was typically root stressed, but had *o*-grade rather than *e*-grade vocalism. The perfect plural, on the other hand, had stress on the affix. The vowel of the root, in the absence of stress, dropped out, yielding zero-grade vocalism. GMC incorporated a similarly suffix-stressed verbal adjective into the verbal system as the past participle in verbs of these types, so that the past participles of these verbs, as well as the preterite plurals, usually exhibit reflexes of zero-grade vocalism. Verbs of this pedigree have been known since their description by Jacob Grimm as "strong verbs." The basic pattern for strong verbs just described (*e*-grade in the present, *o*-grade in the preterite singular, zero-grade in the preterite plural and the past participle) is reflected in the GO examples in (5.8). It is customary in grammars of at least the early GMC languages to represent the ablaut of the strong verb classes by citing these four "principal parts." (These examples are drawn from only two of the traditional seven classes of strong verbs, but they are sufficient for the present purpose of illustrating the kinds of secondary changes which have affected the subsequent shape of strong verbs in the GMC languages.)

(5.8)   *Present*   *Pret Sing*   *Pret Pl*   *PP*
          hilpan 'help'   halp   hulpum   hulpans   (GO)
          singwan 'sing'   sangw   sungwum   sungwans   (GO)
          kiusan 'choose'   kaus   kusum   kusans   (GO)

          helpfan   halpf   hulpfum   gi-holpfan (OHG)
          singan   sang   sungun   gi-sungan   (OHG
          kiosan   kōs   kurum   gi-koran   (OHG)

          helfen   half   halfen   geholfen   (GE)
          singen   sang   sangen   gesungen   (GE)
          frieren 'freeze'   fror   froren   gefroren   (GE)

Even in GO, the inherited pattern is already represented in a rather altered form. We may begin by noting that in some of the present forms, the vowel of the root is *i*, not *e*. This is because of later sound changes which turned /e/ to /i/ in front of a nasal followed by a consonant (everywhere but GO), or in all environments (GO). Note also the presence of /u/ in the zero-grade forms of *hilpan* and *singwan* in GO. In IE, since this was a zero-grade form, there would have been no vowel here. The *l* itself would have functioned as a syllabic nucleus. However, early GMC systematically dispreferred such syllabic resonants, and "resolved" them by introducing an epenthetic /u/ to serve as the syllable nucleus, which was lowered by umlaut to /o/ in languages other than GO when followed in the next syllable by a low vowel, as in past participles like *giholpfan*. The second thing to note is the alternation between /s/ and /r/ in the preterite of *kiosan* in OHG. This is a reflex of Verner's Law, under which voiceless fricatives turned into voiced fricatives in zero-grade forms – /s/ becoming /z/ in the present example, which in turn became /r/ by a later change. Note, though, that there is no similar alternation in GO between /s/ and /z/ in *kiusan*. This is a reflection of a strong tendency in GMC, instantiated early on in GO, to eliminate the redundant alternation between Verner's Law consonants and their non-Verner's Law counterparts in the strong-verb system. Relic survivals strongly indicate that GO underwent Verner's Law with the rest of GMC, but all of the resultant alternations have been leveled out in the strong-verb system, in favor of the voiceless alternant. This tendency toward paradigm leveling is carried even farther in the Modern GE examples. Here, not only is the Verner's Law difference between the preterite singular and the preterite plural leveled out, but so is the vowel difference. GE no longer shows any of the inherited variation in root shape between singulars and plurals in the past tense of strong verbs. (Etymologically identical alternations do survive in GE and elsewhere in GMC in the present tense of "pretero-present" verbs, whose *present* tense forms are based on IE perfects (GE *darf* 'I may'/ *dürfen* 'we may').) What is true of GE is also true of the less richly inflected modern languages (EN, continental Scandinavian, DU, for example), where little trace of former singular/plural vowel differences remains in the preterites of strong verbs. Among the modern languages, such alternations are found only in IC and FA, and even these languages have given up the Verner's Law contrasts between singular and plural preterites:

(5.9)	Present	Pret Singular	Pret Plural	PP
	njósa 'sneeze'	neys	nusu	nosið (FA)

Strong verbs like these stand in contrast to a second type – the "weak" verbs – which form their preterites by suffixing a past-tense morpheme with a dental consonant (/t/ or /d/) rather than by means of ablaut alternations. There are some weak verbs in which the difference between tenses is signaled secondarily by vowel alternations, for example, GO *bringan~brāhta*. These are still weak verbs, though irregular, since the past tenses exhibit a dental suffix. The dental preterite of weak verbs is a distinctive GMC innovation. The source of the dental past tense suffix has been the subject of extended controversy, but it appears likely that it originated in some way from a form of the IE 'do' root. Weak paradigms attracted a different verbal adjective, also characterized by a suffix with a dental consonant (*-*to*), as their past participles. Weak verbs are the productive pattern in GMC, while strong verbs are a relic class. From earliest times, when new verbs are added to GMC languages, through derivation from other word classes or through borrowing, they are added as weak verbs. Exceptions to this generalization (such as the borrowed YI *šextn* 'to ritually slaughter', whose past participle is *gəšoxtn* (Jacobs 2005: 214), and the borrowed EN verbs *thrive* and *strive* – pointed out to me by Roger Lass) are rare. Moreover, when verbs switch inflectional type, they change from strong to weak and, again with marginal exceptions, not the other way around. This difference in productivity can be viewed in part as a manifestation of a GMC preference for affixation, instead of internal modification, as a way of signaling grammatical contrasts, and in part as a consequence of the increasing complexity of the strong verb alternations that resulted from secondary changes of the sort discussed above. In Early Modern EN, such shifting from the highly varied and increasingly atomistic strong classes to the more uniform and regular weak patterns took place on a large scale. A partial list of verbs which shifted from strong to weak in Early Modern EN is given in (5.10). Some patterns (e.g., that of *write/wrote/written* and *sing/sang/sung*) resisted this trend more successfully than others.

(5.10)   bow, brew, creep, flee, lie, lose, reek, rue, seethe, burn, burst, carve, climb, delve, help, melt, mourn, starve, swell, yield, flay, gnaw, shave, wash, step, flow, fold, mow, sow, weep

Interestingly, while individual verbs have shifted from strong to weak in other GMC languages, no other language has experienced such a large-scale defection. By my count, there are only about 70 basic strong verbs remaining in EN, compared to roughly 180 in DU, for example, and about an equal number for GE (cf. Booij 2002b: 59f.; Messinger 1973: 17f.). However, it appears likely that the wholesale abandonment of simple past forms in a number of GMC languages (AF, PG and YI, as well as various GE dialects) in favor of the periphrastic present perfect as the sole exponent of past tense is an alternative reaction to the same growth in complexity of the strong-verb system. This is argued to be the case in GE in Born 1979. In some of these languages, the weak/strong distinction continues to be signaled in spite of the elimination of simple past tense, since there is still a contrast in past participles between those which are formed by a dental suffix and those which are formed by ablaut (e.g., PG *gəmaxt* 'made-PP', *gənumə* 'taken-PP' (van Ness 1994: 431), YI *geshikt* 'sent-PP', *gekumen* 'come-PP' (Jacobs *et al*. 1994: 407)). In AF, however, this difference too has been neutralized through loss of the participle suffix, resulting in the complete disappearance of the strong/weak verb distinction (Donaldson 1994: 495).

278   5 *The verbal systems of Germanic*

5.1.2.2   *Mood: indicative, subjunctive, and imperative*

5.1.2.2.1 **Subjunctive**   GMC has three moods: the indicative, the imperative and an "irrealis" mood used for talking about contrary-to-fact scenarios and eventualities with low probability of occurrence. There is a certain amount of terminological confusion involved in labeling the latter. In grammars of the older languages, it tends to be called "optative." In grammars of the modern languages, on the other hand, it is usually referred to as "subjunctive" (GE "Konjunktiv"). From the standpoint of etymology, the former is more accurate, since the forms in question derive from IE optative forms. In their use, however, they conflate the functions of the IE optative and the subjunctive, which does not survive formally in GMC. Adding further to the terminological confusion is the coexistence in GMC of two different inflectional paradigms for this optative/subjunctive mood. These are most standardly referred to as present subjunctive and past subjunctive (or present optative and preterite optative) respectively. It is important to keep in mind, however, that these terms are based on the morphological shapes of the forms in question, and not on their meanings. There is not, and never has been, a contrast in time reference between the two (but see below for an important qualification). Some grammatical traditions have dispensed with these labels altogether. For example, in GE grammatical descriptions, they are generally known respectively as subjunctive I (for "present subjunctive") and subjunctive II (for "past subjunctive"). I will continue to use the traditional terms, and we will turn shortly to evidence indicating that the labels "present subjunctive" and "past subjunctive" are not wholly inappropriate.

Present subjunctives are so-called because their stem resembles that of the present tense indicative – that is, the *e*-grade form of the root in strong verbs. Past subjunctives are so-called because they are typically formed from the same root as that used in the preterite plural – that is, the zero-grade root in the case of strong verbs. The following examples, from GO and GE, show these similarities:

(5.11)   a. biudand 'command'   biudaina   (GO)
             3PlPresIndicative   3PlPresSubjunctive
             budun   budi
             3PlPretIndicative   3SgPretSubjunctive

          b. steht 'stand'   stehe   (GE)
             3SgPresIndicative   3SgPresSubjunctive
             stunden   stünden
             3PlPretIndicative   3PlPretSubjunct (archaic)

In each of these cases, we see that the vowel of the present subjunctive is like that of the present singular indicative, while the vowel of the past subjunctive is like that of the past plural indicative, aside from differences introduced by later sound changes, such as the umlaut in *stünden* produced by the former front vowel of the subjunctive suffix. This alignment between present and past tense and the two types of subjunctives appears to have been accidental in origin – reflecting two different modes of forming optatives in IE (athematic and thematic) which had no original temporal significance, and simply happened to line up in a particular way with GMC present/past paradigms (Beekes 1995: 246). However, GMC has systematized and reinforced this link between the two subjunctive formations and tense. For example, those strong verbs which introduced a long /e:/ in place of zero grade in the preterite plurals also did so in the past subjunctive of the same verb classes (GO *bērun* 'they bore-PastIndic', *bēreina* 'might they bear-PastSubjunct'), thus continuing the formal correspondence between the two. Over time, the two types of subjunctives have become progressively less distinct from the formally corresponding tenses in the indicative. Present subjunctives have become less distinct from present indicatives, and past subjunctives from past indicatives. So, for example, while GO systematically differentiated past subjunctive from past indicative in weak as well as strong verbs (*habaida* 'he had' /*habaidedi* 'he might have'), past indicatives and past subjunctives have become identical for regular weak verbs even in such relatively conservative modern languages as GE and IC (GE *hörte*, IC *heyrþe* 'heard (3SgPastSubjunct/Indic)'. Both languages keep the two distinct only in the subclass of weak verbs exhibiting "*Rückumlaut*" – that is, umlaut in the indicative present but not the indicative past tense. With these verbs, the past indicative has an unumlauted vowel, while the past subjunctive has an umlauted vowel (GE *brannte* 'burned-PastIndic'/ *brennte* 'burned-PastSubjunct'). The increasing tendency toward identity between the subjunctive and indicative has led to a virtually complete formal merger of past indicative and past subjunctive in some modern GMC languages.

Both types of subjunctive are used to express a (lesser or greater) disavowel on the part of the speaker of the truth of the proposition. To the extent that there are clear-cut differences in meaning between them, they tend to involve a notion like "degree of potentiality for the proposition to be(come) true." So, for example, in GO, GE, IC and EN, present subjunctive is used for "fulfillable wishes," while past subjunctive is used for wishes whose likelihood of fulfillment is small. This contrast between two different irrealis forms, based on a greater or lesser degree of realizability, appears to be a GMC innovation.

(5.12) a. Es lebe der König!
it live-PresSubjunct the king
'Long live the King!'
(GE, Schulz and Griesbach 1960: 73)

b. Käme mein Vater doch!
came-PastSubjunct my father!
'If only my father came!'
(GE, Schulz and Griesbach 1960: 75)

c. Nu fraleitais skalk þeinana
now release-2SgPresSubjunct servant your
'Now may you release your servant'
(GO, Luke 2:29, Streitberg 1920: 204)

d. jah wainei þiudanodedeiþ
and I-wish reign-2PlPastSubjunct
'and I-wish you-might-reign'
(GO, I Cor. 4:8, Streitberg 1920: 204)

e. Guð fyrirgefi þér!
God forgive-3SgPresSubjunct you
(IC, Kress 1982: 237)

f. Væri ég kominn til tunglsins!
were-1SgPastSubjunct I come to moon-the
'If only I were on the moon!'
(IC, Kress 1982: 237)

Because of the implied possibility of fulfilling the wish, present subjunctive in this use comes close in meaning to an imperative, and is very often used with imperative force. So, for example, in the GO Bible translation, Greek second person imperatives are often translated as subjunctives, for reasons that are not always evident, but that may have to do with differing degrees of assumed controllability of the action.

(5.13) Hauseiþ mis allai jah fraþjaiþ
hear-2Pl-Imper me all and understand-3PlPresSubjunct
= Greek Imperative = Greek Imperative
'Hear and understand me!'
(GO Mark 7:14, Krause 1968: 217)

In all of the GMC languages except GO, the third person imperative has disappeared as a distinct form, and present subjunctive has taken over the function of a command

5.1 Historical prelude 281

form for third person (see, e.g., Einarsson 1945: 150 on IC). In GO, where there is still a third person imperative, both it and the corresponding present subjunctive forms are used to translate Greek imperatives, depending on the degree to which the speaker wishes the outcome. Third person imperative is used only when it is clear that the speaker does not do so, as in the following:

(5.14)   a. atsteigadau   nu   af   þamma galgin...
            climb-down-3SgImper now from the   cross
            'Let him now climb down from the cross'
            (GO, Matt. 27:42, Krause 1968: 218)

Compare the following, in which the Greek imperative is translated as a present subjunctive:

(5.14)   b. weihnai   namo þein
            be-sanctified-3SgPresSubjunct name your
            'May your name be sanctified'
            (GO, Matt. 6:9)

In other uses, the difference between present and past subjunctive is not so sharp. For example, GE uses subjunctive in reported speech, to distance the speaker from commitment to the truth of the speech being reported. In principle, either subjunctive can be used basically interchangeably here, though where one of the forms is non-distinct from its indicative counterpart there is a tendency to prefer the other.

(5.15)   a. Ich habe gehört, daß er krank sei/wäre
            I   have heard   that he sick   is-PresSubj/PretSubj

GE does not exhibit the tense shift that characterizes indirect reporting of speech in EN. In the GE example in (5.15a), the present tense verb of the reported utterance is simply replaced by one or another subjunctive form to indicate the reporter's lack of commitment to the truth of the utterance s/he is reporting. The two subjunctive forms are interchangeable for this purpose, and, crucially, whichever is chosen, this is still understood to be a report of a present tense assertion. In EN, on the other hand, indicative, not subjunctive, is used in indirect reporting of speech, but the "sequence of tense" rule requires that the tense of the verb of the original utterance be shifted to conform to that of the main clause verb:

(5.15)   b. I heard that he was sick

That these two treatments of reported speech are not mutually exclusive is shown by IC, in which an original present tense utterance like (5.15c) adjusts to the tense of the main verb (sequence of tenses), but as in GE assumes subjunctive form, thus either appearing as a present subjunctive (5.15d) or as a past subjunctive (5.15e) (Kress 1982: 236).

(5.15)   c. Hún fer heim á morgun
                 she goes home tomorrow
                 (IC, Einarsson 1945: 157)

               d. Hann segir, að hún fari heim...
                 he says that she go-PresSubjunct
                 (Einarsson 1945: 157)

               e. Hann sagði, að hún færi heim...
                 he said that she go-PastSubjunct
                 (Einarsson 1945: 157)

This is significant, since it indicates the two different subjunctive forms do have contrastive tense values for some purposes. It is not a difference in meaning, though. This is shown by the fact that, when the original utterance has a past tense verb, it must be reported in indirect discourse by means of a periphrastic perfect construction with 'have' in one or another subjunctive form (depending on the tense of the main clause).

(5.15)   f. Hún kom heim í gær
                 She came home yesterday
                 (Einarsson 1945: 157)

               g. Hann segir, að hún hafi komið...
                 He says that she have-PresSubjunct come....

               h. Hann sagði, að hún hefði komið...
                 He said that she have-PastSubjunct come...

Here, the perfect construction is what signals that the proposition refers to a reported event in past time. The contrast between present subjunctive and past subjunctive is without meaning, being automatically predicted by the tense of the main clause verb. Nonetheless, the fact that *fari* and *færi* in (5.15d) and (5.15e) are differentially selected by the tense of the main clause shows that for certain purposes (such as tense agreement) "present" and "past" subjunctives do count as present and past forms respectively.

In the modern GMC languages other than IC and GE, present subjunctive is still distinctly marked only in the third person singular, if at all (EN *live* vs. *lives*). In these languages, moreover, it can be regarded as a fossil form, since it no longer occurs productively, but is restricted to fixed formulaic wishes, as the contrast between (5.16a) and (5.16b) shows.

(5.16)   a. Long live the King!

b. *Long last the meeting!

c. ólukka   slái   hann!
misfortune strike him
(FA, Barnes 1994: 205)

d. Gud velsigne dig!
God bless   you
(DA, Allan *et al.* 1995: 303)

e. Leve konungen!
live king-the
(SW, Holmes and Hinchcliffe 1994: 297)

f. het ga u   goed
it go you good
'May all go well for you'
(DU, Donaldson 1981: 160)

As a productive device, however, it has been superseded in this function by modal plus infinitive constructions.

(5.16)   g. Ja, må hon leve...!
long may she live
(SW, Holmes and Hinchcliffe 1994: 295)

In some of these languages, the present subjunctive survives in a somewhat more productive way as a substitute for third person imperatives in such contexts as recipes (cf. Donaldson 1981: 160).

The past subjunctive, too, aside from GE and IC, is in the process of becoming wholly non-distinct from the indicative preterite. To the extent that differences survive, they are restricted to strong verbs (e.g. DU *kwam* 'came-PastIndic', *kwame* 'came-PastSubjunct)' and irregular verbs. So, for example, in EN, the formally distinct subjunctive is restricted to the singular of the verb *be*, and even this is in the process of replacement by the indicative past: 'If I was rich. . .' appears to be universally preferred by my students, notwithstanding the fact that it is stigmatized in prescriptive grammar. A similar development is in progress in SW, where Holmes and Hinchcliffe (1994: 298) report that a form identical to the indicative past is replacing the distinctive subjunctive form in sentences like:

(5.17)   a. Om jag vore/var ung   igen
if   I   were/was young again
(SW, Holmes and Hinchcliffe 1994: 298)

In DA (Allan *et al.* 1995: 304) and in DU (Donaldson 1981: 160), only the indicative-like form is possible in this context:

(5.17)   b. als ik rijk was....
         if I rich were
         (DU, Donaldson 1981: 160)

         c. Hvis jeg var dig...
         if I was you
         (DA, Allan *et al.* 1995: 304)

Although these languages are sometimes described as "losing" the subjunctive, it is arguable that the subjunctive is still a distinct inflectional category from past tense in such languages as EN, even when the two are formally identical, since a different mapping of form and meaning is involved in each case. Not everyone agrees on this point, however. Jannsen (1994: 111) and Fabricius-Hansen (1994: 51) claim that in such languages as DA, NO, EN and DU, where the subjunctive has ceased to exist productively as a formally distinct inflectional category, there is now only a single "past tense," whose meanings have accordingly been enlarged to encompass non-past counterfactual as well as past time reference. The complexity of the result does little to recommend this approach.

5.1.2.2.2 **Imperative** For the most part, the GMC imperative has forms distinct from those of the indicative only in the singular. Plural imperative forms are identical to the corresponding indicatives, distinguished from them only by whether or not they have a subject pronoun and their order with respect to that pronoun.

(5.18)   a. Ihr hört 'you hear'   Hört! 'Hear!'
         (GE)

         b. Sie kommen 'you come'   Kommen Sie! 'Come!'
         (GE)

(The occurrence or non-occurrence of subject pronouns in imperative constructions is discussed in detail in Section 4.12.3.)

GO, however, distinguishes third person plural imperative, for example, *nimandau* 'let them take', from third person indicative *nimand* 'they take'. GO is, in fact, the only GMC language to exhibit distinctive third person imperative forms at all, and it has them in both singular and plural (though not dual). The distinct imperative forms of GO are the following:

(5.18)   c. Singular 2   nim-0 'take'/ nasei-0 'save!'
                      3   nim-adau 'let him take'
            Plural   3   nim-andau

Table 5.1 *Inflectional endings of active strong verbs in selected Germanic languages*

		Gothic				Icelandic				Frisian		Swedish		Afrikaans
		PRES		PAST		PRES		PAST		PRES	PAST	PRES	PAST	
		IN	SU	IN	SU	IN	SU	IN	SU					–
Sg	1	a	au	–	jau	–	i	–	i	–	–	er	–	
	2	is	ais	t	eis	ur	ir	st	ir	st				
	3	iþ	ai	–	i	ur	i	–	i	t	–			
Pl	1	am	aima	um	eima	um				e	en			
	2	iþ	aiþ	uþ	eiþ	ið		uð						
	3	and	aina	un	eina	a	i		u					
Infin		an				a				e		a		

5.2 Modal auxiliaries

The treatment of modal verbs is complicated by the fact that the semantic, morphological, selectional and syntactic criteria for their identification do not converge exactly on a single set of elements. On the morphological side, most modal verbs are, historically, "pretero-present" (or perfect-present) verbs – that is, verbs whose present tense is formed on the IE perfect, rather than on the IE present (a fact related to their generally stative meanings). This results in present tense forms which resemble the past tense forms of basic strong verbs with respect to their vocalism and endings. Thus, for example, the GO *kunnan* 'to know' has a present tense which looks like the past tense of a corresponding regular strong verb of the same class:

(5.19)   ik kann 'I know'   cf.   ik band   'I bound'
         is kann 'he knows'   is band   'he bound'
         weis kunnum 'we know'   weis bundum   'we bound'

Because of this origin, unlike regular verbs in the present tense, they are endingless in the first and third person singular – a characteristic of strong verb past tenses. Thus, for example, in GE, *ich kann* 'I can' differs from *ich singe* 'I sing'.[2] From a synchronic morphological standpoint, this gives modal verbs the appearance of inflectional defectiveness, since they lack the full range of person inflectional endings and contrasts exhibited by other verbs in the singular present, for example (EN *he sings* versus *he can*, DA *jeg singer* versus *jeg kan*). This property does not pick out all and only modal verbs, since other verbs (EN *dare* and OE *witan* 'to know', for example – also of pretero-present origin) share the anomalous inflection

---

[2] For the same reason, pretero-present verbs have a different vowel in the singular present than in the plural present (GE *ich kann/wir können*), like past tenses of strong verbs. Not having recourse to IE perfect forms for the purposes of past tense formation, pretero-present verbs formed weak preterites, adding the dental suffix directly to the zero grade of the root (GO *ik kunþa*, GE *ich konnte*). The infinitive forms of pretero-present verbs are formed on their present plural stems, and thus also show the reflexes of the zero-grade vocalism that was characteristic of plural perfects in IE (GO *kunnan*, GE *können*).

but fail to pattern as modals with respect to other criteria, including meaning (see below). There is, though, a historical tendency to adjust the morphology in such a way as to maximize the correspondence between this distinctive pretero-present inflectional pattern and modal meaning. Thus, on the one hand, *dare*, historically a pretero-present but with a non-modal meaning, now occurs with the regular 3Sg -*s* in at least some syntactic circumstances ('He dares to do that', vs. 'He dare not do that'). Conversely, *need*, originally a regular weak verb, not a pretero-present, but with a modal meaning, now tends to appear without the -*s* under some circumstances ('He needs to do that', but 'He need not do that'). Note that it has also assimilated to modals with respect to syntactic properties, such as the ability to precede the clausal negator, and the ability to appear with prepositionless infinitives, which will be discussed below. Developments comparable to one or another of these are also found in other GMC languages. YI *flegn* 'used to' and *kern* 'ought to', originally non-pretero-present with modal-like meanings, have come to inflect as a pretero-present in some varieties of YI (Birnbaum 1979: 263; Jacobs 2005: 216), while GE *taugen*, 'be of use, avail', and *gönnen* 'to not begrudge', original pretero-presents with non-modal meanings, have ceased to inflect as preteropresents. Moreover, as Denison (1993: 296f.) points out, other members of the class of pretero-presents without modal meanings have tended to disappear over time in EN (e.g., *unnan* 'to grant', *dugan* 'avail', *witan* 'to know' and all other non-modal pretero-presents in OE), thus further increasing the correspondence. While the correspondence between this morphology and membership in the modal category is not complete, it is the most distinctive characteristic of the class across the GMC languages, and one which seems to have become more strongly aligned with semantic properties over time. Other morphological properties include participation in the GE double-infinitive construction in perfect tenses discussed in note 12. However, this is again not exclusive to modal verbs, since it is also found with verbs of perception. In EN, modals are also characterized by defectiveness with respect to tense, connected in part with the general conflation of preterite and conditional forms (see Denison 1993: 294).

Semantically, modals are auxiliaries which take verb phrases headed by other verbs (the "main" or "lexical" verb) as arguments, and add to them an additional assertion of, roughly, modality. Modality is of two basic types. On the one hand, the modal may assert something about the possibility, probability, necessity, permissibility or desirability of the event described by the other verb phrase (the "root" meaning of the modal). In some of these cases, for example, 'You may leave', the modal serves as a speech-act verb. Uttering the sentence amounts to bestowing permission. On the other hand, the modal may assert something about the source and quality of the speaker's information for the factuality of that event ("epistemic" meaning). Individual modals normally admit either root or epistemic meanings.

(5.20) a. Er soll verhaftet werden (ROOT: desirability)
         he should arrested become
         (GE)

       b. Er soll verhaftet worden sein (EPISTEMIC: hearsay)
         he should arrested become be
         'He is supposed (alleged) to have been arrested'

Root meanings are sometimes further categorized as deontic (obligation and permission) and dynamic (those having to do with possibility and intent).

Epistemic and root interpretations of modals are found in all of the modern GMC languages. However, epistemic interpretations seem to be less frequent in the earlier languages, largely restricted in OE, for example, to 'may/might' (Denison 1993: 298).

(5.20) c. þæt hit mihte bīon þrēora mīla brād
         that it might be three miles wide
         (OE, Orosius, Ohthere)

       d. heyrir hann, at Skrýmir mun sofnat hafa
         hears he that Skrymir may slept have
         (ON, Edda)

Goossens (1982) claims that they are in large part a secondary development in EN. If so, then their distribution across the modern languages would appear to be another case of similarity by convergence.

The semantic argument of the modal is the entire predication ('he is arrested' in (5.20a, b), for example). The first one asserts that that proposition is desirable. The second asserts that it is hearsay. In neither one is there a direct, semantic connection between a modal and the subject 'he', whose semantic role is instead determined entirely by the nonfinite "lexical" verb. This property is sometimes referred to as "transparency."

These semantic criteria for identifying modals, again, do not line up perfectly with morphological and syntactic critera. *Appear*, for example, would seem to resemble modals semantically, but does not conform to the recognized class of modals inflectionally. Nor does it share with the modals another widespread syntactic characteristic; unlike other verbs taking infinitive complements, modals typically take infinitives without a prepositional complementizer (*to, zu, at*). This syntactic criterion seems to recur at least as a necessary condition for modals across most GMC languages (though not as a sufficient condition, since there are non-modal verbs which take bare infinitive complements – see Section 6.7.1). Thus, in FR, for example, all modal verbs take bare infinitives:

(5.21) a. Hja kin/mei/moat/sil/wol dat boek lêze
         she can/may/must/shall/want that book read
         (FR, Hoekstra 1997: 4)

The verb *doare* 'dare', on the other hand, another pretero-present verb which used to take bare infinitives but which has a non-modal meaning, has now begun to appear with a prepositional infinitive (as is also the case with EN *dare*).

(5.21)   b. Hy doar dat net te sizzen / Hy doar dat net sizze
         he dare that not to say
         (FR, Hoekstra 1997: 4)

In IC (where the various characteristics of modals converge less than elsewhere), some verbs with pretero-present morphology and modal meanings take *að* infinitives, rather than bare infinitives. This is true of *kunna* 'know (how to)', *eiga* 'be supposed to', and *þurfa* 'need to', though not of *mega* 'be allowed to', and *vilja* 'want'.

(5.21)   c. Ég þarf (ekki) að fara
         I need (not) to go
         (IC, Einarsson 1945: 166)

Therefore, modals resist identification as a unitary, exhaustive semantic morphological or syntactic category. In fact, in the great majority of the GMC languages, it would seem that they can be regarded as simply a subset of verbs which happen to share a cluster of semantic, morphological and selectional peculiarities, some of which are shared by non-modal verbs. Modern EN is a very clear exception, however. In EN, modal verbs have come to exhibit unique syntactic patternings which do set them apart from all lexical verbs, and which indicate that they are in fact instances of a separate word type. First of all, they, unlike lexical verbs, can appear in a special Aux(iliary) position to the left of the sentential negator and frequency adverbs.

(5.22)   a. He may not/often leave

         b. *He leaves not/often

They are also able precede the subject of the clause in main clause questions ("subject-aux inversion"), unlike lexical verbs with which an auxiliary verb 'do' must be used.

(5.22)   c. May we leave now?

         d. *Left they at 3:00?

They share these properties with the aspectual auxiliaries *have* and *be*, as well as the "dummy auxiliary" *do*, though not with lexical verbs:

(5.22)   e. He is {not/often} leaving

         f. He has {not/often} left

However, the modal verbs differ from *have* and *be* in that they can *only* occur to the left of the negator, and of medial frequency adverbs. *Have* and *be*, on the other hand, can occur to the right of sentence adverbs, in a nonfinite form (present or past participle or infinitive), just in case another finite verb occupies the leftward Aux position.

(5.22)   a. He must not have left

b. He must not be leaving

c. He has not been studying

d. He may not have been leaving

Probably to be connected with this is the fact that EN modals, unlike those of other GMC languages, lack nonfinite forms; they do not have present and past participles and infinitives. In contexts where we might expect nonfinite forms of modals, we instead get nonfinite forms of unrelated non-modal verbs, or verb plus adjective combinations, with equivalent meaning. This is in contrast to GE, for example, where all modals have infinitives (and other nonfinite forms).

(5.23)   a. *musting, *musted, *to must → having to, had to, to have to

b. *shoulding *shoulded *to should → being supposed to, etc.

Other differences between EN modals and those in other GMC languages follow from this. EN modals cannot be "stacked," as they can in GE, for example – that is, they cannot appear as nonfinite complements of other modals or aspectual auxiliaries. EN modals also cannot appear in infinitive clauses, as they can in GE.[3]

(5.23)   c. *I hate to must wait   I hate to have to wait.

d. Ich hasse, warten zu müssen
I hate wait to must
(GE)

e. *He is supposed to must stay home.

f. *He has musted stay at home

g. Er hat zu Hause bleiben   müssen
He has at home to-remain musted

h. Er soll   zu Hause bleiben müssen
he should at home remain must
'He is alleged to have had to stay home'

---

[3] Restricted apparent exceptions to the prohibitions against stacking of modals and nonfinite uses of modals appear in some nonstandard dialects of EN, e.g., Appalachian EN – *might could, useta could, musta didn't* (Wolfram and Christian 1976: 90) – and Scots EN (Brown 1991; Miller 2004: 53).

(i)   You'll have to can do it whether you like it or not
(Scots, Brown 1991: 75)

In at least some cases of stacking, these authors note that the first modal can often be paraphrased as an adverb (*might could* = 'perhaps could'), and suggest that this may be the best analysis for them.

Arguably further evidence of a different status for modals in GE than in EN is the fact that in GE (and in other GMC languages), modals need not always be auxiliary verbs, but can be the sole verb in the clause, as in the following cases, with understood but unexpressed verbs of motion:

(5.24) a. Ich muß nach Hause [ ]
         I must [ ] home
         (GE)

       b. Jeg må [ ] på arbejde
          I must [ ] to work
          (DA, Allan *et al.* 1995: 292)

This whole cluster of differences between EN modals on the one hand and modals in GE and elsewhere on the other follows from the more or less standard view that GE modals are members of the lexical category verb, and therefore have a distribution not unlike other verbs, while EN modals are members of the lexical category Aux, and can only appear in the unique Aux position reserved for the finite verb of the clause. GE modals (as well as the auxiliaries *have* and *be* in EN and elsewhere) are verbs which take bare VPs as their complements. Like other verbs, they can move into the auxiliary position of the sentence just in case it is not already occupied (e.g., by a higher modal). If the Aux position is occupied, then they will, like other verbs, stay within the verb phrase, appearing in the appropriate nonfinite form. EN modals, on the other hand, are "native" auxiliaries. They can only appear in the Aux slot. Thus, they will never appear to the right of the sentential negator for example, nor in a nonfinite form. Further, since each sentence has a unique Aux position, there will be only one modal per clause in EN. In GE, on the hand, modals, since they are verbs, can head verb phrases which are selected by higher modals, and they can in turn select VPs of their own. Stacking will thus be a possibility.

The situation is perhaps more complicated than this, however. In the GE stacked modal example in (5.23h), we observe that the uppermost modal has an epistemic interpretation, but the lower one has a root interpretation, and, in fact, it appears to be impossible to construct examples in which the lower modal has an epistemic interpretation. The same applies to cases like:

(5.25) a. Er muß das gemacht haben
         'he must have done   that' (epistemic)
         (GE)

       b. Er hat das machen müssen.
          'he had to do   that' (root only)

In the first of these, but not in the second, the modal may have the epistemic meaning of 'conclusion from indirect evidence'.

Similarly, modals in infinitive clauses admit only root meanings – not epistemic ones. (For GE, compare Fagan 1996; Abraham 2001a: 102.) Vikner (1988: 35) points out that this is true in DA, van Kemenade (1992) reports the same distribution of interpretations for DU and Brown (1991) for Scots. This being the case, we can perhaps conclude that all epistemic modals are Aux elements in the other GMC languages, as well as standard EN, and therefore restricted to finite positions, non-stackable and so on, and that the difference between EN and these other languages is that EN assigns the same status to root modals as well, whereas root modals elsewhere in GMC are assigned to the category Verb. Abraham (2001a: 113) offers an analysis along these lines.

How did EN come to be different on this point from other GMC languages? Earlier investigators of the syntax of modals in Old and Middle EN claimed that, as in GE, they had the syntactic distribution of verbs in pre-modern EN, citing, among other things, the fact that they occur in syntactic frames other than in front of bare VPs – taking direct objects, locative complements, finite clausal complements or no complements at all, for example – and that, unlike their Modern EN counterparts, they do exhibit nonfinite forms.

(5.26) a. Yet I can Musick too
(Early Mod EN, cited in Denison 1993: 307)

b. þatt I shall cunnenn cwemenn Godd
that I shall can   please   god
'That I shall be able to please God'
(Early ME, Denison 1993: 310)

The fact that they can no longer do so indicates that they have shifted categories, from verbs to Aux elements, between Early Modern and Modern EN. (See Denison 1993 for an overview of such analyses, and, more recently, Roberts and Roussou 2002.) Other recent and systematic studies, on the other hand, have concluded that no such category change has occurred; the appearance of category change results from the fact that in earlier EN these forms existed as doublets of homophonous lexical verbs and auxiliaries. The lexical verbs were lost and the auxiliaries retained. In OE, for example, in addition to its modal meaning, *cunnan* 'can' also functioned as a lexical verb meaning 'know'. Allan (1987:151) claims that it was only in these non-modal meanings that these verbs could show verb-like syntactic behavior, such as appearing with direct objects and in nonfinite forms. When they appear in meanings equivalent to Modern EN modals, they are always finite, and only take bare VP complements. (See also van Kemenade 1992 for a similar claim that modals were already syntactically distinct from other verbs in OE.) Warner (1993: 146), on the basis of very detailed and systematic examination, comes to a comparable (though somewhat less categorical) conclusion, claiming that by the time of ME, "pretero-present verbs subcategorized for plain infinitives which denote necessity, obligation and related notions of futurity are finite only." According to this view, the impossibility of sentences like (5.26a) in Modern EN does not reflect a change in the syntax of modals but a loss of the corresponding homophonous lexical verbs. Modal verbs have always been distinct syntactically from regular verbs; the difference between OE and Modern EN is that a series of changes have taken place which make the distinction more salient. The changes include loss of these lexical verb homophones of true modals, loss of non-modal pretero-present verbs (leaving the modals inflectionally isolated), the replacement of bare infinitive complements of non-modal verbs by *to*-infinitive complements, and, in relatively recent times, the loss by lexical verbs of the ability to appear in the Aux position, and to participate in subject-aux inversion, leaving only modal verbs and aspectual auxiliaries with that ability. Against the background of this reevaluation of syntax of modals in OE, it will be interesting to take a closer look at anomalies in the behavior of modals in the other GMC languages. In SW, for example, not all modals have infinitive forms (Holmes and Hinchcliffe 1994: 292), though it is not clear that this breaks down in the same way as in ME, nor that the division falls along root/epistemic lines. *Skola* 'shall', *kunna* 'be able' and *vilja* 'want to' have infinitives and participles, but *må* 'may, must', *tör* 'is probably' and (literary) *lär* 'is said to' do not.

5.3 Developments in the expression of tense in Germanic

As we have seen, GMC had only two inflectionally signaled tenses: "present" and "past." This minimal system was subsequently supplemented by the development of periphrastic expressions for other tense/aspect distinctions, involving a combination of various auxiliary verbs with nonfinite verbal forms: infinitives, past participles and present participles. So, for example, individual GMC languages have developed present perfect and pluperfect, future and progressive constructions, as well as combinations of these – for example, future perfect progressives like:

(5.27) Ég mun hafa verið að lesa
'I shall (may) have been reading'
(IC, Einarsson 1945: 143)

None of these developments is traceable to the parent language, and they are absent or underdeveloped in the older languages. GO, for example, has no systematic periphrastic expression of future tense, perfect tense or progressive. Thus, the extensive use of auxiliary verbs plus nonfinite verb forms across GMC languages, rather than inflection,

5.3 Developments in the expression of tense in Germanic

to express distinctions in tense and aspect (and, as we will see, voice and mood) is a late development, though not one which is unique to GMC; similar periphrastic constructions have arisen in the neighboring Celtic and Romance languages.

5.3.1 Identifying periphrastic tense/aspect constructions

A discussion of periphrastic tenses necessarily confronts the vexed question of how they are to be delimited. For example, the following GO construction appears to be a progressive construction, contrary to the claim that early GMC did not have these, since, like the EN one, it consists of 'be' plus an apparent present participle.

(5.28)   was   kunnands
         he-was knowing
         (GO, Sk. Ib:13)

Note, however, that stative verbs like 'know' in general resist participation in progressive constructions in languages which have such constructions. Moreover, the nonfinite verbal forms of GMC are ambiguous with respect to category. Thus, participles, in addition to being parts of verbal paradigms, can also function as adjectives, or even as nouns. Therefore, it is likely that the participle in this GO example is to be interpreted as a predicate adjective, rather than a form of the verb. It thus means something like 'he was knowledgeable that. . .'. The problem illustrated by this example is a general one, and the existence of such look-alike constructions can make it difficult to identify and date the beginnings of periphrastic aspect and voice constructions. (Compare Visser 1963: 1929ff. for a discussion of how this complicates the dating of the EN progressive, for example.) Similar problems arise with respect to the identification of perfect constructions in GMC. In their origins, the GMC perfect constructions are often claimed to have been predications of states, in which the past participle functions as a predicative adjective. Constructions like the GE

(5.29)   Ich habe es gebrochen
         I   have it broken

are usually regarded as arising from resultative constructions involving a transitive verb *haben* with a direct object, of which the participial adjective, for example, *gebrochen* is predicated, the whole thing meaning something like 'I have it in a state of brokenness'. From here, according to the standard story, the perfect construction emerges by way of a process of grammaticalization in which *haben* ceases to function as a lexical verb of possession and becomes an aspectual auxiliary, the participle ceases to be a stative adjective and begins to function as a part of the verbal paradigm, and the whole comes to describe an event, rather than a state. Exactly when such a transition takes place in individual languages is hard to pinpoint. 'Have' has clearly become a perfect auxiliary, rather than a lexical verb of possession when it starts appearing with intransitive verbs in constructions with no objects, as in the following:

(5.30) a. þet hē hæfde gebēon on þes cynges swicdōme
           that he had   been   at the king's betrayal
           (OE, AS Chr. 1096)

        b. oðþæt folcgetrume   gefaren   hæfdon
           until   with-an-army gone   they had
           (OE, Gen.1987, Visser 1963: 2059)

These examples show that by late OE 'have' had made that transition at least in past perfect constructions, though not all investigators are willing to grant that it had a full-fledged perfect construction. See the reservations expressed in Mitchell (1985: I, 298).[4]

In a somewhat similar vein, it is observed in Einarsson 1945: 141 that intransitive verbs of motion in IC participate in two different periphrastic constructions – one with the helping verb *vera* 'be' and a participle which agrees with the subject and one with the helping verb *hafa* 'have' and a non-agreeing participle (appearing with a default neuter ending). These are illustrated in (5.31).

(5.31) a. Hann er kominn
           he   is come

        b. Hann hefur komið
           he   has come
           (IC, Einarsson 1945: 141)

The two differ in that the former means, roughly, 'he is in a state of having come (and is therefore still here)', while the latter has an actional interpretation ('He has come in the past, but is not necessarily here now'). See Yamaguchi and Pétursson 2003 for a more exact characterization of the semantic difference. The construction in (5.31a) differs in this respect from 'be' perfects in other GMC languages, such as DU (5.31c), which do not imply a continuing state.

---

[4] Brinton (1988: 99), on the other hand, places the origin of the EN perfect in prehistorical times, stating that "the development of the perfect in GMC is primarily preliterary," and challenges the traditional derivation from stative possessive constructions, stating that "there is no reason to believe that these collocations originally expressed possessive meaning. . ." (Brinton 1988: 102).

(5.31)   c. De brief is   met de tweede post gekomen
the letter arrived with the second post
(DU, Sorace 2000: 858)

Kress (1982: 147ff.), like Einarsson, treats both of the IC constructions as distinct periphrastic verbal aspect constructions, both of which belong to verbal paradigms, classifying them respectively as "Resultative/Situative" and "Perfect" conjugations. It is not obvious, however, in view of its stative meaning, that the former might not be better analyzed as a predicate adjective construction with a participial adjective, rather than a verbal construction with a verbal past participle. See Mitchell 1985: I, 303ff. for a similar reservation about whether there was a true perfect with 'be' in OE.

A similar set of questions arises with respect to progressive, or continuous tense, constructions. As noted above, EN has a progressive construction, consisting of two components: an auxiliary and a nonfinite verb form. The *-ing* gerund in (5.32) behaves like a verb in, for example, taking adverbial modifiers and NP complements.

(5.32)   I am slowly finishing this chapter

Since it is built up from the same types of elements as other periphrastic tense/aspect constructions in the language, regarding it as a part of the tense/aspect system of EN, that is, as a part of the verbal conjugation (in a sense appropriately enlarged to include periphrastic constructions), seems unproblematic. IC also has a construction which signifies continuous tense, called "progressive" by Thráinsson (1994: 163) and "kursiv" by Kress (1982: 159). This construction, too, is formed with an auxiliary 'be' plus a nonfinite form of the verb – in this case, the infinitive. However, it also includes a third element, the infinitive marker *að*.[5]

(5.33)   a. hún er að   borða
she is *að* eat-Inf
'She is eating'
(IC, Thráinsson 1994: 163)

In IC grammars, this construction is also treated as a part of the verbal paradigm; Kress regards it as constituting a "cursive conjugation" (cf. also Einarsson 1945: 143).

---

[5] This construction is one of a family of aspectual constructions found exclusively in Icelandic, which Haugen (1976: 307) reports have been attributed to Irish influence. The others include inchoative constructions with *fara* 'go' (*Ég fer að hlæja* 'I begin to laugh') and perfective with *vera búinn* (lit. 'be lived') (*Ég er búinn að gleyma* 'I have forgotten'). The latter, according to Kress (1982: 155), is similar in meaning to the present perfect, but differs from it in implying the continued existence of a resultant state.

Farther toward the margins is the construction in DA (5.33b) and FA (Barnes 1994: 211), and the YI construction in (5.33c), which includes, besides the auxiliary, the nonfinite verb and the complementizer, a preposition.

(5.33)   b. han var ved at skrive   et brev
                he was with at write-Inf the letter
                'He was writing the letter'
                (DA, Haberland 1994: 334)

           c. ikh halt   in shraybn
               I   hold in write-Inf
               'I am writing'
               (YI, Ebert 2000: 633)

Farther still from the canonical structure of a periphrastic tense/aspect is the construction in AF (5.33d) that Lockwood (1965: 210) refers to as "continuous tense" (see also Donaldson 2000: 114).

(5.33)   d. Ek is   aan die skryf
                I   am on   the write
                'I am writing'
                (AF, Lockwood 1965: 210)

The meaning of this construction again overlaps with that of the EN progressive, but here we would be on more solid ground in denying it status as a part of the tense/aspect marking paradigms of AF, since *skryf* is not a form of a verb at all, but a noun.

Ebert (2000: 607) extends the umbrella of "progressive constructions" far enough to include paraphrases like (5.33e), found in a number of modern GMC languages, and concludes that all of the modern languages have progressive constructions (see also Donaldson 1993: 220).

(5.33)   e. Hi sät än löst et bläär
                he sits and reads the newspaper
                (NF, Ebert 2000: 608)

Again, these constructions are functionally equivalent to the progressives of EN, for example, since, as Ebert notes, they are the ones that are elicited by asking, "What is X doing right now?", but they deviate sufficiently from the canonical shape of periphrastic verbal constructions to make their inclusion in verbal paradigms a highly doubtful step. Some guidelines for distinguishing "true progressive" constructions from look-alike constructions, specifically with respect to EN progressives, are offered in Denison 1993: 372ff., but in general the boundaries between those constructions which actually warrant treatment as part of the inflectional paradigms of verbs and those which do not are not sharp. Drawing a possibly arbitrary line, I will limit my attention in this chapter to just those periphrastic constructions consisting of no more than a (verbal) form of the lexical verb (infinitive, participle or gerund), an auxiliary, and an infinitive marker such as *to* and *að*. Excluded by this criterion are such constructions as the "singulative aspect" construction used in Yiddish to express one-time action (Jacobs 2005: 222), as in *er tut a kuk* 'he gives a glance', since it appears to involve a noun, rather than a nonfinite verb form, though as Jacobs points out, the situation is not quite so clear-cut as this.

5.3.2 Future

GMC lacks an inflectional future. All of the GMC languages allow the use of "present" tense forms in reference to future time. This is the normal expression of future in GO, for example (Streitberg 1920: 201). GO makes marginal use of the perfective prefix *ga-* to reinforce the future meaning of present tense forms with durative verbs, though always with an accompanying sense of perfectivity. So, for example, in the following, the first verb translates a Greek future, and the second a Greek present.

(5.34) gaarma þanei arma
pity-1Sg.Pres whom pity-1Sg.Pres
'I will pity whom I pity'
(GO, Rom. 9:15)

Some (though possibly not all) of the modern languages have developed periphrastic future constructions. Even in languages where a periphrastic future has developed, present forms can be used to convey future meanings, and there are some contexts where only the present, not the periphrastic future, can be used in reference to future time. So, for example, present tense stands in for the future quite generally in subordinate time and condition clauses (see Abraham 1989: 348f. for discussion).

(5.35) a. When the semester begins we will be busy

b. Når semestret begynder, vil vi få travlt
when the semester begins will we be busy
(DA, Allan *et al.* 1995: 269)

The possibility of using simple present in future meaning is more circumscribed in EN than in other GMC languages. Thus, for example, (5.35c) is possible in SW (and other languages), but its translation into EN with a simple present tense is not.

(5.35) c. Jag ringer till di i morgen
I call you tomorrow

If intended as a plain assertion about a proposed future action, the corresponding EN sentence requires a *(wi)ll*:

(5.35)   d. I'll call you tomorrow

(The use of present for future is not unrestricted elsewhere, however. Allen *et al.* (1995: 269) point out that in DA, present-as-future is frequent with telic verbs (those which imply a goal or end-point), such as 'stop', 'come', but not generally with atelic verbs (which do not imply a goal or end-point), such as 'live', 'read', 'eat', with which a future auxiliary is normally used.)

The present tense EN gloss on (5.35c), however, is possible in a situation with intended future reference if uttered in a context where the speaker is offering a reminder/asking for a confirmation of a pre-existing plan:

(5.35)   e. So it's settled. I call you tomorrow and then you call John.

In general, it seems to be the case that simple presents used as futures are possible only where this requirement of referring to an already scheduled future event is satisfied.

(5.35)   f. The train leaves on Friday

This restriction has to do with more general differences between EN and other GMC languages with respect to the meaning of the simple present – in particular, it is related to the general fact that the EN simple present does not point to specific instants in time, but rather is used in predications of a generic, habitual, timelessly true nature, with present progressive being used to locate events in the immediate now. Correspondingly, present progressive can be used to express future tense in EN without the limitations imposed on simple future.

(5.35)   g. I'm seeing the new Star Wars film tomorrow

This present-progressive-as-future shares with present-as-future in other GMC languages the property that it is limited to the near future.

(5.35)   h. The world is ending tomorrow/ !!in four billion years

Abraham (1989: 352) also claims that EN, alone among the modern languages, uses its future auxiliary in statements of habitual action, such as the following:

(5.35)   i. She'll sit there for hours just staring at the wall
           (Abraham 1989: 352)

In addition to using present for future under some circumstances, each of the GMC languages has developed future constructions involving auxiliary verbs of one sort or another. These are relatively late developments, and in some respects highly individual. They differ from each other in terms of the source of the auxiliary, and in terms of how much of the original meaning of the auxiliary carries over (Abraham 1989). Abraham distinguishes three types of sources for future auxiliaries.

5.3 Developments in the expression of tense in Germanic

(5.36)   a. Inchoative verbs ('become' futures)

               b. Verbs of motion
                  'go' ('andative' futures)
                  'come' ('venitive' futures)

                c. Modal verbs

Not taken into account in this typology is the striking use of *haban* 'have' as a future auxiliary in GO for durative verbs (Streitberg 1920: 201), reflected in (5.37a), for instance, where *tauja* and *taujan haba* translate a Greek present and future respectively.

(5.37)   a. þatei   tauja   jah taujan haba
                 which do-1SgPres and do-Inf have-1SgPres
                 'what I do and will do'
                 (GO, 2 Cor. 11:12)

This is unique in GMC, though it has an interesting analogue in most Romance languages, where the future suffix is derived from Latin *habere* (Roberts and Roussou 2002: 36).

Case (5.36a) is instantiated in GE (and in perhaps part in YI – see below), which has adapted the inchoative verb *werden* 'become' to use as a future auxiliary. Interestingly, DU, AF and FR failed to develop a future of this type, even though the cognate of this verb (DU *worden*, FR *wurde*) is used as an auxiliary in other constructions, for example, passive (Abraham 1989: 362).

Case (5.36b), in which verbs of motion become future auxiliaries, is found in a variety of West and North GMC languages. 'Come' as a future auxiliary is primarily associated with continental Scandinavian (NO and SW but not DA), though it also appears in Alemannic High GE (Abraham 1989: 362).

(5.37)   b. Eg kjem til å reise   i morgen
                 I   come to   depart tomorrow
                 'I will depart tomorrow'
                 (NO, Abraham 1989: 374)

                c. Es kunt   ga   regna
                  it comes against raining
                  'It is going to rain'
                  (Alemannic, Abraham 1989: 361)

Most West GMC languages, on the other hand, including EN, tend to employ 'go' along with infinitives as a future auxiliary.

(5.37)	d. Nou gaan wij iets		anders doen
		now go	we something other	to-do
		(DU, Abraham 1989: 367)

This is not universal among these languages, though. WF, for example, lacks such 'go'-future construction, aside from cases in which actual motion is involved, as does GE.

(5.37)	e. *No geane wy wat		oars dwaan
		now go	we something other	to-do
		(WF, Abraham 1989: 367)

In general, the 'go' future is used for proximate future, for example, in EN, DU and YI.

Finally, in case (5.36c), future auxiliaries derive from modal verbs. All modal verbs are inherently future-oriented, since the sentences in which they occur describe potentialities. In fact, though, only the modal 'will', with its original volitional meaning, and 'shall', with its original meaning of obligation, evolve into future auxiliaries. All of the modern GMC languages except for GE, which has chosen the inchoative *werden* as its future auxiliary exclusively, and IC, which has developed no true future auxiliary at all, have turned one or the other of these two modals into a future auxiliary (while sometimes also retaining it in its modal functions). In earlier stages of GE, too, 'shall' was the most usual choice for the expression of future, occurring with regularity in OHG, though generally retaining some of its earlier modal meaning (Erdmann 1874: 5). Abraham (1989: 368) notes that FR, lacking the 'go' future of other West GMC languages and the *werden*-future of GE and YI, is unique among the GMC languages in having only the modal type, with the auxiliary *sille*. There is wide variation across modern GMC with respect to the choice between these two modals as the future auxiliary. Some dialects of EN use both, and eighteenth-century prescriptive attempts at regulating their distribution led to the notorious *shall/will* rule (cf. Crystal 2003: 194). Other varieties of EN (Irish, Scottish and American) have only *will*, *shall* surviving only marginally, for example, in formulaic polite requests like 'Shall we go?' DA *ville* has become a pure future marker, while *skulle* retains more modal force, implying that the future event being asserted is a matter of agreement/arrangement or promise (Allan *et al.* 1995: 269). On the other hand, in SW (Holmes and Hinchcliffe 1994: 283), only *skola* has come to be a purely temporal marker of future tense in the third person (while continuing a separate existence as a modal of obligation); *ville* still only occurs as a modal verb of volition. In other persons, however, *skola* too retains modal force, signaling intention or suggestion (Bandle *et al.* 2005: 1622), in contrast to the modally neutral venitive future *komma att*. DU uses *zullen* alone as a future auxiliary, while Low GE uses *willen* as a future auxiliary in reference to events in the immediate future (Lindow *et al.* 1998: 104), alongside *warrn* 'become' (for future events about which there is certainty (Lindow *et al.* 1998: 102)) and *schölen* 'shall'.

(5.37)   f. De Bahn will Klock dree na Hamborg föhrn
             The train will clock three to Hamburg go
             (Low GE, Lindow *et al.* 1998: 104)

YI, too, uses the 'want' verb (*veln*) as a future auxiliary, at least through part of its paradigm.

(5.37)   g. ikh vel shraybn 'I will write'
             du vest shraybn 'you will write'
             er vet shraybn 'he will write'
             mir/zey veln shraybn 'we/they will write'
             (YI, Lockwood 1965: 253)

The first person forms here are identical to those of the corresponding forms of the modal *veln*. However, forms with no /l/ appear in the second person and in the third person singular. In this respect the future auxiliary is different from the modal verb, which has /l/ throughout. Historically, this is because the future auxiliary is actually a conflation of the original *veln* 'want' paradigm and the original *vern* 'become' paradigm (Lockwood 1965: 253). It is not clear, though, that it is so understood synchronically. YI grammatical descriptions, including Jacobs *et al.* 1994: 406 and Katz 1987: 138, identify all of these forms with a single future auxiliary, *veln*.

The transition from modal to future auxiliary is least far along in IC. Einarsson (1945: 137) offers *munu* 'may' as a future auxiliary in his paradigms (*ég mun berja* 'I shall (may) beat'), but this identification is called into question by Kress (1982: 166) and others (cf. Abraham 1989: 375f.).

5.3.3 Perfect tenses and past tenses

The perfect constructions of the GMC languages are unconnected with (and semantically quite distinct from) the IE perfect. In fact, in early GMC translations, perfect and pluperfect in other IE languages are treated as the translational equivalent of GMC simple past tense.

(5.38)   a. ni-u Iesu Xristau...saƕ?
             not-Q Jesus Christ...saw?
             'Have I not seen Jesus Christ?' (Greek has perfect)
             (GO, 1 Cor. 9:1)

           b. Thode intfieng ther heilant then ezzih
             when received the savior the vinegar (Latin has pluperfect)
             (OHG, Tatian (Sievers) 208:4)

302   5 *The Verbal Systems of Germanic*

The periphrastic perfect constructions (present perfect, past perfect or pluperfect and future perfect) occur in all of the modern GMC languages, and in the medieval languages aside from GO, but it is still unclear to what extent they are a common inheritance and to what extent they are of medieval origin, and therefore reflect parallel developments in individual languages. They occur, for example, in OHG, OE (see the preceding section) and abundantly in OS, for example (see Watts 2001):

(5.39)   a. sô wir eigun nû   gisprochan
             as we have now spoken
             (OHG, Otfrid I, 25, 11, Erdmann 1874: 229)

         b. thie hebbiad iro   herta gihrênod
             who have   their heart purified
             (OS, Arnett 1997: 59)

Even in these closely related languages, though, there are individual differences in their formation: OHG uses both *haban* and *eigan* as perfect auxiliaries, for example, and EN from the earliest period uses 'have', not 'be', as the perfect auxiliary with the copula, in contrast with the continental West GMC languages. The constructions nonetheless share features in common across these languages, including the use of two different auxiliaries, 'have' and 'be' (even in EN, until recent times), and arguably their basic meaning as well.

5.3.3.1   *The form of the perfect*

In the usual case, the perfect tenses of GMC employ a combination of an auxiliary – in either its present tense form (present perfect), its past tense form (pluperfect), or its future tense form (future perfect) – plus a past participle. In the Upper GE dialects, where the simple past forms have been lost even for the perfect auxiliary (see Section 5.1.4.4), past perfect is now expressed by means of a present perfect of a present perfect (see Grebe *et al.* 1966: 105, Curme 1952: 283 and Behaghel 1924 II: 272).

(5.40)   a. Ich hab's ganz   vergessen gehabt
             I   have-it completely forgotten had-PP

         b. ich bin eingeschlafen gewesen
             I   am slept   been
             (Behaghel 1924: II, 272)

YI, too, has lost the simple preterite, leaving only the present perfect as a "past" tense, and this has led to a similar development in the past perfect:

(5.40) c. ex hob gyhat gyhailt
I have had-PP healed
'I had healed/ had been healing'
(Birnbaum 1979: 269)

In some of the older languages, the participle exhibited variable agreement with a co-occurring NP (the subject in case the perfect auxiliary was 'be', or the object in case it was 'have'). The former case is illustrated in (5.41e). The latter is illustrated in (5.41a). It was also possible to have a non-agreeing participle, however, even in these early languages (5.41b).

(5.41) a. swīþe wel þū mē hæfst ārētne
very well you me have cheered-MSgAcc
(OE, Sol. 180:32, cited in Wülfing 1901: II, 55)

b. þonne hē hine gefangen hafað
when he him caught-0 has
(OE, Ps. 9:30, cited in Wülfing 1901: II, 55)

In these older languages, the uninflected participle is decidedly the more frequent (Watts 2001: 129). It is not clear that this variation is connected directly with the assumed transition from adjectival participles to verbal ones. Participle agreement in GMC perfect constructions has tended to disappear over time. So, for example, Einarsson (1945: 163) notes that in Modern IC, the participle in perfect construction with *hafa* 'have' takes an invariant singular neuter ending, as in (5.41c), but he notes that in earlier stages, the participle could agree with the object, as in (5.41d):

(5.41) c. hann hefur aukið   eldana
he has stoked-PP-SgNeut fires-the

d. hann hefur aukna   eldana
he has stoked-PP-Pl fires-the
(IC, Einarsson 1945: 163)

Similarly, in OHG there was participle agreement with the subject when 'be' was the perfect auxiliary, as in (5.41e), but agreement has disappeared by MHG (Paul 1989: 294).

(5.41) e. tho   argangana   warun ahtu tagu
when gone-PP-Pl were eight days
(OHG, Tatian 7:1, cited in Paul 1989)

This seems to reflect the more general treatment of predicate adjectives.

In NO, there is a split between BN, which has invariant non-inflecting participles, and NN, in which participles of most strong verbs and a subset of weak verbs taking *være* as their helping verb, inflect for agreement (Bandle *et al.* 2005: 1592).

In SW, the distinction between default-neuter participles in perfect constructions and agreeing participles elsewhere (e.g., in passives and in adjectival uses) has led in relatively recent times to a further formal elaboration between invariant supine forms and inflected past participle forms (see Section 5.5.3 and Holmes and Hinchcliffe 1994: 287 for discussion).

5.3.3.1.1 **Omission of the perfect auxiliary** SW, NO (Bandle *et al.* 2005: 1592) and pre-twentieth-century Modern GE allow the omission of the perfect auxiliary in subordinate clauses.

(5.42) a. Han sa, att hann varit sjuk
    he said that he been sick
    (SW, Holmes and Hinchcliffe 1994: 287)

    b. Wenn er diesen Brief selbst geschrieben, so will ich ihn anstellen
     if he this letter self written, so want I to-employ him
     'If he has written this letter himself, I want to hire him'
     (GE, Curme 1952: 283)

    c. Det ville vært fint
     it would been fine
     (NO, Bandle *et al.* 2005: 1592)

This construction was apparently borrowed into SW from GE in the seventeenth century, but then lost from GE while it was retained in SW (Haugen 1976: 377).

5.3.3.2 *Perfect auxiliary choice*

With the exception of the OHG experiment with *eigan*, perfect auxiliaries in the GMC languages have been limited to the cognates of *have* and *be*. GMC shares this characteristic – the choice of these two auxiliaries as well as the criteria for selection, to a large extent – apparently exclusively with the Romance languages. The GMC languages divide themselves into several groups with respect to how the two auxiliaries are distributed. In some languages, only a single auxiliary has survived. In SW and some varieties of NO (Haugen 1976: 80; Bandle *et al.* 2005: 1592), as well as Modern Standard EN and some varieties of YI (Jacobs 2005: 217), 'be' has been given up altogether, and 'have' occurs as the perfect auxiliary in all cases.

(5.43) a. Vi har varit i Grekland förr
    we have been in Greece before
    (SW, Holmes and Hinchcliffe 1994: 279)

    b. De skulle ha kommit
     they would have come
     (SW, Granberry 1991: 60)

5.3 Developments in the expression of tense in Germanic 305

Whether IC belongs in this group depends on the proper analysis of *vera*-perfects, discussed in Section 5.1.4.1. In some varieties of AF, too, 'have' is used as the perfect auxiliary with all verbs, although, more usually, 'be' is still used for the perfect of the verb *wees* 'be' (Donaldson 1993: 237).

The opposite case is represented in Shetlands EN, where, as reported in Robertson and Graham 1991 and Melchers 1992, only 'be' occurs as a perfect auxiliary (a situation apparently unique in the GMC languages, though Melchers discusses reports of apparent highly sporadic idiolectal parallels in southwestern NO).

(5.43)   c. Fifty Voars I'm   dell'd an set da taaties
            fifty springs I'm (= 'I've') dug and set the potatoes
            (Shetlands EN, Robertson and Graham 1991: 11)

Other languages have alternations in auxiliary choice; in DA, Northern Low GE and, variably, OE and ME (Visser 1963: 2044; Mustanoja, cited in Mitchell 1985: I, 302), 'be' is selected by intransitive motion verbs and change of state verbs as a perfect auxiliary, though the verb 'be' itself selects 'have':

(5.43)   d. Jeg har læst bogen
            I have read book-the
            (DA, Allan *et al.* 1995: 264)

          e. Brevet er forsvundet
            letter-the is disappeared
            (DA, Allan *et al.* 1995: 264)

          f. Vi har været i Italien
            we have been in Italy
            (DA, Allan *et al.* 1995: 264)

          g. Ik bün na den Koopmann lopen
            I am to the merchant run
            (Low GE, Lindow *et al.* 1998: 99)

          h. Korl hett hüüt hier west
            Karl has today here been
            (Northern Low GE, Lindow *et al.* 1998: 99)

In these languages, we can characterize the class of verbs admitting 'be' as '(intransitive) verbs of change of position or state'.

Modern GE and DU also use 'be' not only with verbs of directed motion/change of state, but also with some intransitive verbs of location and continued existence, which do not involve change, such as GE *sein* 'be', *liegen* 'lie' and *bleiben* 'remain' (though not *existieren* 'exist' and *verweilen* 'stay, linger'. (See Lieber and Baayen, 1997, appendix, for an extensive list of verbs in DU categorized by auxiliary choice.) Here, however, variability begins to manifest itself not only in the form of differences between near synonyms, but also between speakers. In GE, for example, verbs of position may take either auxiliary, depending on the speaker, and Ponelis (1993: 446), Lieber and Baayen (1997) report both dialect variation and historical competition between 'have' and 'be' as the perfect auxiliary with *zijn* 'be' in DU.

(5.43)   i. Der Zug ist spät angekommen
            the train is late arrived
            (GE, Sorace 2000: 864)

         j. Die Zwillinge sind im April geboren
            the twins   are in April born
            (GE, Sorace 2000: 866)

         k. Das Buch ist/hat auf dem Boden gelegen
            the book is/has on the ground lain
            (GE, Sorace 2000: 870)

         l. Peter ist lange Zeit im Ausland gewesen
            Peter is long time   abroad been
            (GE, Sorace 2000: 870)

In those languages in which verbs of motion can take 'be' as an auxiliary, they do so only in cases where the motion is "telic" – that is, motion toward a goal. In atelic uses, the verbs of motion take 'have' as an auxiliary. Thus, for example, 'run' in Low GE takes 'have', as in (5.44a), unless a goal of motion is specified (as in 5.43g).

(5.44)   a. Ik heff den ganzen weg lopen
            I have all the   way run
            (Low GE, Lindow *et al.* 1998: 99)

         b. Jan heeft gelopen
            Jan has run
            (DU, Lieber and Baayen 1997: 807)

How best to analyze the nature of perfect auxiliary choice has been one of the more extensively discussed problems in GMC and Romance linguistics over the past few decades, and it is impossible to do justice to that extensive literature here. The reader is referred to Sorace 2000 and Lieber and Baayen 1997 for a discussion of some of the research on the problem. The fundamental question is whether auxiliary choice is determined by syntax or by semantics. A prominent early analysis of the former type is the Unaccusative Hypothesis of Perlmutter (1978) (cf. also Burzio 1986; Rosen 1984),

5.3 Developments in the expression of tense in Germanic

discussed further in Section 4.9.4.1.2.5. Under that hypothesis, the surface subjects of the "intransitive" verbs which take 'be' as their auxiliary are in fact underlyingly direct objects, while those which take 'have' are underlyingly subjects. This makes the former look much like passive sentences, and the claim is that 'be' appears as a perfect auxiliary in these cases for the same reason that it appears as a passive auxiliary in some of these languages. More refined versions of this hypothesis have been advanced. Other investigators have argued that the determinants of auxiliary choice are fundamentally semantic, and not reducible to syntactic structure. Investigators espousing a position of this type are divided about whether there are multiple semantic determinants of auxiliary selection, leading to irreducible scalarity in auxiliary selection (e.g., Shannon 1995) or whether it is possible to identify a single semantic determinant (Lieber and Baayen 1997). Sorace (2000), on the basis of facts from some Romance and GMC languages, advances the following descriptive Auxiliary Selection Hierarchy to characterize the variation. Languages differ with respect to how far down the hierarchy 'be' extends.

(5.45)   Change of location (selects BE (least variation))
             Change of state
             Continuation of a pre-existing state
             Existence of a state
             Uncontrolled process
             Controlled process (motional)
             Controlled process (non-motional) (selects HAVE)

5.3.4 The meaning of the (present) perfect and the past

What exactly the perfect means, whether it is an aspect or a tense, and whether it has a common meaning across the GMC languages are also matters of substantial and ongoing debate. This debate has been particularly vigorous in the case of GE, with special focus on what sets the perfect apart from the simple past in that language. Before returning to this case, I will establish a framework by discussing what makes the present perfect distinctive in languages where such differences are more robust.

Both present perfect and past tense are used to describe events which took place in the past. The main difference in interpretation between present perfect constructions and simple past constructions in at least some languages is that the former but not the latter suggest that the past action decribed is relevant, in some sense, to the situation at (or beyond) the moment of speaking. Thus, for example, it may be that the action has been completed immediately before the moment of speaking, as in (5.46a) (the "proximate past" case). Or it may be that the past action is one of a possible series of actions, which have occurred in the past but to which others of the same type may be added in the future, as in (5.46b) (the "open time frame" case). Present perfect (5.46c) is anomalous because the time frame in which the past events occurred is understood to have been concluded.

308   5 The Verbal Systems of Germanic

(5.46)   a. He has just left

          b. I have only seen three Mel Gibson movies (this year)

          c. !!In London in the 70s, I have seen Big Ben three times

There are rather remarkable differences across the GMC languages, though, with respect to how this "present relevance" requirement is construed. On the one hand, in (Standard) EN, DA and SW, for example, present perfect is also used to express durative events which started in the past but continue on into the present, whereas in GE, DU, AF and Irish EN these are typically expressed as simple present events.[6]

(5.47)   a. They have been married for three years.

          b. Jeg har   ventet paa dig i mange timer
             I   have waited for you a long   time
             (DA, Ehrich and Vater 1989: 114)

          c. De   har   varit gifta   i   många år
             they have been married for many years
             (SW, Holmes and Hinchcliffe 1994: 279)

          d. Ich warte auf dich seit   vielen Stunden
             I   wait for you since many hours
             (GE, Ehrich and Vater 1989: 114)

          e. Ik woon nu   tien jaar   in Amsterdam
             I live   now ten years in Amsterdam
             (DU, Boogaart 1999: 151)

          f. Sy bly   al jare op Springfontein
             she remains years in Springfontein
             'She's been living in Springfontein for years'
             (AF, Donaldson 1993: 227)

          g. We're living here seventeen years
             (Irish EN, Harris 1993: 161)

---

[6] Correspondingly, GE uses simple past tense to refer to an event that started before some reference point in the past and continued through the time of that reference point, while English once again uses a perfect construction:

(i)   Ich wartete schon eine Stunde
          I had been waiting for an hour
          (GE, Russon and Russon 1965: 64)

5.3 Developments in the expression of tense in Germanic

Boogaart (1999: 151) notes that DU can use either present tense or present perfect in such contexts, as can GE (Hendricks (1981: 40), though with a subtle meaning difference. Interestingly, the EN, DA and SW sentences here lose the "continuing into the present" sense when the time phrase is omitted, while retaining "present relevance." Example (5.47h) can be interpreted to mean that they are no longer married.

(5.47) h. They have been married

However it differs from

(5.47) i. They were married

in that (5.47h) still suggests that the time frame is still open, and that they may therefore remarry at some point in the future, whereas (5.47i) does not. This indicates that the default interpretation of present perfect is 'event/ state existing prior to the present, but with present relevance', but that in some languages, the presence of duration phrases allows the stretching of the event itself into the present.

In DA and SW, but not in EN, the requisite "present relevance" can be supplied by the simple continued existence of an object/state created by a past event, as in (5.48):

(5.48) a. Heiberg har skrevet *Elverhøj*
Heiberg has written *Elverhøj*
(the author is dead but the book still exists)
(DA, Allan *et al.* 1995: 266)

b. Vem har skrivet *Röda rummet*
who has written *Red Room-the*?
(SW, Holmes and Hinchcliffe 1994: 280)

This extended sense of "present relevance" is not just of importance for perfects in these languages, but also for (structurally similar) passive constructions, which can be in the present tense even when describing past events, just in case the objects resulting from those events still exist:

(5.49) a. När är ni född ?
when are you born ?
(SW, Holmes and Hinchcliffe 1994: 275)

But

(5.49) b. Strindberg föddes 1849
Strindberg was-born 1849
(SW, Holmes and Hinchcliffe 1994: 276)

(5.49) c. Slottet er opført omkring 1450
the castle is built around 1450
(DA, Allan *et al.* 1995: 260)

Variation is found with respect to present relevance even in dialects of a single language. British EN, for example, requires present perfect in *I've already eaten*, whereas American EN and Irish EN admit *I already ate* (Harris 1993: 162).

Various means have been advanced for capturing this difference between perfect and past formally. Many investigators have attempted to characterize the difference in fundamentally temporal terms, involving the basic oppositions anteriority/ non-anteriority and simultaneity/non-simultaneity. See Musan 2001 for a summary of such accounts. In these accounts, which typically start out from the schemata first advanced by Reichenbach (1947), tenses are characterized by reference to three different points on the timeline along which they occur. [E] is the time of the event itself. [S] is the time of the speaker's utterance of the sentence. [R] is a "reference time" – a third point along the timeline, which may or may not be distinct from the first two – by reference to which the event is localized in time. Thus, for example, in Andersson's account (1989: 41), past tense means simply [E < S] – that is, that the time of the event is anterior to the time of speaking. Perfect, on the other hand, shares with the past that component of meaning, adds the additional component [R, S] – that is, R is simultaneous with S – introducing the notion of present relevance. Andersson thus maintains (1989: 45) that the perfect tenses of GMC are fundamentally tenses, completely characterizable in terms of points along a timeline (see, however, Musan 2001 for an alternative view). Past perfect, in this scheme, is used to assert the occurrence of an event E prior to a reference point R which is also prior to the time of the utterance S [E<R<S]. Past perfect is thus a "relative past tense."

The question of whether the two-part meaning of the present perfect ([E < R], [R, S simultaneous]) can in turn be related to the two-part syntax (present auxiliary plus participle) of the construction used to express it has also been a matter of debate. Some investigators claim that it is compositional in this way. For a recent and detailed discussion of this question, see Musan 2001. Thus, for example, Ballweg (1989), along with others, claims that the present perfect involves the embedding of one tense operator under another, that is, a perfect operator denoting anteriority with respect to a reference time embedded under a present operator: (Pres (Perf (p))). Present perfect sentences are thus a kind of present tense sentence. Present tense, as we have noted earlier (Section 5.3.2), varies in its interpretation across the GMC languages. In some of them, present tense forms can readily appear with future meaning, in the presence of future adverbs. This is true of GE and the Scandinavian languages, for example, as pointed out by Andersson (1989: 32), but much less so in EN:

(5.50) a. Nächste Woche ist er in Groningen
Next week is he in Groningen
(GE, Andersson 1989: 32)

b. Nästa vecka är han i Groningen
(SW, Andersson 1989: 32)

c. Next week he will be in Groningen
(Andersson 1989: 32)

This is also, according to Andersson (1989: 31), related to the fact that in GE and SW, present tense indicative can be used in commands (*Du är tyst nu!*), but not in EN, where a future is required (*You will be quiet*). Ballweg (1989: 89) claims, in fact, that "present tense" in these languages imposes no restrictions at all on the reference time [R]. This is why so-called present tense can be used in reference to past time ("narrative present") as well as future. The idea that present perfect sentences are a kind of present sentence is supported by the fact that in these same languages, present perfect has the same unrestricted time reference as present sentences do; as Ehrich and Vater (1989: 115) point out, it is possible for present perfect sentences in GE and SW to contain future time phrases, and to refer to future events (anterior to a reference time in the future). This is again not possible in EN.[7]

(5.51) a. Jeg har læst bogen (indtil) i morgen
I have read book-the by tomorrow
(DA, Ehrich and Vater 1989: 115)

b. Morgen Mittag habe ich das gemacht
Tomorrow noon have I that done
(GE, Zifonun *et al.* 1997: 1705)

c. I will have done that by tomorrow noon

The fact that present perfect is compatible with future adverbs just in those languages where present tense is also compatible with such adverbs is readily understandable if we interpret the present perfect as a type of present tense. On the other hand, Boogaart's contrastive investigation of perfect constructions in DU and EN

---

[7] Perhaps related is the observation by Haugen (1976: 80) that the present perfect in Scandinavian but not English can convey a meaning of inferred probability of past events.

(i) Han har vært syk da han sa det
he has been sick when he said that
'He must have been sick when he said that'
(Dano-NO, Haugen 1976: 80)

(Boogaart 1999) suggests that the interpretation of the present perfect construction cannot be simply a matter of the meaning of its components, but must be at least in part a function of the availability of other tense/aspect forms in the system.

The special problem posed by GE and DU for the position that the meanings of present perfect constructions are built up from the meanings of their components is that the "present perfect" in those languages is apparently not always subject to a present relevance requirement in the same way as in the other languages, and that therefore, in a wide range of contexts, in GE, at least, it gives the appearance of being semantically equivalent in sentences like (5.52a) to the simple past:

(5.52)   a. Ich bin gestern gekommen
            I am yesterday come
            'I came yesterday'

          b. Ich kam gestern
            I came yesterday
            (GE)

          c. Ik heb gisteren een brief geschreven
            I have yesterday a letter written
            (DU, Boogaart 1999: 64)

These languages seem to be quite different from EN and other languages on this point, where sentences like !*I have come yesterday* are not possible.

Perfect sentences like (5.52a, c) tend to appear in GE and DU in non-narrative (and therefore mainly in spoken language) excepting only for auxiliary and modal verbs. The simple past is largely restricted to narrative discourse (and is therefore more frequent in written language). This distribution is apparently old, being found, for example, in OS, the ancestor of DU (see Watts 2001: 131).

In DU, the difference between simple past and present perfect involves more than the type of discourse. The distribution and interpretation of the two is in fact highly complex, and the reader is referred to Boogaart 1999 for details. In Boogaart's description, the interpretation of the perfect is not simply a matter of its compositional meaning, but in part a function of the other forms with which it competes. Boogaart (1999: 24) makes a further distinction in past tenses between imperfective past ([E, R< S]), in which the event described is simultaneous with a reference event in the past, and perfective past ([R<S]). These two subcases are differently realized in different GMC languages. In EN, the progressive is available to represent imperfective past, and because of its availability, according to Boogaart (1999: 24), the simple past cannot have this interpretation of simultaneity (the "inclusion" reading) in non-narrative discourse:

5.3 Developments in the expression of tense in Germanic 313

(5.53)   a. When John entered, Mary was writing/wrote a letter

In DU, on the other hand, the simple past is employed as the exponent of the imperfective past in such cases.

(5.53)   b. Toen Jan binnenkwam, schreef Marie een brief
              when Jan came in,   wrote Mary a   letter
              'When John came in, Marie was writing a letter'
              (Boogaart 1999: 23)

Further illustration of the equivalence of EN simple past and DU present perfect as expressions of the perfective past is provided by (5.53d), the DU translation of (5.53c), uttered in a context of after-the-fact realization. DU present perfect constructions thus have, in addition to present perfect meanings, perfective past meanings – the latter being unavailable to the present perfect constructions of EN. (For an apparently similar claim for GE, see ten Cate 1989.)

(5.53)   c. I didn't turn off the stove

           d. Ik heb het gas niet uitgedraad
              I have the gas not off-shut
              (Boogaart 1999: 25)

Boogaart suggests in fact that the different distribution of simple past and present perfect in DU according to discourse types is also not just a stylistic matter, but an aspectual matter, having to do with the different role of tense in non-narrative and narrative contexts; the restriction of present perfect to non-narrative discourses is viewable in a very weak way as a "present relevance" effect. Statements made in non-narrative discourse describe events as "viewed from the perspective of the here-and-now" (Boogaart 1999: 25).

We see, therefore, that the perfect construction in DU has taken over a part of the former territory of the simple past: that of perfective past meaning. GE perfects, according to Boogaart, have developed yet further in the direction of overlap in meaning with the simple past; unlike DU, for example, GE present perfect is compatible with imperfective, as well as perfective past interpretations. Thus, the "inclusion" reading is possible in (5.53e).

(5.53)   e. Sie hat gearbeitet als   ich anrief
              she has worked   when I   called
              'she was working when I called'
              (GE, de Vuyst 1983, cited in Boogaart 1999: 155)

Schematically, Boogaart (1999: 156) represents the difference in the interpretation of the perfect construction in EN, DU and GE (in non-narrative contexts) in the following way:

(5.53) f.   Perfect Perfective past Imperfective past

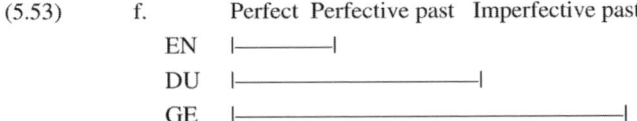

Extensively debated in GE is whether the present perfect has thus become simply an alternative expression of past tense. The question takes on particular interest in connection with the fact that in some GE dialects, particularly in the south (e.g., Swiss GE, Keller 1961: 67), as well as southern dialects of DU (de Vooys 1957: 42), YI (Jacobs 2005: 217) and AF (Ponelis 1993: 383), the simple past tense has disappeared aside from relics, and the present perfect is the only means remaining of talking about past time. At one extreme is the view that even in standard GE, simple past and perfect are simply two morphologically different expressions of past tense (see ten Cate 1989: 141 for references). Lindstedt (2000: 371) claims that when a perfect construction can be used as a narrative tense it has ceased to be a perfect; that this is what has happened in South GE, as well as other adjacent languages, including North Italian and spoken French, in what he views as an areal development. Others hold that simple past and present perfects are always semantically distinct, though the two meanings are not always distinguishable in practice. There is no room here to examine all of these views, much less to attempt to arbitrate among them. The reader is referred especially to Abraham and Janssen 1989 for a good representation of opinions.

Ballweg (1989: 94) and Zifonun *et al*. (1997: 1706ff.) propose a pragmatically based account for the interpretation of the two tenses; while the meaning of "past" is computable in one step ([E<S], in our terms – that is, 'look for an event time prior to the time of speaking'), the computation of the meaning of "perfect" is a two-step process. The perfect operator signals an event which is anterior to a reference time (in our terms, [R]). Further, however, the reference time [R] must be identified by equating it with the time provided by the higher tense operator, for example, present, which, in the default case, is interpreted as 'moment of speaking ([S])'. Thus, the interpretation of present perfect (in the absence of contradictory time phrases) is [E<R=S]. Ballweg suggests that languages can deal pragmatically with this extra computational step in two different ways. They can ignore it, in which case the present perfect will "mean" the same thing as the simple past, as it does in the relevant dialects and registers of GE. Or they can interpret it in terms of Grice's Maxim of Quantity, and assume that the speaker would not have gone to the extra effort of using the more complex form without purpose. Such a pragmatic calculation puts [S] into special focus, inducing the "quasi-aspectual" sense of "present relevance." In fact, it is possible to envision why speakers might follow these different pragmatic paths. In EN and like languages, the present perfect and the simple past both belong to the same

5.3 Developments in the expression of tense in Germanic

discourse types, and, therefore, choice of one over the other will always have salient pragmatic consequences. In GE, on the other hand, the selection of one over another is an automatic consequence of the discourse type in which it is being used (conversation versus narrative), and therefore less pragmatically significant. In Southern GE, where there is no contrast, these pragmatic considerations will not be active (Zifonun *et al.* 1997: 1706). Compare Musan 2001: 398 for an alternative view, in which the variability in the interpretation of the GE present perfect is a matter of which component of its structure is in focus. Note that present perfect is also routinely used to describe a past event with present relevance in GE, in the presence of appropriate time adverbs, such as *schon* 'already' (labeled "Up-to-Now" adverbs in Hendricks 1981). Thus, even in GE, the present perfect is preferentially used in contexts of present relevance.

(5.54)   Sie hat schon oft   angerufen
         she has   often called
         (GE, Hendricks 1981: 37)

5.3.5 Progressive

As observed in Section 5.3.1, various GMC languages have ways of describing continuous action, but not all of these can be plausibly regarded as integral parts of the tense/aspects systems of those languages. The two constructions which may most probably be identified as genuine progressive aspect constructions are the EN *be* + V-*ing* construction and the IC *vera* + *að* + infinitive construction:

(5.55)   a. She is eating

         b. hún er að borða.
            she is *að* eat-Inf
            'She is eating'
            (IC, Thráinsson 1994: 163)

The history of the EN construction is considered in detail by Denison (1993). It is interesting to note that the progressive, continuous or ongoing action meaning associated with the construction in the modern language was not a consistent feature of the presumably ancestral OE 'be' plus present participle constructions (Quirk and Wrenn 1955: 80; Mitchell 1985: I, 274). Mitchell concludes that in OE the progressive and the simple present were only stylistic variants.

Both the EN and the IC constructions, since they describe ongoing action, are incompatible with stative predicates such as *vita/know*, *elska/love*, *hata/hate*. In IC, however, this restriction applies more rigorously than in EN. EN stative verbs like *live*, *dwell*, *sit*, *lie*, *remain*, *sleep* allow the progressive, but their IC equivalents *búa*, *dvelja(st)*, *sitja*, *liggja*, *verða*, *sofa* do not (Einarsson 1945: 144).

The development of progressive as an alternative to the simple present has given rise to the possibility for expression of contrasts which go beyond mere aspectual ones. In EN, for example, the simple present/progressive contrast has come to signal a range of often subtle pragmatic contrasts. For example, in (5.55c), the choice of progressive suggests an impermanence to the state described.

(5.55)   c. I live/am living in Chicago

In (5.55d) the choice of simple present over present progressive for future action conveys more strongly a sense of plan, intent or agreement. In adhortative questions the choice of the progressive serves the purpose of softening and greater politeness (5.55e). Other such pragmatic contrasts can no doubt be isolated.

(5.55)   d. We leave/are leaving for Rome tomorrow
         e. Shall we go/be going?

By contrast, in IC the progressive is used as an alternative to the simple present for making the utterance more emphatic. According to Einarsson (1945: 144), "[t]his is common in half-angry or surprised questions, exclamations or commands" (cf. also Kress 1982: 161). Interestingly, as Einarsson points out, in these non-aspectual uses, the *vera+að+*infinitive construction is possible with stative verbs like *búa* 'live'.

(5.55)   f. til   hvers ertu að búa   á Ási?
            wherefore are-you   *að* living at Ás?
            'Why are you living at As?'
            (IC, Einarsson 1945: 145)

The Modern EN progressive construction has no equivalent function, though emphasis was perhaps among the functions of its precursor in OE (Quirk and Wrenn 1955: 80).

5.4 Voice inflections and voice auxiliaries

Middle and passive voice constructions are distinct from the corresponding active constructions in two ways. First, they involve a different mapping from semantic argument structure to syntactic positions. Thus, in a typical case, the subject of a passive sentence corresponds to the object of its active counterpart. Second, these voice constructions (sometimes) differ from the active by virtue of containing distinctive morphological markers, in the form of auxiliaries or affixes, for example. This section will discuss the morphological/syntactic means used to signal passive and middle voice. Those properties relating to their effects on valency/argument structure have been discussed in Section 4.9.4.

5.4.1 Passive

IE did not have an inflectionally distinct passive as such, though the middle voice forms could be used with passive force (Fortson 2004: 83). In some of the languages descending from it, including GMC (GO), these developed into distinctively passive meanings. As we will see, this tendency of middle voice forms to develop passive meanings is not an uncommon development, and it recurs at various stages in the histories of the GMC language. In Greek, the middle voice and passive meanings coexist, resulting in middle voice and passive voice paradigms which overlap considerably in form. In GMC, reflexes of IE middle endings with middle meanings show up in GMC only in relic forms, for example, in ON *haiti* 'I am called', OE *hātte* (Krause 1968: 262). In GO, the original middle meanings have been lost, and forms coming from this source have only passive value.

(5.56) a. saei   gabairada weihs haitada
            he-who is-born   holy is-called
            'He who will be born will be called holy'
            (GO, Luke 1:35)

Inflected passives built with these inherited affixes are also clearly relics in GMC; they occur only in GO, and only in the present tense, where the surviving forms have been substantially reduced through paradigm leveling. Even in the present, they are not the only means used for translating Greek passive forms. GO makes extensive use of intransitive-inchoative *-nan* verbs for this purpose, such as *hailnan* 'to become healed':

(5.56) b. gahailniþ   sa þiumagus meins
            become-healed-3SgPres the servant   my
            'My servant will be healed'
            (GO, Matt. 8:8)

There are no inflected passive forms in the preterite. Instead, GO exhibits the periphrastic mode of passive formation found in the other languages, consisting of an auxiliary verb *wairþan* 'become' or *wisan* 'be' plus a past/passive participle. In this regard GO is not unlike Latin, which has inflected passives in the present, but periphrastic passives with a past participle plus auxiliary in the perfect.

(5.56) c. insandiþs was aggilus Gabriel
            sent   'was' angel   Gabriel
            'The angel Gabriel was sent'
            (GO, Luke 1:26)

(5.56) d. jah sa frawrohiþs warþ du imma
and that-one accused 'became' to him
'And that one was accused to him'
(Luke 16:1)

The remaining GMC languages form passives in all tenses in this way, with the past/passive participle plus a passive auxiliary deriving from an intransitive predicate of existence ('be', 'become', 'remain'). In some dialects of Southern GE, on the other hand, the passive auxiliary *cho*, from the verb 'come', is used (Hodler 1969: 473f.). GE, DU and FA make use of both *sein/zijn/vera* 'be' and *werden/worden/verða* 'become' with past participles in passive-like constructions. The two types of passives differ in meaning, however. 'Be' passives (5.57a–c) are predications of a state, rather than an event ('statal' passives), and do not imply an agent. 'Become' passives (5.57d–f), on the other hand, are predications of events ('actional' passives) and do imply an agent.

(5.57) a. Die Flasche ist (*plötzlich) gebrochen
the bottle is (*suddenly) broken
(GE)

b. De deur is gesloten
the door is closed
(DU, Donaldson 1981: 163)

c. Alt er uppskrivað
all is written down
(FA, Lockwood 1964: 134)

d. Die Flasche wurde (plötzlich) gebrochen
the bottle 'became' (suddenly) broken
(GE)

e. De deur wordt gesloten
the door 'becomes' closed
(DU, Donaldson 1981: 163)

f. hann var vorðin hongdur ólögliga
he was become hanged unlawfully
'He had been hanged unlawfully'
(FA, Lockwood 1964: 134)

It is widely accepted that only the second of these is a true passive, and that the first is simply a predicate adjective construction with a participial predicate adjective.

(In Standard DU, and in AF, this opposition breaks down somewhat, since in the perfect tenses, the past participle of the passive auxiliary *worden* is omitted, and the passive construction thus resultantly contains the perfect auxiliary *zijn* plus a passive participle, thus leading to a formal neutralization of the statal passive/actional passive distinction in these tenses. See van der Wal 1990 for a discussion of the origin of this construction.)

(5.57)   g. het raam   is (door hem) gewassen (*geworden)
                the window is (by him)   washed
                'The window has been washed by him'
                (DU, Donaldson 1981: 162)

The cognates of *worden* and *zijn* are used to form passives in other GMC languages as well, for example, OE, GO, OHG, and Old and Modern IC, but in these languages, unlike Modern GE and Modern DU, no corresponding state/event meaning contrast has emerged. Compare the GO examples in (5.56c, d) and the following examples from OE:

(5.58)   a. Hēr Ōswine cyning wæs   ofslægen
                here Oswine king   'was' slain
                (OE, van der Wal 1990: 496)

                b. Her Onna cyning weard   ofslægen
                here Onna king   'became' slain
                (OE, van der Wal 1990: 496)

See also Mitchell 1985: 332. Van der Wal (1990) demonstrates that Old FR, OHG and Middle DU also used both 'be' and 'become' for actional passives, as does NN, where the GMC *werþan 'become' shares the function of passive auxiliary with its newer synonym *bli* 'become' (from an older meaning 'remain'):

(5.58)   c. Katta   blir/vert sett av oss
                cat-the becomes seen by us
                (NN, Åfarli 1992: 10)

                d. Veggen er måla   av Marit
                wall-the is painted by Marit
                (NN, Åfarli 1992: 13)

Thus, the earliest accessible state of affairs in GMC seems to have involved periphrastic passives with competing auxiliaries which overlapped functionally. Some languages (GE and DU) have apparently resolved this competition by segregating the two, and adapting the formal distinction between them to the expression of the statal/actional opposition. Others, including Modern IC (and to a large extent, ON) and

Modern EN, have resolved it by disposing of 'become', and using 'be' as the general passive auxiliary in actional as well as statal passives.

(5.59)   a. við erum barðir
            we are   struck-3Pl
            (IC, Kress 1982: 148)

           b. var hann vegenn
            was he   slain-MascSg
            (ON, Heusler 1967: 136)

In EN, the inherited verb *werþan* 'become' had disappeared not only from passive constructions, but from the language in general by the fourteenth century. It is still found in Old Modern IC, but functions as a passive auxiliary only in certain special senses. In Modern IC, for example, *verða* passives are modal, implying possibility (and, by extension, futurity):

(5.59)   c. það verður ekki tekið alvarlega
           that can't be   taken seriously
           (IC, Kress 1982: 150)

Kress (1982: 151) points out, though, that the distinction between actional and statal passives is formally signaled in IC when the verb involved is one which takes objects in cases other than accusative. In such instances, the object retains its oblique case in the actional passive construction, while in the statal passive construction, the participle is construed with a nominative NP (see also Barðdal and Molnár 2000).

(5.60)   a. Dyrunum   er   lokað
            doors-the-Dat is (being) closed

           b. Dyrnar   eru   lokaður
            doors-the-Nom are (in a) closed (state)
            (IC, Kress 1982: 151)

This is consistent with the idea that the actional passive involves a verbal participle, which shares in the case-governing properties of its active counterpart, while the participle in the statal passive is simply a predicate adjective, which, like other predicate adjectives, is predicated of a nominative subject. Thus, the superficial identity between statal and actional passives conceals a covert structural difference.

In continental Scandinavian (SW, BN and DA, and, under the influence of the latter, NN and FA), the inherited 'become' verb (GMC *werþan-*) has tended to be replaced, since the fifteenth century, by another actional passive auxiliary, *bli(ve)* 'become', with regional survivals in SW (Holmes and Hinchcliffe 1994: 312). This may be due ultimately to Middle Low GE influence (Braunmüller (1991: 205n).

(5.61) a. Katta blir sett av oss
cat-the becomes seen by us
'The cat is seen by us'
(NN and BN, Åfarli 1992: 10)

b. Zebraen bliver jaget af løven
zebra-the becomes chased by lion-the
(DA, Allan et al. 1995: 314)

c. Han blev påkörd av en bil igår
he became hit by a car yesterday
(SW, Holmes and Hinchcliffe 1994: 311)

d. seglini verða (blíva) slitin
sails are being torn
(FA, Lockwood 1964: 134)

5.4.1.1 *Other passive-like constructions*

Besides the GO inflectional passives and the periphrastic passives with 'be, become', which are found in all of the GMC languages, there are other constructions across the family which have been described as passive-like. Most interesting among these is the *s*-passive of continental Scandinavian, discussion of which, however, will be deferred until after middle voice constructions have been introduced, since the two are very closely connected historically. The so-called passive infinitives in GMC are discussed in Section 5.5.1.1.

Other constructions sometimes mentioned as alternative passives are EN *get* passives, GE *bekommen* passives, DU *krijgen* passives and DA *få* passives. The latter three, however, qualify as passive only in the sense that they can be paraphrased by means of passive sentences, and are best analyzed as simply active sentences in which the direct object of the verb is modified by a past participle with resultative meaning.

(5.62) a. Ich bekomme einen Zahn gezogen
I get a tooth pulled
(GE, Berger et al. 1972: 115)

b. Jeg fik min bil repareret med det samme
I got my car repaired immediately
(DA, Braunmüller 1991: 101)

The EN *get* passive is a more likely candidate as a passive construction, since in these the subject of *get* does correspond to the logical direct object of the participle.

(5.62) c. He got arrested ~ He was arrested

There are numerous differences between the two, however. Most significantly, *get*, unlike *be*, in passive sentences imposes some selectional restrictions on its subject, which cannot be an expletive element, for example:

(5.62) d. There were three men arrested *There got three men arrested

5.4.2 Middle voice

As noted in the preceding chapter, the label "middle voice" is applied to a heterogeneous set of constructions. On the one hand, in languages like Greek, middle voice forms, in their core uses, signal reflexive or self-directed action in which the subject of a transitive verb is understood to represent both the actor and the patient of the action. Thus, *eloúsato* means 'she bathed (herself)/he bathed (himself)'. On the other hand, constructions like the EN (5.63) are also called middle voice constructions.

(5.63) These books sell well

Here, the subject of the verb is understood to represent its theme argument – the things which one sells, in the present case. This is not an instance of self-directed action carried out by an entity on itself. The actor – the seller of the books – is implied but unexpressed. With respect to the semantic roles of their subjects, middle voice constructions of this kind are much closer to passives. In the previous chapter (Section 4.9.4.2), these were labeled Type I middles and Type II middles respectively. The two types of middle voice constructions are quite distinct, but the fact that the same label is applied to both types of construction perhaps involves more than a simple matter of terminological confusion. There does seem to be a connection between them, as reflected in the fact that many languages use the same means for expressing both. Thus, IC *setjast* 'to sit down' (literally, 'to set oneself down') is an instance of the 'reflexive action' middle, in which the normally transitive verb *setja* 'to set' is construed with only one argument, understood to represent both actor and patient. *Hræðast* 'to be afraid', on the other hand, is an instance of the more passive-like middle, in which the subject argument is understood to be associated only with the semantic role of object of the corresponding transitive, *hræða* 'to frighten'. *Ég hræðast* thus does not mean 'I frighten myself', but 'something frightens me/I am frightened'.[8] Compare GE *sich baden* 'to bathe (oneself)' and *sich fürchten* 'to be frightened'.

---

[8] 'Middle voice' morphology can be associated with still other semantic effects. Holmes and Hinchcliffe (1994: 308) also make note of what they term an "absolute" use:

(i)   Deras hund bits
          their dog bites (as a general rule)

The GMC languages can be partitioned into those which mark middle voice constructions (of both types) with a reflexive pronoun or an affix which derives from one and those which do not employ such marking.⁹ EN and DU are of the latter type; their middle voice constructions do not include the reflexive pronoun:

(5.64) a. Dit boek leest (*zich) gemakkelijk
this book reads (*self) easily
(DU, Fagan 1992: 173)

In general, it appears that languages which employ reflexives or vestigial reflexives in their (productive) derivations of unaccusative verbs (see Section 4.9.4.1.2.5) also employ them in their middle voice constructions (see Fagan 1992: 200).

(5.64) b. The door opened. The books sell well
(EN)

c. Die Tür öffnete sich. Die Bücher lesen sich leicht
(GE)

d. Dyrnar opna-st. Jón gref-st
door-the opens-ST. Jón bury-ST (= John gets buried)
(IC, Kissock 1997: 4)

In the Scandinavian languages, the reflexive of the middle voice construction has undergone a number of formal changes which made its identity as a reflexive pronoun increasingly opaque. It was first reduced to -*sk*, in which form it appears in ON, and then transformed to -*st* in Modern IC (see Ottósson 1992 for detailed discussion). Correspondingly, it ceased by stages to participate in the inflectional alternations characteristic of reflexive pronouns. First, whereas the reflexive pronoun *sik* was exclusively accusative, and in contrast with the dative *sér*, the clitic -*sk* of ON neutralized the accusative/dative opposition, as the following alternations show (the second example being notable as well for the stranding of the preposition):

---

⁹ Vater (1988) identifies a third sort of possible middle construction – that illustrated in (i) – which occurs without a reflexive in DA and GE, as well as English.

(i) The pencil writes well
Der Bleistift schreibt gut
Blyanten skriver godt

They are not canonical middle voice constructions, since it is not the theme of the verb which appears as an instrumental subject, but they have some of the characteristics of middle constructions – referring to potentialities, rather than specific events, and requiring the manner modification characteristic of middle constructions.

(5.65) a. hann brásk   (for...hann brá   sér
         he   changed   he   changed self-Dat)
         (ON, Heusler 1967: 138)

     b. hann aétlaþesk   fyrer (for hann aétlaþe fyrer sér
        he   thought-self for   he thought for self-Dat)
        'He made up his mind'
        (Heusler 1967: 138)

Second, whereas the clitic -*sk* of ON was exclusively third person, and in opposition to first person singular -*mk*, for example (5.65c), the -*st* of Modern IC is used for all persons and numbers, thus having become fully indeclinable, losing all pronominal features and becoming a pure voice marker (5.65d).

(5.65) c. kǫllomk   ek nú eiga   England
         pronounce-myself I now to-own England
         (ON, Heusler 1967: 138)

     d. ég (þú, hann) kallast
        I (you, he) call-self/am called, etc.
        (IC, Kress 1982: 145)

Eythórsson (1995: 235ff.) presents arguments that the reanalysis as voice marker had already taken place in ON. His arguments include the striking contrast between (5.65e), where the predicate nominal exhibits accusative case in agreement with the (full) reflexive object in this still-transitive construction, and (5.65f), where the predicate nominal exhibits nominative agreement, indicating that this is a middle voice construction, which no longer contains an object for that predicate nominal to agree with:

(5.65) e. Hann nefndi sik   Gestr
         he   named self-Acc Gestr-Acc
         (ON, Eythórsson 1995: 237)

     f. Hann nefndisk   Gestr
        he   named-sk Gestr-Nom
        (ON, Eythórsson 1995: 237)

Kissock (1997) claims that IC -*st* has not yet acquired the status of an inflectional suffix, however. Her arguments include the fact that it follows clear inflectional affixes (5.65g) and that it can be separated from the verb stem by a clitic subject in some dialects (5.65i).

(5.65) g. við heyr-ð-um-st
we hear-past-1Pl-ST
'we were heard'
(IC, Kissock 1997: 4)

h. se-st-u ← se-st þú
sit-ST-you
(informal IC, Kissock 1997: 5, citing Ottósson)

i. sett-u-st
(IC dialect, Kissock 1997: 5, citing Ottósson)

On the other hand, Einarsson (1945: 100) and Kemmer (1993: 189) point out that in colloquial IC the order *-ust-um*, with the middle marker preceding the person affix, is sometimes found instead of *-um-st* in cases like (5.65g), suggesting perhaps yet another step toward inflectional affix status.

Where both the *-st* form and a construction with a full reflexive pronoun coexist in IC, the two are not equivalent in meaning. Kissock (1997: 6) notes that *brennast* 'get burned' is accorded a passive-like interpretation relative to *brenna sig* 'burn oneself'. Kress (1982: 144) notes that the former tend to take on a special, semi-idiomatic meaning. Thus, *baða sig* means 'bathe oneself', but *baðast* means 'to bask (in water or sunshine)' (see also Birkmann 1997). In contrast, GE and DA exhibit Type II middle constructions with full-fledged reflexive pronouns.

(5.66) a. Das Buch liest sich leicht
the book reads itself easily
'The book reads easily'
(GE, Vater 1988: 403)

b. Bogen læser sig let
book-the reads self easily
(DA, Vater 1988: 403)

Semantically, the dissociation of the actor role from the subject argument – crucial in the transition from Type I to Type II middles – may have started out from such pragmatically uncertain cases as (5.65d). The change is fully carried through in Type II middles such as IC (5.66c), which approximate passive meanings:

(5.66) c. Í Afríku finnst gull
in Africa gold is (= can be) found
(Kress 1982: 144)

5.4.2.1 Other middle voice constructions

Most GMC languages, EN excepted, admit a periphrastic middle voice construction with the verb 'let', which makes explicit the modal meaning of potentiality:[10]

(5.67) a. Das Buch läßt sich leicht lesen
the book lets self easily read
'The book reads easily'
(GE, Vater 1988: 403)

b. Bogen lader sig let læse
book-the lets self easily read
(DA, Vater 1988: 403)

c. Stolen lader sig godt sidde på
chair-the lets self good sit on
(DA, Vater 1988: 404)

d. det lader sig ikke gøre
that lets self not do
'That can't be done'
(DA)

e. det låter göra sig[10]
that lets do self
'That can be done'
(SW)

f. dit boek laat zich gemakkelijk lezen
the book lets itself easily read
'The book can be easily read'
(DU, Fagan 1992: 173)

---

[10] The word order difference between DA and SW in these reflexive middles mirrors that found with 'passive infinitive' complements of 'let'. In DA, the logical object of the infinitive precedes the infinitive, while in SW it follows it. NO allows both orders (Åfarli 1992: 34).

(i) Hun lod huset bygge/*bygge huset
she let house-the build
(DA, Platzack 1986: 130)

(ii) Hon lät bygga hyset/*huset bygga
(DA, Platzack 1986: 130)

Fagan notes that in DU, as in the other languages, the reflexive is required in these paraphrases, even though it is not required in plain middle constructions in DU.

5.4.3 The Scandinavian *s*-passive

In addition to the periphrastic passives with 'be', 'become', and 'remain', some of the Scandinavian languages have developed a new inflectional passive, expressed by a morpheme -*s(t)*, in origin identical to the IC middle voice marker discussed in the previous section. In ON and in IC, the -*st* suffix is used in some instances with clearly passive force, but this is not the usual use. Thus, Heusler (1967: 138) notes such instances as

(5.68)   a. skip búask
          (the) ships prepare themselves (= are prepared)
          (ON, Heusler 1967: 138)

and *spyriask*, 'be learned (by inquiry)', *føþask* 'be born', but points out that few predicates in 'pure' Old IC have strictly passive sense. Similarly, Kress (1982: 143) notes that reflexives are sometimes used in Modern IC to indicate that the subject undergoes an action involuntarily, but observes that these translate into GE more felicitously as reflexive [middle] verbs than as passives. In some instances, they are associated with modal meaning of possibility, as in the following example.

(5.68)   b. Í Afríku finnst gull
          in Africa gold finds-ST (= can be found)
          (IC, Kress 1982: 144)

In continental Scandinavian, on the other hand, this formerly reflexive suffix has become a productive marker of passive voice, though it remains restricted in terms of tense and register, in ways which vary from language to language. While the *s*-passive is very common in the preterite in SW (Holmes and Hinchcliffe 1994: 310), it is infrequent in the past in DA (Allan *et al.* 1995: 317). SW uses these *s*-passives much more extensively than NO or DA (Afårli 1992: 15), and indeed there are a few verbs which allow only an *s*-passive (Braunmüller 1991: 57). Afårli (1992: 16), who considers them structurally parallel periphrastic passives in NO (BN and NN), notes that they are restricted, with some exceptions, to the present tense, or to infinitives (and in NN, to the infinitive alone), while periphrastic passives are not restricted in this way.

(5.68)   c. Maten bør kjopes (BN)/kjøpast (NN) av deg
          food-the will-be bought   by you
          (Åfarli 1992: 14)

d. ??Jon advartes i går
   John was warned yesterday
   (Åfarli 1992: 15)

All investigators of the phenomenon point out that there is a tendency to use *s*-passives to describe habitual events or potentialities, and to use periphrastic passives for the reporting of specific events, in cases where both are possible (cf. Åfarli 1992: 15; Allan *et al*. 1995: 316, 319; Holmes and Hinchcliffe 1994: 310f.; Bandle *et al*. 2005: 1633).

(5.68)   e. Posten udbringes hver dag
         post-the deliver-S every day
         (DA, Allan *et al*. 1995: 319)

         f. Posten bliver udbragt nu
         post-the becomes delivered now
         'The post is being delivered now'
         (DA, Allan *et al*. 1995: 319)

The tendency for *s*-passives to be used in timeless statements, and their customary modal force, reminds us in a general way of what was said about the meaning of (Type II) middle voice constructions in the preceding section, and more fully in Section 4.9.4.2. Åfarli notes this resemblance, but goes on to observe that there are several reasons for continuing to regard these as passives, not as middles, in spite of it. First, the characterization just given of the semantic difference between the two kinds of passives is just a rough tendency; it is possible to use *s*-passives in reporting specific events (5.68g) (and to use periphrastic passives to describe habitual action: cf. Allan *et al*. 1995: 319). Second, unlike middles, *s*-passives need not contain manner phrases, and they may contain overt agent phrases (5.68h) – a possibility which is unavailable in middle constructions.

(5.68)   g. hun idømtes en bøde
         she was given a fine
         (DA, Allan *et al*. 1995: 315)

         h. Zebraen jages/bliver jaget af løven
         the zebra chase-S/becomes chased by lion-the
         (DA, Allan *et al*.1995: 314)

Other (somewhat muddled) tendencies toward complementarity in the distribution of the two types of passive have been observed as well. Allan *et al*. (1995: 316) state that in DA, *s*-passives are rare in compound tenses (e.g., perfect), but this does not seem to be the case in SW. See Holmes and Hinchcliffe 1994: 313 for a list of factors serving to condition the distribution of the two in that language.

In both languages periphrastic passives tend to occur with concrete/human subjects, and in statements with obvious future time reference. Among the more striking differences is a reported distribution dependent on the interpretation of governing modal verbs. Allan *et al.* (1995: 318) report that periphrastic passives with *blive* generally occur after modals in their epistemic meanings, while *s*-passives tend to occur after modals in their root meanings:

(5.68) i. Han kan blive afskedigt
    he may be sacked (= surmise)
    (DA, Allan *et al.* 1995: 318)

  j. Han kan afskediges
    he may sack-S
    'He can be sacked (= assertion of possibility)'

It would be interesting to investigate to what extent these differences in preferred distribution can be viewed as vestiges of the origins of the constructions in question (i.e., the resultative origins of the *bli(ve)* construction (Braunmüller 1991: 57), and the middle voice origins of the *s*-passive), and to what extent it involves simple arbitrary assignment of the two to mutually exclusive contexts by way of functionalizing an emerging formal contrast, but of course such an undertaking is not possible here.

5.5 Nonfinite verbal forms

The original inventory of verbal nouns in GMC consisted of an infinitive and two participles – a present participle and a perfect participle. These were nominal elements in IE, but, with the rise of periphrastic tenses and voices in GMC, they have come to be incorporated in varying degrees into verbal paradigms as well, functioning as principal parts of verbs, in addition to their roles as adjectives or nouns (see Section 5.3.1 for some discussion of this categorial ambiguity).

5.5.1 The infinitive

The GMC infinitive derives from IE deverbal nouns with the suffix **-no-*, added to the present stem of the verb, appearing as *-Vn* in GMC, the vowel being determined by the verb class (IE accusative **deik-o-no-m* → GO (*ga*)*teihan* 'to announce'). Infinitives still end in *-n* in GO, OE, OS, Old and Modern High GE, Modern Low

GE, YI and DU. However, due to the erosion of final syllables, other GMC languages have lost the nasal. So, for example, infinitives end in -e (/ə/) in DA, FR and Swiss GE, -a in SW and IC. Some GMC languages, including EN and AF, have given up infinitive affixes altogether, and there is no formal difference (with marginal exceptions, largely limited to the verb 'be' and, in AF, 'have') between finite and nonfinite verbs. In AF, even the special forms of the infinitives of 'be' and 'have' tend to be replaced by the corresponding finite bases in many areas (Ponelis 1993: 411).

In GMC, infinitives are used to represent the untensed verb in construction with modals and future auxiliaries, in nonfinite subject and complement clauses, in purpose clauses and other adverbial clauses, and in infinitival relative clauses and questions, where these are possible (see Section 6.5.1.11).

(5.69) a. þatei Helias skuli qiman
        that Elias should come
        (GO, Mark 9:11)

        b. þarei ik im, þaruh sa andbahts meins wisan habaiþ
        where I am, there the servant my be have (Fut Aux)
        (John 12:26)

        c. ni skuld ist lagjan þans in kaurbaunan
        not lawful is to-lay those in treasury
        (Matt. 7:6)

        d. gawaurhta twalif du wisan miþ sis
        he caused twelve to be with him
        (Mark 3:14)

        e. urrann sa saiands du saian
        went-out the sower to sow
        (Luke 8:5)

        f. I found a man to fix the sink

        g. I don't know how to fix the sink

5.5.1.1 *The voice of the infinitive*

The infinitive has been claimed by some to have been neutral in voice in early GMC, having either active or passive force depending on the context. In the older GMC languages and some of the modern ones, including GE, it seems to admit a passive interpretation after verbs of command, permission and causation. In the

GO example in (5.70a) (and others like it) the infinitive translates a Greek passive infinitive.

(5.70)   a. Peilatus uslaubida giban þata leik
'Pilate allowed the body to be given'   or
'Pilate allowed (someone) to give the body'
(GO, Matt. 27:58)

        b. Anabauþ briggan haubiþ is
he-commanded to-bring his head
'He commanded his head to be brought'   or
'He commanded (someone) to bring his head'
(GO, Mark 6:27)

        c. Se cyning hēt his sunu ofslēan
the king commanded his son to slay
'The king commanded his son to be slain' or
'The king commanded (someone) to slay his son'
(OE, Orosius, cited in Kageyama 1992: 113)

        d. Der König ließ seinen Sohn töten
the king let his son kill
'The king let his son be killed'   or
'The king let (someone) kill his son'

As the alternative glosses suggest, however, it is possible to analyze these as active infinitives, whose non-specific subject is not expressed. This is a fairly standard analysis (cf. Callaway 1913: 30ff.; Mitchell 1985; Kageyama 1992; Lightfoot 1991), but, to the contrary, Åfarli (1992: 34) takes these to be passive constructions, following Taraldsen (1983), as does Platzack (1986). This view is supported by the fact that in at least some of these languages they may contain agent phrases:

(5.71)   a. Han lod hende male af en kendt kunstner
he let her paint by a known artist
(DA, Platzack 1986: 131)

        b. Er ließ sie von der Polizei verhaften
he caused them by the police arrest
(GE)

Infinitives also appear with apparent passive meaning in some GMC languages in "retroactive infinitive" constructions like (5.72) (see van der Gaaf 1928b, Mitchell 1985: I, 394 and Kageyama 1992 for some discussion):

(5.72) a. Hwæt is ūs tō dōnne
what is to us to do
(OE, Ælfric, CHom., Mitchell 1985: 395)

b. Diese Bücher sind noch zu lesen
these books are still to read
(GE)

Modern EN differs from OE in lacking both of these types of apparently passive uses of infinitives without passive marking. Thus, in Modern EN we say:

(5.72) c. The king let his son be killed

d. These things are to be done

This difference is attributed by some to a reanalysis occasioned by the shift from OV to VO in EN (cf. Lightfoot 1991). However, NO, also a SVO language, still exhibits such constructions as (5.72e) without passive morphology.

(5.72) e. Han let barnet slå/slå barnet
'He let the child be beaten'
(NO, Åfarli 1992: 34)

Interestingly, both relative orders of object and verb are allowed here, though the NP-V order is preferred. In this connection, Platzack (1986: 130) points out a striking contrast between DA and SW with respect to the ability to use bare infinitives with passive meaning. DA requires the object to precede the infinitive in such constructions, while SW requires that they follow:

(5.72) f. Hun lod huset bygge/*bygge huset
she let house-the build/*build house-the
(DA, Platzack 1986: 130)

g. Hon lät bygga huset/*huset bygga
she let build house-the/*house-the build
(SW, Platzack 1986: 130)

In SW, if the object of the infinitive precedes that infinitive, then the infinitive must be overtly marked as passive. Compare SW (5.72h) with DA (5.72i):

(5.72) h. Jag har hört honom nämnas/*nämna
I have heard him be-named/*name
(SW, Platzack 1986: 130)

(5.72)   i. Jeg har hørt ham nævne
         I have heard him name (= 'be named')
         (DA, Platzack 1986: 130)

After modal verbs, overtly passive infinitive constructions are consistently used even in those languages which allow "active infinitives with passive meaning" after verbs of causation and command.[11]

(5.73)   a. skal sunus mans...uskusans fram sinistam wairþan
            shall son man's   tried   by priests   become
            'The son of man will be tried by the priests'
            (GO, Luke 9:22)

         b. Er soll   verhaftet werden
            he should be   arrested
            (GE)

5.5.1.2 *Bare infinitives and prepositional infinitives*

All of the GMC languages distinguish between "bare" infinitives and prepositional infinitives – that is, infinitives preceded by prepositions. It is not clear whether this opposition can be reconstructed for the parent language, since the different dialects use different prepositions in the latter, and differ from each other as well with respect to whether the infinitive inflects for case after the preposition. The Scandinavian languages use prepositions going back to Old IC *at* as an infinitive marker, while the West GMC languages use reflexes of *tō. GO uses *du*, which, in spite of its resemblance to *tō, cannot be related to the latter for phonological reasons.

The earlier West GMC infinitives inflect for dative case after the preposition (the so-called "West GMC gerund"; e.g., OHG *zi tuonne* 'to do'), whereas they are uninflected in Scandinavian and in GO (GO *du fiskon* 'to fish'). This formal contrast between (preposition-dependent) inflected infinitives and uninflected infinitives has largely disappeared in the modern West GMC languages (e.g., EN and GE), but is still reflected vestigially in FR (Hoekstra 1997), where in the wake of phonological

---

[11] It appears not to have been possible for conjoined active and passive infinitives to depend on a common modal verb. When faced with translating such constructions, the Gothic translator consistently rendered the passive infinitive as a finite verb. This appears to have been true of other older dialects as well. See Harbert 1978: 115 and the references cited there.

(i)   ibai   mag   in wamba...aftra galeiþan jag gabairaidau?
         perchance can-he into womb later   go-Inf   and be-born-Subjunct
         (GO, Sk. IIc:10)

reductions formerly uninflected infinitives now end in *-e*, while those formerly inflected for dative case now end in *-en*. As shown in example (5.74), after the semi-modal *doare* 'dare' either type of infinitive can occur.

(5.74) a. Dat sil   er wol nit sizze doare/doare te sizzen
that shall he well not   dare   to say
(FR, Hoekstra 1997: 4)

The *-en* infinitives of Modern FR have a second historical source, the gerund (*-en* ← *-ande*), in which cases they do not co-occur with the preposition *te*, so that there is now a tripartite distinction in FR between *-e* infinitives, *-en* infinitives and *te...-en* infinitives.

(5.74) b. Hy giet/bliuwt   op 'e stoel sitten
he goes/remains on the chair sit[ting]
(FR, Hoekstra 1997: 6)

The distribution of the two types of infinitives (bare and prepositional) shares at least a common core across the individual dialects. In GO, *du*-infinitives seem to be restricted, with few exceptions, to subject infinitives, purpose infinitives and infinitives dependent on nouns and adjectives. In each of these cases independence from the Greek model for translation can be demonstrated:

(5.75) a. iþ þata du sitan af taihswon meinai...nist mein du giban
but the   to sit   at right   my...not-is mine to give
(GO, Mark 10:40)

b. þatei atgaft mis du   waurkjan
which you-gave to-me to do [Greek has a finite clause here]
(John 17:4)

c. skaftida   sik du galewjan ina
he-prepared self to betray   him
(John 12:4)

d. hlauts imma urrann du saljan
(a) lot to-him fell   to sacrifice
(Luke 1:9)

e. ausona du hausjan
ears   to hear
(Luke 8:8)

f. ufjo   mis   ist du meljan izwis.
superfluous for-me is to write   to-you
(2 Cor. 9:1)

In other functions, for example, in infinitival complements of lexical verbs, as well as infinitives dependent on modal verbs and auxiliaries, bare infinitives occur.

(5.76)   a. jah anabauþ   þizai managein anakumbjan ana airþai
           and he-commanded the multitude to-sit   on earth
           (GO, Mark 8:6)

        b. unte   ni magt   ain tagl hweit aiþþau swart gataujan
           because not you-may one hair white or   black make
           (GO, Matt. 5:36)

In SW, the distribution of the two is quite similar. Bare infinitives are used with modals, perception and causation verbs as in (5.77a-c), as well as with a diverse list of verbs characterized by Holmes and Hinchcliffe (1994: 268) as "modal equivalents," some of which are listed in (5.77d.):

(5.77)   a. Måste du göra det?
           must you do that?
           (SW, Holmes and Hinchcliffe 1994: 268)

        b. Vi såg honom göra det
           we saw him   do   that
           (SW, Holmes and Hinchcliffe 1994: 269)

        c. Han lät kaffet   kallna
           he let coffee-the cool
           (SW, Holmes and Hinchcliffe 1994: 269)

        d. *behöva* 'need to', *besluta* 'decide to', *bruka* 'usually do', *tänka* 'intend to', *börja* 'begin to', *försöka* 'attempt to', *nödgas* 'be forced to', *lova* 'promise to', *vägra* 'refuse to', *önska* 'wish to'

Prepositional infinitives with *att* are used, as in GO, with subject infinitives (5.78a), infinitives qualifying nouns or adjectives (5.78b) and purpose clauses (5.78c).

(5.78)   a. Att spela   piano är svårt
           to   play the piano is hard
           (SW, Holmes and Hinchcliffe 1994: 270)

        b. Har du tid   att göra det?
           have you time to do   that?
           (SW, Holmes and Hinchcliffe 1994: 270)

        c. Han reste sig för att   kunna se bättre
           he   got up in order to   see better
           (Holmes and Hinchcliffe 1994: 552)

The basic difference between SW and GO is that SW has a group of control verbs which take *att*-infinitive complements (optionally, according to Platzack 1986: 127):

(5.79)   a. Hon älskar att   åka bil
she loves to-drive the car
(SW, Holmes and Hinchcliffe 1994: 270)

b. Jag föredrar att avgå
I prefer to resign
(SW, Holmes and Hinchcliffe 1994: 270)

c. Otto försöker (att) vissla
Otto tries to whistle
(SW, Platzack 1986: 127)

Similarly, in OE, according to Quirk and Wrenn (1955: 86), bare infinitives were still usual after modals and as complements of verbs of causation, intention, inception and motion. *Tō* was the norm with subject infinitives (5.80a), infinitival purpose clauses (5.80b), infinitival cause clauses and infinitival modifiers of nouns (5.80c) and adjectives (5.80d). Something like this thus may well have been the original distribution[12] (see Miller 2002 for extensive discussion of OE infinitive constructions).

(5.80)   a. dereð...summum monnum...þæt sōð tō gehīerenne
hurts to some men the truth to hear
'to hear the truth hurts some people'
(OE, Quirk and Wrenn 1955: 87)

b. ūt ēode se sǣdere his sǣd tō sāwenne
out went the sower his seed to sow
(OE)

c. gierd mid tō þrageanne
(a) rod with (which) to chastise
(OE)

d. geornful tō gehīerenne
eager to hear
(OE)

---

[12] Mitchell (1985: I, 389) makes note of the fact that when two infinitives are conjoined in a context where *to*-infinitives would be expected, the first one is often equipped with a preposition, while the second is a bare infinitive:

(i)   mē is nēod to farene and ðone gesēon
to-me is need to go and that one see
(OE, Ælfric Cath. Hom. ii: 372.18)

5.5 Nonfinite verbal forms

The main deviation from this distribution elsewhere in GMC involves the extension of the prepositional infinitive (at the expense of the bare infinitive) in some languages, for example, DA, GE and EN, to a wider range of infinitival object complements. Thus, for example, many of the GE counterparts to the SW verbs in (5.77d) also took bare infinitives in MHG, but require *zu*-infinitives in Modern GE. These include *pflegen* 'to usually do', *beginnen* 'to begin', *wænen* 'to hope', *biten* 'to ask', *gern* 'to desire' (see Paul 1962: 319 for discussion). (On the other hand, GE does not require *zu* with (unextraposed) subject complements.)

Many of the SW verbs listed in (5.77d) as taking bare infinitives have counterparts in DA which take *at*-infinitives (Allan *et al.* 1995: 277):

(5.81)   a. Jag hoppas kunna komma
           I hope be-able come
           (SW, Holmes and Hinchcliffe 1994: 268)

           b. Jeg håber at komme til festen
           I hope to come to party-the
           (DA, Allan *et al.* 1995: 278)

According to Platzack, whereas *att* is optional with SW control infinitive constructions, *at* is obligatory in the corresponding DA constructions:

(5.81)   c. Otto forsøger at/*0 fløjte
           Otto tries to whistle
           (DA, Platzack 1986: 127)

(For a discussion of other significant differences between *at* and *att*, see Section 6.4.2.)

In IC, prepositional infinitives even occur with some apparent modal verbs:

(5.82)   a. kanntu að keyra bíl?
           can you drive a car?
           (IC, Kress 1982: 245)

           b. Þú þarft ekki að borga leigu
           you need not pay the rent
           (IC, Kress, 1982: 245)

In some marginal instances, a single verb may occur with bare or prepositional infinitives. This is true, for example, in EN with the quasi-modal *dare*, where the bare infinitive tends (though not strictly) to go along with other "modal" features, such as the absence of 3Sg -*s* and occurrence to the left of the sentential negator.

(5.82)   c. He dare not do that

           d. He doesn't dare to do that

In GE *helfen* 'help', *lehren* 'teach', *lernen* 'learn' and a few other verbs take bare infinitives or not, depending largely on the weight of the infinitive phrase.

(5.82) e. Er lehrt ihn schreiben
he teaches him to-write
(GE, Berger *et al.* 1972: 440)

f. Er lehrt ihn ein Pferd (zu) satteln
he teaches him a horse to saddle
(GE, Berger *et al.* 1972: 440)

Other alternations are more complex. Thus, in EN, the verb *see* takes a bare infinitive complement in active voice, but a prepositional infinitive in passive:

(5.82) g. I saw him (*to) leave

h. He was seen *(to) leave

There are also dialectal differences. While causative *have* takes bare infinitives in Standard EN, in Appalachian EN it can appear with prepositional infinitives:

(5.82) i. He had the blacksmith to make him a pair of forceps
(Appalachian EN, Wolfram and Christian 1976: 98)

5.5.1.2.1 **Split infinitives** The nature of the syntactic relationship between the preposition and the infinitive in prepositional infinitive constructions also appears to vary across the GMC languages. In some, including GE and OE, the preposition is always immediately adjacent to the verb, and nothing – not even verbal particles – can intervene:

(5.83) a. Er verspricht, morgen abzufahren
he promises, tomorrow off-to-drive
(GE)

b. dēofolsēocnessa ut tō adrīfanne
possession out to drive
(OE, Mark 3:22, Kageyama 1992: 95)

In these languages the preposition appears to be morphologically associated with the verb. In other languages the preposition exhibits a higher degree of independence, being separable from the verb by intervening constituents (so-called "split infinitives"). These are possible in SW, for example, as well as EN (where it is mildly stigmatized in prescriptive grammar). In EN, these emerged in EME (Miller 2002: 229). DA, on the other hand, does not allow split infinitives, as (5.83e) shows.

(5.83) c. Vi uppmanade dem at aldrig göra om det
we urged them AT never do that again
(SW, Holmes and Hinchcliffe 1994: 522)

d. Jag hoppas att snart få träffa dig igen
I hope AT soon get-to see you again
(SW, Holmes and Hinchcliffe 1994: 554)

e. Jeg var besluttet på rigtigt at more mig
I was determined really to enjoy myself
(DA, Allan *et al.* 1995: 277)

A more complex situation in WF and NF is reported and analyzed by Hoekstra (1997: 103ff.). Hoekstra distinguishes between two types of infinitive constructions with the infinitive marker *tu* – "verbal *tu*-infinitives" and "sentential *tu*-infinitives." In the former, as illustrated in (5.83f) from the Fering dialect of NF, the infinitive marker is immediately adjacent to the verb, as it is in DU and GE. Not even verbal particles can intervene. In the sentential *tu*-infinitive constructions of (5.83g) and (5.83h), on the other hand, the *tu* is separated from the infinitive by both particles and other constituents, such as object nominals. This is impossible in DU and GE.

(5.83) f. dat't beslood [(am) a dörnsk man ens apturedin]
that-she decided for the livingroom but once up-to-tidy
'that she decided to tidy up the livingroom only once'
(NF, Hoekstra 1997: 110)

g. dat at taag begant [tu apweiein]
that the roof begins to up-blow
(NF, Hoekstra 1997: 112)

h. dat'f begand [tu bruad üübkliamen]
that-we began to bread butter
'that we began to butter bread'
(NF, Hoekstra 1997: 114)

EN *to* shows a degree of freedom not found elsewhere in GMC, in that it can be stranded by the ellipsis of the rest of the infinitive construction:

(5.83) i. You can come if you want to

5.5.1.3 *Preterite infinitives*

ON developed preterite infinitives, whose occurrence was conditioned by agreement with the past tense of the verb governing the infinitive (see Haugen 1982: 162 for discussion).

(5.84) a. Skírnir lézt ganga mundu
Skírnir said-himself to-go to-would
(ON, SnE Gylf ch. 3, cited in Haugen 1982: 162)

These preterite infinitives are normally identical with the 3Pl preterite of the verb, just as the present infinitive is identical with the 3Pl present, and Haugen suggests that this was the analogical basis for their development. The form was restricted in ON primarily to AcI constructions. It persists in Modern IC (but not elsewhere in North GMC), where it is limited to the two modal forms *mundu* and *skuldu*.

(5.84) b. Hann sagðist það gera skuldu
he said-himself that to-do to-would
'He said that he would definitely do that'
(IC, Kress 1982: 164)

To these, though, should be compared the unusual substitution of the past participle for the infinitive in FA after past tense verbs, as discussed in Bandle *et al.* (2005: 1582).

(5.84) c. Eg havi biðið hann gjørt tað
I have asked him done-PP that
'I have asked him to do that'
(FA, Bandle *et al.* 2005: 1582)

5.5.1.4 *Yiddish tautological infinitives*

YI has a construction in which an infinitive-like form is used as a clause-initial topic, and is resumed by a finite form of the same verb later in the clause:

(5.85) a. šraijbn šrajbt er a briv
to-write writes he a letter
'As far as writing is concerned, he is writing a letter'
(YI, Jacobs 2005: 213)

However, as Jacobs points out, these forms are formed by attaching an *-n* to a finite form, and are thus not always identical with the infinitive – particularly in the case of irregular verbs. Accordingly, they seem to represent a distinct type of nonfinite verb.

(5.85) b. izn (/*zajn) iz er a šnajdər
being *to-be is he a tailor
'What he is is a tailor'
(YI, Jacobs 2005: 213)

5.5.2 The present participle and the English gerund

The present participle in GMC is based on an IE suffix *-o-nt*, added to the present stem; GO *bairands* 'bearing (Nom. Sg.)' ←**bher-o-nt-os*. It inflects as an adjective and has a distribution like that of adjectives occurring in attributive, predicative and substantivized roles.

(5.86)   a. Xristus, sunus gudis libandins
Christ, son of-God-Gen living-Gen
(GO, John 6:69)

        b. wilja þis sandjandins mik
will of-the-Gen sending-Gen me
'the will of the one who sent me'
(GO, John 6:40)

        c. ains wisands þize twalibe
one being of-the-Gen twelve
(GO, John 6:71)

When functioning as nominals, these participles are generally interpreted as agent nouns. As discussed in Section 4.2, it is necessary to distinguish between participles functioning as nouns, which retain adjectival inflections (5.86d), and nouns derived from participles (5.86e), which inflect as nouns:

(5.86)   d. (gudis) þis nasjandins uns
of God of-the-Gen saving-Gen us
'of God, the one saving us'
(GO, 2 Tim. 1:9)

        e. jah nasjand usbeidam
and savior-Acc we-await
(GO, Phil. 3:20)

The two also differ with respect to case governance in GO; present participles which have been lexicalized as nouns, for example, *fijands* 'enemy' (←*fijan* 'to hate') govern the genitive, regardless of the case governed by the related verb, while present participles functioning as occasional substantives have the same case assigning properties as the related verbs (Streitberg 1920: 214).

In the following GO participial absolute construction, the participle takes a full array of arguments, appearing with an accusative object and a (dative) subject argument.

(5.86)   f. [þata imma rodjandin]   managai galaubidedun imma
          that him-Dat speaking-Dat many   believed   him
          'When he spoke that, many believed him'
          (GO, John 8:30)

In these uses, GE grammars refer to "satzwertige" (roughly, 'sentence-equivalent') participles, and it is clear that they in some sense stand in for finite verbs here. With the exception of EN, however, participles have this sentence-equivalent function only in modifying (adjectival or adverbial) phrases. Only in EN are they fully integrated into the verbal system of the language, participating in the formation of verbal aspects (e.g., progressives) and representing the verb in nonfinite subject or complement clauses.

5.5.2.1   The English gerund

The participle of Middle and Modern EN has parted company from the rest of GMC with respect to both its form and its syntax. On the formal side, the GMC participle in -*nd* has been replaced by a distinct affix, -*ung*/-*ing* (see Denison 1993: 403, Lass 1992: 144ff. and especially Miller 2002: 315ff. for discussion of the development of this construction). On the syntactic side, the new -*ing* forms were incorporated into the verbal system in two different ways. They came to be used, together with 'be', in the progressive construction, which in this form is unique to EN (see Section 5.3.5). Mitchell (1985: I, 280) reports a proposal by Nickel (1967) that the progressive in OE derives in part from agent nouns ending in -*end*. Thus, (5.87a) becomes (5.87b), where it happens that *ēhten* takes genitive objects.

(5.87)   a. Hē wæs ēhtend   cristenra manna
          he was a persecutor of Christian men

         b. Hē wæs ēhtende   cristenra manna
          he was persecuting Christian men

Second, these present participles began to overlap with the inherited infinitive as the exponent of the verb in nonfinite subject and complement clauses:

(5.88)   a. I continued/stopped/tried/remembered reading the book

         b. I continued/stopped/tried/remembered to read the book

         c. Reading this book would difficult

         d. To read this book would be difficult

It is customary to label the -*ing* forms occurring in these latter contexts 'gerunds', reserving the label 'present participle' for the fully homophonous -*ing* forms occurring in adjectival uses, and in progressive constructions (see, e.g., Lass 1992: 144). In cases where they contrast, the differences in meaning between infinitives and gerunds are sometimes quite sharp. Thus, (5.88e) presupposes that the book has been read, while (5.88f) does not. In other cases, however, the differences are very subtle, involving at most slight aspectual differences:

(5.88) e. Did you remember reading the book?

f. Did you remember to read the book?

g. I continued reading the book/continued to read the book

There are, on the other hand, contexts in which only gerunds, not infinitives, can appear. So, for example, while 'begin', 'start' and 'cease' can take either infinitive or gerund complements, 'stop' and 'finish' can only take gerundive complements.

Moreover, EN infinitive phrases cannot appear as complements of prepositions, while gerund phrases can:

(5.89) a. He left without saying goodbye/*without to say goodbye
b. He was worried about falling down/*about to fall down

This may suggest that, in EN, gerunds are more "noun-like" than infinitives (as does the fact that they allow genitive "subjects," as in (5.88g)). Interesting in this connection is the fact that, in EN, nominalizations of verbs which occur with the definite article take the shape of gerunds, while other languages employ infinitives in this context.

(5.90) a. iþ þata du sitan af taihswon meinai...nist mein du giban
but the to sit   at left-hand my... is not mine to give
(GO, Mark 10:40)

b. das Lesen   von Büchern
the to-read of   books
(GE)

EN gerunds in fact exhibit an extensively discussed ambiguity with respect to their categorial status, behaving variously as verbs or as nouns. On the one hand, they may co-occur with definite determiners and plural markers, and take complements with *of*, just as nouns do. In these cases, they also take adjectival modifiers, just as nouns do.

(5.91) a. the repeated readings of the book

On the other hand they may take bare (accusative) complements, just as verbs do, in which case they do not behave like nouns in other ways. They do not admit definite determiners (although they do allow possessives), they do not pluralize, and they take adverbial, rather than nominal modifiers. See Chomsky 1970 for a classic discussion of these contrasts.

(5.91)   b. (His/*the) repeatedly reading (*-s) books

The situation is further complicated by the fact that even the "verbal" gerund can appear variously with a genitive or an accusative subject, as in the following examples.

(5.91)   c. I hate his/him loudly singing bawdy ballads

          d. His/him loudly singing bawdy ballads annoys me

The remaining GMC languages, lacking a gerund, employ the infinitive in a wider range of contexts. Thus, for example, in SW and DA the infinitive does appear as complement of a preposition, as in the following examples:

(5.92)   a. Han gick utan   att säga adjö
            he left without to say goodbye
            (SW, Holmes and Hinchcliffe 1994: 553)

          b. Han var bange for at falde ned
            he was afraid for to fall down
            (DA, Allan *et al.* 1995: 278)

          c. Efter att ha   ätit   lunch, gick vi   på en promenad
            after to have eaten lunch, we went for a walk
            (SW, Holmes and Hinchcliffe 1994: 273)

Similarly, infinitive complements are possible in these languages after verbs like 'stop':

(5.92)   d. Det har slutat   regna
            it has stopped to-rain
            (SW, Holmes and Hinchcliffe 1994: 272)

In other cases – particularly in factive contexts (those in which the truth of the embedded proposition is presupposed) – other languages must sometimes resort to finite clauses to convey the meaning expressed by a gerundive phrase in EN:

(5.92)   e. Att jag är hans bror   har ingenting med saken att   göra
            that I am his brother has nothing to do   with it
            'My/me being his brother has nothing to do with it'
            (SW, Holmes and Hinchcliffe 1994: 273)

          f. Vi tackade honom för att   han kom
            we thanked him   for that he came
            'We thanked him for coming'
            (SW, Holmes and Hinchcliffe 1994: 273)

The syntax of the EN gerund and its historical development are discussed in great detail in Miller 2002.

5.5.3 The past participle and the supine

The GMC "past/passive" participles (or "second participles" (Mitchell 1985: I, 413)) are, historically, verbal adjectives, formed by adding either of two IE adjective suffixes, *-no- or *-to, to the (zero-grade of the) verbal root. These came to be associated with strong verbs and weak verbs respectively (*broken*, *cried*), presumably due to the similarity between *-to and the dental preterite suffix of weak verbs. Not all verbs originally had past participle forms. In GO, intransitive durative verbs such as 'stand' and 'be' lacked PPs (Streitberg 1920: 215).

In continental West GMC (GE, DU, YI and AF), the originally perfectivizing prefix *ge-* has been grammaticized as a secondary past participle marker, attached to verbs with stressed initial syllables (GE *ge-séhen* 'seen' but *erínnert* 'remembered', *spaziert* 'walked'). This may have been general West GMC. It is often missing in OE, but apparently the circumstances of its (non)occurrence are at least partially predictable (Denison 1993: 414). In AF and some varieties of DU, the prefix is extended even to verbs with atonic initial syllables (Ponelis 1993: 421). AF has lost the participle suffixes, and the prefix thus remains as the sole morphological marker of the participle.

As adjectives, past/passive participles occur in both predicate and attributive positions, inflecting for agreement or not according to the rules determining adjective agreement in general. As was the case with the present participle, they can also appear as the main predicate of absolute participial constructions in GO, for example.

(5.93) at andanahtja þan waurþanamma
       at night   then become-PastPrt-Dat
       'night having come...'
       (GO, Matt. 8:16)

It is arguably only when they come to be incorporated into the system of verbal voice (in the "actional" passive) or aspect (in perfect constructions), however, that they undergo category shift, becoming a "principle part" of the verb. This category shift is not necessarily accompanied by morphological changes, that is, loss of inflection for agreement (cf. Mitchell 1985: I, 294, 302 for OE). In general, agreement morphology remains on the participle in passive constructions, whether stative or actional, better than in perfect constructions. So, for example, in SW, predicate adjectives inflect for agreement with the subject (with interesting exceptions discussed by Holmes and Hinchcliffe 1994: 86ff.), and so do participles in actional (as well as stative) passives:

(5.94) a. Rosor är vackra
roses are lovely-Pl
(SW, Holmes and Hinchcliffe 1994: 88)

b. Herrarna blev afbrutna av servitrisen
gentlemen-the were interrupted-Pl by waitress-the
(SW, Holmes and Hinchcliffe 1994: 311)

On the other hand, there is no longer agreement between the object and a past participle in perfect constructions, as in Old SW and ON. Rather, in Modern SW the nonfinite verb in perfect constructions appears in an invariant form based on the neuter singular, regardless of the gender and number of the object.

(5.94) c. stæin hafiR rettan
stone he-has raised-AccSg
(Old SW, Haugen 1982: 135)

d. Jag har plockat kantereller
I have picked-NeutSg chanterelles
(SW, Holmes and Hinchcliffe 1994: 278)

Modern SW has in fact developed this contrast between agreeing and non-agreeing participial forms yet further, by developing a formal distinction in some paradigms (primarily Class IV, which includes most historically strong verbs) between (non-agreeing) supine forms, which occur in perfect constructions, and (agreeing) participial forms, which occur in periphrastic passive constructions (both actional and statal). Example (5.94e) shows a passive construction with a participle inflected for (neuter) agreement, and (5.94f) shows an invariant supine form in a perfect construction. This elaboration of the system of non-finite verbal forms is unique to SW.

(5.94) e. England blev slag-et 2-3 av Sverige i finalen
England became beat-PP-NeutSg two to three by Sweden in final-the
(SW, Holmes and Hinchcliffe 1994: 311)

f. Vem har skriv-it *Röda rummet?*
who has write-Supine *Red Room*-the?
(Holmes and Hinchcliffe 1994: 280)

Agreement of the participle was optional in OE passives. In BN the participle does not agree, but in NN it does.

(5.95) a. hī   ymbseald wǣron
        they-NomPl surrounded-0 were
        (OE, Bede)

    b. Hestane   vart drepne
       horses-the were killed-MPl
       (NN, Åfarli 1992: 11)

    c. Hestene ble   drept
       horses-the became killed
       (BN, Åfarli 1992: 11)

5.6 Verbal valency

Verbal valency is to be understood, for present purposes, as the number and type of arguments required by a particular predicate, and the syntactic roles to which those arguments are assigned. In general, the configuration of syntactic arguments in which a predicate appears is a function of its semantic structure and the rules for mapping between semantic arguments and syntactic positions (see Levin 1993 for discussion). The latter are fairly uniform, at least across the GMC languages. So, for example, all of the GMC languages have 'put' type verbs, which take a subject argument, a direct object argument and a locative phrase (adverbial or prepositional phrase) argument, since all of them contain predicates which describe an action by an agent on an object which involves the movement of the object to a location, and all of them share mapping rules which assign agent roles to subjects, location roles to locative PPs or adverbs, and so on.

Given the definition, though, there are at least two ways in which languages might vary on this point. First, they might "package" the semantic building blocks of actions into lexical items differently. It is imaginable, for instance, that a language might lack 'put' verbs, and instead express equivalent ideas periphrastically with a sequence of more elementary predications, involving 'cause', 'move' and 'be'. Or they might have a multiplicity of 'put' verbs, which are more specific because they incorporate particular secondary predicates ('put in a vertical position', etc.). One interesting systematic instance of crosslinguistic differences of this sort involves whether a given language packages "manner of movement" or "goal of movement" together with the primary predicate of motion in its movement verbs (French *entrer dans la maison en courant* vs. EN *run into the house*. Cf. Talmy 1991). According to König (1996) the GMC languages are almost without exception languages in which the expression of manner is incorporated into the verb. Second, they might vary with respect to which syntactic roles are assigned to which arguments. Variation of both sorts is found in the GMC languages. With respect to the first, for example, Plank (1984) and Fischer (1997: 267) point out with respect to GE, and van Voorst (1996: 236) with respect to DU, that, while EN uses verbs like 'paint' and 'dig' without differentiation in both describing the action of 'creation by painting/digging' and 'affecting by painting/digging' (effected vs. affected objects), GE and DU sort the two out, using different verbs in the two cases:

(5.96) a. paint a   picture   paint a   wall
           ein Bild malen   die Wand streichen
           (GE, Fischer 1997: 267)

        b. dig a   grave   dig the   ground
           ein Grab graben   den Boden ausgraben
           (GE, Fischer 1997: 267)

        c. een boek schrijven   een check uitschrijven
           write a book   write a check
           (DU, van Voorst 1996: 237)

Other generally similar one-to-many correspondences are found in cases like *know*: *wissen* 'know (a fact)', *kennen* 'know (a place or person)', *können* 'know (how to)'; and EN *put*, which variously corresponds to GE *setzen*, *stellen* or *legen*, depending on the orientation of the placed object. There may be more systematic tendencies at work here. Plank (1984) and König (1996) propose that EN verbs tend to be less semantically specific than their GE counterparts. Going along with this is the observation by Abraham (2001a: 96) that in very many cases where EN uses a single verb form for both transitive and intransitive (*melt, grow*), DU and GE systematically have two distinct forms – *melt* versus *es schmiltzt* 'it melts (intransitive)'/*es schmeltzt* 'it melts (transitive)', *grow* versus *wachsen* 'grow (intransitive)'/*anbauen* 'grow (transitive)'.

Second, the GMC languages sometimes vary with respect to how individual argument roles are realized syntactically. A much-discussed case is that of non-agentive subjects, which are allowed to a considerably greater extent in EN than in closely related languages such as DU and GE. We can isolate a couple of different apparent manifestations of this generalization. First, EN, relative to GE and DU, much more readily allows instrumental, patient and locative subjects (cf. Rohdenburg 1974; Hawkins 1986: 57ff.; van Voorst 1996; Fischer 1997: 98; König 1996: 36ff., for example).

(5.97) a. *Dieses Hotel verbietet Hunde
           this   hotel forbids   dogs
           (GE, Hawkins 1986: 58)

        b. *Der Prozeß kann nicht fortfahren
           the   trial   cannot   proceed
           (GE, Hawkins, 1986: 58)

c. *Heyerdahl's Boot (zer)brach am ersten Tag das Ruder
Heyerdahl's boat broke a rudder on the first day
(Hawkins 1986: 59)

d. *Dieses Zelt schläft vier
this tent sleeps four
(GE, Hawkins 1986: 59)

e. *Vijf dollar koopt een maaltijd bij McDonalds voor je
five dollars buys you a meal at McDonalds
(DU, van Voorst 1996: 231)

f. *Het steentje heeft de voorruit gebroken
the rock broke the windshield (on the instrumental reading)
(van Voorst 1996: 229)

Instead, in such cases, these languages often encode such arguments as prepositional phrases. Compare (5.97a) with (5.97g), for example.

(5.97) g. In diesem Hotel sind Hunde verboten
in this hotel dogs are forbidden
(Hawkins 1986: 61)

Another phenomenon of this sort – the most widely discussed one – involves experiencer subjects in EN, which often correspond to dative objects in GE.

(5.98) a. I feel sick
mir ist schlecht
to-me is bad
(GE, Fischer 1997: 97)

b. He lacks a good friend
Ihm fehlt ein guter Freund
to-him lacks a good friend
(Fischer 1997: 97)

Similar differences are found with object arguments, though none quite so systematic as these. Van Voorst notes contrasts between EN and DU like the following:

(5.99) a. chew one's gum
op zijn kauwgom kauwen
on one's chewing-gum chew
(DU, van Voorst 1996: 236)

(5.99)	b. bite one's tongue
op zijn tong bijten
on one's tongue bite
(DU, van Voorst 1996: 236)

Both these and the subject cases, according to van Voorst, can be analyzed as results of a general difference between EN and DU: the use of the transitive frame NP V NP in DU is reserved for strongly transitive events, in which an agent performs an action on an object which is wholly affected by that action. Where the action described does not meet this threshhold, alternative constructions are used. This is the case, for example, when the actor is not an agent, as in the instrumental subject cases, or when the object is not fully affected by the action, as with predicates of experience, or, in the cases just illustrated, when the action does not result in the consumption of the object: one can chew meat in DU, but not gum. For a discussion of valency differences between EN and GE, see Frense and Bennett 1996. Hawkins (1986) offers an alternative general interpretation of facts like those under discussion as a reflection of a general typological difference; subjects and objects in EN are more semantically diverse than in GE, which observes a more restricted mapping from semantic roles to grammatical roles, and is therefore more semantically transparent (see Fischer 1997: ch. 5, for discussion).

5.7 Head, complement and adjunct placement in the verb phrase

Verb position has always been without doubt the most extensively discussed and debated issue in GMC syntax, and variation in the positions of verbs, both between languages and within languages, is among the more striking features of the family. Much early discussion of the crosslinguistic differences was framed within the rubric Verb–Object (VO) versus Object–Verb (OV) languages. As traditionally construed, though, this rubric conflated what have turned out to be a number of separate issues, which require separate treatments. To see how, consider the facts of GE. GE has clauses in which verbs precede their objects and other complements. This is the case, for example, in main clauses, such as (5.100a). On the other hand, it also has clauses in which the verb is in final position, following its complements. This occurs, for example, in subordinate clauses, or when the verb is in a nonfinite (infinitive or participial) form, as in (5.100b-e).

(5.100)	a. Der Dichter **las** gestern Abend leider nicht seine Gedichte
the poet read yesterday evening unfortunately not his poems

b. daß er gestern leider nicht seine Gedichte **las**
that he yesterday unfortunately not his poems read

c. Ich will eines Tages **diese Länder besuchen**
   I want someday these countries to-visit

d. Ich habe letztes Jahr **diese Länder besucht**
   I have last year these countries visited

e. der **seine Gedichte lesende** Dichter
   the his poems reading poet

This poses a typological dilemma. Given that GE has (at least) two different verb positions – one for declarative main clauses and one for subordinate clauses – can one of them be singled out as the basic verb position, and, if so, which one and on what grounds? Is GE "basically" an OV language, or a VO language, for example? In some typological studies, the question has been decided on functional/statistical considerations; declarative main clauses are taken as basic because they are usable in a wider range of contexts/less marked and perhaps more frequent than other sentence types (such as questions or topic sentences). This was, for example, the procedure followed by Greenberg (1963) in his seminal typological study of constituent order. But these considerations are not based on grammatical structure in any way, and from a structural point of view, there is no special reason why declarative sentences should a priori be more basic than others; in fact, there turn out to be a number of reasons for taking the verb-final order of embedded clauses to be more basic. A simple one is the fact that in that order, the verbs are typically adjacent to their complements – the things they are understood to go together with semantically – while in the verb-second order of main clauses, they are often separated from their complements by one or more intervening constituents, as the examples in (5.100) show.

In fact, there is evidence in at least some of these cases that the verb and the complements adjacent to it do form a single syntactic unit, a verb phrase, since they can be "moved around" together as a single entity – for example, to the clause-initial topic position. Note that in these cases, the verb follows its complement.

(5.101) a. [Nach Bonn fahren] will er am Freitag leider nicht
            to Bonn to-go wants he on Friday unfortunately not

         b. [Nach Bonn gefahren] ist er am Freitag leider nicht
            to Bonn gone is he on Friday unfortunately not

Generative grammarians have built up a number of other arguments for the by now widely accepted claim that verbs in the V-2 position do not originate there, but are moved to that position from within the VP further to the right. The starting point of these is, often at least, that this idea harmonizes with our expectation that things which go together semantically should go together structurally. So, for example, in a pioneering study which laid the foundation for many of these arguments, Koster (1975) began with what we have been calling phrasal verbs, such as GE *aufhören* 'to stop', or DU *afmaaken* 'finish'. As noted in Section 2.4, these form, in some sense, a single lexical item, but differ from ordinary lexical items in that the verb and the associated particle can, under some circumstances, be separated from each other. Koster demonstrated that the position of the particle in V-2 sentences mirrors exactly that of final (finite or nonfinite) verbs in non-V-2 sentences. The simplest initial assumption for accounting for this state of affairs, he argues, is that verbs (including those with associated particles) are introduced as a unit in their rightmost position, and that they remain in that position as finite verbs in subordinate clauses, or when they are dependent nonfinite verbs. In main clauses, finite verbs are moved out of that final position to the V-2 position, stranding the associated particle. This analysis satisfies our expectation that the two components of particle verbs should form a unit, and it also accounts in a straightforward way for the parallels in the possible positions of inflected verbs in subordinate clauses on the one hand and particles and nonfinite dependent verbs on the other. Thus, GE (and DU) are basically OV languages, since that is the position of the verb within the verb phrase, when it has not undergone leftward displacement.

Koster's initial proposal has undergone extensive elaboration in the intervening decades, and some of it (including the claim that subordinate clause verbs and nonfinite verbs can be relied on to reflect the "basic" position of the verb) has been called into question. It is nonetheless serviceable as a framework for our discussion of variation (crosslinguistic and grammar-internal) in verb position in GMC. Given such an analysis, we have seen that the problem of verb position in the GMC languages factors into (at least) two separate problems. The first of these is what the position of the verb is in a given language when it is *in situ* in the verb phrase, under the facilitating (but controversial) assumption that this is reflected in the position of nonfinite verb forms relative to other elements in the VP. The second is the cluster of problems surrounding verbs which have been displaced from their basic positions, including what positions they are moved to, which types of verbs are moved, and under what circumstances such movement is possible/required. Because of the way in which this volume is organized, these two questions will be considered separately. The question of the basic position of the verb within the verb phrase will be addressed in the current chapter. The syntax of displaced verbs (the "verb-second" phenomenon) will be treated as a part of the syntax of the clause, in the next chapter.

5.7.1 The relative order of the verb and its complements within the VP

The modern GMC languages fall into two main groups with respect to the relative positions of nonfinite verbs and their complements/modifiers. In one group, represented by Low GE, nonfinite verb forms follow their dependents:

(5.102)   a. De Bahn will Klock dree na Hamborg **föhrn**
            the train will clock three to Hamburg go
            (Low GE, Lindow *et al.* 1998: 104)

         b. Ik warr mit de Arbeit fardig **worrn sien**
            I will-be with the work finished been be
            'I will have been finished with the work'
            (Lindow *et al.* 1998: 102)

         c. Ik heff den ganzen Weg **lopen**
            I have the whole way run
            (Lindow *et al.* 1998: 99)

Similarly, the verb is final in subordinate clauses in Low GE:

(5.102)   d. De Arbeid, wo he veel Geld för **kregen harr**, hett sik nich lohnt
            the work, where(fore) he much money gotten has, has self not rewarded
            'The work, for which he got much money, wasn't worth it'
            (Lindow *et al.* 1998: 296)

To this "OV" group of languages belong most of the continental West GMC languages (GE, DU, AF and FR). In the "VO" group of languages, consisting of Modern EN, YI and all of the Scandinavian languages, old and new, nonfinite verbs precede their complements, as in the following FA examples.

(5.103)   a. Eg havi ikki **sæð** bókina enn
            I have not seen book-the yet
            (FA, Lockwood 1964: 131)

         b. Vit kunnu ikki **fáa** meira
            we cannot get more
            (FA, Lockwood 1964: 138)

It is generally assumed that the OV order is the older of the two, and that some of the GMC languages have undergone a historical shift in word order from OV to VO. See, for example, Kiparsky 1995b, who proposes an account of this diachronic development (which is not limited to GMC, but is found in other families as well). Eythórsson

(1995: 20ff.) demonstrates that in GO, independent of the Greek model, OV order is the norm; where a single verb with a complex meaning in the Greek text is translated as a sequence of complement plus verb, the two elements uniformly appear in the order complement–verb (except in the presence of an element which forces movement to the verb-second position – see Section 6.3).

(5.104)   a. dwala **gatawida**
foolish made   (= Greek emóranen)
(GO, 1 Cor 1:20, Eythórsson 1995: 20)

b. batizo **ist**
better is   (= Greek sumphérei)
(GO, Matt. 5:29, Eythórsson 1995: 20)

c. haubiþwundan **brahtedun**
head-wounded brought   (= Greek ekephalaíōsan)
'They wounded (him) in the head'
(GO, Mark 12:4, Eythórsson 1995: 20)

d. saei liban **taujiþ**
which life makes   (= Greek to zōopoioũn)
(GO, John 6:63, Eythórsson 1995: 21)

And in Runic GMC, nonfinite verb forms seem to have followed associated phrases:

(5.104)   e. Frawaradaz, ana hahai **slaginaz**
Frawaradaz, on horse slain
(Runic GMC, Möjbro, Antonsen 1975: 33)

This suggests the possibility that GMC was originally an OV language, though the truth may have been more complex than this, as we will see below.

5.7.1.1 *Variation in verb position in OV languages: verb raising and extraposition*

In the GMC OV languages, to a substantially greater extent than in other OV languages, such as Japanese and Turkish, it is possible for some constituents to follow a verb in "clause-final" position (i.e., a dependent nonfinite form, or the verb in a subordinate clause). These exceptions are customarily attributed to local reorderings of elements at the ends of clauses – the subject of the present section.

5.7.1.1.1 **Verb raising** In general, it is expected that in verb-final order in sentences containing multiple verb forms, the order of verb forms in an OV language will reflect the relative depth of syntactic subordination of the verbs involved, since in OV languages verbs follow their complements and modifiers. That is, for example, infinitives dependent on finite verbs will precede those finite verbs, and nonfinite verb forms dependent on other nonfinite verb forms will precede the latter. These expectations are borne out in some cases, as in the Low GE sentences cited in the preceding section and in the following FR example, from den Besten and Edmondson (1981).

(5.105)   a. dat er it boek lêze kent hat
            that he the book to-read been-able has
            'that he has been able to read the book'
            (FR, den Besten and Edmondson 1981: 12)

Here, the infinitive 'read' is dependent on the modal 'be able', which takes dependent infinitives, and the modal in turn is a past participle dependent on the tense/aspect auxiliary, which takes past participles as its complements. This hierarchy of dependency is reflected in the order of the verb forms.

However, this is not always the case. In the GE example in (5.105b), the finite verb is not last, but precedes both of the nonfinite verbs.[13]

(5.105)   b. daß er das Buch hat lesen können
            that he the book has to-read be-able
            'that he has been able to read the book'
            (GE, den Besten and Edmondson 1981: 12)

Since Evers 1975, constructions of this type, in which a governing verb precedes one or more dependent forms rather than appearing in the expected final position in a subordinate clause, have been referred to as "verb-raising" constructions, reflecting a widely assumed analysis of them under which the final verb cluster undergoes a reanalysis into a single complex verb, by way of "raising" the embedded nonfinite verbs and adjoining them successively to the next higher verb in the syntactic structure. The branches of the resulting verbal complex can (and sometimes must) then be reordered relative to each other by an "inversion" operation under specific circumstances, yielding structures in which the hierarchy of subordination is no longer directly reflected in the word order. So, for example, in (5.105b) the branch of the tree containing the perfect auxiliary has been inverted with the remainder of the verb complex. In the following DU example, the same thing has happened, but the lexical verb and the modal have been inverted with each other as well.

---

[13] Note that the modal here does not show up in the past participle form normally governed by the perfect auxiliary, but rather as an apparent infinitive. Constructions like those in example (5.105b), in which an expected past participle assumes the form of an infinitive in the presence of another infinitive, are referred to as double infinitive constructions, or *Infinitivus pro Participio* constructions. There is variation across GE dialects with respect to which verbs govern this double infinitive construction. See den Besten and Edmondson 1981: 24 and Broekman 1993.

(5.105)   c. dat hij het boek heeft kunnen   lezen
that he the book has   been-able to-read
(DU, den Besten and Edmondson 1981: 13)

For the case in which a finite perfect auxiliary takes a modal verb as its complement and the modal verb in turn selects a dependent infinitive of a lexical verb, Broekman (1993: 120) notes the following patterns: in Low GE and in WF, the order is Lexical Verb–Modal (Participle)–Perfect Auxiliary.

(5.105)   d. dat he dat book lesen kunnt hett
that he the book read could has
'that he could read the book'
(Low GE, Broekman 1993: 120)

In High GE, on the other hand, the order is Perfect Auxiliary–Lexical Verb–Modal (Infinitive), and in Standard DU it is Perfect Auxiliary–Modal (Infinitive)–Lexical Verb. In both of these languages, the modal appears as an infinitive, rather than in the past participle form expected of dependents of perfect auxiliaries – an instance of the Double Infinitive Construction discussed in note 13. AF exhibits yet another possibility, according to Broekman (1993: 29): Modal Verb–Main Verb–Perfect Auxiliary, while PG exhibits the fixed order Lexical Verb–Perfect Auxiliary–Modal Verb:

(5.105)   e. Ich wees, as   er lese het kenne
I   know that he read has be-able
'I know that he could read'
(PG, Louden 1990: 472)

Thus, the attested orders come close to exhausting the logically possible permutations. The relative order of verbs also depends on the nature of the verb (modal versus tense/aspect auxiliary and the number of verbs involved) in ways which vary widely from language to language in continental West GMC. (The reader is referred to Maurerer 1926, den Besten and Edmondson 1981, Haegeman and van Riemsdijk 1986, Rutten 1991, Haegeman 1993: 109ff. and Zwart 1996 for extended discussion.) For example, Standard DU allows inversion in instances in which a simple infinitive is dependent on a modal while Standard GE does not:

(5.105)   f. dat ik hem zien wil ~ wil   zien
that I him see want want see
(DU, Haegeman and van Riemsdijk 1986: 426)

In GE, inversion takes place only if the verb dependent on the modal or aspectual auxiliary in turn has an infinitive complement of its own. This is one of the parameters of variation for inversion in a partial typology offered by Haegeman and van Riemsdijk (1986). The others include whether inversion is obligatory or optional (as in the present case), and whether the verb inverting with its complement must be a modal or auxiliary or not. These parameters interact with each other. So, for example, modals may optionally invert in GE if they have a dependent infinitive and are in turn embedded under an aspectual auxiliary, resulting in variation like that in (5.105g, h). In (5.105h), the modal *können* is inverted relative to its complement:

(5.105)   g. daß er hätte kommen wollen können
that he had   to-come   to-want to-be-able
'that he could have wanted to come'
(GE, Haegeman and van Riemsdijk 1986: 427)

h. daß er hätte können   kommen wollen
that he had   to-be-able to-come   to-want
'that he could have wanted to come'
(GE, Haegeman and van Riemsdijk 1986: 427)

Among the analytical controversies involving verb-raising constructions, beginning with Evers (1975), is whether they are monoclausal or biclausal constructions – that is, roughly, whether they have the syntax of simple or complex sentences. The considerations that arise are discussed in detail in Haegeman 1992.

Haegeman and van Riemsdijk (1986), among others, observed that in many continental West GMC languages, including Swiss GE and West Flemish, it is possible for an object NP to appear interspersed among the verbs in the final verb cluster.

(5.106)   a. das er **en arie** hät wele chöne   singe
that he an aria   has want be-able sing
'that he wanted to be able to sing an aria'
(Swiss GE, Haegeman and van Riemsdijk 1986: 428)

b. das er hät **en arie** wele chöne   singe
that he has an aria   want be-able sing
'that he wanted to be able to sing an aria'
(Swiss GE, Haegeman and van Riemsdijk 1986: 428)

c. das   er hät wele **en arie** chöne   singe
that he has want an aria   be-able sing
'that he wanted to be able to sing an aria'
(Swiss GE, Haegeman and van Riemsdijk 1986: 428)

d. das er hät wele chöne   **en arie** singe
that he has want be-able an aria sing
'that he wanted to be able to sing an aria'
(Swiss GE, Haegeman and van Riemsdijk 1986: 428)

Haegeman and van Riemsdijk argued (1986: 428) that these constructions also involve some version of verb raising, in part because they are constrained identically by the same conditions as verb-raising constructions in the same language. They therefore conclude that some of the OV GMC languages make use of an extended version of verb raising, in which a subordinate verb together with its object complement, rather than just the verb by itself, can be joined by verb raising with the higher verb to form a verbal complex. Applying inversion to various branches of this verbal complex will yield variation like that seen in (5.106). They call this extended version of verb raising "verb-projection-raising." Languages vary with respect to whether only nonfinite verbs can be raised, or whether the verbs plus their direct complements can be raised (the VPR case). Others, however, including Rutten (1991), Haegeman (1992) and Louden (1990), argue against the existence of VPR, and even of verb raising itself, and in favor of an analysis involving a process more like extraposition, as discussed in the next section. The arguments are too technical to pursue here. Louden's argument is based on a previously overlooked (though not unique) word-order possibility found in PG, in which the finite verb appears sandwiched in between two nonfinite verbs in a position not straightforwardly derivable from any combination of verb raising and inversion.

(5.107) Ich wees as   er gehe hot welle schwimme
         I   know that he go   has want swim
         'I know that he wanted to go swimming'
         (PG, Louden 1990: 472)

5.7.1.1.2 **Extraposition** Subordinate clause verbs and dependent nonfinite verbs in main clauses may fail to appear absolutely finally for yet another reason: some clausal constituents may – and, in some instances, must – be displaced to the right of these otherwise clause-final verbs, a phenomenon generally known as extraposition. So, for example, finite object clauses in GE, unlike other object complements, must appear to the right of the verb:

(5.108)   a. *Er hatte, daß er nicht lange leben würde, gewußt
             he had,   that he not long live would, known
             (GE, Hawkins 1986: 145)

Extraposition can also apply to infinitive clauses. Hawkins (1986: 145f.) notes that extraposition of infinitive clauses in GE is optional if the infinitive clause is the sole argument of the verb, but obligatory when the verb has another argument. Example (5.108d) is fine if the bracketed phrase is moved to the right of the verb:

(5.108) b. Er hat die Frau   zu gewinnen gehofft
he has the woman to win   hoped
(GE, Hawkins 145)

c. Er hat gehofft, die Frau zu gewinnen

d. *Ich werde meinem Sohn [morgen den späteren Zug zu nehmen]
empfehlen
I will my son [tomorrow the later train to take] recommend
(GE, Hawkins 1986: 146)

Extraposition in these instances is not restricted to OV languages; EN has obligatory extraposition of clausal direct objects, for example, as the following sentences show:

(5.108) e. *I said [that they should leave the room] to the children

f. I said a word to the children.

It is also possible for non-clausal constituents to appear in the extraposition position to the right of final verbs, but they are severely constrained in terms of both category and function. In the modern OV languages only adverbial phrases, including prepositional phrases with adverbial functions, are allowed this possibility:

(5.108) g. Ich erzähle dir gleich,   was ich gehört habe [bei Müllers]
I   tell   you immediately what I   heard have [at Müllers]
(GE, Hawkins 1986: 148)

Arguments of the verb, including prepositional phrases which are required to complete its meaning, are not allowed to extrapose:

(5.108) h. *Die Gelegenheit wird ihn bestimmt verleiten [zu einem
voreiligen Schritt]
the opportunity will him certainly lead [to a premature step]
(GE, Hawkins 1986: 148)

Strikingly, in the predecessors of the modern OV languages, the appearance of constituents after the finite verb was not so strictly limited. Weerman (1989) notes that it was possible for even such constituents as direct object NPs to follow nonfinite verbs, and inflected verbs in subordinate clauses, in the ancestors of DU and GE. This is illustrated by the following examples from Middle DU and OHG. In each case, the order illustrated is entirely impossible in the modern language. See also Weerman 1997, Davis and Bernhardt 2002: 138, as well as Ramat 1987: 102ff. for OV~VO variation in Runic GMC.

(5.109) a. Ic sal   sendan minen ingel vor   dijn anschin
I shall send   my   angel before your face
(Middle DU, cited in Weerman 1997: 434)

b. dhasz dhu firstandes   heilac chiruni
that   you understand holy   secret
(OHG, Isidor, Weerman 1989: 19)

On the basis of such alternations, Weerman proposes a rather different scenario from the one traditionally assumed; early GMC was prevailingly but not strictly OV. It also allowed VO as a secondary order – a possibility which Weerman links to its relatively rich case inflection (the order VO being "licensed" by case morphology). The erosion of case inflection, however, undercut the basis for such OV~VO alternations, forcing individual languages to settle on one of the two alternants. Some became (strictly) VO, while others became (strictly) OV. Thus, rather than a linear development from OV to VO, Weerman posits a development of the form OV (~VO)→OV *or* VO.

YI stands out among the modern languages in exhibiting a similar indeterminacy with respect to basic word order. The original order of YI was presumably that of MHG – that is, (predominantly) OV. However, VO order has become increasingly frequent through time, so that by now the order nonfinite verb–object is overwhelmingly the most frequent order (Santorini 1993: 234; Birnbaum 1979). Both OV and VO orders sometimes remain possible, though:

(5.109) c. Ix hob Moišn gezen
I have Moiše seen
(YI, den Besten and Moed-van Walraven 1986: 125)

d. Ix hob gezen Moišn
I have seen Moiše

In bitransitive sentences, both objects can follow the verb (if both are NPs), but, according to den Besten and Moed-van Walraven, they cannot both precede it:

(5.109) e. Er hot gegebn Moišn dos bux
he has given Moiše the book
(YI, den Besten and Moed-van Walraven 1986: 125)

f. Er hot Moišn gegebn dos bux

g. ???Er hot Soren dos bux   gegebn
he   has Soren the book given
(den Besten and Moed-van Walraven 1986: 126)

This raises the question of which of these orders is basic in the grammar of contemporary YI. On the one hand, one could assume VO and account for OV orders by way of scrambling of the object to the left of the verb. On the other hand, one could assume OV and account for VO orders through rightward extraposition of the object. Both positions have been argued for. For a review of the literature, see Santorini 1993. Santorini's conclusion is that the question is not decidable on the basis of grammatical argumentation. Instead, she offers a statistical approach, demonstrating that, on the one hand, OV orders occur more frequently than would be predicted under the scrambling hypothesis, given the rate of occurrence of scrambling generally in YI, and that, conversely, VO orders occur more frequently than would be predicted under the extraposition hypothesis, given the general rate of extraposition in YI. She concludes that it is unlikely that either order is derived, proposing instead that YI simply has two distinct base orders, competing with each other in the synchronic grammar (a conclusion which seems to be anticipated by den Besten and Moed-van Walraven 1986: 126).

Pintzuk (1993) makes a partially, though not entirely, similar claim for OE. OE exhibits both verb-final and non-verb-final orders in embedded clauses. It has been claimed by van Kemenade (1987) and others that OE was an OV language in subordinate clauses, and that apparent failure of finite verbs in subordinate clauses to appear clause-finally are due to the obscuring effect of verb raising and extraposition. Assuming OV order, for example, the order VO in the subordinate clause in (5.109h) would have to result from extraposition (necessarily, extraposition of the liberal sort also found in OHG and Middle DU, which allows even direct objects to be moved rightward across the nouns):

(5.109)   h. þonne wind styreð lāð   gewidru
              when wind stirs   grievous storms
              (OE, Beow. 1374f., cited in Pintzuk 1993)

Pintzuk, however, argues that not all instances of nonfinal verbs in subordinate clauses can be accounted for, starting from the assumption of verb-final order, by such auxiliary assumptions, and concludes that OE was a "double base" language in which two competing clausal structures coexist (the difference having to do with whether the Aux slot (Infl), to which the verb moves from its position within the VP, occurs to the left of the VP or to its right). Compare also Mitchell 1985: I, 405f., who notes alternations in verb position in OE which he relates to an ongoing transition from OV to VO.

Another apparent instance of a relic OV order in a language which has generally developed VO syntax is found in ON, where objects can also precede nonfinite verbs – an order not possible in modern North GMC languages:

(5.109)   i. ef nokkurir vilji land hennar kaupa
              if some   will land her   buy
              (ON, Bandle *et al.* 2005: 1154)

5.7.2 The order of objects

When both nominal objects of a bitransitive verb in the GMC languages are full NPs, the indirect (recipient) object precedes the direct object in the unmarked case:

(5.110)   a. Ik joech de kat in bal
I gave the cat a ball
(FR, Tiersma 1999: 94)

b. I gave the boy the book

c. Jag lånade studenten min bok
I lent student-the my book
(SW, Holmes and Hinchcliffe 497)

d. Han gav gentuni matin
he gave girl-the food-the
(FA, Lockwood 1964: 154)

As noted in Section 4.1.2.3.1, Kiparsky (1997: 461) reports that this order is fixed in case-poor languages such as EN, FR, DU, SW and West Flemish. So, for example, reordering of the IO and DO NPs in Flemish results in ungrammaticality:

(5.110)   e. da Valère Marie dienen boek nie gegeven eet
that Valere Marie those books not given has
(West Flemish, Haegeman 1993: 140)

f. *da Valère dienen boek Marie nie gegeven eet
(West Flemish, Haegeman 1993: 140)

This restriction applies only to nominal IOs. Where the IO role is expressed as a PP, it follows the direct object in the unmarked case, as other PPs do:

(5.110)   g. I gave the book to the boy

h. Jag lånade min bok till studenten
I lent my book to student-the
(SW, Holmes and Hinchcliffe 498)

i. da Valère dienen boek nie an Marie gegeven eet
that Valere your book not to Marie given has
(West Flemish, Haegeman 1993: 140)

In the West Flemish example in (5.110e), both the indirect and the direct object come (obligatorily) in front of the clausal negative marker *nie*, while in the NO example in (5.110k), both of them follow the negative marker:

(5.110) j. *da Valère Marie nie dienen boek gegeven eet
(Haegeman 1993: 140)

k. Ola ga ikke Marit appelsinen
Ola gave not Mary orange-the
(NO, Hellan and Platzack 1999: 126)

Since the clausal negator is outside the VP, the objects in the West Flemish examples, unlike those in NO – must also be outside the VP. This difference is attributed to different conditions for the operation of Object Shift. Interestingly, though, the relative order IO – DO is conserved in both cases.

5.7.2.1 Scrambling

The relative order of objects is harder to pin down in some GMC languages than in others, due to the possibility of "scrambling." Scrambling is the local reordering of argument and adjunct phrases. GE, for example, allows either order of IO and DO (and, for that matter, even allows these objects to precede the subject):

(5.111) a. daß Jan das Buch seinem Vater gibt
that Jan the book his father-Dat gives

b. daß Jan seinem Vater das Buch gibt

c. daß das Buch seinem Vater Jan gibt
(GE, Kiparsky 1995b: 143)

Because of scrambling, the relative order of arguments in GE is not fixed on the basis of their grammatical roles, but may be varied to reflect the information structure of the utterance, with thematic/old information tending to appear leftward of rhematic/new information. Even in GE, however, Lenerz (1977) and Hawkins (1986: 44) conclude that the basic order of arguments is IO–DO, based on observations like the following:

a. When theme/rheme distinctions are neutralized, for example, by choosing DOs and IOs with indefinite articles, reflecting that they are both being introduced into the discourse for the first time, the arguments appear in the fixed order IO–DO:

(5.112) a. Ich habe einem Schüler ein Buch geschenkt

b. A rhematic IO may precede a thematic DO, in contravention of the theme/rheme ordering principle, but the converse is not possible:

(5.112) b. *Ich habe ein Buch dem Schüler geschenkt
I have a book to-the-pupil given
(Hawkins 1986: 45)

c. Ich habe einem Schüler das Buch gegeben
I have to-a-pupil the book given

Hawkins (1986: 44) makes the methodological point that "basicness is established by showing that one order is free from grammatical restrictions which affect the other." Similarly, den Besten and Moed-van Walraven (1986: 126) point out that, while one object can precede the verb in a YI bitransitive sentence while the other follows it, it is distinctly odd for the DO to precede the verb while the IO follows it.

Kiparsky (1995b, 1997) claims that there is a unidirectional correlation between richness of morphological case among the GMC languages and the possibility of reordering nominal arguments by scrambling; in languages which are case poor (DU, Flemish, FR, continental Scandinavian, EN and Afrikaans), the direct nominal arguments of the clause must occur in a fixed order, which cannot be altered by scrambling (see also Weerman 1997: 433). Scrambling is not excluded in case-poor languages; according to Weerman (1997: 430), all of the OV West GMC languages allow it, whether they have morphological case or not (to which list we can add one VO language, YI – see Kiparsky 1997: 462). In DU sentences like (5.112d), for example, the adverbs *waarschijnlijk* 'probably' and *vaak* 'often' can appear in any order, relative to each other or either of the objects. That is, DU, a case-poor language, has scrambling, but unlike GE the two objects cannot be reordered relative to each other:

(5.112)   d. dat de vrouw waarschijnlijk vaak de mannen de film toont
            that the woman probably   often the men   the film shows
            (DU, Weerman 1997: 430)

          e. *dat Jan het boek zijn vader geeft
             that Jan the book his father gives
             (DU, Kiparsky 1995b: 143)

In the VO languages other than YI (that is, EN and Scandinavian), on the other hand, even this limited possibility of scrambling is unavailable; verbs and objects cannot be separated from each other by adverbs, and the two objects of double object constructions cannot be separated from each other by adverbs (Kiparsky 1995b: 173n.).

The correlation between case morphology and fixed order of nominal arguments does not work in the other direction. Kiparsky points out (1995b: 173n.; 1997: 462) that some GMC languages with rich case systems nonetheless require fixed Subject–IO–DO order. These include IC[14] and the Grisons dialect of Swiss GE, in which direct

---

[14] Kiparsky (1997: 483f.) observes that DOs and IOs are not reorderable in Icelandic with the exception of those occurring with a small class of verbs including 'give', 'show' and 'sell'. Kiparsky concludes that this variation is not a consequence of constituent reordering (scrambling), but of the coexistence of two distinct argument frames for such verbs – a "recipient-oriented" frame and a "transfer" frame.

5.7 Head, complement and adjunct placement

objects and indirect objects cannot be reordered, for example, as they can in Standard GE, even though the two languages are equivalently rich in case marking:

(5.112) f. und den het dr. dogdor S. em Bbuur   de KB erklärt
and then has the doctor S. the farmer-Dat the artificial-insemination explained
(Grisons Swiss GE, Kiparsky 1997: 462)

g. *und den het dr. dogdor S. de KB em Bbuur erklärt

Kiparsky concludes that, while case-poor languages have only syntactic position available as a means of encoding argument relations, case-rich languages may use either case or position or both for this purpose, and may therefore either be free-constituent-order languages or (if they make use only of the latter) fixed-constituent-order languages.

The uniform IO–DO order of GMC for full NP objects cuts across the divide between OV languages and VO languages. However, when the objects are weak pronouns, the distinction between VO and OV languages possibly reemerges as a significant one in determining order of arguments. In bitransitive constructions in VO languages, the order of pronouns, like that of non-pronominal arguments, is IO–DO:

(5.113) a. He gave him it

b. Ola ga   henne den ikke
Ola gave her   it   not
(NO, Hellan and Platzack 1999: 126)

c. Jeg lånte ham den
I   lent him it
(DA, Allan et al. 1995: 485)

In OV languages, though, the usual order for pronoun objects appears to be DO–IO:

(5.114) a. ik joech it har
I gave it her
(FR, Tiersma 1999: 94)

b. Ich gab es ihm
I   gave it him
(GE)

c. Hij heeft hem haar gegeven
he has   it   her given
(DU, Abraham and Wiegel 1993: 38)

Thus, in at least some of the OV languages, the normal order of pronoun objects is the opposite of that found with NP objects. Abraham and Wiegel (1993: 38) refer to this as "the puzzle of inverse clitic-order."[15]

In some of these languages, the opposite order is possible as well. In West Flemish, for example (Haegeman 1992: 63; 1993: 146), clitic object pronouns may appear in either order relative to each other (though they must always follow subject clitics, as in the following example, where the subject clitic is doubled by a full pronoun).

(5.114) d. da-me t ze/ze   t wunder gezeid een
            that we it them/them it we said   have
            'that we said it to them'
            (West Flemish, Haegeman 1992: 63)

5.8 Phrasal verbs

Highly characteristic of the GMC languages are "particle verbs," or "phrasal verbs," that is, verbs which co-occur with morphemes, often homophonous with adverbs or locative prepositions, forming with them a semantic unit. The lexical aspects of these were discussed in Section 2.4. Examples include EN *look out*, GE *annehmen* 'accept', SW *resa av* 'depart', FR *stilstien* 'stand still', GO *innatgaggan* 'go in', AF *aantrek* 'put on'. As noted, the meaning of a phrasal verb is sometimes compositional – computable from the meanings of its constituent parts – but very often not, as in the case of EN *come around* 'revive' versus AF *omkom* 'to die' (literally, 'to come around'), and some particles make more or less consistent semantic contributions to the phrasal verbs in which they participate which are not obviously related to their meanings as independent words. Syntactically, what stands out about them is that the verbal particle and the verbal root are sometimes contiguous and sometimes not, depending on the syntactic circumstances. This is most strikingly evident in the modern OV languages, such as AF, DU and GE, in which, when the verb is final, either as an infinitive or a finite verb in a subordinate clause, the particle immediately precedes the verb (separable from it at most by the infinitive marker 'to' and the participle prefix *ge-*), but when the verb is nonfinal, it is separated by arbitrarily many other elements from the particle, which remains in final position:

---

[15] Whether this is true of all pronouns (weak and strong) in all OV languages is unclear. Weiß states that in Bavarian when both IO and DO are clitic pronouns (thus controlling for differences in pronoun weight) the normal order is IO–DO, and DO–IO is at best highly marked, but see Abraham and Wiegel 1993: 38f. for an apparently conflicting claim.

(i)   das'a'ma'n geem hod
            that he me it given has
            (Bavarian, Weiß 1998: 89)

(5.115) a. **Skakel** jy die lig **af**?
shut you the light off?
(AF, Donaldson 1993: 374)

b. Ek sal die lig **afskakel**
I shall the light off shut
(AF, Donaldson 1993: 374)

c. Het jy die lig **afgeskakel**?
have you the light off shut?
(AF, Donaldson 1993: 374)

d. Ek het vergeet om die lig **af te skakel**
I have forgotten the light off to shut
(AF, Donaldson 1993: 374)

e. dat ek nou **opstaan**
that I now upstand
(AF, Donaldson 1993: 263)

This pattern, quite robust in the modern OV languages, is seen as at least incipiently present in early GMC by Eythórsson (1995: 39).

In general, verbal particles consistently follow the verb in VO languages, even when the verb is a nonfinite form, though, as Jacobs (2005: 238) notes, YI is an exception in this regard:

(5.116) Er vet **avek-šikn** dem briv
he will away send the letter
(YI, Jacobs 2005: 238)

No consensus has been reached on the syntactic status of GMC phrasal verbs or the status of the verbal particles which they include. At the center of inquiry has been the problem of reconciling the fact that they are clearly syntactically complex, consisting of two syntactically independent components, with the fact that they behave for some purposes like single lexical items. As noted, verbal particles form semantically atomic units with the associated verb, the two of them constituting a single lexical item in some sense. Particles, moreover, can change the valency of the verb – a property usually associated with derivational affixes. Thus, while DU *bel* 'to phone' is optionally transitive, *opbel* 'to phone (someone)' requires an object (Booij 2002b: 211). Booij also notes (p. 210) that verbal particles are not capable of independent modification. For example, when negating a sentence with the phrasal verb *huishouden* 'keep house', in which the verbal particle is originally a noun, it is impossible to use the negative determiner *geen* as one normally would in a sentence with an indefinite object. Rather, the sentential negator *niet* is used:

(5.117) Jan kan niet/*geen huishouden
Jan can not /*no   house-hold
'Jan cannot keep house'
(DU, Booij 2002b: 210)

The fact that verbal particles behave neither like bound morphemes nor like other phrasal accompaniments of verbs (such as adverbs, objects or prepositions) thus also requires explanation. Recent approaches to this complex of problems are represented in Dehé *et al.* 2002. According to one recent analysis (Farrell 2005), they do not constitute a unitary syntactic phenomenon even within individual languages.

In the VO languages, Holmberg and Rijkhoff (1998) note interesting variation with respect to the relative order of the particle and various objects. In one group – EN, NO, IC and FA – lexical noun objects may precede or follow the particle, while pronominal objects must precede the particle, intervening between it and the verb.

(5.118)   a. Vi slapp ut   hunden/*den
we let   out dog-the/it
(NO, Holmberg and Rijkhoff 1998: 86)

b. Vi slapp hunden/den ut
we let   dog-the/it   out

In DA, on the other hand, objects of all sorts precede the particle (5.118c), while in SW objects of all sorts follow it (5.118d).

(5.118)   c. Vi lod hunden/den ud
we let dog-the/it   out
(DA, Holmberg and Rijkhoff 1998: 86)

d. Vi släppte ut   hunden/den
we let   out dog-the/it
(SW, Holmberg and Rijkhoff 1998: 86)

6

The syntax of the clause

In this chapter we will examine those aspects of the grammar (morphology and syntax) of the clause which are not readily subsumed under the (internal and external) syntax of noun phrases or verb phrases. Much of the discussion will relate to the very dynamic syntax of the left periphery of the clause in GMC – such things as the syntax of auxiliaries, complementizers, verb-second word order, subject-verb inversion, clausal negation, topicalization, relative clause formation, interrogation and left-dislocation. A large part of the recent literature on the syntax of the clause in the GMC languages – perhaps the majority of that work – is framed in terms of what is sometimes referred to as "extended X-bar theory," and I will adopt a bare-bones version of that approach here. I will assume throughout the chapter that sentences may be represented by syntactic trees of the following general form.

(6.1)

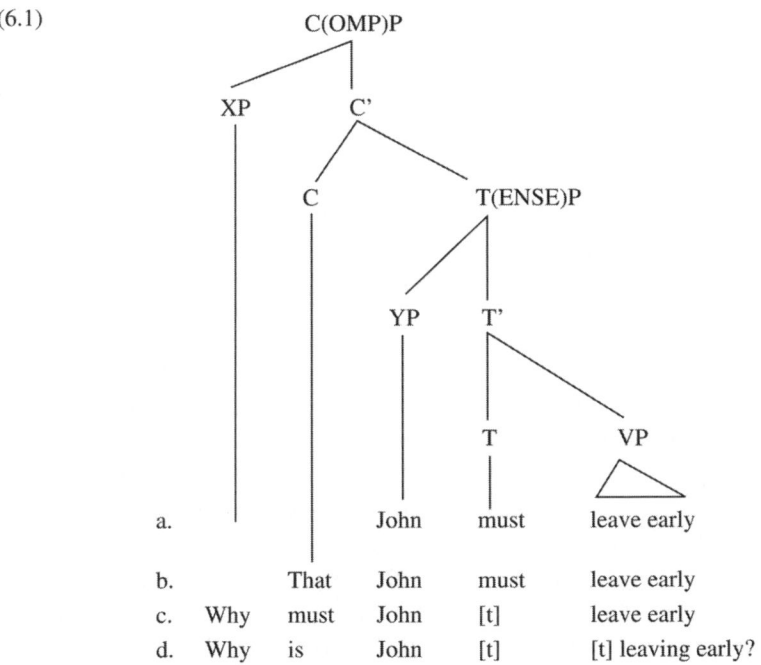

This tree and the associated examples reflect the claim that sentences in the GMC languages consist minimally of a verb phrase, containing the lexical verb and its modifiers and arguments, a position for a tensed element, such as a modal or auxiliary, which is outside the verb phrase, and a Subject position. It also makes the claim that the position occupied by the tensed element is the head of the clause (and that therefore, the clause is a "Tense Phrase"). The subject occurs immediately to the left of this head, in the "Specifier" position of the TP. Complementizers, such as the sentential subordinating element *that*, when they occur, are held to be the heads of yet another layer of clausal structure, the "Complementizer Phrase" (CP). As in the case of the TP, the architecture of this phrase makes available exactly one slot to the left of its head – the Specifier of the CP position – and this is held to be the position occupied by clause-initial question phrases, for example. Much of the variation in constituent order within the clause in GMC can be accounted for straightforwardly by statements referring to a tree of this shape, which specify which elements can/must occupy which of these positions under various circumstances. For example, the verb-second/subject-aux inversion phenomenon characteristic of WH-Questions in the GMC languages can be captured by assuming that when there is a question phrase in the Spec CP position, the head of the next phrase down – the T element – must be moved into the head position of the CP (the complementizer position), thereby occurring just to the right of the question phrase, and in front of the clausal subject. More elaborate variants of the tree representation of clausal structure have been advocated in recent literature, but the basic structural assumptions implicit in (6.1) will be sufficient to facilitate my description of such things as co-occurrence and relative order of constituents, scope of adverbs and operators, and variation in the position of the finite verb within and across the GMC languages.

6.1 Sentence adverbs

It is not universally agreed that the traditional label "adverb" describes a unitary category. Adverbs are not distinguished inflectionally from other lexical classes. In the sole inflectional category in which they participate, comparison, they are inflected in the same way as adjectives. Nor are they distinguished systematically by their derivational morphology. Some of the GMC languages have affixes which productively derive adverbs (both VP adverbs and sentence adverbs) from adjectives (EN *obvious-ly*, *quick-ly*, GO *gatemi-ba* 'fittingly', *unwenigg-o* 'unexpectedly', *glaggwu-ba/glaggw-o* 'meticulously'). Other GMC languages, such as GE, DU, and the Scandinavian languages and Appalachian EN (Wolfram and Christian 1976: 105; Montgomery 2004: 269), on the other hand, make less systematic use of special affixes for this purpose; instead, they frequently use the same form for both adjective and adverb. In languages in which predicate adjectives take inflectional endings, the same forms in adverbial use take an invariant neuter adjective ending, as in (6.2a). These languages do, however, have suffixes for deriving adverbs from other categories. For example, DA *-mæssig* is used productively to derive adverbs from nouns: *regelmæssig* 'regularly'.

(6.2)   a. Barnet   kan ikke stave rigtig-t
                child-the can not   spell correctly
                (DA, Allan *et al.* 1995: 336)

Syntactically, adverbs are distinguished by virtue of being the one lexical category which does not take complements of its own:

(6.2)   b. see [the student]
              c. to [the student]
              d. humiliation [of the student]
              e. proud [of the student]
              f. *proudly [of the student]

Adverbs are often treated as members of a more inclusive class of "adverbials," which we may define as 'adverbs and phrases of other category types, such as noun phrases and prepositional phrases used in similar adjunct functions'. For example, noun phrases are used frequently as time phrases, appearing in the particular case required by this "adverbial" role. The case in question varies from language to language, and sometimes even within languages (GO *himma daga* 'today' (lit. 'this day-DSg'), *gistradagis* 'tomorrow-GSg'). Similarly, prepositional phrases are frequently used as time phrases and location phrases, in which uses they also overlap functionally with adverbs. I will not employ the label "adverbial" here, though, since first of all it involves an undesirable confusion of lexical category with function, and second, because in fact adverbs and other "adverbials" do not have the same distribution even when they serve similar functions, as the following example shows.

(6.3)   I then/*[$_{NP}$yesterday]/*[$_{PP}$in the winter] visited Paris[1]

---

[1] Haider (2004) claims that such "phrasal adverbials" are disallowed medially in VO languages such as EN, as in (i) but not OV languages.

(i)   He will {very soon/*without any difficulties} find an appropriate solution
        (Haider 2004: 788)

However, there appears to be variation even within individual languages on this point:

(ii)   We'd all the time get in fights
        (Appalachian EN, Wolfram and Christian 1976: 99)

It is customary to distinguish broadly between two types of adverbs – VP-adverbs and sentence adverbs. This distinction embodies a syntactic and a semantic claim. VP-adverbs are syntactic constituents of the VP, and they are understood to have *scope* over (only) the VP – that is, their meanings combine with that of the VP, and they are understood to qualify the action described by that VP. Manner adverbs, for example, are a type of VP-adverb. Sentence adverbs, on the other hand, are syntactically constituents of the clause, and outside of the verb phrase. Semantically, they have scope over the clause – their meanings combine with the meaning of the proposition asserted by that clause. (The notion of scope will also be of importance in the next section, on the syntax of negation.) The different syntactic positions of the two types of adverbs can be demonstrated in a variety of ways. For example, in EN, VP-adverbs but not sentential adverbs can intervene between the verb and its complement, as in (6.4a), and VP-adverbs but not sentential adverbs can be moved to the front of the clause along with the rest of the VP, as in (6.5a).

(6.4)   a. He ran completely up the hill
         b. *He ran obviously up the hill

(6.5)   a. He said he'd completely run up the hill and [completely run up the hill] he did

         b. *He said he'd certainly run up the hill and [certainly run up the hill] he did

The partitioning of adverbs into the two groups "sentence adverbs" and "VP-adverbs" is probably not sufficiently fine-grained, however. In semantic terms, at least, sentence adverbs are of a heterogeneous sort, and have been subjected to a variety of classificatory schemes. Kotova (1986: 1) observes a major distinction between sentence adverbs with "full-fledged lexical semantics," such as *frankly*, *shortly*, *probably*, which can often be paraphrased as a higher predicate ('It is probable that. . .'), and adverbs which do not exhibit full-fledged lexical semantics, such as *only*, *also*, *at least*, which are not paraphrasable in this way, and are logically operator-like. Ramat and Ricca (1998: 192), focussing on the former type, distinguish speech-act adverbs such as *briefly* and *frankly*, domain adverbs such as *technically* and *linguistically*, modal adverbs such as *probably*, *allegedly* and *hopefully*, evaluative adverbs such as *unfortunately* and *wisely*, and event adverbs such as *yesterday* and *often*, among other types. Ramat and Ricca (1998: 192) assign them to a hierarchy of discrete functional/semantic "layers," with speech-act adverbs representing a relatively high stratum, while time and place adverbs occupy a relatively low one. They view this hierarchy as a functional one, rather than a syntactic one, but other recent accounts claim that different types of sentence adverbs, too, appear at different levels in the syntactic tree, depending on their type. Many of the restrictions on relative ordering of adverbs of different types show some constancy across languages. Some investigators (e.g., Travis 1988; Cinque 1999; Nilsen 2000), have proposed that this fixity of relative order reflects hierarchical syntactic structure: clauses are composed of several discrete phrasal layers (more than the three assumed here), each of which is home to a different subset of "sentence adverbs" (see Nilsen 2000:21f. for a critical discussion of the ordering differences on which such claims are based). So, for example, the following NO sentence shows the only admissible order of the adverbs it contains. All other permutations are disallowed.

(6.6) a. Han hadde fortsatt alltid nettopp nesten helt klart det
he had still always just almost completely made it
(NO, Nilsen 2000: 29)

In spite of parallels in adverb order from one language to the next, though, there is at least some crosslinguistic variation in adverb position in GMC. In SW and DA, for example, the order is (manner adverb – place adverb – time adverb):

(6.6) b. Han reste plötsligt bort igår av någon anledning
he travelled suddenly away yesterday for some reason
(SW, Holmes and Hinchcliffe 1994: 514)

GE and DU, on the other hand, perhaps because they are OV languages, prefer the opposite relative order: time adverb – (manner adverb)–place adverb:

(6.6) c. Er wird heute hier arbeiten
he will today here work
(GE)

Ramat and Ricca (1998: 206ff.) note that in European languages the same form can often be used as either a VP-adverb or a sentence adverb, and derivational suffixes which are exclusive to the one or the other are rare. So, for example, in the following sentences, *frankly* can function either as a (VP-level) manner adverb or as a (sentence-level) speech-act adverb, and *wisely* can function either as a manner adverb or an evaluative adverb, the difference between the two being signaled by word order:

(6.7) a. He often speaks frankly
b. He frankly often says too much
c. He seldom acts wisely
d. He wisely seldom acts

They point out, though, that a subset of the GMC languages does exhibit a derivational affix (GE -*erweise*, Swiss GE -*erwiis*, DU -*erwijs*, DA and SW -*vis*), which is used exclusively to derive sentence adverbs. In GE, where it is most productively employed, for example, there are contrasts like the following:

(6.8)   a. Er hat mir klugerweise geantwortet
        'Cleverly he answered me'
        (GE, Ramat and Ricca 1998: 204)
     b. Er hat mir klug geantwortet
        'He answered me cleverly'
        (GE Ramat and Ricca 1998: 204)

Other lexical devices are also used to signal the difference between sentence adverbs and VP adverbs. In SW, NO, IC and DA, the modifying particle *nog/nok* occurs obligatorily when one of these 'two-way' adverbs is used as a sentence adverb.

(6.8)   c. Klokt   *(nog) svarade   han inte mig
           cleverly enough answered he   not me
           'Cleverly, he did not answer me'
           (SW, Ramat and Ricca 1998: 209)

Ramat and Ricca (1998: 210) propose that this particle is on its way toward grammaticalization as a derivational morpheme for sentence adverbs.

DA also exhibits a striking inflectional difference between sentence adverbs and VP adverbs. In general, sentence-level adverbs ending in *-lig*, such as *følgelig* 'consequently', *navnlig* 'namely', *rettelig* 'rightfully', *sandelig* 'indeed', *visselig* 'assuredly', do not take the 'neuter' *-t* suffix, while *-lig* adverbs used as manner adverbs (the canonical VP adverb) do, often with sharp meaning contrasts (Allan *et al.* 1995: 336, 348ff.):

(6.8)   d. han udførte arbejdet antagelig-t
           he did   job-the satisfactorily
           (DA, Allan *et al.* 1995: 349)

        e. Han har antagelig udført arbejdet
           he has presumably done   job-the
           (DA, Allan *et al.* 1995: 350)

        f. Vi kan ikke rigtig(t) finde en løsning på problemet
           we can not really   find a solution to problem-the
           (DA, Allan *et al.* 1995: 353)

        g. Vi kunne ikke løse problemet rigtig-t
           we could not solve problem-the correctly
           (DA, Allan *et al.* 1995: 353)

As the optionality of -*t* in example (6.8f) indicates, this contrast is not now fully intact.

Sentence adverbs can in general appear initially in the GMC languages. This position is less readily available to VP-adverbs. Some, but not all of the latter, are allowed to appear initially:

(6.9) a. Carefully he took the book out of the box
       b. *Completely he took the book out of the box

In EN, initial adverbs are followed by the subject, except for those adverbs which have the force of sentential negation, with which the subject and the auxiliary must be inverted:

(6.10) a. Unfortunately I must leave
       b. Seldom have I seen that

In the remaining modern GMC languages, initial sentential adverbs behave like other initial constituents, occasioning subject-verb inversion in all instances.[2] In all cases, these initial adverbs appear in the same position as topic phrases in a given language, and they are generally incompatible with the preposing of other topics, suggesting that they are in the topic position of the clause. The difference between EN and the rest of modern GMC with respect to inversion can be attributed to the fact that it alone among these languages is a non-strict V-2 language (see Section 6.3.2). Also attributable to this cause is another difference between EN and the other languages with respect to adverb position; EN is alone in allowing sentential adverbs to intervene between the subject and the auxiliary in main clauses:

(6.11) a. He obviously/fortunately has worked hard on this

The position of these adverbs may be identified with the postverbal 'clausal adverbial position' of the other GMC languages, for example, SW (Holmes and Hinchcliffe 1994: 519), if the effects of V-2 on verb position are taken into account:

(6.11) b. Han är tyvärr dum
          he is alas dumb
          (SW, Holmes and Hinchcliffe 1994: 501)

---

[2] Exceptional in this respect is SW *kanske* 'perhaps', whose appearance at the front of the clause may fail to trigger inversion, and which is in fact followed by subordinate clause word order, as in (i), though inversion is also possible, as in (ii):

(i)   Kanske han redan har gjort det
      perhaps he already has done that
      (SW, Holmes and Hinchcliffe 1994: 542)
(ii) Kanske har han redan gjort det
      (SW, Holmes and Hinchcliffe 1994: 542)

There is an etymological explanation for its anomalous behavior (Holmes and Hinchcliffe 1994: 542).

In addition, lower level sentence adverbs such as time and location adverbs can appear at the end of the VP, following nonfinite verbs and objects, in VO languages (6.12a) but not in OV languages (6.12b).

(6.12)   a. Per tänker inte laga mat ikväll
Peter thinks not to-make dinner tonight
(SW, Holmes and Hinchcliffe 1994: 522)

          b. *Peter will nach Berlin fahren morgen
Peter wants to Berlin to-drive tomorrow
(GE)

6.2 The syntax of negation

6.2.1 Some definitions: negation, scope and polarity

Negative words (like other semantically similar elements) have scope – defined here as that part of the sentence with which they are understood to combine semantically, and to which they add negative meaning. Sometimes the whole clause is understood to be negated. Sometimes it is a single constituent within the clause.

(6.13)   a. I did not open the can
           b. He opened the can with [no difficulty]

In (6.13a), the whole clause is understood to be in the scope of negation, hence negated; there was no event of can-opening. In (6.13b), the negation does not apply to the predicate, but only to the noun phrase headed by *difficulty*. Thus, this sentence asserts that there was an event of can-opening, denying only that it involved difficulty. The former case will be of primary concern here. We will refer to it as sentential negation, as opposed to constituent negation – the difference between them being one of scope.

The determination of the scope of a negator is made easier by the fact that all of the GMC languages have a class of elements which we can call polarity items, which share with each other the property of having to occur in the scope of negation (or some semantically similar operator, such as an interrogative word or a conditional complementizer). Thus, for example, such elements as EN *any, ever, even* and OS *êniga* 'any' can only appear in these contexts:[3]

---

[3] EN *any* has a non-polarity use, roughly equivalent to *every*, in addition to its use as a polarity item with an interpretation essentially like that of *some*.

(6.14) a. *I have seen him yet
        b. I have not seen him yet
        c. Have you seen him yet?
        d. *I have seen any cars
        e. I have not seen any cars
        f. Have you seen any cars?
        g. te huuî habas thu thes êniga mêda fon gode?
           how do you have for-that any reward from God?
           (OS, Heliand (Behaghel) 1547)

A still more restricted behavior is exhibited by another set of items, which for the moment we will consider as polarity items (though see Section 6.2.3) – for example, *neouuiht* 'nothing' and *neo* 'never' in OS. These appear only in sentences with clausal negation, not in questions or conditional sentences. We can call the type represented in (6.14) A-type polarity items, and the type represented in (6.15) N-type polarity items (cf. Bernini and Ramat 1996: 120ff. on this distinction).

(6.15) huuand imu **n**is biholan **neouuiht**
        because to-him is hidden nothing
        (OS, Heliand (Behaghel) 1578)

Note that OS *neouuiht* is not only an N-polarity item, in the sense that its occurrence is dependent on a sentential negator; it is also overtly negative in form, incorporating an identifiable negative morpheme. The class of such negative-incorporating polarity items and the class of N-polarity items (those which are restricted to negative contexts) are not coextensive. The former is a morphological category. The latter is a syntactic category. While it seems to be true that negative-incorporating polarity items are always N-polarity items, there are polarity items which do not incorporate negative morphology but which are nonetheless N-polarity items, occurring only in negative contexts, as we will see.

The existence of items which must be in the scope of negation gives us a structural test for our intuitions about negative scope. In (6.16a), the negative, whose scope is restricted to the bracketed adjective phrase, fails to license a polarity item contained in another phrase elsewhere in the sentence, in contrast with (6.16b).

(6.16) a. She's a [not unattractive] woman (*in any respect)
           (Quirk *et al.* 1985: 791)

        b. She isn't an unattractive woman in any respect

6.2.2 Scope, polarity and syntactic position

As we observed earlier, it appears that there is a general relationship between semantic scope and syntactic structure. In the general case, the negator has to be higher up in the syntactic tree than the polarity item, in order to license it. An interesting illustration of this in EN is found in the following contrast: polarity items in subject phrases or topic phrases in EN main clauses cannot be licensed by the sentential negator, while polarity items contained in object NPs can. The same facts hold elsewhere in GMC, though, as we will see, not all GMC languages exhibit this asymmetry.

(6.17) a. I didn't see [any students]
        b. *[Any students] didn't come
        c. *[Anything], I didn't buy

There are reasons for thinking that this is because the subject noun phrase (as the specifier of TP), and the topic phrase (as the specifier of CP) in EN are higher up in the syntactic tree than the negative element *n't*, and therefore cannot be licensed by it. Observe, first of all, that when a clause like (6.17b) is embedded in turn in a larger clause which contains sentential negation, the subject of the embedded clause can contain a polarity item.

(6.18) I don't think that [any student] came

Similarly, in dialects of EN which allow the fronting of the auxiliary + *n't* in declarative sentences (presumably to the C(OMP) position in tree (6.1)), polarity *any* can again appear in the subject phrase.

(6.19) Ain't anybody going to bother you

In these cases, but not in (6.17b), the sentential negator is high enough in the clausal structure to license the negative polarity item.

Interestingly, the observed exclusion of negative polarity items from the subject positions and topic positions of negated clauses as in (6.17) is not universal in the GMC languages. Some of the older languages, such as GO, OS and OHG, seem to have systematically allowed sentences equivalent to (6.17b, c), in which a polarity item in subject position or topic position is licensed by sentential negation.

(6.20) a. jah waiht   ni andhof
           and anything not he-answered
           (for Greek kaì oudèn [ ] apekrínato
           and nothing he-answered)
           (GO, Mark 14:61)

        b. jah ainshun us izwis ni   fraihniþ mik
           and any   of you not asks   me
           (for Greek kaì oudeìs ex hymôn [ ] erōtâi me
           and none of you asks me)
           (GO, John 16:5)

c. that ênig liudo   ni scal farfolgan is friunde
   that any of-people not shall follow his friend
   (OS, Heliand (Behaghel) 1493)

d. sô siu iru   uuiht ni farlêt
   so she of-them any   not left
   (OS, Heliand (Behaghel) 3775)

e. antat iro   thar ênig ni uuas thes fiundo folkes
   until of-them there any not was of the enemies' people
   (OS, Heliand (Behaghel) 3880)

f. that gi neo   ni suerien suuîðoron êðos
   that you never not swear stronger oaths
   (OS, Heliand (Behaghel) 1518)

g. wiht ni fórahtet ir   iu
   a-whit not fear   you yourselves
   'Do not fear a whit'
   (OHG, Otfrid III.8:29, cited in Ramat 1987: 176)

h. thie líut   es wiht   ni duáltun
   these people of-it a-whit not hesitated
   'These people have not hesitated in it a whit'
   (Otfrid I.1:58, cited in Ramat 1987: 176)

(In these languages, of course, polarity items can also appear in object phrases in negative sentences.) Jespersen (1917: 58) and Traugott (1992: 269) report cases in OE similar to those in (6.20). The facts of early GMC and modern GMC are contrasted in Harbert 2002, where it is argued that the occurrence of these kinds of constructions, with polarity items in subject position, and topic position in the older languages but not in the modern ones, is related to the position of the sentence negator. This will be discussed further below. In this connection, observe the following French example, which appears to be like those in early GMC.

(6.21)   Aucun chaussure ne me va
         any   shoe   not me fits
         (French, van der Wouden 1997: 165)

6.2.3 Polarity items, negative concord and multiple negation

In the preceding section, we looked briefly at polarity items like EN *anything*, GO *waiht*, which I identified as polarity items because they are dependent on a co-occurring negator (or other operator). I also labeled the dependent negative *neouuiht* in the old Saxon example in (6.16a) a polarity item. It is different from these other polarity items in that it incorporates a negative morpheme (which lacks independent negative force, and whose appearance is conditioned by the presence of the clausal negator). Behaghel (1924: II, 76) refers to these two types respectively as "negative summierende Glieder" and "positive summierende Glieder." In early GMC the two coexisted, sometimes alternating in the same texts, as in the following OS examples:

(6.22)   a. ni uuas im   tueho <u>nigiên</u>
not was to-them doubt no
(OS, Heliand (Behaghel) 2904)

b. nis   thes   tueho <u>ênig</u>
not-is of-that doubt any
(OS, Heliand (Behaghel) 3190)

In still other languages, only the negative-incorporating forms are found, So, for example, in YI, all non-specific arguments in the scope of sentential negation must be negative in form.

(6.23)   Er vaist   kain zax   niśt
he knows no   thing not
(YI, Birnbaum 1979: 302)

Such so-called "double negative" constructions were also the norm in earlier EN and GE, and they are still the norm in some dialects.

(6.24)   a. Ni batut ir   niouuihtes in minemo namen
not asked you nothing   in my   name
(OHG, Tatian (Sievers) 175: 2)

b. Es isch nie   ke Möntsch i   das Wirtshus 'gange
it is   never no man   in the pub   gone
(Bernese GE, Hodler 1969: 145)

c. Ik heff keen Geld   nich
I   have no   money not
(Low GE, Lindow *et al.* 1998: 284)

However, they have in relatively recent times become stigmatized by prescriptive grammar in the standard languages, on the basis of the dictum that "two negatives make a positive" (cf. Behaghel 1924: II, 80). The idea behind this prescriptive rule – that sentences like (6.24c) involve "double negatives" or "multiple negatives" – is of course inaccurate from a semantic viewpoint. (6.24c) involves only the simple negation of an affirmative proposition. The difference is made clear in an interesting way by the following contrast in IC (Thráinsson 1994: 187): IC has two different "negative" indefinite determiners, *neinn* 'any' and *enginn* 'no'. *Neinn* (the only one with an original negative etymology, involving the GMC *ne*) is an N-polarity item. It has no negative force of its own, and can only occur with a real negative element. *Enginn* (which was not originally a negative word – see below) has independent negative force, as in (6.25c) – an instance of true "double negation."

(6.25)   a. ég á   engan/*neinn bíl
            I have no car/*any   car
            (IC, Thráinsson 1994: 187)

          b. ég á   ekki neinn bíl
            I don't have any   car
            (IC, Thráinsson 1994: 187)

          c. ég á   ekki engan bíl
            I don't have no   car   (It is not the case that I have no car)
            (IC, Thráinsson 1994: 187)

Some recent investigators have concluded that what I have labeled negative-incorporating polarity items are not simply another type of negative polarity item. Rather, they are related to the clausal negator by a distinct relationship, that of negative concord, through which their negative form "spreads" to them from the clausal negator, under conditions which can differ from those in which a polarity item is licensed by a clausal negator. *Anyone* and *no one* in (6.26) are thus related to the sentential negation by different processes.

(6.26)   a. I didn't see anyone   (polarity licensing)
          b. I didn't see no one   (negative concord)

Languages like YI, in which all apparent negative polarity items are of the negative incorporating type, are thus sometimes said to have "obligatory negative concord."

(6.26)   c. Er vil   guuer-niśt   visn
            he wants absolutely-nothing (not) to know
            'He doesn't want to know absolutely anything'
            (YI, Birnbaum 1979: 302)

          d. Kain méńć vaist   ys niśt
            no   one   knows it not
            'Nobody knows it'
            (YI, Birnbaum 1979: 302)

382   6 *The syntax of the clause*

(6.26) e. Er vaist   niśt kain sax ~ Er vaist   kain sax niśt
              he knows not nothing   he knows nothing not
              (YI, Birnbaum 1979: 302)

        f. Keyner hot nist gezen ire trern
           no-one has not seen her tears
           'No one has seen her tears'
           (YI, Lockwood 1995: 130)

For discussion of the syntax of negative concord in GMC, and specifically for arguments that negative polarity items and elements involved in negative concord have different distributions, the reader is referred to Haegeman and Zanuttini 1996, Horn and Kato 2000: 6 and van der Wouden 1997: part 2.

6.2.4 Negative complementizers and pleonastic negation

The following sentence would seem to indicate that polarity items need not depend on a clausal negator, but may depend instead on an implied negation which is a part of the meaning of a lexical verb; *anything* here seems to depend on *doubt*.

(6.27) a. I doubt that anything will come of it

As Laka (1990) points out, though, this is not the correct analysis of such examples. *Doubt* cannot license polarity items in its own clause (6.27b). It can apparently only license polarity items in a clausal complement.

(6.27) b. *I doubt anyone

Laka (1990: 185) observes that we can account for this by assuming that, while *doubt* cannot by itself license polarity items, when it takes a clausal complement, it selects a complementizer with the abstract feature [+NEG], and that feature, as a type of clausal negation, can license a polarity item within its scope. Interesting in this connection is the fact that in several GMC languages (as well as Romance languages), when a verb with a meaning of 'hindrance', 'precaution', 'prevention' or 'prohibition' takes a clausal complement, the complement clause actually exhibits an overt clausal negator that lacks any independent negative force – a pleonastic negation. Van der Wouden (1997: 196) refers to negation of this sort, following Jespersen (1917: 75ff.), as Paratactic Negation. For discussion of its syntax and interpretation, see Van der Wouden (1997: 200ff.).

(6.27) c. iþ is...faurbauþ ei mann   ni qiþeina þata
           but he forbade that anyone not he-might tell that
           'But he forbade him to tell anyone that'
           (GO, Luke 9:21)

       d. Min muoter hat verbotten mir, das ich nicht ushin kam ze dir
           my mother has forbidden me, that I   not out   came to you
           'My mother has forbidden me to come to you'
           (Middle Bernese GE, Hodler 1969: 147)

       e. Men hindre dat   hier niet die weiflaers 't zamenrotten
           (let) some prevent that here not the hesitant come together
           (seventeenth-century, DU, cited in van der Wouden 1997: 198)

       f. nature...forbedeth that no man make hymself riche
           (ME, Chaucer, cited in van der Wouden 1997: 196)

6.2.5 Constituent negation with sentential scope

As established in Section 6.2.3, the scope of a negator is normally determined by its syntactic position, and polarity items have to be in the scope of the negative element on which they are dependent – hence, lower than the negative element in the syntactic tree. However, both the generalization that polarity items have to be licensed by negative elements occurring higher up in the syntactic tree and the distinction between sentential negation and constituent negation in terms of scope are clouded by the fact that, under some circumstances, negative elements which we would identify as constituent negation (because they are syntactically parts of noun phrases, prepositional phrases or other constituents of a clause) nonetheless have the force of sentential negation – that is, they seem to have scope over the whole sentence, as indicated by their ability to license polarity items/tag questions higher up in the syntactic tree, as in (6.28).

(6.28) a. [No salesperson] will bother you at any time
       b. He will speak [with [no undergraduate]] at any party/ever/will he?

Here, even though the negation is constituent negation from a syntactic standpoint, since it is contained within the bracketed NP, it appears to have scope over the whole sentence, so it can license polarity items which are outside of the phrase containing it. We can refer to this phenomenon descriptively as "constituent negation with sentential scope (CNSS)." (Jespersen 1917: 56ff. discusses this phenomenon under the label "negative attraction.") Because of CNSS, there are two roughly equivalent ways in EN of expressing negation in sentences like:

(6.29) a. He will see no student (CNSS)
b. He will not see any student

In the subject phrase example in (6.30a), however, only the CNSS option is available. The sentential negation option is unavailable here, as we noted above, because the polarity item in the subject position is too high up to be in the scope of the clausal negator.

(6.30) a. *Any salesperson will not bother you at any time
'No salesperson will bother you at any time'

Even if we use an indefinite article, rather than a polarity item, the sentence remains odd.

(6.30) b. A salesperson will not bother you at any time
c. No salesperson will bother you at any time

CNSS is apparently preferred over the use of clausal negation here, too, where the alternative sentence (6.30a) would contain a NP with a non-negative indefinite determiner outside of the scope of the clausal negator.

There is crosslinguistic variation among the GMC languages involving the choice between ordinary sentential negation and CNSS negation. GE differs from EN with respect to sentences like (6.29a,b); in GE, only the CNSS option is possible. Ordinary sentential negation is ruled out with indefinite objects (6.31c), and constituent negation of the NP has to be used instead, as in (6.31b).

(6.31) a. Ich will den Studenten nicht sehen
I want the student not to-see

b. Ich will keinen Studenten sehen
I want no student to-see

c. ??Ich will einen Studenten nicht sehen
I want a student not to-see

Santelmann (1994) claims that this is connected with the fact that GE, unlike EN, has object shift (as discussed in Section 4.8.1.2.1), which moves the object leftward out of the VP, and thus out of the scope of the clause-level negator. As a result, constituent negation is required, for the same reason that (6.30b) is odd. Further evidence that there is a typological connection between the position of indefinite NPs relative to that of clausal negators on the one hand and the choice between CNSS and clausal negation on the other may be found in the contrasts between DU and AF pointed out in Ponelis 1993: 463. In DU, objects (as well as sentential adverbs) precede the negative marker. In AF, on the other hand, they follow the negative marker, unless emphasis is intended.

(6.32) a. ze hadden de brand niet kunnen blussen
they had the fire not be-able put-out
'They were not able to put out the fire'
(DU, Ponelis 1993: 463)

b. Maria kan nie die gebou sien nie
Maria can not the building see not
'Maria cannot see the building'
(AF, Ponelis 1993: 463)

Correspondingly, DU requires that sentences containing an indefinite object be negated through CNSS – that is, by means of a negative article, which has the force of sentential negation. The corresponding AF sentences, on the other hand, have sentential negation together with an object NP with an indefinite article.

(6.32) c. hij heeft geen jas
they have no coat
(DU, Ponelis 1993: 465)

d. hy het nie 'n jas nie
they have not-a coat not
(AF, Ponelis 1993: 465)

Other GMC languages supply some further evidence for such a connection between object position and the possibilities for expressing sentential negation. Holmes and Hinchcliffe (1994: 524) point out contrasts in SW like those in (6.33a) and (6.33b); sentential negation with an indefinite object is expressed in either of two ways. In (6.33a), we find a 'not...any' construction. The ordinary sentential negator (*inte*) is used here in conjunction with a noun phrase whose determiner is a polarity item (*några* 'any'). In (6.33b), on the other hand, the sentential negator *inte* does not appear; negation is conveyed instead by a negative determiner (*inga*) on the object NP (which again has sentential scope because of CNSS). Note, though, that the object NPs in the two constructions do not occupy the same positions. In the CNSS construction, the object occurs to the left of the verb, while in the ordinary sentential negation construction, it occurs to the right. In subject position, on the other hand, apparently the CNSS option with *ingen* is available, while the 'any...not' option is not (6.33e).

(6.33) a. Han sa att han inte hade [några pengar]
he said that he not had any money
Holmes and Hinchcliffe 1994: 524)

b. Han sa att han [inga pengar] hade
he said that he no money had

(6.33)   c. Jag har [inte] hört [någonting] om detta
I have not heard anything about that
(SW, Holmes and Hinchcliffe 1994: 524)

d. Jag har [ingenting] hört om detta
I have nothing heard about that

e. [Ingen] har sett mig
no one has seen me
(SW, Holmes and Hinchcliffe 1994: 190)

(The availability of these two possibilities also depends on register, and on whether the clause has a lexical verb alone or a lexical verb plus auxiliary. See Holmes and Hinchcliffe 1994: 189ff, 523ff. for discussion.) Unlike GE, SW does not have ordinary object shift, except for unstressed pronouns (see Bobaljik and Jonas 1996a: 206), so objects normally follow their verbs. However, negative object NPs can be moved to the left of the verb, as in (6.33b), yielding exceptional OV order (see Bandle 2005: 1155). When the objects are shifted to the left in this way, the sentential negative marker is suppressed, and the constituent negation of the shifted object acquires sentential force. Similar facts are found in DA (Allan *et al*. 1995: 516):

(6.33)   f. Jeg havde ikke sagt noget
I have not said anything
(DA, Allan *et al*. 1995: 516)

g. Jeg havde ingenting sagt
I have nothing said

Similar facts are also reported for GE and West Flemish (Haegeman 1995: 167ff.), NO (Christensen 1991) and Later ME (Ingham 2000). In the following, a negative indefinite object whose negation has sentential force is preposed to the left of the verb.

(6.34)   For I may no leysour haue
for I may no leisure have
(Late ME, Paston Letters, Ingham 2000)

Since such leftward shift of objects in Late ME appears to involve negative objects in the overwhelming number of instances, Ingham argues that it is not ordinary object shift, but a special leftward displacement linked to their status as negated phrases. Thus we see that in the GMC languages, constituent negation can have sentential force under some circumstances. The negated phrase in such cases is often shifted leftward in the clause, relative to its basic position. This leftward shift of negative objects happens even in languages which do not generally have object shift, such as SW, DA and Late ME. The observed asymmetries find a straightforward explanation under the NegP hypothesis of Haegeman (1995), to which the interested reader is referred.

A rather different state of affairs is reflected in the older GMC languages (see Harbert 2002 for detailed illustrations and discussion). In all of the modern languages, as we have seen, a negated indefinite object NP can convey the force of clausal negation (the CNSS phenomenon). In some of these languages, CNSS is the only possibility for negating a clause which contains an indefinite object. In GO, OE and at least some dialects of OHG, though, CNSS was apparently possible only under more limited circumstances than in the modern languages. In GO, for example, where the Greek Bible has sentences with CNSS, the GO translation systematically adds a sentential negator *ni* whenever the negated indefinite object or subject follows the finite verb, as in (6.35). This suggests that GO did not allow CNSS when the negated constituent was postverbal (though a counterexample is found in John 10:41).

(6.35)   a. jah in mis **ni** bigitiþ **waiht**
            and in me...not will-find anything
            (GO, John 14:30)

            b. kaì en emoì [ ] heurḗsei   **oudén**
            and in me   he-will-find nothing
            (Greek)

            c. jah **ni** qeþun   **mannhun waiht**
            and not they-said to-anyone anything
            (GO, Mark 16:8)

            d. kai [ ] **oudenì oudèn** eîpon
            and   no-one nothing they-told
            (Greek)

Only when the indefinite NP preceded the finite verb (as a subject or a topicalized nonsubject), as in (6.36), could it carry the force of sentential negation by itself, without the need for the clausal negator.

(6.36)   a. [ni waiht] nimaiþ   in   wig
            nothing   may-you-take in the way
            (GO, Luke 9:3)

            b. mēdèn aírete eis tèn hodón
            nothing take   in the way
            (Greek)

(6.36) c. [ni waiht] auk ist gahuliþ
no thing for is hidden
'for nothing is hidden'
(GO, Matt. 10:26)

d. oudèn gár estin kekalymménon
nothing for is hidden
(Greek)

In the following example, in fact, the GO word order is changed, relative to the Greek, in order to place the negated constituent preverbally.

(6.36) e. jah... [ni ainnohun] kaurida
and...not anyone I-burdened
(GO, 2 Cor. 11:8)

f. kaì...ou katenárkēsa oudenós
and not I-burdened no one
(Greek)

A similar distribution is found in OE. When a negative noun phrase or adverb phrase precedes the main verb (primarily in subordinate clauses) it can negate the clause by itself, without the need for a clausal negator, as in (6.37). However, where the negative phrase follows the finite verb (primarily in main clauses), as in (6.38), there is clausal negation, rather than CNSS.

(6.37) a. 7 him nænig wiþstōd
and none him withstood
(OE, Bede (Miller) 52:25)

b. þæt hēo nænigne incan to him wiston
that they no enmity toward him knew
(OE, Bede (Miller) 348:7)

(6.38) a. **ne** bið hēo mid **nænigne** synne byrðenne ahefigad
not is she with no sin's burden afflicted
= Latin nullo peccati pondere grauatur
(OE, Bede (Miller) 76:12)

b. **ne** mihton hī **nænigne** fultum æt him bigitan
not might they no help at him find
= Latin neque hæc tamen agentes quiquam...
(OE, Bede (Miller) 48:9)

And the same is true of at least some varieties of OHG. In the OHG *Tatian*, there is a strong tendency to use the clausal negator *ni* not only when the negated indefinite phrase is postverbal, as in (6.39a), but even when the indefinite phrase is preverbal, as in (6.39b). However, there are at least a few examples showing that it could be dispensed with in the latter case, as in (6.39c, d). Some of these are pointed out by Behaghel (1924: II, 77), who also observes a connection with verb position. Thus, CNSS was again apparently possible just in case the negative indefinite preceded the finite verb (though it was apparently not preferred even then).

(6.39)   a. inti sie **ni** quedent imo **niouuiht**
and they not say to him anything
= Latin et nihil [ ] ei dicunt
(OHG, Tatian (Sievers) 104:7)

     b. [niouuiht] **ni** gifiengumes
nothing not we-took
= Latin nihil [ ] coepimus
(OHG, Tatian (Sievers) 19:6)

     c. [**nioman**] thoh uuidero offano sprah fon imo
no-one though again openly spoke of him
= Latin nemo tamen palam loquebatur de illo
(OHG, Tatian (Sievers) 104:3)

     d. inti **nēuuiht** unōdes ist iu
and nothing impossible is to-you
= Latin nihil impossibile erit vobis
(OHG, Tatian (Sievers) 92:8)

What appears to be a strong tendency in OHG toward avoiding CNSS in favor of clausal negation appears to have the force of a requirement in OS, where there is no single clear case of CNSS, even when the indefinite NP precedes the verb (and lots of missed opportunities to deploy it) (cf. Behaghel 1924: II, 76).

(6.40)   a. that iru thar **nioman** thurh thes neriandan hêlaga helpa harm **ne** gifrumidi
that to-her there no one through the Lord's holy help harm not did
(OS, Heliand (Behaghel) 3889)

     b. that thar **nênig** gumono **ni** ginas
that there no man not was-saved (Ms. C has *enig gumo*)
(OS, Heliand Ms. M (Behaghel) 4369)

(6.40) c. **neo** gi umbi iuuam   meti (**ni**) sorgot
never shall you about your food not worry (*ni* missing in Ms. M)
(OS, Heliand (Behaghel) 1858)

For the remainder of the older dialects, though, the generalization seems to hold that a negative indefinite constituent can carry the force of clausal negation by itself, without the need for a clausal negator, only in preverbal, not in postverbal position. In this latter restriction they are different from the modern GMC languages. They are also different from the modern languages in another, and probably related, way; all of the early GMC languages express clausal negation by means of a preverbal negative particle (*ni, ne*), rather than by a "medial" (postverbal) negator like GE *nicht*, IC *ekki*. or EN *not*.

The connection between the possibility of CNSS and the position of the clausal negator was pointed out in Haegeman and Zanuttini 1996, on the basis of modern Romance and GMC languages. They claim (1996: 120) that in languages where the clausal negator precedes the verb, constituent negation can take clausal scope only if the negated consituent is "in a position c-commanding INFL" (that is, for our purposes, in a position in front of the inflected verb), while languages in which the clausal negator is not preverbal are not restricted in this way. Thus, for example, Zanuttini (1997: 8f.) points out for the Romance languages that the kind of asymmetry we have observed in older GMC (CNSS only when the negated constituent is preverbal) is characteristic of those Romance languages which express clausal negation by means of a preverbal particle, such as Italian, but not languages which have medial (postverbal) clausal negators, such as Piedmontese. In Piedmontese, CNSS can be controlled by postverbal negative indefinite phrases as well, just as in modern GMC (6.41d).

(6.41) a. Non ha   detto niente
not s/he-has said nothing
(Standard Italian, Zanuttini 1997: 8)

b. A l'ha   pa dit   gnente
s/he-has not said nothing
(Piedmontese, Zanuttini 1997: 8)

c. *Ho   visto nessuno
I-have seen no-one
(Standard Italian, Zanuttini 1997: 8)

d. I l'hai vist gnun
I have seen no-one
(Piedmontese, Zanuttini 1997: 9)

Further support for such a typological connection is provided by the facts of ON. ON gave up the GMC clausal negator *ni* early on, in favor of postverbal negative markers (through a process to be discussed in a subsequent section). In fact, it developed two postverbal negators in succession: a negative suffix, *-a(t)*, restricted for the most part to the archaic poetry of the poetic *Edda*, and a more modern one, the free-standing negative adverb *ekki* (identical to the clausal negator of Modern IC). The former is illustrated in (6.42):

(6.42)   Em-k-**at** ek álfa   né ása   sona
         am-I-not I elves' nor Æsir's son
         (ON, Skírnismál (Dronke) 18:1)

(The origins of these will be discussed in a later section. See also Eythórsson 1995 for more detailed treatment.) Significantly, in both of these stages of ON, contrary to the other older languages, but like the modern ones, a negative indefinite object in either a preverbal or a postverbal position could convey the force of clausal negation.

(6.43)   a. En **ekki vopn**   höfðu þeir
             but no weapon had they
             (ON, Heimskringla, Kristjánsdóttir *et al.* 1991: 22)

         b. Eftir orustu þessa fékk Haraldur konungr **enga mótstöðu** í Noregi
             after this battle got King Harald   no resistance   in Norway
             (ON, Heimskringla, Kristjánsdóttir *et al.* 1991:73)

         c. **mangi** er þér   í orði   vinr
             no one is to-you in words (a) friend
             (ON, Lokasenna (Dronke) 2:6)

         d. lífs tel ek   [vón **ǫnga**]
             of life count I hope no
             (ON, Atlamál in Groenlenzko (Dronke) 88:8)

         e. þó   hann **æva** hendr
             washed he   never hands
             (ON, Voluspa (Dronke) 33:1)

         f. Mun **engi** maðr ǫðrum   þyrma
             shall no   man to-another show-respect
             (ON, Voluspa (Dronke) 44:11)

         g. þá   var [kostr **engi**]
             then was choice no
             (ON, Atlamál in Groenlenzko (Dronke) 62:2)

392   6 *The syntax of the clause*

Thus, ON patterns with modern GMC in both respects predicted by Haegeman's and Zanuttini's generalization: it has postverbal clausal negators, and it allows CNSS with negative indefinite phrases in postverbal position.

6.2.6 On formal differences between sentential negators and constituent negators

There is extensive overlap in the GMC languages in the forms used for sentential negation and constituent negation. GO was the most uniform of the GMC languages in this respect, using the same morpheme, *ni*, for all types of negation.

(6.44)   a. Iudas, ni sa Iskarjotes
Judas, not the Iscariot
(GO, John 14:22)

         b. ni sakuls, ni faihufriks
not quarrelsome, not greedy
(1 Tim. 3:3)

         c. ni bi himina
not by heaven
(Matt. 5:34)

         d. ni qam hveila is
not came time his
(John 8:20)

         e. ju [ni ik] waurkja ita
but not I do it
(Rom. 7:20)

It differs from the other GMC languages in that it does not show the results of lexical incorporation, or fusion, of the negative particle with a following indefinite pronoun, noun or adverb to yield intrinsically negative indefinite pronouns and adverbs such as GE *nie, niemand, nirgends, nichts, kein*. The negative and the indefinite element remain independent in GO, and can occur separately from each other (Behaghel 1924: II, 76).

(6.45)   a. ni ainshun
not anyone
(Luke 16:13)

         b. jah ni aiw ainshun mag frawilwan þo
and not ever anyone may snatch-away those
(John 10:29)

c. ni waiht ~ ni... waiht
   not a-thing not...a-thing
   (1 Tim. 4:4) (John 6:63)

In all of these cases, the GO *ni. . .ainshun*, *ni. . .waiht* translate a single Greek word, *oudén* 'nothing' or *oudeìs* 'no one'.

The development of such lexically incorporated negative indefinite forms is well under way in other early languages, and they are widespread in the modern GMC languages. One special case of this process of negative-indefinite incorporation has been the development of distinctive negative determiners in noun phrases for constituent negation of indefinite noun phrases (e.g., EN *no*, GE *kein*, DU *geen*, AF *geen/g'n*, YI *keyn*). For a discussion of the similar development of ON *engi*, SW *inga*, see the next section. These apparently functioned originally as polarity items without independent negative force, dependent on the clausal negation marker. As the differences in these forms show, they are the outcomes of a number of apparently independent lexical developments. EN *no* and GE *kein*, for example, come from combinations of 'not' and 'one', but two different negative morphemes are involved. This is thus a further instance of convergence of individual developments in modern GMC.

For constituent negation of other categories, however, including prepositional phrases, pronouns and adjectives, as well as those noun phrases which already have determiners, or which do not admit determiners (pronouns and proper names, for example), all of these languages use the same negative form used in sentential negation.

(6.46) a. ikke vi ønsker dette
           not we wished that
           (NO, Askedal 1994: 256)

       b. inte i något fall, kan vi tillåta dette
          not in any case can we allow that
          (SW, Andersson 1994: 296)

       c. I will drink not a drop

       d. He should fear not his enemies but his friends

       e. Nicht müde bin ich, sondern zermürbt
          not tired am I, but exhausted
          (GE)

       f. Inte alla pojkar ljuger
          not all boys lie
          (SW, Holmes and Hinchcliffe 1994: 523)

That is, aside from negative determiners and other products of negative-indefinite incorporation, the forms used for constituent negation are the same as those used for sentential negation. There are some sentential negators, though, which are not also found as constituent negators, including OE *ne*, MHG *en*, West Flemish *en* and Modern EN *n't*. These are all clitic-like forms which require a finite verb as a host, and it is most likely on that account that they are limited to sentential negation.

6.2.7 On the typology of sentential negation in Germanic

6.2.7.1 The "cycle of negation"

As we have noted, in GO, and in other early GMC languages, a sentence could be negated solely by an unstressable negative particle (GO *ni*, OE *ne*, OHG *ni*, Middle DU and MHG *en*). These particles typically appeared immediately in front of the verb.

(6.47)   a.   þarei ik im, jus ni   maguþ qiman
                 where I am, you may not   come
                 (GO, John 7:34)

In some of these languages the negative particle seems to "attract" the verb, causing it to appear farther to the left in sentential structure than it would otherwise (see Section 6.3.2 below). This shows up very clearly in OE, for example, where a pronominal subject, which precedes the finite verb in main clauses, follows both the negative and the verb in a negative sentence, as in (6.47c.).

(6.47)   b.   þā tēþ   hīe brōhton sume þǣm cyninge
                 the teeth they brought some to-the king
                 (OE, Voyage of Ohthere)

                c.   Ne mētte   hē ǣr   nān gebūn land...
                     not encountered he before any settled land...
                     (OE, Voyage of Ohthere)

Similarly, in GO, as Eythórsson (1995) has established, the normal order of the verb is final in affirmative main clauses, but in negative main clauses it appears systematically to the left of objects and other dependents of the verb, and adjacent to the negator *ni*.

(6.47)   d.   unte   ni nimiþ   arbi
                 because not he-takes inheritance
                 = Greek ou gàr mề klēronomḗsēi
                 (GO, Gal. 4:30)

e. ju ni drigkais　　þanamais　　wato
　 yet not you-may-drink thenceforward water
　 = Greek mēkéti hydropótei
　 (1 Tim. 5:23)

f. ni wairþam usgrudjans
　 not let us-become dispirited
　 = Greek ouk ekkakoûmen
　 (2 Cor. 4:1a)

And in ON poetry, while subjects normally precede the verb in affirmative main clauses, they invariably follow V + negative morpheme *a(t)* in main clauses.

(6.47)　　g. Þrymr sat á　　haugi
　　　　　　Þrymr sat on (a) mound
　　　　　　(ON, Þrk 6, cited in Eythórsson 1995: 194)

　　　　　h. kemr-a　　nú　Gunnarr
　　　　　　 comes-not now Gunnarr
　　　　　　 (ON, Gðr III:8, cited in Eythórsson 1995: 193)

In GO, the clause-initial *ni* appears to be closely affiliated with other elements of the left periphery, hosting clitic conjunctions and question markers, for example (*nih*←*ni* + *uh* 'and', *ni-u*←*ni* + *-u* '?'). In other languages, however, it often forms a phonological unit with the verb.[4]

(6.48)　　　nis　eo　sô sâlig　man...
　　　　　　not-is ever so happy man
　　　　　　'there is never so happy a man...'
　　　　　　(OS, Heliand (Behaghel) 1655)

Where sentences with the negative particle also happened to contain nonspecific arguments or adjuncts, these elements could be realized as polarity items. In GO, they often bear the suffix *-hun*, which was restricted to (A/S-)polarity items.

(6.49)　　a. jah　　ni mannhun skalkinodedum aiw ƕanhun
　　　　　　　and we not-anyone we-served ever at-any-time (lit., 'when-hun')
　　　　　　　(GO, John. 8:33)

---

[4] However, it is also possible for the negative particle to appear as an enclitic on a preceding element in some languages:
(i)　　　　　wirn　　 kunnen leider　　　baz
　　　　　　w :-not can　unfortunately better
　　　　　　(MHG, Iwein 7684, cited in Paul 1989: 399)

396   6 The syntax of the clause

Aside from these, the negative particle was the only exponent of negation in older GMC. However, some of these languages developed an additional marker of sentential negation, which eventually supplanted the unstressed preverbal negative particle in some of them. These secondary negative markers arose by way of a process which is standardly held to have proceeded in three steps. Through a process of semantic bleaching, the polarity form of a nonspecific nominal lost its lexical meaning, and came to be able to appear even in clauses where there were no argument positions for it to represent, as a simple reinforcer of the negative particle (for the purpose of expressing emphatic negation) in sentences containing no other stressable polarity item which could be emphasized. We may think of these as "dummy" polarity items: they did not contribute thematic meaning to the sentence. This is illustrated in the following GO example, where *waiht* has no counterpart in the Greek text.

(6.49)   b. iþ   faur mik silban ni   **waiht** ƕopa
             but for myself   not 'thing' boast-1Sg
             'I will not AT ALL boast on my own behalf '
             (GO, 2 Cor. 12:5)

Eventually, in precursors of all of the modern GMC languages, these in turn lost their emphatic character, and became simply a structurally necessary part of sentential negation, co-occurring with the preverbal particle even when no emphasis was intended. At this point, the expression of sentential negation was discontinuous, involving a negative particle which preceded the inflected verb immediately and the phonologically heavier former polarity item, which typically followed the verb in main clause word orders. Some examples are given in (6.49c, d).

(6.49)   c. Annd icc ne mihte nohht mīn ferss ā33 wiþþ
                           goddspelless wōrdēss well fillenn all
             and I   not might not   my verses ever with
                           gospel's words well fill all
             (Early ME, Orm. II:16)

         d. er'n   hat uns niht getân niwan guot und êre
             he-not has us   not done except good and honor
             (MHG, Nib. 868:1)

Finally, the preverbal particle itself disappeared in most of the modern languages, leaving the other element (typically referred to as a "negative adverb") as the sole realization of negation, though FR and southwestern dialects of DU (Ponelis 1993: 464) have retained the preverbal negative particle *en*. Haegeman and Zanuttini (1996) discuss the syntax of *en* in West Flemish, a Belgian dialect of DU, in detail. They point out that it is now optional there, that it can only occur with another negative constituent, and that it seems to have no independent negative force, serving rather solely as a marker of negative scope. In consequence of these changes, both negative-incorporating polarity forms (EN *not*, GE *nicht*) and N-polarity forms of other origins (e.g., SW *inte*, DA *ikke*, IC *ekki*, FA *ikki*, which come from the neuter pronoun *eit* plus a generalizing suffix *-gi*, cognate with the GO *hun* in *hvas-hun* 'anyone', etc.) have come to replace the original negative particle as the basic marker of sentential negation. Old West Norse poetry exhibits the negative suffixes *-a* and *-(a)t*, which originated respectively from the masculine and neuter forms of the word 'one' (**aina*, **ainata*) (Eythórsson 1995: 229). They could originally co-occur with *ne*, with restrictions; *ne* was excluded from clause-initial positions, and in these cases *at* was the sole negator from the earliest period. Subsequently, however, *ne* disappeared from all contexts, leaving only *at* as a sentential negator (see Eythórsson 1995: 218ff. for discussion). *At* is interestingly different from the other cases of polarity items becoming negators, since it behaves as an enclitic, rather than a free morpheme, from the beginning.

Jespersen (1917) observed these parallel developments, which have counterparts in French and Welsh, and they have been much discussed in later literature under the name of "Jespersen's cycle of negation." Frisch (1997) presents a detailed study of the internal staging of the process in ME, interesting especially for its methodology, which focuses on the relative chronology of the rise of what he calls the "postverbal negator" and the decline of the preverbal negator. Donhauser (1995) challenges Jespersen's cycle as a misleading simplification of a more complex reality. As noted in Section 6.2.5., these changes in turn were related to changes in the syntax of CNSS.

6.2.7.2 *Afrikaans final negation*

AF has developed a rather striking variation on the two-part negation structure. It has developed an obligatory clause-final negative marker (the "associated negative," in Ponelis' terms), which serves as a sort of signal of scope, following all constituents which are in the scope of negation. This marker appears in clauses with the sentential negative morpheme *nie* and in CNSS clauses.

(6.50)   a. Dit is nie duidelik wie kwalifiseer nie
            it is neg clear   who qualifies   *nie*
            (AF, Ponelis 1993: 456)

            b. Jy sal nêrens kom nie
            you will nowhere get *nie*
            (AF, Ponelis 1993: 453)

The final negative is obligatory except when other negative elements appear clause-finally. In that case, it is optional when the other negative element is a negated constituent (6.50d), and disallowed when it is the sentential negator *nie* (6.50c).

(6.50) c. Die honde blaf nie
           the dogs bark *nie*
           AF, (Ponelis 1995: 453)

        d. Ek weet niks   (nie)
           I know nothing (*nie*)
           (AF, Donaldson 1994: 502)

This construction is discussed at length in Donaldson 1993, Ponelis 1993, Roberge 2000 and Bell 2004.

6.3 The syntax of the left periphery: topics, verb-second and subject/verb inversion

The patterning of elements at the left periphery of the clause – in particular, the so-called V-2 phenomenon – has been treated as the central problem of GMC syntax in recent years, and its analysis has been the subject of a vast literature. Most of this literature has focussed on the proper theoretical interpretation of the facts, which are themselves relatively straightforward.

Descriptively speaking, the V-2 phenomenon is the requirement, apparently holding under at least some circumstances in all of the GMC languages, that the finite verb of the clause be no further from the beginning of the clause than second position (not counting conjunctions). In subject-initial main clauses, most of the modern GMC languages, as well as most of the medieval languages, typically have verb-second order, with the inflected verb occurring immediately after the subject NP. Declarative main clauses with verb-final order are also found in early medieval GMC: Runic GMC, GO, OE (particularly in second conjuncts of coordinate sentences (cf. Kiparsky 1995b: 147f.)), OHG and Middle DU (Weerman 1989: 182ff.), but this order is in competition from the earliest times with subject-verb order, and has disappeared across the board by later medieval times.

EN has V-2 order with a more limited extent than other GMC languages in subject-initial main clauses. When the sentence contains only a lexical verb (as opposed to an auxiliary verb), the verb follows not only the subject but also such elements as frequency adverbs (*He often left early/*He left often early*). Only modals, *have*, *be* and the dummy auxiliary *do* routinely precede such elements (*He will often leave/has often left early*). That is, lexical verbs in declarative sentences in EN do not seem to occur as far to the left as in other languages. We can account for this in terms of the tree structure in (6.1) by claiming that in Modern EN, only modals and auxiliaries can appear in the T(ense) position. Lexical verbs, such as *left*, remain within the VP and thus follow frequency adverbs, for example, which mark the leftward boundary of the VP. Similarly, modals, *have* and *be* but not lexical verbs can precede the clausal negative marker *not* (*He is not leaving/*He left not*). When there is no modal or auxiliary available to precede the negative marker, a dummy auxiliary, *do*, must be supplied to represent the T(ense) position (*He did not leave*). The prohibition against lexical verbs appearing in this leftward position is a recent one in EN, dating from the Modern EN period, and is connected historically with the development of a syntactically distinct class of modal verbs (see Section 5.2). It sets EN apart from the other GMC languages.

When a sentence element other than the subject begins an independent sentence, all of the GMC languages require the finite verb to follow that initial element immediately in at least some circumstances with the subject coming third. This "subject-verb inversion" is thus a hallmark of the GMC languages, though it is not exclusive to them; Roberts (1993: 6) reports that Old French was a (strict) V-2 language, with subject inversion, as are a number of other Romance varieties, medieval and modern, and it may perhaps be interpreted as an areal phenomenon. The main parameters of variation in GMC with respect to this second subcase of V-2 involve:

a. whether all verbs or only auxiliaries are subject to the V-2 requirement,
b. whether the effect holds in subordinate as well as main clauses, and, if so, whether there are restrictions on the type of subordinate clause, and
c. what sorts of clause-initial constituents trigger (or are exempted from) V-2.

For a systematic overview of the variation, the reader is referred to Vikner 1995.

Variation in parameter (a) can be summed up in a few words: contemporary EN stands out among all the GMC languages in that only modals, *have*, *be* and the "dummy" auxiliary *do* show the V-2 property of having to precede the subject, for example, in word questions, where the clause-initial position is occupied by a question phrase. In (6.51a), the subject and the auxiliary of the sentence stand in the order Aux-Subject, rather than in the order Subject-Aux which is found in declarative sentences.

(6.51) a. What must I read?

In sentences in which there are no auxiliaries, but only a lexical verb, the dummy auxiliary *do* appears in these "Subject-Aux inversion" cases.

(6.51) b. I read this. What did I read?

That is, the kinds of verbs which can precede the subject in EN inversion questions are precisely the same as those which can appear in the T(ense) position in ordinary declarative sentences, thus preceding such elements as frequency adverbs and the clausal negator. In the other GMC languages, where lexical verbs precede frequency adverbs and clausal negators in declarative sentences, they also precede the subject in questions. That is, all and only those elements which can appear in the T(ense) position in (6.1) in a given language can invert with the subject in questions.

6.3.1 Main-clause/subordinate clause asymmetries in verb position

The GMC languages partition themselves into two groups with respect to the second of the parameters above. Standard EN is among the group which shows asymmetries between main clauses and subordinate clauses. In subordinate clause questions in standard EN, unlike main clauses, the subject and the auxiliary remain in that order, rather than inverting. (Not all dialects of EN show such an asymmetry between main and subordinate clause questions, though. Some varieties which do not will be discussed further in Section 6.5.2.)

(6.51)   c. I wonder what I must read. I wonder if I must read this.

Most other GMC languages exhibit similar asymmetries (though with lexical verbs, as well as auxiliaries), as the SW examples in (6.52) show. In main clause questions, but not in subordinate clause questions, the verb is obligatorily the second element. Thus, in (6.52a), the finite verb must precede the subject, while in the subordinate clause question in (6.52b), it must follow the subject (as well as the clausal negator *inte*). In GE and DU, the alternation between main and subordinate clauses is still more salient, since the main clause V-2 order contrasts with clause-final verb position in subordinate clauses.

(6.52)   a. Varför öppnade han inte brevet
           why opened he not letter-the?
           (SW, Platzack 1985: 50)

           b. Jag undrar varför han inte öppnade brevet
           I wonder why he not opened letter-the
           (SW, Platzack 1985: 50)

           c. Er muß zu Hause bleiben
           he must at home stay
           (GE)

           d. Seine Mutter sagt, daß er zu Hause bleiben muß
           his mother says that he at home stay must

OE, too, has V-2 in main but not in subordinate clause questions.

(6.52)   e. Hwæt sægest þū, yrþlingc?
           what say you, ploughman?
           (OE, Ælfric)

           f. ac hē nyste hwæt þæs sōþes wæs
           but he not-knew what the truth was
           (OE, Ohthere)

6.3 The syntax of the left periphery 401

Note that in the GE examples in (6.52c, d), the verb appears in the V-2 position in the main clause, where there is no complementizer, and appears finally in the subordinate clause, where there is a complementizer. Similarly, in (6.51a) in EN, the auxiliary precedes the subject in the main clause yes/no question, where there is no complementizer, but it follows the subject in the embedded clause question in (6.51c), where the clause is introduced by the complementizer *if*. The following examples illustrate the same kind of complementarity for conditional clauses in GE and EN:

(6.53) a. Wenn ich reich wäre, kaufte   ich mir   einen neuen Wagen
            if   I rich were, would-buy I myself a   new   car
        (GE)

        b. Wäre ich reich, kaufte   ich mir   einen neuen Wagen
           were I rich, would-buy I myself a   new   car

        c. If I had only said something!

        d. Had I only said something!

This complementarity between leftward occurrence of the verb and the presence of a complementizer is the foundation of the standard analysis of such constructions in the generative framework, under which the V-2 position of the verb is identified with the C(OMP) position. In questions, the verb must move to that position from the T position when the C(OMP) position is not already occupied by a complementizer. When it does so, it comes to precede the subject. The tree in (6.1) provides for only one position still further to the left in clausal structure: the Specifier position of CP. Therefore, the verb, when in COMP, can occur no later than in second position. In cases where the verb is clause-initial, as in yes/no questions or conditional sentences, we may assume that the SpecCP position is occupied by a non-phonological element – an abstract question operator. Some of the GMC languages also allow the clause-initial to remain empty in declarative sentences too, yielding V-1 declarative order.

As a diachronic sidenote, Kiparsky (1995a) argues that the rise of V-2 in GMC was a consequence of the development of subordinating complementizers (and therefore of the CP architecture underlying V-2), as the language shifted from adjunction to syntactic subordination as a means of expressing semantic relationships between clauses. The interested reader is referred to that work for further discussion.

6.3.1.1 *Absence of main/subordinate asymmetries*
Such main/subordinate clause asymmetries in verb position are not always found in the GMC languages, however. An exception of a rather trivial sort is found in GO, where, unlike SW and Standard EN, verb fronting was possible in indirect questions, as well

402   6 *The syntax of the clause*

as main clause questions, as Eythórsson (1995: 49) notes. The following example shows the verb in initial position in the subordinate clause, in contrast with the Greek order, even though -*u*, the translational equivalent of *if*, is present.

(6.54)   witaidedun   imma hailidedi-u   sabbato daga
          they-watched him   he-might-heal-Q sabbath day
          'They watched him, whether he would heal on the Sabbath'
          (GO, Mark 3:2, cited in Eythórsson 1995: 106)

However, this does not necessarily contradict the account of V-2 offered here. We need only assume that, because of its clitic status, the complementizer -*u* 'if', unlike its EN counterpart, does not "fill" the COMP slot, but, like other clitics, co-occupies that slot with the verb which precedes it (and in fact depends on the verb to support it).

A second class of restricted exceptions to the main clause/subordinate clause asymmetry in V-2 involves the phenomenon of "embedded root clauses." Compare the following examples from DA, for instance:

(6.55)   a. Vi ved, at   denne bog har Bo ikke læst
             we know that this book has Bo not read
             (DA, Vikner 1995: 67)

          b. *Johan beklager at denne bog har jeg læst
             John   regrets that this book have I read
             (DA, Vikner 1995: 72)

In the first of these examples, there has been topic fronting in the subordinate clause, and the inflected verb precedes the subject, as well as the negative adverb. In these respects, this subordinate clause resembles a main clause. The label "root clause" has been devised to unite descriptively the set of main clauses and those subordinate clauses which behave like them in showing V-2 order and topic fronting, for example. Thus, (6.55a) involves an "embedded root clause." Not all embedded clauses admit this behavior. It is limited to 'that' clauses, and in fact only a subset of these. The second example shows that this order is not possible under a verb such as *beklager* 'regrets'. Embedded root behavior (verb fronting and fronting) cannot occur in embedded questions or relative clauses:

(6.56)   a. Jeg ved ikke, hvorfor koen   alltid står   inde i huset
             I   know not, why   cow-the always stands inside in house-the
             (DA, Vikner 1995: 73)

          b. *Jeg ved ikke, hvorfor koen   står alltid inde i huset
             I   know not, why   cow-the stands always inside in house-the
             (DA, Vikner 1995: 73)

c. *Jeg ved ikke, hvorfor i værelset har koen stået
   I know not, why in room-the has cow-the stood
   (DA, Vikner 1995: 74)

OE also exhibits this "restricted embedded V-2" (Kiparsky 1995a: 164n.).

(6.56) d. Ic secge þæt behefe ic eom ge cingce ge ealdormannum
   I say that useful I am both to-king and to-aldermen
   (ÆColl. 150, cited in Kiparsky 1995a: 145)

Continental West GMC forms a still more restrictive subgroup, in which embedded root behavior is found only in 'that'-type complements from which the complementizer has been omitted. In GE, only when an embedded 'that' clause lacks a complementizer does it behave like a main clause, with verb fronting and topicalization.

(6.57) Er sagt, morgen fahre sie ab
   he says tomorrow goes she away
   (GE)

The subset of main verbs which admit embedded root clauses in SW overlaps extensively with the verbs that allow 'that' complementizer drop (and therefore embedded root behavior) in GE.[5]

By contrast with these languages, two of the modern GMC languages, YI and IC, exhibit what Vikner (1995: 80) terms "general embedded V-2" behavior. In these languages, topicalization and subject-verb inversion are not limited to certain types of 'that'-clauses, but can occur generally in embedded clauses. So, for instance, in the following YI examples, the subject is preceded by both a fronted topic and a fronted verb, even in the complement of a main clause verb 'regret' (6.58a), and even in embedded questions (6.58b). The possibility of topic fronting in embedded questions and relative clauses is severely limited, however (see Vikner 1995: 74).

(6.58) a. Jonas bedoyert az dos bukh hob ikh geleyent
   John regrets that this book have I read
   (YI, Vikner 1995: 72)

---

[5] In particular, a comparison of the list of verbs provided by Vikner which allow complementizer drop in GE (e.g., 'hint', 'indicate', 'answer', 'claim', 'report', 'learn', 'hope', 'think', 'say') with his list of verbs which do not ('be sorry', 'confirm', 'regret', 'prove') suggests that factivity is involved in the distinction. Compare also Kiparsky 1995a: 164n. and Roberts 1993: 58. The correspondence between factivity and the possibility of complementizer drop is not completely sound, however; 'remember', a factive verb, allows complementizer-drop, while 'doubt', a non-factive verb, does not. See Vikner 1995: 72 for a discussion of the difficulty of finding a natural class distinction between the two groups of verbs.

(6.58) b. oyb ofyn veg vet dos yingl zen a kats
if on-the way will the boy see a cat
(YI, Santorini 1995: 54)

Because the word-order possibilities in YI and IC subordinate clauses more closely resemble those of main clauses, they are sometimes referred to as "symmetrical" V-2 languages, as opposed to "asymmetrical" V-2 languages like GE, in which the main clause/subordinate clause differences are greater. YI and IC are the two languages which allow expletives of the clause-initial type to appear in embedded clauses (Vikner 1995: 70 and Section 4.9.2 of the present volume). Among the approaches to explaining the difference between symmetrical and asymmetrical languages has been one of roughly the following sort: in asymmetrical languages, topics are in the same position as questions phrases, for example, and therefore impossible in embedded questions such as (6.56c) in SW because the (SpecCP) position in which those topics would occur is occupied by the question phrase. Symmetrical V-2 languages such as YI, on the other hand, allow the topic phrase to occur in the position normally reserved for the subject of the clause instead (SpecTP). Thus, the topic may co-occur with a question phrase in a subordinate clause, since the two are not competing for the same structural slot, but when it does, the subject of the clause must be postverbal since the preverbal position in which it would otherwise occur is occupied. The interested reader is referred to Kroch and Taylor 1997 for a discussion of these two types of V-2, and a defense of the striking claim that both the YI type of V-2 and the SW type of V-2 were represented in two different regional varieties of ME. This same constellation of facts has been addressed in a rather different way, making more articulated assumptions about structure, by other investigators. See Roberts 1993: 58ff., Vikner 1995: 80ff. and Thráinsson 1996: 264ff. for three rather different theoretical implementations of these alternatives.

6.3.2 The triggers of verb-second order and the typology of V-2

The final one of our three parameters has to do with the types of main clauses in which V-2 appears. All of the GMC languages exhibit V-2 constructions under some circumstances. However, it has been usual in recent literature to propose a typological distinction between "strict V-2 languages," including all of modern GMC except EN, and "residual-V-2 languages" (a term originating with Rizzi 1991), represented, among modern GMC languages, at least, only by EN. EN resembles the strict V-2 languages in having inversion in questions, in imperative sentences, in complementizerless conditional sentences, and in sentences in which a negative phrase with sentential scope has been preposed, as the examples in (6.59) show.

(6.59) a. Why must you leave so soon?
b. Hear ye! (archaic)

c. Had we only known, we could have helped
d. At no time can you leave the building
e. Not one piece of chocolate did she eat

EN differs from the strict V-2 languages like GE, however, in that in GE, but not EN, preposing of ordinary, non-negative topics is also accompanied by inversion, so that the verb in GE is in second position, but in EN it comes third.

(6.60)   a. Yesterday the man left early

b. Gestern   ist der Mann früh abgefahren
yesterday is the man   early left
(GE)

If the extent of the differences between EN and the strict V-2 languages were limited to only a single triggering environment, then it would hardly constitute the basis for proposing a fundamental typological distinction. (As we will see, older GMC had triggering environments for V-2 which are not found in either Modern GE or Modern EN). However, advocates of the strict V-2/residual V-2 typology propose that the differences are more extensive than this. In particular they claim that the two types of language differ even with respect to the structure of superficially similar sentences which begin with unemphatic subjects, such as the following pair.

(6.61)   a. Er hat mir geholfen
he has me helped
(GE)

b. He has helped me

It is claimed that the subjects in these two types of sentences are in different positions; in GE, but not EN, the subject is displaced to the "topic" position (SpecCP), and the verb is also moved leftward, to the C(OMPLEMENTIZER) position on the left periphery of the clause. More generally, the verb is in the C position in every main clause in a strict V-2 language, but is only in the C position in a residual V-2 language such as EN when the presence of a specific trigger, such as a question phrase or a negative phrase, requires it to be. See Rizzi 1991, among many others, and Travis 1991 and Zwart 1993, for a conflicting view.

Recent investigations of the older GMC languages (in particular, Kiparsky 1995a and Eythórsson 1995) have shown that V-2 syntax was already to be found in the earliest representatives of the family, but in a form that in some respects seems to resemble Modern EN more than the other modern languages. Like all of the modern GMC languages, the earlier ones all have V-2/subject-verb inversion in main clause questions, as Eythórsson observes. It is, for example, present in GO:

(6.62) a. hʋa skuli þata barn wairþan?
        what shall that child become ?
        (GO, Luke 1:66, Eythórsson (1995: 25))

In fact, in yes/no questions, GO provides us with a boundary marker which lets us pin down more closely the position to which the verb moves, in the form of the interrogative affix -*u*. Eythórsson (1995: 104) claims that -*u* is an interrogative complementizer, which, because of its clitic nature, does not block the verb from moving to COMP, but in fact depends on the verb to serve as a host for it in that position.

(6.62) b. wileiz-u   ei   qiþaima...
        you-want-Q that we-might-say
        'Do you want that we might say...?
        (GO, Luke 9:54)

There can be little doubt that this was the pattern of common GMC. The only modest deviation on this point is the one noted by Taraldsen (1986a: 20), that Northern NO dialects lack V-2 in certain cases of "light" (monosyllabic) question words (cf. also Nordgård 1986; Vikner 1995: 53; Westergaard 2003):

(6.62) c. Kor studentan ska bu/   *Kor ska studentan bu?
        where student-the shall live ?   where shall student-the live?
        (Northern NO, Taraldsen 1986: 21)

We also saw above that preposed negative constituents are among the V-2 triggers in Modern EN (6.59d). It goes without saying, of course, that they also occasion verb fronting in the modern strict V-2 languages, as do all clause-initial constituents. Eythórsson (1995: 24ff.) demonstrates that clause-initial negation triggered V-2 in the earliest GMC for which we have evidence. In GO, as in EN, a clause-initial negative "attracts" the verb to the left periphery. Eythórsson's demonstration involves cases where the GO order can be shown to be independent of the Greek. In non-negative declarative sentences, as was demonstrated in (5.104), where GO translates a single verb form in Greek with a verb-plus-complement sequence, the GO verb follows its complement, showing that GO was not a strict V-2 language with V-2 in all main clauses. However, when the sentence in question begins with a negative element, the order verb-complement is found, showing that such negative elements also cause leftward displacement of the verb in GO:

(6.63) a. unte ni nimiþ   arbi
        for not he-receives inheritance
        = Greek ou gàr mề klēronomḗsēi
        (GO, Gal. 4:30, Eythórsson 1995: 24)

b. ju   ni drigkais   þanamais wato
   now not may-you-drink thenceforth water
   = Greek mēkéti hydropótei
   (GO, 1 Tim. 5:23, Eythórsson 1995: 24)

c. ni was wulþag
   not it-was glorious
   = Greek ou dedóxasti
   (GO, 2 Cor. 3:10, Eythórsson 1995: 24)

In summary, GO shows V-2, but of a sort which is more reminiscent of the "residual V-2" of Modern EN than the "strict V-2" of the rest of modern GMC, since it is not in all main clauses that the verb appears in a leftward position, but only in clauses beginning with certain specific "triggers," such as interrogative or negative elements.

The evaluation of the evidence of the other early languages, and in particular OE, has turned out to be more complicated, and more controversial. Unsurprisingly, OE shows V-2 in all of the cases in which Modern EN (as well as the rest of GMC) does – in questions and negative sentences, for example.

(6.64)   a. Ne mētte hē ǣr   nan gebūn   land...
            not found he before any inhabited land...
            (OE, Orosius, Voyage of Ohthere)

         b. Nis   Angelcynn   bedǣled Drihtnes hālgena
            not-is English-kind deprived of-lord's saints
            'The English people are not lacking in the Lord's saints'
            (OE, Ælfric, St. Edmund)

         c. Hwæt sprycst þū ?
            what speak you?
            (OE, Ælfric, Colloquy)

         d. Hwæt cunnon þās   þīne gefēran?
            what know these your companions ?
            (OE, Ælfric, Colloquy)

The question of whether it is a strict V-2 language, like Modern DU or SW, or a residual V-2 language, like Modern EN, would therefore seem to hinge on its behavior in main clauses which begin with ordinary topics. These show inversion in the modern strict V-2 languages, but not in Modern EN. Surprisingly, we get different answers depending on which sorts of subjects we look at. If we restrict our attention to topic-initial clauses with pronoun subjects, we find the order Topic-Subject-Verb, like Modern EN, as Eythórsson (1995: 294) and Kiparsky (1995a) point out.

(6.64) e. [Ēasteweeard] hit mæg bīon syxtīg mīla brād
eastward   it may be   sixty miles broad
(OE, Orosius, Voyage of Ohthere)

f. [Ond ealle ðā hwīle] hē sceal seglian be lande
And all the   while   he shall sail   by land
(OE, Orosius, Voyage of Ohthere)

g. [þyder] hē cwæð þæt man ne mihte geseglian on ānum mōnþe
thither he said that one not might sail   in one   month
(OE, Orosius, Voyage of Ohthere)

h. þā tēð   hie brohton sume þǣm cyninge
the teeth they brought some to-the king
(OE, Orosius, Voyage of Ohthere)

i. þā dēor   hī   hātað hrānas
the animals they call   reindeer
(OE, Orosius, Voyage of Ohthere)

A comparison of these examples with question sentences like (6.64c) reveals an asymmetry very much like what we find in Modern EN: subject/verb inversion in questions, but none in topic sentences. The facts are complicated somewhat by the fact that not only subject pronouns, but also object pronouns can precede the verb in topic-initial sentences, as in:

(6.64) j. on þæt stēorbord him   bið   ǣrest Īraland
on the starboard to-him will-be first Ireland
(OE, Orosius, Voyage of Ohthere)

Nonetheless, they support the view that the verb is in a lower position in topic sentences than in questions. We can accommodate these facts by assuming that (a) the verb is in the auxiliary position (T in tree 6.1) in topic-initial sentences, and (b) the subject and object pronouns of GMC are clitics in a position somewhere to the left of the Aux position, but to the right of the C position. They will thus precede the verb in these topic-initial sentences. In questions, however, and in negative-initial sentences, the verb will be attracted still further to the left, to license the question element or negative element in SpecCP, and will thus precede these clitics.

Kiparsky (1995a) and Tomaselli (1995) point out similar facts for OHG. In the very early Isidor translation, noted for its independence from the Latin model, subject (and other) pronouns appear between the topic and the verb, just as in OE:

6.3 The syntax of the left periphery

(6.65)   a. [erino portun] ih firchnussu
            brass doors I break
            = Latin portas aereas conteram
            (OHG, Isidor (Eggers) 157)

         b. [fone reue aer lucifere] ih dih chibar
            from womb before Lucifer I you bore
            = Latin ex utero anteluciferum genui te
            (Isidor (Eggers) 409)

However, as in OE, in sentences with initial negatives and in questions the verb did precede the subject (see above).

(6.65)   c. Nalles sie dri goda
            not at all may-be three gods
            = Latin nec tres dios
            (Isidor (Eggers) 259)

         d. ni uueizs ih einigan chuninc
            not know I any king
            = Latin nesciam quem regem
            (Isidor (Eggers) 591)

         e. Huuemu ist dhiz nu zi quhedanne
            to whom is this to be said?
            = Latin Cui ergo dicitur?
            (OHG, Isidor (Eggers) 189)

In the OE examples adduced so far, the syntax of OE seems to be like that of Modern EN. Pronoun subjects follow the inflected verb in nonsubject questions, but precede the verb in sentences with nonsubject initial topics. When sentences with subjects other than pronouns are considered, however, this similarity breaks down. In OE sentences with topics and non-pronominal subjects, the attested order is almost exclusively Topic-Verb-Subject.[6]

(6.66)   & of hēom twam is eall manncynn cumen
           and of those two is all mankind come
           (OE, WHom, cited in Kroch and Taylor (1997: 302))

---

[6] Kroch and Taylor (1997: 304) note that the order Topic-Subject-NP-Verb is possible in OE when the topic phrase is a "scene-setting" time adverbial:

(i)   On þisum gēara Willelm cyning geaf Raulfe eorle Willelmes dohtor
            in this year William king gave Ralph Earl William's daughter

See Kroch and Taylor 1997 and van Kemenade 1997 for further discussion of the still problematic status of OE V-2.

6.3.2.1 *Some additional environments for verb fronting*

In addition to negatives, questions and imperatives, Eythórsson lists a few other environments for verb fronting in GO. While verbs ordinarily follow their complements, as we have seen, they appear systematically in front of their objects when those objects are pronouns, just in case the pronouns are not preceded by complementizers. If there is a complementizer, the verb remains in the position following the pronoun. The following pair of sentences illustrate this contrast:

(6.67)   a. ushaihah sik
               hanged   himself
               = Greek apégxato
               (GO, Matt. 27:5, cited in Eythórsson 1995: 29)

         b. jabai mik frijoþ
               if   me you-love
               = Greek eàn agapâté me
               (John 14:15, cited in Eythórsson 1995: 31)

Given the general tendency for pronouns to appear to the left in GMC clauses, it is highly unlikely that they are postposed here. Eythórsson proposes rather that object pronouns in GO are clitics, which must be supported by an element to their left; fronting of the verb is used to satisfy this requirement, in case there are no other candidates. Similar behavior is found in other older GMC languages (as well as elsewhere); in many (though not all) OE texts, pronouns do not occur clause-initially. In the OE Bede translation, for example, when no other constituent is clause-initial, the verb must precede pronominal subjects in declarative sentences.

(6.68)   a. Hæfde hē his dohtor   him   tō wīf beweddad
               had   he his daughter for-himself as wife wed
               (OE, Bede 168:4, Miller 1890)

         b. Wæs hē gerȳnlico word sprecende
               was   he mystic   words speaking
               (OE, Bede (Miller) 94:22)

Again, the motivation for verb fronting here seems to be to support the clitic subject pronoun. The verb follows the subject pronoun when it is preceded by a conjunction, or by some other clause-initial constituent, so verb fronting seems to be a last resort.

(6.68) c. Ond hē sōna þāra gerisne andsware onsende
and he soon sent to-those (an) answer suitable
(Bede (Miller) 64:4)

d. Caldran ic geseah
(a) colder (one) I saw
(Bede (Miller) 436:12)

Similarly, Eythórsson (1995: 184) accounts for the Verb-Subject pronoun order found in some early runic inscriptions in the older *futhark* as involving the same sort of verb fronting to support a subject clitic (see also Hopper 1975: 36):

(6.69) hait-ika farauisa
am-called-I travel-wise
(Runic GMC, Sjælland bracteate 2, Antonsen 1975: 65)

Compare GO (6.70a):

(6.70) a. im ik
am I
= Greek egṑ eimí 'I am'
(GO, John 8:58)

Roberts (1993: 96) notes the existence of a similar restriction on subject clitics in Old French as well as other Romance languages (the "Tobler-Mussafia Law").

Eythórsson also proposes that the verb is fronted in (6.70b), since it appears to the left of the clitic conjunction *-uh*. Since *-uh* in GO is only used in clausal coordination, Eythórsson identifies it as a complementizer element, and concludes that the verb to its left has been moved to C in these cases as well:

(6.70) b. iþ Filippus qaþ-uh du imma
but Philip said-and to him
= Greek légei autôi Phíllipos
(GO, John 14:8, Eythórsson 1995: 94)

It is not to support the *-uh* that the verb is fronted here, however, since, as Eythórsson notes, where a nonsubject constituent is clause-initial, as in (6.70c, d), it is possible for *-uh* to lean on that clause-initial constituent, and fronting of the verb is not required.

(6.70) c. þan-uh was maurgins
then-and was morning
(GO, John 18:28, Eythórsson 1995: 93)

(6.70) d. þat-uh samo jah þai waidedjans ...idweitidedun imma
that-and same [way] also the evil-doers reviled him
(GO, Matt. 27:44)

Eythórsson concludes (1995: 72) that definite, contrastive subjects are obligatorily topicalized in GO, as in (6.70b), and that the verb is required to move to C just in the case of subject topicalization, in order to satisfy a special licensing requirement on subject movement. The fact that *-uh* attaches to the verb is accounted for by assuming that (a) it is associated with the complementizer position, and (b) as a clitic it attaches to the closest head to its left.

Other, inversion triggers found among the GMC languages include the OE *þā* 'then', which triggered obligatory inversion even into the ME period (Lightfoot 1995: 41).

(6.71) a. ðā wunade hē ðær sum fæc tīde
then remained he there some amount of time
(Bede (Miller) 264:30)

b. Þā sceolde hē ðær bīdan ryhtnorþanwindes
then should he there await due-north-wind
(OE, Voyage of Ohthere)

The idiosyncracy of this remarkably stable and invariant case is underscored by the fact that other time phrases behaved like ordinary topics here, not forcing V-2 order.

(6.71) c. Æfter þon hē gewāt to sumum medmiclum ēalonde
after that he went to a certain middle-sized island
(OE, Bede (Miller) 272:25)

In (6.71b), therefore, we have an apparent topicalized adverb in a non-strict V-2 language which is exceptional in that it obligatorily triggers V-2. Conversely, Vikner (1995: 46) observes that there are some apparent adverbs in the (strict V-2) Continental Scandinavian languages which appear exceptionally not to trigger inversion, at least obligatorily. These include SW *kanske* 'probably', FA *kanska* 'perhaps' (Lockwood 1964: 154) and DA *mon* 'I wonder'.

(6.72) Kanske Lena inte köpte en ny bok igår
perhaps Lena not bought a new book yesterday
(SW, Vikner 1995: 46)

Vikner accounts for these by proposing that they are in fact complementizer elements, and, as such, block the fronting of the verb.

What most of the instances of verb fronting to the V-2 position discussed so far have in common is the fact that the fronting of the verb is related to the presence of some other constituent in the clause-initial position (a question phrase, a negative element or a clitic pronoun, for example). We may presume that the preposing of the verb is needed to "license" this initial sentence element. This analysis can be extended in a fairly straightforward way to a class of other cases, in which there is no overt element, such as yes/no questions and 'if'-less conditional clauses. For these, we may posit an abstract, non-phonological element (an interrogative or conditional operator) in clause-initial position, whose presence is the trigger for verb fronting (an analytical assumption which is defensible on other grounds). Also explainable in such terms is the phenomenon of "Topic-drop" (Huang 1984) in some GMC languages. In colloquial Modern GE, for example, object pronouns may be omitted in conversational contexts in which their referent has been established as the topic of discussion, but only with inverted word order, indicating that this possibility is limited to the topic position, SpecC.

(6.73) a. [ ] hab' ich schon gesehen
           have I   already seen
        'I have already seen him/her/it'
        (GE, Huang 1984: 547)

Huang argues that these are possible in GE (but not in EN, for example) because GE has a "zero-topic" available. Instances of "spontaneous" verb-first order in declarative sentences arguably go here as well. In many of the GMC V-2 languages, old and modern, the verb can appear initially in a declarative clause even though none of the triggering elements is present, giving the impression of spontaneous V-1 order. (These kinds of sentences tend to occur most frequently in lively narration.)

(6.73) b. Kom Ólafur seint heim
           came Olaf   late home
        (IC, Sigurðsson 1990, cited in Vikner 1995: 87)

Vikner claims that such sentences are possible only in strict V-2 languages (though not in all of those). This, however, seems to be true only of the (accidental) set of modern GMC languages, since V-1 declaratives are also found in OE, which, as we have seen above, was not a strict V-2 language (see Kiparsky 1995a: 142f.). There is no independent evidence for "spontaneous" declarative V-1 in GO.

(6.73) c. Hæfde se cyning his fierd on tū   tōnumen
           had   the king   his army in two   divided
        (OE, AS Chr. 863, Kiparsky 1995a: 143)

In any case, Vikner proposes further that the presence or absence of V-1 declaratives in the modern languages does not correlate with any other structural feature of these languages, concluding that:

the possibility of V-1 declaratives is determined by some property, maybe a lexical one, which is entirely unrelated to other differences between V-2 languages. It is hard to see what Yiddish, Icelandic, colloquial Dutch, colloquial German, and Malmö Swedish would have in common that is not found in, for example, Danish, standard German, and standard Swedish (Vikner 1995: 90).

6.3.2.2 *Quotative inversion*

Given what has been said about V-2 in EN so far, sentences like (6.74) are unexpected in at least three ways.

(6.74) "Good luck," said his father

First, the verb which appears in front of the subject is not a modal or aspectual auxiliary, but a lexical verb, even though lexical verbs cannot in general precede the subject in EN. Second, inversion is always optional in these cases. The verb can follow the subject as well as precede it. Finally, inversion takes place even though the fronted constituent (the quotative complement) is not the type of element (e.g., a question phrase or a negative adverb) that triggers V-2 in EN. It appears, rather, to be an ordinary fronted topic, of a sort which is not otherwise associated with inversion. "Quotative Inversion" therefore seems to be a type of inversion process distinct from those involved in the V-2 phenomenon. The syntax of such constructions has been analyzed by Collins and Branigan (1997) and in later work by Collins. Establishing the antiquity of this phenomenon poses some difficulty. In strict V-2 languages, where all constituents appearing at the beginning of a main clause trigger V-2 order, it would not seem to be possible to distinguish quotative inversion from the more general case. It is possible to establish that it existed as far back as OE, however. An exhaustive examination of the OE translation of Bede's *Historia ecclesiastica gentis Anglorum* gives evidence of the following robust patterns. First, pronoun subjects preceded their verbs in non-interrogative non-negative sentences, so long as there was at least one element in front of them to give them the syntactic support which they required as clitics (Section 4.8.1.4). Thus, the pronoun subject and the verb were not inverted, for example, in sentences beginning with coordinating conjunctions, as in (6.75a). Nor, crucially, were they inverted in sentences which began with ordinary topics, as in (6.75b, c). That is, as I have mentioned, OE, like Modern EN, was not a strict V-2 language. Topic fronting did not cause inversion, at least with pronoun subjects. Nonetheless, pronominal subjects always followed the verb when the latter was the quotative verb *cweðan* and the sentence-initial position was occupied by (all or part of) its quotative complement (6.75d, e). Thus, as in Modern EN, OE does not show inversion in cases where there is a preposed topic and the subject is a pronoun in the general case, but it does show inversion of verb and pronominal subject when the preposed material is a direct quotation. OE, therefore, had quotative inversion.

(6.75) a. ond hē þā ongān
and he then began
(OE, Bede (Miller) 98:16)

b. sōð þū sagast
truth you say
(Bede (Miller) 354:10)

c. þæt wīf hē onfēng fram hyre yldrum
that wife he got from her parents
(Bede (Miller) 58:13)

d. "Nese," cwæð hē, "Ne onfēng hē his gōdum gitsiende"
"No," said he, "He didn't receive his goods out-of-covetousness"
(Bede (Miller) 216:5)

e. "Mē is," cwæð hēo, "þīn cyme on miclum ðonce"
"To me is," said she, "your coming very gratifying"
(Bede (Miller) 290:15)

6.4 Complementizers

6.4.1 That-clauses

Some verbs take clauses as subjects or objects. In the GMC languages, clauses used in these roles are preceded by a complementizer, which marks them as syntactically subordinate to the clause in which they function as arguments. The employment of syntactic subordination as the means for expressing relationships between clauses in such cases is argued in Kiparsky 1995a to have been a GMC innovation, as was the development of a lexical category of complementizers. Kiparsky argues that IE employed parataxis (or coordination) rather than hypotaxis (or syntactic subordination) to encode such relationships among clauses. Other IE families, including, Italic, Hellenic, Slavic and Celtic, have also developed complementizers as markers of clause subordination, but there is reason to think that these developments have taken place independently; whereas the Romance languages derive their finite clause complementizers from the interrogative pronoun $*k^wo$, as does Gaelic (gu), the GMC languages are united in employing reflexes of the demonstrative pronoun $*tod$ for this purpose.

GO makes use of the particle ei, apparently also a pronoun in origin, as its basic complementizer for finite clauses. Ei may appear by itself in introducing both subject and object clauses, as in:

(6.76) a. þugkeiþ im   auk **ei**   in filuwaurdein seinai andhausjaindau
        seems   to-them for that in verbosity   their they-may-be-heard
        (GO, Matt. 6:7)

   b. qiþa izwis **ei**   ni fraqisteiþ   mizdon seinai
      I-tell you that not they-will-lose treasure their
      (GO, Matt. 10:42)

More frequently, however, *ei* occurs in combination with a second element, *þat(a)*, which originates from the same source as the homophonous neuter demonstrative *þata* (←*tod*), yielding a new, compound complementizer *þat-ei*.

(6.76) c. hausideduþ **þatei** qiþan ist þaim airizam: ni maurþrjais
        you-heard that   said   is by the ancestors: not kill-Imp
        (GO, Matt. 5:21)

   d. qiþanuh þan ist **þatei** ƕazuh saei afletai qen, gibai izai afstassais bokos
      said-and then is that whoever who might-divorce a woman, give her divorcement book
      (GO, Mark 5:31)

The pronominal origins of the first part of this compound complementizer are reflected in the fact that it occasionally inflects for case when the subordinate clause it introduces is the complement of a verb which assigns oblique (dative or genitive) case:[7]

(6.76) e. jah gatraua þamm-ei   mahteigs ist   þata anafilh   mein fastan
        and I-trust that-Dat-*ei* able   he-is that commission my to-keep
        (GO, 2 Tim. 1:12)

GO *ei* and *þatei* are largely complementarily distributed, the former occurring in subjunctive counterfactual clauses after verbs of wishing and command, for example, while the latter occurs in the main in indicative clauses after verbs of thinking and saying, for example. No other GMC language exhibits such a distinction in complementizers.

---

[7] Arguments are presented in Harbert 1982, 1992 that, even though *þamm-* in this example receives its dative case from the main clause verb, it is a part of the subordinate clause. As Streitberg (1920: 239) points out, such case inflection of complementizers is apparently no longer productive in attested GO, since in other examples one finds the invariant (historically accusative) form *þat-ei* even when the clause occurs as a complement of a verb like *fraþjan* 'understand' which assigns dative case:

(i)   froþun   **þat-ei** du im þo gajukon qaþ
        they-knew that   to him the parable spoke
        (GO, Mark 12:12)

The West GMC languages share with GO the use of a neuter demonstrative (*that*, *daß*, *dat*, etc.) as a complementizer, though not in combination with other complementizer elements. Also apparently from the same source are the Scandinavian complementizers *að*, *at*, *att*, in spite of their different appearance (Vigfusson 1874: 28).

(6.77) a. hêt   that he im ni andrêdi
he-commanded that he him not fear
(OS, Heliand (Behaghel) 116)

The *that* complementizer appears to be omissible in the GMC languages from most object clauses, but not from subject clauses:

(6.77) b. and cwæþ hē wolde   wiðsacan his criste
and he-said he wanted to renounce his Christ
(OE, Æl. S. 3.373, cited in Mitchell 1985: II, 30).

c. Han sagde, (at) han arbjedede hårdt
he said (that) he worked hard
(DA, Allan *et al.* 1995: 464)

6.4.2 Infinitive complements

The shape of infinitive complements is more varied than that of finite complements. EN has the most articulated set of different nonfinite complement types, and will therefore serve as our starting point. We may distinguish first of all between bare infinitive complements and *to*-infinitive complements, the former now restricted to occurrence with a small set of verbs of perception and causation:

(6.78) a. I let/ helped/ saw him leave

All other types of infinitive complements involve the infinitive marker *to*. Among the constructions with these "prepositional infinitives," we may distinguish between Control constructions, such as (6.78b), Accusative with Infinitive, or Subject-to-Object Raising constructions, such as (6.78c) and (6.78d), and *for*-NP-*to* constructions, such as (6.78e):

(6.78) b. I tried to leave
c. I forced him to leave
d. I believe him to have left
e. I would hate/prefer for him to lose

As discussed in Section 5.5.1.2, *to*-infinitives have tended historically to be generalized in control constructions like (6.78b) and (6.78c) in some GMC languages, EN included, at the expense of bare infinitives.

The constructions in (6.78d, e) are of late origin. The *for*-NP-*to* construction in (6.78e), according to Fischer (1990: 29), is first unambiguously attested in the sixteenth century. In this construction, the *for* appears before all constituents of the infinitival clause, including the subject, just as *that* does, and is standardly analyzed as a complementizer.[8] Some other GMC languages have apparent analogues to these *for-to* constructions. So, for example, West Flemish has *vu. . .te*, and DU has *om. . .te*, where in each case the first element is optional.

(6.78) f. Valère prebeerdige (vu) dienen boek te kuopen
Valère tried (for) that book to buy
(West Flemish, Haegeman 1992: 47)

The existence of such infinitival constructions, with both an overt complementizer (*for/vu*) and an infinitive marker (*to/te*), raises a question of analysis in other cases, in which only a single marker is involved. Is *att* in (6.79a), for example, the counterpart of *to* in EN or of *for* – that is, an infinitive marker or a prepositional complementizer?

(6.79) a. Jag föredrar att avgå
I prefer *att* resign
(SW, Holmes and Hinchcliffe 1994: 270)

Here, unlike EN, we cannot use its position relative to the subject to help decide, because infinitival *att* clauses in SW never have overt subjects. Platzack (1986: 123) argues, however, that it is possible to apply other tests to make this determination, and arrives at the striking result that the "infinitive marker" has a different status in

---

[8] In this respect, it is different from another construction, earlier in occurrence and of arguably separate origin – the *for-to* construction, exemplified by the following examples from (early) ME and Irish EN.

(i) Hit by-comeþ for clerkus [crist for to seruen]
it becomes for clerks Christ for to serve
(ME, Piers Plowman, cited in Fischer 1990: 32)

(ii) I was sorry [for to hear the death of Mr. O'Connors]
(Irish EN, Filppula 1999: 185)

In these constructions, there are no overt subjects in the infinitive clauses to mark the boundary of these and thereby pin down the position of the *for* and *to*, but, as van Gelderen (1993: 87) notes, in the earliest ME cases, at least, *for-to* is preceded by constituents of the infinitive phrase in examples like (i), suggesting that the *for* of *for-to* is not a complementizer on the left periphery of the infinitive phrase. Both Fischer and van Gelderen analyze *for-to* as a complex infinitive marker here, not a complementizer.

different Scandinavian languages. In SW, it is a complementizer, and as such can never be preceded by constituents of the infinitive clause, such as a subordinate clause negator, for example. In DA, on the other hand, it is an infinitive marker or tense element, and therefore can be preceded by negation belonging to the infinitive clause:

(6.79) b. Han hadede ikke at have noget at tage sig til
   he hated not *at* have anything to do
   'He hated not to have anything to do'
   (DA, Platzack 1986: 123)

   c. Han hatade att inte ha något att göra
   he hated *att* not have anything to do
   (SW, Platzack 1986: 123)

Cf. also Thráinsson (1998: 355ff.), who notes that NO allows either order.

Platzack claims that a number of other contrasts in the distribution of *at/att* follow from this difference in syntactic status. For example, *at* appears in DA Subject Raising constructions, but *att* may not appear in SW Subject Raising constructions.

(6.79) d. Han siges at tale svensk flydende
   he is-said *at* speak Swedish fluently
   (DA, Platzack 1986: 127)

   e. Han sägs tala svenska flytande
   he is-said to speak Swedish fluently
   (SW, Platzack 1986: 127)

There are also apparent differences in the West GMC languages with respect to the status of the infinitive marker 'to', as noted in Section 5.5.1.2.1. In some of them, including GE and OE, the preposition is always immediately adjacent to the verb, and nothing – not even verbal particles – can intervene. In Modern EN, and in FR, on the other hand, it is possible for adverbs to intervene between the *to* and the infinitive (the so-called "split infinitive"). On the basis of this difference, Kageyama (1992) argued that *to* changed between OE and ME from a part of the verbal morphology – a nonfiniteness marker on the verb – to a syntactically independent nonfinite tense marker in the clause – essentially, the nonfinite counterpart to auxiliaries – which occupies the T slot in the tree in (6.1). The reader is referred to Thráinsson (1998) for a review of the literature on the complex question of the syntactic status of infinitive markers in GMC. Thráinsson suggests, among other things, that a simple distinction between complementizers and nonfinite tense markers may be insufficient to account for the range of variation, whose description might require a more articulated syntactic tree.

6.5 Relative clauses, questions and other fronting constructions

All of the GMC languages share a class of constructions in which a clause containing a gap or a pronoun is preceded by a constituent which completes the meaning of that clause, by "substituting in for" the gap or pronoun. Schematically, such Filler-Gap constructions have the following shape.

(6.80) XP_i [$_S$. . ...0_i/ pron$_i$. . ...]

This class of constructions – relative clauses, WH-word questions, topic sentences and various types of left dislocated sentences – will be the subject of the present section. Though they differ from each other in various ways, they tend to exhibit parallels in behavior in individual languages – with respect to whether or not they admit preposition stranding, the amount of syntactic distance allowed between the filler and the gap and so on. By way of attempting to highlight these commonalities while at the same time following the construction-by-construction approach of the present volume, I will proceed as follows: I will describe the constructions one at a time, starting with relative clauses. However, when stranding and other phenomena of similarly general relevance are encountered for the first time in the course of these discussions, I will take a slight detour in order to subject them to a general treatment.

6.5.1 A typology of Germanic relative constructions

6.5.1.1 *The Germanic type*
Relative clauses are clausal modifiers of NPs. The NP and the clause taken together will be referred to as a relative construction, and the NP (or its head noun) as the head of the relative construction. The examples in (6.81) illustrate some types of relative construction found in GMC:

(6.81)   a. I know [the man [who(m) you said hello to [t]]]

           b. I sog's [dem Mõ   [wo [e] im Gartn arwat]]
              I tell-it to-the-man *wo* in-the garden works
              (Bavarian, Bayer 1984a: 216)

The relative clause is typically defective, missing an argument or adjunct constituent, and we link the head noun to the clause by interpreting it as if it were in the position of the missing constituent – that is, as a filler for the gap. I will refer to the position of the gap in the relative clause as the relativized position. Thus, in (6.81a), the noun phrase *the man* is understood to be linked to the position of the object of the preposition *to*. We may say that the object of a preposition has been relativized here.

6.5 Relative clauses, questions and other fronting constructions   421

Under some circumstances the relativized position is not realized as a gap, but filled with an overt "resumptive" pronoun understood to be coreferential with the head NP. In some cases a relative pronoun appears between the head and the gap, on the left periphery of the relative clause. This pronoun typically (with some exceptions, to be discussed below) exhibits the case marking expected of the relativized position, and is therefore a more plausible candidate for "filler" than the head noun. We can imagine that it originates in the position of the gap, where its case is determined, and is then displaced from that relativized position, to the left periphery of the relative clause ("WH-Movement"). Since the landing site for this movement is the position immediately to the right of the head noun, we may imagine that this movement is motivated by the need to place the relative pronoun in a position sufficiently local to the head that the two can be "linked" or identified with each other. Thus, in relative constructions with relative pronouns, at least, the relationship between the head and the gap is not a direct but a mediated one, and there are two separate relationships to deal with in these constructions: the local relationship between the head and the relative pronoun, and the relationship between the relative pronoun and the position relativized.

In the usual case in the GMC languages (and in fact in Western IE languages in general), the verb of the relative clause is finite, the clause and the head noun form a single NP constituent, the noun precedes the relative clause, and the latter is introduced by a relative marker of some sort – in (6.81a), the relative pronoun *who*. This is not the only form which relative clauses take in the IE languages. Two other types of relative clauses are also widely attested: participial relative clauses and correlative clauses. In the former, the verb of the relative clause is not finite but appears in a nominalized form, as in (6.82a). These kinds of relative clauses typically precede the head noun and are not introduced by relative pronouns or particles.

(6.82)   a. mãiNE naactii huii ek   laRkiiKO dekhaa
            I-Erg   dance-Part one girl-Acc   saw
            'I saw a girl who was dancing'
            (Hindi, Srivastav 1991: 641)

The GMC languages have, from the earliest times, made use of "participial relative constructions" which show these same properties.

(6.82)   b. de [in boek lêzende] frou]
            the a book reading   woman
            (FR, Tiersma 1999: 123)

         c. bi   [þans [usþriutandans izwis]]
            concerning those accusing   you
            (GO,   Matt. 5:44)

The relative order of the head and the participial relative phrase varies from language to language. In GE, a participial relative of this type precedes the head, while in EN it follows the head. This difference can be derived from the general preference mentioned in Section 4.2.3.2.1 that heads and modifiers within NPs be ordered in such a way that the head of the modifer occurs on the periphery of its own phrase which is closest to the modified head.

The participial "relativization strategy" is more restricted than the finite relative strategy in GMC in one important way: the head noun can only be understood to stand in a subject relation to the participial verb. Thus, relativization of the direct object position cannot be effected by this strategy (except indirectly, by replacing the active participle with a passive participle). In the remainder of this chapter, these participial relative constructions will be left out of consideration.

In the remaining type of IE relative construction, the correlative type, the relative clause is an independent clause, rather than a subordinate clause, which occurs adjoined to the left of the main clause, as in (6.83a).

(6.83) a. jo   laRkii khaRii   hai vo   lambii hai
           REL girl   standing is **DEM** tall   is
           'which girl is standing, that one is tall'
           (Hindi, Srivastav 1991: 639)

Note also that the "head" is not external to the relative clause, but contained in it – as shown by the fact that it is preceded by a relative particle. We may therefore speak of this as an "internally headed" relative construction. The head is linked to the main clause by means of a coreferential demonstrative pronoun in the latter. For a discussion of the semantic interpretation of correlatives (and in particular, for a demonstration that they are very different semantically from embedded relatives, and do not actually involve noun modification), see Srivastav 1991.

Kiparsky (1995a) argues that these correlatives are the earliest type of relativization in IE. (Outside of Indic, they are found in other early IE languages – Hittite, for example.) In GMC, only a few traces of them remain. They are to be found, for example, in OE generalizing ('whoever')-type relative clauses, for example, as in (6.83b).

(6.83) b. And tō swā hwilcere lēode   swā wē cumað, we cunnon ðǣre gereord
           and to whichever   people as we come,   we know   their language
           (OE, Alc. Th. v. 2, p. 474.2, cited in Allen 1980a: 119)

Here again, the "head" noun is inside of the relative clause, which is therefore internally headed. The evidence for this is that it is preceded by a preposition which belongs to the relative clause. The relative construction precedes the main clause and the main clause contains a demonstrative pronoun (ðǣre), coreferential with the head.

Thus, these OE constructions exhibit all of the characteristic properties of the Hindi correlative, and may therefore be regarded as a continuation of that type in GMC. Such constructions are not limited to the medieval languages. Dal (1966: 205) cites examples from Early Modern GE.

Kiparsky (1995a: 155) suggests as well that this correlative syntax underlies the phenomenon known in classical philology as "Inverse Attraction" found in some medieval GMC languages (as well as elsewhere – see Grimm 1866; Hahn 1964). This phenomenon is illustrated in (6.83c).

(6.83)   c.   [den schaz   [den in ir vater lie]]   der wart mit ir geteilet hie
                the treasure-ACC which them her father left it was with her
                                                                                            shared here
                (MHG, Gregorius 635)

Here, we see that the head of the relative clause (*den schaz*) again behaves in one respect as if it belongs to the relative clause, rather than to the main clause; it appears in accusative case determined by the role of the relative pronoun in the relative clause. Again, this seems to be restricted to cases in which the relative construction occurs on the left periphery of the main clause, and the latter contains a resumptive pronoun – that is, in a structure which resembles the correlative type. "Inverse attraction" is not widespread, even in medieval GMC. It occurs in native compositions in MHG (see especially Grimm 1866) but is avoided in GO, even when it occurs in Greek (e.g., Luke 20:17) and is found in OE apparently only in literal translations from the Latin.

The dominant relative construction type in GMC, however, has always been one which involves an "external" head, not contained within the relative clause. This head is modified by an embedded clause which has a finite verb and which is introduced by some form of relative marker – a complementizer or relative pronoun. Normally, the relative clause follows the noun immediately, and forms with it a single NP constituent, though in all of the GMC languages, it is also possible for the relative clause to be separated from the modified head noun by a limited string of constituents, including nonfinite verbs in clause-final position ("Extraposition").

(6.84)   ik wol   [in koekje] ite   [dat krekt út 'e oven komt]
            I   want a   cookie   to-eat   that just out-of the oven comes
            (FR, Tiersma 1999: 121)

6.5.1.2 *Types of relative markers: 'that'-relatives, 'WH'-relatives and others*

What I have referred to loosely as "Relative Markers" in fact seem to be of at least two distinct types: relative pronouns and relative "particles" or complementizers.

Individual languages in the GMC family make use of one or both of these devices, alone or in combination. The distinction between these two is in some instances a matter of ongoing controversy. In the following, I will take a particular position, not universally agreed upon, about ways in which the two can be told apart, and I will discuss the distribution of these two types of markers in GMC. I will also argue, though, that the issue is clouded by the existence of a third variety of relative marker, an inflected complementizer, which shares features of both of the other two types.

As a working principle I will adopt the position that a relative marker can be identified as a pronoun if it shows a subset of the characteristic inflectional or distributional properties of pronouns. So, for example, relative pronouns can be identified as pronouns first of all by virtue of the fact that they inflect as pronouns do, at least for case, and in some of the GMC languages for number and gender as well. This is illustrated by (6.85) from GE.

(6.85)   a. Die Kinder, denen   er geholfen hat, waren dankbar
                the children whom-DPl he helped   has were grateful
                (GE)

           b. Das Kind, dem   er geholfen hat, war dankbar
                the child whom-DSgNeut he helped   has was grateful

In some cases, the inflectional characteristics are highly reduced. So, for example, in languages such as EN, where the relative pronouns are based on interrogative forms, they do not reflect number distinctions, just as interrogative pronouns do not. *Who* is both singular and plural. Moreover, in all but formal registers of EN, the contrast between objective case and nominative case has been leveled, leaving only a minimal case contrast between genitive (*whose*) and non-genitive (*who*). Nonetheless, the fact that they participate in case contrasts demonstrates their status as pronouns.

In addition to showing at least a subset of the inflectional characteristics of pronouns, relative pronouns can also be identified as pronouns by virtue of the fact that they exhibit some (though not all) of the distributional characteristics of pronouns. They cannot appear in subject or object positions in a clause, since they are always obligatorily leftward displaced, occurring at the beginning of the relative clause. In this respect, they are different from other pronominal forms with which they are homophonous (i.e., question pronouns or demonstrative pronouns – see below) since the latter can appear *in situ* in non-initial positions within their clause (e.g., in 'Who gave what to whom?'). However, while they never appear in argument positions within the clause because of this property, they can bring a bit of their local syntactic environment along with them to the front of their clause by carrying along, or "pied-piping," the phrases containing them, and this allows us to observe their pronoun-like distribution within those phrases. All of the GMC languages allow pied-piping under at least

6.5 Relative clauses, questions and other fronting constructions

some circumstances. Thus, as illustrated in (6.86) from DA, for example, relative pronouns of the *hv*-paradigm can occur as prenominal genitives within noun phrases and as objects of prepositions within prepositional phrases, just as ordinary pronouns can. (Pied-piping of the preposition is optional and literary in DA. See below for further discussion.) The fact that they occur in positions characteristic of pronouns here (possessive modifier, object of preposition) allows us to identify them as pronouns.

(6.86)   a. Mr. Petersen, [hvis [broder]] forsvandt i Amerika
             Mr. Petersen, whose brother   disappeared in America
             (DA, Koefoed 1958: 176)

           b. Hans er en ven,   [på hvem] man kan stole
             he   is a friend on whom one can rely
             (DA, Koefoed 1958: 176)

Many GMC languages also allow relative clauses to be introduced by what are sometimes termed "relative particles," or "relative complementizers" – non-pronominal markers of subordination which occur instead of or in combination with relative pronouns. The distinction between these and relative pronouns has been the subject of confusion and controversy in the literature. I will start with the most clear-cut instances, by way of establishing the criteria for distinguishing them from relative pronouns, and then proceed to some instances which are more controversial. GO *ei* and *þei* are particularly clear cases of elements introducing relative clauses which are not relative pronouns. These elements can introduce relative clauses by themselves under restricted conditions, as in (6.87a, b). One of them (*ei*) also co-occurs systematically with the overt relative pronouns of GO, always following the pronouns (6.87c).

(6.87)   a. fram þamma daga   ei hausidedum
             from   the   day   *ei* we-heard
             (GO, Col. 1:9)

           b. und   þata hveilos þei miþ im   ist brudfaþs.
             during the while *þei* with them is bridegroom
             (GO, Matt. 9:15)

           c. þo waurda þo-ei   ik rodida izwis
             the words which-*ei* I   spoke to you
             (GO, John 6:63)

To my knowledge, no one has ever analyzed them as relative pronouns. There are several reasons for this. First of all, they do not show any of the distributional or inflectional characteristics of pronouns. They do not inflect for case and number, for example, and they are never preceded by a pied-piped preposition. Moreover, they do not resemble any of the uncontroversial pronouns in GO. Rather, they are identical in shape with elements which introduce nonrelative subordinate clauses, as in (6.87d) (cf. Section 6.4).

(6.87)   d. ufkunnand   allai, þei meinai siponjos sijuþ
will-recognize all   that my   disciples you-are
(GO, John 13:35)

Furthermore, they are not in complementary distribution with uncontroversial relative pronouns, but sometimes co-occur with them, as in (6.87c). Thus, the GO case provides us with evidence that GMC introduced relative clauses in at least two different ways: with a relative pronoun (P-relatives) or with a complementizer-like element (C-relatives). Moreover, the GO examples provide us with a cluster of properties by reference to which we can at least provisionally begin to distinguish the two. Relative complementizers do not have the inflectional or distributional properties generally exhibited by pronouns. They do not inflect for case, for example, or pied-piped prepositions. Since they do not occupy the same positions as relative pronouns, they may under some circumstances co-occur with relative pronouns. Moreover, in the GO cases discussed so far, at least, they are identical with elements that introduce nonrelative subordinate clauses, and they show no resemblance to pronouns occurring elsewhere in the language (unlike the *þo* of example (6.87c), for example, which is homophonous with the demonstrative pronoun).

Consider the Scandinavian *sem/som* and its predecessor, *er*:

(6.88)   a. Jag känner en man som är stark
I   know a man that is strong
(SW, Allwood 1982: 17)

    b. land,   er hann kom frå
the land that he   came from
(ON, Vigfusson 1874: 131)

Informal treatments, at least (e.g., Holmes and Hinchcliffe 1994: 220 and Granberry 1991: 42), all characterize *som* as a "relative pronoun." Einarsson (1945: 127) also identifies IC *sem* as a relative pronoun. Applying our criteria, however, we find that, like GO *ei*, *þei*, and unlike the clear relative pronouns of other GMC languages, *som/sem* never inflects, is never preceded by a preposition belonging to the subordinate clause, never occurs as a part of a larger NP, does not come from a pronoun historically but a comparative/predicative particle equivalent to EN 'as', and is not restricted to relative clauses. Most revealingly, it also introduces embedded questions, for example, where it co-occurs with, rather than taking the place of, the interrogative pronoun:

(6.88) c. Vi vet hvem som har gjort dette
we know who that has done this
(NO, Taraldsen 1986: 11)

d. Jag vet inte vem som äger den
I know not who that owns it
(SW, Anward 1982: 57)

Again, therefore, we have reason to regard these as C-relative constructions, not P-relative constructions.

An apparently quite similar case is that represented by OE/Early ME *þe*, as well as its cognates in other West GMC languages. *þe* can introduce a relative clause by itself, as in (6.88e), or together with a relative pronoun, as in (6.88f).

(6.88) e. on þǣm ǣhtum þe heora spēda on bēoð
in those possessions that their wealth in is
(OE, Voyage of Ohthere)

f. tō eorðan of ðǣre ðe ðū genumen wǣre
to earth, out-of which that you were taken
(OE, Gen. 3:19, cited in Seppänen 2004: 72)

þe has all of the properties enumerated for *ei* and *som*, except that it does not occur as a complementizer in non-relative clauses. First, it is invariant – never inflected for any of the categories for which pronouns are inflected. In this respect, it is different from the clear relative pronouns of OE, such as the co-occurring *ðare* of example (6.88f), which does inflect for case, number and gender. Second, it does not appear in any of the positions characteristic of pronouns. Pied-piping of prepositions was obligatory in the case of the undisputed relative pronouns of OE, as in (6.88f); the preposition could not be left behind. *þe*, on the other hand, occurs exclusively at the left edge of the clause – that is, in the position to which complementizers are restricted, and can never be preceded by a pied-piped preposition. In (6.88e), as elsewhere, the preposition is necessarily stranded. Moreover, like GO *ei*, OE *þe* can be preceded by an overt relative pronoun, as in (6.88f), in which case it is clearly not itself the relative pronoun. It is also, unlike the undisputed relative pronouns of OE, not formally similar to any of the other pronouns (demonstrative or interrogative) of the language. This array of facts has led many investigators (including, for example, Jespersen 1927; Allen 1980a) to conclude that OE *þe* is not a relative pronoun, but a relative complementizer, though this view has been disputed.[9]

---

[9] In a recent paper, Seppänen (2004), while agreeing that *þe* is a complementizer in cases where it occurs with another relative pronoun, as in (6.88f), claims that it has a different categorial

6 The syntax of the clause

The distinction still becomes somewhat more problematic in the case of relative particles which are etymologically related to (and therefore resemble) pronouns in a given language, since the formal similarity can predispose one to think of them as pronouns. Of this type are YI *vos* and Bavarian *wo*, both deriving from interrogative forms, and, perhaps most controversially, EN *that*, which is homophonous with the demonstrative pronoun.

status in cases like (6.88e), where it introduces the relative clause by itself. In these cases, according to Seppänen, *þe* is itself a relative pronoun. I reject this view in the present treatment, in favor of the view that *þe* is a complementizer in all of its uses, though it is not possible in the present context to justify that choice in detail. Seppänen's view requires us to suppose that OE had a relative pronoun *þe* which happened to be homophonous with a complementizer and (unlike the other relative pronouns of OE) not homophonous with any of the other pronouns in the language. Further, unlike any of the other relative pronouns of the language, the proposed pronoun had none of the inflectional or distributional properties which allow us to identify pronouns of other types as belonging to that category, such as marking for case and the ability to pied-pipe prepositions. Seppänen points out correctly that there are other items generally considered pronouns which lack one or another of these characteristics. However, *þe*, in its usual uses, lacks *all* of the characteristic inflection and possibilities of occurrence which would lead us away from the default assumption that it is always a complementizer, and toward the alternative conclusion that it is sometimes a (highly defective) pronominal. Under the view that *þe* is sometimes a pronoun, its systematic un-pronoun-like behavior in inflection and distribution would apparently have to be stipulated, while they follow without stipulation from the default view that *þe* is a complementizer, not a pronoun, in all of its uses. This is an especially important consideration in view of the fact that this cluster of "minor idiosyncratic properties" (Seppänen 2004: 75) is not unique to *þe*, but is shared by a whole class of relative markers in the GMC languages, including GO *ei*, *þei* and Scandinavian *som/sem*. These too are inflectionally invariant, do not pied-pipe and are identical with complementizers occurring elsewhere in the language, though not with pronouns. Identification of these elements as belonging to a unitary class of (relative) complementizers allows for a natural account of these properties. See Seppänen 2004 for the opposing view, and van der Auwera 1985, Seppänen 1993, 2000 and Seppänen and Kjelmer 1995 for arguments intended to show that, contrary to the position taken here, Modern EN relative *that*, the successor to *þe*, is also a pronoun rather than a complementizer. There is at least enough uncertainty in the situation, though, that native speakers (as well as linguists) occasionally treat relative *þe* and *that* in a way which clearly shows that they regard them as pronouns. Seppänen (2000) points out a few cases in OE in which *þe* exhibits the pronoun-like property of being able to precede the relative complementizer *þe*, as in (iii) (see also Wülfing 1894: I, 411, who characterizes it as "rare"). Similarly, as pointed out in van der Auwera 1985 and Seppänen and Kjellmer 1995, speakers of Modern EN have at various times in various places extended possessive -'s to relative *that*, as in (iv). This is in fact standard in Scots (Roger Lass p.c.), as well as Appalachian EN (Montgomery 2004: 266).

(iii)   Crist, þe þe is trēowe wisdom and sawle līf
        Christ, *þe þe* is true   wisdom and soul's life
        (OE, Ælfric, Seppänen 2000: 31)

(iv)   The dog that's leg was run over
        (Seppänen and Kjellmer 1995)

(6.88)   g. The woman that I saw was very busy

        h. die froy   vos ikh ze zi, iz zeyer farnumen
          the woman that I   see her is very busy
          (YI, Lowenstamm 1977: 206)

Lowenstamm (1977) argues that *vos* is a relative particle/complementizer in (6.88h), as does Jacobs (2005: 236ff.), while Lockwood (1995: 124) calls it a relative pronoun. The argument that *vos* is a relative complementizer, and not a relative pronoun, is complicated by the fact that a homophonous form does still serve as a relative pronoun in the language, as in (6.88i). We know that *vos* is a relative pronoun in this example because, like relative pronouns elsewhere, it can appear in construction with a preposition, which it has pied-piped to the front of the relative clause. The ability to be preceded by a preposition is distinctly a (pro)nominal property.

(6.88)   i. di alte shtub, in vos   mayne eltern   hobn gevoynt
          the old room in which my   parents have lived
          (YI, Lockwood 1995: 125)

However, Lowenstamm points out that when the antecedent of the relative clause is animate, as in (6.88h), *vos* is inflectionally invariant, always on the clausal periphery, and cannot appear inside of pied-piped PPs or NPs. When the relativized position is contained in a PP or an NP, *vos* occurs at the beginning of the clause and the PP or NP is left *in situ* (with a resumptive pronoun marking the relativized position).

(6.88)   j. der yid   vos ikh farloz zikh af im, iz mayn shokhn
          the man that I   rely [self] on him is my   neighbor
          (YI, Lowenstamm 1997: 206)

        k. der bokher vos zayne shpilkhlekh valgern zikh, iz mayn shvesterkind
          the boy   that his toys are-lying-around   is my   cousin
          (YI, Lowenstamm 1977: 206)

Moreover, in such uses, the relative particle *vos* does not carry over the semantic features of the pronouns from which they derive historically. YI *vos* is etymologically a neuter/inanimate question word, but in (6.88j, k) it introduces relative clauses on animate, masculine heads, and in (6.88h) it introduces a relative clause on an animate, feminine head. Thus, it does not show any type of pronominal behavior: pied-piping of prepositions, inflectional variation, or agreement with features of its antecedent. Further evidence that *vos* is a complementizer comes from the fact that it is used elsewhere in YI as a complementizer introducing non-relative clauses:

(6.88) l. a marokhe vos es regnt
         a good thing that it is raining
         (YI, Lowenstamm 1977: 203)

Finally, Lowenstamm supplements these arguments with others based on co-occurrence. First of all, note that in (6.88j) and (6.88k), there is no gap in the relative clause. Rather, the relativized position is occupied by a resumptive pronoun. Resumptive pronouns are normally found only in relative constructions with particles, not those with relative pronouns. The explanation for this is straightforward. In relative constructions with relative pronouns, the relative pronoun is itself the relativized argument, which is moved to the front of the clause, leaving behind a gap. There is thus no place for a resumptive pronoun. Relative particles, on the other hand, do not originate in the relativized position, but are generated in clause-initial positions. In such cases, the relativized position can be realized independently as a pronoun *in situ*.

The categorial status of EN *that* has been a matter of prolonged debate even among linguists. Much of the literature on both sides of this issue is summarized in van der Auwera 1985, and the reader is referred there for the argumentation. The case for *that* as a complementizer, rather than a relative pronoun, is again a cumulative one; it fails to behave in a pronoun-like way in any respect. Not only does it not follow prepositions or occur with genitive/possessive marking – in standard EN, at least, but see note 9 – (neither of which is probative in itself, as van der Auwera notes), but it does not encode animacy and number, unlike the corresponding demonstrative pronoun. In short, there seems to be no convincing evidence for treating it as a pronoun, aside from its homophony with the demonstrative, though the latter fact is mitigated by the fact that it is also homophonous with the declarative complementizer.

Finally, as we will see in Section 6.5.1.3, the relative *that* of ME, like many of the relative particles listed above (GO *ei*, OE *þe*, NO *som*) actually co-occurs with (relative or interrogative) pronouns in some cases. The fact that it co-occurs with relative pronouns makes it particularly clear that it cannot be a relative pronoun itself (at least in these particular constructions), but must belong to some other category.

A particularly problematic additional case is posed by the GO relativizers *izei* and *sei*, exemplified in (6.89) and (6.90).

(6.89)   a. saƕazuh izei usqimiþ izwis
            whoever *izei* kills   you
            (GO, John 16:2)

         b. saƕazuh izei þiudan sik silban taujiþ
            whoever *izei* (a) king himself makes
            (GO, John 19:12)

6.5 Relative clauses, questions and other fronting constructions 431

    c. mannan izei sunja izwis rodida
       (a) man *izei* truth to-you spoke
       (GO, John 8:40)

    d. ahman sunjos izei fram attin urrinniþ
       spirit of truth *izei* from father proceeds
       (GO, John 15:26)

    e. þana ize ni kunþa frawaurht
       the-one *izei* not knew sin
       (GO, 2 Cor. 5:21)

(6.90) a. managei sei stoþ hindar marein
       multitude *sei* stood beyond sea
       (GO, John 6:22)

    b. in baurg Galeilaias sei haitada Nazaraiþ
       in town of Galilee *sei* is-called Nazareth
       (GO, Luke 1:26)

    c. izai sei haitada stairo
       to-her *sei* is-called sterile
       (GO, Luke 1:36)

On first consideration, there are at least a couple of reasons for interpreting these forms as relative pronouns. First of all, unlike the relative particles considered so far, they are sensitive to some of the features of the head of the relative construction; *izei* appears only in relative clauses modifying masculine nouns, and *sei* only in relative clauses modifying feminine nouns. Such sensitivity to gender is the kind of behavior that we would expect of relative pronouns. Second, they look like relative pronouns. The uncontroversial relative pronouns in GO are formed by appending the complementizer *ei* to pronouns. In the third person, the pronouns in question are demonstratives (Masculine $sa + ei \rightarrow saei$, Feminine $so + ei \rightarrow soei$, Neuter $pata + ei \rightarrow patei$). In the first and second person, they are formed on personal pronouns (e.g., 1Sg $ik + ei \rightarrow ikei$).

(6.91)   ik...ik- ei   ni im wairþs ei haitaidau   apaustaulus
        I   1SgNom-*ei* not am worthy that I-might-be-called apostle
        (GO, 1 Cor. 15:9)

If there were counterparts to the latter in the third person – that is, relative pronouns formed on personal pronouns, rather than on demonstrative pronouns – the results ($is + ei \rightarrow izei$) and ($si + ei \rightarrow sei$) would look essentially like the relativizers actually attested in (6.89) and (6.90). This is the prevailing opinion of the etymologies of these forms – espoused by Eckhardt (1875), Delbrück (1900), Feist (1923: 223) and Krause (1968) – though there is a second view, held by Streitberg (1920: 228) and Klinghardt (1877), according to which they come from indeclinable complementizers, and their association with pronominal gender features is a secondary development.

Even if *izei* and *sei* are etymologically relative pronouns, though, there are several reasons for suspecting that they are at least not to be so analyzed in the synchronic grammar of GO. In particular, as noted by Streitberg, unlike the clear relative pronouns of GO, they are indeclinable. Unlike the demonstrative-based third person forms, or for that matter the personal-pronoun-based first and second person relative pronouns, *izei* and *sei* have no oblique forms. They are used only in subject relativization. Perhaps more revealing, they have no distinct plural forms, even when used with a plural head, as in the examples in (6.92). Here, we do not find the form **eiz-ei* (from *eis* (3PlNom) + *ei*), which we would expect were *iz-ei* in fact a productive relative pronoun. Similarly, there is no corresponding neuter, **itei*. These gaps would all be surprising if *izei* were in fact a productive relative pronoun.

6.92   a. faura liugnapraufetum þaim izei qimand
       before false-prophets, those *izei* come
       (GO, Matt. 7:15)

       b. þai   ize ni kausjand dauþaus
       those *izei* not they-taste death
       (GO, Mark 9:1)

       c. þai   ize...þata waurd gahaband
       those *izei*...that word keep
       (GO, Luke 8:15)

Second, if *izei* were a relative pronoun based on the third person personal pronoun, we would have to wonder why this relative pronoun should not be able to originate in nonsubject positions, as well as subject positions, pied-pipe prepositional phrases to the front, and so on, just as the clear relative pronouns in GO are. Such restrictions on relative pronouns would at least require exceptional stipulation.

Thus, there are several respects in which the analysis of *izei* in the synchronic grammar as a third person pronoun /is/ plus the complementizer *ei* appears to be insufficient. Klinghardt (1877) also noted that *izei* tended to undergo phonological reduction of a type to which the productive relative pronouns of the language were not subject (appearing as *ize* in seven of eighteen occurrences), and interpreted the phonetic instability of the final vowel here as further evidence that *izei* was not perceived, by the time of attested GO, at least, as a compound of a pronoun plus the complementizer *ei*.

6.5 Relative clauses, questions and other fronting constructions 433

I therefore conclude, as Klinghardt, Streitberg and von der Gabelentz did, that *izei* is in fact a relative particle – a complementizer of some sort, rather than a relative pronoun – possibly arising, as did the relative complementizer of YI, through fossilization of an original relative pronoun. It is less far along on this trajectory than its YI counterpart, since it still preserves one vestigial pronoun-like feature, in its sensitivity to the gender of the head. We may regard it, therefore, as an "agreeing complementizer." Agreeing complementizers – complementizers which participate in formal alternations conditioned by co-occurring NPs – have been posited for other languages as well. This has become a more or less standard analysis for the well-known *que/qui* alternation in French, illustrated in (6.93a).

(6.93)   a. l'homme que tu crois   qui (*que) [ ] viendra
            the man that you believe that   will-come
            (French, Bennis and Haegeman 1984: 36)

Qui is clearly not a relative pronoun, since it does not have to appear on the periphery of the relative clause, adjacent to the head, as seems to be required of relative pronouns crosslinguistically. In (6.93a) it appears in what seems to be the complementizer position of a more deeply embedded clause, adjacent to the subject "gap." Nonetheless, it manifests at least one pronoun-like property, in its sensitivity to the grammatical role of the relativized argument. *Qui* appears only in instances of subject relativization (a restriction which, interestingly, it shares with GO *izei*).

An essentially parallel case is found in West Flemish, as reported in Bennis and Haegeman (1984). The general strategy for relativization in West Flemish is a complementizer-initial strategy, using the invariant complementizer *da*, which is homophonous with the 'that' complementizer of the language. This is in fact the only possibility if the object is being relativized. However, when subjects are relativized, another option becomes available, as shown in (6.93c):

(6.93)   b. den vent da   Pol getrokken heet
            the man that Pol met   has
            (West Flemish, Bennis and Haegeman 1984: 34)

            c. den vent da/die   gekommen is
            the man that/who come   is

As in French, the appearance of the special relative form *die* is restricted to cases of subject relativization. Further, as in French, this special form always appears adjacent to the subject gap, even when that gap is in an embedded clause, as in (6.93d). Again, the fact that it does not move to the front of a relative clause like a relative pronoun suggests that it is not one, but rather an agreeing complementizer (though see Bennis and Haegeman 1984 for an alternative view).

(6.93)   d. den vent da Pol peinst die [ ] gekommen is
the man that Pol thinks that/who come is
(Bennis and Haegeman 1984: 35)

In summary, therefore, in addition to relative pronouns and invariant relative particles, the class of relative markers appears to include a "hybrid" category of agreeing complementizers. The assumption of such a category enables us to accommodate the existence of relative markers like *izei*, which exhibit a certain amount of sensitivity to nominal features but not the full paradigms of the true pronouns of the language, and which lack entirely the distributional properties of relative pronouns. One significant distributional characteristic shared by all of the candidates for this status which we have discussed (the inflected complementizers of French and West Flemish, as well as GO *izei* and *sei*) is the fact that they are only deployed in the case of subject relativization. Given this characteristic, the *der* which occurs in DA subject relative clauses (Section 6.5.1.9) also comes under consideration.

6.5.1.3 *Co-occurrence of relative pronouns and relative particles*

Some of the GMC languages allow (or require) both relative pronouns and relative particles/complementizers to co-occur at the beginnings of relative clauses. Such co-occurrence is found in GO, OS, early OHG, Middle DU, FR, OE and ME. The last two have to be treated as two independent cases, since there is no continuity between them; ME uses different lexical items than OE for both the relative pronoun (*se* vs. *who*) and the particle (*þe* vs. *that*), and according to Allen (1980a: 204), the OE construction died out before the ME one arose, indicating that the latter is not a simple relexification of the former. Note also that the particle used in GO (*ei*) is not etymologically connected to the ones found in West GMC (*þe/(da)t*), suggesting again that the common inheritance is not the particular construction, but the template.

(6.94)   a. þā ān **þā** **þe** tō æfæstnesse belumpon
those alone which that to piety were-suited1
(OE, Bede (Miller) 342:17)

         b. twalib, **þanz-ei** jah apaustuluns namnida
twelve, whom-that and apostles he-named
(GO, Luke 6:13)

         c. In een uutgehouwen graf, in **dien dat** noch niemant gheleit was
in a hollowed-out grave, in which that still no-one laid was
(Middle DU: Stooet 1923, cited in Allen 1980a: 264)

         d. îogewelihhemo **ther-de** habet wirdit gegeban
to whomever who-that has it-will-be given
(OHG, Tatian 149:8, cited in Behaghel 1928: III, 714)

e. He **which that** hath no wyf
   he which that has no wife
   (ME, Chaucer, cited in Fischer 1992: 302)

f. Sikkema is de boer by **wa't** ik ûngetiidzje sil
   Sikkema is the farmer by whom-that I harvest shall
   (FR, Tiersma 1999: 122)

g. dea Hund **dea wo** gestern d'Katz bissn hot
   the dog which that yesterday the cat bit has
   (Bavarian, Bayer 1984: 24)

Among the modern GMC languages, this possibility seems to be found only in FR (where the complementizer *(da)t* appears to be required) and Bavarian. Some of the medieval languages which allowed the construction (e.g., ME and Middle DU) have lost it. It is unrepresented in Scandinavian relative clauses, but complementizers do co-occur with question pronouns in Modern SW (6.95a) and Belfast EN (6.95b).

(6.95) a. Jag vet inte vem som äger den
   I know not who that owns them
   (SW)

b. They asked which book that I had chosen
   (Belfast EN, Henry 1995: 120)

In GO, the relative pronoun cannot occur without the complementizer *ei* (though the converse is possible). The complementizer also seems to be required in FR. Elsewhere, the pronoun can occur by itself. When both occur, pronouns and complementizers appear in that order. We can account for this by assuming the following structure for such doubly introduced relative clauses. The complementizer is the head of CP, while the relative pronoun phrase is the phrasal specifier of CP.

(6.96)

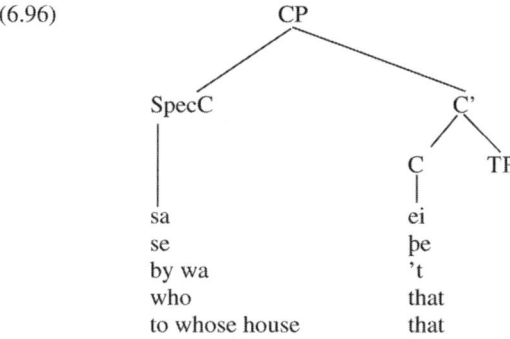

Although this assumption about phrasal architecture allows for a straightforward description of the possibility of doubly introduced relative clauses, it does not explain why some languages allow both positions to be filled while others do not, and I am unaware of any fully satisfying answer to this question. When only the relative pronoun phrase is present the construction will be called a P-relative. This case will be further divided into D-relatives and W-relatives, depending on whether the relative pronoun is etymologically connected to the demonstrative pronoun paradigm or the interrogative pronoun paradigm (see below). When only a relative complementizer or particle appears, the construction will be called a C-relative. Where both positions are filled, it will be termed a P/C-relative. Where neither is filled, it will be termed a 0-relative.

6.5.1.4 *Types of relative pronouns: demonstratives and interrogatives*

Paul (1962: 358) and Dal (1966: 198) claim that "asyndetic" (0-relative) clauses, such as the OHG (6.97), represent the oldest type in GMC, but there seems in fact to be little basis for this claim. These are in fact sparsely attested in the early dialects.

(6.97)   in droume si   in   zelitun then weg sie   faran scoltun
          in dream they them told   the way they go   should
          (OHG, Otfrid V, 9, 37, cited in Erdmann 1874: 128)

GO and OE do not admit them. It is only in OHG that they are found with frequency among the early dialects. There is also no evidence for Dal's claim (1966: 198) that the relative pronouns were a late development, and that C-relative clauses preceded them historically. In GO again, the overwhelming majority of relative clauses are introduced by relative pronouns; the C-relatives are restricted to certain special cases, as will be seen below in Section 6.5.1.5.1. Moreover, the particular form of relative pronouns in the early languages would seem to point back to a common inheritance; the fact that OE, OHG, OS and GO all agree in having relative pronouns based on the demonstrative paradigm (as opposed to the interrogative paradigm found in Latin, for example), followed (optionally or obligatorily) by complementizers, suggests that this is a common pattern inherited from the parent language. There is no evidence for the "growth" of relative pronouns within GMC proper. I also see no compelling reason to accept the common claim (also made in Dal 1966: 198; Paul 1962: 258) that these relative pronouns started out as demonstrative heads of relative constructions – that is, as constituents of the main clause – and that they were reanalyzed as belonging to the relative clause. GMC has had D-relative pronouns (based on the *to paradigm of IE) apparently as far back as we are able to discern (see also Behaghel 1928: III, 713). They are the basic type in GO, OE, GE and DU. They set GMC apart from its neighbors (Celtic, Italic and Slavic) and seem to be a GMC innovation.

In addition to these D-relatives, some of the GMC languages have developed relative pronouns based on the interrogative paradigm, at different times and in different distributions. There is general agreement among the modern languages in the use of W-relative pronouns when the phrase modified by the (nonrestrictive) relative clause is not a NP but a clause.

(6.98) a. Peter kom for sent, hvad der var synd
Peter was late, which was a pity
(DA, Koefoed 1958: 176)

b. to make pes betwen the kynges After the lawe of charite
Which is the propre duete Belongende to the presthode
to make peace between the kings, after the law charity
which is the proper duty belonging to the priesthood
(ME, Gower, Confessio Amantis (Peck) Prologue 256–259)

c. Peter kam spät, was uns sehr geärgert hat
Peter came late, which us very-much annoyed has
(GE)

This seems to be a late usage, however. The OED lists 1390 as the earliest occurrence in EN. Behaghel (1928: III, 757f.) cites only one example from Late OHG and attributes its existence to Latin and French models. It thus represents another instance of similarity by convergence, rather than by inheritance.

W-forms have also come to be used even in languages which use D-relatives or C-relatives in the usual case, in relative clauses on quantificational heads like 'everything', 'something' and 'nothing', as well as on demonstrative heads.

(6.99) a. Alles/das/nichts, was er sagt, ist wahr
all/that/nothing what he says is true
(GE)

b. Hingað kemur allt hvað heiti hefur
thence comes all what has a name
(Archaic Mod. IC, Kress 1982: 252)

c. Hon ger allt vad hon äger till de fattiga
she gives all what she can to the poor
(Formal SW, Holmes and Hinchcliffe 1994: 225)

Another widepread occurrence of W-forms in relative constructions involves their use in so-called "Free Relatives." I will defer discussion of these to Section 6.5.1.10.

In addition to these uses, some of the GMC languages have also come to use W-forms as relative pronouns in relative constructions headed by lexical nouns. This usage is not original, apparently – it is missing in GO, OHG and OE, for example – but it has developed to at least some degree in the great majority of the modern languages. In many of them, this has remained a restricted strategy, limited to certain syntactic contexts, or stylistically constrained. So, for example, Kress (1982: 252) characterizes its use in IC as generally archaic:

(6.100) a. þær kristallsár, á hverjar sólin gljár
         the crystal rivers, on which the sun shines
         (IC, Kress 1982: 252)

In some languages, though (YI, AF and EN), W-relatives have completely displaced D-relatives. In YI, one of these W-forms has in turn gone on to become an invariant particle, *vos*. In addition to *vos*, YI also has two sets of inflected W-relative pronouns: *ver/vemen/vemens* (human only) and *velkh* – the latter belonging to the written language, according to Lockwood (1995: 126). AF will be discussed in the next section.

(6.100) b. di froyen velkhe ikh ze, zeynen farnumen
         the women whom I   see are   busy
         (YI, Lowenstamm 1977: 199)

6.5.1.5   *The distribution of D-relatives, W-relatives and C-relatives in Germanic*
In the following sections, I will discuss the various patterns of distribution of C-relatives, D-relatives and W-relatives. The particular interest of the coexistence of these different types of relative construction is that they are frequently not interchangeable, but complementarily distributed. There are circumstances in which only one can be used. The situation is made more interesting by the fact that, in many cases, particular patterns of distribution recur across the individual languages, and more interesting still by the fact that these patterns sometimes appear to be the result of parallel developments, rather than common inheritance.

6.5.1.5.1 **The Gothic type** As noted above, in GO, relative clauses are overwhelmingly introduced by D-relative pronouns, with attached complementizers.

(6.101) þo waurda þo-ei   ik rodida izwis
         the words which-Comp I spoke to you
         (GO, John 6:63)

6.5 Relative clauses, questions and other fronting constructions

C-relatives are restricted essentially to two cases: they occur (with the complementizer *ei*) in modifying time or manner heads, as in (6.102), and they occur (with the complementizer *þei*) in relative clauses modifying generalizing pronoun heads (the 'whoever' type) (6.103). *Ei* and *þei* can be shown to be complementizers because they are also used to introduce non-relative clauses, including object clauses.

(6.102)   a.   fram þamma daga ei   hausidedum
                  from the   day   that we-heard
                  (Col. 1:9)

            b.   þamma haidau ei   Jannes jah Mambres andstoþun Moseza
                  in-the   manner that Jannes and Mambres resisted   Moses
                  (2 Tim. 3:8)

(6.103)   a.   bidei mik þisƕizuh þei wileis
                  ask   me whatever   that you-want
                  (Mark 6:22)

            b.   þisƕammeh   þei wiljau   giba   þata
                  to-whomever that I-want   I-give that
                  (Luke 4:6)

None of the other GMC languages restricts the distribution of C-relatives in this way, but it is interesting to note that even in some other GMC languages which do not make general use of a C-relative strategy, it is still possible to use a C-relative precisely in the case of relative clauses on heads which are time words. So, while OHG does not generally introduce relative clauses with the complementizer *thaz/daz*, it does so in (6.104a). (We know that the *thaz* here has to be a complementizer, not a relative pronoun, since it does not agree in gender with the head.) Curme (1952: 202) cites a number of similar instances from Modern GE, including (6.105b).

(6.104)   a.   after   thero ziti thaz her suohte   fon   then magin
                  according to the time that he   ascertained from the   wise-men
                  (OHG, Tatian (Sievers) 10:1)

            b.   das letzte Mal, daß ich ihn   sah...
                  the last   time that I   saw him...
                  (GE, Curme 1952: 202)

An apparently similar case is reported from AF by Ponelis (1993: 294ff.). In AF, relative clauses are virtually always introduced by a WH-form (e.g. *wat*). Exceptionally, however, relative clauses on temporal heads do not require *wat*, but allow *dat* (the 'that' complementizer of AF) instead. That is, apparently, C-relatives are allowed in AF too, just in case the head is a noun denoting time.[10]

(6.104)   c. Daar was wel   'n tyd dat/wat ek op 'n plaas gebly het
               there was indeed a time that   I on a farm stayed
               (AF, Ponelis 1993: 295)

And van der Auwera (1985: 162) cites the following example from DU:

(6.104)   d. In de week dat Jan toekwam was iedereen bezig
               in the week that Jan arrived   was everyone busy
               (DU)

Similarly, in OE, while the specifically relative complementizer þe was widely used in relative constructions of all types, the "general purpose" that-complementizer þæt, as reported by Allen (1980a: 102ff.), introduces relative clauses when the head is a time phrase, or when it was the universally quantified pronoun eall 'all' – an interesting point of comparison with the GO examples in (6.102) and (6.103).

(6.104)   e. Nū is se tīma ðæt þēos woruld is gemæncged mid meanigfealdan māne
               now is the time that this world is mixed   with manifold   evil
               (Wulfstan, cited in Allen 1980a: 103)

6.5.1.5.2 The German pattern

Modern GE lacks C-relatives; relative constructions are always introduced by relative pronouns. The relative pronouns are of the W-type when (a) the modified head is a clause (cf. Section 6.5.1.4 above), or (b) when the modified head is an inanimate quantificational pronoun or demonstrative (e.g., *alles* 'everything', *nichts* 'nothing', *etwas* 'something', *das* 'that'). In relative

---

[10] In fact, Ponelis treats these cases in a fundamentally different way. He takes the bracketed clause in (i) to be a NP complement clause, not a relative clause:

(i)   die tyd [dat/wat   si   werk]
           the time that/'what' she works
           'the time that she works'
           (Ponelis 1993: 296)

and claims that the originally relative *wat* is expanding into non-relative functions, gradually replacing the complementizer *dat* even in complement clauses. He notes, however, that this cannot occur with 'non-temporal NP complements,' as in (ii):

(ii)   die idee/besef   dat/(* wat) niks   verkeerd kan gaan nie
           the idea/realization that/*'what' nothing wrong   can go
           (AF, Ponelis 1993: 296)

6.5 Relative clauses, questions and other fronting constructions 441

constructions on lexical heads, D-relative pronouns are used virtually exclusively, as in (6.105):

(6.105) Das Kind, mit dem ich sprach
the child with whom I spoke
(GE)

There is one systematic exception to this, involving the relativization of objects of prepositions. When the object of the preposition is inanimate, the D-relative construction alternates with a W-relative construction, involving a '*wo*-compound', in which, descriptively speaking, the object of the preposition is replaced by an etymologically interrogative form, *wo*, which is prefixed to the preposition, with a linking consonant -r- in case the preposition begins with a vowel. Because of the latter property, the resultant forms are often called "R-compounds." The two possibilities are illustrated in (6.106a, b).

(6.106) a. der Stuhl, auf dem ich saß
the chair on which I sat

b. der Stuhl, wo-r-auf ich saß

We see here a very modest encroachment of W-forms on the relative functions of the D-forms. It may be important as a sort of "foot in the door" – a special context of occurrence from which W-forms might subsequently have been generalized at the expense of D-forms in some GMC languages (e.g., DU) (cf. Ponelis 1993: 190f. for discussion of staging in the spread of W-relative forms).

FR represents the mirror-image of GE here. When relativizing objects of prepositions, FR uses a W-form *following* the preposition, but uses a D-form preceding the preposition (which is usually stranded). Both of these are possible with animate antecedents.

(6.107) a. Sikkema is de boer by wa't ik ûngetiidzje sil
Sikkema is the farmer by whom-that I harvest-hay shall
(FR, Tiersma 1999: 122)

b. Sikkema is de boer dêr't ik by ûngetiidzje sil

6.5.1.5.3 The Early Middle English type

What I am calling the EME pattern (because it originates there earlier than elsewhere apparently) is also found in at least one other GMC language, AF, as I will argue. Let us start with the AF case.

In DU, relativization involves two distinct types of relative pronouns: D-forms and W-forms. Ponelis (1993: 190) claims that the W-relative forms of DU arose under

442   6 *The syntax of the clause*

Romance influence. In Standard DU, only D-forms can be used to relativize direct arguments (NPs whose role in the relative clause is that of subject or object), while only W-forms can be used to relativize prepositional objects and possessives.

(6.108)   a. de vraag   die   zij stelde
             the question which she asked
             (DU, Ponelis 1993: 191)

          b. het vlees dat hij kocht
             the meat that he bought
             (DU, Ponelis 1993: 191)

          c. de auto waarin wij reisden
             the car wherein we travelled
             (DU, Ponelis 1993: 191)

          d. de student aan wie   de brief word gericht
             the student to whom the letter was addressed
             (DU, Ponelis 1993: 191)

          e. de man in wiens stoel ik zit
             the man in whose chair I sit
             (DU, Donaldson 1981: 65)

Burridge (1993: 243) describes a system apparently like this for Middle DU as well, noting, though, that sometimes the D-form used in direct case relativization failed to inflect, and observing that in this regard it seems to have behaved like the invariant relative marker *þe* in OE – that is, as a C-relative particle.

From this foothold in oblique case contexts, there has been a historical tendency for the W-forms to work their way up the hierarchy of grammatical relations, occurring eventually in direct cases as well (Ponelis 1993: 190). Ponelis points out that, while D-forms are still preferred in Standard DU for direct relatives, neuter *dat* is largely replaced by *wat* colloquially.

(6.108)   f. het vlees wat hij kocht
             the meat that he bought
             (DU, Ponelis 1993: 191)

This displacement was carried even further in AF; according to Donaldson (1994: 493) and Ponelis (1993: 188), AF (having eliminated D-forms entirely) now makes use of W-relative pronouns in all positions:

6.5 *Relative clauses, questions and other fronting constructions* 443

(6.109) a. 'n beleid wat verander
a policy that is-changing
(AF, Ponelis 1993: 188)

b. spelers op wie   ons reken
players on whom we count
(AF, Ponelis 1993: 189)

c. beginsels waa-r-op ons reken
principles whereon we count
(AF, Ponelis 1993: 189)

Note that in the relativization of prepositional objects, we find an alternation based on animacy which is very much like the one we observed in the GE examples in (6.106). Consider now the syntactic status of *wat* in (6.109a). If we analyze the direct relative *wat* as a relative pronoun, as suggested by Ponelis and Donaldson, we have to ask why it should fail to have special forms for use when the relativized subject or object is animate, as W-relative pronouns in EN do, for example. In AF, the relative form introducing direct relative clauses is an invariant *wat*, regardless not only of whether the head noun is singlar or plural, but also of whether it is animate or inanimate.

(6.109) d. joernaliste wat gereageer het
journalists who reacted   have
(AF, Ponelis 1993: 188)

We can, of course, simply state that the animacy contrast is neutralized in direct case forms of the relative pronoun, but this begs the question of why just there.[11] For one thing, the distinction between animate and inanimate is still signaled in the interrogative pronouns in AF (*wie* 'who' vs. *wat* 'what').

(6.110) a. wie is jy?
who are you?
(AF, Ponelis 1993: 482)

b. wat wil die kinders nou doen?
what want the children now to-do?
(AF, Ponelis 1993: 482)

---

[11] Ponelis (1993: 193), while continuing to label the W-relativizers of AF as pronominal, does make note of their invariance, and attributes these developments to a combination of creolization and the consequent loss of gender (facilitating the extension of the originally neuter *wat* to original common gender heads) and the influence of the model Portuguese, with its invariant relative complementizer *que* (also historically interrogative and neuter).

If the animacy contrast is leveled out in the case of the invariant "direct" relative pronoun – as a consequence of creolization, let us say – we might ask why it was not leveled out here, too. The answer, of course, is that animacy contrasts on interrogative pronouns are semantically contentful, whereas in relative pronouns they are redundant and dispensable, since their semantic content is recoverable from the head. Still, formal correspondence between W-relative pronouns and W-interrogative pronouns is usual in languages that have both, and gratuitous divergence from this pattern in AF would at least be a puzzle. And the puzzle would be compounded by the fact that the putative W-relative pronoun of AF does not lack an animacy contrast in all positions in its paradigm, but only in the direct case. The relative pronoun does have a special animate form, *wie*, contrasting with inanimate *wat*, when it occurs as object of a preposition, and as a genitive modifier of a NP, as shown in the examples in (6.111)-(6.112) (though Ponelis notes (1993: 189) that in colloquial AF, the invariant *wat* strategy is tending to encroach on these positions, too):

(6.111)   a. lede   met wie   sy gepraat het
                   people with whom she spoken has
                   (AF, Ponelis 1993: 188)

             b. sakkies   waarin   alles gebêre word
                   little-bags wherein all   stored is
                   (AF, Ponelis 1993: 188)

(6.112)   a. ouers   wie se   kinders kwalifiseer
                 parents whose (literally, who their) children qualify
                 (AF, Ponelis 1993: 189)

             b. die tafel wat se   poot stukkend is
                 the table whose (literally, what its) leg   broken   is
                 (AF, Ponelis 1993: 188)

If the animacy distinction was simply given up in direct case relative pronouns, why was it not given up in the case of the oblique ones too? In fact, the paradigm in question would be a typological oddity in the GMC languages, where, in general, contrasts in animacy, number and the like are generally more robustly signaled in direct cases than in oblique cases (think of EN *who/what* versus *whose*, for example). And the puzzle would deepen in the face of contrasts like the one in (6.113):

(6.113)   a. lede   met wie   sy gepraat het
                   members with whom she spoken has
                   (AF, Ponelis 1993: 189)

6.5 Relative clauses, questions and other fronting constructions

    b.   lede   wat sy mee gepraat het
        members *wat* she with spoken has
        (AF, Ponelis 1993: 189)

When objects of prepositions are relativized in AF the preposition can be pied-piped or stranded. Stranding of the sort reflected in (6.113b) ("plain" preposition stranding, as opposed to R-stranding) is very frequent in AF relative clauses, according to Ponelis. Note, however, that if we construe *wat* in (6.113b) as a relative pronoun which has been fronted out of its prepositional phrase, we must also reckon with the mysterious change in form which this movement imposes on it. Why should *wie* become *wat* just in case it is moved? Why should the fronting of a relative pronoun be accompanied by a formal change, resulting in the loss of its specification for animacy?

These problems disappear if we take the *wat* of direct relatives in AF to be something other than a fronted pronoun – a relative complementizer, for example, like the *izei* of GO or the *som* of DA or (to cite some etymologically closer examples) the cognate *vos* in YI or the *qui* of French. As a complementizer, its formal invariance, and its reduced sensitivity to features of the head, are expected.

As further corroborative evidence, we may note that *wat* appears as a complementizer even outside relative contexts, as in the cleft construction in (6.114):

(6.114)   Dit was 'n bietjie gou dat/wat   die lorrie gekom het
               it   was a bit   soon that/'what' the truck come has
               (AF, Ponelis 1993: 295)

The arguments for relative particle status are very much like those introduced by Lowenstamm (1977) for YI. I conclude, therefore, that the most plausible analysis of the AF facts is that the relative pronoun (*wie*) is restricted to relativization of the positions of objects of prepositions and possessors, and that the *wat* employed in direct relativization is not a relative pronoun any longer, but an invariant relative particle, or complementizer. A pattern strikingly similar to this is to be found in ME, in its very early stages, which arrived at it by a quite different route. The introduction of this pattern is documented in prodigious detail by Chevillet (1981). In OE, relative clauses were introduced by a D-relative pronoun (*se*-relatives) or by an invariant relative complementizer (*þe*-relatives) or by both in combination (*se-þe*-relatives). It was impossible for both to be absent – that is, there were no 0-relatives. This pattern continued on into the EME period, and is reflected, for example, in the twelfth-century Vespasian Homilies in Chevillet's data, and in contemporary texts, such as the Bodley Homilies. It should be noted, since it will become important, that the D-relatives predominated here, occurring almost twice as often in this text as the C-relatives.

(6.115) a. hēo hæfde ān oðre dohter,   sēo was ēac genæmd Maria
         she had   an other daughter, who was also called   Maria
         (Vesp. D. 14: 139/9, Chevillet 1981: ex. 26)

  b. þone Ælmihtigne God, sē   þe āne is God...
     the Almighty   God, who that alone is God
     (Vesp. D. 14: 90/ 30, Chevillet 1981: ex. 19)

  c. sēo hæfde āne suster þe   was genæmd Maria
     she had   a sister that was named   Maria
     (Vesp. D. 14: 154/8, Chevillet 1981: 26)

At the end of the twelfth century, however – perhaps even earlier in some dialects – two changes took place quite abruptly, and from all appearances, simultaneously. W-relative pronouns were introduced, but apparently only in the position of prepositional objects. And the D-pronouns of OE disappeared. In the *Trinity Homilies* of c. 1200, for example, all of the direct relatives are introduced by bare complementizers (*þe* or *þat*), while W-pronouns appear in oblique object position. The contemporary *Vices and Virtues* exhibits at most two possible instances of an old D-relative pronoun in direct cases, as opposed to many others with bare complementizers:

(6.116) a. helende þat is Crist   þe lauerd
         savior   that is Christ the Lord
         (Trinity Homilies VIII/49, Chevillet 1981: ex. 56)
  b. ure drihten on wam we bileuen
     our Lord   in whom we believe
     (Trinity Homilies XXXI/199, Chevillet 1981: ex. 59)
  c. tach me godnesse, ðurh   wan ich god muʒe bien
     teach me goodness, through which I good might be
     (Vices and Virtues 127/22, Chevillet 1981: ex. 97)

At this point, objects of prepositions are relativized with W-pronouns, but subjects and direct objects are relativized with C-relatives (cf. also Allen 1980a). In the still earlier and more northerly Ormulum (1180), we find this same pattern, though in addition to objects of prepositions, the W-forms were also used in relativizing (soon-to-disappear) dative arguments of verbs like 'follow', and possessors.

(6.117) a. Her iss whamm   ʒuw   birrþ   follʒhenn
         here is whom-Dat to-you it-behooves to follow
         (Orm. 12887, Chevillet 1981: ex. 105)

  b. Crist, whas moderr ʒho wass wurrþenn
     Christ, whose mother she was become
     (Orm. 3424, Chevillet 1981: ex. 106)

C-relatives continued to be possible in relativizing objects of prepositions, and when they were used, the preposition was stranded. Thus, two possibilities existed for relativizing these positions: pied-piping, with a W-pronoun, as in (6.116b), and stranding in C-relatives. The stranding possibility is illustrated in (6.118).

(6.118) þatt tun   þatt he wass borenn inne
         that town that he was born   in
         (Orm. 3290-91, Chevillet 1981: ex. 120)

This EME pattern was relatively short lived, but robust while it lasted. It is, in the main, the same pattern as attested in AF, though arrived at in yet another way – through the virtually simultaneous adoption of WH-relative pronouns, exclusively in oblique contexts, and the elimination of the inherited relative pronouns across the board, leaving the C-strategy as the only one available for direct case relativization.

The EME pattern is of course also the same pattern found in French, and many investigators (e.g., Traugott 1972: 154) attribute the rise of W-relative pronouns in EN to French influence. If this is correct, one is led to wonder what language-internal factors might have made this particular bit of French morphosyntax sufficiently attractive to prompt its repeated borrowing into GMC. A comparable pattern is also found in Scottish Gaelic, where relative pronouns exist (unlike Irish), but are restricted to relativization of prepositional objects, a C-relativization strategy with an invariant particle *a* being used in relativization on direct case positions.

We see, therefore, that what appears to be a new pattern – C-relatives for direct cases and P-relatives for objects of prepositions – has arisen at opposite ends of the GMC world, and apparently from opposite directions, structurally speaking: in the one case, by supplementing an original C-relative strategy with a P-strategy, just in the oblique cases, and in the other, by reanalyzing direct relative pronouns as relative complementizers, thus restricting an original P-strategy to oblique contexts.

Some descriptions of the continental Scandinavian languages suggest a similar pattern there. Koefoed observes that in DA, subjects and objects are relativized by the invariant relativizer *som*, but that P-relatives with WH-pronouns can be used in relativizing possessors and prepositional objects, with or without pied-piping (though in both cases C-relatives are also available).

(6.119) a. Her er drengen, som reddede sin søster fra at drukne
            here is boy-the that saved   his sister from to drown
            (DA, Koefoed 1958: 176)

         b. Hr. Petersen, hvis   broder forsvandt i Amerika
            Mr. Petersen, whose brother disappeared in America
            (DA, Koefoed 1958: 176)

(6.119) c. Hans er en ven, på hvem man kan stole
he is a friend on whom one can rely
(DA, Koefoed 1958: 176)

d. Hans er en ven, som man kan stole på
he is a friend that one can rely on
(DA, Koefoed 1958: 176)

e. jeg kender en mand som hans søster har været gift med
I know a man that his sister has been married to
(DA, Haberland 1994: 345)

Similarly, in SW, Granberry (1991) claims that whereas relativization of direct argument positions involves the invariant particle *som*, W-forms can be used in relativizing possessor and prepositional object positions:

(6.120) a. flickan, vars vän han var, sade adjö
girl-the whose friend he was said goodbye
(SW, Granberry 1991: 42)

b. familjen i vars hus vi bor kommer snart tillbaka
family-the in whose house we live are soon coming back
(SW, Holmes and Hinchcliffe 1994: 224)

c. staden, til vilken jag kom, är stor
town-the to which I came is large
(SW, Granberry 1991: 42)

However, the situation here is rather murky, and different descriptions seem to contradict each other. Anward (1982: 58) gives examples of W-relatives in SW even in relativization of direct case positions, for example. Matters are still further complicated by questions of register. Some sources (e.g., Allan *et al.* 1995: 201 for DA and Holmes and Hinchcliffe 1994: 222 for SW) characterize the use of W-forms as restricted to formal registers. A detailed account of areal and register variation in usage for all of the languages we have been looking at is of course not possible, and the reader is referred to the relevant individual descriptions. Again, though, there seems to be at least a tendency in these languages, where both strategies coexist, to prefer the C-strategy for direct relativization and the W-strategy for oblique relativization.

6.5.1.6 *The expression of person in relative pronouns*

Since relative pronouns based on demonstratives and interrogatives are inherently third person, a problem arises when the head of the relative construction is a pronoun in the first or second person. Different languages have addressed this problem

6.5 Relative clauses, questions and other fronting constructions 449

differently. The most straightforward resolution of this conflict is offered by GO, in which the appropriate personal pronoun is used as a relative pronoun on non-third person heads (independent of the Greek, which uses a third person relative pronoun here).

(6.121)   a. þu is sunus meins sa liuba, in þuz-ei waila galeikaida
             you are son my the beloved in you-that well I-am-pleased
             (GO, Mark 1:11)

          b. jus juz-ei simle wesuþ fairra
             you you-that once were far
             (Eph. 2:13)

A more usual treatment has been to introduce the relative clause in the usual way – either with a D-pronoun or a relative complementizer – but to inflect the verb of the relative clause for first or second person agreement:

(6.121)   c. I who am...

          d. vér, er hér erom komner
             we, that here are-1Pl come
             (ON, Behaghel 1928: III, 752)

          e. ik, die heer veertig jaar gewerkt heb...
             I, who here forty years worked have-1Sg...
             (DU, Geerts *et al.* 1984: 240)

          f. Gabriel bium ic hêtan, the gio for goda standu
             Gabriel am I called, who always before God stand-1Sg
             (OS, Heliand (Behaghel) 119)

In Modern GE, such agreement mismatches between the relative pronoun and the verb are avoided; third person agreement is the rule in such constructions:

(6.121)   g. Du, der ja nicht alles wissen kann...
             you, who not all know can-3Sg...
             (GE, Engel 1988: 295)

Remarkably, though, since the sixteenth century the D-relative in such constructions in GE has come to be optionally reinforced by a following personal pronoun, in which case the agreement is with the personal pronoun, and not with the D-pronoun.

(6.121)   h. Er hat uns, die wir ihm gefolgt haben, verdankt
             he has us, who we him followed have, thanked
             (GE, Schulz and Griesbach 1960: 156)

450   6 *The syntax of the clause*

> i. Ich, der ich schon   zehn Jahre hier wohne...
>   I,   who I   already ten   years here live...

Not clear is whether this pronoun is a resumptive pronoun in subject position within the relative clause, or whether the *der* and the *ich* form a single, complex relative pronoun.

6.5.1.7   *Correlates and non-correlates of the P-relative/C-relative distinction*
It has been noted in individual languages in which both constructions co-occur that particle relatives and pronoun relatives are subject to different syntactic restrictions. This section will present a catalogue of the differences which have been pointed out, with a view toward attempting to determine what crosslinguistic generalizations can be made.

6.5.1.7.1   **Distribution in restrictive and non-restrictive clauses**   First of all, it has been claimed for Modern EN that P-relatives and C-relatives differ in their ability to introduce nonrestrictive relative clauses (NRRELs). Nonrestrictive relative clauses are relative clauses which provide incidental information about a NP whose referent is already assumed to be sufficiently established. They contrast with restrictive relatives (RRELs), in which the relative clause plays a role in the identification of the referent of the noun phrase – predicating information about it which helps the hearer to narrow down the possible referents. Relative clauses modifying heads which are unique-referent nouns or proper names are thus normally nonrestrictive.

(6.122)   a. John, who/*that I believe you met at the party, by the way...
           b. The sun, which/*that is almost a hundred million miles from Earth...
           c. The man that you met at the party...

NRRELs are parenthetical, and are thus set off by pauses – reflected orthographically in EN through the use of commas. It has been claimed that in EN, only relative pronouns, not the complementizer *that*, can introduce NRRELs. Thus, the versions of (6.122a, b) with *that* are ungrammatical for most speakers (though see Jacobsson 1994 and van der Auwera 1985 for counterexamples). However, among the languages which allow C-relatives, this restriction seems only to hold for Modern EN. It did not hold of OE (Allen 1980a: 91), and in the Scandinavian languages, *som* can introduce NRRELs:

(6.122)   d. De   eleverna, som   är mycket unga förresten, är mycket otrevliga
              those pupils   who are very young by the way, are very unpleasant
              (SW, Holmes and Hinchcliffe 1994: 536)

NRRELs and RRELs are still distinguished in the Scandinavian languages, though, in that while relative *som* is omissible in cases of nonsubject relativization in RRELs in NO, for example, it is not omissible in such cases in NRRELs (Askedal 1994: 263).

6.5 Relative clauses, questions and other fronting constructions 451

6.5.1.7.2 Stranding differences In Modern EN, when the constituent being questioned is the object of a preposition, the preposition may be treated in either of two ways. It may be carrried along to the left periphery of the clause, along with the leftward-displaced question phrase or relative phrase (the pied-piping case), or it may be left in its normal position within the clause, while the relative pronoun appears by itself at the front of the relative clause (the "preposition-stranding" case).

(6.123) a. the man to whom I spoke
         b. the man who/that I spoke to

The availability of the pied-piping and stranding options is connected in part with the type of relative clause. This is true at least in the obvious sense that in C-relatives there is no relative pronoun to carry the PP along to the clausal periphery, so that stranding is the only option. In this section, we examine the variation in the distribution of these two options across GMC, by way of seeing whether a closer connection can be established between the type of relative clause and the choice of pied-piping or stranding.

In OE, at least, the connection appears to have worked in both directions. Allen (1980a) observed that in OE, C-relatives with *þe* allowed (and required) stranding of the preposition when a prepositional object was relativized, but that, on the other hand, in D-relatives stranding was not possible; rather, the preposition had to be pied-piped to the front of the clause, along with the relative pronoun.

(6.124) a. wætan...ðe druncennysse   ðurh cōme
           liquid that drunkenness through might come
           'liquid...through which drunkenness might come'
           (OE, St. Guthlac, cited in Allen 1980a: 77)

         b. ðā claðas   his hādes, of ðǣm wæs ūre gekind geedneowod
           the clothes of his estate, by which was our race renewed
           (OE, Blickling Homilies, cited in Allen 1980a: 83)

In fact, Allen states this more generally for OE: in constructions involving the fronting of any constituent, not just relative pronouns, stranding of a preposition is disallowed. Thus, pied-piping is required in the question fronting case of (6.124c) and the topic fronting case of (6.124d) as well.

(6.124) c. Tō hwǣm lōcige ic buton tō ðǣm ēaðmodum?
           to whom look I but to the humble?
           (OE, Cura Pastoralis, cited in Allen 1980a: 122)

         d. Tō ðǣm sōðum gesǣlðum ic tiohige ðæt ic ðe lǣde
           to the true happiness I intend that I you lead
           (OE, Boethius, cited in Allen 1980a: 51)

It is only in the case of C-relative clauses and similar constructions (see Allen 1980a) where there is no (overt) leftward-displaced constituent, such as a relative pronoun, question phrase or topic phrase, that stranding is possible in OE. Allen's account for this is that two fundamentally different syntactic processes are involved. P-relatives in OE involve movement of the relative pronoun, but C-relatives, with no overt relative pronouns, involve deletion of the relativized argument in place. Movement out of prepositional phrases, stranding the preposition, is not allowed, but deletion of the prepositional object is. This accounts for the asymmetries observed. Kiparsky (1995a: 150) takes up this non-movement analysis of C-relatives as well, and claims that a number of differences between C-relatives and P-relatives in OE, with respect to preposition stranding, the possibility of resumptive pronouns, differences in the size of the syntactic domain over which they can operate, and others, support such an analysis.

Letting the OE asymmetry guide our expectations, we might expect that P-relatives elsewhere in GMC will disallow stranding, and that C-relatives, on the other hand, will allow it. These expectations are only partially borne out, failing, in some languages, in both directions (see Allen 1980b: 313). On the one hand, it does seem to be the case that other languages sharing with OE a set of relative pronouns derived from demonstratives (the D-relative languages) do not allow stranding, but require pied-piping. This was true of GO, for example, and still appears to be true of Modern GE and Modern DU. On the other hand, as we shall see, it is not true in general of those languages in which D-relatives have been supplanted by W-relatives.

Correspondingly, stranding in C-relatives, which was quite generally possible in OE, also appears in some other languages with C-relatives.

(6.125) a. Hunden som vi så   på
            the dog that we looked at
            (BN, Haugen 1982: 172)

         b. ek skal fá þér annat, þat er þú megir vel fara á til Íslands
            I shall get you another, that ER you may well go on to Iceland
            (ON, Heusler 1967: 162)

         c. Teir funnu eitt reiður, sum trý   egg   vóru í
            they found a   nest   that three eggs were in
            (FA, Lockwood 1964: 122)

However, as Allen (1980b: 313) notes, this does not hold true for YI. YI, as noted above, has C-relatives, in which the complementizer derives from a former relative pronoun (Lowenstamm 1977). Here, when the relativized constituent in a relative clause introduced by *vos* is the object of a preposition, the preposition cannot be stranded, but must take a resumptive pronoun in its complement position.

(6.125) d. der mentsh, vos mit im hob ikh geredt, iz meyn khaver
the person *vos* with him have I spoken is my friend
(YI, Weinreich 1971: 331)

In this respect, YI is different from AF. The *wat*-relatives of AF, which were argued, like YI *vos* relatives, to involve a complementizer derived from a W-relative pronoun, do allow stranding.

(6.125) e. lede wat sy mee gepraat het
members *wat* she with spoken has
(AF, Ponelis 1993: 189)

Conversely, an innovative group of modern GMC languages has come to allow stranding as a general option not only in C-relatives, but also in P-relatives, as well as other "fronting" constructions, such as questions and topic sentences. This group consists of EN, AF and the Scandinavian languages.

(6.126) a. king Alla, which I spak of yore...
king Alla, which I spoke of before...
(ME, Chaucer, Allen 1980a: 229)

b. en ven, hvem man kan stole på
a friend that one can rely on
(DA, Koefoed 1958: 176)

c. Vem bodde han hos?
who stayed he with?
(SW)

d. Watter vakke is jy voor verantwoordelik?
which subjects are you for responsible?
(AF, Ponelis 1993: 354)

Thus, while there may have been a correlation in GMC between C-relatives and stranding on the one hand and pied-piping and P-relatives on the other, in modern GMC we find both C-relatives in which stranding is disallowed and P-relatives in which stranding is possible.

While OE did not generally allow stranding in question and topic constructions like those in (6.124c, d), there was a marginal exception, apparently common to all West GMC languages. While it was impossible to strand prepositions when topicalizing a full NP, as in (6.124d), it was allowable to strand them when topicalizing a pronoun, as in:

(6.127) a. and him man gebrōhte ðā tō fela bedridan menn
and him one brought then to many bedridden men
'And him, one brought many bedridden men to'
(OE, Ælfric, Allen 1980a: 53)

This, as Allen notes (1980a: 53ff.), correlates with another difference between these two kinds of prepositional objects; full noun phrases occurring as objects of prepositions obligatorily follow their prepositions. On the other hand, personal pronouns occurring as objects of prepositions are allowed to precede those prepositions. Both of these cases are illustrated in (6.127b). Allen concludes that stranding is possible for just those prepositional objects which can precede their prepositions.

(6.127) b. oð   ðæt hī   ealle becōmon <u>ðurh ða clypunga</u>   <u>him tō</u>
              until that they all   came   through the calling   him to
              'until they all came to him because of the calling'
              (OE, Ælfric, St. Edmund)

OE is not alone in admitting stranding under these circumstances. Other West GMC languages like DU, GE and FR, while not allowing preposition stranding as a general possibility, do allow it in the case of prepositional objects which precede the preposition. So, for example, in DU, question pronouns of a type which follow their prepositions, as in (6.127d), are not separated from those prepositions, while those which precede their prepositions in "R-compounds," as in (6.127c), can be separated from their prepositions (Vat 1978).[12] See also the FR example in (6.107b).

(6.127) c. Waar denk je an?
             what think you about?
             (DU, Hoekstra 1995: 96)

---

[12] FR, unlike DU and GE, appears to allow stranding not just in the R-stranding case, as in (ii), but even when the fronted pronoun is not of the sort which follows the associated preposition, as in (iii), and even when the fronted phrase is a full NP, as in (iv).

  (i)   Njonken wa   hast   justerjûn sitten?
         next-to whom have-you yesterday sat?
         (FR, Tiersma 1999: 107)

  (ii)   Wêr   hast   justerjûn njonken sitten?
         who-R have-you yesterday next-to sat?
         (FR, Tiersma 1999: 1)

  (iii) Wa hast   justerjûn njonken sitten?
         who have you yesterday near   sat?
         (FR, Tiersma 1999: 107)

  (iv)   Hokker kandidaat stimme jimme op?
         which candidate vote   you   for?
         (FR, Hoekstra 1995: 97)

Such sentences are impossible elsewhere in continental West GMC. Hoekstra argues that cases like these in FR do not actually involve preposition stranding, but rather an empty resumptive pronoun in the position of object of the preposition.

d. *Wie heb je mee gepraat?
   who have you with talked?
   (DU, Hoekstra 1995: 105)

Because of the special morphological shape such pre-prepositional pronouns sometimes take (e.g., *waar* instead of *wat* in 6.127c), Ponelis calls such stranding of prepositions "R-stranding," to distinguish it from "plain stranding" – the more general possibility of stranding found in some languages in which even post-prepositional objects are separated from their prepositions. R-stranding appears to be a common West GMC possibility. OE allows R-stranding in all sorts of fronting constructions, including questions and topic-initial sentences, while plain-stranding is limited to C-Relatives, as in (6.124a).[13]

Among the modern languages, EN, AF and the Scandinavian languages allow 'plain stranding,' while DU, YI and GE either do not allow stranding in P-relatives at all or allow only R-stranding. The more complicated case of FR is discussed in note 12. Hoekstra (1995) concludes that it, too, allows only R-stranding, appearances notwithstanding. Are there generalizations to be made about this distribution? One fact we have noted is that the original D-pronouns of GMC do not seem to allow plain stranding (e.g., in OE and GE). This generalization only works in one direction, however, since there are also some languages (e.g., DU) in the non-stranding group which have introduced W-forms in the position of object of preposition, and yet still do not allow stranding. Second, we note that the languages which do not allow plain stranding in P-relatives have in some cases preserved the OV subordinate clause order of early GMC, while the languages which allow plain stranding include those which have become systematically VO in subordinate clauses. In fact, under some accounts, the shift in word order is claimed to be an essential step in the development of the stranding possibility (e.g., Lightfoot 1991: 120). However, YI has also undergone the OV to VO shift, yet it does not allow stranding of prepositions, so the shift in verb order is apparently not a sufficient condition for the development of stranding. Conversely, AF retains embedded-clause OV word order, and yet allows plain stranding. Ponelis attributes the rise of stranding in AF to EN influence, though, so we may be dealing with a contact phenomenon here. Finally, we note that (again excepting AF) the languages with plain stranding are ones whose ancestors had a long-standing, robust C-relative strategy (OE *þe*, ON *som*), which could also be used for relativizing objects of prepositions, and in which stranding has always been possible (and in fact required). It may therefore be that stranding in the

---

[13] Vat (1978) argues that these cases too are in fact covert instances of R-stranding. The interested reader is referred to that paper.

P-relatives and questions in these languages was an analogical generalization from the C-relative constructions to which it is native. That is, 'the man who you talked to' was licensed analogically by 'the man that you talked to'. Cf. Dekeyser 1990: 92, who gives an early example of stranding with a P-relative from the thirteenth-century text of Layamon's *Brut*, but claims that stranding with P-relatives was rare until Late ME.

6.5.1.7.3 **Alternation with 0-relative clauses** Many of the GMC languages allow 0-relative clauses – that is, relative clauses which are not introduced by either a relative pronoun or a complementizer.

(6.128)   a. Gevið hesum manni tann ans,   hann eigur uppibornan
                  give this   man   the attention he   has   earned
                  (FA, Lockwood 1964: 122)

            b. Sir, be þe faith i haue to yow
               sir, by the faith I have to you
               (EME, Cursor M. , Fischer 1992: 308)

            c. den bog som/0 du gav mig
               the book that/0 you gave me
               (DA)

This is possible in SW, DA, NO and Middle and Modern EN. Unintroduced relatives are not possible, on the other hand, in Modern GE or DU. One generalization that possibly emerges here is that 0-relatives tend to appear in languages which have C-relatives, and not in those which do not, and from this it appears reasonable to conclude (as many investigators do) that the 0-relative is not a separate type, but simply a C-relative in which the complementizer is deleted (see Dekeyser 1990: 100, for example). Again, however, the correlation is not seamless. On the one hand, there are some languages in which I have argued that C-relatives exist, but in which 0-relatives do not. These include first of all the three languages in which it has been claimed that relative complementizers have arisen in fairly recent times from W-forms, namely, Bavarian, YI and AF. The list also includes OE, however, where C-relatives (with þe) existed from the earliest times, but where 0-relatives are virtually unattested.

    Conversely, 0-relatives, while not frequent in any of the older GMC languages, seem to be much more abundant in some texts in OHG (particularly the poetry of Otfrid) than in ON or OE, even though OHG has no developed complementizer strategy for relativization (see Behaghel 1928: III, 742).

(6.128)   d. thiu thing wir hiar nu sagetun
               the things we here now said
               (OHG, Otfrid, Erdmann 1874: 127)

6.5.1.7.4 **Resumptive pronouns** In some languages, under some conditions, the position relativized can be realized as a resumptive pronoun rather than a gap, and it has been claimed for some of these languages that the availability of the resumptive pronoun option depends on whether the relative clause is a C-relative or a P-relative. Traugott (1992: 229) and Kiparsky (1995a: 151) point out that in OE, resumptive pronouns seem to be restricted for the most part to C-relatives, as in (6.129a) (where they occur with some frequency). Kiparsky uses this as one of his arguments that OE C-relatives do not involve movement of a relative pronoun. Resumptive pronouns are not wholly unattested in relative clauses of the *se(-þe)* type (see Wülfing 1894: I, 410; Seppänen 2004: 84), but they are quite rare there.

(6.129)   a. se god þe þis his bēacen wæs
               the god that this his sign   was
               'the God whose sign this was'
               (OE, cited in Kiparsky 1995a: 151)

Thus, at least in OE, there seems to be a correlation between C-relatives and the possibility of resumptive pronouns. In fact, this state of affairs seems to have continued throughout the ME period (cf. Visser 1963: 58ff.):

(6.129)   b. Our Lord that jn hevene ne Erthe he hath non pere
               our Lord that in heaven nor earth he has no   peer
               (ME, Merlin, Visser 1963: 59)

Looking across the family, we find such a correlation in at least one other language. Resumptive pronouns are fully grammatical in the YI *vos*-relatives in (6.88j, k), for instance, though apparently disallowed in relative constructions with *velxn*, *vemen* (Jacobs 2005: 236). The possibility of the resumptive pronoun was presented in that section as one of the arguments that *vos* is a particle and not a fronted relative pronoun.

Resumptive pronouns are also usual in *som*-relative clauses in SW (Zaenen and Maling 1982), though under quite different syntactic circumstances. The difference has to do with how deeply embedded the relativized position must be before it can be realized as a resumptive pronoun. OE and YI allow resumptive pronouns in very "shallow" positions – objects, and even subjects, of the relative clause – while in SW,

458   6 *The syntax of the clause*

according to Zaenen and Maling, the resumptive pronoun cannot be closer than two clauses away from its antecedent.

(6.129)   c.   *Här är boken   som jag läste den
                 here is book-the that I   read it
                 (SW, Zaenen and Maling 1982: 224)

In SW, moreover, the possibility of a resumptive pronoun does not correlate with the absence of pronoun fronting, since it is possible to get resumptives in W-questions:

(6.129)   d.   Vem undrade   alla om han skulle komma i   tid?
                 who wondered all   if   he would come   on time?
                 (SW, Zaenen and Maling 1982: 224)

This suggests that there are two different types of resumptive pronoun in GMC: the shallow type, found in YI and in OE, which appears to be freely available even in simple relative clauses, and the deep type found in SW, which is restricted to complex constructions – particularly in those where the position relativized or questioned is found in a "syntactic island," such as the embedded question in (6.129d). In these cases, the pronoun has been claimed to serve a specific function: facilitating the processing of complex structures (cf. Zaenen and Maling 1982).

The situation of Modern EN differs from that of SW essentially only in degree. As in SW, resumptive pronouns in shallow positions, as in (6.129d), are entirely ill formed, while the deep kind are not infrequently heard, though generally judged as marginal. Again, the judgments seem to be independent of whether the construction is a P-relative or a C-relative. Both are equally well (or ill) formed.

6.5.1.7.5 **Boundedness differences**   It has long been recognized that relativization is sometimes subject to restrictions on the types of syntactic boundaries that are allowed to intervene between the head/relative pronoun on the left edge of the construction and the relativized position (the gap). For example, in EN it is not possible for the relativized position to be inside a more deeply embedded relative clause.

(6.130)   a.   *This is the car which I know the [the man [that bought [ ]]

Beginning with Ross (1968), these restrictions have been known as island constraints, and the configurations from within which relativization is prohibited are called syntactic islands.

On the other hand, it has also long been noted that these constraints do not apply in a uniform way across languages. In the modern Scandinavian languages, for example, sentences like (6.130b, c) are fully well formed. For a full discussion of

6.5 Relative clauses, questions and other fronting constructions 459

(the absence of) island constraints in Scandinavian, see the papers in Engdahl and Ejerhed 1982.

(6.130)   b. I går såg jag en film som jag redan glömt vem som __regisserat__
yesterday saw I a film that I have already forgotten who that_directed_
(SW, Engdahl 1982: 153)

            c. her er en bok som jeg ikke har møtt noen som __ har lest__
here is a book that I not have met anyone that __has read__
(NO, Taraldsen 1982: 205)

In at least one case, it has been claimed that sensitivity to syntactic islands depends on the P-relative/C-relative difference; Kiparsky (1995a: 150) has claimed that in OE it was possible to relativize positions within syntactic islands, such as relative clauses, but only in C-relatives.

(6.130)   d. Ac for þǣm hē genēðde swīðost over þone munt ðe hē wiste þæt
Flamineus se consul wiende þæt hē buton sorge mehte on þǣm
wintersetle gewunian
but because he ventured most quickly over the mountain that he knew
that Flamineus the consul thought that he might dwell on in winter
quarters without care
(OE, Orosius 188:30, cited in Kiparsky 1995a: 151)

And, in fact, it seems that the correlation holds up in certain cases; in languages with only P-relatives, relativization is constrained by island constraints. However, the correlation breaks down in Modern EN, where C-relatives, as well as P-relatives, are sensitive to island constraints. Thus, replacing the pronoun *which* in (6.130a) with the complementizer *that* still results in ungrammaticality.

6.5.1.8   *Other cases of pied-piping and stranding*

Section 6.5.1.7.2 considered variation across GMC with respect to whether, in the case of relative or interrogative pronouns which function as the understood objects of prepositions, the preposition appears together with the pronoun at the front of the clause (the pied-piping case) or whether only the pronoun appears at the front of the clause, separated from the preposition (the stranding case). More generally, we speak of pied-piping when a movement operation moves not only the specified element X (a relative pronoun or question phrase, for example) in a configuration like [$_{YP}$...X...], but also the phrase YP which contains it. When only X is moved, leaving the containing phrase behind, we speak of stranding. Besides the case where YP is a prepositional phrase, there are several others, and the possibility of stranding or pied-piping varies across languages and across syntactic categories. Stranding appears to be the more usual possibility. So, for example, when the relative pronoun is understood to be the complement of an adjective, the adjective phrase is always stranded, not pied-piped.

(6.131)   a. *This is the boy/John, [proud of whom] his father is

            b. *Hier ist der Junge/Hans, [stolz auf den]   sein Vater ist
                here is the child/Hans   proud of whom his father is
                (GE)

Besides the case of prepositional objects discussed above, in fact there are only two other cases in which pied-piping is found, and in which, therefore, the pronoun appears at the left periphery of the clause not by itself, but contained within a larger phrase. Van Riemsdijk (1982) observes that GE infinitival clauses can appear along with their objects at the front of the clause in (non-restrictive) relative clauses of the following sort (cf. also Ross 1968: 113). Pied-piping here is optional.

(6.132)   Jetzt hat er sich endlich den Wagen, [den zu kaufen] er sich schon lange
            vorgenommen hatte, leisten können
            now he has finally the car [which to buy] he had planned for a long
            time afford been-able
            'Now he has finally been able to afford the car which he had been
            planning to buy for a long time'
            (GE, van Riemsdijk 1982)

The only other instances of pied-piping involve cases where the containing phrase is a NP. The behavior of NPs with respect to stranding or pied-piping is quite complicated, and depends on both the position in the NP that the relative pronoun or question word occupies, and the position of that NP in the sentence. There are also differences between relative clauses and questions with respect to pied-piping in these cases. In most GMC languages, relatives or question words occurring as prenominal possessors within NPs must pied-pipe the NP containing them. Stranding is disallowed:

(6.133)   a. *[Whose] did you see [[]pictures]?

In GO, stranding was arguably possible here, as in (6.133b), though we cannot tell for sure that this is a native GO construction, since the constituent order corresponds exactly to that of the Greek.

(6.133)   b. [ƕis]   habaiþ [[ ] manleikan]?
                whose has-it   image?
                (GO, Luke 20:24)

6.5 Relative clauses, questions and other fronting constructions

However, native texts in other early GMC languages seem to confirm that possessors were more readily separable from the nouns they modified than they are in the modern languages. They are often separated from the associated NP in OE, for example:

(6.133)   c.   nā þū [mīnne] þearft [[ ] hafalan] hȳdan
               not you my   need   head   to-hide
               (OE, Beowulf 445)

           d.   [ende [ ]] gebīdan [worulde līfes]
               end   to-await of-worldly life
               (OE, Beowulf 2342)

Stranding of NPs in relative clauses is more generally possible when the relative pronoun is associated with a complement position inside the NP:

(6.134)   a.   die vestings   [waarvan] 'n mens   vandag nog [die mure] kan sien
               the fortresses whereof   a person today   still the walls can see
               (AF, Ponelis 1993: 190)

           b.   Reports [which] the government prescribes [the height of the [lettering on the [covers of...]]]
               (Ross 1968: 109)

In these cases, pied-piping of the containing NP is also possible, and in the case of constructions like (6.134d), where the relative pronoun is contained in multiple NPs, any of the containing NPs can be pied-piped.

(6.134)   c.   die vestings, [die mure waaarvan] 'n mens vandag nog kan sien
               (Ponelis 1993: 190)

           d.   Reports [the lettering on the covers of which] the government prescribes the height...

Pied-piping in questions is much more constrained than pied-piping in relative clauses. Neither GE infinitive pied-piping nor NP pied-piping like that in (6.134 c, d) is possible in questions:

(6.135)   a.   *[Was zu kaufen] hatte er sich schon lange vorgenommen?
                  What to buy   had   he for a long   time   intended?

           b.   *[Covers of what] does the government regulate?

In general, question phrases may pied-pipe a NP in the GMC languages only if they are in the pre-head genitive position within that NP (*Whose pictures did you see?*, but not **Pictures of whom did you see?*). Pied-piping is generally obligatory in the former case, and stranding is disallowed. There is, however, one unusual but rather widespread phenomenon in GMC in which movement of a question element in the pre-head position in a NP results in stranding of that NP. Following den Besten (1985), we can call this phenomenon *wat-voor*-split. GE and DU exhibit complex interrogative specifiers consisting of an interrogative pronoun (*wat/was*) and an etymological preposition (*voor/für*), the latter having apparently lost its status as a preposition, since it no longer determines the case of the following NP. The two elements together mean 'what kind of'.

(6.136)   a.   [Wat voor romans] heeft hij geschreven?
               what for novels has he written?
               (DU, den Besten 1985: 34)

As (6.136a) shows, this interrogative specifier can pied-pipe its NP, but, in contrast with the general impossibility of extracting an element from a prenominal position within a NP, the *wat/was* can also be extracted here, stranding the NP:

(6.136)   b.   [Wat] heeft hij [voor romans] geschreven?
               (Du, den Besten 1985: 34)

In addition to DU and GE, the construction is also found in YI (Jacobs *et al.* 1994: 413) and Low GE (Lindow *et al.* 1998: 296). A similar construction is also found in SW (Anward 1982: 53) and NO (Lie 1982: 195). Lie characterizes it as a loan from Middle Low GE, still dialectically restricted in NO.

(6.136)   c.   [Vad för (en) soffa] sov han i?
               what for (a) sofa slept he in
               'What sofa did he sleep in?'
               (SW, Anward 1982: 54)

               d.   [Vad] sov han i för (en) soffa?
                   What slept he in [for (a) sofa]?
                   'What sofa did he sleep in?'
                   (SW, Anward 1982: 53)

6.5.1.9 *Special properties of subject relativization*

Across the GMC languages, one frequently encounters special syntactic behavior when the gap in a relative clause is in subject position, adjacent to a complementizer. We may divide these into two types. On the one hand, there are special forms which can be employed only when relativizing subjects. We have seen at least one instance of this type: in GO, the special relative markers *izei* and *sei*, which I have identified as agreeing complementizers, are used only for subject relativization (as are their

6.5 Relative clauses, questions and other fronting constructions

apparent counterparts, West Flemish *die* and French *qui*). Possibly also to be included here is the DA *der* 'there', homophonous with the presentational subject expletive, which can appear only when the subject is being relativized. It is optional, but when it is used, the relative complementizer *som* is not used:

(6.137) a. Her er drengen, som/der reddede sin søster fra   at drukne
             here is boy-the that/*der* saved   his sister from to drown
             (DA, Koefoed 1958: 176)

The temptation here is to take *der* to be either a relative pronoun or a resumptive pronoun in the subject position (under a non-movement analysis). However, both of these are counterindicated by the fact that it also shows up in embedded questions, where it co-occurs with a fronted question pronoun (again, just in the case of questioning the subject):

(6.137) b. Vi ved hvem der taler   med Marit
             we know who   *der* speaks with Marit
             (DA, Taraldsen 1986b: 153)

The fact that it can co-occur with a pronoun fronted from subject position, but cannot co-occur with the complementizer *som*, suggests the possibility that it too is a member of the class of agreeing complementizers, deployed just in case of subject gaps.

On the other hand, there are numerous instances of options which exist for the relativization of all nonsubject positions, but which are disallowed exactly in the case of subject relativization. One such case is found, for example, in GO, in relative clauses modifying universal pronouns of the 'whoever/whatever/wherever' type. When nonsubject positions are relativized in these, the relativized clause is normally introduced by the invariant complementizer *þei*:

(6.138) a. bidei mik þishvizuh þei wileis
             ask me whatever that you-want
             (GO, Mark 6:22)

         b. þishvaduh þei gaggaiþ   in   gard ...
             wherever that you-may-go into house...
             (GO, Mark 6:10)

         c. þishvammeh **sa**-ei   habaiþ gibada imma
             to-whomever who-that has   is-given to-him
             (GO, Mark 4:25)

         d. þishvah **þat**-ei   ist sunjein...
             whatever which-that is true...
             (GO, Phil. 4:8)

The nativeness of this pattern is supported by its independence from the Greek model for translation. Thus, it appears that in GO, subject relativization required either a relative pronoun or an agreeing complementizer, as *izei* has been argued to be. An ordinary complementizer could not appear adjacent to the position of the relativized subject. Applying the label by which this phenomenon has been known descriptively for many years, we may say that GO exhibits (a version of) the "*that*-trace effect." The phenomenon is so called because of the observation that in many languages, the gap (a "trace" of movement, in some analyses) in a relative or topic or question construction cannot be adjacent to (certain kinds of) complementizers. The phenomenon is evident in EN in asymmetries like the following, for example.

(6.138)   e. The   man who I think he saw [t] was your father
          f. *The man who I think that [t] saw him was your father

Descriptively, the gap in the relative clause cannot be in the subject position, adjacent to a *that* complementizer. (Omission of the *that* makes the sentence well formed.) While sharing something in common, these special requirements for subject relativization demonstrate intriguing variation across languages. For example, the EN facts are not quite parallel to those of GO. In EN, the effect disappears if the complementizer is in turn adjacent to the head of the relative construction. Thus, there is no *that*-trace effect in (6.138g).

(6.138)   g.   The man that [] saw him was your father

In GO, on the other hand, a bare complementizer apparently could not introduce a relative clause with subject relativization even when it would be adjacent to the head of the construction. Overt relative pronouns were apparently required even in that position, as in (6.138c, d). Moreover, in the EN case the ill-formedness can be eliminated by dropping the complementizer, while GO apparently did not allow complementizer-drop.

A comparable, though still different, subject/nonsubject asymmetry shows up in the Scandinavian languages; in SW (as well as other Scandinavian languages) *som* is freely omissible in nonsubject relativization, as in (6.138h).

(6.138)   h. Vi talade on   människor som/0 vi inte längre umgås med
             we talked about people   that   we no longer see
             (SW, Anward 1982: 58)

          i. Vi talade om   upplevelser som/*0 trotsar all beskrivning
             we talked about experiences that   defy   all description
             (SW, Anward 1982: 58)

However, the *som* cannot be left out in the case of subject relativization, as in (6.138i). Similar facts obtain in other continental Scandinavian languages, and, as the following examples show, the pattern holds true of questions as well as relative clauses:

(6.139)   a. Vi vet   hvem som/*0 snakker med Marit
                We know who   that/ *0 speaks   with Marit
                (NO, Taraldsen 1986b: 150)

               b. Vi vet   hvem som/0 Marit snakker med
                We know who   that /0 Marit speaks   with

FA, by contrast, allows deletion even in the case of subject relativization:

(6.139)   c. tær konurnar, 0   heima skuldu vera, eru burturstaddar
                the women   should be at   home are away
                (FA, Lockwood 1964: 122)

The continental Scandinavian restriction on *som* deletion next to a subject gap in a relative clause seems to find a close parallel in Modern Standard EN, though one of rather recent origin; relative *that* (the *that* introducing the relative clause) can be deleted freely in instances of nonsubject relativization, as in (6.139d), but it cannot be deleted in instances of subject relativization:

(6.139)   d. The man (that) you saw is his father
               e. The man *(that) saw you is his father

That drop was possible here in ME and into the Modern EN period (6.139f, g). It is now impossible for most speakers of Standard EN, however, though still possible in various EN dialects (6.139h). (See Bever and Langendoen 1972 for further discussion on the history of this construction.)

(6.139)   f. He sente after a cherl was in the toun
                (ME, Chaucer, C.T., cited in Bever and Langendoen 1972: 56)

               g. I had several men died in my ship
                (eighteenth-century EN, Swift, cited in Bever and Langendoen 1972: 58)

               h. I got some kin people lived up there
                (Appalachian EN, Wolfram and Christian 1976: 121)

Finally, we should make mention again of the fact that the W-relative pronouns of ME were first introduced only in oblique positions, spreading from there to object positions, and then, only toward the end of the ME period, to subject positions. Thus, there was a (relatively brief) period in the history of the language during which subjects were the only arguments which could not be relativized by means of relative pronouns.

In summary, we see the following special treatments of subject relatives in GMC: some languages have forms which can only be used for subject relativization. These include GO *izei/sei*, West Flemish *die*, and DA *der*. In some, subject relativization is prohibited from positions adjacent to (non-relative) complementizers. This *that*-trace effect shows up, though in rather different ways, in GO and in EN. Finally, the Modern Scandinavian languages, as well as Modern EN, prohibit the omission of (relative) complementizers in cases of subject relativization.

6.5.1.10 *Free relatives and attraction*

As we have seen, relative constructions usually have NP heads, which the relative clause is understood to modify. Demonstrative pronouns, like other NPs, can serve as the heads of relative constructions. In case the language in question has D-relatives, demonstrative heads will be homophonous with the relative pronoun, as in:

(6.140)   a. ak bi þans þanz-ei atgaft mis
                but for those who-that you-gave to-me
                (GO, John 17:9)

All of the GMC languages, however, also exhibit constructions in which one of the two pronouns is unexpressed, as in:

(6.140)   b. jah athaihait þanzei wilda is
                and he-called who-*ei* wanted he
                'And he called whom he wanted'
                (GO, Mark 3:13)

Such constructions are often called free relative constructions. They are also sometimes referred to as headless relative constructions, though the question of whether the sole pronoun in such constructions (for which I will adopt the neutral label "pivot") is a relative pronoun inside the relative clause or a demonstrative head belonging to the main clause has been a matter of controversy (Bresnan and Grimshaw 1978; Groos and van Riemsdijk 1981; Harbert 1982, for example). The details of the relevant argumentation, especially for the modern languages, are too complex to pursue here, and the correct answer may in fact vary from one language to another. For example, the pivot in GO free relatives clearly seems to belong to the relative clause, since it is routinely preceded by prepositions belonging to the relative clause, as in (6.140c), and can show up in a case determined by its role in the relative clause, as in (6.140d).

6.5 Relative clauses, questions and other fronting constructions 467

(6.140) c. ushafjands ana þammei lag,   galaiþ in gard seinana
                picking up on what-*ei* he-lay, went into yard his
                'Picking up what he was lying on, he went into his yard'
                (GO, Luke 5:25)

   d. þammei   leitil fraletada   leitil frijod
      whom-Dat-*ei* little is-forgiven little loves
      'The one to whom little is forgiven loves little'
      (GO, Luke 7:47)

On the other hand, in OE, the pivot in free relatives does not appear in the case appropriate to the role of the relative pronoun in the relative clause, but always in the case appropriate to a demonstrative head of the relative construction, as determined by the role of the NP which it heads in the main clause (see Allen 1980a:108).[14]

(6.140) e. befæste hē ðā lāre þǣm   þe   [ ] his wordum ne gelīefan
                confirm he the teaching to-those-Dat that [ ] his words not believed
                'Let him confirm his teaching to-those that didn't believe his words'
                (OE, CP 25, 2, cited in Allen 1980a: 108)

Thus, it appears that the pivot in free relatives in GO is a relative pronoun, and not a demonstrative head (for further arguments, see Harbert 1992), while in OE, it appears to be the demonstrative head of the relative construction.

The status of the pivot in GO as a relative pronoun, however, is obscured somewhat by the phenomenon of attraction; while the pivot does often appear in the case appropriate to the lower clause, as in (6.140d), it can, under specific circumstances, appear instead in the case appropriate to the role of the whole NP in the main clause, as in (6.141a).

(6.141) a. þaimei   iupa   sind fraþjaiþ
                which-Dat-*ei* upwards are think-on
                'Think on those things which are above'
                (GO, Col. 3:2)

---

[14] When the free relative construction is in "Left-Dislocated" position, the pivot does show up in the case appropriate to the role of the relative pronoun in the relative clause:

(i)   And ðone   ðe ðū hæfst, nis   sē   ðīn were
         and that-one-Acc that you have not-is he-Nom your husband
         (OE, Alc. P.V. 37, Allen 1980a: 111)

It is likely that such instances of apparently Left-Dislocated relative constructions are in fact correlative constructions, of the sort discussed in Section 6.5.3.

468   6 The syntax of the clause

Which of the two competing cases appears on the pivot is determined as follows: when the case appropriate to the whole NP, as determined by its role in the main clause, and the case expected of the relative pronoun, by virtue of its role in the subordinate clause, are different, the pivot in GO free relative constructions appears in whichever of those two cases is rightmost on a Case Hierarchy of the form Nom<Acc<Dat/Gen. In (6.140d), the subordinate clause verb requires dative case and the matrix clause requires nominative case, since the whole relative construction is the subject of the main clause. Dative case, the more oblique of the two, appears on the pivot. In (6.141a), the subordinate clause requires nominative case, since the relativized position is that of subject of the relative clause, while the main clause requires dative case, since the relative construction is the object of the main clause verb, *fraþjan*, which assigns dative case. In Harbert 1992, arguments are presented showing that the pivot is still a relative pronoun even when it appears in a matrix-clause-determined case, indicating the need for a rule which assigns the matrix case "down into" the relative clause when the Case Hierachy condition requires it. The existence of such a process is confirmed by the fact that it applies in headed relative clauses elsewhere in GMC, for example, in MHG, as in (6.141b), where both the head NP and the relative pronoun are separately represented, and the constituency of the affected relative pronoun is therefore not in doubt. Here, both the head NP and the relative pronoun show up in the genitive appropriate to the role of the head NP. (In GO, attraction is found only in free relatives.)

(6.141)   b.   daz ir   iemer êre   müezet han [des dienstes [des   iu wirt getan]
              that you always honor might have the service-G which-G to-you is done
              (MHG, Karl 9665-6, Bartsch 1857: 255)

Attraction of the sort illustrated is primarily a characteristic of early GMC (though not found in OE), but it has a functional equivalent among the modern GMC languages in the form of matching conditions – a requirement, roughly speaking, that the pivot simultaneously satisfy the case and category requirements of both the main clause and the relative clauses. Under this restriction, for example, in GE, if the relative construction is in a matrix context requiring nominative case but the role of the relativized position in the relative clause is an accusative position, as in (6.142a), the choice of either case on the pivot yields ill-formedness. On the other hand, when both clauses require the same case, as in (6.142b) the result is well formed.[15]

---

[15] This is a constraint that is sensitive only to superficial case forms; where a neuter pivot appears in a context in which the matrix clause requires nominative and the embedded clause accusative, it can satisfy both since the two forms are homophonous:

(i)   Was er kaufte, dauerte nicht lange
            what he bought lasted   not   long
            (GE)

(6.142) a. *Wen/*Wer   du siehst ist gerade eingekommen
             whom-Acc/who-Nom you see   is just   come in
             'The one whom you see has just come in'
             (GE)

         b. Ich nehme, wen   du   empfiehlst
             I   take   whom you recommend
             (GE)

When the relativized argument in the embedded clause is a prepositional phrase but the relative construction is the object of a transitive main clause verb, which requires NP objects, the sentence is also bad. The phrase containing the pivot must satisfy the category requirements of both the lower verb and the higher clause. Thus, (6.142c), the literal translation of GO (6.140c) is ungrammatical in GE (or EN). Note that (6.142d), in which the preposition has been stranded and only the relative pronoun has been fronted, is good.

(6.142) c. *Er nahm, auf was/worauf er lag
             *he took   on what   he lay
             (GE)

         d. He picked up what he was lying on

The pivot thus appears to have to satisfy both the requirements of the main clause (as if it were the head of the relative construction) and the embedded clause (as if it were the relative pronoun). This apparent split allegiance of course contributes to the difficulty of determining which clause it belongs to syntactically, and arguments have been mounted for both analyses. The syntax of these matching constraints is discussed in detail in Bresnan and Grimshaw 1978, Groos and van Riemsdijk 1981, Harbert 1982, Suñer 1984, Grosu 1996 and Vogel 2001, 2002. Both attraction and matching can be understood functionally as strategies for insuring that grammatical information about both the relative head and the relative pronoun will be signaled, even though only one of them is overtly represented.

As we can see from the above examples, another way in which free relatives differ from each other across the GMC languages involves the etymology of the pivot. Some of them, like GO and OE, use D-forms as pivots, while others, including all of the modern languages, have W-forms.[16]

---

[16] FR is a bit odd here in that the choice of demonstratives or interrogatives in these free relative constructions is dependent on the animacy of the head.

(i)   dy't in misdied docht, moat straft wurde
         who a crime   does should be punished
         (FR, Tiersma 1999: 122)

(ii)   Wat men net te plak bringt, wurd gau wei
         what you don't put away   is   soon lost
         (FR, Tiersma 1999: 123)

470   6 *The syntax of the clause*

(6.143) a. Þú lætr aldre þinn hlut, viþ huern sem þú átt um
you never surrender your portion, with whomever you are dealing
(ON, Heusler 1967: 157)

b. wat men net te plak bringt, wurdt gau wei
what one doesn't put away is soon lost
(FR, Tiersma 1999: 123)

c. vi gör vad vi kan
we do what we can
(SW, Granberry 1991: 42)

d. hva du ikke vet, har du ikke vondt av
what you don't know won't hurt you
(BN, Askedal 1994: 264)

In at least some of the latter, the W-forms appear to have arisen historically by successive reduction of generalizing ('whatever') type relative constructions of the form 'so what so', which appear to have been common to the West GMC languages:

(6.143)

e. Fæder and Mōder mōtan heora bearn to swā hwylcum cræfte gedōn
father and mother may their children to whichever craft put
swā him lēofost byð
as to-them most preferable is
(OE, Ælfric, P. XIX 54, Allen 1980a: 114)

f. só uúer só izzit fon thesemo brote
so who so eats of this bread
(OHG, Tatian (Sievers) 82, 10)

The W-form here appears to belong to the matrix clause, as indicated by the fact that it can be preceded by a preposition of matrix clause origin, as in (6.143e), but never by one of embedded clause origin. (Cf. Allen 1980a: 114, Dal 1966: 200, Behaghel 1923: I, 369, all of whom concur that the relative clause proper begins with the second *swā/ so*.) The development from these constructions to the W-form free relatives of Modern GE is schematized by Behaghel in the following way:

(6.143)   g. so wer so → so wer → swer → wer

These W-form free relatives have in part inherited the generic meaning of the earlier 'so-what-so' constructions, and are accordingly used in gnomic statements like (6.143h, i). However, they can also have individual reference, as in (6.143j):

6.5 Relative clauses, questions and other fronting constructions 471

(6.143)   h. Who(ever) steals my purse steals trash
              i. I take what(ever) I can get
              j. I like what you are wearing

6.5.1.11 Infinitival relative and interrogative constructions

Modern EN admits relative clauses with infinitive verbs:

(6.144)   a. I found a topic about which to write

These Modern EN infinitival relatives admit overt relative pronouns only in the case of relativization of a prepositional object, and only when the preposition is pied-piped, rather than stranded. Infinitival relatives involving the relativization of "direct-case" positions – subjects, direct objects and prepositional objects with stranding – do not allow relative pronouns. The distribution of relative pronouns in these is thus reminiscent of the pattern found in EME finite relative clauses (6.5.1.5.3) – relative pronouns in prepositional object positions, but not in direct case positions. Relativization of possessors does not appear to be possible at all in infinitival relatives (6.144e).

(6.144)   b. I found a man (*who) to fix the sink
              c. I found a man (*who) to hire
              d. I found a man (*who) to talk to
              e. *I found a man whose car to borrow

These contrast with infinitival questions, which are also found in Modern EN, in a variety of ways. When the direct object is being questioned in an infinitival question, the interrogative pronoun, unlike the relative pronoun, appears obligatorily (6.145a). In infinitival questions, moreover, unlike infinitival relatives, the pronoun may occupy a possessor position (6.145c), while infinitival questions about the subject of the infinitive are not possible, with or without a question word (6.145b).

(6.145)   a. I don't know what to fix
              b. *I don't know who to fix the sink
              c. I don't know whose father to invite
              d. I don't know who to talk to/to whom to talk

Christensen (1984) notes the existence of what appear on first consideration to be infinitival relatives in NO. These always lack relative pronouns, and prepositions in them are always stranded.

(6.146)   a. Vi har   funnet en ekspert til å reparere bilen
                we have found an expert to   repair   car-the
                (NO, Christensen 1984: 75)

(6.146)   b. Vi har funnet en bok å lese for barna
we have found a book to read to the children
(NO, Christensen 1984: 75)

c. Vi har funnet en kniv til å skjære brød med
we have found a knife to slice bread with
(NO, Christensen 1984: 75)

d. *Vi har funnet en kniv med hvilken å skjære brød
we have found a knife with which to cut bread
(NO, Christensen 1984: 82)

However, she argues that these are in fact not infinitival relatives but purpose phrases. First of all, they are not admissible in contexts where interpreting them as a purpose clause modifying the action of the main clause is unavailable.

(6.146)   e. *Vi har lest om en ekspert til å reparere bilen
we have read about an expert to repair car-the
(NO, Christensen 1984: 77)

Second, the *til*-phrase in (6.146a) is in fact a constituent of the VP, not of the NP, as evidenced by its distribution in sentences like the following:

(6.146)   f. Til å reparere bilen har vi funnet en ekspert
to repair car-the have we found an expert
(NO, Christensen 1984: 77)

g. *En ekspert til å reparere bilen har nettopp kommet
an expert to repair car-the has just come
(NO, Christensen 1984: 77)

The same considerations would seem to apply to other languages as well. Thus, while GE has sentences like (6.146h), which look like candidates for infinitival relatives, such an analysis is counterindicated by the impossibility of (6.146i), with an infinitival relative on a lexical head in subject position (though GE does allow corresponding constructions with indefinite pronoun heads, as in (6.146j)).

(6.146)   h. Er gab ihr Medizin zu trinken
he gave her medicine to drink
(GE, Tappe 1984: 230)

i. *Ein Mann die Spüle zu reparieren ist an der Tür
a man the sink to fix is at the door
(Tappe 1984: 227)

j. Etwas   zu trinken ist im   Kühlschrank
    something to drink   is in-the refrigerator
    (GE, Tappe 1984: 230)

OE, too, exhibits apparent infinitival relatives (Allen 1980a: 105; Kageyama 1992).

(6.147)   Ic haebbe [mete [tō etenne]] ðone ðe gē nyton
           I have   meat to eat   which that you not-know
           (OE, Alc.P.V.72, cited in Allen 1980a: 105)

The OE constructions differed from those of Modern EN in two ways. First, relative pronouns were never allowed in them. Thus, when the relativized position was object of a preposition, the preposition was always stranded (Allen 1980a: 105). Second, according to Kageyama (1992: 121), citing Visser (1963: 979), there were no infinitival relatives with subject relativization in OE. Miller (2002: 221ff.) argues that these apparent infinitival relatives in OE, too, are in fact infinitival purpose clauses, and that true infinitival relatives emerged only in ME.

Infinitival questions are absent in both GE and the continental Scandinavian languages, but they occur in EN and in AF.

(6.148)   a. *Ich weiß nicht, [wen anzurufen]
              I   know not   whom to call
              (GE, McDaniel 1989: 574)

           b. *Det er unklart [hva å gjøre]
              it is unclear what to do
              (NO, Christensen 1984: 82)

           c. Ek het   nie geweet [wat om te   doen] nie
              I have not known what COMPL to do not
              (AF, Donaldson 1993: 328)

According to Allen (1980a: 212), they did not exist in OE, and became possible only in EME:

(6.149)   ant nuste   hwet seggen
           and not-knew what to-say
           (EME, St. Katherine 1535, Allen 1980a: 213)

6.5.2 Questions

Several aspects of the syntax of questions have been treated earlier, in conjunction with the discussion of the syntax of relative clauses. For example, infinitival questions are discussed in conjunction with infinitival relatives in Section 6.5.1.11, pied-piping/ stranding of prepositions in questions is treated in conjunction with stranding in relative clauses in Section 6.5.1.7.2, and co-occurrence of complementizers and question words is treated in Section 6.5.1.3. The present section will be devoted only to such aspects of interrogative constructions as are unique to those constructions.

Characteristic of all GMC languages is the occurrence of subject/verb or subject/ Aux inversion in questions in at least some contexts. Inversion normally takes place in main clause questions, though Katz (1987: 195) and Lockwood (1995: 122) note that in YI it is more usual than elsewhere to convey interrogative force without inversion, through intonation alone.

In the case of yes/no questions, inversion is usually the only syntactic signal of the interrogative. GO, however, employs a special clause-initial particle -*u* as an interrogative marker in such questions, along with verb fronting. This particle attaches to the right of the first element in the clause (whether main or subordinate), and is treated in Eythórsson 1995: 104ff. as a complementizer.

(6.150)   a. wileiz-u ei qiþaima?
want-2Sg-U that say-1PlSubjunct
'Do you want that we tell?'
(GO, Luke 9:54)

YI, too, often exhibits a yes/no interrogative particle *tsi*, borrowed from Slavic (Lockwood 1995: 122; Jacobs 2005: 229).

(6.150)   b. tsi bistu meshúge gevorn?
Q are you crazy become?
(YI, Lockwood 1995: 122)

It is optional in main clause questions, but obligatory in indirect yes/no questions (Jacobs 2005: 229f.), where it may be translated as *if*.

A question particle could also introduce yes/no questions in ON:

(6.150)   c. hvárt elskar þú mik?
Q love you me?
(ON, Bandle *et al.* 2005: 947, 1157)

The other GMC languages exhibit overt yes/no interrogative complementizers only in subordinate clauses.

(6.150)   d. Vi undrar, om det är möjligt
we wonder if it is possible
(SW, Holmes and Hinchcliffe 1994: 533)

6.5 Relative clauses, questions and other fronting constructions

In most of the family the interrogative complementizer is distinct from other conjunctions, but in EN (*if*) and SW (*om*), it is homophonous with the conjunction used for conditional clauses. In West Flemish (unlike DU, for example), the interrogative conjunction used in indirect yes/no questions can co-occur with the complementizer *dat* (*of dat* 'if that') (Haegeman 1992: 46). In some varieties of EN, including Irish EN, South African EN, African American EN and Appalachian EN, yes/no questions are signaled by inversion rather than by conjunctions even in subordinate clauses:

(6.150)   e. He came to see would we set up a shop
(Irish EN, Harris 1993: 168)

f. I asked him could I come downstairs
(Appalachian EN, Wolfram and Christian 1976: 129)

Main clause WH-questions in GMC languages typically begin with a question phrase followed by a verb or auxiliary, followed by the subject, while in subordinate clauses the order is typically WH-phrase–Subject–Verb. In Irish EN, African American EN and Appalachian EN, however, and optionally in AF, inversion also takes place in subordinate WH-questions:

(6.151)   a. I asked what had she done
(Irish EN, Henry 1995: 116)

b. Momma asked me where have I been
(Appalachian EN, Wolfram and Christian 1976: 129)

c. Ek weet waar bly jy nou/jy   nou bly
   I know where live you now/where you now live
(AF, Donaldson 1993: 371)

Some languages allow (and in fact sometimes require) a complementizer after the question word in subordinate clauses. In DA, for example, the question word must be followed by *der* in the case of subject questions.

(6.151)   d. Ved du, hvem   der har boet i det hus?
       do you know who DER has lived in that house?
(DA, Allan *et al.* 1995: 193)

In general, exactly one question phrase appears at the front in an interrogative clause. In instances in which a single clause contains multiple WH-phrases, only one of them is at the beginning of the clause, while the others remain *in situ*.

(6.152)   a. Who bought what where?

Exceptional in this regard are multiple WH-questions in YI, where more than one such phrase may be fronted to the same clausal periphery. Jacobs *et al.* (1994) note that this feature is shared with many languages of eastern Europe, and so may be an areal feature. This possibility is not found in all dialects of YI. Those that do allow it differ with respect to whether it is allowed in both direct and indirect questions, or only in indirect questions (Jacobs 2005: 231; see also Diesing 2003).

(6.152)　　b.　hot zi nit gekent　　farshteyn　　ver　mit　vemen es shlogt zikh
　　　　　　　　had she not been-able to-understand who with whom it fought self
　　　　　　　　(YI, Jacobs *et al.*1994: 414)

A rather different instance of multiple question phrases is the phenomenon of "partial WH-movement" in FR and some dialects of GE, in which, in a question containing multiple embedded clauses, each of the clauses begins with a WH-phrase. The one beginning the most deeply embedded clause is the "real" question phrase – the one whose form is appropriate to the gap in that clause. Each of the higher clauses in turn begins with a dummy or placeholder WH-form, which is typically the invariant question word 'what'.

(6.153)　　a.　Wat tinkst　　wa't　dien hat?
　　　　　　　　what think-you who-it done has?
　　　　　　　　'Who do you think did it?'
　　　　　　　　(FR, Tiersma 1999: 108)

　　　　　　b.　Was glaubt　Hans mit　wem　Jakob jetzt spricht
　　　　　　　　what believes Hans with whom Jakob now speaks?
　　　　　　　　'With whom does Hans believe that Jakob is speaking now?'
　　　　　　　　(GE, McDaniel 1989: 569)

　　　　　　c.　Was glaubst du　was　Hans meint mit wem Jakob gesprochen hat?
　　　　　　　　what think　　you what Hans believes with whom Jakob spoken　has
　　　　　　　　'With whom do you think Hans believes Jakob spoke?'
　　　　　　　　(GE, McDaniel 1989: 575)

The GE construction has been widely discussed, for example, in van Riemsdijk 1983a, McDaniel 1989 and Sternefeld 2002. McDaniel (1989: 570), for example, presents arguments from intonation and word order that these constructions do form a single syntactic unit, and are not two separate questions, one of which is parenthetical (*'What do you think? Who did it?'*). Note, for example, that the second clause in (6.153b) has subordinate word order, indicating that it is an embedded clause. McDaniel suggests that the construction serves to make possible the questioning of relatively deeply embedded positions in the northern dialects of GE, in which the direct fronting of argument question phrases out of finite clauses is prohibited.

In addition to alternative questions and specification questions, the GMC languages also exhibit what we may term "confirmation" questions or "tag" questions, in which a declarative statement is made, followed by an interrogative codicil, or "tag," which invites the hearer to confirm the correctness of the proposition. Tag questions have a different shape in EN than elsewhere in GMC. In EN, the tag consists of a copy of the auxiliary of the main clause (a dummy auxiliary *do* being supplied if the main clause lacks an auxiliary) and a pronominal copy of the subject of the main clause. A clausal negator may be included or not, depending on the degree of the speaker's certainty about the truth of the proposition:

(6.154)   a. You saw him, didn't you? / (So) you saw him, did you?

These "copy tags" are not shared by the other GMC languages, and, indeed, seem to be restricted to EN and the Celtic languages. Other GMC languages use the more common device of an invariant tag element. Some languages have tags of different polarity, depending on the expected answer (6.154e, f).

(6.154)   b. Er kommt morgen, nicht wahr?
                 he comes tomorrow, not true?
                 (GE)

             c. Du kommer hem till mig i kväll, eller hur?
                 you will be coming back to my place tonight, or what?
                 (SW, Holmes and Hinchcliffe 1994: 349)

             d. Du har inte gjort det, eller hur?
                 you have not done that, or what?
                 (SW, Holmes and Hinchcliffe 1994: 349)

             e. Do bist siik, net?
                 you are sick, no?
                 (FR, Tiersma 1999: 108)

             f. Do bist net siik, wol?
                 you are sick, yes?
                 (FR, Tiersma 1999: 108)

There are no examples of tag questions in GO, but GO does have some interrogative particles which are functionally similar to tags to a certain extent in that they express the speaker's presuppositions about the truth of the proposition. For example, questions begin with *ibai* when the speaker presupposes a negative answer.

(6.154)   g. ibai jah weis blindai sijum?
            ibai also we blind may-be
            'Are we also blind?'
            (GO, John 9:40, Streitberg 1920: 219)

6.5.3 Topic constructions and left dislocation constructions

The GMC languages exhibit two other construction types besides relative clauses and WH-Questions of the form XP_i [$_S$] in which a phrase (typically but not necessarily a NP) is followed by a clause. These are Topic constructions and Left-Dislocation (LD) constructions. In both of these, the leftward XP is understood to establish the topic of the following clause, which in turn is a statement about that topic. The most obvious difference between the two is that there is a gap in the topic construction but not in the left-dislocation construction, which instead contains a resumptive pronoun understood to refer back to the leftward constituent.

(6.155)   a. Those books I refuse to read
            b. Those books, I refuse to read them

In (6.155b), the resumptive pronoun is itself not displaced leftward, but appears in the position in the clause appropriate to its grammatical role. This type (the 'Hanging Topic' LD-construction (HTLD)) is the only type that exists in EN, but we will shortly be contrasting it with another type which prevails in other GMC languages. There are other well-known differences between Topic constructions and LD constructions. See Zaenen 1994 for some discussion of these. Among other things, topic phrases and left-dislocated phrases seem to be in different positions. The former, but not the latter, are incompatible with question phrases.

(6.156)   a. *These books who reads ?
            b. These books, who reads them?

Moreover, in IC, as in other strict V-2 languages, the Topic phrase counts as the clause-initial constituent for the purpose of V-2, while the LD phrase does not.

(6.157)   a. Þessum hring hefur Ólafur lofað   Maríu
               this ring-Acc has   Olaf   promised to Mary
               (IC, Zaenen 1994: 122)

            b. Þessi hringur, Ólafur hefur lofað   Maríu honum
               this ring-Nom Olaf   has   promised Mary it
               (IC, Zaenen 1994: 122)

Such differences have led some investigators to an analysis under which the leftward phrases in LD constructions are introduced in that position, whereas Topic phrases are moved to their position by the same sort of operation which fronts Question phrases. Consonant with this claimed difference in derivation are a number of other differences between the two which have been discussed generally under the label of "connectedness phenomena." Topic phrases behave in a number of respects in ways appropriate to the position of the gap – the two positions are thus "connected," whereas (Hanging Topic) LD constructions do not exhibit such connectedness between the leftward NP and the resumptive pronoun. So, for example, in languages with morphological case, NP Topics exhibit the case appropriate to the position of the gap, whereas Hanging Topics in HTLD constructions appear in nominative case regardless of the case of the resumptive pronoun, as in (6.157b). Similar connectedness effects, involving pronoun interpretation, idiom chunks and quantifier scope, are discussed in Zaenen 1985, 1994, Vat 1994 and van Riemsdijk (1994) and the references cited there.

However, the GMC languages other than EN exhibit a second type of LD construction, first labeled by Zaenen "Contrastive Left Dislocation (CLD)," which has an interesting tendency to pattern with Topic constructions, rather than HTLD constructions, with respect to connectedness properties. In the CLD construction, the resumptive pronoun does not appear in its usual position in the clause, but at the left edge of the clause, adjacent to the LD constituent. Sometimes the fronted resumptive element assumes the same form as a relative pronoun.

(6.158) a. Den Hans/ ??der Hans, den kenne ich schon seit zwölf Jahren
the Hans-Acc/??the Hans-Nom, that-one I know already since 12 years
'Hans, I have known him for 12 years'
(GE, van Riemsdijk 1994: 5)

Sometimes, however, in IC and SW, it appears as a personal pronoun, thus resembling the HTLD construction aside from word order.

(6.158) b. Peysuna   sína,   hana finnur Ólafur hvergi
sweater-Acc self's, it-Acc finds Olaf   nowhere
(IC, Zaenen 1985: 48)

As these examples show, these constructions also differ from HTLD constructions in that the LD phrase in them exhibits case connectedness effects; it appears in the same case as the fronted demonstrative or pronoun, unlike the HTLD constructions like (6.157b).

Such contrasts in case connectedness are supported by parallel contrasts involving reflexives and reciprocals, for example (though the contrasts are often not sharp (cf. van Riemsdijk 1994: 7)). Thus, the LD phrase in the IC CLD in (6.158b) can contain a reflexive, whose intended antecedent is the subject of the following clause. On the other hand, the LD phrase in the HTLD construction cannot (6.158c). Similar contrasts are found in other languages (see Vat 1994 for DU and GE).

(6.158) c. *Peysan sín,   Ólafur finnur hana hvergi
              sweater self's, Olaf   finds it   nowhere
              (IC, Zaenen 1985: 7)

The HTLD type of LD construction appears to be distributed widely across languages. The CLD construction, on the other hand, is more restricted. Among Western European languages, it seems to be limited to GMC, though it has been noted that with respect to connectedness phenomena it resembles another type of LD, the Clitic LD construction, found in other European languages. See the papers in Anagnostopoulou *et al.* 1994 for details. Both HTLD and CLD constructions are found in early GMC languages, as the following examples from OE illustrate:

(6.159) a. Ðāra īglanda...þāra sindon   þrēo & fiftig
            the islands-Gen... of-them-Gen are three and fifty
            'The islands, there are fifty three of them'
            (OE, Oros. 1 1.26.35, cited in Traugott 1992: 280)

        b. Þās Godes þegnas... hwyder   gescyt þonne heora endebyrdnys?
           the God's servants-Nom...whither falls then   their order?
           (OE, Ælfric, Catholic Homilies I, 24, 346.1, Traugott 1992: 280)

In some of the early languages, notably OHG and MHG, connectedness effects in the CLD construction take an unusual form. When the LD phrase in MHG contained a relative clause, it was the relative pronoun in that relative clause, rather than the resumptive demonstrative in the main clause, which determined the case of the LD NP, as in the following example – an instance of what is referred to in grammars of the classical languages as "inverse attraction."

(6.159) c. Den schaz den in ir vater lie der wart mit ir geteilet hie
           the treasure-Acc which-Acc them their father left, it-Nom was
           with her shared here
           (MHG, Gregorius 635)

Case agreement of this sort appears to have been quite standard in MHG (see Grimm 1857). GO, however, systematically goes out of its way to avoid imitating such inverse

6.5 Relative clauses, questions and other fronting constructions

attraction when it appears in the Greek model for translation (Grimm 1857: 412). The following example is representative. In the Greek version, 'stone' is accusative.

(6.159) d. [stains [þammei uswaurpun þai timrjans]],
  sah warþ du haubida waihstins
  stone-Nom that-Dat threw out the builders,
  that-one became head of-corner
  'The stone that the builders threw out,
  it became the head of the corner'
  (GO, Mark 12:10)

REFERENCES

Abraham, Werner. 1989. Futur-Typologie in den germanischen Sprachen. In Werner Abraham and Theo Janssen, eds., *Tempus-Aspekt-Modus: Die lexikalischen und grammatischen Formen in den germanischen Sprachen.* Tübingen: Max Niemeyer. 345–390.
   1991. *Discourse Particles.* Amsterdam: John Benjamins.
   1995. Adjektivrektion. In Werner Abraham, ed., *Deutsche Syntax im Sprachenvergleich.* Tübingen: Gunter Narr. 241–280.
   1997. The Interdependence of Case, Aspect and Referentiality in the History of German: The Case of the Verbal Genitive. In Ans van Kemenade and Nigel Vincent, eds., *Parameters of Morphosyntactic Change.* Cambridge: Cambridge Uninversity Press. 29–61.
   2000. Modal Particles in German: Word Classification and Legacy beyond Grammaticalization. In Petra Vogel and Bernard Comrie, eds., *Approaches to the Typology of Word Classes.* Berlin: Mouton de Gruyter. 321–350.
   2001a. Peculiarities of Verbal Classes in German, Particularly in Relation to English and Dutch. In Sheila Watts *et al.*, eds., *Zur Verbmorphologie germanischer Sprachen.* Tübingen: Max Niemeyer. 83–116.
   2001b. How Far Does Semantic Bleaching Go? In Jan Terje Faarlund, ed., *Grammatical Relations in Change.* Amsterdam: John Benjamins. 15–64.
Abraham, Werner and Theo Janssen, eds. 1989. *Tempus-Aspekt-Modus: Die lexikalischen und grammatischen Formen in den germanischen Sprachen.* Tübingen: Max Niemeyer.
Abraham, Werner and Anko Wiegel. 1993. Reduktionsformen und Kasussynkretismus bei deutschen und niederländischen Pronomina. In Werner Abraham and Josef Bayer, eds., *Dialektsyntax.* Opladen: Westdeutscher Verlag. 12–49.
Åfarli, Tor. 1992. *The Syntax of Norwegian Passive Constructions.* Amsterdam: John Benjamins.
Aijmer, Karin. 1996. Swedish Modal Particles in a Contrastive Perspective. *Language Sciences* 18: 393–427.
Allan, Robin, Philip Holmes and Tom Lundskær-Nielsen. 1995. *Danish: A Comprehensive Grammar.* London: Routledge.
Allan, W. Scott. 1987. Lightfoot noch einmal. *Diachronica* 4: 123–157.
Allen, Cynthia L. 1980a. *Topics in Diachronic English Syntax.* New York: Garland.
   1980b. Movement and Deletion in Old English. *Linguistic Inquiry* 11: 261–324.
   1986. Dummy Subjects and the Verb-Second "Target" in Old English. *English Studies* 6: 465–470.
   1995. *Case Marking and Reanalysis.* Oxford: Clarendon Press.
Allwood, Jens. 1982. The Complex NP Constraint in Swedish. In Elisabet Engdahl and Eva Ejerhed, eds., *Readings in Unbounded Dependencies in Scandinavian Languages.* Umeå: Almqvist and Wiksell. 15–32.
American Heritage Dictionary of the English Language, 4th edn. 2000. Boston: Houghton Mifflin.

Anagnostopoulou, Elena, Henk van Riemsdijk and Frans Zwarts, eds. 1994. *Materials on Left Dislocation*. Amsterdam: John Benjamins.
Andersson, Eric. 1994. Swedish. In Ekkehard König and Johan van der Auwera. *The Germanic Languages*. London: Routledge. 271–312.
    2000. How Many Gender Categories Are there in Swedish? In Barbara Unterbeck *et al.*, eds., *Gender in Grammar and Cognition*. Berlin: Mouton de Gruyter. 545–559.
Andersson, S.-G. 1989. Zur Interaktion von Temporalität, Modalität, Aspektualität, und Aktionsart bei nichtfuturischen Tempora im Deutschen, Englischen und Swedischen. In Werner Abraham and Theo Janssen, eds., *Tempus-Aspekt-Modus: Die lexikalischen und grammatischen Formen in den germanischen Sprachen*. Tübingen: Max Niemeyer. 27–50.
Andrews, A. 1990. The VP Complement Analysis in Modern Icelandic. In Joan Maling and Annie Zaenen, eds., *Modern Icelandic Syntax* [Syntax and Semantics 24]. San Diego: Academic Press. 165–186. [first published 1976]
Andvik, Erik. E. 1992. *A Pragmatic Analysis of Norwegian Modal Particles*. Arlington: SIL and the University of Texas at Arlington.
Antonsen, Elmer. 1964. Zum Umlaut im Deutschen. *Beiträge zur Geschichte der deutschen Sprache und Literatur* 86: 177–196.
    1969. Zur Umlautfeindlichkeit des Oberdeutschen. *Zeitschrift für Dialektologie und Linguistik* 36: 201–207.
    1975. *A Concise Grammar of the Older Runic Inscriptions*. Tübingen: Max Niemeyer.
    1981. On the Syntax of the Older Runic Inscriptions. *Michigan German Studies* 7: 50–61.
Anward, Jan. 1982. Basic Swedish. In Elisabet Engdahl and Eva Ejerhed, eds., *Readings on Unbounded Dependencies in Scandinavian Languages*. Umeå: Almqvist and Wiksell. 47–76.
Apelt, O. 1874. Über den Accusativus cum Infinitivo im Gotischen. *Germania* 19: 280–297.
Arndt, Walter. 1960. "Modal Particles" in Russian and German. *Word* 16: 323–336.
    1970. Nonrandom Assignment of Loanwords: German Noun Gender. *Word: Journal of the International Linguistic Association* 26: 244–53.
Arnett, Carlee. 1997. Perfect Auxiliary Selection in the Old Saxon Heliand. *American Journal of Germanic Linguistics and Literatures* 9: 23–72.
Askedal, John Ole. 1994. Norwegian. In Ekkehard König and Johan van der Auwera, eds., *The Germanic Languages*. London: Routledge. 219–270.
    1996. Ergativity in Norwegian. *Nordic Journal of Linguistics* 9: 25–46.
Bach, Adolf. 1965. *Geschichte der deutschen Sprache*, 8th edn. Heidelberg: Quelle & Meyer.
Ballweg, Joachim. 1989. Preterite, (Present-) Perfect and Future. In Werner Abraham and Theo Janssen, eds., *Tempus-Aspekt-Modus: Die lexikalischen und grammatischen Formen in den germanischen Sprachen*. Tübingen: Max Niemeyer. 85–102.
Bammesberger, Alfred. 1986. *Der Aufbau des germanischen Verbalsystems*. Heidelberg: Carl Winter.
    1990. *Die Morphologie des urgermanischen Nomens*. Heidelberg: Carl Winter.
Bandle, Oskar *et al*. 2002–2005. *The Nordic Languages*. 2 vols. Berlin: Walter de Gruyter.
Barbier, Isabella. 1996. On the Syntax of Dutch *er*. In Rosina Lippi-Green and Joseph Salmons, eds., *Germanic Linguistics: Synchronic and Diachronic*. Philadelphia: Benjamins. 65–84.
Barðdal, Jóhanna and Valéria Molnár. 2000. Passive in Icelandic—Compared to Mainland Scandinavian. *Working Papers in Scandinavian Syntax* 65: 109–146.
Barnes, Michael P., with Eivind Weyhe. 1994. Faroese. In Ekkehard König and Johan van der Auwera, eds., *The Germanic Languages*. London: Routledge 190–218.
Bartsch, Karl. 1857. *Karl der Grosse von dem Stricker*. Leipzig: Gottfried Basse.
Basbøll, Hans. 2003 Prosody, Productivity and Word Stress: The *stød* Pattern of Modern Danish. *Nordic Journal of Linguistics* 26: 5–44.

Bayer, Josef. 1984a. Toward an Explanation of Certain *That*-t Phenomena: The COMP-Node in Bavarian. In W. de Geest and Y. Putseys, eds., *Sentential Complementation*. Dordrecht: Foris 23–32.
Bayer, Josef. 1984b. COMP in Bavarian Syntax. *The Linguistic Review*. 3: 209–274.
Beekes, Robert. 1995. *Comparative Indo-European Linguistics*. Amsterdam: John Benjamins.
Behaghel, Otto. 1923–1932. *Deutsche Syntax: Eine geschichtliche Darstellung*. 4 vols. Heidelberg: Carl Winter.
 1965. *Heliand und Genesis*. 8th edn., revised by Walther Mitzka. Tübingen: Max Niemeyer.
Bell, Arthur. 2004. Bipartite Negation and the Fine Structure of the Negative Phrase. PhD dissertation, Cornell University.
Bennis, Hans and Liliane Haegeman. 1984. On the Status of Agreement and Relative Clauses in West Flemish. In W. de Geest and Y. Putseys, eds., *Sentential Complementation*. Dordrecht: Foris 33–54.
Berger, Dieter *et al.*, eds. 1972. *Duden Zweifelsfälle der deutschen Sprache*. (Der Grosse Duden vol. 9). Mannheim: Bibliographisches Institut Mannheim.
Bernini, Giuliano and Paolo Ramat. 1996. *Negative Sentences in the Languages of Europe*. Berlin: Mouton de Gruyter.
Bever, T. G. and D. T. Langendoen. 1972. The Interaction of Speech Perception and Grammatical Structure in the Evolution of Language. In Robert P. Stockwell and Ronald K. S. Macaulay, eds., *Linguistic Change and Generative Theory*. Bloomington: Indiana University Press. 32–95.
Birkmann, Thomas. 1997. Das neuisländische Mediopassiv: Flexion oder Wortbildung? In Thomas Birkmann *et al.*, eds., *Vergleichende germanische Philologie und Skandinavistik: Festschrift für Otmar Werner*. Tübingen: Max Niemeyer. 81–90.
Birnbaum, Solomon. 1979: *Yiddish. A Survey and a Grammar*. Toronto: University of Toronto Press.
Blevins, Juliette. 1995. The Syllable in Phonological Theory. In John Goldsmith, ed., *Phonological Theory*. Cambridge: Blackwell Publishers. 206–244.
Bloomfield, Leonard. 1933. *Language*. London: Allen and Unwin.
Bobaljik, Jonathan and Dianne Jonas. 1996. Subject Positions and the Roles of TP. *Linguistic Inquiry* 27: 195–236.
Boekx, Cedric. 2002. On the Co-occurrence of Expletives and Definite Subjects in Germanic. In Werner Abraham and C. Jan-Wouter Zwart, eds., *Issues in Formal German(ic) Typology*. Amsterdam: Benjamins. 45–64.
Bonebrake, Veronica. 1979. *Historical Labial-Velar Changes in Germanic: A Study of the Counterdirectional Sound Changes in English and Netherlandic*. Umeå: Umeå University.
Boogaart, Ronny. 1999. Aspect and Temporal Ordering: A Contrastive Analysis of Dutch and English. PhD dissertation, Vrije Universiteit.
Booij, Geert. 1995. *The Phonology of Dutch*. Oxford: Clarendon Press.
 2002a. Separable Complex Verbs in Dutch: A Case of Periphrastic Word Formation. In Nicole Dehé *et al.*, eds., *Verb-Particle Explorations*. Berlin: Mouton de Gruyter. 21–41.
 2002b. *The Morphology of Dutch*. Oxford: Oxford University Press.
Born, Renate. 1979. Disintegration and Reintegration—the History of the Verbal Ablaut from Proto-Germanic to Modern German. PhD Dissertation, Cornell University.
Braune, Wilhelm. 1874. Die altslovenischen Freisinger Denkmäler in ihrem Verhältnisse zur althochdeutschen Orthographie. *Beiträge zur Geschichte der deutschen Sprache und Literatur* 1: 527–35.
 1963. *Althochdeutsche Grammatik*, 11th edn., revised by Walther Mitzka. Tübingen: Max Niemeyer.
 1973. *Gotische Grammatik*, 18th edn., revised by Ernst Ebbinghaus. Tübingen: Max Niemeyer.

Braunmüller, Kurt. 1991. *Die skandinavischen Sprachen im Überblick*. Tübingen: Francke.
2000. Gender in North Germanic: A Diasystematic and Functional Approach. In Barbara Unterbeck *et al.*, eds., *Gender in Grammar and Cognition*. Berlin: Mouton de Gruyter. 25–54.
Bresnan, Joan and Jane Grimshaw. 1978. The Syntax of Free Relatives in English. *Linguistic Inquiry* 9: 331–391.
Brinton, Laurel. 1988. *The Development of English Aspectual Systems*. Cambridge: Cambridge University Press.
Broekman, Henny. 1993. Verb Clusters in Germanic: The Non-Existence of the Third Construction. In Thomas F. Shannon and Johan P. Snapper, eds., *The Berkeley Conference on Dutch Linguistics 1993: Dutch Linguistics in a Changing Europe*. Lanham: University Press of America. 117–130.
Brown, Keith. 1991. Double Modals in Harwick Scots. In Peter Trudgill and J. K. Chambers, eds., *Dialects of English: Studies in Grammatical Variation*. London: Longmans.
Bruce, Gösta and Ben Hermans. 1999. Word Tone in Germanic Languages. In Harry van der Hulst, ed., *Word Prosodic Systems in the Languages of Europe*. Berlin: Mouton de Gruyter. 605–658.
Buccini, Anthony. 1988. Umlaut Alternation, Variation, and Dialect Contact: Reconditioning and Deconditioning of Umlaut in the Prehistory of Dutch. In Thomas J. Walsh, ed., *Synchronic and Diachronic Approaches to Linguistic Variation and Change*. Washington, DC: Georgetown University Press. 63–80.
Bures, Anton. 1993. There is an Argument for a Cycle at LF, here. *CLS* 28. *Volume* 2: *The Parasession*. Chicago: Chicago Linguistic Society. 14–35.
Burridge, Kate. 1993. *Syntactic Change in Germanic*. Amsterdam: John Benjamins.
Burzio, Luigi. 1986. *Italian Syntax: A Government-Binding Approach*. Dordrecht: Foris.
1988. On the Non-Existence of Disjoint Reference Principles. Paper presented at LSA Annual Meeting.
Butler, Milton C. 1977. The Reanalysis of Object as Subject in Middle English Impersonal Constructions. *Glossa* 11: 155–170.
Callaway, Morgan. 1913. *The Infinitive in Anglo-Saxon*. Washington, DC: Carnegie Institution.
Cardinaletti, Anna. 1998. On the Deficient/Strong Opposition in Possessive Systems. In Artemis Alexiadou and Chris Wilder, eds., *Possessors, Predicates and Movement in the Determiner Phrase*. Amsterdam: John Benjamins. 17–54.
1999. Pronouns in Germanic Languages: An Overview. In Henk van Riemsdijk, ed., *Clitics in the Languages of Europe*. Berlin: Mouton de Gruyter. 33–82.
Cardinaletti, Anna and Michal Starke. 1999. The Typology of Structural Deficiency: A Case Study of the Three Classes of Pronouns. In Henk van Riemsdijk, ed., *Clitics in the Languages of Europe*. Berlin: Mouton de Gruyter. 145–234.
Carstensen, Broder. 1980. The Gender of English Loan-Words in German. *Studia Anglica Posnaniensia: An International Review of English Studies* 12: 3–25.
Casaretto, Antje. 2004. *Nominale Wortbildung der gotischen Sprache: Die Derivation der Substantiva*. Heidelberg: Carl Winter.
Chevillet, François. 1981. Les relatifs au debut du Moyen-anglais. PhD dissertation, Université de Lille 3.
Chomsky, Noam. 1970. Remarks on Nominalization. In Roderick Jacobs and Peter Rosenbaum, eds., *Readings in English Transformational Grammar*. Washington, DC: Georgetown University Press. 184–221.
Chomsky, Noam and Morris Halle. 1968. *The Sound Pattern of English*. New York: Harper and Row.
Christensen, Kirsti Koch. 1984. Infinitival (Pseudo-)Complementation of Noun Phrases in Norwegian. In W. de Geest and Y. Putseys, eds., *Sentential Complementation*. Dordrecht: Foris 75–82.

1985. Complex Passives and Conditions on Reanalysis. *Working Papers in Scandinavian Syntax* 19: 1–49.

1986. Complex Passives, Reanalysis and Word Formation. *Nordic Journal of Linguistics* 9: 135–162.

1991. AGR Adjunction and the Structure of Scandinavian Existential Sentences. *Lingua* 84: 137–158.

Cinque, Guglielmo. 1999. *Adverbs and Functional Heads*. Oxford: Oxford University Press.

Clements, George N. 1975. The Logophoric Pronoun in Ewe: Its Role in Discourse. *Journal of West African Languages* 10: 141–177.

Clements, G. N. 1990. The Role of the Sonority Cycle in Core Syllabification. In John Kingston and Mary Beckman, eds., *Between Grammar and Physics of Speech*. Cambridge: Cambridge University Press. 283–333.

Cole, Peter, Wayne Harbert, Gabriella Hermon, and S. N. Sridhar. 1980. On the Acquisition of Subjecthood. *Language* 56: 719–743.

Collins, Beverley and Inger M. Mees. 1996. *The Phonetics of English and Dutch*, 3rd edn. Leiden: E. J. Brill.

Collins, Chris and Phil Branigan. 1997. Quotative Inversion. *Natural Language and Linguistic Theory* 15: 1–41.

Comrie, Bernard. 1995. Sprache und Sprachen: Universalien und Typologie. In Ewald Lang and Gisela Zifonum, eds., *Deutsch—Typologisch*. Berlin: Walter de Gruyter. 16–30.

Corbett, Greville. 1991. *Gender*. Cambridge: Cambridge University Press.

Crystal, David. 1987. *The Cambridge Encyclopedia of Linguistics*. Cambridge: Cambridge University Press.

2003. *The Cambridge Encyclopedia of the English Language*, 2nd edn. Cambridge: Cambridge University Press.

Curme, George. 1952. *A Grammar of the German Language*, 2nd edn. New York: Frederick Ungar.

Dal, Ingerid. 1966. *Kurze deutsche Syntax auf historischer Grundlage*, 5th edn. Tübingen: Max Niemeyer.

Davidsen-Nielsen, Niels. 1996. Discourse Particles in Danish. In Elisabeth Engberg-Pedersen et al., eds., *Content, Expression and Structure: Studies in Danish Functional Grammar*. Amsterdam: John Benjamins. 39–64.

Davis, Garry W. and Gregory K. Iverson 1994. Thl- in Gothic. *Historische Sprachforschung/ Historical Linguistics* 107: 155–164.

1996. Gothic *thl*-: A Response to Woodhouse. *Historische Sprachforschung/Historical Linguistics* 109: 276–278.

Davis, Graeme and Karl A. Bernhardt. 2002. *Syntax of West Germanic: The Syntax of Old English and Old High German*. Göppingen: Kümerle.

de Boor, Helmut, Hugo Moser and Christian Winkler, eds. 1969. *Siebs deutsche Aussprache*, 19th edn. Berlin: de Gruyter.

de Schutter, Georges. 1994. Dutch. In Ekkehard König and Johan van der Auwera, eds., *The Germanic Languages*. London: Routledge. 439–377.

de Vooys, C. G. N. 1949. *Nederlandse Spraakkunst*, 2nd edn. Groningen: J. B. Wolters.

Dehé, Nicole, Ray Jackendoff, Andrew McIntyre and Silke Urban, eds. 2002. *Verb-Particle Explorations*. Berlin: Mouton de Gruyter.

Dekeyser, Xavier. 1990. Preposition Stranding and Relative Complementizer Deletion: Implicational Tendencies in English and the Other Germanic Languages. In Sylvia Adamson, Vivien Law, Nigel Vincent and Susan Wright, eds., *Papers from the 5th International Conference on English Historical Linguistics*. Amsterdam: John Benjamins. 87–109.

Delbrück, Berthold. 1900. *Vergleichende Syntax der indogermanischen Sprachen*. Strassburg: Karl Trübner.

Delsing, Lars-Olof. 1998. Possession in Germanic. In Artemis Alexiadou and Chris Wilder, eds., *Possessors, Predicates and Movement in the Determiner Phrase*. Amsterdam: John Benjamins. 87–108.
Demske-Neumann, Ulrike. 1994. *Modales Passiv und "Tough Movement."* Tübingen: Max Niemeyer.
den Besten, H. 1985. The Ergative Hypothesis and Free Word Order in Dutch and German. In Jindrich Toman, ed., *Studies in German Grammar*. Dordrecht: Foris. 23–64.
   1996. Associative DP's. In Marcel den Dikken and Crit Cramers, eds., *Linguistics in the Netherlands 1996*. Amsterdam: John Benjamins. 13–24.
den Besten, Hans and Jerrold Edmondson. 1981. The Verbal Complex in Continental West Germanic. *Groninger Arbeiten zur generativen Linguistik* 19.
den Besten, Hans and Corretje Moed-van Walraven. 1986. The Syntax of Verbs in Yiddish. In Hubert Haider and Martin Prinzhorn, eds., *Verb Second Phenomena in Germanic Languages*. Dordrecht: Foris. 111–135.
den Besten, Hans and Gert Webelhuth. 1990. Stranding. In Günther Grewendorf and Wolfgang Sternefeld, eds., *Scrambling and Barriers*. Amsterdam: John Benjamins. 77–92.
Denison, David. 1981. The Origins of Completive *Up* in English. *Neuphilologische Mitteilungen* 86: 37–61.
   1993. *English Historical Syntax: Verbal Constructions*. London: Longman.
Diesing, Molly. 2003. On the Nature of Multiple Fronting in Yiddish. In Cedric Boekx and Kleanthes K. Grohmann, eds., *Multiple Fronting*. Amsterdam: John Benjamins. 51–76.
Donaldson, Bruce. 1981. *Dutch Reference Grammar*. The Hague: Martinus Nijhoff.
   1993. *A Grammar of Afrikaans*. Berlin: Mouton de Gruyter.
   1994. Afrikaans. In Ekkehard König and Johan van der Auwera, eds., *The Germanic Languages*. London: Routledge. 478–504.
   2000. *Colloquial Afrikaans*. London: Routledge.
Donhauser, Karin. 1995. Negationssyntax in der deutschen Sprachgeschichte: Grammatikalisierung oder Degrammatikalisierung? In Ewald Lang and Gisela Zifonum, eds., *Deutsch—Typologisch*. Berlin: de Gruyter. 201–217.
Dresher, B. Elan and Aditi Lahiri. 1991. The Germanic Foot: Metrical Coherence in Old English. *Linguistic Inquiry* 22: 251–286.
Dronke, Ursula. 1969–1997. *The Poetic Edda, Edited with Translation, Introduction, and Commentary*. 2 vols. Oxford: Clarendon Press.
Dryer, Matthew S. 1986. Primary Objects, Secondary Objects, and Antidative. *Language* 62: 808–845.
Ebbinghaus, Ernst. 1970. Gothic L̩, R̩, M̩, N̩? The Evidence Reviewed. *Journal of English and Germanic Philology* 69: 580–583.
Ebert, Karen H. 2000. Progressive Markers in Germanic Languages. In Östen Dahl, ed., *Tense and Aspect in the Languages of Europe*. Berlin: Mouton de Gruyter. 605–654.
Ebert, Robert. 1975. Subject-Raising, the Clause Squish, and German *scheinen*-Constructions. In Robin E. Grossman, L. James San and Timothy J. Vance, eds., *CLS 11*. Chicago: Chicago Linguistic Society. 177–187.
Eckhardt, E. 1875. Über die Syntax des Relativpronomens. PhD dissertation, Halle.
Eggers, Hans, ed. 1964. *Der althochdeutsche Isidor nach der Pariser Handschrift und den Monseer Fragmenten*. Tübingen: Max Niemeyer.
Ehrich, Veronika and Heinz Vater. 1989. Perfekt im Dänischen und Deutschen. In Werner Abraham and Theo Janssen, eds., *Tempus-Aspekt-Modus: Die lexikalischen und grammatischen Formen in den germanischen Sprachen*. Tübingen: Max Niemeyer. 103–132.
Einarsson, Stefán. 1945. *Icelandic*. Baltimore: The Johns Hopkins Press.
Eisenberg, Peter. 1994. German. In Ekkehard König and Johan van der Auwera, eds., *The Germanic Languages*. London: Routledge. 349–387.

Elenbaas, Marion. 2003. Particle Verbs in Early Middle English: The Case of Up. In Leonie Cornips and Paula Fikkert, eds., *Linguistics in the Netherlands 2003*. Amsterdam: Benjamins 45–57.
Elmer, Willy. 1981. *Diachronic Grammar: The History of Old and Middle English Subjectless Constructions*. Tübingen: Max Niemeyer.
Engdahl, Elisabet. 1982. Restrictions on Unbounded Dependencies in Swedish. In Elisabet Engdahl and Eva Ejerhed, eds., *Readings in Unbounded Dependencies in Scandinavian Languages*. Umeå: Almqvist and Wiksell. 151–174.
Engdahl, Elisabet and Eva Ejerhed, eds. 1982. *Readings in Unbounded Dependencies in Scandinavian Languages*. Umeå: Almqvist and Wiksell.
Engel, Ulrich. 1988. *Deutsche Grammatik*. Heidelberg: Julius Groos.
Engh, Jan. 1984. On the Development of the Complex Passive. *Working Papers in Scandinavian Syntax* 10: 1–23.
Erdmann, Oskar. 1874. *Untersuchungen über die Syntax der Sprache Otfrids*. Volume 1. Halle: Verlag der Buchhandlung des Waisenhauses.
Esau, Helmut. 1972. Form and Function of German Adjective Endings. *Folia Linguistica: Acta Societatis Linguisticae Europaeae* 6: 136–145.
Evans, Eston. 1975. Psychological Process Experiencer Verb-Impersonals: A Case Grammar Approach. PhD dissertation, University of Texas, Austin.
Everaert, Martin. 1980. Inherent Reflexive Verbs and the "zich"/ "zichzelf"-Distribution in Dutch. *Utrecht Working Papers in Linguistics* 10: 1–50.
    1986. The Syntax of Reflexivization. PhD dissertation, University of Utrecht.
    1991. Contextual Determination of the Anaphor/ Pronominal Distinction. In Jan Koster and Eric Reuland, eds., *Long-Distance Anaphora*. Cambridge: Cambridge University Press. 77–118.
Evers, Arnold. 1975. The Transformational Cycle in Dutch and German. PhD dissertation, University of Utrecht [reproduced by the Indiana University Linguistics Club].
Eythórsson, Thórhallur. 1995. Verb Position and Verb Movement in Early Germanic. PhD dissertation, Cornell University.
    2002. Changes in Subject Case Marking in Icelandic. In David Lightfoot, ed., *Syntactic Effects of Morphological Change*. Oxford: Oxford University Press. 196–212.
Eythórsson, Thórhallur and Jóhanna Barðdal. 2005. Oblique Subjects: A Common Germanic Inheritance. *Language* 81: 824–881.
Faarlund, Jan Terje. 1990. *Syntactic Change: Toward a Theory of Historical Syntax*. Berlin: Mouton de Gruyter.
    1994. Old and Middle Scandinavian. In Ekkehard König and Johan van der Auwera, eds., *The Germanic Languages*. London: Routledge. 38–71.
Fabricius-Hansen. 1994. Das dänische und norwegische Tempussystem im Vergleich mit dem Deutschen. In Rolf Thieroff and Joachim Ballweg, eds., *Tense Systems in European Languages*. Tübingen: Max Niemeyer. 49–68.
Fagan, Sarah M. B. 1989. Geminates in Intensive and Iterative Germanic Class II Weak Verbs. *Beiträge zur Geschichte der deutschen Sprache und Literatur* 111: 35–58.
Fagan, Sarah. 1992. *The Syntax and Semantics of Middle Constructions*. Cambridge: Cambridge University Press.
    1996. The Epistemic Use of German and English Modals. In Rosina Lippi-Green and Joseph Salmons, eds., *Germanic Linguistics: Synchronic and Diachronic*. Amsterdam: John Benjamins. 15–34.
Farrell, Patrick. 2005. English Verb-Preposition Constructions: Constituency and Order. *Language* 81: 96–137.
Feist, Sigmund. 1923. *Etymologisches Wörterbuch der gothischen Sprache*. 2nd edn. Halle: Max Niemeyer.

Fertig, David L. 1996. Phonology, Orthography and the Umlaut Puzzle. In Rosina Lippi-Green and Joseph Salmons, eds., *Germanic Linguistics: Syntactic and Diachronic*. Amsterdam: John Benjamins. 169–184.
Filppula, Markku. 1999. *The Grammar of Irish English: Language in Hibernian Style*. London: Routledge.
  2004. Irish English: Morphology and Syntax. In Bernd Kortmann *et al.*, eds., *A Handbook of Varieties of English*. Berlin: Mouton de Gruyter. 73–101.
Fischer, Klaus. 1997. *German–English Verb Valency*. Tübingen: Gunther Narr.
Fischer, Olga. 1990. Syntactic Change and Causation: Developments in Infinitival Constructions in English. PhD dissertation, University of Amsterdam.
  1992. Syntax. In Norman Blake, ed., *Cambridge History of the English Language*. Volume 2. Cambridge: Cambridge University Press. 207–408.
Fishman, Joshuah. 2001 A Decade in the Life of a Two-in One Language. In J. Fishman, ed., *Can Threatened Languages be Saved?* Buffalo: Multilingual Matters. 74–100.
Foolen, Ad. 1995. Dutch Modal Particles: The Relevance of Grammaticalized Elements. In Thomas Shannon and Johan P. Snapper, eds., *The Berkeley Conference on Dutch Linguistics 1993*. Lanham, MD: University Press of America. 57–70.
Fortson, Benjamin. 2004. *Indo-European Language and Culture: An Introduction*. London: Blackwell.
Freidin, Robert and Rex Sprouse. 1991. Lexical Case Phenomena. In R. Freidin, ed., *Principles and Parameters in Comparative Grammar*. Cambridge, MA: MIT Press.
Frense, J., and P. Bennett. 1996. Verb Alternation and Semantic Classes in English and German. *Language Sciences* 18: 305–317.
Frisch, Stefan. 1997. The Change in Negation in Middle English: A NEGP Licensing Account. *Lingua* 101: 21–64.
Fudeman, Kirsten. 1999. Topics in the Morphology of Balanta, An Atlantic Language of Senegal. PhD dissertation, Cornell University.
Geerts, G. *et al.*, eds. 1984. *Algemene Nederlandse Spraakkunst*. Noordhoff: Wolters.
Giusti, Giuliana. 1990. Floating Quantifiers, Scrambling, and Configurationality. *Linguistic Inquiry* 21: 633–641.
Goblirsch, Kurt. 1994. A Comparative Study of the Scandinavian Consonant Shift. *General Linguistics* 34: 195–202.
Goossens, L. 1982. On the Development of the Modals and of the Epistemic Function in English. In A. Ahlqvist, ed., *Papers from the Fifth International Conference on Historical Linguistics*. Amsterdam: John Benjamins. 74–84.
Gordon, Raymond G., Jr., ed. 2005. *Ethnologue: Languages of the World*, 15th edn. Dallas: SIL International. Online version: http://www.ethnologue.com/.
Görlach, Manfred. 1991. *Introduction to Early Modern English*. Cambridge: Cambridge University Press.
Gorter, Durk, Alex Riemersma and Jehannes Ytsma. 2001. Frisian in the Netherlands. In Guus Extra and Durk Gorter, eds., *The Other Languages of Europe*. Buffalo: Multilingual Matters. 103–118.
Granberry, Julian. 1991. *Essential Swedish Grammar*. Dover: Constable.
Grebe, Paul *et al.*, eds. 1966. *Der große Duden Grammatik der deutschen Gegenwartssprache*. Mannheim: Bibliographisches Institut Mannheim.
Greenberg, Joseph. 1963. Some Universals of Grammar with Particular Reference to the Order of Meaningful Elements. In Joseph Greenberg, ed., *Universals of Language*. Cambridge, MA: MIT Press. 73–113.
Gregor, Bernd. 1983. *Genuszuordnung: Das Genus englischer Lehnwörter im Deutschen*. Tübingen: Max Niemeyer.
Grewendorf, Günther. 1989. *Ergativity in German*. Dordrecht: Foris.

Grimm, Jacob. 1857. Über einen Fall der Attraction. *Germania* 2: 410–418.
  1866. Über einige Fälle der Attraktion. In *Kleinere Schriften*. Volume 3. Berlin. 312–347.
Grimshaw, Jane. 1990. *Argument Structure*. Cambridge, MA: MIT Press.
Grohmann, Kleanthes. 1997. Pronouns and the Left Periphery of West Germanic Embedded Clauses. In Werner Abraham and Elly van Gelderen, eds., *German: Syntactic Problems—Problematic Syntax*. Tübingen: Max Niemeyer. 163–190.
Groos, Anneke and Henk van Riemsdijk. 1981. Matching Effects in Free Relatives: A Parameter of Core Grammar. In A. Belletti, L. Brandi and L. Rizzi, eds., *Theory of Markedness in Generative Grammar*. Pisa: Scuola Normale Pisa. 171–197.
Grosu, Alexander. 1996. The Proper Analysis of "Missing-P" Free Relative Constructions. *Linguistic Inquiry* 27: 257–293.
Gussenhoven, Carlos. 1999. Dutch. In *Handbook of the International Phonetic Association: A Guide to the Use of the International Phonetic Alphabet*. Cambridge: Cambridge University Press. 74–77.
  2000. On the Origin and Development of the Central Franconian Tone Contrast. In Aditi Lahiri, ed., *Analogy, Levelling and Markedness: Principles of Change in Phonology and Morphology*. Berlin: Mouton de Gruyter.
Gussenhoven, Carlos and Gösta Bruce. 1999. Word Prosody and Intonation. In Harry van der Hulst, ed., *Word Prosodic Systems in the Languages of Europe*. Berlin: Mouton de Gruyter. 233–272.
Haberland, Hartmut. 1994. Danish. In Ekkehard König and Johan van der Auwera, eds., *The Germanic Languages*. London: Routledge. 313–348.
Haegeman, Liliane. 1992. *Theory and Description in Generative Grammar: A Case Study in West Flemish*. Cambridge: Cambridge University Press.
  1993. Some Speculations on Argument Shift, Clitics and Crossing in West-Flemish. In Werner Abraham and Josef Bayer, eds., *Dialektsyntax*. Opladen: Westdeutscher Verlag. 131–160.
  1995. *The Syntax of Negation*. Cambridge: Cambridge University Press.
Haegeman, Liliane and Henk van Riemsdijk. 1986. Verb-Projection Raising. *Linguistic Inquiry* 17: 417–466.
Haegeman, Liliane and Raffaella Zanuttini. 1996. Negative Concord in West Flemish. In Adriana Belletti and Luigi Rizzi, eds., *Parameters and Functional Heads*. Oxford: Oxford University Press. 117–180.
Hahn, E. Adelaide. 1964. Relative and Antecedent. *Transactions and Proceedings of the American Philological Association* 95: 111–141.
Haider, Hubert. 2004. Pre- and Postverbal Adverbials in OV and VO. *Lingua* 114: 779–807.
Hale, Mark. 1994. Recovering the Prosody-Syntax Interface in Notker. Paper presented at the Berkeley/Michigan Germanic Linguistics Roundtable, Berkeley, April 8, 1994.
Harbert, Wayne. 1978. Gothic Syntax: A Relational Grammar. Dissertation, University of Illinois.
  1982. On the Nature of the Matching Parameter. *The Linguistic Review* 2: 237–284.
  1985. Markedness and the Bindability of Subject of NP. In Fred R. Eckman, Edith A. Moravcsik and Jessica R. Wirth, eds., *Markedness*. New York: Plenum Press. 139–154.
  1992. Gothic Relative Clauses and Syntactic Theory. In Irmengard Rauch, Gerald Carr and Robert L. Kyes, eds., *On Germanic Linguistics: Issues and Methods*. Berlin Mouton de Gruyter. 109–146.
  1999. Erino portun ih firchnussu. In Gerald Carr et al., eds., *Interdigitations: Essays for Irmengard Rauch*. New York: Peter Lang. 257–268.
  2002. The Syntax of Indefinite Phrases in Negative Sentences in Germanic. *International Journal of Germanic Linguistics and Semiotic Analysis* 7: 101–126.
Harris, John. 1993. The Grammar of Irish English. In James Milroy and Lesley Milroy, eds., *Real English: The Grammar of English Dialects in the British Isles*. London: Longman. 139–186.

Haspelmath, Martin. 1998. How Young is Standard Average European? *Language Sciences* 20: 271–287.

1999. External Possession in a European Areal Perspective. In Doris L. Payne and Immanuel Barshi, eds., *External Possession*. Amsterdam: John Benjamins. 109–135.

Haugen, Einar. 1976. *The Scandinavian Languages: An Introduction to their History*. Cambridge, MA: Harvard University Press.

1982. *Scandinavian Language Structures*. Tübingen: Max Niemeyer.

Hawkins, John. 1986. *A Comparative Typology of English and German: Unifying the Contrasts*. Austin: University of Texas Press.

Heffner, R.-M. S. 1950. *General Phonetics*. Madison: University of Wisconsin Press.

Heidermanns, Frank. 1993. *Etymologisches Wörterbuch der germanischen Primäradjektive*. Berlin: de Gruyter.

Heinrichs, Heinrich M. 1954. *Studien zum bestimmten Artikel in den germanischen Sprachen*. Giessen: Wilhelm Schmitz.

Hellan, Lars. 1983. Anaphora in Norwegian and the Theory of Syntax. *Working Papers in Scandinavian Syntax 5*. Trondheim: University of Trondheim.

1984. A GB-Type Analysis of Complex Passives and Related Constructions. *Working Papers in Scandinavian Syntax 10*. Trondheim: University of Trondheim.

Hellan, Lars and Christer Platzack. 1999. Pronouns in Scandinavian Languages: An Overview. In Henk van Riemsdijk, ed., *Clitics in the Languages of Europe*. Berlin: Mouton de Gruyter. 123–142.

Helthoft, Lars. 2001. Recasting Danish Subjects: Case System, Word Order and Subject Development. In Jan Terje Faarlund, ed., *Grammatical Relations in Change*. Amsterdam: Benjamins. 171–204.

Hendricks, Ronald V. 1981. Aspect and Adverbs in German. PhD dissertation, Cornell University.

Henry, Alison. 1995. *Belfast English and Standard English: Dialect Variation and Parameter Setting*. Oxford: Oxford University Press.

1996. Imperative Inversion in Belfast English. In James Black and Virginia Motapanyane, eds., *Microparametric Syntax and Dialect Variation*. Amsterdam: John Benjamins. 79–94.

Herslund, Michael. 1986. The Double Object Construction in Danish. In Lars Hellan and Kirsti Koch Christensen, eds., *Topics in Scandinavian Syntax*. Dordrecht: Reidel. 125–148.

Hestvik. A. G. 1990. LF-Movement of Pronouns and the Computation of Binding Domains. PhD dissertation, Brandeis University.

Heusler, Andreas. 1967. *Altisländisches Elementarbuch*, 7th edn. Heidelberg: Carl Winter.

Hickey, Raymond. 2000. On the Phonology of Gender in Modern German. In Barbara Unterbeck, Matti Rissanen, Terttu Nevalainen and Mirja Saari, *Gender in Grammar and Cognition*. Berlin: Mouton de Gruyter. 621–664.

Hock, Hans. 1986. *Principles of Historical Linguistics*. Berlin: Mouton de Gruyter.

Hodler, Werner. 1969. *Berndeutsche Syntax*. Bern: Francke.

Hoekstra, Jarich. 1995. Preposition Stranding and Resumptivity in West Germanic. In Hubert Haider, Susan Olsen and Sten Vikner, eds., *Studies in Comparative Germanic Syntax*. Dordrecht: Kluwer. 95–118.

1997. The Syntax of Infinitives in Frisian. PhD dissertation, University of Groningen.

Hoekstra, Jarich and Peter Meijes Tiersma. 1994. Frisian. In Ekkehard König and Johannes van der Auwera, eds., *The Germanic Languages*. London: Routledge. 505–531.

Hoekstra, Teun. 1984. *Transitivity: Grammatical Relations in Government Binding Theory*. Dordrecht: Foris.

Hogg, Richard. 1992. *A Grammar of Old English. Volume 1: Phonology*. Oxford: Blackwell.

Holmberg, Anders and Jan Rijkhoff. 1998. Word Order in the Germanic Languages. In Anna Siewierska, ed., *Constituent Order in the Languages of Europe*. Berlin: Mouton de Gruyter. 75–104.

Holmberg, Anders and Görel Sandström. 1996. Scandinavian Possessive Constructions from a Northern Swedish Viewpoint. In James Black and Virginia Motapanyane, eds., *Microparametric Syntax and Dialect Variation*. Amsterdam: John Benjamins. 95–120.

Holmes, Phillip and Ian Hinchcliffe. 1994. *Swedish: A Comprehensive Grammar*. London: Routledge.

Holthausen, Ferdinand. 1921. *Altsächsisches Elementarbuch*, 2nd edn. Heidelberg: Carl Winter.

Hopper, Paul. 1975. *The Syntax of the Simple Sentence in Proto-Germanic*. The Hague: Mouton.

Horn, Laurence and Yasuhiko Kato. 2000. *Negation and Polarity: Syntactic and Semantic Perspectives*. Oxford: Oxford University Press.

Howe, Stephen. 1996. *The Personal Pronouns in the Germanic Languages: A Study of Personal Pronoun Morphology and Change in the Germanic Languages from the First Records to the Present Day*. Berlin: de Gruyter.

Howell, Robert. 1991. *Old English Breaking and its Germanic Analogues*. Tübingen: Max Niemeyer.

Howell, Robert, Paul Roberge and Joseph Salmons. forthcoming. *The History of the Germanic Languages*. Cambridge: Cambridge University Press.

Howell, Robert B. and Joseph C. Salmons. 1997. Umlautless Residues in Germanic. *American Journal of Germanic Linguistics and Literatures* 9: 83–111.

Huang, C.-T. James. 1984. On the Distribution and Reference of Empty Pronouns. *Linguistic Inquiry* 15: 531–574.

Ingham, Richard. 2000. Negation and OV Order in Late Middle English. *Journal of Linguistics* 36: 13–38.

Iverson, Gregory K. and Joseph C. Salmons. 1995. Aspiration and Laryngeal Representation in Germanic. *Phonology* 12: 369–396.

1999. Glottal Spreading Bias in Germanic. *Linguistische Berichte* 178: 135–151.

2003. Laryngeal Enhancement in Early Germanic. *Phonology* 20: 43–74.

Jackendoff, Ray. 2002. English Particles Constructions, the Lexicon, and the Autonomy of Syntax. In Nicole Dehé, Ray Jackendoff, Andrew McIntyre and Silke Urban, eds., *Verb-Particle Explorations*. Berlin: Mouton de Gruyter. 67–94.

Jacobs, Neil. 2005. *Yiddish: A Linguistic Introduction*. Cambridge: Cambridge University Press.

Jacobs, Neil et al. 1994. Yiddish. In Ekkehard König and Johan van der Auwera, eds., *The Germanic Languages*. London: Routledge. 388–419.

Jacobsson, Bengt. 1994. Nonrestrictive Relative *That*-Clauses Revisited. *Studia Neophilologica* 66: 181–195.

Jaeggli, Osvaldo and Kenneth Safir. 1989. The Null Subject Parameter and Parametric Theory. In Osvaldo Jaeggli and Kenneth Safir, eds., *The Null Subject Parameter*. Dordrecht: Kluwer. 1–44.

Janssen, Theo A. J. M. 1994. Tense in Dutch: Eight "Tenses" or Two Tenses? In Rolf Thieroff and Joachim Ballweg, eds., *Tense Systems in European Languages*. Tübingen: Max Niemeyer. 93–118.

Jespersen, Otto. 1917. *Negation in English and Other Languages*. Copenhagen: Bianco Lunos.

1927. *A Modern English Grammar on Historical Principles*. Volume 3. Copenhagen: Munksgaard.

Jessen, Michael. 1996. Phonetics and Phonology of the Tense and Lax Obstruents in German. PhD dissertation, Cornell University.

1998. *Phonetics and Phonology of Tense and Lax Obstruents in German*. Amsterdam: John Benjamins.

Jessen, Michael and Catherine Ringen. 2002. Laryngeal Features in German. *Phonology* 19: 189–218.
Jonas, Dianne. 1996a. Residual V-to-I. In David Lightfoot, ed., *Syntactic Effects of Morphological Change*. Oxford: Oxford University Press. 251–270.
  1996b. Clause Structure, Expletives and Verb Movement. In Werner Abraham *et al.*, eds., *Minimal Ideas: Syntactic Studies in the Minimalist Framework*. Amsterdam: John Benjamins. 167–188.
Jones, Charles. 1988. *Grammatical Gender in English: 950 to 1250*. London: Croom Helm.
Josefsson, Gunlög. 1998. *Minimal Words in a Minimal Syntax: Word Formation in Swedish*. Amsterdam: John Benjamins.
Kageyama, Taro. 1992. AGR in Old English to-Infinitives. *Lingua* 88: 91–128.
Karagjosova, Elena. 2003. Modal Particles and the Common Ground: Meaning and Functions of German *ja, doch, eben, halt*, and *auch*. In Peter Kühnlein *et al.*, eds., *Perspectives on Dialogue in the New Millennium*. Amsterdam: John Benjamins. 335–350.
Kastovsky, Dieter. 1992. Semantics and Vocabulary. In Richard Hogg, ed., *The Cambridge History of the English Language*. Volume 1. Cambridge: Cambridge University Press. 290–408.
  1994. Typological Differences between English and German and their Causes. In Toril Swan *et al.*, eds., *Language Change and Language Structure: Older Germanic Languages in a Comparative Perspective*. Berlin: Mouton de Gruyter. 135–158.
  2000. Inflectional Classes, Morphological Restructuring and the Dissolution of Old English Grammatical Gender. In Barbara Unterbeck *et al.*, eds., *Gender in Grammar and Cognition*. Berlin: Mouton de Gruyter. 709–727.
Katz, Dovid. 1987. *Grammar of the Yiddish Language*. London: Duckworth.
Keller, R. E. 1961. *German Dialects: Phonology and Morphology*. Manchester: Manchester University Press.
Kemmer, Suzanne. 1993. *The Middle Voice*. Amsterdam: John Benjamins.
King, Robert D. 1969. *Historical Linguistics and Generative Grammar*. Englewood Cliffs, NJ: Prentice-Hall.
King, Robert D. and Stephanie A. Beach. 1998. On the Origins of German Uvular [R]: The Yiddish Evidence. *American Journal of Germanic Linguistics and Literatures* 10: 279–90.
Kiparsky, Paul. 1995a. Indo-European Origins of Germanic Syntax. In Adrian Battye and Ian Roberts, eds., *Clause Structure and Language Change*. Oxford: Oxford University Press. 140–170.
  1995b. The Shift to Head-Initial VP in Germanic. In Höskuldur Thráinsson, Samuel Epstein and Steve Peter, eds., *Studies in Comparative Germanic Syntax II*. Dordrecht: Kluwer. 140–179.
  1997. The Rise of Positional Licensing. In Ans van Kemenade and Nigel Vincent, eds., *Parameters of Morphosyntactic Change*. Cambridge: Cambridge University Press. 460–494.
Kissock, Madelyn. 1997. Middle Verbs in Icelandic. *American Journal of Germanic Linguistics and Literatures* 9: 1–22.
Klaeber, Fr. 1950. *Beowulf and the Fight at Finnesburg*, 3rd edn. Lexington, MA: D. C. Heath.
Klinghardt, H. 1877. Die Syntax der gotischen Partikel ei. *Zeitschrift für deutsche Philologie* 8: 142–180, 289–329.
Kluge, Friedrich. 1913. *Urgermanisch: Vorgeschichte der altgermanischen Dialekte*, 3rd edn. Strassburg: Trübner.
Koefoed, H. A. 1958. *Danish*. London: Hodder and Stoughton.
König, Ekkehard. 1996. Kontrastive Grammatik und Typologie. In Ewald Lang and Gisela Zifonum, eds., *Deutsch—Typologisch*. Berlin: Walter de Gruyter. 31–54.
König, Ekkehard and Johan van der Auwera, eds. 1994. *The Germanic Languages*. London: Routledge.

Köpke, Klaus-Michael and David Zubin. 1995. Prinzipien für Genuszuweisung im Deutschen. In Ewald Lang and Gisela Zifonun, eds., *Deutsch—Typologisch*. Berlin: de Gruyter. 473–491.
Koptjevskaya-Tamm, Maria. 2003. Possessive Noun Phrases in the Languages of Europe. In Frans Plank, ed., *Noun Phrase Structure in the Languages of Europe*. Berlin: Mouton de Gruyter. 621–722.
Koster, Jan. 1975. Dutch as an SOV Language. *Linguistic Analysis* 1: 111–136.
Koster, Jan and Eric Reuland. 1991. Long-Distance Anaphora: An Overview. In Jan Koster and Eric Reuland, eds., *Long-Distance Anaphora*. Cambridge: Cambridge University Press. 1–26.
Kotova, Eva. 1986. *Sentence Adverbials in a Functional Description*. Amsterdam: John Benjamins.
Krahe, Hans. 1967. *Historische Laut- und Formenlehre des Gotischen*, 2nd edn, revised by Elmar Seebold. Heidelberg: Carl Winter.
Krause, Wolfgang. 1966. *Die Runeninschriften im älteren Futhark*. Volume 1. Göttingen: Vandenhoeck & Ruprecht.
1968. *Handbuch des Gotischen*. Munich: C. H. Beck.
Kress, Bruno. 1937. *Lautlehre des modernen Isländischen*. Leipzig: Otto Harrassowitz.
1982. *Isländische Grammatik*. Munich: Max Hueber.
Kristjánsdóttir, Bergljót et al. 1991. *Snorri Sturluson Heimskringla*. Volume 1. Rejkjavík: Mál og mennig.
Kristoffersen, Gjert. 2000. *The Phonology of Norwegian*. Oxford: Oxford University Press.
Kroch, Anthony and Ann Taylor. 1997. Verb Movement in Old And Middle English: Dialect Variation and Language Contact. In Ans van Kemenade and Nigel Vincent, eds., *Parameters of Morphosyntactic Change*. Cambridge: Cambridge University Press. 297–325.
Kufner, H. 1985. The Case of the Conjugating Conjunctions. *Orbis* 31: 87–100.
Kuriłowicz, J. 1964. *The Inflectional Categories of Indo-European*. Heidelberg: Carl Winter.
Lahiri, Aditi, Tomas Riad and Haike Jacobs. 1999. Diachronic Prosody. In Harry van der Hulst, ed., *Word Prosodic Systems in the Languages of Europe*. Berlin: Mouton de Gruyter. 335–424.
Laka, Itziar. 1990. Negation in Syntax: On the Nature of Functional Categories and Projections. PhD dissertation, MIT.
Lanouette, Ruth. 1996. The Attributive Genitive in the History of German. In Rosina Lippi-Green and Joseph Salmons, eds., *Germanic Linguistics: Synchronic and Diachronic*. Amsterdam: John Benjamins. 85–102.
Larson, Richard. 1995. Olga is a Beautiful Dancer. Paper presented at the Winter Meeting of the Linguistic Society of America, New Orleans.
Lass, Roger. 1988. How to Do Things with Junk: Exaptation in Linguistic Evolution. *Stellenbosch Papers in Linguistics* 17: 33–61.
1992. Phonology and Morphology. In Norman Blake, ed., *The Cambridge History of the English Language. Volume 2: 1066–1476*. Cambridge: Cambridge University Press. 23–155.
1994. *Old English: A Historical Linguistic Companion*. Cambridge: Cambridge University Press.
Lehmann, Winifred. 1986. *A Gothic Etymological Dictionary*. Leiden: Brill.
1994. Gothic and the Reconstruction of Proto-Germanic. In Ekkehard König and Johan van der Auwera, eds., *The Germanic Languages*. London: Routledge. 19–37.
Lenerz, Jürgen. 1977. *Zur Abfolge nominaler Satzglieder im Deutschen*. Tübingen: Gunter Narr.
Levin, Beth. 1993. *English Verb Classes and Alternations*. Chicago: University of Chicago Press.
Leys, Odo. 1979. Zur Systematisierung von Es. *Deutsche Sprache* 1/79: 28–34.
Liberman, Anatoly. 1982. *Germanic Accentology. Volume 1: The Scandinavian Languages*. Minneapolis: University of Minnesota Press.
1992. Vowel Lengthening before Resonant + Another Consonant and Svarabhakti in Germanic. In Irmengard Rauch, Gerald F. Carr and Robert L. Kyes, eds., *On Germanic Linguistics: Issues and Methods*. Berlin: Mouton de Gruyter. 163–215.

Lie, Sven. 1982. Discontinuous Questions and Subjacency in Norwegian. In Elisabet Engdahl and Eva Ejerhed, eds., *Readings in Unbounded Dependencies in Scandinavian Languages*. Umeå: Almqvist and Wiksell. 193–204.

Lieber, Rochelle and Harald Baayen. 1997. A Semantic Principle of Aux Selection in Dutch. *Linguistics* 42: 327–357.

Lightfoot, David. 1991. *How to Set Parameters*. Cambridge, MA: MIT Press.

— 1995. Why UG Needs a Learning Theory: Triggering Verb Movement. In A. Battye and I. Roberts, eds., *Clause Structure and Language Change*. New York: Oxford University Press. 31–52.

Lindauer, Thomas. 1998. Attributive Genitive Constructions in German. In Artemis Alexiadou and Chris Wilder, eds., *Possessors, Predicates and Movement in the Determiner Phrase*. Amsterdam: John Benjamins. 109–140.

Lindow, Wolfgang *et al*. 1998. *Niederdeutsche Grammatik*. Bremen: Verlag Schuster Leer.

Lindstedt, Jouko. 2000. The Perfect-Aspectual, Temporal and Evidential. In Östen Dahl, ed., *Tense and Aspect in the Languages of Europe*. Berlin: Mouton de Gruyter. 365–83.

Lockwood, W. B. 1964. *An Introduction to Modern Faroese*. Copenhagen: Munksgaard.

— 1965. *An Informal History of the German Language*. Cambridge: W. Heffer and Sons.

— 1968. *Historical German Syntax*. Oxford: Clarendon Press.

— 1995. *Lehrbuch der modernen jiddischen Sprache*. Hamburg: Helmut Buschke.

Louden, Mark. 1990. Verb Raising and the Position of the Finite Verb in Pennsylvania German. *Linguistic Inquiry* 21: 470–477.

Lowenstamm, Jean. 1977. Relative Clauses in Yiddish: A Case for Movement. *Linguistic Analysis* 4: 197–216.

Lutz, Angelika. 1991. *Phonotaktisch gesteuerte Konsonantenveränderungen in der Geschichte des Englischen*. Tübingen: Max Niemeyer.

Maddieson, Ian. 1984. *Patterns of Sounds*. Cambridge: Cambridge University Press.

Maling, Joan. 1983. Transitive Adjectives: A Case of Categorial Reanalysis. In Frank Heny and Barry Richards, eds., *Linguistic Categories: Auxiliaries and Other Puzzles*. Dordrecht: Reidel. 253–289.

— 1984. Non-Clause-Bounded Reflexives in Modern Icelandic. *Linguistics and Philosophy* 7: 211–241.

Maling, Joan and Annie Zaenen. 1990. Preposition Stranding and Passive. In Joan Maling and Annie Zaenen, eds., *Modern Icelandic Syntax*. San Diego: Academic Press. 153–164. [First published 1985]

Mallén, Enrique. 1989. The Internal Structure of Determiner Phrases. PhD dissertation, Cornell University.

Marsden, Richard. 2004. *The Cambridge Old English Reader*. Cambridge: Cambridge University Press.

Masica, Colin. 1991. *The Indo-Aryan Languages*. Cambridge: Cambridge University Press.

Mauerer, Friedrich. 1926. *Untersuchung über die deutsche Wortstellung in ihrer geschichtlichen Entwicklung*. Heidelberg: Carl Winter.

McArthur, Tom. 2002. *Oxford Guide to World English*. Oxford: Oxford University Press.

McCormick, Susan. 1981. A Metrical Analysis of Umlaut. *Cornell University Working Papers in Linguistics* 2: 126–137.

McDaniel, Dana. 1989. Partial and Multiple WH-Movement. *Natural Language and Linguistic Theory* 7: 565–604.

McWhorter, John. 2002. What Happened to English? *Diachronica* 19: 217–272.

Melchers, Gunnel. 1992. "Du's no heard da last o' dis"—on the Use of *be* as a Perfective Auxiliary Dialect. In Matti Rissanen *et al*., eds., *History of Englishes: New Methods and Interpretations in Historical Linguistics*. Berlin: Mouton de Gruyter. 602–610.

Messinger, Heinz. 1973. *Langenscheidt's New College German Dictionary*. Berlin: Langenscheidt.
Miller, D. Gary. 2002. *Nonfinite Structures in Theory and Change*. Oxford: Oxford University Press.
Miller, Jim. 2004. Scottish English: Morphology and Syntax. In Bernd Kortmann *et al.*, eds., *A Handbook of Varieties of English*. Berlin: Mouton de Gruyter. 47–72.
Miller, Thomas, ed. 1890. *The Old English Version of Bede's Ecclesiastical History of the English People. Part I*. London: N. Trübner.
Minkova, Donka. 2003. *Alliteration and Sound Change in Early English*. Cambridge: Cambridge University Press.
Mirto, Ignacio. 1995. *The Syntax of the Meronymic Construction*. Pisa: Edizioni ETS.
Mitchell, Bruce. 1985. *Old English Syntax*. 2 vols. Oxford: Clarendon Press.
Montgomery, Michael. 2004. Appalachian English: Morphology and Syntax. In Bernd Kortmann *et al.*, eds., *A Handbook of Varieties of English*. Berlin: Mouton de Gruyter. 245–280.
Montgomery, Michael and Curtis Chapman. 1992. The Pace of Change in Appalachian English. In Matti Rissanen *et al.*, eds., *History of Englishes: New Methods and Interpretations in Historical Linguistics*. Berlin: Mouton de Gruyter. 624–646.
Mørck, Endre. 1994. The Distribution of Subject Properties and the Acquisition of Subjecthood in the West Scandinavian Languages. In T. Swan, E. Mørck and O. Jansen Westvik, eds., *Language Change and Language Structure: Older Germanic Languages from a Comparative Perspective*. Berlin: Mouton de Gruyter. 159–194.
Moulton, William G. 1954. The Stops and Spirants of Early Germanic. *Language* 30: 1–42.
    1973. Vowel System with Five Heights. In Harald Scholler and John Reidy, eds., *Lexicography and Dialect Geography: Festgabe for Hans Kurath*. Wiesbaden: Steiner. 187–194.
Murray, Robert W. and Theo Vennemann. 1983. Sound Change and Syllable Structure in Germanic Phonology. *Language* 59: 514–528.
Musan, Renate. 2001. The Present Perfect in German: Outline of its Semantic Composition. *Natural Language and Linguistic Theory* 19: 355–401.
Nickel, E. 1997. An Example of a Syntactic Blend in Old English. *Indogermanische Forschungen* 72: 261–274.
Nielsen, H. 1989. *The Germanic Dialects: Origins and Early Dialectal Relations*. Tuscaloosa: The University of Alabama Press.
Nilsen, Øystein. 2000. *The Syntax of Circumstantial Adverbials*. Oslo: Novus Press.
Norde, Muriel. 1995. Grammaticalization vs. Reanalysis: The Case of Possessive Constructions in Germanic. In Richard Hogg and Linda van Bergen, eds., *Historical Linguistics. Volume 2: Germanic Linguistics*. Amsterdam: John Benjamins. 211–222.
    2001. The Loss of Lexical Case in Swedish. In Jan Terje Faarlund, ed., *Grammatical Relations in Change*. Amsterdam: John Benjamins. 241–272.
Nordgård, Torbjørn. 1986. COMP-Features and Word Order. In Östen Dahl and Anders Holmberg, eds., *Scandinavian Syntax*. Stockholm: University of Stockholm. 113–122.
Oftedal, Magne. 1952. On the Origin of the Scandinavian Tone Distinction. *Norsk Tidsskrift for Sprogvidenskap* 16: 201–225.
Orel, Vladimir. 2003. *A Handbook of Germanic Etymology*. Leiden: Brill.
Orr, Robert. 1982. The Twofold Adjective Declension in Germanic and Slavic (with some consideration of Baltic): A Contrastive/Comparative Analysis. *Zeitschrift für vergleichende Sprachforschung* 96: 104–118.
Ottósson, Kjartan. 1989. VP-Specifier Subjects and the CP/IP Distinction in Icelandic and Mainland Scandinavian. *Working Papers in Scandinavian Syntax* 44: 89–100.
    1992. *The Icelandic Middle Voice: The Morphological and Phonological Development*. Lund: Lund University.
Padgett, Jaye. 1995. *Stricture in Feature Geometry*. Stanford, CA: CSLI Publications.

Page, Richard. 1997. On the Origin of Preaspiration in Scandinavian. *American Journal of Germanic Linguistics and Literatures* 9: 167–190.
Paul, Hermann. 1962. *Kurze deutsche Syntax*, 3rd edn., revised by Heinz Stolte. Tübingen: Max Niemeyer.
 1989. *Mittelhochdeutsche Grammatik*, 23rd edn., revised by Pieter Wiehl and Siegfrid Grosse. Tübingen: Max Niemeyer.
Peck, Russell, ed. 1968. *Confessio Amantis*. New York: Holt, Rinehart and Winston.
Penzl, Herbert. 1949. Umlaut and Secondary Umlaut in Old High German. *Language* 25: 223–240.
Pereltsvaig, Asya. In press. Small Nominals. *Natural Language and Linguistic Theory* 24.
Perlmutter, David. 1978. Impersonal Passives and the Unaccusative Hypothesis. *Berkeley Linguistics Society* 4: 126–70.
Philippi, Julia. 1997. The Rise of the Article in the Germanic Languages. In Ans van Kemenade and Nigel Vincent, eds., *Parameters of Morphosyntactic Change*. Cambridge: Cambridge University Press. 69–93.
Pintzuk, Susan. 1993. Verb Seconding in Old English: Verb Movement to Infl. *The Linguistic Review* 10: 5–35.
Plank, Frans. 1984. Verbs and Objects in Semantic Agreement. Minor Differences between English and German that Might Suggest a Major One. *Journal of Semantics* 3: 305–360.
 2003. Double Articulation. In Frans Plank, ed., *Noun Phrase Structure in the Languages of Europe*. Berlin: Mouton de Gruyter. 337–396.
Platzack, Christer. 1985. A Survey of Generative Analyses of the Verb Second Phenomenon in Germanic. *Nordic Journal of Linguistics* 8: 49–73.
 1986. The Structure of Infinitive Clauses in Danish and Swedish. In Östen Dahl and Anders Holmberg, eds., *Scandinavian Syntax*. Stockholm: University of Stockholm. 123–137.
Polo, Chiara. 2002. Double Objects and Morphological Triggers. In David Lightfoot, ed., *Syntactic Effects of Morphological Change*. Oxford: Oxford University Press. 124–142.
Ponelis, Fritz. 1993. *The Development of Afrikaans*. Frankfurt am Main: Peter Lang.
Postal, Paul. 1974. *On Raising: One Rule of English Grammar and its Theoretical Implications*. Cambridge, MA: MIT Press.
Prince, Ellen. 1997. Yiddish Subject-Prodrop: Languages in Contact and the Syntax–Discourse Interface. Paper presented at the LSA Institute.
Prokosch, E. 1938. *A Grammar of Comparative Germanic*. Baltimore: Linguistic Society of America.
Quirk, Randolph, Sidney Greenbaum and Geoffrey Leech *et al*. 1985. *A Comprehensive Grammar of the English Language*. London: Longmans.
Quirk, Randolph and C. L. Wrenn. 1955. *An Old English Grammar*. London: Methuen.
Ramat, Paolo. 1987. *Linguistic Typology*. Berlin: Mouton de Gruyter.
Ramat, Paolo and Davide Ricca. 1998. Sentence Adverbs in the Languages of Europe. In Johan van der Auwera ed., *Adverbial Constructions in the Languages of Europe*. Berlin: Mouton de Gruyter. 187–276.
Reed, Carroll E. 1942. The Gender of English Loan Words in Pennsylvania German. *American Speech: A Quarterly of Linguistic Usage* 17: 25–29.
Reichenbach, H. 1947. *Elements of Symbolic Logic*. New York: Macmillan.
Reskiewicz, Alfred. 1966. Split Constructions in Old English. In M. Brahmer, S. Helsztynski and J. Krzyzanowski, eds., *Studies in Language and Literature in Honour of Margaret Schlauch*. Warsaw: Polish Scientific Publications. 313–326.
Riad, Tomas. 2000. The Origin of Danish Stød. In Aditi Lahiri, ed., *Analogy, Levelling and Markedness: Principles of Change in Phonology and Morphology*. Berlin: Mouton de Gruyter. 261–300.
Rickford, John R. 1999. *African American Vernacular English: Features, Evolution, Educational Implications*. Malden, MA: Blackwell.

Ringen, Catherine O. 1999. Aspiration, Preaspiration, Deaspiration, Sonorant Devoicing and Spirantization in Icelandic. *Nordic Journal of Linguistics* 22: 137–56.

Ritt, Nikolaus. 1994. *Quantity Adjustment: Vowel Lengthening and Shortening in Early Middle English.* Cambridge: Cambridge University Press.

Rizzi, L. 1991. Residual Verb Second and the WH-Criterion. In Andrea Belletti and Luigi Rizzi, eds., *Parameters and Functional Heads.* Oxford: Oxford University Press. 63–90.

Roberge, Paul T. 1983. Those Gothic Spirants again. *Indogermanische Forschungen* 88: 109–155.

2000. Etymological Opacity, Hybridization, and the Afrikaans Brace Negation. *American Journal of Germanic Linguistics and Literatures* 12: 101–176.

Roberts, Ian. 1993. *Verbs and Diachronic Syntax: A Comparative History of English and French.* Dordrecht: Kluwer.

Roberts, Ian and Anna Roussou. 2002. The History of the Future. In David Lightfoot, ed., *Syntactic Effects of Morphological Change.* Oxford: Oxford University Press. 23–56.

Robertson, T. A. and John J. Graham. 1991. *Grammar and Usage of the Shetland Dialect.* Lerwick: The Shetland Times. [First published 1952].

Rohdenburg, G. 1974. *Sekundäre Subjektivierung im Englischen und Deutschen: Vergleichende Untersuchung zur Verb- und Adjektivsyntax* [PAKS-Arbeitsbericht 8]. Bielefeld: Cornelson-Velhagen und Klasing.

Rohrbacher, Bernhard. 1994. The Germanic VO Languages and the Full Paradigm Theory. PhD dissertation, University of Massachusetts.

Romaine, Suzanne. 1994. Germanic Creoles. In Ekkehard König and Johan van der Auwera, eds., *The Germanic Languages.* London: Routledge. 566–603.

Rosel, Ludwig. 1962. *Die Gliederung der germanischen Sprachen.* Nuremberg: Hans Carl.

Rosen, Carol. 1984. The Interface between Semantic Roles and Initial Grammatical Relations. In David Perlmutter and Carol Rosen, eds., *Studies in Relational Grammar 2.* Chicago: University of Chicago Press. 38–80.

Ross, John Robert. 1968. Constraints on Variables in Syntax. Reproduced by Indiana University Linguistics Club. (1967 MIT dissertation).

Russom, Geoffrey. 2002. A Bard's Eye View of the Germanic Syllable. *Journal of English and Germanic Philology* 101: 305–328.

Russon, A. and L. J. Russon. 1965. *Advanced German Course.* New York: David McKay.

Rutten, Jean. 1991. Infinitival Complements and Auxiliaries. PhD dissertation, University of Amsterdam.

Samuels, M. L. 1972. *Linguistic Evolution, with Special Reference to English.* Cambridge: Cambridge University Press.

Sandström, Caroline. 2000. The Changing System of Grammatical Gender in the Swedish Dialects of Nyland, Finland. In Barbara Unterbeck and Matti Rissanen, eds., *Gender in Grammar and Cognition.* Berlin: Mouton de Gruyter. 793–806.

Santelmann, Lynn. 1994. Evidence for NegP and Object Shift in German. *Cornell Working Papers in Linguistics* 12: 154–182.

Santorini, Beatrice. 1993. Jiddisch als gemischte OV/VO Sprache. In Werner Abraham and Josef Bayer, eds., *Dialektsyntax.* Opladen: Westdeutscher Verlag. 230–244.

1995. Two Types of Verb Second in the History of Yiddish. In Adrian Battye and Ian Roberts, eds., *Clause Structure and Language Change.* New York: Oxford University Press. 53–79.

Schlick, Werner. 1984. Die Kriterien für die deutsche Genuszuweisung bei substantivischen Anglizismen. *German Quarterly* 57: 402–431.

Schrijver, Peter. 2003. Early Developments of the Vowel Systems of North-West Germanic and Saami. In Alfred Bammesberger and Theo Vennemann, eds., *Languages in Prehistoric Europe.* Heidelberg: Carl Winter. 195–226.

Schulz, Dora and Heinz Griesbach. 1960. *Grammatik der deutschen Sprache.* Munich: Max Hueber.

Schwink, Frederick W. 2000. The Velar Nasal in the Adaptation of the Runic Alphabet. *American Journal of Germanic Linguistics and Literatures* 12: 235–249.
Sells, Peter. 1987. Aspects of Logophoricity. *Linguistic Inquiry* 18: 445–479.
Seppänen, Aimo. 1993. The Relative "That" Reconsidered. In André Crochetière, Jean-Claude Boulanger, Conrad Ouellon, and Pierre Auger, eds., *Actes du XVe Congrès International des Linguistes, Québec, Université Laval, 9–14 août 1992: Les langues menacées/Endangered Languages*. Laval: Sainte-Foy. 369–372.
  2000. On the History of Relative *that*. In Ricardo Bermúdez-Otero, David Denison, Richard M. Hogg and C. B. McCully, eds., *Generative Theory and Corpus Studies*. Berlin: Mouton de Gruyter. 27–52.
  2004. The Old English Relative *þe*. *English Language and Linguistics* 8: 71–102.
Seppänen, Aimo and Göran Kjellmer. 1995. The Dog that's Leg Was Run over: On the Genitive of the Relative Pronoun. *English Studies: A Journal of English Language and Literature* 76: 389–400.
Shannon, Thomas. 1987. On Some Recent Claims of Relational Grammar. In Jon Aske *et al.*, eds., *Proceedings of the Thirteenth Annual Meeting of the Berkeley Linguistic Society*. Berkeley: University of California at Berkeley. 247–262.
  1990. The Unaccusative Hypothesis and the History of the Perfect Auxiliary in Germanic and Romance. In Henning Andersen and Konrad Koerner, eds., *Papers from the 8th International Conference on Historical Linguistics*. Amsterdam: John Benjamins. 461–499.
  1995. Explaining Perfect Auxiliary Variation: Some Modal and Aspectual Effects in the History of Germanic. *American Journal of Germanic Linguistics and Literatures* 7: 129–63.
Shorrocks, Graham. 1996. The Second Person Singular Interrogative in the Traditional Vernacular of the Bolton Metropolitan Area. In James Black and Virginia Motapanyane, eds., *Microparametric Syntax and Dialect Variation*. Amsterdam: John Benjamins. 169–188.
Sievers, Edward, ed. 1892. *Tatian, Lateinisch und Altdeutsch*, 2nd edn. Paderborn: Ferdinand Schöningh.
Sievers, Edward. 1898. *Angelsächsische Grammatik*. Halle: Max Niemeyer.
Sigurðsson, Halldór. 1986. Moods and (Long-Distance) Reflexives in Icelandic. *Working Papers in Scandinavian Syntax* 25: 1–53.
  1989. Verbal Syntax and Case in Icelandic in a Comparative GB Approach. Dissertation, University of Iceland.
  1990. Declaratives and Verb Raising in Icelandic. In Joan Maling and Annie Zaenen, eds., *Modern Icelandic Syntax*. San Diego: Academic Press.
Smith, Henry. 1994. 'Dative Sickness' in Germanic. *Natural Language and Linguistic Theory* 12: 675–736.
Smith, J. R. 1971. Word Order in the Older Germanic Languages. PhD dissertation, University of Illinois.
Smith, Michael B. 2001. Why Quirky Case Really Isn't Quirky: Or, How to Treat Dative Sickness in Icelandic. In Hubert Cuyckens and Britta E. Zawada, eds., *Polysemy in Cognitive Linguistics*. Amsterdam: John Benjamins. 115–159.
Sorace, Antonella. 2000. Gradients in Auxiliary Selection with Intransitive Verbs. *Language* 76: 859–90.
Sportiche, Dominique. 1988. A Theory of Floating Quantifiers and its Corollaries for Constituent Structure. *Linguistic Inquiry* 19: 425–449.
Sprouse, Rex. 1989. On the Syntax of the Double Object Construction in Selected Germanic Languages. PhD dissertation, Princeton University.
Srivastav, Veneeta. 1991. The Syntax and Semantics of Correlatives. *Natural Language and Linguistic Theory* 9: 637–686.

Stearns, MacDonald. 1978. *Crimean Gothic: Analysis and Etymology of the Corpus*. Saratoga, CA: Anma Libri.
Steinmetz, Donald. 2001. The Great Gender Shift and the Attrition of Neuter Nouns in West Germanic: The Example of German. In Irmengard Rauch and Gerald Carr, eds., *New Insights in Germanic Linguistics, II*. New York: Peter Lang. 201–224.
Stellmacher, Dieter. 1983. Neuniederdeutsche Grammatik, Phonologie und Morphologie. In Gerhard Cordes and Dieter Möhn, eds., *Handbuch zur niederdeutschen Sprach- und Literaturwissenschaft*. Berlin: Eric Schmidt. 238–278.
Sternefeld, Wolfgang. 2002. WH-Expletives and Partial WH-Movement: Two Non-Existing Concepts? In Werner Abraham and C. Jan-Wouter Zwart, eds., *Issues in Formal German(ic) Typology*. Amsterdam: J. Benjamins. 285–306.
Stockwell, Robert P. 1977. Motivation for Exbraciation in Old English. In Charles N. Li, ed., *Mechanisms of Syntactic Change*. Austin: University of Texas Press. 291–314.
Stoett, F. A. 1923 [1968]. *Middelnederlandsche Spraakkunst: Syntaxis*, 3rd edn. The Hague: Martijnus Nijhoff.
Streitberg, Wilhelm. 1920. *Gotisches Elementarbuch*. Heidelberg: Carl Winter.
Streitberg, Wilhelm, ed. 1960. *Die gotische Bibel*, 4th edn. Heidelberg: Carl Winter.
Suñer, Margarita. 1984. Free Relatives and the Matching Parameter. *The Linguistic Review* 3: 363–387.
Suzuki, Seichi. 1991. Germanisch /sp/, /st/, /sk/ und /skw/als Lautgruppen. *Amsterdamer Beiträge zur älteren Germanistik* 33: 1–8.
Talmy, L. 1991. Path to Realization: A Typology of Event Conflation. *Berkeley Linguistics Society* 17: 480–519.
Tappe, Hans Tilo. 1984. On Infinitival Clauses without COMP. In W. de Geest and Y. Putseys, eds., *Sentential Complementation*. Dordrecht: Foris. 227–238.
Taraldsen, Knut T. 1982. Extraction from Relative Clauses in Norwegian. In Elisabet Engdahl and Eva Ejerhed, eds., *Readings in Unbounded Dependencies in Scandinavian Languages*. Umeå: Almqvist and Wiksell. 205–222.
   1983. *Parametric Variation in Phrase Structure: A Case Study*. Dordrecht: Foris.
   1984. Remarks on Complex Passives. In B. Brendemoen and E. Hovdhaugen, eds., *Riepmoćala: Essays in Honour of Knut Bergsland*. Oslo: Novas Forlag.
   1986a. On Verb Second and the Functional Content of Syntactic Categories. In Hubert Haider and Martin Prinzhorn, eds., *Verb Second Phenomena in Germanic Languages*. Dordrecht: Foris. 7–26.
   1986b. *Som* and the Binding Theory. In Lars Hellan and Kirsti Koch Christensen, eds., *Topics in Scandinavian Syntax*. Dordrecht: Reidel. 149–184.
   1996. Reflexives, Pronouns and Agreement in Icelandic and Faroese. In James Black and Virginia Motapanyane, eds., *Microparametric Syntax and Dialect Variation*. Amsterdam: John Benjamins. 189–212.
ten Cate, Abraham P. 1989. Präsentische und präteritale Tempora im deutsch-niederländischen Sprachvergleich. In Werner Abraham and Theo Janssen, eds., *Tempus-Aspekt-Modus: Die lexikalischen und grammatischen Formen in den germanischen Sprachen*. Tübingen: Max Niemeyer. 133–154.
Thieroff, Rolf and Joachim Ballweg, eds. 1994/1995. *Tense Systems in European Languages*. 2 vols. Tübingen: Max Niemeyer.
Thiersch, Craig. 1978. Topics in German Syntax. PhD dissertation, MIT, Cambridge, MA.
Thorrell, Olaf. 1973. *Svensk Grammatik*. Stockholm: Esselte Studium.
Thornburg, Linda. 1984. The History of the Prepositional Passive in English. In Vassiliki Nikiforidou, Mary VanClay, Mary Niepokuj and Deborah Feder, eds., *Proceedings of the Eleventh Annual Meeting of the Berkeley Linguistics Society*. Berkeley: Berkeley Linguistics Society. 327–336.

Thráinsson, Höskuldur. 1976a. Some Arguments against the Interpretive Theory of Pronouns and Reflexives. *Harvard Studies in Syntax and Semantics* 2: 573–624.
  1976b. Reflexives and Subjunctives in Icelandic. *Proceedings of the Northeast Linguistic Society* 6: 225–239.
  1991. Long-Distance Reflexives and the Typology of NPs. In Jan Koster and Eric Reuland, eds., *Long-Distance Anaphora*. Cambridge: Cambridge University Press. 49–76.
  1994. Icelandic. In Ekkehard König and Johan van der Auwera, eds., *The Germanic Languages*. London: Routledge. 142–189.
  1996. On the (Non-)Universality of Functional Categories. In Werner Abraham *et al.*, eds., *Minimal Ideas: Syntactic Studies in the Minimalist Framework*. Amsterdam: John Benjamins. 253–281.
  1998. Infinitival Complements in Some Old and Modern Germanic Languages. In John Ole Askedal, ed., *Historische germanische und deutsche Syntax*. Bern: Peter Lang. 335–363.
Tiersma, Pieter. 1999. *Frisian Reference Grammar*, 2nd edn. Ljouwert: Fryske Akademy.
Tomaselli, Alessandra. 1995. Cases of V-3 in Old High German. In Adrian Battye and Ian Roberts, eds., *Clause Structure and Language Change*. Oxford: Oxford University Press. 345–369.
Toon, Thomas. 1982. Variation in Contemporary American English. In Richard W. Bailey and Manfred Görlach, eds., *English as a World Language*. Ann Arbor: University of Michigan Press. 210–250.
Traugott, Elizabeth, 1972. *The History of English Syntax*. New York: Holt, Rinehart and Winston.
  1992. Syntax. In Richard M. Hogg, ed., *The Cambridge History of the English Language. Volume 1: The Beginnings to 1066*. Cambridge: Cambridge University Press. 168–289.
Travis, Lisa. 1988. The Syntax of Adverbs. *McGill Working Papers in Linguistics, Special Issue on Comparative Germanic Syntax*. 280–310.
  1991. Parameters of Phrase Structure and Verb-Second Phenomena. In Robert Freidin, ed., *Principles and Parameters in Comparative Grammar*. Cambridge, MA: MIT Press. 339–364.
Trnka, B. R. 1936. General Laws of Phonemic Combination. *Travaux du Cercle Linguistique de Prague 6:* 294–300. [Reprinted (party revised) in Vilém Fried, ed., *Bohumil Trnka: Selected papers in Structural Linguistics*. Berlin: Mouton, 1982. 113–118.]
Tryon, Darrell. 1987. *Bislama: An Introduction to the National Language of Vanuatu*. Canberra: Research School of Pacific Studies, Australian National University.
Twaddell, W. Freeman. 1938. A Note on Old High German Umlaut. *Monatshefte* 30: 177–181.
van Coetsem, Frans, Ronald Hendricks, and Peter Siegel. 1981. On the Role of Function in Sound Change. *Cornell Working Papers in Linguistics* 2: 166–185.
van der Auwera, J. 1985. Relative "*that*"—A Centennial Dispute. *Journal of Linguistics* 21: 149–179.
van der Gaaf, Willem. 1928a. The Post-Adjectival Passive Infinitive. *English Studies* 10: 129–138.
  1928b. The Predicative Passive Infinitive in English. *English Studies* 10: 107–114.
van der Hulst, Harry, ed. 1999. *Word Prosodic Systems in the Languages of Europe*. Berlin: Mouton de Gruyter.
van der Wal, Marike. 1990. Passive Constructions in Old Frisian. In Rolf Bremmer *et al.*, eds., *Aspects of Old Frisian Philology*. Amsterdam: Rodopi. 495–505.
van der Wouden, Ton. 1997. *Negative Contexts: Collocation, Polarity and Multiple Negation*. London: Routledge.
van Gelderen, Elly. 1993. *The Rise of Functional Categories*. Amsterdam: John Benjamins.
van Kemenade, Ans. 1987. *Syntactic Case and Morphological Case in the History of English*. PhD dissertation, University of Utrecht.
  1992. Structural Factors in the History of English Modals. In Matti Rissanen *et al.*, eds., *History of Englishes: New Methods and Interpretations in Historical Linguistics*. Berlin: Mouton de Gruyter. 287–309.

1997. V2 and Embedded Topicalization in Old and Middle English. In Ans van Kemenade and Nigel Vincent, eds., *Parameters of Morphosyntactic Change.* Cambridge: Cambridge University Press. 326–352.
van Ness, Silke. 1994. Pennsylvania German. In Ekkehard König and Johan van der Auwera, eds., *The Germanic Languages.* London: Routledge. 420–438.
van Riemsdijk, Henk. 1982. On Pied-Piped Infinitives in German Relative Clauses. In Jindrich Toman, ed., *Studies in German Grammar.* Dordrecht: Foris. 165–192.
  1983a. Correspondence Effects and the Empty Category Principle. In Yukio Otsu *et al.*, eds., *Studies in Generative Grammar and Language Acquisition.* Tokyo: International Christian University. 5–16.
  1983b. The Case of German Adjectives. In Frank Heny and Barry Richards, eds., *Linguistic Categories: Auxiliaries and other Puzzles.* Dordrecht: Reidel. 223–232.
  1994. Left Dislocation. In Elena Anagnostopoulou *et al.*, eds., *Materials on Left Dislocation.* Amsterdam: John Benjamins. 1–12.
van Voorst, Jan. 1996. Some Systematic Differences between the Dutch, French and English Transitive Construction. *Language Sciences* 18: 227–245.
Vance, Barbara. 1996. Verb-Second, Null Subjects and Syntactic Change in Medieval French. Ms., Indiana University.
Vat, Jan. 1978. On Footnote 2: Evidence for the Pronominal Status of þær in Old English. *Linguistic Inquiry* 9: 695–716.
  1994. Left Dislocation, Connectedness and Reconstruction. In Elena Anagnostopoulou *et al.*, eds., *Materials on Left Dislocation.* Amsterdam: John Benjamins. 67–92 [first published 1981].
Vater, Heinz. 1988. Mittelkonstruktionen im Englischen, Dänischen und Deutschen. In Pavica Mrazović and Wolfgang Teubert, eds., *Valenzen im Kontrast.* Heidelberg: Julius Groos. 398–417.
Vennemann, Theo. 1984. Hochgermanisch und Niedergermanisch. Die Verzweigungstheorie der germanisch-deutschen Lautverschiebungen. *Beiträge zur Geschichte der deutschen Sprache und Literatur* 106: 1–45.
  1988. *Preference Laws for Syllable Structure and the Explanation of Sound Change. With Special Reference to German, Germanic, Italian and Latin.* Berlin: Mouton de Gruyter.
  2003a. Languages in Prehistoric Europe North of the Alps. In Alfred Bammesberger and Theo Vennemann, eds., *Languages in Prehistoric Europe.* Heidelberg: Carl Winter. 319–332.
  2003b. Syntax und Sprachkontakt: Mit besonderer Berücksichtigung der indogermanischen Sprachen des Nordwestens. In Alfred Bammesberger and Theo Vennemann, eds., *Languages in Prehistoric Europe.* Heidelberg: Carl Winter. 333–364.
  2003c. Zur Frage der vorindogermanischen Substrate in Mittel- und Westeuropa. In Theo Vennemann, ed., *Europa-Vasconica-Europa Semitica.* Berlin: Mouton de Gruyter. 517–590.
Vigfusson, Guðbrand. 1874. *An Icelandic–English Dictionary.* Oxford: Clarendon Press.
Vikner, Sten. 1985. Parameters of Binder and Binding Category in Danish. *Working Papers in Scandinavian Syntax* 23: 1–61.
  1988. Modals in Danish and Event Expressions. *Working Papers in Scandinavian Syntax* 39: 1–33.
  1994. Finite Verb Movement in Scandinavian Embedded Clauses. In David Lightfoot and Norbert Hornstein, eds., *Verb Movement.* Cambridge: Cambridge University Press. 117–148.
  1995. *Verb Movement and Expletive Subjects in the Germanic Languages.* Oxford: Oxford University Press.
Visser, F. Th. 1963–1973. *An Historical Syntax of the English Language.* 3 vols. Leiden: E. J. Brill.
Visser, Willem. 1997. *The Syllable in Frisian.* Holland Institute of Generative Linguistics. (PhD dissertation, Free University of Amsterdam).

Vogel, Ralf. 2001. Case Conflict in German Free Relative Constructions: An Optimality Theoretic Treatment. In Gereon Müller and Wolfgang Sternefeld, eds., *Competition in Syntax*. Berlin: Mouton de Gruyter. 341–375.
    2002. Free Relative Constructions in OT-Syntax. In Gisbert Fanselow and Caroline Féry, eds., *Resolving Conflicts in Grammars: Optimality Theory in Syntax, Morphology, and Phonology*. Hamburg: Buske. 119–162.
Voyles, Joseph. 1971. The Problem of West Germanic. *Folia Linguistica: Acta Societatis Linguisticae Europaeae* 5: 117–50.
    1992. On Old High German Umlaut. In I. Rauch and G. Carr, eds., *On Germanic Linguistics: Issues and Methods*. Berlin: Mouton de Gruyter. 365–377.
Warner, Anthony R. 1993. *English Auxiliaries: Structure and History*. Cambridge: Cambridge University Press.
Watts, Sheila. 2001. How to Become an Auxiliary: Progressive and Perfect in Old Saxon. In Sheila Watts, Jonathan West, and Hans-Joachim Solms, eds., *Zur Verbmorphologie germanischer Sprachen*. Tübingen: Max Niemeyer. 117–136.
Wauchope, Mary Michelle. 1991. *The Grammar of the Old High German Modal Particles Thoh, Ia, Thanne*. New York: Peter Lang.
Wedel, Alfred. 1997. Verbal Prefixation and the "Complexive" Aspect in Germanic. *Neuphilologische Mitteilungen* 98: 321–332.
Weerman, Fred. 1989. *The V2 Conspiracy: A Synchronic and a Diachronic Analysis of Verbal Positions in Germanic Languages*. Dordrecht: Foris.
    1997. On the Relation between Morphological and Syntactic Case. In Ans van Kemenade and Nigel Vincent, eds., *Parameters of Morphosyntactic Change*. Cambridge: Cambridge University Press. 460–494.
Weinreich, Uriel. 1971. *College Yiddish*, 5th edn. New York: YIVO Institute for Jewish Research.
Weiß, Helmut. 1998. *Die Syntax des Bairischen*. Tübingen: Max Niemeyer.
Westergaard, Marit. 2003. Word-Order in WH-Questions in a North Norwegian Dialect: Some Evidence from an Acquisition Study. *Nordic Journal of Linguistics* 26: 81–109.
Williams, Joseph. 1975. *Origins of the English Language: A Social and Linguistic History*. New York: The Free Press.
Wolfram, Walt. 2004. Rural and Ethnic Varieties in the Southeast: Morphology and Syntax. In Bernd Kortmann *et al.*, eds., *A Handbook of Varieties of English*. Berlin: Mouton de Gruyter. 281–302.
Wolfram, Walt and Donna Christian. 1976. *Appalachian Speech*. Arlington, VA: Center for Applied Linguistics.
Wülfing, Ernst. 1894. *Die Syntax in den Werken Alfreds des Großen*. Volume 1. Bonn: P. Hanstein's Verlag.
    1901. *Die Syntax in den Werken Alfreds des Großen*. Volume 2. Bonn: P. Hanstein's Verlag.
Wurzel, Wolfgang. 1987. *Inflectional Morphology and Naturalness*. Dordrecht: Kluwer.
Yamaguchi, Toshiko and Magnús Pétursson. 2003. The Speaker and the Perfect Auxiliaries *Hafa* and *Vera* in Icelandic. *Language Sciences* 25: 331–352.
Zaenen, Annie. 1985. *Extraction Rules in Icelandic*. New York: Garland.
    1987. The Place of *bevallen* (Please) in the Syntax of Dutch. Unpublished paper, CSLI, Stanford.
    1994. Contrastive Dislocation in Dutch and Icelandic. In Elena Anagnostopoulou *et al.*, eds., *Materials on Left Dislocation*. Amsterdam: John Benjamins. 119–150.
Zaenen, Annie and Joan Maling. 1982. The Status of Resumptive Pronouns in Swedish. In Elisabet Engdahl and Eva Ejerhed, eds., *Readings in Unbounded Dependencies in Scandinavian Languages*. Umeå: Almqvist and Wiksell. 223–230.
    1990. Unaccusative Passive and Quirky Case. In Joan Maling and Annie Zaenen, eds., *Modern Icelandic Syntax* [Syntax and Semantics 24]. San Diego: Academic Press. 137–152.

Zaenen, Annie, Joan Maling, and Höskuldur Thráinsson. 1990. Case and Grammatical Functions in the Icelandic Passive. In Joan Maling and Annie Zaenen, eds., *Modern Icelandic Syntax* [Syntax and Semantics 24]. San Diego: Academic Press. 95–136 [first published 1985].

Zanuttini, Raffaella. 1997. *Negation and Clausal Structure*. Oxford: Oxford University Press.

Zifonun, Gisela, Ludger Hoffmann and Bruno Strecker. 1997. *Grammatik der deutschen Sprache*. 3 vols. Berlin: de Gruyter.

Zonneveld, Wim, Mieke Trommelen, Michael Jessen, Gösta Bruce and Kristjan Árnason. 1999. Word-Stress in West-Germanic and North-Germanic Languages. In Harry van der Hulst, ed., *Word Prosodic Systems in the Languages of Europe*. Berlin: Mouton de Gruyter. 477–604.

Zwart, Jan Wouter. 1993. Dutch Syntax: A Minimalist Approach. PhD dissertation, University of Groningen.

  1996. Verb Clusters in Continental West Germanic. In James R. Black and Virginia Motapanyane, eds., *Microparametric Syntax and Dialect Variation*. Amsterdam: John Benjamins. 229–258.

Zwicky, Arnold M. and Geoffrey K. Pullum. 1983. Cliticization vs. Inflection: English *n't*. *Language* 59: 502–13.

INDEX

Note: The major Germanic languages (AF, BN, DA, DU, EN, FA, FR, GE, GO, IC, ME, MHG NN, NO, OE, OHG, OS, SW, YI) are cited with such great frequency throughout the book that citing each mention of them in the index is not practicable. Rather, the index only lists the discussions of these languages in the introductory chapter.

ablaut 6, 22, 89, 271, 275
accusative-with-infinitive constructions 261–264
adjectives, in adjective phrases 171–175; agreement on predicate adjectives 219–221; in comparative constructions 11, 174–175; complements of 171–174; position in noun phrase 127–130; weak and strong inflection of 6, 130–137
adverbs 370–376; order of 373; sentence adverbs and VP adverbs 372–376
African-American English 273, 475
Afrikaans 17
affricates 47–48; and constraints on clusters 71
Aktionsart see verbal aspect
Albanian 11
alliteration in Germanic verse 69
anaphors 196–213; short-distance and long-distance 204–211; very-long-distance anaphors vs. logophors 211–213; with inherently reflexive verbs 13, 205–209
anticausative prominence 10
Appalachian English 115, 182, 194, 196, 218, 228, 370, 475
Armenian 11, 141
articles 9, 137–155; co-occurrence with genitive phrases 150–155; definite 6, 141–146; indefinite 139–141, 146–148; omission of 145–148; proprial article 160, 162; weak quantifiers 137–139
aspiration 44–45; preaspiration 45

assibilation 49
associative NPs 162–163
attraction 467–468
auxiliary position 288–291

Bala 137
Balkan languages 11
Balto-Slavic 11
Basque 10, 11
Bavarian 48, 146, 218, 366, 456
Bislama 13
Bokmål 20
breaking; in Gothic 55; in Modern Frisian 64; in Old English 55
Breton 140

case 103–122; alternatives to 107–111; in experiencer constructions 116–122; instrumental 104; lexical and structural case 112–122, 245; loss of the accusative/ dative distinction 105–107, 121, 177–179; loss of lexical case 114–122
Celtic 6, 9, 22, 167, 273, 415, 436, 477
Chinese 222
circumflex accent in Norwegian 86
complementizers 415–419; sources of 415–417; with infinitives 417–419
compounding 29–32; genitive compounds 31; genuine and non-genuine compounds 30; linking morphemes in 31–32; root compounds 30

505

conjunction(s) 11; clitic 395, 402, 406, 411; interrogative 406, 475
continental Scandinavian languages 19
control constructions 257–258
Crimean Gothic 14
Czech 10

Danish 20; loanwords in Faroese 23
Dano-Norwegian 20
dative movement 109
dative sickness in Icelandic 117
definiteness; and expletives 233–234; and impersonal passives 246
deflection 90–91
derivational morphology 26–29; borrowed suffixes 26, 29; category shift/ zero derivation 29; *Kompositionssuffixe* 29; in loanwords 25; non-cohering suffixes 29; prefixes 13, 27, 40; stem-based and word-based lexicon 29, 30
diphthongs 63–65; centering 64
discourse particles 32–36; down-graders and up-graders 34; evidentials and 33
double object constructions; and dative movement 109; order of objects in 365–368; passive and 240–242
doubly filled comp 434–436
DP-hypothesis 160
Dutch 17

East Germanic 7, 14
East Norse 19
English 18–19; as a typological outlier 13
Estonian 40
Ewe 212
exceptional case marking *see* accusative-with-infinitive constructions
experiencer constructions 6, 10, 116–122, 214
expletive arguments 224–236; and definiteness 233–234; S-initial expletives 231; in transitive expletive constructions 214, 235; valency and 234–235
extraposition 361–363, 423; and expletives 226

factivity 403
Faroese 19, 20
Finland Swedish 85
Finnish, 11
Frankish 48, 52

French 10, 12, 55, 315, 397, 434, 437, 447; Norman French loan words in English 23
fricatives 45–53
Frisian 13, 17–18
front-rounded vowels 63; inward and outward rounding 63 *see also* umlaut
futhark see writing systems
future 297–301; future auxiliaries with 298–301; use of present tense in expressing 297–298; the *shall/will* rule 300

geminate consonants 74–77; degemination of 75–76, 78–79; High German Consonant Shift and 75; Holtzmann's Law 74; *Verschärfung* 74; West Germanic gemination 74–75
gender 93–103; agreement on adjectives 95–96, 98–100; common 101–102; in loanwords 25–26; loss of gender distinctions 13; and noun classes 93–95; relative frequencies of 102–103; syntactic and semantic agreement with pronouns 96–98
genitives; double in English 158; group 163; Saxon 156
Germanic languages; distinctive characteristics of 6–7; genetic relationships among 7–8; typological classification 12–13
Germanic foot 80–81
Goedelic 46, 213
grammaticization 22
Great Vowel Shift 64
Greek 10, 11, 22, 141
Grimm's Law 42

Hanseatic League 9, 18, 23
Hebrew; influence on Yiddish compounds 29, 30; loanwords in Yiddish 23
Hebridean English 213
Heliand and Genesis 18
Hellenic 415
High German 15–16; influence on Scandinavian 23
High German Consonant Shift 47–48, 52, 71; and geminate consonants 75
Hungarian 11, 40

Icelandic 19
imperative *see* mood
inalienable possession *see* meronymic constructions
infinitives 6, 331–342; bare and prepositional 287, 336–340, 417–419; double infinitive construction 286, 355; *for-to* 417–419; preterite 342; split 340–341, 419; tautological 342; voice of 332–335
inflection; inherent and contextual 90; nominal 89–122; prefixes 272; verbal 270–284
Ingvaeonic *see* North Sea Coast Germanic
Insular North Germanic 19
inverse attraction 423
Irish English 213, 218, 273, 310, 311, 418, 475
island constraints 458–459
Italic 22, 415, 436
Italian 12, 315

Japanese 222, 358

kennings 26, 30

Landsmål 20
Latin 22, 437; loanwords in Old English 24
left-dislocation 478–481; connectedness effects in 479–481
length 74–79; closed syllable shortening and 76; of consonants *see* geminate consonants; foot-final lengthening and 77; great quantity shift and 77; homorganic lengthening and 76; open syllable lengthening and 78; trisyllabic shortening and 78
Limburger 13
linguistic convergence 8–12
Lithuanian 10
loanwords 22–26; gender assignment and 25–26; nativizing 24–26; loan-translation 24–25
logophors *see* anaphors
long object shift 188–189, 192–195
Low German 8, 18; loanwords in Scandinavian 23
Luxembourgish 13, 16

Maxim of Quantity 315
maximize onset 72
meronymic constructions 164–167

meteorological constructions 226, 232
middle constructions 251–255, 323–328; in Icelandic 255, 324–327; '*let*'-middles 327; middle voice in Indo-European 318, 323; reflexive suffix in 255, 324–328; in West Germanic 252–255
minimal rhyme constraint 66
modal passive constructions 268–269
modal verbs 285–292; and the auxiliary position 288–291, 398; root and epistemic meanings of 286–287, 290–291; as speech act verbs 286
mood 6, 273, 278–284; imperative 280–281, 284; subjunctive 278–284

negation 376–398; constituent negation with sentential scope 11, 383–392; cycle of negation 394–397; final negation in Afrikaans 397–398; the NegP hypothesis 387; scope of 376–379; sentential negators and constituent negators 392–394
negative complementizers and pleonastic negation 382
negative concord and multiple negation 379–382
negative-indefinite incorporation 394
negative polarity items 376–382, 395–396
nominalization 123–124
nominal phrases 122–171; complements in 126; determiners in 137–155; discontinuous NPs 168–171; genitive phrases in 148–167; headed by lexical nouns 126; without nominal heads 122–124; position of adjectives in 127–130; with pronoun heads 124–126
nominative-with-infinitive construction *see* subject raising
non-finite verb forms *see* infinitives, participles
North Germanic 7, 19–20; influence on English 9, 23; mutual influences in 9
North Sea Coast Germanic 7–8, 17–19; characteristics of 179, 203
Northwest Germanic 7, 14–15
Norwegian 20
number 91–93; dual 93, 179, 195; plural marking in loanwords 25; pluralia tanta 92
Nynorsk 20

objects, order of 365–368; weak pronouns and 368
object shift 183, 384–387
obstruents 41–53; biases in voicing assimilation 44–45; final devoicing of 50–51; laryngeal features of 43–45; postvocalic voicing/lenition of 51–52, 53; place features of 42–43
Olang Tirolese 186
Old French 399
Old Norse 19
Old Saxon 18

palatalization 48–49; in Yiddish 54
paradigm leveling 91
participles 6, 343–349; in absolute constructions 344; the English gerund 344–347; past/passive participle 275, 276, 347–349; present participle 343–344; supine 349
particles *see* phrasal verbs
passive constructions 10, 318–323; auxiliary choice in 12, 13, 319–322; complex in NO 244; in ditransitive sentences 240–242; expression of the agent in 238–239; '*get*'-passive 322–323; inflectional in Gothic 274, 318; intransitive and unaccusativity 247–251; impersonal 245–246; nonlocal 244–245; periphrastic 6, 274; prepositional 242 243; Scandinavian *s*-passive 328–331
Pennsylvania German 13, 16, 361
perfect constructions 10, 302–316; choice of the auxiliary with 13, 294–295, 302, 305–308; omission of the auxiliary in 304; in Indo-European 302, 275; loss of simple past tense and 12, 303, 315–316; and past tense 309–316; present relevance and 309–316
phrasal verbs 36–40, 366, 368
pied-piping 424, 427, 429, 445, 451, 456, 459–462; of infinitive clauses 460; of noun phrases 460–462
possessive constructions; dative possessors 11; external possessors 13, 165, 167–168 *see also* meronymic constructions; postnominal periphrastic 160–161; prenominal periphrastic 158–160; proper name possessive markers, 161–162

preaspiration *see* aspiration
predeterminers 165, 167–168
preposition stranding 445, 454, 456
present tense, meaning of 298
pretero-present verbs 285–286, 292
pro-drop 221–223
progressive 295–296, 316–317
pronouns 175–213; atonic and clitic 181–192, 368, 408; loss of case distinctions in 177–179; personal 175–203; possessive 148–149, 151–153, 155–157, 195; predicate possessive 195; referential properties of 196–213; reflexive *see* anaphors; loss of reflexive 179–181; resumptive *see* resumptive pronouns; and verb-fronting 410–411; T/V 192–195
proper names as possessors 155–157, 160–162
psych-shift 120–122

quantifier stranding and quantifier float 169–170
questions 473–477; infinitival 471, 473; multiple-WH-questions 475–477; partial-WH-movement questions 476–477; question markers in 395, 474; tag questions 477
quotative inversion 414

R-compounds 441, 454; R-stranding 456
reduplication 69, 272
relative clauses 11, 420–473; agreeing complementizers in 430–434; attraction in 467–468; correlative 421–423; C-relatives, P-relatives, D-relatives and W-relatives 436–459; expression of person in 448–450; free relative constructions 466–470; generalizing relative constructions 470; infinitival 471–473; matching effects in free relatives 468–469; non-restrictive 437, 450; participial 421–422; relative markers in 423–434; relative particles/complementizers 425–434, 445; relative pronouns 7, 12, 423–425, 436–459; typology of 420–448; unintroduced 436, 456–457, 465; with subject relativization 462–466
replacive morphemes 89
resumptive pronouns 430, 457–458
retroflex consonants 42, 54

Rhenish Fan 47
Riksmål 20
Romance 6, 9, 10, 11, 44, 140, 273, 299, 305, 308, 390, 411, 415
Romanian 10
Rückumlaut 279
Russian 10

Scandinavian dialect continuum 3, 19
Schwyzertütsch 13, 16, 360; Grisons dialect of 367
Scottish Gaelic 10, 140, 415, 447
scrambling 366–368; richness of case morphology and 367–368, 108
Shetlands English 46, 216
Skeireins 14
Slavic 10, 11, 415, 436, loanwords in Yiddish 23
sonorants 53–56; liquids 54–56; nasals 53–54
sonority hierarchy 65–71
South African English 475
Spanish 222
Standard Average European 9–12, 164
spread glottis *see* aspiration
state and non-state languages 13–14
stem-based and word-based morphology 91
stød 86–87
stops 41–45
stress 79–84; ablaut and 271; in derived forms 84; Germanic accent shift and 6, 79; the Germanic foot and 80–81; effect of Latinate vocabulary on 81–82; prefixes and 81; three-syllable window and 82
strong verbs 271, 274–276
subject agreement 214–224; asymmetries in subject-verb agreement 217–218; with complementizers 218–219; concord with nonverbal predicates 219–221, 303–304; with expletives 235; Northern Subject Rule 218; and pro-drop 221–223; between subject and verb 214–218; syntactic correlates of richness of agreement morphology 221–224; thematic and athematic endings 270; and verb position 223–224
subject raising 259–260; infinitival complementizers in raising constructions 419

subjects 214–255; derived subjects in passive constructions 237–251; in imperative clauses 236–237; in middle constructions 251–256
subjunctive *see* mood
supine *see* participles
suprasegmental phonology 65–88
Swedish 20
syllable boundaries 72–73; Gothic word division and 72; maximize onset and 72; minimal rhyme and 72; preference for bimoraic syllables 72
syllable codas 73–74; epenthesis in 73; preference for coronal consonants in 73
syllable onsets 66–73; in Gothic 66–71; place-based restrictions on 69–71; sonority-based restrictions on 68–69; in Yiddish 72–73
syllable structure 65–74

tense 6, 272, 274–276; periphrastic expression of tense and aspect 6, 292–317; in reported speech 281–282; sequence of tenses 281–282
that-trace effect 464
Tok Pisin 13
tone *see* word tone
topic constructions 478–479
topic drop 413
tough-movement constructions 264–269
Turkish 10, 358
two-reflexive languages *see* anaphors, short-distance and long-distance

umlaut 28, 58–63, 89, 271; a-umlaut 59; i-umlaut 59–63; u-umlaut 63; primary umlaut 59; secondary umlaut 60–63
unaccusative hypothesis 256; and auxiliary selection 307; and intransitive passives 247–251
unrounding 63

verb-first order; in conditional sentences 413; in declarative sentences 413–414; in yes/no questions 413
verb fronting 11, 354 *see also* verb-second order; in conditional clauses 413; in yes/no questions 413

verb-object and object-verb languages 12, 353–368; and preposition stranding 455
verb phrase, order of elements in 353–368
verb-projection raising *see* verb raising
verb-raising 12, 358–361
verb-second order 7, 370–376, 398–414; exceptions to V-2 412, 406; in embedded root clauses 402; strict V-2 and residual V-2 languages 404–410; and subject-verb inversion 398–399; symmetrical and asymmetrical 400–404; triggers of 404–414
verbal aspect 39–40, 297; present verbs with future meaning and 298
verbal valency 350–353; and expletives 234–235
Verner's Law 42, 49–50, 271, 276
Vlaams 17 *see also* West Flemish
voice *see also* obstruentsfinal devoicing of; obstruents, laryngeal features of; biases in voicing assimilation 44–45, 274, 318–331
vowels 56–65; tense/lax contrasts in 58

was-für split 170, 462
weak verbs 276–277; dental suffix in 276; shift from strong to weak 277
Welsh 140, 218, 397
West Flemish 12, 23, 108, 183, 184, 188, 219, 229, 237, 360, 365, 368, 386, 394, 396, 418, 433, 434, 475
West Germanic 7, 15–19
West Germanic dialect continuum 3
West Norse 19
word order *see* adverbs, order of; object shift; objects, order of; scrambling; verb-first order; verb-second order; verb phrase, order of elements in
word tone 84–88; in Dutch and German 87–88; in Swedish and Norwegian 85–87
writing systems; Gothic 14; Runic *futhark* 14–15, 19; Yiddish 16
Wulfila 14

X-bar syntax 369–370

Yiddish 16
Yorkshire English 194